Liturgy and Music

Lifetime Learning

Robin A. Leaver
and
Joyce Ann Zimmerman, C.PP.S.

Editors

A Liturgical Press Book

 THE LITURGICAL PRESS
Collegeville, Minnesota

Cover design by David Manahan, O.S.B. Illustration: detail of woodcarving from an organ panel, ca. 1350, Erfurt Cathedral, Germany.

ISBN 13: 978-0-8146-2501-9
ISBN 10: 0-8146-2501-0

	4	5	6	7	8

Library of Congress Cataloging-in-Publication Data

Liturgy and music : lifetime learning / Robin A. Leaver and Joyce Ann Zimmerman, editors.
    p.   cm.
  Intended primarily for professional liturgical musicians in the Christian mainline sacramental denominations.
  Includes bibliographical references and index.
  ISBN 0-8146-2501-0 (alk. paper)
  1. Church music—Instruction and study. 2. Liturgics.
I. Leaver, Robin A. II. Zimmerman, Joyce Ann, 1945– .
MT88.L57   1998
264'.2—dc21
                                                       98-12229
                                                        CIP
                                                        MN

Contents

Acknowledgments

Earlier versions of chapters 3–4, 6–9, 11, 18–19, and 25 appeared in *Liturgical Ministry,* a thematic quarterly also published by The Liturgical Press.

Chapter 16 is a revision and expansion of an article first appearing in *Reformed Liturgy & Music* 23 (Spring 1989) 61–65.

The chart "The Evolution of African American Music" on page 368 is reproduced by kind permission of Dr. Portia K. Maultsby, Ph.D.

Introduction

Robin A. Leaver and Joyce Ann Zimmerman, C.PP.S.

Psalm 147 proclaims "How good it is to sing praises to our God; for he is gracious, and a song of praise is fitting" (v. 1, NRSV). This is only one of over a score of psalms that explicitly connect singing with praising God. If liturgy is to praise God, then surely music amplifies that praise and, indeed, connects us with that whole heavenly choir constantly offering hymns of praise to God. As that golden-tongued preacher John Chrysostom said so long ago: "Above, the hosts of angels sing praise; below, men [sic] form choirs in the churches and imitate them by singing the same doxology. . . . The inhabitants of heaven and earth are brought together in a common solemn assembly; there is one thanksgiving, one shout of delight, one joyful chorus."[1] What marvelous affirmation of the use of music during worship! What encouraging endorsement of those dedicated to church music ministry!

That music is an essential element of worship is predicated by its inexorable presence—in the religious practices of antiquity to the present, cutting across all cultures. Even those persuasions that cultivate a kind of quietism in their worship still "sing praise" to God in their very silence, attesting to the many contours music can take. Speaking with one voice together as assembly soon takes on a cadence and tonality that reminds us more of singing than speaking. The rhythms of processions and the fluidity of gestures are embodied expressions of the heart's song. Everything about worship elevates us to a realm where full-throated praise is the only fitting utterance. But beyond these very important, broader considerations of music and worship loom the more narrow genre of liturgical music as such. Hymns, service music, preludes and postludes, devotional music, and various forms of chant all find their place in worship, and these are the focus of this volume.

The title *Liturgy and Music* delimits the subject, structure, and intended primary audience of this volume. The contributors all come from Christian mainline, sacramental denominations. Although some of the theory and principles addressed may well apply to non-Christian religions or non-sacramental Christian ones—and, hence, make the volume useful to a wider audience—the discussion is intentionally more restricted. This choice allowed the contributors to be more focused, more nuanced, and more specific in the development of their chapters. Although the primary audience is professional liturgical musicians or those preparing to be so, nonetheless pastors, liturgy planners, liturgy committee members, professional liturgists, and anyone who takes their worship seriously would all benefit from perusing these chapters. The preference for "liturgy" rather than "worship" in the title underscores the ritualized, sacramental nature of the worship we are exploring.

The book is divided into two parts with the individual chapters in the two parts roughly paralleling each other. Part 1, as the title indicates, offers a basic introductory knowledge of various issues in liturgy. Part 2 is a solid introduction to the scope and role of liturgical music and musicians in Christian sacramental denominations. Each part concludes with a bibliographic chapter (the reader should, however, also take note of the bibliographical citations, either in the text and/or notes, in other chapters since not all the bibliographic sources are repeated in the summary bibliographies). By this means we hope to underscore the intent of the subtitle, that coming to an appreciation and understanding of musical liturgy is a lifetime learning process, both for those professionally responsible for the planning and execution of music during liturgy and for all members of the liturgical assembly. Each chapter can be studied or read on its own, independent of the others. There has been no attempt by the editors to smooth out denominational references and differences in practices. One of the blessings of ecumenical dialogue has been that we have emphasized the convergences rather than the divergences, and have come to appreciate the fact that we can all learn much from each other and from the differing ways of interpreting and implementing liturgical tradition. This is perhaps one of the most unique contributions of the volume.

The reader will notice that many of the contributors draw on references from *Sacrosanctum Concilium,* "The Constitution on the Sacred Liturgy," from the Second Vatican Council. This was a Roman Catholic Church Council and, therefore, its proceedings reflect this tradition; nevertheless, *Sacrosanctum Concilium* has served as a blueprint and impetus for liturgical renewal among virtually all Christian sacramental denominations. So much so, that we can rightfully say *Sacrosanctum Concilium* has become, truly, an ecumenical document. If the reader has not studied this document, we strongly urge her or him to do so and believe that this would be time well spent.

Some of these chapters (especially in the first part on foundations of liturgy) originally appeared in *Liturgical Ministry,* a thematic quarterly periodical published by The Liturgical Press. This volume grew out of the desire of the editors to make more readily accessible the theology and pastoral applications contained in those original articles. Drawing together this foundational material and paralleling it in the musical domain also guided the development of the second part, most of which is newly written material for this volume. This points to another unique feature of this work: Liturgy and music are not presented as two domains isolated from each other but rather are interpreted from the premise that foundational issues in liturgy have their interrelated counterpart (and counterpoint) in music. So much so, that we can rightfully say we have *musical liturgy* rather than music during liturgy. In practice, approaching liturgy as *musical liturgy* encourages liturgical music ministers to take their legitimate place alongside and be as important as all the other liturgical ministers. It dispels any notion of a hot summer's Sunday liturgy being "quiet and barebones, let's finish and beat the heat" (with the implication that the whole choir doesn't go on vacation during the summer months). It means that the choir, organist, cantor, and other musicians are not there to entertain, but to help lead the liturgical prayer. *Musical liturgy* uniquely highlights not only the importance of the use of music at worship, but also the intimate bond between making music and praying.

Our desire is to offer a comprehensive theological approach to liturgical music. Obviously, not every topic important for the practicing liturgical musician is covered. For example, anyone working professionally with a worship community today must be knowledgable about and sensitive to the inclusive language issue. Another example: it is assumed that the liturgical musician is competent musically, so no issues regarding building musical skills are included. The bibliographic chapters suggest readings in some of these other areas, knowledge of which is essential to good ministry and good music practice.

We are excited in that we believe this volume breaks new ground for both a theology of liturgy and a theology of liturgical music. It is a lifetime learning process continually to discover new ways that musical liturgy can raise us up to encounter our God in praise and thanksgiving. We editors will be grateful if this volume leads liturgical music professionals and others to a more full-throated expression of their worship of God. We editors will be humbled if this volume leads those whose ministry is music—together with those to whom they minister—to sing with the psalmist:

> My heart is steadfast, O God,
> my heart is steadfast.
> I will sing and make melody.
> Awake, my soul!
> Awake, O harp and lyre!
> I will awake the dawn.
> I will give thanks to you, O Lord,
> among the peoples;
> I will sing praises to you among
> the nations. (Ps 57:7-9)

Note

1. *Homilia I in Oziam seu de Seraphinis I; PG* lvi, 97 quoted in James McKinnon, ed., *Music in Early Christian Literature,* Cambridge Readings in the Literature of Music, John Stevens and Peter le Huray, gen. eds. (Cambridge/New York: Cambridge University Press, 1987) 89.

Part I

Worship/Liturgy

Chapter 1

What Is Liturgical Worship?

Mary M. Schaefer

Introduction

The experience of encounter with the holy, awe-provoking yet fascinatingly attractive, is known from the history of religions.[1] This experience invites engagement with a transcendent "holy mystery" or "ground of being" who at once is utterly beyond all created personal beings and is very near (immanent) to them. In both Judaism and Christianity God is the Holy One and Creator of all that exists (Gen 1; Deut 6:4; John 1:1-3).

By their very existence created things praise their Creator; God is glorified by all the creatures God has made. Human beings, endowed with reason and will, have been created according to God's image and likeness (Gen 1:27). They are free to choose the way of life or the way of death. When they choose the good, their lives acknowledge God as personal source and goal and God is glorified. When human beings contradict God's purposes they sin, "miss the mark." The glorification of God which is worship's content expresses and deepens the relation between God and creatures. Corporate worship orients human beings toward their own full personhood and instructs them in right relationship to all creation. Their sanctification is accomplished by correspondence with God's project, one which began before the ages and has cosmic dimensions.[2]

Christian worship is adoration of God by the community of disciples of Jesus Christ, Word of God enfleshed. Christians are animated

3

by the Holy Spirit in their witness to Christ, service of their fellow human beings, and worship of God. Their worship is rooted in the Paschal Mystery, the events of Jesus Christ's life, death, resurrection, and ascension to God's right hand. In the power of the Holy Spirit Jesus preached the coming of God's reign. In all things Jesus was God's faithful servant, referring his whole life to the God whom he called by the special and intimate title *Abba*, Father. Faithful to the end to the mission given him, through his obedience and in his person Jesus restored humankind together with all of creation to right relationship with God and modeled free acceptance of God's offer of self-giving love. Through, with, and in Christ and empowered by the Holy Spirit, acceptable worship is offered to God.

The Christian scriptures testify that God, active in the world as Word and Spirit, pours out self for us in love. The personal relational names Father, Son, and Holy Spirit, favored in the Johannine literature, speak of the dynamic interrelationships of these three persons in their mutual sharing of the one divine life.

I. The Church as Praying Community

The whole of the life of faith lived by Jesus' followers can be subsumed under three aspects: witness (preaching of the gospel by life, word, and deed), service in love, and worship.[3] The Church as community of faith witnesses to its neighbors. It serves them with love; its members together with all of humanity will be judged on their loving deeds (Matt 25:31-46). However, the specific character of the Church's relationship to God for the world is best articulated when it worships.

The Church at worship is a people which prays. Prayer is the raising of the mind and heart to God; that God initiates the dialogue is presumed. Already the Church prays when individual members follow the Lord's command to pray to God "in secret" (Matt 6:5-6). When gathered for public worship the Church shows itself to be an assembly constituted by and responding to God's call.[4] Then the Church proclaims the scriptures and interprets them, intercedes for the world, and gives praise and thanks to God. In response to God's promise and offer of loving relationship, the assembly expresses its faith by corporate prayer and the celebration of sign-actions ("sacraments") symbolizing a new relationship to God. These symbolic rituals act as transparency for the mystery at the depths of existence: God's loving will to save. Having recalled, prayed for, and experienced anew God's saving activity and having been invited to deepen their commitment, believers are sent out to participate in the world's renewal.

A. Terminology: Worship or Liturgy?

Worship and liturgy are terms used interchangeably in some circles; in others, one term is strongly preferred to the other. Although *worship*[5] may refer to relations between human beings and also to objects which are idolized, its application to religious behavior is common. In this last instance worship is the reverence human beings, individually or communally, pay to God. Christian public worship is one sphere where such homage is expressed externally. The term *liturgy*[6] refers especially to those forms of public corporate worship which follow a set structure or series of *rites* (procedures required or usual in a solemn celebration). The specific form or formularies used in public worship are also designated as liturgy.

1. Some Protestant traditions use exclusively or prefer the term *worship* (as in "service of worship") because it denotes the inner dimension of public homage paid to God while deemphasizing the external forms. Liturgy, the external form ("shape") or formula of worship in a tradition, may be awarded lesser value or even viewed as dangerous to authentic worship "in spirit and in truth" (see John 4:23). Respect for "objective" content carried by outer forms (e.g., "God-talk" handed on in inherited categories) is offset by the notion that authentic worship arises only from an individual's inner self.

2. Preferring the term *liturgy,* Catholic traditions may not distinguish linguistically between outer forms and their inner content. Practice or theory may imply that liturgical forms carry and convey their content, God's self-communication, *ex opere operato* (by the very fact of the "work being worked"). In these traditions "objective" content may be well expressed, but adequate place for and expression of the subjectivity of the worshipers who participate *ex opere operantis* ("by reason of the work of the one working") may be deficient.

3. *Liturgical worship* is the term chosen in this chapter to describe worship which follows a customary pattern or ritual structure rooted in identifiable Jewish and early Christian traditions. It invites conscious and active participation as a way of engaging with the divine action, is oriented toward the expression of the depth-dimension of human experience through use of symbols, and expresses the shared faith of communities which can be designated churches.

B. Critical Reflection on Liturgical Worship

The object of the formal study of liturgy is the Church at prayer. Prayer is not a spiritual transaction which takes place apart from the body or contrary to the dynamics of human communication. Corporate prayer—God's communication with us and our response to God in community—makes full use of both verbal and non-verbal means of human communication. Corporate prayer takes place within a context of song, story, and choreographed gesture and movement. Through shared symbol-making which incorporates elements of creation, Christian worship enables its participants to remember, to experience, and to anticipate that time when God's project of salvation will be realized. Christian worship animates its participants to give themselves to God's project. At the end of time, faith maintains, God will be all-in-all and the purpose of creation will have been fully realized: return to God through Christ risen and active in the Spirit.

Study of the Church at prayer should draw on contributions which the human sciences—anthropology, sociology, and psychology—can make. As Christian worship is a response to the mystery-dimension of life, phenomenology (especially study of where the holy is experienced), the meaning communicated by the aural and visual arts, qualitative studies (esthetics, or appreciation of the beautiful), the science of signs (semiotics), and the interaction of human beings with their environment (proxemics) throw light on worship as a human cultural phenomenon engaged in by those who seek communion with the divine.

Theological reflection about the praying Church (liturgical theology) turns to a whole range of sources—scripture, doctrines and their evolution, history and tradition, historical and comparative liturgical studies, conciliar decisions, spirituality, the various ways faith is expressed in different cultures—in order to analyze and interpret corporate worship as a first-order (that is, immediate, unreflected) expression of communal faith. Liturgical studies has also a critical function: to critique present practice in light of past forms, thereby envisioning what better expresses the Church's faith. Critical reflection on and correction of liturgical worship prevent its becoming narcissistic and self-serving, captive to ideology, or remote from life and cultures.

Theology of liturgy uses the tools of systematic theology to analyze the dynamics of worship. What takes place in this event of divine-human communication? What qualifies (or disqualifies) a particular liturgy for communication of the faith within its culture? What structures underlie liturgical worship? Since the God whom Christians worship is triune, do the trinitarian relationships (immanent or among the Persons and economic, i.e., interacting with creation to effect the plan of salvation[7]), shape the Church's worship so as to inform and instruct praxis?

Any in-depth critique of liturgical worship needs to view the many elements which have an impact on worship: its anthropological basis, biblical sources, the historical development and disintegration of rites, and doctrinal and theological content. Evaluation of liturgy as event of human communication, pastoral outcomes, and the theology of Church which shapes the symbolic form are involved. No analysis of liturgical-sacramental worship is complete which fails to account for the presence and action of the Trinity as originator of, active agent in, and final goal of Christian liturgical worship.

C. Liturgical Worship: Emotional, Cerebral, or Affective?

Traditional liturgical worship may give greater emphasis to (1) an emotional or (2) a cerebral mode of expression. Contemporary liturgical praxis, in which theory interacts constructively with practice and practice with theory, strives for (3) an affective mode, that is, one which integrates the affections with the intellect so as to balance emotional expression and intellectual content.

1. Emotionally driven worship puts a high value on personal, private devotion. Discomfort with liturgical forms may be expressed. Worship is viewed as primarily a matter of the individual's "subjectivity" even when it transpires in public assembly. Remembering is a mental exercise. Emotional experience is to the fore; "He [Jesus] walks with me, he talks with me." The worshipful person is friend of Jesus but passive before God. Alternatively, behavior outside the ordinary may be attributed to God's Spirit. Worship in an emotional mode is likely to phrase prayers, preaching, and hymnody in the first-person singular and place the person of the leader(s) in the foreground, although theology may downgrade the role of appointed leadership. Music and hymnody may border on the sentimental. Conversely, music may make peace with secular values so as to offer little challenge to enter into a converted way of seeing and feeling. The person who understands worship as engaging the subjective emotions may feel threatened when asked to share corporate symbols as a way of expressing faith.

2. Cerebral or intellectualized worship attempts to express in words the full content of adoration of God. The word functions literally, as sign rather than symbol. So embarrassed are we before the Holy One, so unable to express emotions, that we cannot stop talking. There are as many instructions as prayers. The presider leaps from the role of prayer-leader to that of master of ceremonies and commentator. "Our next hymn is found in. . . ." The preacher instructs

the untaught. There's not a moment of silence. God has no chance to get a word in edgewise.

The symbolic language and symbols chosen are for God's edification rather than the participants'. In this highly rationalized worship there is little room to bring our own life-experiences, joys, and problems to the liturgy; the affective life of individuals is neither expressed nor alluded to. If the tradition is Protestant the value of frequent sacramental participation may be downplayed. Conversely, Catholic traditions may act as though sacraments are effective—indeed the only kind of worthwhile worship—because they are "done by the book" by a properly equipped agent, the ordained leader. Intellectualized worship resorts to law in order to avoid mistakes and control gestures and emotions. The community's role is to be audience.

3. Affective worship seeks a balance between the mind and the emotions of the participants, all of whom are involved in the action as "celebrants." Word and symbolic gesture are each given their due. Narrative theology involves the hearers in the history of God's chosen people. Preaching is practiced as the uncovering and sharing of faith-experience. Informative language is limited to what is needed to facilitate the experience and language of communion, that interchange with God and with one's fellow worshipers where the deepest human values are shared.

Bodiliness is valued as real symbol of the human spirit. Each person is unique; each has gifts to give the community and gifts to receive. Therefore there is a certain pluralism in the celebration. In the presence of God a sense of wonder (appreciative consciousness) is at play. Symbols and symbolic actions have a surplus of meaning; since they disclose life's depth-dimension, their shared meaning is not fully explicable. Moreover, the community understands these symbols to be "real"; both the leaders and the assembly as co-celebrants believe in what they are doing.

The media of human communication include word, symbol, gesture, movement, silence, and music. Instead of being treated as decoration and extraneous to the "real business" of worship, music is integral to the expression of liturgical content and bodily engagement. Text and music together—musical liturgy or sung prayer—are appreciated for their power to illumine the mind and move the heart. The ultimate inspiration for those who sing as well as for the text and music of liturgy is understood to be the Holy Spirit.

Finally, in affective worship the connection between liturgy and life becomes clear. The community has taken to heart the exhortation, "But be doers of the word, and not merely hearers who deceive themselves" (Jas 1:22, NRSV). The community with its leaders is attuned to the task of acknowledging and overcoming alienation and marginalization through the proclamation of the scriptures, preaching, prayers, and use of inclusive language and symbol. The assembly itself with its mutuality of ministries is recognized as the primary liturgical mode by which Christ is actively present among believers.

Critical analysis and evaluation of the worship of particular faith communities must be undertaken with respect for the community's traditions, culture, and charisms. What are the ways God calls this particular community to express its faith at this point in history, in this culture? Because liturgical worship utilizes external symbols to reveal the depth-dimension it confesses, avoidance of ongoing evaluation and renewal of liturgies signifies, in some way, an unwillingness to enter into the lifelong process of conversion. Sooner or later such a stance leads to a crisis in the life of the community.

D. A Problem for Liturgy Today

There is ample evidence that many Christians have been acclimatized to change everywhere in life but in the worship event. They equate an invariable liturgy with an immutable God who ensures a secure point of stability in a world otherwise in flux. Many Christian communities face the crisis of rapidly diminishing numbers. Who needs public worship? What happens in corporate worship that differs qualitatively from the homage offered God by individuals in the secrecy of their room or amidst the beauty of creation? Since liturgical worship is guided by rubric and threatened by rote repetition, is not private worship more sincere and authentic?

These questions confront liturgical worship as celebrated in both catholic and reformed traditions. In many aspects Reformation traditions originating in the sixteenth century were continuations or reforms of the Roman rite, whether they reduced liturgical worship to older and simpler patterns or preserved secondary elements. It is not surprising, then, that the conclusions drawn by both parties were similar. Between the sixteenth and mid-twentieth centuries, both Protestant and Catholic traditions grounded the worship of God on natural law. According to this way of thinking worship is a duty which obligates the creature to give due homage to its creator.

The obligation to participate in liturgical worship might be enforced, e.g., by a law of the Church which required attendance at Mass on Sundays and holydays "under pain of mortal sin." From the Protestant side the individual's pious act took precedence; attendance at worship was a free expression of subjective piety or devotion towards God. When not balanced by a theology of God's prior invitation and present activity, such piety could degenerate into a Pelagian (works-righteousness) stance. In either case, worship was an exercise of the virtue of religion. It focused on what humans do rather than on what God has done and continues to do in Christ.

Emptying pews are eloquent witness that, for large numbers of today's cultural Christians, neither legalism nor individual permissiveness carry sufficient conviction to promote regular attendance at communal worship. By contrast, under torture the lay martyrs of Abitina in North Africa (d. 303) explained why they persisted in assembling for worship despite imperial edict prohibiting such assemblies: "We cannot live without our Lord's Day celebration." Corporate worship supported their faith; if there were no assembly in which faith could be expressed personally, faith would wither![8]

II. The Human Person, Worshiper and Symbol-Maker

The human body is symbol of a unique individual. A symbol is a sign of the created world which not only points beyond itself to some ultimate reality, but already in some sense "contains" that reality. As "embodied spirit" the human person is a "real symbol": identity between the symbol and the thing symbolized is realized. A true symbol has prior meaning which awaits recognition. Human beings "make" symbols and rituals (sequences of patterned behavior) in the sense that they construct meaning from them as they construct sentences.

Human beings are creatures of ritual. Psychologists have shown the necessity of rituals for integration into and growth in human community. Rituals enable persons to confront creatively and acceptingly "boundary situations" which cannot be changed, manipulated, or avoided such as birth, illness, and death. The history of religions provides ample evidence of the importance of symbol and ritual in the formation and continuance of cultures as well as of a certain commonality of religious experience wherever questions of ultimate meaning are raised. The Hebrew and Christian scriptures are products of cultures in which symbol and ritual played a central role in giving coherence to life and conveying religious meaning.

A. Liturgical Worship in the Hebrew Scriptures

Everywhere the Hebrew scriptures display God's life-creating initiative inviting dialogue. God's initiative occurs in the midst of everyday life as well as in celebratory events. In Genesis chapter 1 God speaks a creative word and creation comes to its fullness. The prophets speak in God's name *(in persona Dei)*, often in the context of ritual activity or some seasonal festival (e.g., Amos 5:21-24; 8:9-10). Their prophetic utterance demands a reciprocal action from the hearers. An individual's religious experience in a sacred place, e.g. on a mountaintop (Exod 19:3-6; 24:1-2, 9-11) or Temple (Isa 6), exhibits the underlying structure of religious worship. In a vision Isaiah experiences God as the awe-inspiring yet fascinating revelation *(mysterium tremendum et fascinans)* which has its parallel in many religions. This transcendent God, insistently present and involved in human history, is object of worship by virtue of active engagement in the world.

The Hebrew scriptures cite blessing and petitionary prayers, songs, and hymns of praise; some of these are accompanied by celebratory actions. The laudatory Song of Moses and the Israelites (Exod 15:1-18) is followed immediately by Miriam's song of praise and her dance to the beat of the tambourine in company with all the Israelite women (Exod 15:20-21). The Hebrew scriptures also offer patterns for communal worship. Exodus 24 combines the reading of the Law with performance. The setting of the prayer of Solomon is the dedication of the Temple in Jerusalem where the whole people are assembled at a time of festival (1 Kgs 8). A solemn procession and animal sacrifices are the action-elements accompanying the blessing and petitionary prayer uttered by the king.

Psalm 117 expresses the universal call to worshipful praise of God:

> Praise the LORD, all you nations!
> Extol him, all you peoples!
> For great is his steadfast love
>   toward us,
>   and the faithfulness of the LORD
>   endures forever.
> Praise the LORD!

Psalm 118, which may have been chanted in the procession entering the temple on the feast of Tabernacles (see Neh 8-9), begins by calling the people to thanksgiving. Each day the Law of Moses is read and interpreted so that the people can understand (Neh 8).[9] A ritual pattern for common worship on a feast day is found in the "national confession" or atonement liturgy of Nehemiah 9. This ritual takes place on the eighth day of the Feast of Tabernacles. The service contains features continued in Christian liturgical worship: the people assemble (v. 1) and confess their sins (v. 2); this is followed by reading from the Book of the Law (v. 3). Then the Levites, exercising a "diaconal" role, call on the people to bless God (vv. 4-5), and God is blessed by recounting the great events of salvation history (vv. 6-31).

The pivotal verse (32) acknowledges God's covenant faithfulness and admits the people's infidelity. Then the signatories to the renewed covenant are listed in chapter 10 and the obligations taken on by the people spelled out (vv. 28ff.). In summary, the reading of God's word leads to confession and a personal-communal renewal of the covenant which is attested by visible signs.

B. Sources for Liturgical Worship in the Christian Scriptures

In the Acts of the Apostles the preaching of God's mighty salvific deeds culminating in the death and resurrection of Jesus Christ leads to praise and thanksgiving on the part of the hearers and the response of faith in baptism. Initially the Christian scriptures show the community of Christ's followers worshiping in the Jerusalem Temple, synagogue, and home (Acts 2:46; 3:1; 9:20). This life of faith is nourished in the Lord's Supper (1 Cor 11:23-29). Sunday, the first day of the week and the day on which Christ rose (John 20:1, 19, 26; 1 Cor 16:2; Acts 20:7), is the privileged day for assembly even though in Judaism the Sabbath was holy and in the Roman Empire the "day of the sun" was an ordinary workday.

For Christians liturgy and life in the world are inseparable; the bodily and the spiritual are integrated (Rom 12:1-3). The whole of Christian worship can be brought back to three commands: "Pray always" (1 Thess 5:17; 2 Thess 1:11; Col 1:9); "Baptize all nations" (Matt 28:19-20); and "Do this in memory of me" (1 Cor 11:25). Although exhortations to prayer (Col 4:2-3) and fragmentary elements such as confessions and acclamations abound (Rev 4:11; 5:13-14; 19:4-9; 22:20-21), the Christian scriptures provide no order of service. However, Christian prayer, the "sacrifice of praise," is directed to God and mediated through Christ (Heb 13:15) in the Spirit.

The later New Testament strata incorporate hymnody, e.g., the christological hymns of Philippians 2:6-11 or Colossians 1:15-20. Frequently Christ is the one addressed in hymns and acclamations. Both God and Jesus Christ are adored in the great visions of Revelation (chs. 4–5, 7, 19), where the Lamb as Christ's symbol receives as well as mediates homage. Reaction to gnosticism in the second to fourth centuries led to the exclusion of non-biblical compositions in favor of psalmody.

It was during this formative period as well that church orders, or rules for community life, were composed. Originally, charismatic leadership offices were crystallized, over the course of the second century, in the characteristic triad: bishop, presbyter, deacon. Despite societal constraints a number of churches included women in the diaconate. Although the terminology used for public office is more or less constant, job descriptions varied then as they do now among the churches. The Lord's Supper, as narrated in the Christian scriptures, has two variant shapes: one in which the words of blessing over bread and cup are separated by a meal in the Jewish tradition (Paul in 1 Cor 11; Luke 22:14-23) and a more ritualized form (Mark 14:22-25; Matt 26:26-29). The Jewish-Christian meal prayers in chapters 9 and 10 of the *Didache* may show a primitive Jewish-Christian Lord's Supper prayer of the late first century. Already this early document uses the term "eucharist" (thanksgiving). Colossians 1:12-20 seems to be a precipitate of such a table prayer.

C. Later Developments in Liturgical Worship

The earliest outline of liturgical worship for baptism or the Lord's Supper is provided from Rome by Justin Martyr in the mid-second century. A Word liturgy preceding the Eucharist involves readings from the scriptures and preaching. After this first part of the synaxis, those not baptized are dismissed, the intercessory prayers are said in common, and the kiss of peace exchanged. Then the table is prepared. Eucharistic prayer is said extempore by the presider, with the Amen of the people at its conclusion expressing their consent. After the breaking of the bread, communion in the "eucharistized" bread and wine (that is, elements over which the thanksgiving prayer has been said) is shared among the assembly by the deacons, who also take communion to those who are absent. A collection for the poor extends the love of the community outward.

Justin's Sunday liturgy presumes active participation. The simple outline, in which functional actions and movements have not yet been "covered" by private prayers or song, has inspired pruning of overripe worship structures in many traditions. Comparative analysis of liturgies makes it clear that word and sacrament, each with its distinctive function and movement, belong together. The early third-century church order attributed to Hippolytus of Rome provides a model eucharistic prayer, helping us to identify those elements which are found as standard features in patristic eucharistic prayers of many churches.

In the course of the fourth century the primitive functional structure of worship begins to be filled in and even overburdened. Robert Taft has elucidated how primary rather than secondary elements are discarded or reduced, e.g., readings from the Hebrew scriptures, psalmody, the prayers of the people (general intercessions), the kiss of peace, and the people's communion. Introductory rites are expanded;

biblical texts are replaced by ecclesiastical compositions (antiphons and refrains).[10] Elements migrate from one liturgical unit to another with resulting incoherence in meaning. Loss of content and breakup of structures, discernible across centuries and traditions, characterize ritual disintegration and necessitate liturgical renewal.

In the churches of East and West the rapid growth of Christian communities together with an undereducated clergy led to worship assemblies in which sacramental actions took precedence over preaching. By the sixteenth-century Reformation, a sacred liturgical language, priestly hegemony of liturgical action, and a merely passive participation of laity together with serious pastoral abuses had devalued the word of God and the sacraments. The Reformers set out to restore the reading of the scriptures and preaching together with regular and even weekly celebration of the Lord's Supper including communion by all participants. But habits of eucharistic abstinence ingrained over centuries militated against the restoration of weekly Eucharist in the majority of Reformation churches. The disintegration of the normative Sunday liturgy, with word replacing table or table the word, represented the state of communal worship until the latter part of the twentieth century in many Christian churches.

D. The Unique Contribution of Liturgical Worship

The early churches were realistically anthropocentric. Confessing that the triune God created the world to share the divine goodness, worship which glorified God was understood as actualizing and sanctifying persons. "The glory of God is the human being fully alive," declared St. Irenaeus (d. ca. 200). All prayer which glorifies God opens human beings to God's purposes and signifies their readiness to receive God's gracious offer of self.

What, then, is the specific contribution of liturgical worship? Corporate prayer, inspired by and invoking God's Holy Spirit, enables persons (spirits-in-the-body) to respond to God's gracious act of self-disclosure in Jesus in ways that exceed individual possibility and build up the faith community as witness to and visible body of the risen Christ in the world. Liturgical prayer takes heart from recalling God's gracious activity in the past. It engages human beings in what God is doing even now, and expands the vision and will to embrace what God wants still to do in history.

Of course, individuals do not benefit from corporate worship unless they enter into it personally. Without prayer "in secret," authentic and meaningful corporate worship is impossible. Personal prayer provides the weft necessary if the fabric of ecclesial prayer and symbol-making is to be woven from the warp of tradition and human yearning. The personal-communal symbolic action which is Christian liturgy's has always been a tradition rooted in the cross and resurrection of Jesus Christ, charter event for the Church; and it has a goal, its Lord who comes from the future.

III. Ecumenical Convergence in Patterns of Worship

A half-century's scholarship and dialogue among liturgists and theologians representing a wide range of churches have led to common or at least converging positions on the basic shape and dynamics of Christian worship. The resulting renewed patterns of worship are bringing closer the sought-for goal of mutual recognition of churches, sacraments, and ministries.

A. The Normative Sunday Worship Service: Word and Table

There is ecumenical agreement that the service of Word and Table (as proclamation of Christ's saving work, memorial of the cross, and celebration of the resurrection; that is, the Paschal Mystery) is the most fitting way to celebrate (solemnize, from Latin *celebrare*) the Lord's Day. The Word and Table service is "normative" on Sunday even if not the most frequent in all churches. Its shape draws believers into the dynamic biblical pattern of word, where faith comes through hearing in hope, and sacrament, where faith is expressed and love deepened through active human response. Thus believers are prepared to answer lovingly the demands of God and neighbor as met in daily life.

---

1. Table of the Word

WORD	leading	INTERPRETATION	concluded by
proclaimed	to	in the preaching, which names God's active presence in the world	PRAYERS OF THE PEOPLE extending community concern to the world

RECONCILIATION through confession or exchange of the peace[11]

2. Table of the Eucharist

TABLE PRAYER	leading	TABLE SHARING	concluded by
of praise, thanks, and offering[12]	to	in bread and cup	SHARING IN SERVICE TO THE WORLD through witness, loving service, and celebration of the faith

---

Word and Table retell the salvation story in complementary ways. Even though the Word of God is word of faith of the Church and is only known to us thanks to the witness of faith, the Word liturgy represents God's initiating dialogue with human beings. The telling of the story from God's perspective is punctuated by answers or responses by the hearers. The sermon or homily is a pastoral discernment of God's revelatory action in the events of present-day life. It is also an invitation to respond according to the hearers' own circumstances and call. Having been called to discipleship or renewed in commitment through the proclamation and preaching, the community is prepared to enter into sacramental actions whose intent, specified by prayer, is to effect communion between God and God's beloved people. Deepened in this relationship, the community is strengthened to participate in God's project for the world.

B. Prayer of the Hours

Responding to the biblical injunction to pray always, the heart of the daily prayer of the Church (or Liturgy of the Hours) in the early communities was psalmody. Some of these Hebrew prayers inspired by the Holy Spirit were understood as prayed with the "voice" of Christ. Recent scholarship has recovered the praise-structure, the priority given to certain psalms and canticles ("scripture-songs") according to the time of day, and the strong symbols of the so-called "cathedral" office, appropriate for parish and other ecclesial communities and revitalized in the liturgical renewal. This "office" or service is distinct from monastic versions in which the entire psalter is said or sung and symbols and ministries are minimal.[13]

Conclusion

The goal of Christian worship is the return of all created things to God their source and wellspring in order to realize the purpose of creation, communion in the divine life. In Christian worship the mediator is Christ and the mutual bond between Christ and believers is the Holy Spirit, God's Gift of love. Active in the depths of Christian worship is the economic Trinity: the loving God who draws persons into community; the risen Christ whose body is given a qualified visibility in the Church; and the Spirit animating, gifting, and energizing the assembly.

But the full, conscious, and active response of the participants in worship is also required. The measure of divine-human communion is directly related to faithful response by individual persons and community. Therefore worship ministries, exercised with competence and expressing the Church's integral faith, are crucial to the assembly. When God and worshipers act in synergy, the inner event of the offer of grace shapes the worshipful response of liturgy—grace invoked and received—so that persons, individually and corporately, enter into Christ's offering of self to God and for humanity.

Liturgical worship is the shape of God's grace in the form of the assembly's believing response. Gathered about Christ, its leader and the priest of its worship, in his name it prays God to send the Holy Spirit to awaken, strengthen, and energize its members for one or another aspect of life in Christ. It has reason to believe that such prayer, made in faith, is always heard.

Notes

1. See Rudolf Otto, *The Idea of the Holy* (London: Humphrey Milford, 1926).

2. The churches of the West speak of sanctification, those of the East of divinization of the human being by union with God. As well, Eastern Christianity has retained a strong sense of the necessary wholeness of creation's adoring response to God. Western theology is beginning to address that theme, and to keep creation and its care in view.

3. *Martyria, diakonia,* and *leitourgia* in Greek. *Martyr* meant witness; *diakonos* (servant) gives the English word deacon; and *leitourgia* referred to the public office performed gratuitously by an Athenian on behalf of the whole citizenry.

4. The Greek word *ekklesia,* from which the terms "ecclesial" (pertaining to the church) and "ecclesiology" (theology of the church) are derived, is, like many words coopted into Christian usage, secular in origin. Referring to a general assembly of citizens, it translated the Hebrew word *qahal* (assembly), used of the Israelites when they wandered in the desert and gathered for liturgy. *Qahal* emphasized the call by God to assemble.

5. From Old English *weorthscipe* meaning worthiness, merit, recognition given or due, honor, and respect.

6. Greek *leitourgia,* from Greek *leitos,* public + *ergos,* performing, originally the public office or duty performed gratuitously by a rich Athenian citizen on behalf of fellow-citizens.

7. "Economy," from the Greek *oeconomia,* God's plan of salvation, referring to God's active work in the world (see Eph 1:3-14).

8. Participation in the liturgical assembly upbuilds faith, one's own as well as others', by expressing it. In keeping with modern culture and their gifts of grace (charisms), believers need to actively express faith through word and deed, symbol and ritual.

9. Related texts include Psalm 106; Nehemiah 1:5-11; Ezra 9:6-15; Daniel 9:4-19; Baruch 1:15-3:8; Daniel 3:26-45; Jeremiah 32:17-25.

10. For instance, psalmody chanted in procession outside the church may be brought into the body of the service; the antiphons may be retained while the scriptural text drops out.

11. See Matthew 5:23-24 and Justin Martyr's outline in I *Apology* 65–67. Confessional elements occur throughout the classical word and table liturgies; a few place personal confession of sin after the service of the word. Exchange of the sign of peace expresses the need for reconciliation with neighbor without which there can be no forgiveness by God (Matt 6:14-15).

12. How eucharistic offering is to be understood is still a matter of theological difference. But cf. Ephesians 5:1-2 ("Be imitators of God . . . and live in love, as Christ loved us and gave himself up for us, a fragrant offering and sacrifice to God") and Romans 12:1 ("I appeal to you therefore, brothers and sisters, by the mercies of God, to present your bodies as a living sacrifice, holy and acceptable to God, which is your spiritual worship").

13. See chapter 8 for a fuller development of the Liturgy of the Hours.

Chapter 2

The Liturgical Year

Thomas J. Talley

Those charged with the planning of a liturgical music program have a special need to understand the seasons and festivals of the liturgical year. The themes encountered in the prayers and lections are seldom self-explanatory, and are themselves often the result of an evolution that needs to be understood as background to the scripture appointments. That said, an explanation of the seasons and their themes must choose between exposition of that evolution, a complex historical process I sought to unfold in a larger work,[1] and the more immediately useful discussion of the seasons and their themes as they are encountered in the present state of the lectionary. In this chapter we will attempt to follow the latter course, but the reader must be warned that at many points it will be necessary to make a historical excursion that will tie the season under consideration to other feasts or seasons on which it may depend. What is intended in this essay is not a practical guide to the musical articulation of the liturgical year (a goal demanding musical authority that I lack), but an introduction to the understanding of the phenomenon of the liturgical year itself.

Prior to the reforms of Pope Paul VI, the Western eucharistic lectionary, we recall, had but two readings, and the two series, "epistles" (which included many Old Testament passages and readings from other non-gospel New Testament books) and the gospels, had independent histories and related to one another only accidentally, if at all. By contrast, the current triennial lectionary provides readings from the Old Testament and New Testament with an intervenient psalm, all in addition to the reading of the gospel. The gospel series has as its basic schema a course reading of one of the synoptic gospels in each of the three years of the lectionary cycle, while the Gospel of John, with its variant chronology, provides further readings in all three years. The idea of the liturgical course reading of a single gospel, it has been argued, reaches back to the very formation of the gospel tradition, and much of the Christian year can be seen as built upon such a hearing of the gospel proclaimed in the Sunday assembly, a reading running from the beginning of the year (at Epiphany) to the proclamation of the passion narrative at Pascha, the unitive festival of Christ's death and resurrection.

Advent

Our liturgical year, however, no longer begins with Epiphany, the earliest nativity festival in the Eastern empire, nor even with Christmas, the Western nativity feast. Rather, our liturgical books have for centuries now been arranged to begin with the preparatory season that leads to Christmas, the season we know as Advent. We think of Advent as the opening of the liturgical year, however, only because our liturgical books are arranged so. J. Neil Alexander has pointed out that the *Comes* of Würzburg, a list of seventh-century epistle assignments for the liturgical year, begins with Christmas and has at its end five Sundays *de adventu domini*, suggesting that the year was conceived of as running from the celebration of Christ's first advent in the incarnation to his second advent at the eschaton.[2]

Those Sundays of Advent in the Würzburg *Comes* are immediately preceded by appointments for the fast of the tenth month, which we would come to know as the December ember days. These seasonal fasts are older at Rome than any season of Advent, and yet the winter fast seems to have been viewed as concerned with Christ's second coming. Such, at least, is the case in the preaching of Leo the Great, Bishop of Rome in the middle of the fifth century. In his Sermon XIX announcing the Fast of the Tenth Month, he says:

> When the Saviour would instruct His disciples about the Advent of God's Kingdom and the end of the world's times, and teach His whole Church, in the person of the Apostles, He said, "Take heed lest haply your hearts be overcharged with surfeiting and drunkenness, and care of this life." And assuredly, dearly beloved, we acknowledge that this precept applies more especially to us, to whom undoubtedly the day denounced is near, even though hidden, for the advent of which it behooves every man to prepare himself lest it find him given over to gluttony, or entangled in cares of this life.[3]

In Syria, at about that same time, a series of Sundays of Annunciation drew attention to the roles of St. John Baptist and the Blessed Virgin Mary in the incarnation. By the middle of the fifth century, homilies of Antipater of Bostra testify to memorials of John the Forerunner and the Blessed Virgin on the two Sundays before the feast of the nativity, and in the seventh-century calendar of Išo-Yabh III these have been extended to four Sundays. Later West Syrian use has six Sundays of Annunciation.[4] That seems also to be the meaning behind the term *de exceptato* used for the six Sundays before Christmas at Milan. At Milan, the sixth Sunday of this season, the Sunday before Christmas, is observed as the feast of the Annunciation. This throws important light, of course, on the assignments for the Fourth Sunday of Advent in our current lectionary. Above all, our season of Advent testifies, as did Irenaeus and Justin Martyr in the second century, to the two advents of Christ, the two parousias, in the incarnation and in final glory, and the definition of Christian history by those two advents.

Christmas and Epiphany

In the sixth century the Emperor Justinian, evidently in an oblique attack on the Monophysite rejection of Christmas at Jerusalem, decreed that the Annunciation should be universally observed on March 25, but in the following century a council at Toledo in 656, noting that it was difficult to observe the feast on that date since it always fell in Lent, ordered instead that the Annunciation should be celebrated on December 18, one week before Christmas. Although it seems that they did not understand the fast before Christmas to make the celebration of the Annunciation inappropriate, they did so understand Lent. That problem was also addressed a bit later (in 692) in Constantinople at the Council in Trullo. There it was determined that the Annunciation would be accorded the liturgical privileges of a Saturday or Sunday (the only days on which Eucharist was celebrated during Lent in Constantinople), no matter on which day of the week March 25 might fall.

That the date assigned to the Annunciation should always fall in Lent, and often in Holy Week, was no accident. To understand why that was so will require looking at two very early determinations regarding the observance of the crucifixion of the Lord, determinations that would prove significant in setting a date for the nativity. The Gospel of John establishes the Jewish date of the passion as the Preparation of the Passover, 14 Nisan (the first spring month in the Jewish lunar calendar), and that was the original one day of the paschal fast in Asia Minor, a fast concluded with the Eucharist at cockcrow of the following morning. However, that lunar calendar was eleven days shorter than the solar year, and in time the Passover date would fall well before the coming of spring. When the discrepancy between the season and the calendar became too obvious, the authorities in Palestine would order the repetition of the month preceding Nisan, thus moving Passover back into the spring season. For Christians in Asia Minor, separated from the synagogues since the end of the first century, this posed a serious problem since they were no longer able or inclined to depend on the authority of Palestinian sages. Some, at least, seem to have forsaken the lunar calendar for the solar calendar of Asia Minor. This was basically the Julian calendar, but at its adoption in Asia in 9 B.C. the birthday of Augustus, September 23 (in Roman reckoning, the ninth day before the beginning of October), was taken as the beginning of the year and the first day of its first month, Kaisar, assigned the same number of days as October. That meant that from then on every Asian month would begin nine days earlier than its Roman equivalent. The first month of spring, Artemisios, began on the day that Romans knew as March 24, and the fourteenth day of that first spring month, equivalent to the Jewish Preparation of Passover, would be known as April 6 when Roman designations came into use in Asia after Constantinople was established as the New Rome. It was on that fourteenth day of the first month of spring that Christians in Asia Minor celebrated Pascha, at first the only annual festival. As the only annual festival, it celebrated the entire mystery of our salvation by Christ, and paschal homilies of the second century show that the content of the observance included not only the passion, death, resurrection, and glorification of Christ, but also the incarnation in the womb of the Virgin. For that reason, it became customary to think of the conception and the death of the Lord as falling on the same day of the year. (Jewish lore tended to identify the birth and death dates of the patriarchs.) As that association of the conception with a fixed date for Pascha became settled, so it became possible to set the date of the birth nine months later, on the date that the Roman calendar would know as January 6.

That date, which we know as the Epiphany, now seems to have been known already to Clement of Alexandria as the date of the nativity around the turn of the second to the third century, and he knows of those who celebrated the baptism of Jesus in Jordan on the same date. This complex theme becomes even richer with the addition of the wedding feast at Cana, Christ's first miracle in which he "manifested forth his glory." Why should this feast have so many themes? A clue is offered in a later document, the so-called *Canons of Athanasius,* which identifies the Epiphany as the beginning of the year. What was it that began then? If we look at the beginning of the Gospel of Matthew we see that it opens with the nativity story. The Gospel of Mark, on the other hand, begins with the baptism of Jesus in the Jordan; and the Gospel of John, after the prologue, begins with the miracle at the Cana wedding feast. Allan MacArthur suggested long ago that the Epiphany marked the beginning of a course reading of John at Ephesus,[5] and it would be easy to believe that the same was true for Matthew at Jerusalem, where evidences of a course reading of Matthew are still clear in lectionaries of the fifth century. At Alexandria we have testimony for the celebration of Jesus' baptism in the Jordan, the opening of Mark's gospel, and also for a fast of forty days imitating the fast of Jesus beginning on January 7, as his trial in the wilderness followed immediately upon his baptism. In other words, the complex theme of Epiphany can be understood as reflecting the course reading of the locally preferred gospel, beginning on that day, nine months after the paschal date, which had come to be associated as well with the conception at the annunciation to Mary.

The fixed paschal date in Asia Minor had to do with the observance of Pascha on the biblical date, but in Africa and at Rome, where Pascha was kept in the night from Saturday to Sunday rather than a fixed date, a different need called for the determination of the Julian date on which 14 Nisan fell in the year of our Lord's death. The commemoration of the death dates of martyrs must have brought pressure to provide a historical date for the saving event mirrored in their deaths. On the basis of perhaps less than totally reliable data, it was determined that the passion occurred in 29 A.D., and that in that year the lunar date 14 Nisan fell on the Julian March 25, a Friday. Testimonies to this date for the passion appear already in the early third century, and (at a date that cannot be fixed with precision) this, too, came to be associated with the Lord's conception. An African work of the early fourth century says that March 25 "is the day of the passion of the Lord and of his conception." It is this association that lies behind the collect that concludes the Angelus, assigned to the Annunciation in *The Book of Common Prayer:* "that we who have known the incarnation of your Son Jesus Christ, announced by an angel to the Virgin Mary, may by his cross and passion be brought to the glory of his resurrection." As the association of the paschal date April 6 with the conception pointed to January 6 as the nativity date, so the association of March 25 with both the passion and the conception pointed to a nativity date of December 25, and this nativity date is first testified to in a list of martyrs' commemorations compiled at Rome in 336.

The question of the origin of Christmas, however, is complicated by the fact that the emperor Aurelian, seeking to establish a solar monotheism that would bring together, or at least moderate competition among Rome's many religious sects (the rapidly growing Christianity among them), established, in 274 A.D., a new festival of the sun on December 25, the traditional date of the winter solstice. Called *dies natalis solis invicti,* this "birthday of the invincible sun" achieved wide recognition throughout the empire, though not enough to prevent the durable gaffe of Epiphanius who, a century later, erroneously identified the Roman observance on December 25 as the Saturnalia.[6] Since the eighteenth century it has been standard to understand Aurelian's festival of the nativity of the sun to be the basis for the observance of the nativity of Jesus on the same date, December 25. It is pointed out that Christians made this the nativity of "the Sun of Righteousness," though less attention is given to that same appeal to Malachi 4:2 in discussion of the birth of Jesus prior to the accession of Aurelian (albeit not in relation to December 25). Some have suggested that Constantine, a known devotee of the sun before his conversion, played a role in the Christian adoption of Aurelian's feast. That, at least, seems improbable since he spent little time in Rome, and in his new Christian capital of Constantinople the nativity was not celebrated on December 25 until well after his death.

Although its first historical assertion comes from the twelfth century,[7] appeal to the influence of the Roman sun festival continues to be made, but whether the influence was from paganism upon Christianity or *vice versa* is perhaps slightly more ambiguous today than it seemed a few decades ago. Less ambiguous is the impact of the lengthening of the hours of daylight on the human spirit, and in the northern temperate zone (and especially its northern tier) this accorded an enthusiastic welcome to the festival so closely related to the solstice, whatever its relation to a Roman festival of the later third century. This welcome is noted at Rome in a Christmas sermon of Leo in the middle of the fifth century, and he is even then concerned that worshipers focus their attention not on the sun, but on the One who made it, suggesting that the "pagan" element was not forgotten. Whatever is to be said finally of pre-Christian influences on the celebration of the nativity on December 25, parallel attempts to find pagan roots for the Epiphany have been unsuccessful, depending as they do on uncritical claims for a supposedly widespread but unidentifiable festival of Dionysus, calendrical imprecisions, and problematic reminiscences of an aging Epiphanius of his visit to Alexandria as a youth.

In the last quarter of the fourth century a process of integration led to the adoption of Christmas in the Eastern empire and of the

Epiphany in Africa and Rome. At Constantinople and Antioch, where the Epiphany had celebrated both the nativity and baptism of Jesus, the nativity was transferred to December 25 and the January festival continued to celebrate Jesus' baptism in the Jordan. In Africa and Italy, however, the nativity story was divided so that the Epiphany began to celebrate the visit of the Magi. Just a bit earlier, a Christmas sermon of the African Optatus of Milevis makes it clear that the story of the Magi had once been included with the Bethlehem nativity on December 25. This division of the story had the effect of limiting the theme of Epiphany to "the manifestation of Christ to the gentiles," a more narrow concept than had attached to the festival earlier. In Gaul, Eastern influence had introduced the Epiphany before the December celebration of the nativity was adopted, and a richer range of themes continued to be associated with the Epiphany even after the adoption of Christmas. Known as the *tria miracula*, these are the visit of the Magi, the baptism in Jordan, and the Cana wedding feast, celebrated in many Epiphany antiphons and in some modern hymns (see, e.g., hymns 131 and 135 in *The Hymnal 1982*). A solitary testimony by Filastrius of Brescia in the final decade of the fourth century notes among the themes of Epiphany the transfiguration that now brings the Epiphany season to a close in some versions of the lectionary.

Lent

It was once common to say that our earliest reference to Lent was in a canon of the Council of Nicea (325 A.D.) calling for periodic local synods, one of them to be held "before the fortieth" *(pro tēs tesserakostēs)*. Today, that phrase is more likely to be interpreted as referring to the fortieth day of Easter. Nonetheless, the period of the Council of Nicea seems to be something of a watershed in regard to a fast of forty days before Pascha. Before Nicea we have clear evidence of a fast of six days in Syria and Alexandria, and more diffuse suggestions that there may have been a three-week preparation for Easter baptisms at Jerusalem and Rome. After the Council of Nicea, however, evidence for a forty-day fast before Pascha begins to appear, first in a Festal Letter of Athanasius from 330.[8] By the end of the century the fast is found everywhere, always referred to as being forty days, although the actual duration varied between six and seven weeks (and eventually eight weeks). Final catechesis for Easter baptisms took place during some or all of this fast, and it is the common view that this preparation for baptism was the reason for the emergence of the lenten season. Many historians, for that reason, have argued that the association of Lent with the forty-day fast of Jesus was a secondary development, artificially ascribing a scriptural model to the season. Gregory Dix, for example, said that if there were any connection between the fast of Jesus and Lent, we should expect the fast not before Easter but following the Epiphany, after that became the celebration of the baptism of Jesus, since it was immediately following the baptism that he was led by the spirit into the wilderness.

However, in 1967 there appeared an essay by the noted Coptologist, René-Georges Coquin, that for the first time presented an in-depth study of medieval documents of the Coptic Church claiming that in early Alexandria (well before the fourth century) the fast of forty days did, in fact, begin on January 7, the day following the Epiphany. Baptism was conferred in the sixth week of this fast, and the season came to a close on the following Sunday with a "Feast of Palms," celebrating Christ's entry into Jerusalem, still several weeks before the six-day fast leading to Pascha. In a subsequent paper published that same year, Coquin argued that it was as a dimension of the Council of Nicea's settlement of the date of Easter that the Alexandrian fast leading to baptism was adopted, but transferred so that it would connect with the older fast before Pascha, by then the dominant time for baptism in most of the Church. Where, as at Constantinople, the prepaschal fast was six days, Lent occupied the preceding six weeks, for a total of seven weeks. Where, as at Rome, the prepaschal fast was of only two days, Lent was just six weeks, including those two days.[9] Although this transfer of the fast of forty days severed its connection with the celebration of Jesus' baptism, Lent retained its original character as a commemorative imitation of the forty days of our Lord's fast in the wilderness.

For a long while, Lent was simply a continuous period of forty days counted without reference to the actual number of fast days. Sunday was not fasted, nor was Saturday in the East. A unique and difficult statement by the pilgrim Egeria says that Jerusalem in 383 extended the total fast to eight weeks so as to provide the full forty days of fasting. Apart from that unsubstantiated (and evidently contradicted) reference, it was only in the sixth and seventh centuries that the forty-day period was variously extended to make up the number of forty fast days. At Rome, this meant beginning the fast on the Wednesday before the old *Inicium Quadragesimae,* the Sunday that had marked the beginning of Lent, adding four more days to the thirty-six fasted during the earlier six weeks. That preceding Wednesday, *Caput Ieiunii,* became the day for enrollment of penitents, ceremonies that in Germany included sprinkling them with ashes before the beginning of Mass. That ceremony was eventually added to the enrollment of penitents at

Rome, and from the end of the eleventh century this ceremony of "ashing" was extended to all the faithful. It was still performed before the beginning of Mass, and at Mass the old gospel reading from Matthew 6 (from a time when this Wednesday was not yet reckoned to be the beginning of Lent) was retained and is still assigned to Ash Wednesday today. When the marking of the foreheads of the faithful with ashes follows after the reading of this gospel, as is usually the case today, a word of explanation may be required.

The lenten suppression of "Alleluia," although unknown in the Byzantine rite, has long been characteristic of the Western liturgy, but this has not always been limited to Lent itself. According to *The Rule of the Master*, a monastic rule from the early sixth century, a *centesima paschae* began on the day after Epiphany and was characterized by the suppression of the *Alleluia* from that day to Easter. The *Rule of St. Benedict*, while influenced by that earlier rule in other matters, says nothing of this extension of the fast, and orders the suppression of *Alleluia* only during Lent, without further specification. It was in the seventh century that Gregory the Great ordered what seems to be a compromise, the suppression of *Alleluia* from Septuagesima, the third Sunday before Lent. That season of "pre-Lent" has fallen victim to liturgical reform in this century, and now the suppression of the *Alleluia* is limited to the six weeks of Lent. Given the other concerns of that season, the sometimes colorful medieval ceremonies relating to the "Burial of the *Alleluia*" at vespers before the suppression have all but disappeared.

Holy Week

Although "Easter" refers to the feast that celebrates the resurrection, the Aramaic term *Pascha*, used in all the Mediterranean countries, can refer to either the fast day of the crucifixion or the day of the resurrection, or both. The very early celebration of *Pascha* in Asia Minor (on the Old Testament date without regard for the day of the week) included a fast on the Preparation of the Passover, a vigil from sundown, and the celebration of Eucharist at cockcrow. When that pattern was accommodated to the structure of the week elsewhere, the day of the fast was Saturday, and the vigil stretched through the night from Saturday to Sunday. That one-day fast on Saturday fell adjacent to the Friday fast day observed (with Wednesday) every week already attested in *Didache* at the end of the first century. By the time of Irenaeus in the second century it is clear that some kept a single fast day while others fasted two days, joining the Friday and Saturday.

The extension of the two days to six is testified to first in *Didascalia Apostolorum,* a Syrian church order of the first half of the third century. There the first four days are semi-fasts (kept only to the middle of the afternoon), by contrast to the strict fasts of Friday and Saturday. The reason given for this extension raises other interesting questions. We fast on Monday, it is explained, because then Judas made his treasonous compact with the priests. We fast on Tuesday because then the Lord ate the Passover with his disciples! We fast on Wednesday because then the Lord was arrested.

That unusual chronology putting the eating of Passover in the night from Tuesday to Wednesday has been traced by Annie Jaubert to the distinctive calendar followed by the sectaries at Qumran and embedded in *Jubilees,* an intertestamental work from the second century before our era. That calendar gave preeminence to the structure of the week, thus the year consisted of only 364 days (exactly 52 weeks), with the result that any date of any month would in every year fall on the same day of the week. Passover, the fifteenth day of the first month, always fell on Wednesday, the feast being eaten from sundown on Tuesday. If one follows Jaubert's argument that this was, in fact, the historical chronology of the passion, then a nagging problem of gospel chronology would be solved. According to the synoptic gospels, Jesus' last supper with his disciples was indeed the Passover. The gospel of John, on the other hand, makes it clear that Jesus was crucified at the time of the slaying of lambs for the feast at the Temple. The inconsistency is resolved if there were two different Passover dates involved, one followed by Jesus and his disciples and influenced by the calendar of Qumran, and the other the official lunar calendar followed at the Temple.

Although a few sources in the fourth century will explain the regular Wednesday fast as commemorative of the Lord's arrest, as that on Friday is of his death, the variant chronology of *Didascalia* failed to find a broad following, although the extension of the fast to six days did catch on elsewhere. As mentioned above, around the middle of the third century a fast of six days before Easter is announced by Dionysius of Alexandria. A century later a fast of six days before Pascha, known as "Great Week," seems to be general in the Eastern church, but by that time it was preceded by the fast of forty days. As suggested earlier, Rome seems to have retained a fast of but two days, Friday and Saturday, before the paschal feast on Sunday, and these constituted the original *triduum sacrum* at Rome. The original form of Lent at Rome, when it was added to those two days, ran from the Sunday of *Quadragesima* through the Thursday before Easter, and that Thursday (now known to us as "Maundy Thursday") was concerned primarily with the reconciliation of the penitents expelled at the beginning of Lent. A second function assigned to that day was the consecration of the chrism for Easter baptisms.

Today Holy Week opens with the Sunday before Easter, and the day bears a dual title, "Passion Sunday" and also "Palm Sunday." "Passion Sunday" is the older designation, going back to a time before the Church in the West adopted the procession with palms that now precedes the Eucharist. Such a procession down the Mount of Olives was reported at Jerusalem by the pilgrim Egeria in 383, and visitors to the Holy City carried the custom back to their homes in the West, where it was established first in Spain and Gaul. Rome was slow to adopt the palm liturgy, and the entry into Jerusalem was long a theme of the Advent liturgy.[10]

At Rome the Sunday before Easter was kept only as Passion Sunday, characterized by the reading of the Passion according to St. Matthew. In the Middle Ages a complex chant scheme for the passion led to the addition to the text of rubrical indications of tempo and style: "T" for *tarde* marked the words of Christ; "S" for *sonoriter* marked other direct quotations; "C" for *celeriter* indicated the narrative. In time, these were taken to indicate three separate singers, and the three "Passion Deacons" made their appearance. The "T" was transformed into a cross, and one deacon sang the "role" of Christus; the "S" was renamed (however improbably) *Synagoga;* and the "C" was taken to mean *Chronista.* With the coming of the period of *ars nova*, polyphonic choirs were admitted to the role of *Synagoga,* and the stage was set for the massive settings of the passions of Matthew (for Passion Sunday) and John (for Good Friday) that we have from such composers as J. S. Bach. In our own day this dramatic reading of the passion has found increased popularity in parish liturgies and has reinforced the identity of this day as the Sunday of the Passion.

In Byzantine tradition, on the other hand, the Sunday at the head of Great Week is given entirely to the celebration of Christ's entry into Jerusalem. This, like the Feast of Palms in primitive Alexandria, brings to a conclusion the fast of forty days, although in Alexandria that fast fell in the six weeks following the Epiphany. Nonetheless, already in the time of John Chrysostom at the end of the fourth century Palm Sunday at Constantinople was seen as the opening of Great Week. In fact, only the Gospel of John, which is read on Palm Sunday in the Byzantine rite, connects the entry into Jerusalem with the passion. Our present practice, presenting over the three years of the lectionary cycle the accounts of the entry and the passion from the three synoptic gospels, has been well served by the hymn writers who, in such compositions as "All Glory, Laud and Honor," have made the connection between the triumphal entry and the passion not made by the synoptic gospels themselves.

The first days of Holy Week, once characterized by the reading of the passions of Mark and Luke, are today much like other days of Lent. The distinctive rites of Holy Week resume on Maundy Thursday, long reckoned as the first day of a redefined "Paschal Triduum," since the time when the Paschal Vigil slipped back into Saturday, and eventually Saturday morning. The gospel at Mass on Thursday is, like the passion of Good Friday, from John, and therefore makes no mention of the institution of the Eucharist. The commemoration of the Last Supper as institution of the Eucharist, although reflected in the rites at Jerusalem in the late fourth century, came into play in the West only much later, a fact that probably contributed to the perception of a need for such a festival as Corpus Christi. The reforms of this century give some emphasis to that theme by the designation of the principal parish celebration as "The Mass of the Lord's Supper." John's account of the Last Supper describes the Lord's washing of his disciples' feet, and this was imitated by those in authority in monastic and cathedral settings, often as an extra-liturgical ceremony. The "Maundy" ceremony from the antiphon *Mandatum novum* gave this day its popular name. The general inclusion of the Maundy in the parish liturgy of the Latin Rite is a feature of the liturgical reforms of this century.

The Good Friday liturgy is notable chiefly for its archaism, preserving elements of the liturgy of a much earlier time, in keeping with the observation of Anton Baumstark that days of greatest solemnity are most resistant to change. The Prayers of the People, for instance, have retained the form these intercessions had in the patristic period. The passion narrative from the Gospel of John has been associated with this liturgy from our earliest evidences. At Rome, from around the beginning of the eighth century, this simple synaxis was preceded by the veneration (in the Basilica of the Holy Cross in Jerusalem) of a large fragment of the wood of the Cross, a devotion that was already characteristic of the Jerusalem rite in 383. Later in that same century a simple wooden cross was venerated in the *tituli* (local churches) of Rome, but that veneration fell after the Word liturgy and before the distribution of the presanctified Eucharist, as is the case today.

The first major liturgical reform in this century was surely the restoration of the Paschal Vigil, a rite that had been allowed to slip back into Saturday afternoon and, eventually, Saturday morning (giving rise to the once common assertion that Lent ends at noon on Saturday, by which time the first Mass of Easter had ended). Although it was frequently asserted that this anticipation of the Easter Vigil was a peculiarly occidental perversion, it is now recognized that the nocturnal celebration of Easter in the Byzantine rite is itself an anticipation of the morning prayer and Eucharist of Easter morning, and the Easter Vigil is celebrated (if at all) on Saturday morning or afternoon. The restoration of this liturgy to a true night vigil, however highly welcomed, has in fact fallen victim to anticipation again in less than half a century, and it is today common to find Easter Vigil celebrations that are ended well before midnight.

Nonetheless, the recovery of the Paschal Vigil has been a significant achievement of liturgical reform in this century. The rite opens with a Blessing of the New Fire, once characteristic of the evening office of Thursday, Friday, and Saturday. A vestige of that earlier custom was the triple candle carried in the procession at the beginning of the vigil. As the three intertwined candles were lighted, one by one, the deacon sang *Lumen Christi* on each occasion. Now that triple candle has disappeared, and it is the Paschal Candle itself that is carried by the deacon, who still, however, sings *Lumen Christi* three times as the people respond *Deo gratias*.

At the completion of the light ceremony, when other candles have been lighted, the deacon sings the Paschal Praise, or *Praeconium*. Historical sources reveal several texts of this chant, but that which has come down to us from Gallican sacramentaries, known as the *Exultet* from its incipit, is surely one of the jewels of liturgical poetry and chant in Western tradition, in spite of the fluidity of its frequently revised text.

At the heart of the Vigil liturgy is the series of readings from the Old Testament, a series first documented at Jerusalem in the first half of the fifth century. There were twelve readings then, and that number of readings was replicated in many other places, although with some variation. Such a series of twelve readings from eighth-century Gaul was preserved in the Roman Missal prior to the postconciliar reforms and can still be seen as an option in the Lutheran Book of Worship.

The original restoration of the Paschal Vigil reduced the readings to the four assigned at Rome in the time of Gregory the Great (and maintained at Salisbury into the sixteenth century). It has been argued that the establishment of a similar Vigil of Pentecost in the seventh century occasioned the division between the two vigils of an earlier series of seven Old Testament readings (one of them being used at both vigils). In any case, the present Roman Lectionary appoints seven Old Testament readings, while allowing for the use of as few as two of them. The American *Book of Common Prayer* gives nine Old Testament readings, of which at least two must be used, one of which must be (as also in the Roman Lectionary) the *Exodus* account of the delivery at the Red Sea.

From at least the third century, the Paschal Vigil was the occasion *par excellence* for the celebration of baptism. In the patristic age it was during the readings of the Vigil that the rites of Christian Initiation were performed in the baptistry, and the reforms of this century have been concerned to restore the baptismal element in the Paschal Vigil. Such is the major thrust of the Rite for the Christian Initiation of Adults, but even when in a given congregation there are none to be baptized the liturgy provides for a solemn renewal of baptismal vows by all present. The baptismal section of the liturgy leads directly into the Eucharist, which brings the Paschal Vigil to its conclusion. The days of Easter week were in many places given to the *Mystagogia,* instructions to the newly baptized explaining the sacraments they had received in the paschal night.

Pentecost

The earliest writer to refer explicitly to paschal baptism was Tertullian, around the turn of the second century to the third. The passage in his treatise on baptism shows clearly that this was not the only occasion for baptism, and also reveals the association of Passover with the death of the Lord and the Sunday of the resurrection as the beginning of the fifty days of Pentecost. He says, "The Passover provides the day of most solemnity for baptism, for then was accomplished our Lord's passion, and into it we are baptized . . . After that, Pentecost is a most auspicious period for arranging baptisms, for during it our Lord's resurrection was several times made known among the disciples, and the grace of the Holy Spirit first given."[11] He acknowledges, however, that baptism can be conferred at any time, and that the grace is the same, whatever the difference in solemnity.

The celebration of the resurrection over an unbroken period of fifty days reflects a similar period between Passover and the Feast of Weeks in the Old Testament, although in the beginning of our era various Jewish groups began the counting of the fifty differently, some from the morrow of Passover, others from the day following the Sabbath after Passover. The fifty day period, a "week of weeks" plus a concluding festival day, is believed to have been the basic unit of a very ancient West Asiatic calendar antedating the Jewish lunar calendar. This would account for the fact that the Feast of Weeks, unlike the other great Jewish festivals of Passover and Tabernacles, lasted but a single day. Testimonies from the second century show that Christians observed these fifty days in celebration of the resurrection, and during this time they never knelt in prayer, nor was fasting practiced. By the late fourth century there are signs in Jerusalem of a special penitential service at the end of the fiftieth day, during which worshipers once again knelt in prayer. Almost universally, normal fast practice was resumed on the day after the fiftieth day.

Although Tertullian, in the passage cited above, spoke of the pentecost as a period of fifty days, by the opening of the fourth century the final, fiftieth day, was being singled out as being itself the feast of Pentecost. Indeed, the Greek version of the Old Testament in one place uses that Greek word, *pentekostê,* to refer to the Feast of Weeks. As a distinct festival, Pentecost celebrated the ascension of our Lord and the descent of the Holy Spirit upon the Church. By the end of the fourth century, however, some had begun to celebrate the ascension on the fortieth day after Easter, on the basis of the statement in Acts 1:3 that the Lord appeared to his followers during forty days. Such was the case at Brescia in northern Italy, where, contrary to the teaching of earlier authorities, the bishop Filastrius tells us that a preparatory fast preceded the ascension festival. He does not say how long a fast that was, but in the following century Mammertus at Vienne is credited with establishing litany processions with fasting on the three days preceding the ascension.[12] In the course of the fifth century the observance of the ascension on the fortieth day became universal, and tended increasingly to signal the end of Paschaltide through such ceremonies as extinguishing the paschal candle on that day. Slowly, one began to hear less about the fifty days of paschal rejoicing, and more about "the Great Forty Days."

The Council of Nicea in its twentieth canon ruled that prayer should be made standing on Sundays and during the fifty days of Easter, but that canon itself reflects that this custom was not universal at that time. Nonetheless, apart from the question of posture at prayer, a major concern of liturgical reform in this century has been the restoration of the integrity of the fifty days of Easter. The feast of Pentecost has been restored to but a single day's observance, no longer with an octave, and the paschal candle that was formerly extinguished after the gospel on ascension day now burns through the day of Pentecost. Where they are still observed, the Pentecost ember days again solemnize the resumption of normal fast practice after Paschaltide. In general, we may say that Eastertide has now very much the shape it had up to the end of late antiquity.

Festivals after Pentecost

With the termination of Eastertide on the day of Pentecost we may say that the original pattern of the liturgical year is complete. In fact, however, the seasons we have examined occupy only about half the year. Nonetheless, other festivals, not a part of the seasonal cycle, have grown up in the time after Pentecost. The earliest of these is the commemoration of all the martyrs, the earliest All Saints' Day, for which we have a sermon of St. John Chrysostom delivered at Antioch late in the fourth century. This is also reflected in the extension of the suspension of fasting through the Sunday after Pentecost in the Syrian church order, *Apostolic Constitutions* (V.20.14), in the late fourth century. That this date for the celebration of All Saints, still maintained in the Byzantine rite, was for a time observed in the West as well is suggested by an entry for this Sunday in the *Comes* of Würzburg, an old Roman epistle list reflecting practice of the sixth century. Since that reference is unique in the extant occidental evidence, it is impossible to know how long or how widely that commemoration was observed. However, in that epistle list the Pentecost Embertide, marking the resumption of normal fast practice after Eastertide, has been shifted to follow the *Dominica in natale sanctorum,* the Sunday after Pentecost, in much the same way as the resumption of fasting was delayed for a week in the Syria of *Apostolic Constitutions* in the late fourth century.

Early in the seventh century, permission was granted by the emperor Phocas for the conversion to Christian use of the Pantheon, a magnificent temple built by Hadrian in the second century on the site of an earlier foundation by Marcus Agrippa, the first such conversion of a pagan temple in Rome. The consecration as "the Church of the Holy Mother of God and all Christian martyrs" by Boniface IV took place, evidently, on May 13, 609. This dedication date seems to have quickly displaced the Sunday after Pentecost as the occasion for the commemoration of all martyrs at Rome, and hordes of pilgrims began to ascend on the city on that date, placing a strain on food supplies available from the previous harvest, according to one later testimony. Such, at least, was one reason given for the subsequent shift of the commemoration of All Saints by Gregory IV to a date shortly following the harvest, November 1. That had been a Druid feast of the dead, *Samhain,* given a Christian reinterpretation and introduced by Alcuin of York into Germany, where it was widely promulgated from the late eighth century.

Eventually, the Pentecost Embertide was moved back into the week following Pentecost, in spite of the festal octave that had grown up there. The ember Saturday was observed with an all-night vigil at St. Peter's, but this, as we have seen with the Paschal Vigil, began to drift back into Saturday. Since that included the Eucharist that ended the vigil on Sunday morning, that Sunday (like others following ember Saturdays) was designated *Dominica vacat* in liturgical books, inviting improvisation. In some places a votive Mass of the Holy Trinity was being assigned to this Sunday by the end of the first millennium, and the establishment of that Sunday as the Feast of the Holy Trinity came along in time, in spite of some opposition. In England and some religious orders the following Sundays were denominated "after Trinity," rather than "after Pentecost," and that usage was continued in the *Book of Common Prayer* until the revision of 1979.

By the time of the universal promulgation of the Feast of the Holy Trinity (by John XXII in 1334) the following Thursday, the first free Thursday after the Pentecost octave, had been assigned for the celebration of the institution of the Eucharist on the Feast of Corpus Christi, an observance commended to the Church by Urban IV in 1264, but one which became universal only in the following century. Its assignment to Thursday reflects the recognition that the institution of the Eucharist had not been celebrated on Thursday of Holy Week, precluded perhaps by the solemnity of passiontide, but also, as suggested above, by the tradition that assigned to both Thursday and Friday of Holy Week the Gospel of John, in which the account of the Last Supper does not mention the institution of the Eucharist.

The remaining Sundays of the year fall within two neutral zones, Sundays after Epiphany and Sundays after Pentecost. In the Latin rite these are supplied by a single series of Sundays *anni circuli,* a phrase that has defied easy translation but is usually rendered "Sundays in ordinary time" in English. Those are assigned to the Sundays after Epiphany until Ash Wednesday, and the series is resumed after Pentecost. The Episcopal Church, having previously defined the First Sunday of Advent as the Sunday nearest the Feast of St. Andrew (November 30), whether before or after that feast, controls the Sundays after Pentecost by that same convention, assigning a collect and readings to Sundays nearest fixed dates. The Sundays after Epiphany are distinct, leading toward the reading of accounts of the Transfiguration on the Sunday before Ash Wednesday, a Lutheran custom adopted by others as well.

In all Western traditions in this country today the Sundays after Pentecost begin to reflect eschatological themes as they approach Advent, and the final Sunday of the time after Pentecost is the Feast of Christ the King. Assigned to the final Sunday of October at the time of its promulgation by Pius XI, it has been reassigned to the final

Sunday of the liturgical year since 1970, and brings the year to an appropriate conclusion, leading into the eschatological themes of the beginning of Advent.

Such is the seasonal cycle that unfolds the mystery of our redemption in Christ, even as do the gospels that are proclaimed in our celebration of that redemption. Alongside this seasonal cycle is the calendar of saints, the feasts of our brothers and sisters whose lives were spent in the service of Christ. At first only martyrs, but then bishops and others, this company of the holy ones reveals the power of the Cross in all of Christian history, and points us back to the center of our sacred time and all time, the living remembrance of the Paschal Mystery of the Redeemer who has come and who comes, unto the consummation of the age.

Notes

1. *The Origins of the Liturgical Year,* 2nd emended edition (Collegeville: The Liturgical Press, 1991).

2. J. Neil Alexander, *Waiting for the Coming* (Washington, D.C.: The Pastoral Press, 1993) 18–19.

3. Cited here from *Nicene and Post-Nicene Fathers,* Series II, Vol. XII, p. 127.

4. John Moolan, *The Period of Annunciation-Nativity in the East Syrian Calendar: Its Background and Place in the Liturgical Year,* Oriental Institute of Religious Studies, India, Vol. 90 (Vadavathoor, Kottayam, 1985).

5. A.A. MacArthur, *The Evolution of the Christian Year* (London: SCM Press, 1953) 69.

6. The Saturnalia fell on December 17 and marked the beginning of a series of year-end festivals that stretched into January, a period during which a council at Saragossa in 380 urged the constant presence of the faithful in church. The influence of these pagan observances can be seen in the beginning of the Great O Antiphons with *O Sapientia* on December 17 (although an added antiphon in England led to December 16 for *O Sapientia* in English calendars). These are, of course, the antiphons known in verse form as "O Come, O Come, Emmanuel."

7. This is in a Syriac gloss on a work of Dionysius bar Salibi, arguing against the celebration of the nativity on December 25 instead of January 6.

8. These Festal Letters were issued annually on the Epiphany by the Patriarchs of Alexandria, announcing the date of Pascha and the beginning of the prepaschal fast. Earlier letters refer only to the fast of six days, mentioned first by Dionysius of Alexandria in the third century.

9. At Alexandria there were at first only six weeks, even though the older prepaschal fast was of six days.

10. Anglican readers may recall that editions of the *Book of Common Prayer* before the present one had the account of the entry into Jerusalem

as the gospel on the First Sunday of Advent. This had earlier been reckoned the Second Sunday of Advent when the season had five Sundays.

11. *De baptismo* 19. Cited here from E. C. Whitaker, *Documents of the Baptismal Liturgy* (London: S.P.C.K., 1970) 9.

12. These came to be known as the rogation days.

Chapter 3

Liturgical Assembly:
Who Is the Subject of Liturgy?

Joyce Ann Zimmerman, C.PP.S.

It is very surprising to me that more has not been written on the nature and function of the liturgical assembly, since *Sacrosanctum Concilium* and the subsequent renewal it inspired have emphasized so much the active role of the liturgical assembly. Perhaps because we have largely limited our interpretation of "active" to *doing things* (singing, responding, processing, ministering, etc.), as important as that aspect may be, have we really limited the fuller role of the assembly as "co-celebrants" with the presider, united with Christ in offering up the one Sacrifice. We wish in this chapter to explore this fuller participation of the liturgical assembly.

My remarks are divided into four main sections: (1) a review of recent literature and statement of the problematic; (2) a summary exposition of French philosopher Paul Ricoeur's hermeneutics of the subject; (3) application of Ricoeur's theory to the domain of liturgy, addressing the question, "Who is the subject of liturgy?"; and (4) new directions for understanding the nature and function of the liturgical assembly teased out from our exposition and analyses. The middle two sections may seem dense and a bit obtuse for someone not versed in Paul Ricoeur or not used to taking a philosophical approach to liturgical studies. To be sure, this is not the only way to delve into the subject, as a perusal of the literature would bear out. The advantage of drawing on Ricoeur is to show the richness of a hermeneutical approach and to demonstrate an analysis of liturgical matters of import using post-critical methods. In other words, the methodological implications are as significant as the liturgical content and implications.

1. Literature and Problematic

The scant corpus of literature on the liturgical assembly published after Vatican II draws heavily on the achievements of scholars who wrote in the decades immediately preceding the Council and leading up to it. Catherine Vincie ably summarizes this work.[1] She notes that the agenda of the liturgical movement by midcentury was to recover the communal nature of liturgical prayer. To this end, the writers focused on three issues: the fact of liturgical assembling, patterns of the assembly's liturgical participation, and developing a theology of the assembly based on biblical and theological foundations.[2]

Drawing especially on the work of Martimort and Maertens,[3] Vincie points out the main lines of these thinkers' approach to an understanding of the nature and function of the liturgical assembly. The identification of assembly with Church is its earliest biblical and theological expression, but this got sidetracked when the small assemblies (mostly in rural areas) belied this concept in practice. Since the whole assembly gathered around the *episcopoi* was a concretization of "gathering together in one place," when this was no longer possible due to the growth in numbers, the visible manifestation was lost; the problematic of relating the part to the whole developed. As time went on, the assembly as concretization of Church was "reduced to a symbolic presence in the person of the presiding minister."[4] Such was the climate inherited by the liturgical movement, and their agenda was to recapture the symbolic meaning of the assembly itself at the level of self-understanding and pastoral practice.[5] In the very assembling, the Church both instills and strengthens its identity as God's assembly; the liturgical assembly is the Church in *act,* the Church becoming itself and manifesting the fullness of its being.[6]

This is the liturgical climate in which the Council Fathers were guided by the Holy Spirit, deliberated, and made their decisions. Three specific responsibilities of the liturgical assembly stated in *Sacrosanctum Concilium* are consonant with this previous work, notably, liturgy is a public—not private—function, the assembly is a unified body but differentiated in its ministries (SC §26), and the full, conscious, and active participation of the assembly is to be fostered (SC §14).[7] All of the works published after the Council essentially deal in one way or another with the same problematic; that is, the identity of assembly as Church.

Serge Heitz[8] boldly asks the question "What is an assembly?" and offers three components to his answer: it involves the Church, it is summoned by Christ, and it makes us sharers in the eschaton.[9] He gets to the heart of the problem when he writes that "the liturgical assembly is characterized by what I might call the primacy of being. That is, it transcends the psychological, intellectual, volitional and emotive levels, whether individual or social, although it certainly gathers these up and integrates them into the ontological sphere."[10] Heitz never really goes into the ontology of the liturgical assembly, but he intimates his grasp of the implications an ontological approach opens up. He develops his remarks by drawing on the notion of Tradition. Tradition (with an upper case "T") is the handing over of the "divine mysteries," concretized in the liturgical assembly "by means of the historical traditions [with a lower case "t"] which express it."[11] Christian Tradition carries the freight of meaning. Two corollaries follow from this. First, Heitz asserts that the whole is in the parts and the window to the whole is in the parts, and, second, the present liturgical assembly concretizes the mystery of Christ in the here and now.[12]

John Gallen[13] also insists that the assembly is the Church; further, the "assembly is the technical word in general usage to describe the gathered liturgical community."[14] He mentions both the assembly's Christological character and its ecclesiological character,[15] but then develops the rest of his article along practical, pastoral considerations (e.g., the liturgical ministries) and leaves the ontological questions open. Once again we have someone who is asserting an ontological identity but who gives us no clues as to the implications.

Critique. These representative authors and their insights have much to recommend. Let us briefly assess some of their strengths and weaknesses.

Catherine Vincie mentions three major contributions of the pre-conciliar writers. She notes that they considered the assembly in itself apart from its acts or function; this paves the way for the assembly to be considered as a *sign* (to use preconciliar language; today we would use "symbol") of the Church and raises the question of the assembly as the subject of liturgy. Second, these authors all underscore the close relationship between the theology of the liturgical assembly and ecclesiology.[16] Third, they explored characteristics of the liturgical assembly, including its inclusive and communal nature while at the same time recognizing differentiation and ordering of ministries.[17] Vincie also aims three criticisms. First, the preconciliar writers did not employ an interdisciplinary approach, omitting the great contributions sociology, politics, ritual studies, cultural anthropology, and psychology could make to the discussion. Second, these authors, in her opinion, lacked critical suspicion; they presented their theology of the assembly in idealistic, theological terms that inadequately reflect the reality at hand. Third (and flowing from the second criticism), they indiscriminately accepted the hierarchicalization of men and women in the Church, at the expense of women in ministry.[18] In a concluding section to her article, Vincie raises some questions she believes confront the North American Church and its liturgical practice:

> [1] Should we even bother coming together in liturgical assembly and what purpose does it serve? [2] How much diversity is possible in a liturgical assembly and what sort of unity can we achieve? [3] What are the implications for inculturation of the liturgy in light of such diversity? [4] How are we to resolve our conflicts over roles and relationships in our assemblies and in our Church? [5] Does the conflict and the struggle have meaning and value? [6] How ought local assemblies (e.g., parish) to be in relationship with one another and how ought local Churches (e.g., diocesan or regional) to be in relationship with one another?[19]

I readily recognize the intent and value of these questions, but I am fearful that they project contemporary concerns and insights back onto a former era that had very different concerns. Our contemporary sharply-focused problems were not—and, probably could not have been—so sharply focused fifty years ago. This is equivalent to saying that today we are able to ask the questions pertinent to the Church of 2050 C.E. It is always a temptation of a critical method to bring a context that is inappropriate to bear on a text. Actually, then, Vincie's critique is aimed at where she wishes her predecessors' research might have led them rather than aimed at the actual data they presented in the context of the Church of their era. Given their context, their theology of assembly is insightful and quite far reaching. On the other hand, Vincie's questions and critique are appropriate for our own Church and context. The reality that we are not "officially" moving forward with any significant progress on these important questions and challenges will no doubt be content for theologians' critique and comments in the not too distant future.

Vincie rightly comments that more work is needed relating the local and contemporary Church and there needs to be more clarity and reflection on the liturgical assembly as an eschatological presence.[20] However, very important to the overall discussion is her failure to raise specifically the ontological questions. Indeed, Vincie is bound by the same critical methodological limitations as the authors she is analyzing. To really gain new direction and a new perspective on a theology of the assembly—in other words, to plumb the ontological implications of the anticipated identity of assembly and Church—we must look to a different methodology that shifts the methodological limitations. Vincie's work is strong in analyzing available data (which is what her predecessors did) and drawing conclusions from it, but she is limited as well. The two-fold question becomes, How do we capitalize on past insights for our own context? and, How does our own context shape our reading of past insights?

Problematic. The literature both before and after the Council leads us to the central issue: the identity of the liturgical assembly with Church and the concomitant ontological questions that identity presupposes. All of the key issues are raised: identity, the relation of the parts to the whole, the nature of liturgical participation and hierarchy of ministers, the question of time and space and how we make the Paschal Mystery of the past present at the same time that the eschaton of the future is present, the relationship of being and action. All of these issues are rightly raised—and this attests to keen insight—but these authors are methodologically limited in how far they can go in providing answers or new directions.

The data recovered from texts using historical-critical methods are invaluable. Invariably it leads to putting our finger on the central questions and issues. However, too often the questions that arise from our own historical context cannot be addressed by using these methodologies. It is interesting to note that two authors who take the questions in a new direction both employ post-critical methods.

Gail Ramshaw[21] speaks of metaphors of human identity; this language suggests that the ontological domain can be approached only indirectly. Language itself discloses meaning and identity. So, for example, she builds a case that liturgy is corporate, based on evidence that there are few self-reflexive references in the liturgical text. W. Alan Smith,[22] though not speaking to liturgy but to religious education, nonetheless offers us some clues for interpretation when he remarks that "a truly dialogical community cannot be based on inequality, injustice, or dehumanization."[23] The self-disclosure of unity appropriate to the liturgical assembly takes place because liturgy is a dialogue of equal subjects.

We are being teased. We are ever so close to that critical but illusive center. These authors all bring us to a pivotal insight: liturgical assembly is the epiphany of the Church. When the assembly gathers, the Church is visible. The theology is there. What eludes us is any further explication. We need other methodological tools, and the post-critical methods are ready-at-hand. In particular, Paul Ricoeur's work on a hermeneutics of the subject[24] will be our guiding post.

2. Ricoeur's Hermeneutics of the Subject

My purpose in this second section of the chapter is not to summarize Ricoeur's hermeneutics of the subject; this would be unduly long and tedious, and much of it would not relate to the task at hand. Rather, I intend to weave together aspects of his thought that I believe are helpful for getting a handle on a theology of liturgical assembly. Ricoeur's hermeneutics of the subject gives us tools to address a number of knotty problems that have plagued any integral approach to a theology of the liturgical assembly; namely, the ontological underpinnings of the liturgical assembly, its nature and function, dualism, and the relation of liturgy and life. Further, the question, "Whose domain is liturgy?" is also given a different perspective.

Early on in his writings, Ricoeur addressed the notion of subject.[25] So a hermeneutics of the subject is hardly a new theme for Ricoeur. Happily enough, though, it is a seminal enough topic for Ricoeur to have warranted a systematic volume which captures the richness of his later thought.[26] My intent is not to detail the arguments of *Oneself As Another;* this would lead us too far astray from the purposes of this chapter.[27] Rather, I wish to sketch out the main lines of the methodology Ricoeur employs and the important consequences of this approach. In the third section of this essay I will spell out implications for liturgy, especially with respect to the question of the subject of liturgy.

Paralleling the method of his indirect approach to ontology,[28] Ricoeur also approaches his hermeneutics of the subject by rejecting any immediate positing of the subject, whether it be the "exalted subject" of Heidegger or the "humiliated subject" of Nietzsche (pp. 1 and 16). Instead, Ricoeur engages an indirect, triadic method that *describes* (first four studies [chapters]), *narrates* (studies 5 and 6), and *prescribes* (studies 7 to 9). He thus offers four different ways to answer the question, "Who?": "Who is speaking?" "Who is acting?" "Who is telling her or his story?" "Who is the moral subject to whom the right or wrong is imputed?" (pp. 16 and 169). Ricoeur begins his analysis by pointing out identifying textual references to a subject (gleaned from language and action) in order to posit personal identity; then he shows how the temporality particular to narrative identity grants to the speaking or acting subject a history, and, finally, he analyzes the ethical and moral determinations of actions in order to bring his hermeneutics of the subject to bear back on the subject. It is this return to the subject that is so essential to Ricoeur and the final movement in a philosophy of the subject that a semiotics alone cannot deliver. The return to the subject guarantees a shattering of solipsism such that Ricoeur's hermeneutics of the subject is wholly dialectical; self is always mediated by the other.

Three "philosophical intentions" thread their way throughout the volume and give coherent structure to his method: (1) "to indicate the primacy of reflective meditation over the immediate positing of the subject" (p. 1); (2) "to distinguish two major meanings of 'identity,'" namely, identity as *ipse* (self) and identity as *idem* (same) (p. 2); and (3) to show that "*ipse*-identity involves a dialectic complementary to that of selfhood and sameness, namely the dialectic of *self* and the *other than self*," strongly suggesting that "the selfhood of oneself implies otherness to such an intimate degree that one cannot be thought of without the other" (p. 3). Although every one of these three philosophical intentions is included to some degree in each of the ten studies that make up *Oneself As Another*, they veritably outline the three major divisions of his volume: studies 1 to 4 deal with analyses of language and action that focus on personal identity; studies 5 and 6, through the detour of narrative analysis and narrative identity, focus on the dialectic of selfhood and sameness; and studies 7 to 9 focus on a dialectic of self and the other. A final, tenth study sketches out the ontological direction of Ricoeur's hermeneutics of the subject. We now turn in more detail to each of these three methodic moments.

1. Description: Analysis of Language and Action. Ricoeur begins with an analysis of the person from the perspective of identifying reference. By "identify," at this initial stage, Ricoeur simply means that "to identify something is to be able to make apparent to others, amid a range of particular things of the same type, of *which* one we intend to speak" (27). In other words, this first step is simply one of distinguishing "this" from all others. The starting point is language, since language itself has certain "indicators" that posit an identifying reference. These indicators include definite descriptions (for example, the person who presides at liturgy, the cantor), proper names (Lord, Jesus Christ), or pronouns and demonstratives (I, you, this, here, now, etc.; 28–30). Ricoeur adopts the strategy of an "irreducible concept," which he designates "basic particulars" (31, following P.F. Strawson). With respect to identifying reference, Ricoeur equates "basic particular" with the notion of "person." It is important to point out that at this early stage of the analysis all we are identifying is a *person spoken about,* as pointed to in language use. We are saying nothing yet about a *speaking* subject (31 and 32). Further, "person" is a single referent with two predicates, namely, "physical predicates which the person shares with bodies, and mental predicates which distinguish it from bodies" (36). In this way, Ricoeur handily dispels mind-body dualism by demonstrating from semantic analysis how there may be a double attribution without a double reference: "two series of predicates for one and the same entity" (36).

In the first study Ricoeur is careful to avoid any reflexive approach to person. In the second study, however, he introduces a pragmatic approach and moves to where context makes a difference (40). It is the utterance, the act of speaking, which "designates the speaker reflexively" (40). Speech act theory establishes the relationship between an utterance and the interlocutors *in the very act of speaking.* To take a classic example, "I promise" is more than a simple statement of fact; the very utterance binds the speaker to a course of action (to fulfill the promise) as well as binds the speaker to the one spoken to (the one to whom the promise is made).[29] The second study moves our quest for the subject beyond simply positing a person *spoken about* to the subject as a couple made up of both speaker and the one spoken to (52). Ricoeur intersects these initial analyses at the point where, by naming (54), the "I" (subject of the utterance) is assimilated to the person (the basic particular; 52).

Studies 3 and 4 trace out from the viewpoint of a theory of action the relationship of action and agent. Ricoeur parallels these two studies on the analyses of action with the analyses of semantics and pragmatics which he took up in the first two studies. Now Ricoeur approaches the question, "Who acts?" from the purview of two other questions ("What?" and "Why?") that have been the focus of other analytic philosophers. Beginning with a critique of "An Agentless Semantics of Action," Ricoeur shows the logical defect of those who concentrate on the "'what' of action without thematizing its relation to the 'who'" (62). He asserts that these philosophers' over-concern about the truth of the description of an action overshadowed "any interest in assigning the action to its subject" (72). Even with the introduction of the notion of intentionality by a conceptual analysis, the surplus between the "What?" and "Why?" remains illusive. Ricoeur suggests that a phenomenology of attestation leads the "What?" question back to "Who?" and this is what is at stake in his analytical approach.

In the fourth study, "From Action to the Agent," Ricoeur reverses the starting point and asks the question, "Is it possible, basing our inquiry on a pragmatics of discourse, to follow the chain of questions in the opposite direction—in other words, to move back from the pair 'what?-why?' to the pivotal question 'who?'?" (88). The key to this backward movement is Ricoeur's use of the resources of ascription (and the coming to the forefront of the epistemological role of attestation). These resources include the understanding that (1) ascription implies that "an agent must be able to *designate himself or herself* in such a way that there is a genuine *other* to whom the same attribution is made in a relevant manner" (98), so that we move from a semantics to a pragmatics of action whereby the meaning of a proposition varies according to the specific speech situation involving an "I" and a "you"; (2) ascription is not the same thing as description because ascribing has an affinity with prescription whereby the agent is "responsible for actions which themselves are considered to be permissible or not permissible" (99; we will see below where a notion of "imputation" figures importantly in Ricoeur's discussion of ethics and morality); and (3) the "power to act" implies that it is within the agent's power so to act (101), whereby a concept of efficient causality leads to a notion of "basic actions" that is "to the theory of action what basic particulars are to the theory of identifying reference" (103). It is finally in the power to act that the "Who?" of action can be related to "Why?" through the "What?" of the action (110). By not tying a theory of action into distinguishing action from other events (noting that action is not a subset of events), Ricoeur is free to explore a theory of action in relation to the question of the self.

At the end of these four studies, Ricoeur has only been able to show—point in the direction of—a partial and abstract determination of selfhood. He is seeking an ever more concrete (phenomenological) determination of the subject. Thus, we leave his internal critique of semantics and pragmatics (of both person and action) with its focus on personal identity to pursue two pivotal studies that explore narrative identity. Our brief summary draws to a conclusion the initial step in Ricoeur's triadic methodology, that of describing. We now turn toward the middle term of Ricoeur's triadic method, narrating (which can be a mediating term between description [what is] and prescription [what ought to be] "only if the broadening of the practical field and the anticipation of ethical considerations are implied in the very structure of the act of narrating" [115]).

2. Narrativity: Analysis of Temporality and Historicity. Whether we consider the person of whom we are speaking or the agent on whom action depends, both the speaking subject and the acting agent have a history of their own (113). This brings back to the forefront the two notions of identity that Ricoeur introduced early on, identity as *sameness* (*idem*-identity) and identity as *selfhood* (*ipse*-identity; 116). Narrativity, with its inherent temporality and historicity, interjects the possibility of *permanence in time* that is exclusively connected to sameness (116). Ricoeur asks yet another leading question: "Is there a form of permanence in time that is a reply to the question 'Who am I?'" (118). Study 5, "Personal Identity and Narrative Identity," is an initial answer to this question. He posits two models of permanence: *character* ("the set of distinctive marks which permit the reidentification of a human individual as being the same," 119) and *keeping one's word* (118). The study elucidates the dialectic between character, in which *idem*-identity and *ipse*-identity almost coincide (118), and keeping one's word, by which the self is freed from sameness (119).

Study 6, "The Self and Narrative Identity," carries "to a higher level the dialectic of sameness and selfhood implicitly contained in the notion of narrative identity" (140). Narrative's structure, by means of the emplotment of events, permits the integration of permanence in time as well as the possibility of innovation, diversity, difference (see 140). Ricoeur makes the startling statement that "characters, we will say, are themselves plots" (143). Narrative displays a dialectic *between* action and character that parallels the "concordance and discordance developed by the emplotment of action" (147). Interestingly enough, "every action has its agents and its patients" and so "the theory of action is extended from acting to suffering beings" (157). Finally, Ricoeur notes that literary narrative has a recognizable beginning and ending,[30] but life histories differ from literary ones. We neither remember our beginning nor can predict our ending; yet, in spite of the many choices and detours (the stories within our larger life story, so to speak), our life is a totality, a unity (160–61). And, because narrative comes out of life and returns to life (163), it necessarily raises the question of the "good" and the "obligatory," which moves the analysis toward the next three studies.

3. Prescription: Analysis of Ethics and Morality. The next three studies return to the question of self, with its ethical aim (Study 7), its moral norm (Study 8), and the practical wisdom or conviction that mediates these (Study 9). Ricoeur begins by distinguishing between ethics (which has as its aim "the good") and morality (which is concerned with obligation and the articulation of norms; 170). With respect to the self, the ethical aim is directed to self-esteem, and moral obligation concerns self-respect (171). Ricoeur asserts that the primacy of ethics over morality minimizes the distance between what is and what ought to be. The ethical intention is aimed at the good life (self-esteem), with and for others (solicitude), in just institutions (justice) (172). In this way Ricoeur comes to show how any hermeneutics of the subject is necessarily bound up with others. In fact, others are the mediating condition of self, which assures that there is a return to the subject. The term Ricoeur uses here is "imputability," the "ascription of action to its agent, *under the condition of ethical and moral predicates* which characterize the action as good, just, conforming to duty, done out of duty, and, finally, as being the wisest in the case of conflictual situations" (292). These three studies on ethics, morality, and conviction bring into sharp focus the dialectic between self and other. In the closing remarks to the ninth study, Ricoeur chooses the term *recognition* to name the category corresponding to the categories of imputability and responsibility, and says that "recognition is a structure of the self reflecting on the movement that carries self-esteem toward solicitude and solicitude toward justice" (296).

The final, tenth study addresses the question, "What ontology is in view?" Consistent with his earlier work on ontology, Ricoeur rejects positing any direct road to ontology and, rather, embraces the indirect path of reflection and analysis. Both selfhood and attestation have an ontological vehemence, but it is in Ricoeur's conception of otherness whereby he concludes that any existential category that arises from a hermeneutics of the self is that of "thrownness" (327), a being delivered over to oneself, but, nonetheless, a being who also is passive, which opens the way for another being to act on the self. Ricoeur's conception of otherness, then, is two-pronged: "one that does justice in turn to the primacy of self-esteem and also to the primacy of the convocation to justice coming from the other" (331). Ultimately, this links up with the two notions of identity that Ricoeur has traced throughout, that of the same as *idem* and the self as *ipse*.

Ricoeur leads us through many pages of reflection in which he proceeds cautiously and thoroughly through lengthy analytic detours to accomplish his phenomenological analysis of the subject. Ricoeur makes mighty demands on his reader because he draws on a broad spectrum of dialogue partners ranging from Plato and Aristotle among the ancient philosophers, through the medieval philosophers, all the way to the German transcendentalists and the contemporary analytic philosophers. And after ten studies of careful analysis, what have we gained toward a hermeneutics of the subject? Ricoeur has shown us that selfhood is recoverable through a phenomenological analysis of texts; that the phenomenological analysis uncovers a dialectic of sameness and selfhood; that the recovery of selfhood is mediated by others. It remains our task to see what this might say about recovering the subject of liturgy from liturgical texts.

3. Who Is the Subject of Liturgy?

At first glance, the question, "Who is the subject of liturgy?" is a straightforward one, albeit answered variously throughout liturgical history. Early on (see the Letter to the Hebrews), we might have answered "Christ, the high priest." During medieval times we might have asserted "The priest, of course!" The liturgical movement and the vision of Vatican II push us to look to the liturgical assembly for an answer. Indeed, in our contemporary Eucharistic rite, all three proposals about the agent of liturgical action—Christ, the presider, the liturgical assembly—are variously supported. However, like Ricoeur, we wish to avoid positing a subject of liturgy too quickly. We will follow reflective detours, as does Ricoeur, to try to answer the question, "Who is the subject of liturgy?"

1. Description: Analysis of Language and Action. The liturgical text itself supports any number of possible candidates for the subject of liturgy, as evidenced by various textual "indicators" that posit an identifying reference. We noted above three references to a subject of liturgy that we can glean from a historical perusal. An examination of the texts themselves delivers helpful data for our analysis.

Sacrosanctum Concilium asserts Christ is present in his Word (§7), and certainly the dialogue beginning and ending the proclamation of the Gospel ("Glory to *you*, O Lord"; "Praise to *you*, Lord Jesus Christ") suggests a personal presence in the very proclamation. Moreover, use of the second person address followed by the first person singular quotation in the prayer preceding the exchange of a sign of peace ("I leave you peace, my peace I give you") is another textual indication of Christ as interlocutor. Further, the apostolic, trinitarian greeting at the very beginning of the introductory rites is at least an indirect reference to God (the Trinity) as an interlocutor.

There are numerous instances of the presider (priest) as interlocutor. In addition to the several times when the presider prays quietly in the first person singular (e.g., at the washing of hands during the Preparation of the Altar and Gifts: "Lord, wash away *my* iniquity; cleanse me from *my* sin" and during the presider's private preparation for communion: "Lord Jesus Christ, with faith in your love and mercy *I* eat your body and drink your blood . . . "), the presider also specifically addresses the liturgical assembly (e.g., "The Lord be with *you* . . . "), proclaims the homily, prays in the assembly's name (for example, during the presidential prayers and Eucharistic prayer), and greets and dismisses the assembly.

Finally, examples of the liturgical assembly as interlocutor would be indicated by the first person singular address of the *Confiteor* or Creed, the acclamations and responses, and numerous times for silent prayer sprinkled throughout the rite. Further, the Eucharistic rite also includes textual indicators of other ministers as interlocutors (directly, by referring to deacons, readers, musicians, and acolytes; indirectly, by referring to those who take part in the processions, those who prepare the liturgy, etc.).

If we would not get caught in a fallacy of choosing too rapidly one of these three (or more) for the subject of liturgy, or perhaps of looking for another candidate, we need to analyze further the data to address critically our question of "Who is the subject of liturgy?" At this stage of semantic and pragmatic analysis, the key lies in Ricoeur's development of the notion of the person as a "basic particular" that is a single referent with two predicates (physical and mental).[31] If there were three (or more) subjects of liturgy, it would be difficult to maintain any unity of the rite. Is there a name (that gives an identifying reference) that can encompass all the textual indications of a subject for liturgy (for example, Christ, presider, assembly)?

I propose the following thesis: the liturgical assembly can be understood to be the subject of liturgy if we take "liturgical assembly" as a single referent with two predicates (God and liturgical ministers). This thesis sets two tasks before us: to account for all the actants uncovered by the indicators and to show how these indicators are differing predicates for the one referent, the liturgical assembly.

A perusal of all the texts bearing on the Eucharistic rite (Sacramentary or other service book, Lectionary, General Calendar, *General Instruction of the Roman Missal,* pastoral documents, etc.) would yield an even lengthier list of indicators of actants than we briefly listed above. We have already mentioned God, but not the itemized names (from the rite itself): God, Lord, Lord God, Lord Jesus Christ, Holy Spirit, God our Father, Almighty God, Lord Jesus, Christ, Our Father, etc. Specification of various liturgical ministries including (at least) presider, lector, cantor, accompanist, musicians, choir, acolytes, hospitality ministers, and Eucharistic ministers is indicated by the text. Further, the assembly itself is indicated as an interlocutor, and is named as "the people," and addressed as brethren, friends, dearly beloved, brothers and sisters, or other suitable names left to the discretion of the presider. In fact, both the texts and our actual celebrations of liturgy attest to the multiplicity of interlocutors. A number of questions arise: Is it possible to discern a single referent for all of the interlocutors, that we name "liturgical assembly"? Is the liturgical assembly a "liturgical person," a "basic particular," irreducible any further? Does our accounting for the many indicators of interlocutors splinter liturgy into so many subjects that any notion of a single referent is impossible?

At first glance, it might seem as though we have mistaken the liturgical assembly as a classification (which eliminates the singular) rather than a basic particular (which is characterized by individualization).[32] Certainly, the liturgical assembly is made up of many individuals (as indicated by the text itself). But that is not problematic for our investigation. We maintain that liturgy is celebrated by a unique subject, a single "liturgical person," that is, a basic particular. Our phenomenological justification for this claim lies in the fact that liturgy unfolds as a single action, albeit with differing elements or events (but, recall from above, we said that action is not a subset of event). Although some particular elements/events may be omitted at times (for example, the *Gloria* or Creed), an internal deep structure remains that configures liturgy as a single action.[33] We are looking for, then, the subject of this action considered as a whole. We claim that the liturgical assembly is the subject of liturgy, a single referent with various predicates assigned to it. If we acknowledge that the textual indicators we outlined above are predicates, what indicators are there to see the liturgical assembly as a basic particular and, therefore, supporting our thesis that the assembly is the subject of liturgy? We suggest the most compelling indicator is the Communion Rite, particularly with its communion procession (and its symbolism of journeying toward the messianic banquet), act of faith ("Body of Christ," "Amen"), and the actual eating and drinking of the Body and Blood of Christ. The "com-union" of the two predicates (Christ, liturgical ministers[34]) tellingly proclaims the assembly as the common referent.[35]

The key to recognizing the liturgical assembly as the subject of liturgy lies in its identity. In this case, the whole exceeds the sum of its parts. We are suggesting here that the liturgical assembly is a unique presence of God and various members of the community such that, when gathered, concretize *in the here and now* the common referent of the predicates, a communion of the human and divine. The liturgical assembly is the privileged locus of the interconnectedness of God and people. We have suggested that the predicates are God and liturgical ministers.[36] How do they point to the liturgical person as common referent? Liturgy obviously unfolds as an action of various interlocutors, even though the speaker(s) and one(s) spoken to may change as the ritual progresses. But there is an interconnectedness (subjectivity) that suggests none of the interlocutors acts indepen-dently of the others. The "I" of liturgy, then, can be assimilated to both God and the liturgical ministers *at the same time.*[37] The named subject—liturgical assembly—is a couple made up of interlocutors.

Drawing our direction from a pragmatics of action, we might also ask about the "What?" and "Why?" of liturgy in order to ensure a re-turn to the pivotal question "Who?" All classical liturgical texts trace the presence of God to the people and God's mighty deeds of salva-tion history—from creation, through the law and prophets, into the new dispensation of the Good News—that gives us a clue to the "What?" The "Why?" is equally at hand: Because humankind has not remained faithful to the covenant, God is the ever faithful One whose presence varies and deepens (covenantal presence to personal pres-ence to indwelling) as humanity gropes to know the God who reveals self to us. Liturgy carries forward the traces of God's action through-out history and it is through our celebrations that those actions can be recovered. The "What?" and "Why?" of liturgy leads us to the "Who?" as the agent of the action.

2. Narrativity: Analysis of Temporality and Historicity. We men-tioned above how either the person of whom we are speaking or the agent on whom action depends imply a history of their own. Narra-tivity, with its temporality and historicity, interjects the possibility of *permanence in time.* With respect to liturgy, this is a primary concept. Liturgy derives from and gives rise to a Tradition, which establishes a continuity of sameness with respect to our making present the Paschal Mystery. The narrativity of liturgy rescues us from "going back to" or "re-enacting" what Jesus did long ago. The permanence in time ensures us of a sameness; that is, the liturgy we celebrate is an *enacting* of those originary events.

At the same time that the narrativity of liturgy ensures a perma-nence in time, a dialectic of *difference* is also operative. *This* par-ticular celebration by *this* particular liturgical person is also unique as an action insofar as it refigures the liturgical assembly into being an ever more perfect locus of God's presence. It is this dialectic of sameness and selfhood (difference) that always leads us back to the subject. The action is defined by the agents who are the actants.

Liturgical narrativity has a double face: on the one hand, the whole of liturgy itself is the narration of God's presence; on the other hand, the liturgical text includes large sections of narrative genre (espe-cially the Eucharistic Prayer) that stamps it quite clearly with a tem-porality and historicity. Liturgy emplots the events of the Paschal Mystery, but at the same time enables innovation for the here-and-now celebrating assembly. Here again the dialectic between sameness and self—between the Tradition and the liturgical assembly—shows itself and plays out the ongoingness of God's redemptive mystery. Because liturgy is specific to the celebrating assembly, it comes out of life and returns to life;[38] liturgy, therefore, also raises the question of the "good" and the "obligatory."

3. Prescription: Analysis of Ethics and Morality. A return to the subject is possible only through other. Any phenomenology of the subject of liturgy, therefore, will necessarily raise questions about the proximity or distance between what is and what ought to be. To impute living the Paschal Mystery to the liturgical person is to connect the liturgical person to others. What others? Form C of the Dismissal is "Go in peace to love and serve the Lord." The implication is "the Lord *in others.*" The "other" of the liturgical person, therefore, extends beyond the liturgical assembly itself and, indeed, even beyond the cultic occasion.

Liturgy is essentially teleological in that it orients us toward our final end: to be gathered as one at the messianic banquet. This aim at the good life, however, is only obtainable by means of solicitude (with and for others; that is, serving others) and justice (in just institutions). The only return to the subject is through the other. With this final methodic moment, we see liturgy as linking up with life and prescribing right relationships. Without this interconnectedness, liturgy risks being solipsistic[39] with no return to the subject, in which case the liturgical person disintegrates (since God, as one of the predicates, is a God of solicitude and justice). Through solicitude for others and justice, the liturgical assembly exercises its mandate to *live* what it celebrates and actually manifests its identity as liturgical person.

4. New Directions

The ramifications of this hermeneutics of the liturgical assembly as the subject of liturgy are varied and promise rich directions for further analyses. We will first spell out some pastoral implications of our remarks and then outline a theology of liturgical assembly.

1. Pastoral Implications. Perhaps one of the most challenging pastoral liturgy problems these remarks address is the role of the liturgical ministers (including the presider) vis-à-vis the assembly. Often actual pastoral practice suggests by the very configuration of the liturgical assembly itself that the whole is made up of only some of the parts. Our description of the liturgical assembly as liturgical person with two predicates (God and liturgical ministers) challenges the whole notion of who is "part" of the assembly or not. Phenomenologically, each liturgical minister is an agent of the action insofar as she or he contributes to the identifying reference. This underscores the *assembly itself as a liturgical minister.* Too often, the people in the pews don't understand their role as a *ministry.* This approach tends to highlight more a ministry of equals than a hierarchy of ministries. Each member of the assembly functions only in relation to the common referent, the liturgical person or assembly as subject of liturgy. Any role or function outside of this orientation is also outside of the liturgical venue. In such cases, the individual may be functioning, but she or he is not ministering.

Another comment is a corollary of the preceding ones and addresses the question of how the presider prays/speaks *for* or *in the name of* the assembly. If the presider as liturgical minister is a predicate of the liturgical assembly, then when the presider prays it is the whole assembly who prays because they share a common identity.[40] If the presider is considered apart from the assembly, then there is a great risk of the members becoming passive recipients rather than acting agents (which has been a problem of the not too recent history of liturgy). The same comments hold true for all the liturgical ministers. Sacred space, in this context, can be more clearly defined as that delimited by the various liturgical ministers performing their ministries. This, above all, includes the assembly itself (as a whole). A related issue is whether the liturgical ministers are only those people who are visible, deputed, ordained, etc. By and large, most of the members of the liturgical assembly are not so specifically designated in their roles. However, this hardly implies that they have a passive role. In fact, the ministry of the assembly is central and primary; it is to be the visible body of the Church; without the body, the Church cannot celebrate. The ministry of the assembly is one of active identification. The ministry of the assembly is to be epiphany of the Church. This is primary. All other designated liturgical ministries are subordinated to this primary ministry in which all share.

Since Vatican II the Church has struggled to plumb the richness of her identity. *Lumen Gentium* asserted that the Church is the people of God. If we take the position that the liturgical assembly is the subject of liturgy, then we can more easily recognize the import of this richness. In fact, the Church is not only the People *of* God, but also the People *in* God (because of the shared referent of the two predicates, God and liturgical ministers). We noted above how the subject is a couple of the speaker and one spoken to. This suggests a new meaning to the notion of the dialogue of Church with God, since both are predicates of the one subject and both are interlocutors engaged in the liturgical action. Liturgy, then (and, particularly, the liturgical assembly), is an expression of Church manifesting identity.

There are ramifications for the notions of community. "Community" is that reality expressed by the shared identity of the predicates. Community, in other words, is a consequence of the "One Body." While community does imply interconnectedness and right relations (justice) between and among members, these are demands and effects of community, not its cause. Community is a concept that first and foremost operates at the level of identity; only then can we speak rightly of loving and just actions. The latter flow *from* the identity, but do not cause it. True "celebration" is an affirmation of this identity. Far from the popular notion of parties and balloons and good times, liturgical celebration is a surrender to the deepest meaning of who we are and can be. The joy and peace that is proper to this notion of celebration derives from a clearer grasp of ourselves and being interconnected with God and each other, the very source of life and dynamism.

2. Toward a Theology of the Liturgical Assembly. The purpose of analysis is not always to derive something new; it may also give a different conceptual framework for what is already intuited, but the new framework adds richness and depth. Our own analysis does not contradict the insight of the preconciliar theologians who recognized the close connection between the liturgical assembly and Church. We hope that it strengthens and supports it. However, we believe that the insight is now more clearly focused with greater methodological precision.

The first and most fundamental point to be made about a theology of the liturgical assembly is that it is far more than an assemblage of people gathering for a common purpose. Its nature is to be the privileged locus of the presence of God to and in the community and an epiphany of the Church as that presence. Therefore, the nature of the liturgical assembly flows from its *identity* rather than its function. There is an intrinsic relationship implied here between a theology of the liturgical assembly and ecclesiology. The most concrete expression of Church comes from the most basic of its actions: interconnectedness (intersubjectivity) with each other and God in the act of worship. Any other notion of church (for example, as institution) derives meaning only from this fundamental identity.

Further, and not unrelated to the question of identity, the narrative function of liturgy gives it a "sense of an ending." We said above that the teleology of the liturgy directs us toward the messianic banquet. Indeed, we can say more than this: liturgy is wholly eschatological in that it already makes present that for which we wait and long. Liturgy, then, is a bearer of hope for its very celebration brings the liturgical assembly in touch with the promise that is already being fulfilled. This eschatological dimension cannot be emphasized enough. It is a unique element of the Church's identity and a remarkable claim.

If it is the nature of the liturgical assembly to be the epiphany of the Church and the privileged locus of God's presence, it is the function of the liturgical assembly to *gather* in order to be a faithful witness to God's presence. This gathering, however, is more than simply people coming together to pray or offer worship. The liturgical assembly gathers for a select action: the celebration of the Paschal Mystery in and through the Tradition. The function of the liturgical assembly is to do what the Church has done faithfully throughout her Tradition. This is why any celebration of liturgy that incorporates or tolerates idiosyncratic elements (either on the part of preparation teams or liturgical ministers) runs a high risk of being solipsistic and of preventing any return to the subject, the liturgical assembly as a whole. The ritual authoritatively celebrated assures that the gathering is, indeed, a liturgical assembly.

Any individual drawing attention to self or making one liturgical element more important than another at the expense of the whole is misguided. Members of the assembly—even presiders and musicians, acolytes and Eucharistic ministers—must be themselves transparent in order not to diminish the real subject of liturgy itself. Yes, the presider leads the assembly; but transparently so. Yes, the choir's communion meditation is appropriate, but for the sake of fostering the divine/human communion, not for the sake of performing beautiful music in itself.

These considerations of the nature and function of the liturgical assembly still leave us one more point to which we must return: there must always be a return to the subject, and that return occurs only through others. Therefore, liturgy can never be a closed ritual, but always leads the liturgical assembly toward solicitude in just institutions. We conclude, then, on the notion that liturgy always speaks to and celebrates our daily living of the Paschal Mystery. Even though the liturgical assembly is a *privileged locus* of the Church, this does not imply that Church ceases when the liturgical assembly disperses. On the contrary, liturgy *ritualizes* what, in fact, Christian living is all about. Unless each member of the assembly *lives* the ritual moment in their daily lives, the content of the celebration is reduced. This suggests that the referent of liturgy, the Paschal Mystery, is not a past event to which the assembly is passively connected; rather, the Paschal Mystery is a dynamic that is both celebrated *and* lived. The prophets from of old all knew this when they consistently made right relationships a prerequisite for an acceptable sacrifice. This is no less true for our own age. We are reminded of what the prophet Micah has told us about how we shall come before our God: " . . . to do justice, and to love kindness, and to walk humbly with your God" (Mic 6:8).

Notes

1. See her "The Liturgical Assembly: Review and Reassessment," *Worship* 67 (1993) 123–144 and *The Role of the Assembly in Christian Initiation,* Forum Essays No. 1 (Chicago: Liturgy Training Publications in cooperation with The North American Forum on the Catechumenate, 1993).

2. See Vincie, "The Liturgical Assembly," 125.

3. See the references in the footnotes in her article "The Liturgical Assembly: Review and Reassessment" and the bibliography given in her *The Role of the Assembly in Christian Initiation,* 119–22.

4. Vincie, "The Liturgical Assembly," 126.

5. Ibid., 128.

6. Ibid., 129–34, *passim.*

7. See Vincie, *The Role of the Assembly,* 2.

8. See Serge Heitz, "Reflections on the Contemporary Liturgical Assembly," in *Roles in the Liturgical Assembly,* The Twenty-third Liturgical Conference at Saint-Serge, trans. Matthew J. O'Connell (New York: Pueblo Publishing Company, 1981) 155–66.

9. Ibid., 156.

10. Ibid., 160.

11. Ibid., 161.

12. Ibid., 161–62.

13. See John Gallen, S.J., "Assembly," in *The New Dictionary of Sacramental Worship,* ed. Peter E. Fink, S.J. (Collegeville: The Liturgical Press, 1990) 71–90.

14. Ibid., 72.

15. Ibid., 73.

16. It is not insignificant, in this regard, that the first document the Council Fathers ratified was *Sacrosanctum Concilium,* which necessitated and resulted in a major revision of the first schema of *Lumen Gentium* that was presented to them.

17. Vincie, "The Liturgical Assembly," 138–39. I might remark here that the earliest strata of the liturgical movement was wholly pastoral in intent and approach. These writers reflect well that agenda and era.

18. Ibid., 140–41.

19. Ibid., 141.

20. See Vincie, *The Role of the Assembly,* 95.

21. See Gail Ramshaw, *Christ in Sacred Speech: The Meaning of Liturgical Language* (Philadelphia: Fortress Press, 1986); especially Chapter 9, "Sacred Speech About the Assembly," 93–102.

22. See W. Alan Smith, "Intersubjectivity and Community: Some Implications from Gadamer's Philosophy for Religious Education," *Religious Education* 88 (1993) 378–93.

23. Ibid., 389.

24. See Paul Ricoeur, *Oneself As Another,* trans. Kathleen Blamey (Chicago/London: The University of Chicago Press, 1992).

25. See, for example, "Heidegger and the Question of the Subject" in *The Conflict of Interpretations: Essays in Hermeneutics,* ed. Don Ihde (Evanston, Ill: Northwestern University Press, 1974) 223–35; also in the same volume, "The Question of the Subject: The Challenge of Semiology," 278–91; and "The Human Being as the Subject Matter of Philosophy" in *The Narrative Path: The Later Works of Paul Ricoeur,* eds. T. Peter Kemp and David Rasmussen (Cambridge/London: The MIT Press, 1989) 89–101. More generally, in some respects Ricoeur's entire philosophical enterprise has been in pursuit of the subject, beginning with his philosophy of the will and action, then moving into text theory, followed by his concern with narrativity.

26. See Paul Ricoeur, *Oneself as Another.* All references to this volume will simply be indicated in the text with page number.

27. I underscore the tentative and exploratory nature of my remarks. I would like to note, however, that Ricoeur avoids mixing philosophy and theology (see *Oneself As Another,* p. 24), but refrains from denying the obvious connections and applications. I am drawing on aspects of Ricoeur's method without rigorously applying his method in all its detail to the body of data upon which I draw (namely, liturgical texts). Ricoeur's hermeneutics of the subject is a tool for us, but the explication of his philosophy and method is not the main purpose of this essay.

28. See "Existence and Hermeneutics" in Paul Ricoeur, *The Conflict of Interpretations: Essays in Hermeneutics,* 6–11; and "Metaphor and Philosophical Discourse" in Paul Ricoeur, *The Rule of Metaphor: Multi-disciplinary Studies of the Creation of Meaning in Language,* trans. Robert Czerny with Kathleen McLaughlin and John Costello, S.J. (Toronto/Buffalo/London: University of Toronto Press, 1977) 295–313.

29. See chapter 9, "Homily As Proclamation," in this volume for a more extensive discussion of speech acts/performative theory.

30. One of the characteristics of narrativity is that the reader has a sense where the story is going, which draws the reader in and leads the reader on through the action. Ricoeur borrows Frank Kermode's phrase "sense of an ending" to describe this phenomenon, which we will take up in the final section below.

31. Ricoeur's dissolution of the mind-body dualism is as important for our liturgical theology as it is for Ricoeur's anthropology. As long as a basic dualism ensues, it is impossible to overcome a breakdown between liturgy and life. With dualism overcome, the way is paved for understanding the relationship of liturgy and life. On this theme, see my *Liturgy as Living Faith: A Liturgical Spirituality* (Scranton: University of Scranton Press and London/Toronto: Associated University Presses, 1993), *passim.*

32. See Ricoeur, *Oneself As Another,* 28.

33. See my *Liturgy as Living Faith: A Liturgical Spirituality, passim.*

34. Here I am using "liturgical ministers" in a broader sense than the recognized ministries (lector, acolyte, Eucharistic minister, etc.). In a very real sense, every person who gathers is a minister.

35. This is one more argument to support the position that receiving communion cannot be taken out of the context of the whole Eucharistic rite without doing violence to its very meaning. Also, this is a first indication of ontological underpinnings. This analysis suggests that the liturgical assembly, as "liturgical person," is especially unique in that it has both human and divine predicates.

36. We recall that Ricoeur noted two predicates for person: physical predicate and mental predicate. We have noted two predicates for liturgical person: God and liturgical ministers. It is tempting to draw some parallels between the predicates of these two very different domains. The liturgical ministers are visible, physical beings; God, on the other hand, is surely encountered but present in a different mode.

37. It is unfortunate that the contemporary Roman Catholic Eucharistic rite has no ritual provision for indicating this. Elsewhere I have argued (see my *liturgical notes* in *liturgical ministry* 3 [Winter 1994] 35–36; other contributors to this issue on the introductory rites make some of the same points) that one purpose of the introductory rites is to provide time for individuals to *surrender* themselves to the ritual action (that is, give themselves over to being a liturgical person) and recognize that they have been called into God's presence. See also my *Liturgy as Living Faith,* 103–4.

38. In *Oneself As Another* (158–63), Ricoeur raises the question of how to relate the narrative of fiction to the narrative of real life; how do life histories differ from literary ones? He further asks whether in real life the roles of author, narrator, and character are distinct, or are they all three one, as is the case in autobiographical narrative? (160). Fictional narrative has closure because of its "sense of an ending"; real life has no sense of closure (149). Yet, liturgy *does* give us a sense of an ending (because it is wholly teleological; it orients us toward the messianic banquet), which is why it ought to be so motivating toward transformation (the function of ritual). Liturgy's sense of an ending suggests that the author, narrator, and characters of liturgy are not really so distinct. Liturgy is autobiographical in that we place ourselves in the Christian Tradition as authors (with God) of our salvation history.

39. Solipsism is overcome by an interconnectedness that ensures a return to the subject through the other. This interconnectedness is not to be confused with a weak and sentimental notion of "community" that often plagues our liturgical assemblies. Further, it is precisely this interconnectedness that disallows liturgy to be a time for private devotions.

40. Conversely, when any other liturgical minister fulfills her/his function as a minister, it is in and for the whole assembly. For example, the hospitality minister's welcome is really the welcome to the assembly *by the whole assembly.* Liturgically, one can never act solipsistically.

Chapter 4

Putting Heart into Liturgy

William Cieslak, O.F.M. Cap.

> The Church earnestly desires that all the faithful be led to that full,
> conscious, and active participation in liturgical celebrations called
> for by the very nature of the liturgy. Such participation by the
> Christian people as "a chosen race, a royal priesthood, a holy na-
> tion, God's own people" (1 Pt 2:9; see 2:4-5) is their right and duty
> by reason of their baptism. (§14)

This passage from *Sacrosanctum Concilium* ("The Constitution on the
Sacred Liturgy") remains a central challenge to most liturgical assemblies across the United States, that is, if I am understanding the
passage correctly. In what does full, conscious, and active participation consist? How does this manner of participation differ from the
way people used to participate at the Eucharistic liturgy? How does
it differ from the way most people are presently participating? Is
there a way to help a local assembly achieve this goal?

Participation during Mass before Vatican II

Some readers are old enough to remember the kinds of prayer and
participation that took place in church while the priest was celebrating Mass in the days before Vatican II and all of the changes. People
in the pews were engaged in prayer in different ways: some prayed
prayers from prayer books for the needs and intentions of friends
and relatives, living and deceased; others prayed only in their hearts,
using no set texts, with prayers set to memory, just talking with God,

or just kneeling there in quiet. Some followed the prayers that the priest was saying, using missals, while others in the Roman Catholic circle prayed the rosary. Most stopped what they were doing, however, when the *Sanctus* bells called them to attend to the consecration, bowing in adoration, perhaps looking up at the host and chalice, perhaps striking their breasts. Activity again focused on the Mass as those who were receiving communion left their pews in orderly form and returned for private adoration and thanksgiving.

At high Mass or solemn Mass the music and ritual action of the Mass itself provided people with the sight and sound of a truly holy event unfolding before them. The choir's chanting or singing in parts added both solemnity and a sense of celebration. The sound of Latin as the language of official prayer for Catholics contributed its own sense of wonder and mystery in their churches. The appearance of two additional sacred ministers, the deacon and subdeacon, created new coordinated movements that captured the imagination and called for a religious response. The smell of incense and the sound of the chain of the thurible clanking against it added to the drama as did the movements of extra acolytes bearing lighted torches during the Eucharistic Prayer.

Kneeling was the prevailing posture during Mass, especially at low Mass. To this was added brief periods of standing and sitting. The overall result was an attentiveness of the body, poised in adoration, reverence, contrition, and supplication. Hands were generally clasped or folded, heads bowed in prayer. Silence from the worshipers was the expectation; distracting others was to be avoided.

The overall effect that one sensed as he or she walked into the congregation-filled church was that something holy or awesome was taking place. Even if the worshipers could not understand the language being spoken or hear the prayers being prayed quietly or see the complex actions that the priest was performing, they, nevertheless, experienced holy action and holy event. The entire atmosphere or milieu was charged with the presence of the holy, and the prayerful atmosphere created by the worshipers themselves contributed to this environment.

Was this the "full, conscious, and active participation" that the Council Fathers were calling for? But why would they feel obliged to call for it, if it were already happening? Certainly, something very positive was taking place in the church described above. Worshipers were definitely prayerful, and heartfelt worship was taking place. But was this the *type* of worship the Constitution had in mind?

Perhaps this was a wonderful example of *private prayer* in the context of the public prayer of the Church performed by the priest, acolytes, and choir. Because most of the people in the pews seemed to be engaged in prayer, they were, in that sense, participating or actively engaged *in some form* of worship. Indeed, their prayerful presence in the church building at the time of the liturgy contributed to the overall prayerful atmosphere or sense of sacredness of the Mass itself as it was perceived by the worshipers.

Devotion: Praying with the Heart

Another way of describing what was happening then would be to say that those who were praying were engaged "devotionally" in the Mass in some way. In other words, people were attending to God, centering their hearts on God, while the priest was celebrating Mass for them and the acolytes were serving for them and the choir was singing for them. This *centering on God* is what is meant by "devotion." It is a word that describes the drive of the human heart toward God. It identifies the source of the devotion (the person praying), the focus of the devotion (God), and the direction of the devotion (from self to God). "Devotion" includes the whole person: heart, mind, emotions, or feelings. While theologians used to distinguish between the will and the feelings with regard to devotion, such distinctions are more theoretical than real. However, feelings alone are not what evokes devotion, and devotion is not merely concerned with feelings, at least not as the term is used here.

If one accepts this description of devotion, then we see that "The Constitution on the Sacred Liturgy" was actually calling for rich, full *devotional* participation. It is in this sense that the term "conscious" needs to be understood. There is a difference between being aware *that* we are attending a liturgy, and being aware that we are *deeply involved* in liturgical prayer. Consciousness, however, does not need to mean that the worshiper is aware of the meaning and function of every word or religious gesture or action. In fact, attending to those elements can often prevent one from entering more deeply into the liturgical event. The quality of consciousness we are seeking is a deep fundamental awareness, conviction, and desire that enters as fully and as deeply as possible into the communal prayer taking place.

Private Devotion and Liturgical Devotion

What is the difference between the spirit of devotion as it manifested itself before Vatican II and the spirit that "The Constitution on the Sacred Liturgy" is calling for? In the description above we notice that many worshipers' spirit of "devotion" often found expression in prayer formulas and religious practices that had little to do with the actual celebration of the Mass. These religious "devotions" (the practices) became the vehicle for devotion (the spirit). Because the celebration of the Mass was seen to be the priest's responsibility and power, the way people "attended" Mass was by supporting the priest's action by their own prayers and religious practices. To this end, they recited prayers that they had learned by heart or prayers printed in their prayer books; they prayed the rosary for a variety of intentions, or sat in reverent recollection. The focus of these devotions, however, was not necessarily the same focus as the Mass; the Blessed Virgin Mary, St. Anthony of Padua, St. Jude, or any other saint might have been the focus. People engaged in these religious practices were *praying privately* next to each other, actively engaged in the performance of religious devotions, but not directly participating in the celebration of the Mass that was taking place.

An exception to this were those people who were following along with the prayers that the priest was saying. These people were praying in the spirit of the Church's liturgy, in harmony with the priest. Their participation, however, was never acknowledged or encouraged; nor was this form of participation seen as necessary or important. In fact, even the role of the choir was seen as accidental to the Mass: the priest was obliged to voice every word the choir sang, almost as if the choir's song did not count. We could say, in summary, that those who followed the Mass along with the priest participated in the *spirit* of the Mass more than they did in its celebration.

"Liturgical devotion" describes the *spirit of prayer* of those followers of the Mass. It also describes the spirit of members of the choir as they blended their voices in song to serve the Church's liturgy. To the extent that worshipers attempted to enter into the spirit and action of the Church's liturgy, their devotion was liturgical. Liturgical devotion is common devotion, devotion performed *in union with,* devotion done together in the same spirit, ideally using the same words and gestures. Liturgical devotion became the focus of the Church's efforts with Vatican II; not only was prayer to be fostered, but prayed *together,* common prayer that was essential to the rite itself. The intent was to develop a ritual whereby the gathered assembly of believers could participate in the very performance of the Church's Eucharist so that, in truth, the entire assembly, each according to his or her status or function, would actually celebrate the Eucharist. The Church needed new roles for the liturgical assembly (and thus a different role for the presiding minister) and forms for expressing liturgical devotion.

Participation in the Eucharist after Vatican II

The Eucharist is no longer the sole responsibility of the priest *alone.* It is the responsibility of the Church, manifest in the entire local praying assembly. "The Constitution on the Sacred Liturgy" states "The Church, therefore, earnestly desires that Christ's faithful . . . should not be there as strangers or silent spectators; on the contrary, through a good understanding of the rites and prayers they should take part in the sacred service conscious of what they are doing, with devotion and full involvement" (§48). The text goes on to say that the faithful participate in the Eucharistic sacrifice "not only through the hands of the priest, but also with him."[1] This understanding of the Eucharist is revolutionary for people in the pews. It calls them into active involvement in the ritual itself rather than in a supporting private prayer role. It calls the choir and music ministers into similar understandings as well. Such an innovative approach to the Eucharist, however, demands the preparation of the entire Eucharistic assembly: all have roles to fulfill, and those roles interact with each other. As deacon and subdeacon had to rehearse their roles for the solemn high Mass, so does the community gathered for Eucharist have to understand its role and rehearse it so that the Eucharist is celebrated according to the directives of the rite.

What is necessary is the development of a liturgical spirit in the hearts of the worshipers. Because Eucharist is the action of the whole people, new ways need to be found by which the people in the pews can express their "full, conscious, and active participation." To this end those given the responsibility of implementing the new Order of Mass created acclamations, responses, common prayers, postures, gestures, and processions through which the entire liturgical assembly might voice its devotion. Many of the texts were to be musical because music moves the heart and unites worshipers in ways stronger than mere words. What was planned was more in the form of a symphony involving solo instruments (presiding minister, readers, cantors), sections (Eucharistic ministers, ushers, greeters, choir, and musicians), and a chorus (the people in the pews). The goal was a performance directed to God, inspired by the Spirit, in and through and with Jesus Christ.

What Went Wrong?

When all the liturgical changes began to occur, worshipers were greeted with a new form of Mass that was unfamiliar but now required. They were expected to join in singing unfamiliar songs, to answer newly composed prayers, and to pay attention, so that they could learn what this was all about. At the same time they were strongly encouraged to put aside their private devotions and prayers. What many ended up giving up was a *devotional attitude* as well, a real spirit of prayer. Instead of entering into prayer, albeit for the most part, private prayer, they became *audience,* onlooker, spectator. They found little or no time to pray (individually) while Mass was going on, and few experienced sitting, listening, and watching as *prayer.* Neither the music nor the common words or gestures touched their hearts the way their own devotions did. So much was foreign and needed to be learned.

Priests, commentators, and music directors did their best to "teach." Often, however, they taught *about* the liturgy rather than teaching liturgical prayer itself. They provided people with functional rather than spiritual reasons why things were being done. People learned a little about the liturgy, but they weren't being fed and formed by the liturgy, not even as well as they had been before.

Part of the difficulty lay in the newness of the rite. New prayers, gestures, and postures do not become familiar overnight, and yet familiarity with a rite is a prerequisite for that rite being used for liturgical prayer. True devotion is expressed through ritual forms only when those forms are known and even presumed. They become vehicles of expression because they do not call attention to themselves. Only then can they become prayerful.

Part of the difficulty lay in the expectation for a speedy adjustment to the new forms. Although the new order of Mass symbolized the deep change taking place in so many dimensions of the Church, its own ecclesiological and liturgical challenge does not seem to have been understood by many bishops and pastors left with the responsibility for directing the renewal. People in the pews seemed excited about all that was happening in the Church, but were they prepared to change their own attitudes toward worship and their own worship patterns in such a radical way? Rather than expecting change overnight, or in a few months, those in leadership roles needed to think long term: years, even a generation of new patterning and formation. We merely have to recall the decades it has taken to begin understanding the active role of the baptized in the Church and the rights and responsibilities that flow from it. The same is true of such concepts as the "priesthood of Christ's faithful" or "priesthood of all believers" in regard to the Church's liturgy.

Part of the difficulty lay in the very structure of the Eucharistic liturgy itself. While the introductory rites open the possibility of rich *devotional* response, the Liturgy of the Word, for the most part, is *edificational,* i.e., structured to rouse faith in the *hearers.* This means that for a long period, very early in the rite, the worshipers are listeners, receivers of words read, sung, and spoken. If an assembly does not know in what spirit to receive these words, if the words themselves as they are spoken or sung don't inspire, if the responsorial psalm and alleluia don't voice the spirit of hearts joined in praise, then this long period of waiting will work in a counterproductive way to liturgical devotion. When this is followed by a collection and preparation of the table that are hardly devotional moments and then by a Eucharistic Prayer that is largely recited by the presiding minister with the rest of the assembly in a receiving posture (kneeling), we might begin to wonder where the devotional dimension of the liturgy is.

All of this is not caused, however, by the official structures; while the Liturgy of the Word is definitely edificational in structure, the Liturgy of the Eucharist is largely devotional in intent: The entire assembly is to be involved in the Eucharistic Prayer, the Eucharistic sacrifice, and the communion-sharing. The difficulty here is *how* the liturgy is envisaged, planned, and performed. If roles and relationships in worship are not understood by those who form the worship and have power over its direction, the rest of the assembly will receive both their mixed signals and ambiguity. Leaders of prayer must understand the structure of the rite and lead assemblies into the holy experience through rich reverent gestures, translucent presences, faith-filled voices that invoke faith responses from fellow worshipers, and a good dose of mystagogical catechesis. Music ministers must discover that their role is to choose music that finds a place in the heart, music that worshipers carry home with them and bring back. They must recognize that singing is a priestly role, right, and responsibility. Liturgy planners must learn respect for ritual and caution with regard to ritual change. They must find the right postures and gestures for this priestly people to enter into common prayer.

Heartfelt Liturgical Devotion

Although not in the majority, there are churches throughout the country where assemblies have taken on their priestly role and have learned to pray in common, where devotion expresses itself in liturgical form. African American assemblies in Chicago, Washington, DC, Oakland, and San Francisco have discovered the music, rhythms, and gestures that enable their worship to be deeply devotional. Seldom is a music book needed because the songs live in church and at home. The word is preached as Holy Word, alive and forceful, challenging both neighborhood and country.

Churches in Las Vegas, Milwaukee, Boston, and Brooklyn have found the spirit of the Church's liturgy and their assemblies stand as witnesses to liturgical devotion. People come with hopes and expectations, energy to engage in worship. They fill those churches from the front, coming to be led in common prayer. There is a sense of welcome and hospitality that turns to quiet listening and voiced common prayer. Everything from the procession with money offerings to the manner of sharing communion has been thought through and patterned in a style that has become their own. The people are grateful for being there: their faces and voices show it and share it. Participation in mission reaches far beyond the doors to the church.

What is the agenda for promoting heartfelt liturgical devotion? Attitudes and understandings need to change. The priestly assembly must identify itself and take responsibility for its actions. Mystagogical catechesis can help here, since its focus is spiritual understanding and appreciation. Those who prepare and lead liturgy must find ways to help the entire priestly assembly prepare for and enter into liturgical prayer. More attention needs to be given to both the edificational and devotional dimension of the Liturgy of the Word. A fresh look needs to be given to the Eucharistic prayers: to their length, postures, and gestures for the people in the pews, and a more dialogical structure. (Presently only the Lord's Prayer seems to have become a moment of liturgical devotion.) Reflecting on the way an assembly receives and shares communion might also be helpful.

Because it *is* taking place, heartfelt liturgy *can* take place! It is taking place where assemblies of believers understand their full, active role. It is taking place where the ritual structure is solid and appropriate for their action. It is taking place where the prayers, songs, gestures, and postures "fit" the needs of the human heart. It is taking place where the environment acknowledges the holiness of the people gathered and supports the sacredness of their action. It is taking place where usher, greeter, choir, cantor, reader, acolyte, preacher, presider, and Eucharistic minister witness to faith shared and deeply treasured at the service of all.

Is There Room for Private Devotions?

This question brings us full circle. Liturgical devotion differs from private devotion first of all, from the point of view of the subject. In liturgical devotion the subject is a group, an assembly of believers; in private devotion, the subject is the individual. From this basic difference flows others: liturgical devotion is addressed to God, whereas private devotions can be addressed to God, to Mary, or to one of the saints (although ultimately to God as well); liturgical devotion is voiced through gestures and texts chosen by the Church for its common worship, while private devotions include practices of the saints, private revelations, religious-cultural practices, family customs, etc., much more loosely overseen and, at times, not controlled by the Church at all. Some private devotions were inspired by the liturgy or the Church's liturgical year and "customized" for specific groups or situations.

The question here is really not whether there is room for private devotions. History tells us that private devotions have regularly sprung up among Christians and will continue to do so, and the presence of private devotional practices in any age can be a sign of the Spirit. But the multiplication of private devotions in any age is also often a sign that the Church has failed to capture the devotional spirit of its baptized faithful or, for one reason or another, has failed to provide liturgical leadership.

There are, of course, those devotional practices that, in the mind of the Church, go astray in that they lose their focus or begin to attribute magical powers to persons, gestures, or objects. As long as there are believers in this world, the manifestation of the holy will be at times both misunderstood and misrepresented. That in itself is not an argument against devotions; it underscores the necessity for discernment.

Devotional practices are often the product of religious inculturation. Through the religious imagination, practices and beliefs of one religious and cultural tradition are wedded with those of another. The resulting practice can be a testimony to the presence of the Spirit within both cultures. Indeed some of these practices might find their way into the Church's liturgical worship itself and become expressions of liturgical as well as private devotion.

So the dialogue might continue: private devotions arising in response to faith, some being transformed into liturgical devotion, liturgical devotion feeding and perhaps forming private ones. The Church will remain alive if its members nourish a devotional spirit. The Church will grow in its corporate or communal identity to the extent that it discovers a fitting liturgical form for its devotional spirit. But since the baptized faithful gather only on occasion for liturgical prayer, the everyday spiritual life of believers will need other forms of both *edification,* through Scripture, spiritual reading, faith sharing, etc., and *devotion,* through private and family prayers and other sound devotional practices.

Note

1. Something similar is found in the *General Instruction of the Roman Missal,* 4th ed., March 1975, §5.

Chapter 5

Symbolic Actions in Christian Worship

Patrick Byrne

This chapter helps us to understand why we use symbols and symbolic actions in our worship. We do so because we are human, and because we are dealing with mysteries that we cannot fully grasp or explain. Human language is not able to speak about God with the same certainty or in the precise, pragmatic terms that we use about building codes, computer standards, or cubic measures. To speak about God and God's continuing action among us in life and in liturgy, we need to use similes and metaphors, the kind of language God uses to speak to us in the scriptures. To express our faith through our worship, we need to use symbols which say in action who we are and what we believe and do in the deepest levels of our reality; to be even more precise, these symbols express what God is doing in us, and how we are responding in God's grace.

I. Using Images and Symbols in Our Worship

The Hebrew and Christian scriptures use a variety of images to bring God's word into our lives in such a way that we are able to accept its message and allow it to have a positive effect in our daily living. Some of these images are words and some are actions.

A. Words

Some images are descriptive words and phrases. The bible uses both similes and metaphors to describe deeper truths:

A *simile* says that the kingdom of heaven is *like* a banquet given by a king and queen for the marriage of one of their children (see Matt 22:2-14). A simile is simpler to grasp than is a metaphor, and is not as challenging to the imagination.

A *metaphor* says that the kingdom of heaven *is* a banquet (Ps 23:5-6), or that God *is* our rock of safety (Ps 18:31-32, as at Gibraltar), or that Jesus *is* the Lamb of God (John 1:29; Rev 5:6). A metaphor is a figure of speech used to illustrate a deep truth by putting two distinct realities side by side, and letting the appropriate similarities, contrasts, and tensions rub off one another in the hearts and minds of the hearers or readers. A metaphor demands more of the listener or reader than does a simile.

B. Actions

Some actions described in the word of God are *symbolic:* they speak with a power beyond words, and can imprint their message in our hearts and minds if we are open to their way of communicating. A few examples will help us to grasp this more clearly.

When Jesus freely chose to eat with sinners, he was accentuating his mission to save all people, including those who had deliberately turned from their loving God, those who had simply drifted away, and those who had remained faithful. When our Lord conversed with lepers and touched them and healed them—people who were considered by their society to be outcasts, cursed and abandoned by their God—Jesus was telling us that no one is rejected by our loving and forgiving Father. When our savior washed the feet of his apostles at the Last Supper, he was showing them that those sent as leaders must serve others in his Church in practical and humble ways. When Jesus invited Peter, who had denied him three times on the first Maundy Thursday, to declare his love for Jesus three times, our Lord was proclaiming that Peter was forgiven, was reinstated as the rock, and was now being sent forth to look after the Good Shepherd's flock.

C. Symbols

Symbols in the liturgy are actions and signs whose meaning comes from the inspired word of God.[1] Symbols are images in action.

Are symbols empty images, or mere figures of poetic speech? Are they burnt-out light bulbs? Are they empty or hollow promises? *No!* Symbols in our liturgy are pregnant images, living words, hope-filled thrusts. They are nonverbal, even preverbal expressions of our faith.

They are concrete ways of proclaiming what we believe and do as followers of Jesus Christ.

Symbols in our liturgy are not arbitrary images concocted and assigned by PR people at the head office, telling us what will meet or tease current or future tastes. Our liturgical symbols are derived from the scriptures, which are inspired by the Holy Spirit. Our liturgical symbols are, therefore, life-giving for us in our current circumstances and for the rest of our lives, here or anywhere in the world.

At the same time symbols are always ambiguous, for they carry many layers of meaning available to the unlearned and challenging to the theologian.

D. Symbols touch our senses

Christian symbols are not vague intellectual images to be grasped by the mind alone. Rather, they are sights for our seeing (movement, light, colors), sounds for our hearing (singing, music, prayers), scents for our smelling (incense, chrism, beeswax), tastes for our savoring (freshly baked bread, wine), and touches for our feeling (anointing, handshakes) (see "Worshiping with our bodies," at section III.F., below).

E. Prose and poetry

The language we use in our Sunday worship tends to move us away from the ordinary, and calls us to enter a new realm of imagery and mystery. We are invited to leave behind the workaday images of prose (it gets you there directly like railroad tracks), and to enter the world of poetry (like a butterfly on its day off). Imagery is the way God speaks to us in Scripture, in liturgy, in prayer, in our emotions, and in daily living, if we are open to God's voice coming to us in many ways.

F. Accepting our Christian symbols

Some believing communities may not feel comfortable with some or even many of these traditional symbols. In two thousand years of Christianity, many communities have lost touch with one or another symbol because of various historical circumstances. This chapter seeks to reflect the full perspective of symbolism in the liturgy, and encourages all faith communities to look further into our 2,000 years of Christian tradition in order to recover and live its vigorous life more fully.

G. Celebrating symbols well each Sunday

The best way to uncover the depths of meaning in our liturgical symbols is by celebrating them well each week within a community of faith. When believers experience these symbols being celebrated well in their worship week after week, accept their biblical foundation, and reflect on them prayerfully, they will be able to grasp more of the core of the mystery which the symbols both conceal and reveal.

II. Recognizing and Celebrating the Symbols in Our Sunday Worship

To understand our Sunday worship today, we need to recognize that we have inherited the traditions and practices of the Christian Church over the past twenty centuries.

A. Sunday is our day of worship

During the time of the apostles, Christians began to celebrate the first day of the week (Sunday)—rather than the Jewish Sabbath (Saturday)—as the Lord's day, the weekly holy day.[2]

B. Eucharist at the center

From the beginning to the present day, the Catholic, Orthodox, and Eastern Churches have had the unbroken tradition of celebrating the Eucharist on Sundays. In the sixteenth century the churches of the Reformation made a positive and valiant effort to continue this practice and to restore weekly communion by the members in each congregation.

C. Derailment

An overpowering sense of sin, inherited by all Christians from the Middle Ages, led the Protestant churches to drop weekly Eucharist since people were not coming to communion; they began to use a service of the word each Sunday, and celebrated Eucharist only occasionally: yearly, quarterly, or monthly. In the Roman Catholic and Orthodox Churches, the Sunday celebration of the Eucharist remained the practice, but without the communion of the people. Neither practice was ideal, but each tried to retain an important part of the Christian tradition of worship.

D. Returning to our full Christian tradition

In recent decades, the major Reformation churches have begun to return to their early Christian roots and restore the celebration of Eucharist as the normal form of Sunday worship. Since the 1950s Catholics are coming to communion much more frequently, and now most of the people present receive in each celebration. More and more Catholic communities have restored communion from the chalice, which had been neglected for many centuries, but there are still many who have yet to embrace the ideal given to us by our Lord. Gradually the major Christian churches are returning to the ideals of the early Church.[3]

E. Our symbols are permanent

Symbols in our liturgy are best understood not only in terms of *objects* (such as water, bread and wine, or oil), but as *actions* (what we do with the water—cleansing or baptizing; or what we do with the bread and wine—eating and drinking together, in memory of the Lord Jesus Christ; or what we do by anointing—strengthening and healing).

The symbols used in our Sunday worship are actions which are always there. We do not need to invent new ones week by week. These symbols derive their form and meaning from the word of God. When we use these symbols well, we respect both the nature of the symbols and the Spirit of God who inspired the scriptures on which these symbols are based. Symbols can speak to the people in our community at a deeper level than can our words alone. When symbols are used often and well, familiarity helps the community members to penetrate them more fully, and gradually become open to new insights into their meaning.

There are many symbols involved in the Church's liturgy. This chapter looks briefly at some ways in which the symbolic actions are present and active in various Christian congregations' Sunday (and sometimes weekday) worship. We are able to recognize and respect these symbols only when we celebrate and use them well. In this way, we help our community members to become more open to them, and we allow the built-in power of these symbols to touch the hearts and minds of our parish family both in our public worship and in our daily living.

F. Liturgical symbols

A number of primary and secondary liturgical symbols are briefly explored in the next two major sections of this essay. Our understanding of each of these symbols needs to be developed in greater detail than space permits here. Our remarks simply open up these areas for further thought and development in each believing community in the years to come.[4] Certainly, it is paramount that those preparing and leading liturgies have given ample prayer and reflection to a rich use of liturgical symbols and symbolic actions.

III. Looking at Our Primary Symbols

A. Recognizing this assembly as God's people, gathered by our God

Here is the symbol: the people gathering and gathered together in this community in response to God's invitation.

On the Lord's day each week, we accept God's invitation to come together with our sisters and brothers, and to recognize that we are one holy family, an assembly of God's people in this locale. God continued to call Israel to be the holy, chosen, priestly, and royal people, God's *qahal* or assembly (see Exod 19:5-8); their response varied down through the centuries. This invitation is renewed for us in the Christian scriptures (1 Pet 2:5, 9-10; Rev 5:9-10). It is in our Christian initiation (understood today as our baptism, confirmation [in many churches], and Eucharist) that we are made members of the Church, the Christian *qahal,* the assembly of God's people in this place, and so we are able to enter into the fullness of living for the Lord.

Since the Second Vatican Council (1962–1965), Roman Catholic teaching has emphasized that the members of a community come together in each Sunday gathering in response to the Father's invitation, and that this assembly is an image of the Church around the world:

> From age to age you gather a people to yourself,
> so that from east to west
> a perfect offering may be made
> to the glory of your name.[5]

We don't assemble each week as a favor to God; rather, we are responding to God's invitation with our obedience, respect, and love. Like Jesus, we say: "Here I am, Lord; I come to do your will" (see Heb 10:7; Ps 40:7-8; also 1 Sam 3:3-10). At the practical level in a local congregation, the meaning of this symbol of the gathered assembly may be opened up to the members of the community along these lines:

1. A welcoming community: Jesus invites us to welcome those he sends to us in many roles. When we welcome them with faith and love, we are welcoming Jesus who sent them, and God our Father who sent Jesus (see Matt 10:40-42). This principle and its rejection are described in more vivid details in Matthew 25:31-46.

We show this welcoming attitude by what we do before and after the service, thus developing a solid foundation for our ritual welcoming. Members of the community need to be invited to show their spirit of welcome in a variety of ways. Some congregations ask a different family each week to greet people as they come into church for the Sunday service; others invite the ushers to carry out this form of welcome. In many communities, one or more of the clergy and other ministers will be at the door to take part in this welcoming. The variety of ways of welcoming people before the service can prepare us for the liturgical act of welcoming.

2. Liturgical welcoming: The opening rites of our celebration help us as individuals and families to recognize ourselves as Church, as members of this community of God's people, that God is calling together today at this worship service in this assembly. The sincere manner of welcoming people before the service begins can prepare us all for the liturgical act of welcoming. The liturgical rites express this welcoming in a more formal way, but they are anchored in the solid foundation of what this community does all week for God and for people.

We celebrate this liturgical welcoming by the entrance song, which binds us into one community; by the procession of ministers through the singing community, with the book of God's word being held on high; by the liturgical greeting and welcome; and by the opening prayer with its invitation to pray as individuals in silence and to respond as a community with a resounding "Amen!"

A note on *errors:* If the community is not a welcoming one, one of two errors will soon creep into its liturgy: (1) informal practices that belong at the church door (for example, "Good morning, friends," "Good morning, Pastor") will overshadow the liturgical greeting and its important role; or (2) folksy ways (for example, "Y'all turn and tell the next person who you are, where you come from, and the state of your health") will overburden an already crowded entrance rite. In either case, the liturgical symbol of God gathering these people and their responding to this invitation can be torpedoed by local insensitivity to traditional Christian symbolism.

B. Proclaiming God's word in this assembly

Here is the symbol: God is speaking to this gathered assembly, and we are responding in faith by our reflection, by silent and public prayer, by community song, and by the way we live our daily life for God this week.

1. God's word is proclaimed in faith. A woman or man of faith spends some time during the week to read over, reflect on, and pray about the Sunday readings. The readers recognize that they have been chosen by the community to bring the voice and words of God to life in their hearts. Conscientious readers ask the Holy Spirit to deepen their faith, so that God's message may be proclaimed and received well through their work of proclaiming it as well as they can.

2. God's word is heard and received in faith. Some members of the community will spend time during the week, reading the Scripture texts and praying over them. When they come together on Sunday, they will be more open to what God's word is saying to them. All who listen to the reading with faith are assisted by the Spirit to hear God's word being spoken to this assembly, here and now. It is the work of the Holy Spirit to cause the Liturgy of the Word to be alive: It is the Spirit who inspired the men and women who wrote these texts, the Spirit who guides the faith of readers and hearers, the Spirit who turns our human voices and human words into the voice and the word of God.

3. Entering into the power of the symbol. How can we allow this symbol to become more alive in our Sunday liturgy? Going beyond the basics of a good sound system, proper microphone techniques, and adequate lighting, we may suggest some further ideas: (1) Invite all members of the congregation to add dynamism to the liturgy by preparing the readings during the week by their prayer and reflection, so that their hearts will be more attuned to God's word. Think what would happen if even 25 percent of our people came prepared to hear God speak to them! (2) Ask people to pray during the week for the readers and the preachers at next weekend's celebrations. (3) Invite the homilist to preach from the opened book of God's word rather than closing it and replacing it with a typescript. (4) Encourage sick and homebound members of the community to pray each week for the hearers and readers and preachers of God's holy word. (5) Start a small group to reflect on the following week's readings, and if possible, invite those who preach to join them. Early in the week, members of the pastoral team may wish to share prayerfully about the following Sunday's texts and their place in the liturgical year and in the life of this community of faith.

C. Praying for the Church and for the world

Here is the symbol: This assembly of God's priestly people—in union with the Church in heaven and on earth—is called by God to pray for the needs of the Church and of the world, and we respond by our heartfelt petitions.

In restoring the intercessions or prayer of the faithful among Catholics, the Second Vatican Council invited the members of each assembly to pray for the Church, civil authorities, those oppressed by various needs, the whole human family, and for the salvation of the whole world (see Acts 28:28). Other churches call this group of petitions the pastoral prayer, the intercessions, the litany, or by other titles.

While preparing this prayer each week, we may reflect on 1 Timothy 2:1-2, which calls for prayer and thanksgiving to be offered for kings and others in high position, so that believers may lead a quiet and peaceful life; verses 3-4 could also be read with profit by those who prepare and pray these intercessions. Where a pastoral prayer is prepared locally, Jesus' teaching about not piling up words (Matt 6:7-8) always needs to be kept in mind.[6]

D. Expressing repentance and forgiveness

Here is the symbol: As a community we recognize that in baptism, God has cleansed us from our sins; that we are weak and have fallen away from the Lord; that we are always in need of Jesus' strength; and that we are invited to keep coming to the Lord Jesus and asking for his mercy and forgiveness. The magnificent vision of St. Paul (Eph 1:3-14) places our need for forgiveness within God's plan for saving all people in and through Jesus Christ our Lord.

When entering someone's home, it is a natural gesture for us to wipe our feet on the doormat, both as a practical act and as a sign of respect for the people who are welcoming us. In some cultures, people remove their outdoor shoes before entering a building. For us, our church building is a sign of the believing community, and a reminder of God's presence among us at all times. As we recall that we are in the presence of God, we may bow, make the sign of the cross, strike our breast (Luke 18:13), genuflect, or kneel. Like the man at the back of the temple, we often include in our personal prayer a plea for mercy and forgiveness (see Luke 18:13-14). Like Isaiah and Peter, we tend to recognize our imperfection when faced with God's holiness (see Isa 6:1-7; Luke 5:8).

The Church in this community and around the world also includes elements of repentance and forgiveness at various times in the liturgy.

1. Prayers of repentance. Members of the local Church have failed in their Christian living, and have disobeyed God. Now, by God's grace, they admit their sinfulness, ask forgiveness, and pray for strength to do better. These prayers, such as the "Lord, have mercy" *(Kyrie),* are often sung or recited in unison. The presiding minister may pronounce words of absolution, forgiveness, or assurance in the name of God and the Church (see John 20:21-23).

In the Sunday liturgy we find penitential prayers at different points: during the opening rites, at the end of the service of the word, in and after the "Our Father," and immediately before communion. Some traditions use more than one of these moments for expressing sorrow and asking forgiveness.

2. Gestures. The sign of peace is the most common gesture used by Christian communities to express their joyful acceptance of God's forgiving love (see section IV.C., below). Another sign could be a sung acclamation of praise and thanks, brief but joyful. Some churches sing the "Lamb of God" *(Agnus Dei,* based on John 1:29) as a transition between the sign of peace and the rite of communion.

3. Other times to express repentance. Around the year 100 C.E., Christians in Syria fasted twice a week, on Wednesdays and Fridays.[7] Traditional times for repentance include the weekdays of Lent, especially Ash Wednesday and Good Friday. Advent is a season of hope and joy, but we are called to "make straight the way of the Lord" into our hearts (see Luke 3:4-6). Among Roman Catholics, every Friday is still a day for voluntary acts of penance or special works of piety or charity by individuals and families.

Local communities may always invite their members and others to take part in a day of prayer and fasting for local or worldwide concerns. Traditionally, penitential practices are observed on a weekday, since Sunday is always a day of rejoicing because of the rising of the Lord Jesus from the dead.

4. Traditional ways of expressing our repentance. Prayer, fasting, and almsgiving were practices of the Jewish people which Jesus handed on to his followers (see Matt 6:1-18). As well, the local Church community may wish to come together to pray and reflect in some of these ways:

Praying the seven penitential psalms. For many centuries the Christian Church has selected seven of the psalms as most appropriate for penitential seasons and situations. These are Psalms 6, 32, 38, 51, 102,

130, and 143. Some or all of these psalms are appropriate for praying and singing in a penitential season such as Lent, and on days of penance, retreat, or renewal. Many musical versions of these psalms are included in our hymnbooks and in other resources. Depending on the circumstances, one or more or all seven psalms could be sung. It would be good to include the people in the congregation through the use of metrical or responsorial texts for at least some of the psalms.

A service of repentance and forgiveness. Particularly during Lent and Advent, the local community may be invited to listen to God's word calling us to turn back to God; to reflect in biblical terms on what we are called to be and do and avoid; to pray for God's mercy for ourselves and for others; to be invited to resolve to do some practical and positive actions for God and the people of God; to listen to words of assurance of God's love, mercy, and forgiveness; and to be sent forth to walk each day with the Lord Jesus, guided by the Holy Spirit. From the many psalms and hymns in our hymnals, we may select some which are appropriate for this congregation at this time in their spiritual growth.

Like the tax collector in the temple, we ask for mercy, and receive it, because of the unbounded love of our God (Luke 18:9-14). Like the tax collector Zacchaeus, we hear Jesus inviting us to share a meal together (Luke 19:1-10). For Christians, this means coming together in the Eucharist, a foretaste of the eternal banquet in heaven.

E. Giving thanks as a community in Christ

Here is the symbol: The people of this faith community have come together at the Father's invitation to give thanks and praise through Christ and with him, and with all the believers on earth and with the angels and saints of heaven.

1. Called in baptism to be God's priestly people. It is good to spend a few minutes reflecting on and praying about Ephesians 1:3-14, 1 Peter 2:5, 9-10, and Revelation 5:10. As individuals we are called into the family of God's people of praise. United with the angels and saints of heaven, "and in the name of every creature under heaven, we too praise" God's glory.[8]

2. Assembled on the Lord's day. On the first day of the week, the day of creation's beginning, the day of Jesus' resurrection, the day of the sending of the Spirit, God assembles us as his family, gathered around the table of the Word and the table of the Eucharist, and not too far from the font of life: *We* are being called to be and give a very clear image of the Church on earth.[9]

In our assembly, after hearing and responding to God's word, we remember, we give thanks, and we offer. We remember God's work in creation, the saving work of Jesus Christ, and the continuing work of the Spirit among us. We give thanks to God for these wonderful works. We offer ourselves and are caught up in Jesus' total self-offering to our Father. All this we give to the Father, through and with the only Son Jesus, in the Holy Spirit—and in the holy Church (Eph 3:21).

3. Prayer of the whole community. The Eucharistic Prayer (the great thanksgiving, the great prayer of thanks) is a presidential prayer, prayed aloud by the presiding minister in the name of all, for it is the prayer of the whole gathered community. All are invited to lift up their hearts, and to give thanks and praise. The "we" of the prayer includes both the members of this assembly and the Christian people of God around the world and the saints and angels in heaven. The whole community is invited to sing the responses to the preface dialogue, and the acclamations within the prayer. Those present also participate by listening and watching, and especially by their own self-offering in union with Jesus and all his people.

4. Strengthening the symbolism. The celebration of the great prayer of thanksgiving is not appreciated in most communities. Most people revert to a somewhat passive role, listening, maybe reading along, sometimes watching. A strong catechesis is needed to emphasize the community nature of this prayer, the importance of singing the acclamations, and the role of each person's self-offering in union with that of Jesus and his Church. When the prayer has no singing within it, its effectiveness as a symbolic action is lessened.

Presiders have to learn to invite people to enter into the prayer. The presbyter has to proclaim its texts clearly, for the Eucharistic Prayer is the Church's proclamation of its faith. In homilies and in Sunday bulletins, in congregational organizations, and in Sunday schools, all members of the faith community need to be challenged to let their praise and thanks and offering continue to grow and swell throughout the prayer, reaching a climax in a thunderous "Amen!" as they conclude the prayer and make it their own by singing their total assent.

F. Worshiping with our bodies

Here is the symbol: God, who made us in the divine image and likeness (Gen 1:26-27), has made us embodied persons, created through and for Jesus Christ (Col 1:16), and invites us to pray with our body as well as with our mind and heart.

As Christians, we accept that we are embodied souls. We understand ourselves as individuals, persons, who can be known only as living combinations of this embodiment (descended from our ancestors, our family tree), and this spirit (an individual person, chosen, created, and assigned by God to this time and place). The result is that each one of us is a unique reflection of God's qualities of beauty, glory, love, dedication, and wisdom, embodied in this specific person. Each of us reflects God's beauty, love, concern, and wisdom in a unique and wonderful way; and like all creation, God saw that we were "very good" (Gen 1:31).

1. Jesus. The incarnate Son of God, Jesus Christ, our brother and our Lord, saved us by living, suffering, dying, and being raised, in obedience to God our Father; his total self-offering, made in and with and through his fully human body, is his personal gift to God.

2. Action of this assembly. In this assembly, Jesus' sisters and brothers offer worship through their human actions—listening and speaking, singing and keeping silence, praying aloud in unison, and in silence in their heart, making gestures and taking postures, using light and movement and vesture and incense and color.

3. Jesus offers his gift and ours. Our Lord offers this worship to God as the sacrifice of the whole Body of Christ, head and members.[10]

4. Improving our symbolism. We recognize that God has designed us as embodied spirits, here in this time and place for a while; we are designed through and for Christ (Col 1:16). God has taken a personal interest in each of us (see Ps 139:13-16). God has chosen us to be people of praise, and Jesus is singing his praise and is offering thanks and glory to God through our lives and our worship.

5. Are we welcoming? A community of faith will want to look around its place of worship, and see if it is truly a place of beauty reflecting the beauty of God. Is this a welcoming place, where people feel free to come for common worship and personal prayer? Is it accessible to people with physical challenges? Are those who are hearing disadvantaged given assistance during celebrations? Do we advertise our welcoming attitude in local papers, phone books, and other directories?

6. Dancing at particular moments in the liturgy. David danced as the ark of the covenant was being brought to Jerusalem (2 Sam 6). Even today some Jewish people dance during the celebration of *Simchat Torah*. Religious dancing is accepted in many cultures. While this may not be part of our North American, British Isles, Northern European, or Puritan backgrounds, it is part of many other nations and cultures which are becoming part of our mosaic today. While many of us may not be ready for dancing or clapping in our worship services, these gestures may be a way in which we could use our bodies in our worship in the years to come.

G. Praying aloud and in silence

Here is the symbol: As individuals baptized into the community of faith, we are invited to raise our hearts and our voices in prayer; at times we are invited to pray silently, but in union with all the members of the assembly. Jesus continues to pray in us and through us (see Heb 7:25; Matt 18:20).

Prayer in unison unites the action of individuals with the action of the community: we recognize ourselves as the Body of Christ in this place. At the same time, the faith and prayer of those around us can strengthen and encourage us. Jesus invites us to agree on what we are asking for, and is present when two or more gather in his name (Matt 18:19-20). He has given us his Spirit to help us in our prayer (Rom 8:26-27). Jesus teaches us to ask our Father for the gift of the Holy Spirit (Luke 11:13).

Prayer may take the form of a dialogue between a worship leader and the community, or between the two halves of the assembly, alternating sections of a psalm or another text. At times, the dialogue may be between cantor or choir and congregation.

1. Three styles of prayer. In a well-balanced Christian liturgy there needs to be room for at least three styles of prayer:

Prayers said or sung by all: The Lord's prayer and the "Glory to God in the Highest" *(Gloria)* are usually sung or prayed by leader and people together. Many hymns are prayers addressed to God or to Jesus.

Prayers by a leader in the name of all: These are said or sung by the leader, and all respond in words or song. The great prayer of thanksgiving is an example, as are many collects, orations, or other ministerial prayers.

Moments for silent prayer or reflection: These may follow the invitation, "Let us pray," or be included after a reading, a prayer, or preaching. Like the mother of Jesus, we may ponder in our hearts the words and actions of God (Luke 2:19, 31). A service without some pauses for silence can be oppressive. Each assembly needs to become comfortable with adequate silence in its worship.

2. A two-way street. There is an important link between public and private prayer. The Lord who invites us to pray with others (Matt 18:19-20; John 14:13-14; 15:7, 16; 16:23-24, 26-27) is the one who invites us to pray in private, too (Matt 6:5-6). He teaches us not to pile up words (Matt 6:7-8), and gives us the Lord's prayer as an example for us to follow (Matt 6:9-13; Luke 11:2-4).

3. Personal prayer gives life to public prayer. Public prayer on Sunday will lack spirit and strength if those taking part are not praying as individuals all through the week. Each member of the assembly needs to be a woman or man or child of prayer, faithful in daily conversation with God. Public worship offered by those who do not pray regularly will tend to be formalistic or even empty of meaning. Regular, faithful praying during the week enriches our Sunday worship with life and joy and light.

Personal prayer can be aloud or in silence, alone or with others, using prayers from the Christian tradition, psalms and canticles from the scriptures, prayers we make up by ourselves, or prayers written by others. A balanced combination of some or all of these may be helpful to most people.

4. Public prayer guides our personal prayer. Personal prayer without sharing regularly in the community's Sunday worship could lead to a weak or even deformed prayer life. Individuals and families need to be guided to pray in the spirit of the Church's liturgy. The Church's spirit of prayer is positive and formative. Some of its qualities can be helpful to us in our personal daily prayer:

We pray as individual members of the Body of Christ: We are unique individuals, chosen in Christ before time began, and called in our baptism to be members of a community of forgiven sinners (Eph 1:3-14). When we pray alone, it is as an individual member of the wider Church; when we pray with others, it is as members called together in the Body of Christ.

Called to be people of praise and thanks: God has selected us, and set us apart to give praise and thanks (Eph 1:12). As God's beloved children, we are called to voice the praise of all creation, singing the song of the universe with and through the Word of God, Jesus our savior. With the psalmist, we invite all nations (Ps 117) and all the universe to join us in praise and thanks (Ps 148).

Broad horizons of prayer: Christians need to pray about the whole world, all the people God loves (see John 3:16), and all creation that God saw as "very good" (Gen 1:31). Our concerns in prayer should include peace in the world, victims of disasters, people in desperate situations, pollution, dying rainforests, endangered species. . . . Our personal and family prayer should lead us to do something practical for these people who are suffering or in need. (I frequently encourage families and individuals to add a petition for peace in the world to their meal prayers.) There are *no* limits to the horizons of prayer for Christians as individuals, families, or communities of faith.

Praying for our community: As well as praying for thousands or millions affected by flooding or volcanic eruptions or local wars, we have to remember the people in our congregation and community who are affected by sickness, disaster, prejudice, unemployment, poor living conditions, addictions, or other problems. We also need to remember those who are working to make things better or who are promoting positive causes in our community. In our personal prayer each day, it would be good to remember all who were mentioned in our community's pastoral prayer or general intercessions last Sunday.

Praying for forgiveness: We need to pray for forgiveness of our personal sins (Luke 15:18-19, 21; 18:13); of the sins of those who harm us (Matt 18:21-22; 6:12; 5:23-24, 43-45; Luke 11:4); and of the sins of our Christian and human communities (Matt 6:12; Luke 11:4). In their Sunday liturgy, most churches pray for such types of forgiveness. Individuals need to forgive and to pray for forgiveness in their personal prayer, in tune with the spirit of the Church's liturgy.

Generous prayer: We may pray for special people or intentions, but our hearts have to remain open to the needs of all as these become apparent to us each day or week. Our prayer has to be generous, ready to embrace all. If we spend a few minutes recalling the people we are praying for each day, we will be ready to extend to them the love that the Lord Jesus has shared with us.

Times for prayer: Traditional times of public prayer for Christians, dating back to the earliest centuries, are morning and evening; these times are based on Jewish practice in the time of Christ. For Catholics, the Second Vatican Council described these as the "hinge" or major hours for the public prayer of the Church called "Liturgy of the Hours."[11]

In tune with the Church's rhythm of prayer, individuals are invited to begin and end the day's work by personal, family, or community prayer. In the morning, we pray with the risen Lord Jesus, giving praise to God, praying for the worldwide Church, and asking for help to walk with Jesus throughout this day. In the evening, before or after supper, we recall the suffering and death of Jesus on the cross, thank him for the good things he has done in our lives today, and ask for his protection through the night.

In many ways, the prayer and practices of the Church's liturgy can help and guide us in our personal and family prayer.

H. Singing and playing music in our liturgy

Here is the symbol: Christ the singer continues to sing his song of thanks and praise to God through the minds, hearts, voices, lives, talents, and instruments of this gathered community of faith. Jesus is God's Word to us, and our word to God (John 1:1-5, 9-14, 16-18; see also Heb 1:1-4).

1. Music and singing are a symbol and foretaste of heaven. Heaven's liturgy of praise and thanks is often described in terms of angels and saints who sing and play musical instruments. Our present liturgy is to be a foretaste of the heavenly celebration in honor of our loving God.[12] Our singing and music in this assembly are a small but important sign of the great celebration we will join when, at the end of our life and service on earth, we enter fully into the Paschal Mystery of Christ. The liturgy of heaven is going to last forever:

> When we've been there ten thousand years,
> Bright shining as the sun,
> We've no less days to sing God's praise
> Than when we'd first begun.[13]

2. Important role of music in liturgy today. In the sixteenth century, Reformation churches accepted the practice of singing by all members of the congregation in each Sunday celebration. Four centuries later, the Second Vatican Council encouraged Catholics to sing during liturgical celebrations.[14] Full participation by the people is most important, since this is the primary and indispensable source of the true Christian spirit.[15] Sung liturgy is the norm for our Sunday celebrations.

St. Augustine tells us that "Singing belongs to lovers." An ancient axiom reminds us, "Those who sing well pray twice."[16] The symbol of singing and playing music in the liturgy is explored in greater detail in the second part of this book.

IV. Reflecting on Some Secondary Symbols

Secondary symbols may be described as other appropriate actions and signs which play a "supporting role" for the primary symbols. Some of them come from the scriptures, and others from traditional elements of Christian worship.

When the primary symbols are being celebrated well during our Sunday worship, the secondary ones may enhance them and underscore their meaning and importance. Thus, when the gospel is being proclaimed well, the use of candles and incense to show honor to God's word during the proclamation may heighten our sense of welcoming and listening to the Good News with joy and reverence.

When, however, the primary symbols are omitted or minimized or poorly celebrated, the use or enlargement of secondary symbols will not improve the situation. If the gospel is poorly proclaimed or the homily ill prepared, use of incense will not make up for or repair this serious lack. If baptism is celebrated with a few drops of water instead of by immersion or a generous pouring, good liturgical dancing will not camouflage the reversal of values and priorities.

A. Presenting our gifts for God, for the Church, and for the poor

Here is the symbol: Out of gratitude and generosity (graces given to us by our God), we bring gifts to God, to the Body of Christ, and to the poor and needy in our midst. We bring these gifts from the abundance which God has shared with us.

1. Some notes from the New Testament. The New Testament has many references to this type of generous giving: the widow's mite (Luke 21:1-4); the attitude toward almsgiving (Matt 6:1-4, 19-21); the sharing of money and the distribution of food (Acts 4:32-37; 5:1-6); Paul's collection for the poor of Jerusalem (1 Cor 16:1-4; 2 Cor 9:1-15). Jesus tells us that whatever we do for others in need, we are doing for Jesus himself (Matt 25:31-46).

2. Early Church. Around 150 C.E., St. Justin, a lay catechist in Rome, describes the Sunday Eucharist, where bread and wine are brought forward to be used in the Eucharist. He also mentions that those who can afford it bring a donation to the bishop for distribution among those in need.[17] Around 1387 C.E., Chaucer describes the wife from Bath as she proudly takes her place in the procession with the gifts:

> In all the parish not a dame dared stir
> towards the altar steps in front of her,
> and if indeed they did, so wrath was she
> as to be quite put out of charity.[18]

3. Today. We normally bring our monetary offerings to church for our Sunday celebration. Some may prefer to mail a check, but most bring their gift each week. As well, many congregations collect supplies for local food banks, for people in third world countries, or for missionaries. Others support organizations which work with the poor, or work with other churches in the community to assist people in need.

When Eucharist is being celebrated, it is common to have some members of the congregation bring the gifts to the communion table or altar before the great thanksgiving prayer. Bread and wine are used for the Eucharist, and the offerings of money and sometimes food for the needy are placed near the table for distribution later.

When we present our offerings during our worship on the Lord's day, we are recognizing, in effect, that we have received many gifts from God's generous love. Now we are bringing a share of these gifts to be used for God's worship, to support the church community and its works, and to help the poor and needy in our area and elsewhere. Our love for God and neighbor is being shown clearly, especially when we follow up our gifts with practical action for others.

B. Using worthy liturgical books in our celebrations

Here is the symbol: A community which strives to offer the best worship possible will encourage the use of worthy, respectable books by all who read, pray, or sing during the liturgy.

1. God's word. When the Church was discerning which books were to be accepted into the canon of Scripture near the end of the fourth century, a major criterion used was to ask which books were proclaimed during the Church's liturgy. Those traditionally read to the people during worship were recognized as the word of God; other early texts, such as the *Didache* or *The Shepherd* by Hermas, were deemed not to be Scripture.

During the early Middle Ages, many illuminated manuscripts were produced by hand to enshrine God's word in a truly respectful manner. *The Book of Kells,* a lavishly illustrated and gorgeously colored text, contained the four gospels in Latin for proclamation during the liturgy; its inspiring beauty continues to be on display in Trinity College, Dublin.

In those days, a deacon carried an illuminated or ornamental volume of the gospels into the church during the entrance procession. God's holy word, enshrined in this worthy book, was carried reverently through the assembled community as a sign of their respect for what they were about to hear.

In the past, the presence and use of a respectful pulpit bible has been one way of expressing the community's reverence for God's word. In many communities today, it is the practice to have a deacon or other reader hold up the book of God's word as the leaders of worship move reverently through the congregation to the table of the word and the altar table. This book may be a large and dignified volume, such as a pulpit bible or a lectionary.[19] By this symbolic action, all taking part are helped to recognize the respect of this believing community for God's word, about to be proclaimed to them.

The Byzantine Churches have a long tradition of providing lavish covers for their gospel book.

2. Books of prayers. In the earliest Christian communities, bishops who presided at the Eucharist followed the general pattern in use in their area, and extemporized the wording of their prayers. Since some were less talented than others, it was not long before some copied down the more elegant words and phrases, and used them in their own prayers. These booklets helped to keep the standards of Christian community prayer forms at a fairly high level. Around the 390s C.E., churches in North Africa began to require all bishops and presbyters to use only approved formularies of prayer.

Examples of prayers from Rome—texts of papal and parish liturgies—began to circulate during the next few centuries in northern Europe, with many modifications and additions as they were copied by hand. Printing with movable type was not invented in Europe until about 1445 C.E.[20]

Many churches today provide official or semiofficial books or texts for use in their liturgies. Some others offer suggested outlines or models that local congregations may adapt.

A problem of dignity: Sometimes a particular reading, prayer, or hymn is not contained in a worthy book. It is better to type or print it out, and put it in the book with paperclips. Loose sheets of paper should never be used by leaders in a service.

3. Books for singing. Most congregations provide one or two hymnbooks to help people join in the singing. Dilapidated books with pages falling out need to be repaired or replaced. Many denominations have issued modern hymnals in the past few years. Congregations would do well to provide them for all to use, thus enabling their members to remain up-to-date with the fresh insights, deeper social awareness, and other developments in the life of the wider Church.

C. Sharing a sign of peace

Here is the symbol: Cleansed by the penitential rite, the hearing of the word of God with faith, the offering of Christ and themselves in the Eucharistic Prayer, and the fervent praying of the Lord's prayer, God's holy people in this community share a sign of peace and love with their sisters and brothers in Christ. The symbol reminds us of the goal of Christ's rule on earth: "a kingdom of truth and life, a kingdom of holiness and grace, a kingdom of justice, love, and peace."[21]

1. A biblical practice. The sharing of the sign of peace is inherited from the Jewish tradition (see Gen 27:26-27, where Isaac kisses Jacob disguised as Esau; and 1 Kgs 19:20). Jesus mentions a kiss as a normal greeting by a host (Luke 7:45). In the epistles, Christians are told to greet one another with a holy kiss, a kiss of love (Rom 16:16; 1 Cor 16:20; 2 Cor 13:12; 1 Thess 5:26; and 1 Pet 5:14).

2. Its location in the Eucharist. Originally a "seal and guarantee" at the end of the Liturgy of the Word, the sign of peace was moved around 416 C.E. by Pope Innocent I to the end of the Eucharistic Prayer. Gregory the Great (590–604) placed the Lord's prayer after the great *Amen,* and the kiss of peace was considered to be one of the ways of putting "as we forgive those who sin against us" into immediate practice.[22]

The position of the sign of peace in the Roman liturgy today is shortly after the *Our Father* (the proposed revised Sacramentary provides an option of placing it at the conclusion of the Liturgy of the Word). The renewed rites of other Christian churches go back to our common tradition, and choose the opening rite of declaring forgiveness or the end of the Liturgy of the Word as suitable places for the sign of peace. In any one of these three positions, the sign of peace is expressing the same meaning.

3. Meaning of the sign of peace today. English-speaking people in North America found it hard in the late 1960s and early 1970s to break out of their shells and share the greeting of peace in a comfortable way. The term "kiss of peace," so easy to use in Latin, was felt to be too intimate, and the "sign" or "greeting" of peace was soon substituted.

Today we still prefer to use these terms, but the action has become more natural and relaxed. Now, married or engaged couples kiss each other, family members and close friends hug or embrace, and strangers smile, shake hands, and greet one another in a more comfortable manner. Special groups—members of an organization or religious community, people on retreat or at a weekend meeting together, or participants in a course or conference—may be drawn to greater exuberance than is usual in a congregational setting because of their emotional investment in this time together.

Sometimes, however, the greeting of peace dribbles off too far and loses its dynamism when people drift from a sign of Christian love to a type of chitchat best done outside the service: asking about Uncle Joe's appendix operation, or the present ages and occupations of the children. Most people, however, have developed a positive attitude toward this action as a way of expressing our love for one another in Jesus Christ, our saving Lord and loving brother.

Normally, the presiding minister greets the people nearby; as a rule, he or she does not wander through the congregation, since the sign of peace is based on our common baptism rather than on ordination or appointment. It is, however, appropriate in funerals for the presider to share the sign of peace with the immediate family members; in weddings, with the newlywed couple and their attendants; and in other celebrations, with people who are more deeply involved.

D. Receiving communion under both forms

Here is the symbol: Jesus nourishes us with his body and blood, consecrated and offered and received in this celebration of this community.

1. At the Last Supper. Jesus took bread, broke it, blessed God over it, and gave it to his disciples: "This is my body, broken for you. Take it and eat it." He took a cup of wine, blessed God over it, and gave it to them: "This is the cup of my blood, the blood of the new covenant, shed in order to forgive sins. Take it and drink it." Then he commanded them to continue to remember him by doing this: "Do this in memory of me."

2. During the Middle Ages. In the first few centuries, Christians continued to do what Jesus commanded. Then a number of gradual developments over the next thousand years began to affect the Church's Eucharistic practices and beliefs:

Fear of Christ, seen as a severe and distant judge rather than as our brother and our merciful Lord, spread from the Eastern Church to the Western Church in the centuries following the Council of Nicaea. Unleavened white wafers baked by "holy" persons began to replace ordinary leavened loaves of bread made by the people at home and brought to the church. People felt unworthy, and stopped going to communion each time they took part in the Mass; by 1215, the Fourth Lateran Ecumenical Council had to legislate a minimal practice of receiving communion once a year, around Easter.

People no longer received communion from the chalice: Eventually they were forbidden to do this. In the second half of the thirteenth century, forms of Eucharistic devotion outside Mass developed, and put much more emphasis on seeing the consecrated wafer ("staring, not sharing") rather than receiving the body and blood of Christ in communion. Among Roman Catholics, communion from the reserved sacrament in the tabernacle gradually came to be accepted as normal on the rare occasions that they communicated.

In the Roman Catholic Church, these negative trends began to be reversed at the beginning of the twentieth century, when Pope Pius X encouraged communion more frequently, and promoted first communion at an early age (younger than the age of 11–12, prevalent in the 1880s and 1890s).

3. Second Vatican Council. In 1963, the Council encouraged Catholics to return to the tradition of receiving communion by returning to the full sign of eating and drinking.[23]

4. Reclaiming our symbols. Jesus gave his apostles unleavened bread and one cup at the Last Supper. St. Paul spoke of one loaf and one cup (1 Cor 10:16-17; 11:23-29). Through the centuries, some variant practices have been incorporated, for one reason or another, into the celebration of the Eucharist:

Bread: Leavened, unleavened, one loaf, several loaves, wafers, cubes; made from wheat flour, made from another type (see John 6:9);

Wine: Wine, grape juice capable of becoming wine, pasteurized grape juice;

Distribution of the communion bread: In the hand, on the tongue;

Distribution of the communion wine: Drinking from one cup, small thimble cups, intinction; both forms given together by a spoon.

Now may be the time for churches to look at the tradition (which includes the scriptures), dialogue with other churches, and discern what is best today in the light of liturgical convergence in this ecumenical age. *Are we open to the stirrings of the Holy Spirit among us?*

E. Using lights and vestments

Here is the symbol: Our New Testament speaks about Jesus as the light of the world. It also mentions special clothing, vesture, or vestments in its description of heaven. We see candles as reminders of Christ our light. Special vesture in the liturgy can be understood as a sign that we want our worship to be done with beauty and dignity.

1. Light and lights. Jesus calls himself the "light of the world" (John 8:12; 9:5). He is the true light that comes into this world (John 1:9). Our Lord invites us to follow him in being the "light of the world," letting our light shine through our good deeds, and leading others to give glory to God our Father (Matt 5:14-16).

In our baptism, Jesus has rescued us from the kingdom of darkness and brought us into the kingdom of light (Col 1:13-14). Now we are called to walk in the light of Christ as children of light (Eph 5:8-14; 1 Thess 5:5). In the new Jerusalem, God the Father and Jesus are described as everlasting light (Rev 21:22-27; 22:5). (We also remember the words of the Nicene Creed: "God from God, Light from Light.")

In our culture, candles and lights are used at banquets and special occasions. What would a birthday or anniversary be without candles on the cake? Or a Christmas tree without lights?

Some churches use candles during their services. Some keep the tradition of a special Easter candle. On the four Sundays before Christmas, many congregations light the candles on the Advent wreath as a type of countdown before Christmas. Services by candlelight are popular in some congregations.

2. Vesture. The Old Testament described elaborate vestments for Aaron and his sons (Lev 8:5-9; Exod 28:1-43; 39:1-43) and for the high priest (Zech 6:9-14). The New Testament speaks about the white-robed people in heaven, whose garments have been washed clean in the blood of the Lamb (Rev 7:13-14). Other references to white robes are given (Rev 4:4; 6:11; 7:9-10; 19:14). Jesus himself is described as wearing a long robe with a golden rope around his waist (Rev 1:13).

During the early Middle Ages, as Christian congregations and churches grew larger, it became the practice to have bishops, priests, deacons, and other liturgical ministers wear a distinctive form of dress, often normal (or formal) dress from a previous age. (A similar practice in our day has funeral directors wearing morning coats; in the United States, some groups wear 1776-style uniforms in fife and drum units.)

A wide variety: After the Protestant Reformation in the 1500s, a variety of other traditions of vesture began, and still remain. In today's churches we find traditional Roman or Eastern vestments, based on ancient Mediterranean secular styles; Geneva gowns; academic garb; and modern business suits. Members of each community need to understand why their tradition vests its presiders and other ministers as it does, and to share this with members of other churches.

Lights and vesture are part of the Christian tradition of worship. How do they fit into your community's worship on the Lord's day?

F. Burning incense in our worship

Here is the symbol: The aromatic smoke rising from the burning incense is an image of the prayers of the saints on earth. This meaning is found in Scripture. This symbol speaks to us of our reverence toward God and of our prayer.

1. In God's word. We find incense associated with sacrifice and with prayer:

With sacrifice: Every morning and evening, incense was burned outside the veil in front of the ark (Exod 30:1-8; 1 Kgs 6:19-22). Zechariah was doing this "at the hour of incense" when the archangel Gabriel announced the birth of the prophet we know as John the Baptist (Luke 1:8-23). The fragrance of the burning incense recalls the pleasing odors of the Old Testament sacrifices (see Gen 8:21; Exod 29:18).

With prayer: Picking up the imagery of Psalm 141, the final book of the Christian scriptures says the smoke from burning incense is the prayer of the saints, the members of the Church on earth (Rev 5:8). Written in a time when heaven was considered to be "above the earth" (see Rev 3:12; 13:13; Mark 7:34; 16:19), the rising smoke aptly symbolized and accompanied the prayers of those on earth rising to God in heaven (Rev 8:3-4).

Other references: We find one verse which combines both meanings, prayer and sacrifice (Ps 141:2). This psalm is traditionally chosen for evening prayer, preferably with incense and the raising of our hearts in prayer. In their time, the wise men included frankincense among their gifts to the newborn king (Matt 2:11).

God is present: A further image presented by the smoke from burning incense is that of the *shekinah,* the cloud which symbolizes that God is present in a special way (Exod 40:34-38; 1 Kgs 8:10-11). The cloud in the transfiguration scene at Tabor has the same meaning (Mark 9:7). The use of incense in our celebrations can remind us that God continues to be present among us, and that our prayers are being offered to our God.

2. Pagan Rome. During the first three centuries, incense was not part of Christian worship. In pagan Rome, burning incense had three uses: a practical way of masking unpleasant odors when a body was carried to its tomb outside the city; a sign of honor when a senator was moving through the streets; and a sacrifice to one or more of the gods (including the emperor). For a Christian to burn incense before an image was a sign of apostasy, of turning away from Christ and abandoning the faith.

3. In Christian worship. After Constantine ended the official persecutions in 313 C.E., incense was no longer a sign of turning away from Jesus and his Church. The neutral and practical value of burning incense in funeral processions was the means by which the use of incense gradually came into the Christian liturgy. As bishops were given the honors accorded to senators, the use of incense became one of their prerogatives.

A sign with several meanings: The scriptural meanings of this symbol include sacrifice, prayer, recognizing the presence of God, and giving honor and respect to our God. The use of burning incense became a way of honoring important people (bishops, emperors) and the worshiping community, and a gesture for showing reverence and respect for places and objects (such as icons) used in our public worship.

4. Using incense during our public prayer. In the past few decades the use of incense seems to have been hijacked by hippies,

New Age groups, and various faddists. We need not cede the field; instead we should reflect on our tradition, both Jewish and Christian. Incense has an honored place in our scriptures and in our worship practices.

A time for reflection:

*Churches and congregations which use incense in some of their liturgies need to reflect on why, when, and how they use incense. Is it used generously and gracefully? Is there room to improve? Have they thought about this symbol enough to be able to explain it clearly to other Christians who do not use it?

*Those who do not use incense or who shun it need to reflect on our Jewish and Christian tradition, scriptures, and liturgies. Have they considered why they are ignoring or rejecting incense? Even if they are not ready to use incense yet, is there room for some fresh discussion about its values in public worship? Can they discuss this with other churches which use incense regularly or occasionally?

*A concern: One problem, however, about the generous use of incense in today's church buildings is that there are people with serious allergies, individuals who are most sensitive to the chemicals in the smoke. One possible solution may be the development of a more neutral type of incense. In outdoor celebrations, however, the use of incense may continue to be appropriate.

Burning incense can add solemnity and festivity to important celebrations, and an atmosphere of reflection and prayerfulness to evening prayer in large or small groups.

G. Washing of feet

Here is the symbol: Love, but love which is shown in a *practical* way. Jesus washed the feet of his apostles, and told them that he was showing them how they should serve one another (John 13:1-17, 20).

1. A unique approach. John's presentation of the Last Supper (John 13:1-17:26) is unique in the New Testament. The first three gospels present the familiar Eucharistic story, with Jesus giving the apostles his body and blood and commanding them to do this in his memory (Matt 26:17-30; Mark 14:12-26; Luke 22:1, 7-38; see 1 Cor 11:23-26, 27-34). John, however, seems to zero in on practical love, the fruit of our Eucharistic celebration, in the spirit of Matthew 25:31-46. Instead of concentrating on the Last Supper rites, he emphasizes what is at their heart: showing our love for God by showing practical love for our neighbors, our sisters and brothers in Christ. The same message is contained in the first letter of John.

Other New Testament references: Footwashing is also mentioned in a few other references (Luke 7:38, 44; John 11:2; 12:3; 1 Tim 5:10).

2. Restoration in the Roman Catholic liturgy. When the Catholic Church completed its major reform of the Holy Week liturgies for the spring of 1956 C.E., it restored the washing of feet on Holy Thursday as a visible and dramatic sign of the practical love which community members need to show for the poor and the weak in their midst. Twelve members of the community, in memory of the apostles of Jesus, represent the family of God in this area. This symbol of loving service to all speaks both to the clergy of the community and to all its members. The texts of the songs and anthems accompanying the rite echo the message of John 13, which is the gospel reading for this celebration.

Before 1956, the rite of washing the feet took place only at the cathedral or seminary, in the sacristy, usually in the afternoon with twelve seminarians and no gathered community; some monasteries retained the celebration with its full meaning. The renewal in 1956 restored the possibility of this symbolic practice to the public worship life of God's people in each parish and community of faith.

3. Catechesis. The washing of the feet is described in the Gospel of John. In our local communities, twelve people—women and men, grandparents, parents, and children—are invited forward after the homily. The clergy of the parish, priests and deacons, wash the feet of the twelve as a sign of Jesus' service to the community through their ministers. Jesus' words, "If I, your Lord and teacher . . ." (John 13:14-15), continue to be remembered among the members of this family of God's beloved children.

4. Use no substitutes. In the four decades since the Holy Week rites were restored, some parishes or other communities have rejected the symbol of footwashing, and have tried to substitute other actions, such as washing people's hands or polishing their shoes.

The substitution of nonscriptural actions for those described in God's word is not wise, since these actions are not life-giving. The Spirit of Jesus spoke about washing feet in the Bible, and Jesus recommended it to his followers by his actions and words. Dare we refuse to listen?

5. In our community of faith. If we do include the washing of feet in our liturgy, what does it mean for us? If we do not have it, is there openness to discuss it as a possibility?

In either case, are we being challenged to put our love into practice in hands-on ways? Would a yearly celebration of the washing of feet prompt us to discuss our call to care for others, to discern some needs around us, and to do something practical?

H. Exploring other Christian symbols

We may explore other secondary symbolic actions which are mentioned in the scriptures, and which have been part of the worship life of some churches and communities. These symbols would include:

1. Laying on of hands. This gesture was used in various ways: in blessing people (Gen 48:14; Matt 19:15; Mark 10:16); in giving the Spirit (Acts 8:17); in commissioning or ordaining (Acts 6:6; 13:3; 1 Tim 4:14; 2 Tim 1:6).

2. Sprinkling with water. Moses threw blood on the people to seal the covenant which God had made with them (Exod 24:7-8). Water was used for purifying people before offering sacrifice. The laver stood between the altar and the door of the tabernacle (Exod 30:19, 21; 40:30-32), and the priests washed their hands and feet before they offered sacrifices. The psalmist prayed for spiritual cleansing (Ps 51:2, 7, 10).

In the Christian scriptures, water is used for baptism (John 3:5; Acts 8:36, 38) and for footwashing (see section IV. G., above). In later centuries, the practice developed of sprinkling people with blessed water, in memory of their baptism, and offers an opportunity for believers to remember and renew their baptismal promises, to die with Christ to sin, and to live with him for God (see Rom 6:3-11). (This sprinkling may be an echo of the sprinkling with the blood of the covenant in Exodus.)

3. Taking part in outdoor processions. See Matthew 21:1-17, and parallels.

4. Anointing with oil. This was a sign of welcoming a guest (Ps 23:5; Luke 7:46). In the Hebrew Scriptures, prophets (1 Kgs 19:16), priests (Exod 29:7-9; Num 3:3), and kings (1 Sam 9:16 and 10:1) were anointed. Jesus is our *Messiah,* the anointed one; this is the meaning of the Greek word "Christ" (Ps 2:2; Luke 4:18; John 1:41; Acts 9:22;

17:2-3). Christians are anointed by the Spirit (2 Cor 1:21-22; Eph 1:13; 1 John 2:20, 27; Rom 5:5). The good Samaritan is described as using oil and wine to help heal the wounded stranger (Luke 10:33). The apostles were sent by Jesus to anoint and heal the sick (Mark 6:13; see also Jas 5:14-15). The Catholic, Orthodox, and Eastern Churches have a long tradition of anointing when celebrating baptism, confirmation (chrismation), ordination, and the sacrament of the sick.

5. Dancing during worship. See section III.F.6, above.

6. Other symbolic actions? Are there other symbolic actions to be explored in the scriptures and in traditional Christian worship practices?

Musicians, liturgists, pastors, and others who wish to grasp the fullness of liturgical worship celebrated by the Body of Christ on earth over the past 1970 years can benefit greatly from researching the meaning of these symbolic actions in the scriptures and in the history of Christian liturgy. There are many riches to be discovered which could be of benefit to many churches and congregations in our time.

V. Moving Ahead

In the scriptures and in the liturgy, God speaks to us in many ways. When we use traditional symbolic actions in our Sunday worship, we are being invited each week to penetrate a little more deeply into the mystery of God's saving love for us, the chosen people, and to take part in a most human way in the worship of Jesus Christ and his Body, the Church.

When, however, the primary symbols are omitted or minimized or poorly celebrated, the use or enlargement of secondary symbols will not improve the situation. If the gospel is poorly proclaimed or if the homily is ill prepared, use of incense will not repair this serious lack; good liturgical dance will not camouflage the reversal of values and priorities.

The pastoral team and the worship committee of a congregation may wish to explore these symbols one at a time, and see where there is room to improve their Sunday worship in this area. Every year or two, they may ask a member of the wider church (the diocesan or presbytery or district worship commission, or another expert in liturgy) to be present for a normal weekend of their Sunday services. Then this person could meet with the local worship committee to offer frank comments—in the light of the Church's long tradition of Sunday worship and their denomination's current guide-lines for good celebration—on what he or she sees and experiences in these celebrations. As well, this person may offer a variety of positive suggestions for improving their celebration of liturgy with its many rich symbols.

Many of these symbols are referred to in the hymns, psalms, canticles, and anthems that we sing. Wedding these symbolic actions with our singing can make their meaning become more evident.

The power of the Holy Spirit is within our Christian symbols when they are celebrated well in our Sunday assembly. Our task as musicians and leaders in worship is to encourage our people to benefit from the vast spiritual riches God is offering us when we gather to give thanks and praise on the Lord's day.

Notes

1. Scripture is important in the liturgy of the Christian Church. God's word is the source and inspiration for many actions in our worship: We proclaim readings from God's word, and open them up and explain them in the homily; we sing psalms and canticles; our prayers and hymns are often based on scriptural images and phrases. The scriptures give us the meaning of various actions and signs (symbols) that we use in our worship.

2. During the first Christian century, the early Church moved its weekly holy day from the Jewish Sabbath to the first day of the week, our Sunday. Creation began on the first day of the week (Gen 1:1-5), and Jesus was raised on the first day of the week (Mark 16:9). Other references from the Christian scriptures to the first day of the week are Acts 20:7, and 1 Corinthians 16:1-2; in Revelation 1:10, it is called the Lord's day. By the year 100 c.e., the *Didache* (14:1) speaks of the "Lord's day—his special day." See also *Sacrosanctum Concilium* ("The Constitution on the Sacred Liturgy") §106; and chapters 2 and 3, above.

3. *Baptism, Eucharist and Ministry* (Geneva: World Council of Churches, 1982) is a serious statement in which more than 100 theologians from many Christian traditions agree on many basic points in these areas. They outline the common shape and traditional elements in the celebration of baptism (§§17–23) and Eucharist (§27). They also point out areas where churches still do not agree in theory or practice, and invite further reflection and dialogue on all sides of the question. Since this statement was issued, many churches have been responding positively to this liturgical and ecumenical challenge.

4. Different churches have different services, but the component parts are often the same or quite similar. Thus, an opening prayer is a collect or oration in its structure and intent. The Eucharistic Prayer is called the great thanksgiving or the thanksgiving prayer in other churches. A homily, a ser-

mon, and a message belong to the same family. In this chapter we use a variety of terms to reflect the varied denominational backgrounds of those reading this book.

5. *Roman Missal: Sacramentary,* Eucharistic Prayer III; see also *Sacrosanctum Concilium* §§41–42; and the *General Instruction of the Roman Missal* §§74–75.

6. See chapter 10 on the General Intercessions.

7. *Didache,* 8:1. See also Matt 6:16-18; 9:14-15; Luke 18:12.

8. Eucharistic Prayer IV, preface

9. See notes 2 and 5, above.

10. As Eucharistic Prayer III proclaims to the Father, "May he make us an everlasting gift to you."

11. *Sacrosanctum Concilium* §89a. The "hinge" hours are the key hours around which the rest of the day's public prayer are celebrated.

12. See Revelation 4:1-11; 5:9-14. In Psalms 149–150, the songs and hymns and many instruments may be considered as our human imitation and echo of the choirs of heaven. See also *Sacrosanctum Concilium* §8.

13. "Amazing Grace," words by John Newton, 1725–1807; verse 5, above, John Rees, 1828–1900.

14. *Sacrosanctum Concilium* speaks of music in many paragraphs: see §§8, 24, 29–30, 33, 39, 44, 46, 54, 91, 93, 99, and 112–121.

15. Ibid. §§14, 31, and 118.

16. Both are quoted in the *General Instruction of the Roman Missal* §19; see Augustine, *Sermon* 336, 1:PL 38, 1472.

17. See *The First Apology of Justin, the Martyr,* chapter 67, page 287, in *Early Christian Fathers,* translated and edited by Cyril C. Richardson (New York: Macmillan, 1970, 1975).

18. Geoffrey Chaucer, *The Canterbury Tales,* translated into modern English by Nevill Coghill (Harmondsworth: Penguin, 1951, 1959); see The Prologue.

19. "Lectionary" has two related meanings. It was first of all a list of assigned readings for the year, or a longer period; later it came to mean a book containing the excerpted readings (pericopes) indicated in the list. A recent example of the first type is the table of readings given in *The Revised Common Lectionary,* by the Consultation on Common Texts (Winfield, BC: Wood Lake Books, 1992).

20. See S.H. Steinberg, *Five Hundred Years of Printing,* 3rd ed. (Harmondsworth: Penguin, 1974).

21. Preface 51, solemnity of Christ the King.

22. *The Mass of the Roman Rite: Its Origins and Development ("Missarum Sollemnia"),* by Joseph A. Jungmann, S.J. (New York: Benziger Brothers, 1955) vol. II, pp. 321–32.

23. *Sacrosanctum Concilium* §55. Other major reforms in the celebration of the Eucharist are outlined in §§50–54.

Chapter 6

Ritual: Straight Jacket or Dancing Shoes?

Joseph J. Fortuna

As the members of the liturgy committee related their experience, their bewilderment and amusement were apparent. Nevertheless, it was clear from the tone of their description that they considered the rite to have been a disaster. Great care had been taken to prepare for the Holy Thursday liturgy of their church of St. Agatha. Particular attention had been given to the footwashing, since the sanctuary in which this action would take place is small. It was decided that the twelve who would have their feet washed would come up in two separate sets of six. After the homily, the first six would come up to sit in the chairs placed on the wide step in front of the altar. The priest would wash their feet and they would return to their places in the assembly. The second set of six would follow. Everything went according to plan until the second set of six returned to their places. Then, to the surprise of the committee, many others in the assembly—of diverse ages, economic and cultural backgrounds—came up into the sanctuary to have their feet washed as well. Some even helped to do the washing. What happened was very different from what had been planned.

It is one thing to assert that what happened was very different from what had been planned. It is a much more difficult task, however, to say what in fact did happen. Why did so many others in the assembly come up to have their feet washed? Why did others remain in their places? What was it that went wrong with this rite? Or did anything at all go wrong? Perhaps it is better to ask what went right. Just what were the participants thinking and doing? What was happening to the individuals and to the community involved in this celebration? How were they engaged and motivated to participate the way they did? What prompted this event to happen at this particular time and not in previous Holy Thursday celebrations at St. Agatha?

It is clear that this list of questions about what happened in this rite is not exhaustive. The nature of the event is such that many more questions could be asked, many of these prompted by the responses to the initial questions. A review of recent literature about ritual also makes it clear that the variety of observations, questions, and answers that are offered will depend to a great extent upon the particular theory of ritual that we find most compelling. In other words, it is on the basis of our understanding of ritual that we will say what happened here. But that is not all. We are also likely to evaluate this event as "going wrong" or "going right" according to what we think about ritual and its participants.

This chapter explores what happened on that Holy Thursday for the purpose of better understanding this particular ritual event and ritual events in general. Ultimately, it aims to deepen appreciation for Christian liturgy as a ritual event and to provide some parameters within which ritual practitioners—assembly members and ministers, liturgical committees and planners, music directors and presiders— can work to maximize their opportunities for encountering the Holy in the liturgy.

Before going further it is necessary to state a presupposition: The footwashing event described above *is* Christian ritual. This is the non-negotiable starting point of the following discussion. The insights and claims of contemporary theories of ritual are always to be offered with reference to this concrete example. Any claims that they make about the nature of ritual and its relation to Christian liturgy must resonate in some way with this particular instance.

Ritual as an Animal Activity

One of the most obvious answers to the question of why so many others besides the twelve entered the sanctuary to have their feet washed is simply that everyone else seemed to be doing it. Without thinking about what they were doing or about its significance, people simply did what seemed to be the appropriate thing to do at the time. They acted unreflectively, as if by reflex or instinct, as if according to some unwritten rule whose force became compellingly operative while the first twelve had their feet washed.

This response would be comfortable for maverick ritual theorist Frits Staal.[1] It is his contention that ritual as such is not to be understood by looking for meanings in the activity that is performed. He suggests that ritual is primarily sounds and acts, and since "sound" reminds us of language and "acts" seem simple, the tendency is to interpret ritual according to a semantic model, i.e., one that looks for meaning in the sounds and acts.[2] He believes that there is simply too much evidence showing that some rituals seem to occur by chance.[3] It is better, therefore, to think of ritual syntactically, i.e., as rule-governed activity. As with the rules of syntax for a native speaker, these rules may not always be apparent to the observer (or even, it seems, able to be articulated by the participant). It is the task of the social scientist to discover the rules that motivate the activity. From this perspective, Staal is led to consider ritual according to a biological rather than a linguistic model.[4] It seems not too far fetched, then, to think of a row of ducks following one another across a pond and a procession of people into the sanctuary to have their feet washed as part of a single genus, i.e., ritual. As ritual, each is an instance of a rule-governed activity that is not inherently meaningful (but which for human beings could subsequently take on meanings).

Retaining the duck metaphor for a moment, we can say that Staal is here swimming against a stream of ritual theorists who primarily see ritual as meaningful activity. However, he is not alone in pointing out that animals ritualize. Many have pointed out that human ritual activity and the ritualization of many other animals have much in common.[5] Opinion is divided about whether these animal ritualizations can be called ritual in a proper sense of the term, but the commonalities do not seem to be disputed.

From this perspective, then, the footwashing on Holy Thursday can be seen as related to the regular grooming habits of many in the animal kingdom. Indeed, it is not uncommon to see cats or primates groom one another. Somewhere deep within the structure of human being, the action of footwashing touches a common chord of animality that links humans to the rest of nature.

Ritual as an Activity of the Human Animal

That everyone else seemed to be doing it is one of the most obvious reasons others may have entered the sanctuary to participate in the footwashing. Yet the most obvious is not always the most correct. Other explanations are possible. Some might suggest that what happened is that the meaning of the action, together with the words earlier proclaimed, literally moved the hearers to participate. Others might point to the experience of solidarity and egalitarianism felt in the rite. Still others might appeal to previous experience of similar footwashings at other churches. It might even be possible that the community so cared for each other beyond the ritual context that what was happening was a natural expression and reinforcement of the relationships the people shared. Conversely, the thought of the priest washing their feet might have subconsciously appealed to those on the lower rung of a hierarchically constituted Church. And there are even more possibilities. In all of these, however, the attempt to explain what happened in the rite has moved distinctly to the level of the *human* animal.[6]

It is not possible to construct here a taxonomy of the various ritual theories that would support one or more of these various explanations. It is sufficient to note that the variety of theories connected with these explanations makes it very difficult to settle upon a definition of ritual as a distinctively human activity. Each theorist gives his or her own nuance to the definition. For example, Victor Turner has defined ritual as

> . . . a stereotyped sequence of activities involving gestures, words, and objects, performed in a sequestered place, and designed to influence preternatural entities or forces on behalf of the actors' goals and interests. . . .[7]

Another anthropologist, Roy Rappaport, has offered this definition:

> I take the term *ritual* to denote *the performance of more or less invariant sequences of formal acts and utterances not encoded by the performers.*[8]

One of the differences in the definitions of these two anthropologists is that Turner's is functional, indicating the purpose or aim of the ritual, whereas Rappaport's is structural, simply pointing out constituent parts of ritual and their relation to one another. Turner's definition, more explicitly than Rappaport's, makes reference to superhuman forces or entities. This trans-human referent is brought out even more clearly in the definition offered by Blasi:

> Ritual is neither the recapitulation of the profane nor the imprisonment of the sacred, but rather the enactment of a referring-to, orienting-toward, focusing-upon, and opening-to the transcendent sacred. In participating in ritual, the person is neither being profane nor being sacred, but is rather being religious.[9]

What is significant about Blasi's definition is that it not only specifies ritual as distinctly human activity, but as distinctly human *religious* activity.

When we examine each of these definitions in the light of the foot-washing event under consideration, the difficulty of defining ritual becomes readily apparent. Each names something of what happened, but none says it all. With Turner, we can affirm that in the footwashing there is a stereotyped sequence of events performed in a sacred place involving words, gestures, and objects, but it is not immediately clear in what way this rite is making an attempt to influence preternatural powers. With Rapapport, we can affirm that the footwashing is an activity that is not encoded by the individual participants but by another, namely, Jesus Christ, "As I have done, so you must also do." Yet the distinctive characteristic of this event is that the performance of the sequence of formal acts and utterances *varied* from previous footwashing rites. With Blasi, we can affirm that this ritual involves the opening toward an other, but the other toward which we are opening is as much a human other as a transcendent sacred other.

This difficulty in capturing the essence of ritual through definition is one reason why, more often than not, treatments of ritual describe characteristics of ritual rather than offer a definition. An example of such a description is that given by James McCleod, who states that for a series of customary behaviors to be defined as rituals in the traditional sense,[10] they must involve all of the following:[11]

1. They must be *conventionalized,* i.e., they must be performed according to certain rules that are widely understood by those through and for whom they are performed. Variations can be tolerated only within certain limits recognized by the practitioners. In the case of the footwashing, no doubt the manner of washing was performed according to rules that would have been demonstrated in the washing of the feet of the first twelve to enter the sanctuary. Significant variation occurred in the inclusion of those who actively participated in the rite. Judging from the reaction of the committee members, this variation was tolerated, but very near the limit they could endure.

2. They must be *dramatic,* i.e., they must evoke or demand emotional empathy from the group. Such emotional empathy can reasonably be inferred among those who participated in the footwashing. Indeed, this very empathy may have motivated those who had not been pre-selected to join in the action.

3. The actions must be *repetitive.* Repetition is a necessary condition for the performance of a ritual. In the footwashing rite, the repetition of the action for a second group of six may have been a cue for the other members of the assembly, freeing them to engage

in the same repetitive action. It may have been that condition by which the participants were given the necessary cues as to how to enter into the action. If so, repetition freed them to lose themselves in the action and not be distracted by the concern over what was or was not permitted. Too much variation might have worked against participation in the ritual.

4. The action must be *communal*, i.e., it must involve more than just one's own personal experience, even if only one other person is involved. Obviously, the footwashing rite was communal in this sense. Participants were not only in direct physical contact with those whom they washed or by whom they were washed, they also were able to easily identify themselves as part of an assembly that was dramatically taking ownership for the ritual action.

5. The actions must have *higher levels of meaning* associated with the actual performance of the ritual than that normally conveyed by the physical objects or actions connected with the ritual. This is clearly the case in what happened in the footwashing. Although washing our feet is (or ought to be!) a daily occurrence, unless we are caring for small children or a sick or disabled person, it is rare for us to wash the feet of another. Even when this washing is done, it is usually done in a private or quasi-private setting. Usually the caregiver is a parent or sibling, servant (e.g., nurse) or friend, rather than a stranger or someone in authority. What is more, the footwashing that occurs in non-ritual settings generally serves a genuine function, namely, it cleans dirty feet. In the ritual activity, more often than not the participants come with basically clean feet. All these differences help to invest a similar physical act of washing with a heightened sense of meaning.[12]

In addition to these characteristics of the ritual activity itself, McCleod identifies several functions that a series of behaviors must accomplish if they are to be considered ritual in the traditional sense. It must (1) involve anticipated outcomes for the group or individuals involved; (2) be an event of personal or community regeneration; (3) demonstrate aspects of the social order and contribute to their perpetuation over time; (4) link the social order to both past and future through its performance; (5) demonstrate what is in-group symbolically and certify what is out-group symbolically; and (6) link the individuals and the group with a specific set of symbols predicated on some mythological or cosmological basis.[13] To see whether ritual in general and the footwashing in particular performs these functions, it is necessary to turn to the work of Victor Turner, arguably the most significant modern ritual theorist.

Turner himself is indebted to another anthropologist, Arnold van Gennep, who early in this century published a now famous work, *Rites of Passage.*[14] Broadly speaking, rites of passage are those that occur when someone moves from one state, place, and social position to another.[15] Van Gennep showed that although these rites are not all developed in the same way by all peoples or ceremonies, they generally have three characteristic phases: *separation* from the ordinary relations and patterns of the previous state or condition, a period of *transition* from the previous to the new state, and *aggregation,* incorporation or re-incorporation into the group.[16] Turner adopts van Gennep's three-phase description, emphasizing the dynamics and movement from one phase to the next. He was especially concerned to demonstrate that ritual is a process.

One of Turner's most significant contributions has been his attention to the middle, transitional, or liminal phase. (The word "liminal" comes from the Latin *limen,* which means "threshold." This in-between period is a threshold that, when crossed, opens to a new space.) He explains that during this liminal phase, the ritual participants are neither in the old state nor in the new. They are not subject to the rules or conditions of either. They exist in the world opened up to them in the ritual, living in the subjunctive, "as-if," "where suppositions, desires, hypotheses, possibilities, and so forth, all become legitimate."[17]

Turner described the relations among the participants during this liminal period as *anti-structural* and the group itself as *communitas.* These terms are notoriously difficult to define clearly and Turner has been accused of ambiguity, imprecision, and unfoundedly attributing categories that he derived from tribal societies to industrial societies.[18] Nevertheless, it is possible to get enough of a sense or feel for what he is talking about to gain some insight into the ritual process.[19]

The ordinary characteristic of human societies is structure.[20] Social relations proceed according to clearly understood customs, patterns, and institutions. When something such as social conflict happens to disrupt the smooth functioning of the structure, rites are often performed to address the tension. (For example, in the Ndembu society in which Turner worked, when normal reproductive processes went awry through repeated spontaneous abortion or the birth of twins, and disruptive social consequences occurred, rites were performed to address the situation.[21]) During these rites, the participants are separated from the structure and enter into the liminal, "in-between," phase of anti-structure. In anti-structure, the clearly understood customs, patterns, and institutions of the structure are suspended. The distance and formality of relationships change. Hierarchical relating gives way to mutual reciprocity and egalitarian relating. Ordinary differentiation between the sexes, such as distinctive clothing, is minimized. A kind of relational immediacy results from "men in their wholeness wholly attending"[22] to one another not only cognitively but emotionally, bodily, and in other ways as well. People are free to be with and for one another in ways that the structure does not permit. In a sense, they can experiment with relationship and with the "powers that be" to discover new potential and new ways of being. What occurs in anti-structure is often experienced as sacred, as the in-breaking of a new order into an old.[23]

Turner uses the word *communitas* to name the group that is anti-structurally related. For him, communitas emerges where social structure is not.[24] He explicitly avoids the term community, for it does not capture enough for him the sense of the essential and generic human bond that exists in communitas.[25] Communitas is characterized by the concrete, spontaneous, and immediate as opposed to the abstract, institutional, and rule-governed.

In what ways do Turner's categories help to explain what happened in the footwashing ritual at issue? In a variety of ways, it is clear that the participants have separated themselves from their ordinary structures and patterns of relating. They have entered a place of worship that is architecturally clearly distinguished from ordinary places. In addition, on Holy Thursday this place of worship may have distinctive appointments, e.g., flowers, white linens instead of purple, special chairs, and pitchers and towels.

The participants assemble for liturgy on a weeknight when normally most of them would not celebrate liturgy. This assembling takes place at the end of a season that is itself already separate, a period of penance devoted to more intense prayer, fasting, and almsgiving. The memories and traditions of previous experiences of Holy Thursday are particularly strong. These are the high holy days of Christianity. Those who are there are not fulfilling some institutionally prescribed obligation, but are there because they choose to be. This, too, sets this gathering and event apart from others.

In addition to this separation from the ordinary, once the liturgy and in particular once the footwashing begins, the familiar customs about who does what, who has access to where, who is responsible to and for whom, seem to be suspended. The priest removes his usual robe for celebrating and takes up a towel. Those who normally are found in pews at some distance from the sanctuary now enter this holy place. Those who would kneel before him [her] for blessing or forgiveness at other times, who would grant him a clerical discount at their place of business, who would send cookies to his home at Christmas time, who would grant him respect and an image that would normally keep him at a distance, who would submit to his authority in spiritual matters, these now sit before him. He kneels before them and, in a gesture that in its ritual formality is both exceedingly intimate and very public, washes their naked and weathered feet. The warmth of the gesture overcomes the cold of the water.

Two more things were particularly noteworthy in this event. The first was the spontaneity which characterized the communitas that developed. The suspension of the usual order of things was noted by the assembly. They were drawn into the intimacy and power of the event. They looked for no sign, no permission, no rubric that says, "Come higher." They were simply carried away by the rite from their places in the assembly to the action in the sanctuary. The second was that sexual role differentiation was suspended. Rubrics that say it is men who should have their feet washed notwithstanding,[26] both men and women spontaneously approached the sanctuary. Whatever bindings that distance them from one another outside the church building—or even within—were loosed, and they took up their dancing shoes and entered their hands and feet, their whole selves, into a communal dance in which all led and all followed. Somehow in this dance they followed freely in the footsteps of Christ.

With this poetic description of what happened in the rite, it is now necessary to return to what McCleod lists as the functions a series of behaviors must accomplish if they are to be called ritual. Each of these functions has to do with the status of the ritual participants after they have moved from anti-structure back to structure, from the liminal to the incorporation phase of the ritual process. In accomplishing each of these functions as described by McCleod, what ritual does is to reinforce and reinvigorate the prevalent personal, social, and even cosmological orientations and structures. It supports and feeds the status quo by allowing the interplay and dissipation of conflicting social energies in a socially acceptable manner.

It is possible to explain the footwashing event in this way. The social tensions that existed in the assembly—between lay and clergy, between those who exercise authority and those who submit to it, between women and men, between conservatives and liberals, between old time parishioners and new arrivals, between one race or another—all are eased by the temporary foray into the subjunctive, into the "as if" social relations were this way. Energy that was formerly channeled into dealing with the tension can now be fully given to a recommitment to the prevalent social, ecclesial, and perceived cosmological order.

If in fact what followed this rite at St. Agatha parish was a recommitment to the prevalent pre-ritual social, ecclesial, and perceived cosmological orders, then someone might claim that the above explanation is on target. However, it is also possible that if such recommitment ensues, the ritual may have in fact made no difference. Things simply continued after as before. On the other hand, if there are changes in the post-ritual relationships and orientations of the parish, then it might be that the ritual in fact somehow helped to bring them about.

There are a number of possible ways to imagine how ritual might have been an agent of change at St. Agatha, but most compelling is the idea that in the liminal phase of the ritual process, e.g., during the actual washing of the feet, the possibilities for new relationships and new orientations of participants to one another, to the Church, and to God were revealed to them. It might even be that this revelation was empowering and transformative of the participants at any number of levels—intellectual, emotional, relational, spiritual.[27] The ultimate result is that the participants returned to structure as changed people, and therefore their post-ritual relationships and orientations were changed.[28]

Ritual as Christian Human Activity

The above discussion of how, if at all, ritual makes a difference to those who participate in it has not yet given much explicit attention to that which is likely to be of most interest to Christian believers, namely, the theological difference that ritual makes. How is the relationship between the participants and God affected by or shaped by ritual? At root, the response to this question has to do not simply with ritual theory, but with how we understand the possibilities for encounter between the human and the divine. For example, for someone who holds that nature is the primary place in which God is to be found, rituals celebrating the seasons of the year or other natural cycles might be most important. To be in harmony with natural cycles is to be in harmony with God. Ritual that helps to place us in harmony with these cycles thus makes a difference in our relationship with God.

The Christian, while not denying that nature is a possible place where God can be encountered, holds that the primary opportunity for encounter with God occurs in the event of Jesus Christ. This means that if ritual is to make its most significant difference in the relationship between the participants and God, it must not only be rooted in the natural, but also and most importantly it must somehow be integrally related to Jesus Christ. This relationship to Christ has been conceived in various ways by Christians throughout the centuries, but inevitably it involves memory and words.[29] Thus, Christian ritual, in addition to the other characteristics of ritual discussed above, will include words and memory among its integral dimensions.

The naming of memory and words as integral elements of Christian ritual advances the discussion of how Christian ritual makes a difference, but it still leaves room for a variety of interpretations. For example, giving priority to the memory of the words and actions of Jesus as they are recounted in the words of the Christian scriptures, we could focus on the command of Jesus in the Gospel of John 13:14-15:

> But if I washed your feet—
> I who am Teacher and Lord—
> then you must wash each other's feet.
> What I just did was to give you an example:
> as I have done, so you must do.

We could then maintain that the ritual of washing one another's feet makes a difference in the participants' relationship to God because they are acting in fidelity to Christ's command. Moreover, we could argue that the spontaneous approach to the sanctuary by others in the assembly is in fact more faithful to the gospel command than the ritual action of a priest washing twelve men's feet, since Christ's command was to wash *each other's* feet. From the point of view of ritual, the difficulty with this approach is that it is not the actual footwashing which makes a difference. What is important is that we must be faithful to the memory of Christ as given in these particular words, in just the same way as we must be faithful to Christ's commands to do anything else.

A variation on this approach is to broaden the notion of memory to include the memory of the Jesus Christ event as it has been handed on in the Christian tradition throughout the centuries. The very breadth of this tradition requires authoritative teachers to ensure that the authentic memory is preserved and handed on. This authority is globally entrusted to the Church. Thus, over the centuries those in authority in the Church have faithfully interpreted the Jesus event to those in their charge, and in the process identified key or privileged Christian rituals called sacraments. When these rituals are performed as the Church intends, then Christian rituals can make their most important difference in the lives of believing participants.[30]

With respect to the footwashing, this approach raises some additional issues because the footwashing rite is not one which has been identified by authoritative interpreters of the memory of Jesus Christ as one of the privileged ritual encounters called sacrament. In addition, the manner in which this particular footwashing took place, i.e., with the spontaneous approach of both men and women from the assembly into the sanctuary, is at variance with what is intended by the compilers of the present Roman sacramentary. In other words, according to this approach, this ritual event is neither sacramental in the strict sense nor even faithful to the words of those who are ultimately entrusted with handing down the memory (and intention) of Jesus Christ. We might then conclude that as far as making a difference in the relationship between God and the participants, this particular footwashing event cannot have been one of the Christian community's most fruitful events.

This approach and conclusion are uncomfortable. They seem to preclude the spontaneity and free play characteristic of the liminal phase described above. In addition, they seem to restrict the possibilities for fruitful encounter between the human and the divine in a way that at least possibly does not fit the experience of those involved in the footwashing rite at issue.

Still another approach to memory and word as integral to Christian ritual is taken by David Power.[31] In his approach, it is not sufficient to see the function of words and memory in ritual as being the handing on of commands of Jesus to be fulfilled by subsequent generations. Nor is it sufficient to see their function as being a simple recital to keep the memory of the Jesus Christ event alive today. Rather, the words and memory that recount the Jesus Christ event of history need to be completed by a creative reconstrual that relates the promise of this event to other times.[32] The words and memory important in Christian ritual are not only those which have been handed on by others in the Christian tradition, but also those of the participants in the ritual itself. This is important because, in Power's approach, the promise of the Jesus Christ event is made present in the participants' narrating it from the perspective of their own distinctive life experiences.[33] The narrating that takes place in Christian ritual is primarily verbal, but not only so. Narrative remembering and ritual action together are a ritual event in which participants encounter the God of the promise made in the Jesus Christ event.

With respect to the footwashing rite, what is important is not a literal carrying out of the command of the Johannine Jesus to do what he had done. Nor is it the faithful carrying out of the ritual as prescribed by the authoritative interpreters of the Church. Rather, what is important is remembering the fidelity of the God of Jesus Christ in a way that is attentive and responsive to the manner in which the promise of this God is being manifest today in the lives of the believing participants. What is important is that the God who comes in ever new ways to believers comes to the participants in this ritual action done in memory of Jesus Christ in still another new way.

According to this approach, the footwashing event in question is not simply a re-enactment of something that Jesus did at the Last Supper. Especially as it involved the spontaneous approach of many in the assembly to the sanctuary to enter into the ritual action, it was an "event eventing." It was the Jesus Christ event once again making known the promise of God's presence for the participants, in a way that was ever new and therefore ever faithful to its way of being in human history. The social and personal transformations in the participants were at the same time the manifestation of God's promise to continue to be with them and sustain them as they attempted to live what these transformations required.

Some Concluding Comments for Participants in Christian Ritual

Ritual in common contemporary usage is often given a bad name. It is taken to be responsible for those aspects of Christian liturgy that are boring and unexciting. It connotes repetition that does not engage but dulls. It evokes images of formalism which seem to distance Christian liturgy from the experience of the participants. It seems to be less than relevant, restricting the free expression and response of participants as if they were in rubrically designed straightjackets.

In response to these too common experiences of ritual, its practitioners—both participants and planners—often seek to remedy the situation by eliminating such things as repetition, formality, and routine. They attempt to replace them with variety and ever new attempts at stimulation. The experience of the footwashing rite described above suggests caution in such adaptations, for it indicates that the reason so many people spontaneously approached the sanctuary had to do with the very ability of ritual's repetition, routine, and formality to help create a space "in-between" in which the participants could freely, imaginatively, and in faith explore possibilities for their relationships with others and with God. If anything at all, the adaptations which are made to Christian ritual should flow from critical reflection upon experiences such as this footwashing rite, experiences that implement accepted ritual forms but leave room for dancing to break out. These rites should be the point of departure for ritual planning and preparation not only because of what they reveal about the workings of ritual as such, but especially because they may well be "event-eventing" in our communities, making known and drawing believers into the promise of God's presence.

Notes

1. Staal's primary exposition of this thesis is in his book, *Rules without Meaning: Ritual, Mantras and the Human Sciences* (New York: Peter Lang, 1989). Some reactions can be found in a symposium on the work in *Religion* 21 (1991) 207–25.

2. Frits Staal, "The Sound of Religion," *Numen* 33 (1986) 213.

3. Ibid., 216.

4. Ibid., 217.

5. For example, see Ronald L. Grimes, *Beginnings in Ritual Studies* (Lanham, Md.: University Press of America, 1982), especially chapter 3, pp. 35–51, where he distinguishes six modes of ritual sensibility: ritualization, decorum, ceremony, liturgy, magic, and ceremony. See also Tom F. Driver, *The Magic of Ritual* (San Francisco: Harper Collins, 1991), especially chapter 2, "Ritualizing: The Animals Do It and So Do We," 12–31.

6. It should be noted that Staal was not denying that ritual activity could be human. Rather, in his opinion his theory implied a definition of human culture that related it much more directly to nature than do symbolic theories of human culture (Frits Staal, "The Sound of Religion," 219).

7. Quoted in Mathieu Deflem, "Ritual, Anti-Structure, and Religion: A Discussion of Victor Turner's Processual Symbolic Analysis," *Journal for the Scientific Study of Religion* 30 (1991) 5.

8. Roy A. Rappaport, "Ritual, Time, and Eternity," *Zygon* 27 (1992) 5.

9. Anthony J. Blasi, "Ritual as a Form of the Religious Mentality," *Sociological Analysis* 46 (1985) 63.

10. McCleod's reference to a "traditional sense" of ritual implies preconceptions about ritual that this chapter does not necessarily share.

11. The characteristics listed below are given by McCleod in "Ritual in Corporate Culture Studies: An Anthropological Approach," *Journal of Ritual Studies* 4 (1990) 92–93. The applications to the footwashing event are mine.

12. Catherine Bell has indicated that it is characteristic of ritual to be a way of acting that distinguishes it from other ways of acting. See Catherine Bell, "Ritual, Change, and Changing Rituals," *Worship* 63 (1989) 34–35.

13. James McCleod, "Ritual in Corporate Culture Studies," 93–94.

14. Arnold van Gennep, *Rites of Passage,* trans. Monika B. Vizedom and Gabrielle L. Caffee, with an introduction by Solon T. Kimball (Chicago: University of Chicago Press, 1960).

15. See Mathieu Deflem, "Ritual, Anti-Structure, and Religion," 7.

16. Arnold van Gennep, *Rites of Passage,* 11: " . . . although a complete scheme of rites of passage theoretically includes preliminal rites (rites of separation), liminal rites (rites of transition), and postliminal rites (rites

of incorporation), in specific instances these three types are not always equally important or equally elaborated."

17. Victor Turner, *The Ritual Process: Structure and Anti-Structure* (Ithaca, N.Y.: Cornell University Press, 1977) vii.

18. For example, see Tom F. Driver, *The Magic of Ritual,* 227–38.

19. Turner acknowledges these criticisms, but responds simply that "the proof is in the pudding." His categories have been used by scholars in a variety of fields to press their own analyses of ritual (*The Ritual Process,* vi).

20. The discussion of structure, anti-structure, communitas, and liminality that follows in the next few paragraphs is based on chapter 3 of *The Ritual Process,* "Liminality and Communitas," 94–130.

21. Ibid., 1–93.

22. Ibid., 128.

23. Ibid., 128.

24. Ibid., 126.

25. Ibid., 96.

26. *The Sacramentary* (New York: Catholic Book Publishing Co., 1985) 136.

27. In his later years Turner was even exploring the neurophysiological components and consequences of ritual. See Edith Turner, "The Genesis of an Idea: Remembering Victor Turner," *Zygon* 21 (1986) 7–8. Similar explorations into the neurobiology of ritual transformation have been undertaken by Eugene G. d'Aquili, "Myth, Ritual, and the Archetypal Hypothesis," *Zygon* 21 (1986) 141–60.

28. This explanation of how the footwashing could be a change agent finds support in Jeffrey VanderWilt, "Rites of Passage: Ludic Recombination and the Formation of Ecclesial Being," *Worship* 66 (1992) 398–416.

29. Ronald Grimes has raised a justifiable suspicion about the use of words in Christian ritual. In particular, he has raised concern that the claims made for Christian narrative may be inflated and cause people to neglect other dimensions of their humanity and other modes of expression in their lives. "Of Words the Speaker, of Deeds the Doer," *Journal of Religion* 66 (1986) 1–17.

30. This approach seems to reflect concerns articulated by Dr. Lynne C. Boughton in "Sacramental Theology and Ritual Studies: The Influence and Inadequacies of Structuralist and Mythographic Approaches," *Divinitas* 36 (1992) 52–76.

31. See David N. Power, "Ritual and Verbal Image," and "Myth, Narrative, Metaphor," chapters four and five in *Unsearchable Riches: The Symbolic Nature of Liturgy* (New York: Pueblo Publishing Company, 1984) 83–143. See especially David N. Power, "Sacrament: Event Eventing," in *A Promise of Presence: Studies in Honor of David N. Power, O.M.I.,* eds. Michael Downey and Richard Fragomeni (Washington, D.C.: The Pastoral Press, 1992) 271–99.

32. David Power, "Sacrament: Event Eventing," 288.

33. Unfortunately, the philosophical and theological presuppositions of Power's approach, which must be addressed if the full implication of his approach is to be appreciated, cannot be discussed here.

Chapter 7

Must Eucharist Do Everything?

John F. Baldovin, S.J.

The answer to our title question for this chapter is obviously "No," but even asking it implies that it relates to a problem with our celebration of the Sunday Eucharist.

It is difficult to get at the malaise that seems to be gripping so much Sunday worship some twenty-five years after the Second Vatican Council. As a college student in the late sixties and a young religious in the seventies, I can remember very well the exuberance that attended the beginnings of the reform. Lately, however, Sunday Eucharistic liturgy seems to have run out of steam—at least in a good number of places. Perhaps the heady excitement of the reform has worn off like the enthusiasm for ecumenism that gripped the same post-conciliar period. Perhaps, however, there are deeper reasons that the liturgical reform seems not to be so successful—reasons that have to do with the appropriation of liturgical reform itself.

Some of the current disquiet with liturgy has been analyzed in a volume which contains papers given at a colloquium in 1988 to mark the twenty-fifth anniversary of *Sacrosanctum Concilium* ("The Constitution on the Sacred Liturgy" of Vatican II).[1] The state of Catholic Church music and liturgy has been lambasted, at times a bit unfairly, by the book *Why Catholics Can't Sing*, that seems to have hit the mark since it gained great popularity when it appeared.[2] Liturgical theologian Theresa Koernke has suggested that it is time to move away from the excesses of the past few decades and toward a renewed liturgy on the basis of more sound theological and cultural anthropological principles.[3]

I am sure that the "flatness" of much (but by no means all) of our Sunday worship (and I doubt if this is a peculiarly Roman Catholic problem) is due to a number of factors, but I will deal with only one of them in this chapter, because I think it speaks to a fundamental error with regard to the nature of liturgy itself. Namely, the fact that the *liturgy cannot do everything.* I propose to analyze our problem by first discussing the centrality of the Sunday Eucharist envisioned by Vatican II, second describing what liturgy cannot do, and finally outlining what a "successful" Sunday Eucharistic liturgy might look like.

I. Centrality of Sunday Eucharist

One of the most important results in the post-Vatican II liturgical reform has been the emphasis on the pre-eminence and centrality of Sunday Eucharist. The grand architect of the reform, Annibale Bugnini, has outlined the fortunes of the *Missa normativa* (i.e., the model celebration of the Eucharist—with singing and multiple ministers, intended for Sundays and feast-days), the resistance that this concept of participative worship met, and the eventual codification of this model in the *Mass of Paul VI* used by Roman Catholics [and similar service books published by other mainline denominations].[4] We should not underestimate the veritable sea-change that this shift in the model of the Eucharist signified—from the Eucharist understood *mainly* in terms of the activity of the priest alone and of the status of the bread and wine, to the Eucharist understood as the corporate activity of an assembly of baptized Christians, celebrating the profound mystery of the dying and rising of Christ for the life of the world. The paradigmatic celebration of the Eucharist is, therefore, the first given in the *General Instruction of the Roman Missal*—a Sunday Eucharist with singing and the active participation of deacons, acolytes, readers, et al.[5] Furthermore, the norms for the liturgical year treat the Lord's day as "the first holy day of all," making it difficult for Sunday to be replaced by other feasts.[6]

There can be little question, therefore, that on the theoretical level, Sunday Eucharist is central in the life of the Church. Pragmatically speaking, the same holds true, for Sunday is obviously the time when the vast majority of church-going Christians assemble. In fact, given the frenetic pace of life in post-industrial society, Sunday will most likely be the *only* time that most Christians come into formal contact with the church as Church. As I see it, the temptation of the past two decades has been to merge the theoretical centrality of the Eucharist with the pragmatic opportunity to "get everything in" with regard to Christian life and worship in one hour on Sunday morning (or Saturday evening, for all too many Roman Catholics now).

Another factor in this mix consists in the failure to appreciate the nature of liturgical activity. My thesis is that once the liturgy becomes instrumental for other ends (i.e., cannot be appreciated in and of itself), then it loses its fundamental *raison d'être*. This is the case because liturgy is by definition ritual activity, and the ritual nature of celebration suffers when we force the Eucharist to be something it isn't.

Now ritual is a notoriously complex and controversial subject. In the first place it is not easy to discern precisely what function ritual— or better, rituals—play in culture and individual human lives. In his survey of the study of myth and ritual, William Doty catalogues some twelve different functions that rituals play, ranging from consolidating personal and group identity, to the dramatic resolution of social tensions, to the enhancement of just plain enjoyment.[7] Some rituals in some cultures reinforce the status quo, while others criticize the same status quo and act as agents of social change; most (perhaps all) rituals have something to say about relationships of power and authority. The same basic ritual can perform a variety of functions over long periods of time and therefore mean rather different things. The celebration of the Eucharist, with its varying historical emphases on the unity of the community, the role of the priest, and seeing Christ present in the consecrated bread, is certainly a case in point.

I would suggest that today the Eucharist fulfills a number of ritual functions. Let me give a functional definition of the Eucharist as an activity. Please note that this definition is by no means adequate as a complete definition. *The Eucharist is the ongoing and repeatable celebration of Christian initiation.* Understanding the Eucharist in the context of Christian initiation is essential to appreciating it as a ritual activity. Christian initiation incorporates an individual into the community of believers by instruction and by learning to pray and act as a Christian. This incorporation is ritualized by symbolic sacramental acts that conform the individual to the dying and rising of Christ: the baptismal bath, the Church's public affirmation of that dying and rising in chrismation and the imposition of hands with prayer (confirmation), and by quite literally being incorporated into Christ in the act of holy communion. This culminating act, unlike the other two ritual moments, is not a one-time event but rather helps to symbolize that incorporation into Christ is a lifetime process.

We renew our baptismal promises once every year at Easter, but in a real sense our initiation is implicitly renewed each time we meet to celebrate the Eucharist.

This approach to the Eucharist contains within it the seeds of two important ritual functions. In the first place, the repetition of the rite supports, solidifies, and celebrates anew the individual and corporate identity of the assembly as what it already is—the Body of Christ. In the second place, however, this act is a challenge, to paraphrase St. Augustine's famous words, to be what we receive; i.e., to grow more and more into the likeness of Christ as individuals and as communities. From this perspective the Eucharist is both formative and transformative.

The ritual does its work, I would submit, by means of two basic ritual structures: the interplay of proclamation and action, and the four-fold shape of the Eucharistic action itself. The dynamic of proclamation and response (or action) acts as a witness to the priority of God's activity in the assembly. We can only perform sacramental actions or engage in formal liturgical prayer in response to God's gracious invitation and God's activity in our lives and in human history. The four-fold shape of the Eucharist (taking = presentation of the gifts; blessing = Eucharistic Prayer; breaking = fraction; giving = communion) compresses the activity of Jesus at the Last Supper into a ritual that plays out Christ's passion, death, and resurrection as the loving and life-giving surrender of self in faith to God, which I take to be the essence of Christian life. In other words, Eucharistic activity embodies both who Christ is and who we are (or better, who we are on our way to becoming). My hunch is that the ongoing repetition of this ritual is essential to the gradual transformation of individuals and communities into the Body of Christ.

Let me deal with an obvious objection here. Ritual has received a bad name in our time precisely because such repetitious activity can become rote and hollow, meaningless and even hypocritical. Worse, rituals can be used to anesthetize people and render them unconscious of their lack of empowerment. Of course, no ritual activity is immune to misuse, as both the prophets of Israel and Jesus were quick to point out. Rituals can be demonic when they are used to serve evil purposes, like the impressive but chilling ritualized rallies of Nazi Germany. Ritual is never enough. That is why sacraments are always sacraments *of faith.* They require belief and commitment even as they enable both to grow. Belief and interrelated action *(praxis)* are required if any ritual, especially Christian ritual, is to have its intended effect.

But to dismiss ritual, instead of the *context* of ritual, as the problem is to attack the wrong problem. The attitude of surrendering to a purely negative estimation of ritual is what I like to call *ritual embarrassment.* Not only would it be a pity, it would be nothing less than a disaster if mainline Christianity were to lose its rich ritual heritage, its confident and exuberant enjoyment of the material of creation in acted symbols. Ritual embarrassment runs the risk of losing this heritage in favor of something like a religious talk-show.

II. What Eucharist Cannot Do

Sunday Eucharist, then, must be allowed to be precisely what it is— a ritual activity. In the face of Eucharist as ritual activity I have enumerated three basic problems:

1) *the pragmatic temptation:* let's get all the Church's work done while we've got everyone here.

2) *the instrumental fallacy:* liturgy should be producing some tangible results.

3) *ritual embarrassment:* (or, an allergy to liturgy): everything formal smacks of hypocrisy.

When these three factors are combined, as they often are at least subconsciously, then we have a deadly combination. I see four major ways in which the Eucharist is forced to do too much and therefore cannot be what it is.

First, liturgy becomes the time in which to do all of the Church's business. If the financial report must be given or the parish school needs support, then the homily or sermon can be dismissed. People won't miss it anyway. Even the parish announcements can take the place of the homily. No doubt we Catholics still have a rather low estimation of the integral importance of the homily at Sunday and feast-day liturgies. Often enough that is because preaching is so mediocre. The liturgy, however, is not the parish business meeting. It *is* the transaction of business in a way, as Aidan Kavanagh puts it,[8] but the business he means is sacred business—a transaction for the life of the world through the life-giving symbols of our redemption. That we dare not imagine a good percentage of any parish community coming to a separate meeting on parish finances or the parish school speaks volumes about our lack of confidence that the people really have a stake in the parish's life.

Second, the liturgy becomes prime time for religious education. This can happen in several ways. Most obviously, the children's liturgy of the word (in parishes where this is practiced) can become a substitute for catechesis rather than a true celebration of the Word. Surely liturgy of the word with children has to be adapted to their own capacities, but it is still liturgy and should not be used as a kind of catechesis with props. Even with adults the liturgy can become an opportunity for information-oriented catechesis. Now clearly the liturgy of the word conveys information—in the readings, the homily, even in a sense in the general intercessions. But the communication of ideas or information is not the *primary* goal of this aspect of the liturgy. The main goal here is the *celebration* of God's activity—in Christ, now by means of our *anamnesis* or remembering God's deeds in Christ and our sure hope in the Holy Spirit that God will continue to act beneficently toward us and our world.

In an oft repeated but little heeded dictum, liturgy is its own best catechesis. One particularly harmful aspect of ritual embarrassment is our conviction that ritual symbols need to be interpreted. Therefore symbols get talked about—and talked to death. Or, as happens rather frequently still, a theme of some sort is imposed upon the liturgy to make it more meaningful. "Our parish liturgy committee has decided that this Lent is going to be about the desert. We're not quite sure if ashes or the color purple will fit into that scheme." Admittedly I exaggerate—but only a little. If the liturgy is about conveying a message, then the message week after week is the same: our (painfully) slow and gradual growth as individuals and as communities into the Body of Christ. In this sense, deriving a theme *from* the readings or other texts for the feast of a day is secondary to the main purpose of the Eucharistic liturgy: entrance into the Paschal Mystery. I suspect that planning groups who think they are avoiding the trap of "theme" liturgies by going to the scriptures or liturgical texts to find a message for the day are making the same fundamental error others are making: thinking that liturgy is about ideas. Hence much of the *ennui* experienced by so many of our assemblies, who fear that liturgy is an opportunity for them to be manipulated by someone else's agenda. In a real sense, I fear that this is nothing more than a new clericalism—now often engaged in not only by clerics but also by a new class of the "liturgically-conscious."

An objection: The idea that every weekly liturgy is "about" the Paschal Mystery sounds rather boring. Response: It is boring if the liturgy is celebrated without vigor and outside the context of vigorous parish life, if music is not well chosen and well performed, if preaching is lackluster and unimaginative, if members of the assembly are treated as though they really ought to be mute spectators at a performance going on inside of what used to be altar rails.

A third way in which too much weight gets put upon the Sunday Eucharist is when the liturgy is expected to substitute for social action. In a way this is a variant on theme- or message-oriented liturgy.

While our Sunday Eucharistic assembly should mirror social justice—in the treatment of every human being with dignity, in honoring the ministerial gifts of members of the assembly—at the same time worship cannot substitute for social action. Of course the performance of the liturgy itself, and preaching, should inspire people to action for justice and peace, but the liturgy is not a place for plotting that out in detail, nor is it a place for making people feel guilty about their sins of omission. Much more is gained by inspiration and invitation than by condemnation.

The fourth and last area in which I think too much weight is being put upon Sunday liturgy is the most sensitive of all, because it seems to be a sacred cow. This is liturgy as an opportunity for people to get to know one another better. This error in liturgy is so fundamental and so rooted in contemporary North American culture that it is extremely difficult to get at. It is founded on the notion that intimacy is, if not the highest, then at least one of the highest values in human life. Francis Mannion has treated this well in an article on liturgy and contemporary culture.[9] He names the problem "the intimization of society"—the idea being that only intimate relationships are authentic and worthwhile. The problem is that liturgy as a ritual act in which hundreds of people participate is not well suited to intimacy in any serious meaning of that term. We hear all the time: "I don't like those big liturgies where everyone is anonymous." What I fear really lies beneath such statements is: "I don't want to deal with people who are different from me." Now there is nothing wrong with friendliness and warmth. There is no reason in the world why Christian worship needs to be stiff. At the same time, however, ritual always has a formal element. There need be no conflict between friendliness and formality, unless we imagine that the only real relationships are intimate. It seems to me that true intimacy is achieved with a very limited number of people, and that to expect the liturgy to foster such intimacy is a misplaced desire. Truly participative liturgies need to be fostered in a context of community, where much of the getting-to-know-one-another occurs outside of the liturgy.

Somehow we have gotten the notion deep within our bones that the primary reason for worship is our edification, what *we* get out of it. But as Robert Taft has noted so trenchantly, the primary thing one gets out of liturgy is "the inestimable privilege of glorifying God."[10] I fear that a religious faith which begins by being self-centered will end up that way. Perhaps the element of duty needs more emphasis in our preaching and catechesis, not duty as the command of an alien or fearsome God, but rather the inner obligation that comes from the recognition of who God is for us and what God has done for us in Christ. I often think that our major problem in worship today has to do not so much with the liturgy itself as with our lack of faith that what is done when we come together to worship really is "for the life of the world."

Paradoxically an element common to the attempts to use the liturgy for education, social action, and community-building is the failure to allow people to participate according to their individual capacities. How often have we heard a presider mildly scolding the assembly for not responding to "Good Morning" heartily enough? In the first place such a greeting misplaces the focus of worship on the presider, who is prominent enough (perhaps too prominent) in contemporary Christian worship. In the second place, although the assembly should be encouraged by the liturgy itself and by preaching to grow as a community, scolding individuals who may not be capable of much interaction on a given day is counterproductive. There is a sense in which the Eucharist, like every ritual, must be a blank screen on which people can project their own needs and preoccupations. I argue this not to recommend solipsism, but to face the fact that people have always come away from ritual activity with different attitudes. Miri Rubin has argued this brilliantly in a book on the Eucharist in the Middle Ages.[11] Even official explanations and expectations of ritual activity are worked out by individuals and sub-groups in their own ways. And no amount of intimidation or manipulation can change this. After all, what keeps symbols alive is their ability to be interpreted and lived in many different ways. That is part of their inherent richness.

III. What Might Sunday Eucharist Look Like?

It is easy enough to be negative and critical about much of what happens at Sunday Eucharistic celebrations. It is far more difficult to be constructive. If employing the weekly Eucharistic assembly for a parish bulletin board, education, social action, or community-building are all misuses, then what would a proper or non-manipulative Sunday celebration look like?

In the first part of this chapter I suggested that Sunday Eucharist is the ongoing ritual experience of Christian initiation and that its effects are slow and cumulative. The first requirement for weekly Eucharistic celebrations, therefore, should be not to expect too much from any one celebration. Ritual *is* community-building but in a subtle way. I suspect that it takes years for a community to realize its potential for Christian living and celebration in its weekly Eucharist. And so, much patience in addition to hard work is necessary for the formation of the kind of worshiping community that the post-

Vatican II liturgy envisions. This is no doubt a hard saying in a culture that expects very quick results.

Growth in the ritual patterns of proclamation/response and taking/blessing/breaking/giving requires, above all, fidelity to these structural elements of the celebration and the discipline not to interfere with them. In other words, there is nothing wrong with a celebration that has the same ritual shape week by week. On the contrary, such repetition is the essence of ritual experience. To many this will sound boring, but, as I pointed out above, it is not at all boring when celebrated in a rich context of vigorous pastoral life.

Moreover, many aspects of the *content* of the celebration do change from week to week—the music, scripture readings, general intercessions, and preaching. A stable structure provides the necessary framework for new elements of content to be absorbed and experienced in a fresh way. While the structure may be stable (and consistently refer through gesture and symbol to the basic content of every celebration, namely, the Paschal Mystery), the content of the celebration should open up the assembly to a new appropriation of this basic pattern of Christ's (and Christian) life each week. At stake here is the community's ownership of the liturgy. If Sunday worship is the preserve of a cadre of professionals (ordained ministers, musicians, liturgists) then it is likely that the assembly will be alienated by the liturgy even if they are entertained by it.

I suspect that what I am arguing for here is more problematic for professional liturgists and others who are frequently involved in the preparation of liturgy than it is for the majority of church-going Christians. The liturgy is such a potent force for shaping Christian life that the professional will always be tempted to "make it work." I have no doubt that most—perhaps all—liturgical planners bring the best of intentions to this endeavor of making the liturgy work. Further, each assembly does need liturgical planners who can put flesh on what is in the books. After all, the ritual script provided by the official texts of the respective denominations is a script that needs interpretation just as a playwrite's drama needs the interpretation of a director and cast in order to be staged. Each community in every different liturgical environment needs to finds its way in living out the ritual experience of the Eucharist. The worst approach would be to impose stylistic interpretations (e.g., certain kinds of music) upon the varied liturgical assemblies, instead of insisting on the two basic structures outlined above. We could make the same argument, I think, about the Eucharistic Prayer, whose structure could remain the same while its content varied, such as the introductory section (or Preface) of many Roman Catholic Eucharistic prayers changes from celebration to celebration.

Second, the Sunday celebration should look like and feel like what we call it: a *celebration*. Some celebrations, it is true, occur spontaneously and with little planning, and some others fall flat even with a great deal of planning and preparation. On the other hand, a weekly liturgy is not likely to be successful as a celebration unless a good deal of planning and preparation go into it. Of course, this becomes much less demanding when a community's ritual structure does not change from week to week; that is, after it has found a way of enacting the basic structure of the Eucharist that suits it. This does not mean that seasonal variations—a different sort of procession for Lent, for example—are not taken into account.

A third factor in successful Sunday Eucharist that does not try to do too much involves respect for the liturgical year, especially with regard to the relation between initiation and the paschal season (Lent and Easter), which comprises thirteen weeks, a fourth of the year. It has long been argued that in liturgy the more solemn occasions tend to retain the most ancient forms.[12] This "liturgical law" expresses eminent common sense. Memory relates to what remains the same, be it smell, color, gesture, musical tune, or anything else in the panoply of ritual actions and things. The wheel need not be reinvented each Advent or each Ash Wednesday or each Paschal Vigil. Although the liturgical year is more like a spiral than a circle— that is, that together with the world we should be moving toward greater acceptance of the Kingdom in our lives and in the world— preparation calls for sensitivity to the interplay between stable and changing elements in worship and the discernment necessary to know how to balance them. In addition, all of the seasonal elements that make up the liturgical year must be evaluated in terms of the same reality being celebrated every time the assembly gathers for Eucharist: the dying and rising of Jesus.

Finally, I am convinced that liturgy is never enough. All of the things we said liturgy should not try to do in the second section of this chapter—education, social action, community formation—are necessary components of successful pastoral life. A Sunday Eucharist builds on these factors even as it encourages them. All of this requires vigorous pastoral leadership and the development of a community with the profound conviction that there is something to celebrate week by week.

Conclusion

The argument of this essay has been that if the weekly Eucharist is to be successful, it must be allowed to be precisely what it is: the ritual celebration of the dying and rising of Christ. We live in an age where entertainment reigns over all, especially in social and political life. But sustained ritual experience, though it may be entertaining, must always avoid the temptation of mere entertainment. It must be grounded in the conviction that our ritual celebration of the dying and rising of Christ is vital to the welfare of the world. It seems to me that if this is the case, we end up with a paradox—a Sunday Eucharist that does not attempt to do too much will, in the final analysis, do a great deal.

Notes

1. Lawrence J. Madden, ed., *The Awakening Church: 25 Years of Liturgical Renewal* (Collegeville: The Liturgical Press, 1992).

2. Thomas Day, *Why Catholics Can't Sing: The Culture of Catholicism and the Triumph of Bad Taste* (New York: Crossroads, 1990).

3. Theresa F. Koernke, "Toward an Ethics of Liturgical Behavior," *Worship* 66 (1992) 25–38.

4. Annibale Bugnini, *The Reform of the Liturgy 1948–1975,* English trans. by Matthew J. O'Connell (Collegeville: The Liturgical Press, 1990) 337–53, esp. 340.

5. *General Instruction of the Roman Missal*, §§7–57, in *The Liturgy Documents: A Parish Resource*, 3rd ed. (Chicago: Liturgy Training Publications, 1991) 50–62. Note that the same pre-eminence is given to Sunday Eucharist in *Sacrosanctum Concilium* (The "Constitution on the Sacred Liturgy") §49 (*The Liturgy Documents,* 19).

6. *General Norms for the Liturgical Year and Calendar,* §4 (*The Liturgy Documents,* 173–74).

7. William G. Doty, *Mythography: The Study of Myths and Rituals* (Tuscaloosa: University of Alabama Press, 1986) 104–06.

8. Aidan Kavanagh, *On Liturgical Theology* (New York: Pueblo Publishing Company, 1984).

9. M. Francis Mannion, "Liturgy and the Crisis of Culture," in Eleanor Bernstein, ed., *Liturgy and Spirituality in Context: Perspectives on Prayer and Culture* (Collegeville: The Liturgical Press, 1990) 1–25.

10. Robert F. Taft, *Beyond East and West: Problems in Liturgical Understanding* (Washington, D.C.: The Pastoral Press, 1984) 33.

11. Miri Rubin, *Corpus Christi: The Eucharist in Late Medieval Culture* (Cambridge: Cambridge University Press, 1991) esp. 3–11, 243–71.

12. See Anton Baumstark, *Comparative Liturgy,* 3rd ed. by B. Botte, trans. by F.L. Cross (London, 1958) 15–30.

Chapter 8

Theology, Styles, and Structure of the Liturgy of the Hours

Austin H. Fleming

Our parish paschal candle is a piece of art truly worthy of its liturgical service. It rises a little more than five feet out of its handsome solid oak stand, is three and a half inches in diameter and weighs in at twenty pounds. Its ornamentation is simple: a cross, the year's numerals, and an alpha and omega have been carved out of the pillar. The displaced wax has been colored and poured back into the designs' grooves. The one liability of such a great candle is the difficulty we experience in carrying it in procession! Its height and weight make it an awkward burden to heft. We look for broad shoulders and strong arms to provide its solemn arrival at the Easter Vigil, but for the rest of the year we tend to leave it in its stand.

At Sunday Evening Prayer, then, our paschal candle is not carried in procession. Rather, it is lighted and standing in the middle of our darkened church as the people arrive to offer their evening sacrifice of praise. At the door of the church is a basket with individual tapers. Women and men, elders and children arrive in the twilight silence, take a taper from the basket, sit by the light of Christ, and wait for the presider's proclamation of this sacred light and for their tapers to be ignited from its flame and for their hearts to be touched with the warmth of the Lord's love. Sitting and sharing this silence one Sunday evening, I found myself deeply grateful for the opportunity to bask in the light and the moving shadows of this shining paschal presence. It saddened me to realize that so many of our people experience the

128

paschal candle only in the light of day, at Eucharist during the Easter season, and at baptisms and funerals through the course of the year. Only at Evening Prayer might we regularly have the opportunity to experience again what we know at the Easter Vigil: the Light of Christ dispelling the darkness of night as the Church makes its solemn offering, an evening sacrifice of praise.

As I sat in church that evening, I had a strong sense of how powerful a role this liturgy had begun to play in our community's prayer. Our Lenten schedule of Evening Prayer on each Wednesday and Sunday night was strong enough to draw some fifty people to Paschal Vespers on Easter Sunday evening. One out of six who had celebrated the Triduum had returned for this liturgy. Would that all three hundred had joined us—but things take time. Over the past eleven years I have worked to introduce three parish communities to the prayer of the Hours. I am deeply convinced of its meaning, its value, and its depth. I have seen people quickly embrace this prayer, make it their own, and find in it the mystery of the Lord's saving presence. My task in this short chapter is to address the theology that supports this prayer, different styles for celebrating this liturgy, and the liturgical structure of the Hours. My hope is that the reader finds here some support and encouragement to introduce or nourish this beautiful prayer in the worshiping community.

A Theology of the Liturgy of the Hours

> Christ Jesus, high priest of the new and eternal covenant, taking human nature, introduced into this earthly exile that hymn which is sung throughout all ages in the halls of heaven. He joins the entire community of [human]kind to himself, associating with it his own singing of this canticle of divine praise.
>
> For he continues his priestly work through the agency of his church, which is ceaselessly engaged in praising the Lord and interceding for the salvation of the whole world. The church does this not only in celebrating the Eucharist, but also in other ways. (SC §83–85)

This precious pearl of wisdom on worship is found in *Sacrosanctum Concilium* ("The Constitution on the Sacred Liturgy" from Vatican II), but not in its opening pages as its tone might suggest. Though this image of the singing, praising, chorus-gathering risen Jesus might sound an introductory note, the Constitution's reader must work through the document's first eighty-two paragraphs and into its fourth chapter before happening upon this gem. That such a statement opens the section on the "Divine Office" is key to understanding the role of the Liturgy of the Hours in the larger context of worship at large.

A theology of the Liturgy of the Hours begins not with a study of this particular prayer form, but with an understanding of liturgical prayer in the life of the Church. In his essay, "'Thanksgiving for the Light': Toward a Theology of Vespers,"[1] Robert Taft, S.J., leads us first through an overview of the meaning of ritual, then to a sketch of Christian liturgy, on to some thoughts on liturgy and spirituality, and finally to the Liturgy of the Hours in particular. In other words, there is a larger context here in which all matters liturgical must be considered, and against which all things liturgical must be measured.

I enjoy asking the question of Christians, "What do you suppose Jesus has been doing since he ascended into heaven?" Most of the responses I hear reflect more accurately the work of the Spirit, the Advocate whom Jesus promised the Father would send in his name (see John 14:25-26). Those who remember the Apostles' Creed will image the risen Savior "seated at the right hand of the Father." But there is something too passive about the Redeemer seated for eternity. The letter to the Hebrews and its description of the heavenly priesthood of Jesus (see chapters 4, 8, 9) offers a significantly more dynamic post-ascension ministry for the risen One: He stands forever before the throne of the Father making intercession for all.

Thirty years after the publication of *Sacrosanctum Concilium*, we might wonder if any measurable portion of our worshiping population has grasped (through experience or catechesis) this basic Christological teaching and its import for how we pray and how we understand what we do when we pray. Is this basic truth about our prayer a guiding and formational element in our celebration of the Rites of Christian Initiation and all that leads up to them? Does this theological heart of our prayer as Christians inform the ways in which we prepare for celebrating the liturgy? Does this thinking shape and even articulate itself in our preaching? Has this image of Christ singing his canticle of divine praise and associating us with his own singing—has this become the hallmark catechesis for pastoral musicians and the whole assemblies of choral praise whom their ministry is meant to serve? Has our experience of the celebration of the Eucharist and the other sacraments helped lead us to understand that this prayer of praise, thanksgiving, and intercession is offered to the Father, *through Christ, with Christ,* and *in Christ,* in the power of the Spirit?

What we are grappling with here is the ministry of the risen Jesus, the high priest of the new and eternal covenant.

To the very end of his life, when the hour for his Passion drew near, at the Last Supper, throughout his agony and upon the cross, the Divine Master showed that prayer was the vital force behind his messianic ministry and paschal mystery. It is true that "in the days when he was in the flesh, he offered prayers and supplications with loud cries and tears to God, who was able to save him from death, and he was heard because of his reverence" (Hebrews 5:7), and by his perfect offering upon the altar of the cross "he has forever perfected those who are being sanctified" (Hebrews 10:14); having been raised from the dead, he now lives forever to make intercession for us. (*General Instruction on the Liturgy on the Hours*, §4)

Indeed, we no longer look for Jesus among the dead! He is risen! And he has not retired into Trinitarian obscurity. His ministry, the same one he began in the flesh, continues in the reign of his Father. And his is the prayer, the only prayer, the Father hears. If we would have *our* praise and prayers, concerns and contrition, needs and interceding lifted up before God, there is but One to whose heart and voice the Father attends—the voice of him who died that we might live. The Father is attuned to the voice of Jesus—and to all whose voices are joined with his!

Taft sums it up:

So liturgy is just a celebration of Christian reality. The eternally present Christ-event is an everlasting hymn of praise and glory before the throne of the Father. Since it is our vocation to enter into this salvific event and live that Christ-life of priestly praise and glory, the Church, his Mystical Body, associates herself with the eternal priestly prayer of her head. In so doing, she truly participates in the salvific praise of Christ.

Seen from this perspective, Jesus is *not* simply a *model* for how Christians ought to pray. Rather, he *is* the prayer (the One who prays), and it is we who share in his one prayer. Our share in his prayer shoulders the Church with a "grave responsibility. Not only does [the Church] share in the mission of Christ to proclaim and effect the mystery of salvation, but it is also involved in the joyous task of giving endless praise and thanksgiving to the Father."[2]

I rehearse all of this in part because it is so basic to any understanding of Christian liturgical prayer, but mostly because it is so crucial to our understanding of the Liturgy of the Hours. The Hours have a rocky history and it is a real shame that a prayer that enjoys such high theological esteem has fallen so frequently on hard times. The Church indicates clearly and without reservation the import of the Hours when it addresses its anamnetic dynamic and function:

[The Liturgy of the Hours] is "the remembrance of the mysteries . . ." (GILOTH, no. 12). As in the Eucharist, so in the celebration of the Liturgy of the Hours, the community gathers to recall to memory the saving works—the mysteries—of God. In the process of memory, the event becomes *present and effective* for this community in this time and place. To facilitate this memory process within the community gathered to pray, the church calls upon the scriptures to assist it. In the [Hours] that section of the scriptures which is referred to as "psalmody" forms the basic content. In the act of praying, the psalms become the voice and the prayer of the community itself. *God becomes present and praised* for his own sake. . . . In fact, the title "sacrifice of praise" used in reference to the Eucharist is also applied to the [Hours].[3]

These are strong statements indeed. Given the implication of these words it is amazing that while private (solitary) "celebrations" of the Eucharist are proscribed by law, the solitary "celebration" of the Hours is, in theory and practice, taken for granted.

The *General Instruction* makes very clear a connection between the Hours and the Eucharist. Given all that we have previously seen with regard to the theological underpinnings of the Hours, it is clear that the Hours and the Eucharist are rooted in the same theological reality: the prayer of Christ. The Eucharist, of course, is our chief celebration of and participation in the prayer of Christ. Historically, however, the celebration of the Hours did not develop out of or in response or reaction to the Church's celebration of the Eucharist. Though the Hours and Eucharist share some important common elements, they are not structurally related as if they formed some whole that has been broken up to accommodate different moments in the course of the day and night. Eucharist and Hours are best understood to be related in that they manifest the same spiritual reality: our share in the ministry of the risen Christ who intercedes for all, forever before the Father.

To say, however, that the celebration of the Hours "spreads to the various hours of the day the praise and thanksgiving as well as the remembrance of the mysteries of salvation, the prayer and the foretaste of heaven's glory which are found in the eucharistic celebration, which is the center and the culmination of the whole life of the Christian community" (*General Instruction,* §12) may add an emphasis in one place that diminishes in another the weight of the Hours in the arena of liturgical prayer.

With regard to the Hours and their relationship to discrete moments of the day, Taft offers some resistance to the notion that the Hours are intended for the "sanctification of time." He offers evidence that "the earliest tradition of noneucharistic public prayer had nothing to do with theories of the 'sanctification of time,' with *kairos* and *chronos*, with a liturgy of 'time' or 'history' as distinct from the 'eschatological' Eucharist." He warns against anything that might "obscure the original purity of the meaning of primitive Christian morning and evening prayer. . . . Both were and are a praise of the same God for the same reason: Christ."[4]

The *General Instruction* offers sound advice when it tells us that "the celebration of the Eucharist is best prepared for by the Liturgy of the Hours." We celebrate the Eucharist weekly (sometimes daily), but that celebration does not exhaust our desire or need for sharing in the prayer of Christ, nor does it satisfy in one celebration the scriptural injunction to "pray without ceasing" (1 Thes. 5:17).

The Eucharist and Hours complement and in some significant ways mirror each other as we share in the ministry of the prayer of Christ. That theology of the celebration of the Hours that roots us in the prayer of Christ, associating us with his own singing of the canticle of divine praise, is the one most deserving of our attention.

Styles of Praying the Liturgy of the Hours

Key to a pastoral understanding of the Liturgy of the Hours is an appreciation of its origin, history, and development. This is so because the present liturgical books for the Hours in the Roman Catholic communion present something of a problem in terms of the contemporary pastoral situation. (I focus on the Roman Catholic rite because it is, perhaps, most illustrative of both the rich theology and pastoral tension that rises from implementing the Hours in a pastoral setting; other denominations do celebrate the Hours—notably, morning and evening prayer—but do so in a more "cathedral" style, discussed below.) A few years before the English translation of the Latin edition of the Liturgy of the Hours, William Storey referred to the post-Conciliar efforts at reform as "both a precious gift to be received with gratitude and a puzzling problem to be grappled with as reverently, constructively and practically as possible." Although the *General Instruction* (published prior to the reformed books themselves) called for the restoration of the Hours as the prayer of the whole Church and reminded us that the prayer of the Hours is not a preserve of the elite, the four volumes finally placed in our hands proved to be, in Storey's words, "an embarrassment of riches." This was a "reverent" way of indicating that the reform had failed, as Storey would write some years later, by failing to take into account the distinction between the "cathedral" (parochial) and "monastic" traditions of the Hours. It will be helpful for us here, with Storey's help, to trace the development of the prayer of the Hours.

The primitive origins of the Hours predate the Christian community and are rooted in daily prayers of Temple and synagogue usage. The times for prayer were related to the daily sacrifices offered in the Temple and the synagogue practice followed a similar schedule and prayers, minus the physical sacrifices. Though any number of sacrifices might be offered, those at dawn and sunset assumed a particular importance. It was just this round of daily prayer with which Jesus and his followers would have been familiar, and this pattern of prayer passed into the practice of the early Church. Early sources point clearly to established services of communal daily prayer. Evidence for the form and content of these services is less compelling but Storey offers us the following five elements of a pattern for these liturgies.[5]

1) The early Church took seriously the scriptural command to pray always. Tertullian writes: "Concerning the times of prayer no rules have been laid down, except of course to pray at every time and place." On the experiential level this meant at least the *orationes legitimae,* the daily common prayers understood to be binding upon all members of the community. This is the prayer of the whole Church, not just the prayer of its leadership or some particular group.

2) The Hours were "thoroughly Christological in intent and content. Morning prayer was the daily celebration of the Lord's resurrection, and evening prayer the daily commemoration of his burial and descent among the dead." The times for prayer remain the same but the community's understanding of those times has been transformed by their resurrection faith.

3) "The hours were composed of Christological psalms and hymns, a few select Old Testament psalms, also largely Christological, and intercessory prayer on a rather extended scale."

4) The services were both very structured and almost totally invariable. Spontaneity and variation were unknown in this age and form of prayer.

5) The purpose of the celebration of the Hours was not instructional or catechetical. The prayer was "worship for its own sake: praise, thanksgiving, adoration and petition."

Through the fourth and fifth centuries, this pattern of prayer becomes more evident and widespread. Daily prayer (morning and evening) for the community was simply the given. What emerges is a prayer that is well known by all who participate in it, a prayer that is simple to learn (repetition), a prayer that is constant (daily), and a prayer that becomes part of the rhythm of Christian living. Psalms, canticles, and hymns were clearly chosen to suit the Hour of the day being celebrated. It was all quite simple, made sense, and appealed to the assembly of believers.

By contrast, the monastic practice enlarged the number of Hours celebrated, the number of psalms prayed, and introduced a substantial portion of *lectio continua* from the scriptures. Before long the monastic practice made its way into cathedrals and parishes and became the norm for the celebration of the Hours—in spite of the fact that its weight and burden were virtually impossible to support in the parochial environment. Those bound to the Hours by order and vow were relieved of their total responsibility by dispensations and the appointment of others to assume these liturgical burdens. Absence from any communal or choral celebration of the Hours led to private recitation, and private recitation as a norm lay the communal celebration of the Hours to rest, outside monasteries and some religious communities and, later, among some of the Reformation communions (who, in the wake of the present liturgical renewal, have largely abandoned the Hours—especially morning prayer—in favor of Eucharist).

This is all a sad story. And it has not yet found a particularly happy ending. For example, the "reformed" Roman Liturgy of the Hours is still essentially a monastic venture. The four week psalter is certainly an improvement and of benefit to those who make of the Hours a personal prayer, but personal prayer is not the shape or the goal of the Hours. Quite the contrary! The demands made by the reformed books are simply too much to ask of a parish community. Even Roman Catholic clergy bound by the Office and those who live in religious houses and communities (outside monastic families) often find the new Hours to be more than they can or will handle. The appearance and acceptance of *Christian Prayer,* the one-volume edition of the Hours, is a telling reality. When we need to publish simplified versions, we need to reassess our practice!

Storey has suggested that the only way for the Church to redeem this situation consists of the "deliberate abandonment of the monastic principle of the recitation of the entire Psalter and the *lectio continua* of the Bible . . . ; the restoration of the principle of the fixed psalm and of discrete readings . . . ; the restoration of the clear-cut principle that the clergy are responsible for restoring the Hours, for presiding at them, for preaching and teaching about them, for helping people 'understand the psalms in a Christian way . . .'" and the restoration, wherever possible, of a classic cathedral celebration of the Hours.[6] In the last part of this essay we shall look at the structure of a "classic cathedral celebration" of Evening Prayer as an example of his suggestions.

Outline of Structure: Morning and Evening Prayers

	1971 Revised Rite	Book of Common Prayer	Book of Alternative Services
Morning Prayer	Introductory Verse Gloria Patri Hymn Psalm (Antiphon, prayer) O.T. Canticle 2nd Psalm Reading Response Benedictus Intercessions Lord's Prayer Prayer Blessing Dismissal	Versicle or Sacred Scripture Confession Invitatory (Ps 95, 96, 100) Psalms (3) Lessons (2) Canticle Creed Lord's Prayer Suffrages Collect Hymn Intercessions Thanksgiving Blessing	Penitential Rite Introductory Verse Invitatory Reading Psalm Response Silence Canticle Response Anthem Hymn Sermon Affirmation of Faith Intercessions Thanksgivings Collect Lord's Prayer Dismissal
Evening Prayer	Introductory Verse Gloria Patri Hymn Two Psalms (Antiphon, prayer) N.T. Canticle Reading Response Homily Magnificat Intercessions Lord's Prayer Prayer Blessing Dismissal	Scripture or Light Service or Versicle Confession Introductory Verse Gloria Patri Phos Hilaron Psalms (3) Lessons Canticle Creed Lord's Prayer Suffrages Collect Hymn Intercessions Thanksgiving Blessing	Penitential Rite Introductory Verse Invitatory Phos Hilaron or Ps 134 Psalm(s) Reading(s) Sermon Affirmation of Faith Intercessions Thanksgivings Collect Lord's Prayer Dismissal

Structure of the Liturgy of the Hours

As noted earlier, the monastic tradition for the Hours offers a more complex, variable liturgy while the cathedral tradition provides for something simple and fixed. For our purpose here we will compare Evening Prayer from the present Roman liturgical books with a cathedral-based format as found in *Praise God in Song: Ecumenical Daily Prayer*[7] as shown in Table 1.

Table 1	
Liturgy of the Hours	**Praise God in Song**
verse	light proclamation
hymn	hymn*
	thanksgiving*
psalm (psalm prayer)	Psalm 141 and offering of incense (psalm prayer*)
psalm (psalm prayer)	*psalm (psalm prayer)*
NT canticle	Psalm 116
short reading	*short reading*
responsory	quiet reflection
antiphon	
Magnificat	Magnificat and incense
prayers	prayers*
Lord's Prayer	Lord's Prayer
closing prayer	closing prayer*
	blessing/sign of peace

Italicized items are variable on a daily or four-week cycle basis.
*These items are variable on a seasonal basis.

Simply on the basis of variability, we can see a great difference between the two celebrations. Central to both is psalmody.

> In the Liturgy of the Hours, the Church makes extensive use of those outstanding songs composed by the sacred authors of the Old Testament under the guidance of the Holy Spirit. Since (the Spirit) is their source, they have the power to raise (our) minds to God, to stir up thoughts of devotion and holiness, to help (us) obtain God's grace for (our) needs, and to provide encouragement and strength in the face of trouble. The psalms foreshadowed that fullness of time in which Christ the Lord appeared, and from which the Church's prayer draws its effectiveness. Although all Christians consider the psalms with the greatest possible esteem, there is no doubt that they present some difficulty to anyone using these sacred songs as prayer. (*General Instruction*, §§100, 101)

If our model for the Hours includes praying through virtually the whole psalter in a week or even a month, then the *General Instruction's* caution here is well advised. There's a burden—actually two! First there is the burden placed on the psalms of being all things to both the Hebrew and Christian scriptures, and second, the burden placed on those using the psalms to be able to understand and pray them as they pass by us in rapid order. The psalms are, of course, of great import to the celebration of the Hours and can rightly be called a school of prayer for us. But like the sacraments, the psalms are there for us, we do not exist for the psalms (or for the whole psalter!).

The raising of our minds to God, the stirring up of devotion and holiness within and among us, and the finding of encouragement and strength to help us through hard times—all of this may well come to those who celebrate the Hours. But it will come not so much because the words of particular psalms or canticles *convince* us of it. Rather, all this will be ours through our participation; our sharing in the prayer of Christ in this liturgy uncovers it for us. Of course, the word we sing and pray and proclaim and hear at the Hours is a saving and, therefore, indispensable word. But the first step here is not to listen for messages, but rather to enter, to dive into, to immerse ourselves in the prayer of Christ and his Church. Common, well-known, known-by-heart songs and prayers enable this; a parade of constantly changing texts will defeat this. Psalms admitting of obvious Christological interpretation and psalms that resonate with the time of the day they are prayed will best serve the purpose and enhance the dynamic desired here.

Other Elements

It is interesting to note that the cover of the Bishops' Committee on the Liturgy Study Text VII: *The Liturgy of the Hours,* is graced by a stylized sketch of a paschal candle and thurible, against the background of a setting sun. Chapter IV of this same document is an instruction on "Celebrating the Liturgy of the Hours." This instruction is more promising than most of what is found in the *General Instruction.* In a fairly cohesive fashion it addresses the place for the prayer, its physical layout and preparation, the environment, the ministers, and includes this statement:

> In addition to the structure of the [Hours] which provides the movement of each element and text, there are other liturgical gestures and signs that *might be inserted* into the celebration depending on local circumstance and the occasion. Thus, one can use an

entrance procession, incense, lights, etc. at proper times *to enhance the flow* of the celebration. Even the posture of the participants should be looked upon and prepared as ritual movement. Standing, sitting, bowing, and kneeling can all *contribute to the effect* of the celebration and should be carefully studied and prepared.[8]

What is distressing here is that such important elements are treated as "possible insertions" designed to "enhance the flow" and to "contribute to the effect." From a cathedral perspective, light and incense and the posture of the assembly are not nifty doodads to tack on at special times or seasons; rather they are a part of the whole liturgical act. Once again, the door to minimalism seems to be opened by the instruction itself, at a time when fullness of signs and symbols are that for which the liturgy and those who celebrate it hunger.

The early Church needed to light its lamps for illumination at the evening of the day. They were quick to give that moment a Christological interpretation, based on their reading of the Christian scriptures. Today, this service of light might include the entrance of the paschal candle, a sung proclamation ("Light of Christ!"—"Thanks be to God!") and the lighting of tapers. The evening hymn follows and the early classic piece for this time is the *Phos Hilaron* ("O Radiant Light"). A seasonal alternative might also be chosen. The light service ends with a sung thanksgiving, the likes of which is witnessed by Hippolytus of Rome (ca. 215), in the *Apostolic Tradition:*

> When the bishop is present, and evening has come, a deacon brings in a lamp; and standing in the midst of all the faithful who are present (the bishop) shall give thanks, and he shall pray thus, saying: "We give you thanks, Lord, through your Son Jesus Christ our Lord, through whom you have shone upon us and revealed to us the inextinguishable light . . . ." (ch. 25)

This formal declaration of thanksgiving contributes even more to our understanding of the Hours as truly a liturgical act. It concludes with the assembly's "Amen."

The classic evening psalm, Psalm 141, established its place in the vesperal liturgy not only because of its refrain, "Let my prayer rise like incense before you, O Lord; the lifting up of my hands like an evening sacrifice," but also because of the penitential nature of the psalm and the need, at day's end, to ask pardon for any failings. Tossing a few grains of incense on a lighted coal at this time does much more than simply "enhance the flow" of the liturgy. The incense offering becomes an integral part of the act and catches up the assembly, really, in its aroma and wafting clouds. Another use of incense (for honoring assembly, paschal candle, and altar) at the Magnificat highlights the singing of Mary's canticle as a true proclamation of the Gospel.

The intercessions are sung in litany form and include the needs of the Church and the world as well as the needs of the local church. When, in cathedral style, the intercessions are relatively invariable, they do indeed become the prayer of the people, that is to say, a prayer the people can make their own. My own experience has shown me how quickly and easily those who celebrate the Hours are able to enter into free intercessory prayer at other times by using the petitions they have "learned" at Evening Prayer. Some communities have also found that the experience of singing the intercessions at Evening Prayer has paved an easy road for introducing the singing of the intercessions at Sunday Eucharist.

We find ourselves again at intercessory prayer and that image of the risen Jesus, standing eternally before the Father, interceding on our behalf and inviting us to join him in singing his canticle of divine praise. This is the prayer the Father hears: the prayer of the body of Jesus, the Church, gathered in the Lord's name and by the power of the Spirit. This is the Liturgy of the Hours.

It is regrettable that the prayer of the Hours has fallen by the way-side in most parishes and even in the lives of many who are bound to this prayer by orders and vow. It is regrettable that so great a prayer seems just beyond the reach of so many who could spiritually prosper by it. But there is hope. Parish communities and religious houses and campus chapels have dusted off the cathedral Hours and brought them to life. Many have come to see that the best Office is not the longest or the shortest or the newest; rather the best Office is the one faithful to the tradition of the Church that fills the needs of the local community and engages them in the prayer of Christ, for the honor and glory of God, and for the sanctification of God's holy Church.

Notes

1. Robert Taft, S.J., *Beyond East and West: Problems in Liturgical Understanding* (Washington, D.C.: The Pastoral Press, 1984) 127–49.

2. *The Liturgy of the Hours: Study Text VII* (Washington, D.C.: United States Catholic Conference, 1981) 18.

3. Ibid., 20 (emphasis added).

4. Taft, *Beyond East and West,* 135, 144.

5. William Storey, "The Liturgy of the Hours: Cathedral vs. Monastery," in John Gallen, ed., *Christians at Prayer* (Notre Dame, Ind.: UND Press, 1977) 65–66.

6. Ibid., 75–76.

7. William Storey and John Melloh, eds., *Praise God in Song: Ecumenical Daily Prayer* (Chicago: GIA, 1979).

8. *The Liturgy of the Hours: Study Text VII*, 37 (emphasis added).

Chapter 9

Homily as Proclamation

Joyce Ann Zimmerman, C.PP.S.

"Proclamation" is an activity we usually associate with the scriptural Word of God. "Homily" is an activity we reserve for that "soft time" during liturgy when the presider (or someone else) "applies" the readings to our lives today. Often, this application to life takes the form of moral exhortation, stories from the preacher's life, jokes to draw attention, social justice platforms, requests to increase our parish monetary contributions accompanied by the painting of a woeful financial picture, and any number of other imaginative uses for these ten minutes or so of the assembly's time and attention. Seldom is it considered a "sacred" activity in itself. To suggest in this chapter that the homily itself is a kind of proclamation and, therefore, a sacred activity, is to challenge both the popular perception of homiletic activity and its content and performance.

Edward Schillebeeckx, in both the Preface and Introduction to his 1985 work *The Church with a Human Face: A New and Expanded Theology of Ministry*,[1] communicates a pastoral sensitivity in face of very real personal anguish. Two aims of his book in particular bring this out: (1) to shatter any hints of a supernatural/natural dualism between faith and praxis (p. 5); and (2) to clarify that praxis expresses the content of the Gospel and, as such, is an *interpretation* of it (p. 10). These two related aims, *mutatis mutandi,* have important implications for our study of the homily.

First of all, dualism between faith and praxis is challenged precisely because of the relationship God offers through Christ, a relationship that spans time and space and is disclosed through a tradition of liturgical celebration. Since the homily is "the proclamation of God's wonderful works in the history of salvation, which is the mystery of Christ ever made present and active in us, especially in the celebration of the liturgy,"[2] the homily is a privileged moment whereby God's salvific events are contextualized. The homily draws on a faith tradition to ground Christian praxis.

Second, the homily as second-order reflection on Sacred Scripture is always an *interpretation,* but at the same time it is much more than a mere application to everyday life. The interpretation of Sacred Scripture that the homily undertakes is a *lived* interpretation. That is, the homily draws on the experience of Christian faith and praxis as evidenced by the tradition in order to find direction and meaning for present faith and praxis.

The aim of this chapter is to describe how a homily overcomes the dualism between faith and praxis and also interprets Christian tradition appropriate for a particular historical and sociological condition. We do so by drawing on language theory that helps us see the role of the homily as structurally parallel to that of the proclamation of the Gospel and the assembly's acclamations, two activities that take place during Christian liturgy. In this, it becomes obvious that a homily that merely applies Scripture to today's socio-historical situation is inherently dualistic because it implies a break between originary events and today's lived experience of those events. Therefore, any homiletic approach today must begin with the presupposition that the ongoing revelation of God's Word is known only through authentic Christian praxis and which constitutes within the tradition the residual meaning of those originary events. This reversal—from an absolute orthodoxy designating orthopraxis to authentic praxis illuminating faith—is critical for any meaningful homiletic activity.

We organize the chapter into a threefold division. First, there is a general description of homily and some of what we must consider if we are to come to a more adequate expression of what a homily is and is supposed to do. Second, an analytic describes a theory of performative language and interprets the role of homily within the structure of Christian liturgy from that linguistic horizon. Third, evaluative criteria are suggested, against which a homily as authentic proclamation might be measured.

Description

Already in the apostolic Church there is ample evidence to support the supposition that homiletic activity is an important part of living the Good News of Jesus Christ. At least one characteristic of hearing and appropriating the Gospel is a concomitant commitment to the person of Christ such that our tongue is loosed to preach the Good News.

The Acts of the Apostles alone accommodates five "styles" among the many examples of preaching recorded therein.[3] Although circumstances and purposes advise the use of a particular style, they all seem to have in common the very same content: the Paschal Mystery, the Good News of God's salvific presence in Jesus Christ. Even more pointed, Luke's Gospel points to Jesus himself as the very content of preaching when it says "Today this scripture has been fulfilled in your hearing" (Luke 4:21, NRSV).

Further, it is not difficult to detect common characteristics of early Christian preaching: It is Christological, ecclesial, relevant to the time and situation, radical, and personal. Each of these characteristics in its own way serves to mark Christian preaching as unique. Because the content is the person Jesus Christ and his saving deeds (hence, Christian preaching is inherently *Christological*), preaching is always *ecclesial* (for the Church is none other than Body of Christ, to borrow Paul's image). Moreover, our memory of the Jesus event enables that event to transcend historical time and space through its liturgical enactment here and now (*this* historical *situation*) while at the same time remaining grounded in those originary events *(radical)*. Christian preaching is always *personal* because baptism is a commitment to live the Paschal Mystery.[4]

Early evidence of Christian preaching is entirely consistent with the Hebrew perception of God's Word as utterly dynamic. *Dabar,* Hebrew for "word," refers to a kind of speaking that is charged with power effecting divine activity and self-disclosure. God's Word, then, is not merely "listened to." Rather, God's Word evokes a *response* from the hearer that is actually a constituent of the Word itself that is spoken.[5]

All of these remarks point to preaching activity as something far more complex than application to daily life. Indeed, many contemporary scholars who address the topic of preaching and homiletics imply the same thing, especially when they refer to preaching as "proclamation."[6] Since preaching is, above all, a kind of communication, we may suppose that an analysis of its language may open up new avenues of research. What kind of a linguistic event is preaching? Performative language theorists offer a clue that suggests one possible way to respond to this question.

Analytic

Since the advent of language theory during this century, religious scholars have striven to decipher religious events from this purview.[7]

It is no surprise to find homileticians drawing on various language theories to devise new homiletic methods and descriptions.[8]

If we take the position that homily is proclamation, we suggest that more is happening than speaking and listening, in terms of ordinary language of communicating data. This is no less true of the proclamation of the Gospel itself. If mere factual information were all that is at stake, there would be no use for a repetitive cycle of readings. Somehow both speaking and hearing as an encounter between speaker and hearer are indicated by the language event. Let's pursue an analytic description of homily as proclamation.

1. Proclamation. Today "proclamation" is a common word in our religious/liturgical vocabulary. Especially the tendency to use "proclamation" rather than "reading" indicates sensitivity to a larger activity. But like all new insights, it takes time to come to an accurate description of what this proclamatory activity really entails.[9]

"Language," as commonly understood, tends to be limited to verbal communication. But this only describes one kind of language use. Even with that, our tendency to "read between the lines" suggests that we know that usually more is taking place than given by the denotative meaning of the vocabulary. Some language theorists speak of "discourse" when referring to this more comprehensive language event.[10] To speak of a "language event" is to acknowledge the surplus of meaning that is part and parcel of every act of communication.

Proclamation is *language* because it communicates.[11] Proclamation is *event* because rather than a fleeting moment it has a meaning that endures by means of the ritual transformation of the assembly; that is, their lived experience of the Good News. Certainly, it is proclamation as language event that constitutes the assembly as Body of Christ.

Proclamation takes place when the conviction of the speaker makes present God's love in such a way that the hearers are also moved to love. Proclamation, then, ultimately is that which makes present the reality of the Paschal Mystery. It has the power to transform because it engages the assembly in a self-involving response. In other words, proclamation, by its very nature, concerns both speaker and hearer in a dialectic activity that surpasses the ritual moment.

Homiletics scholars may use different vocabulary, but their attempts to say what a homily does (or ought to do), nonetheless grapple with the same linguistic concerns. Walter Burghardt brings together experience, preacher, and assembly: "If you are to do more than parrot the exegete and theologian, if you are to touch God's living word to a living people, you have to hear that word with your own ears, see the risen Christ with your own eyes, experience for yourself the Lord God and the loving work of His hands."[12] According to Burghardt, the preacher's words come alive when the preacher comes alive (40). This suggests that fruitful homilies have far less to do with anecdotes and attention-getting contrivances and much more to do with genuine Christian experience that touches the preacher in such a way that it comes alive, naming and challenging the Christian experience of the assembly as well. The preacher has the luxury of time and interaction with her or his lived experience to bring the Word alive during the proclamation of the homily. If it is indeed proclamation, the homily rings so true and has the force of commitment so vivid that the assembly is drawn into the same Word. Only then will there be sufficient impetus of the proclamation such that the assembly, in turn, is drawn to an intersection of proclamation and *their* lived experience. The assembly's luxury of time to savor the proclamation comes precisely in their living it.

Others, too, have insisted on the same intersection of experience and interlocutors. For example, Robert P. Waznak says, "I suspect the reason why homilies often fail is that we preachers do not pay attention to our own experience of God in our times." He also says, "Preaching seeks to change the way people believe and act."[13] Joseph Fitzmyer, analyzing Paul, makes a similar observation: "For Paul the response to that proclamation was not merely faith as the result of hearing . . . or an assent of lips and heart about the lordship of Christ. It had indeed to begin in this way. But it had to entail eventually . . . 'a commitment of faith,' a dedication of the whole person to God in Christ Jesus."[14]

Speaker, hearer, and content of the preaching intersect when homily is, indeed, proclamation. Performative language theory offers a path to flesh this out in order to elucidate the life-related activity that, ultimately, Christian preaching is.

2. Performativity. Although a great deal of our everyday speech is informational or factual (e.g., "It is raining today"), it is grossly misleading to suggest that all communication is this straightforward. Most of us can recognize the difference between these three statements: "It is raining today," "I wish it would rain today," and "Rain, rain go away." J.L. Austin distinguished these differences and called them "performatives" in order to indicate the close relationship between some communication utterances and a distinct force that they carry to act or "perform"; hence, "speech-*act* theory" or "performative" language.[15]

Speech-act or performative theory distinguishes among three types of communication utterances. There is the propositional, called "locutionary," which is a simple statement of fact; here, the content and force of the speech-act are identical. All communication is locutionary that has simply conveying information as its aim. Some liturgical language (albeit a proportionately small amount) is locutionary; for example, the Scripture reference citation announced by the lector or deacon (or presider) during a liturgy of the word ("A reading from . . .").

Additionally, there are those utterances which obviously are meant to express more than content. In some cases, the force of communication redounds to the speaker. This type of communication is called "illocutionary." Wishes, promises, commitments, statements of belief are all examples of illocutionary statements. Prayer as praise and/or thanksgiving would be liturgical examples of illocutionary communication. Acclamations are perhaps the most important of the illocutionary utterances during liturgy and for this reason they are best always sung. Illocutionary utterances are so significant for liturgy because they are closely aligned with the transformation that is proper to liturgy (ritual). Illocutionary speech captures the intent of the speaker.

In other cases, the force of communication implicates the hearer. This third type of communication is called "perlocutionary." Commands are the most common example. Petitionary prayer is perlocutionary because the import of the linguistic utterance is to "move" God to answer our prayer. "Go in peace to love and serve the Lord" is another example of a perlocutionary liturgical utterance. Perlocutionary liturgical communication tends to break open the celebration so that it has meaning beyond the cultic occasion. It is closely aligned with ministry in that perlocutionary speech most frequently has direct bearing on our everyday living.

Obviously, the verb carries much of the burden for determining the type of speech-*act* an utterance is. Since verbs are "action words," this is entirely understandable. However, interjections and pronouns and other elements of speech contribute important clues for identifying the type of communication that takes place.

Proclamation, as it is liturgically used, is a unique speech-act. While ordinary language is identified as *either* locutionary, illocutionary, or perlocutionary, I believe proclamation alone integrates the import of these three aspects of all communication into a single dynamic of immense moment. Authentic proclamation requires that the force of the speech act clearly include speaker and hearer as well as content without diminishing the self-involving force of any of them.

Proclamation is a blend of content and a bi-directional dynamic, persona and action. Proclamation synthesizes the import of the locutionary, illocutionary, and perlocutionary into one dynamic during the same language event. In other words, liturgical proclamation simultaneously places the force of the communication act on each speaker and hearer as they both give and receive the content, which is none other than Jesus Christ and his salvific message. Proclamation is locutionary, illocutionary, and perlocutionary at one and the same time.

We might say that the homily as proclamation is the intersection of the preacher and assembly's encounter with the person of Christ. In other words, the homilist—the speaker—preaches from her or his experience of and commitment to the Good News (illocutionary) while at the same time the homilist engages the assembly—the hearers—in response to the Word (perlocutionary). The result is an encounter with the presence of God in Christ through the Spirit (content) such that there is a transformation of both preacher and assembly into ever more perfect images of their identity as Body of Christ (locutionary).

The homilist seeks mutual engagement, but this is never entertainment and genuine homiletic activity is even far more than holding or piquing the assembly's attention. It is more than eloquent rhetoric or passionate speech. At stake is nothing less than our own faith expression and fruitful cooperation in the work of redemption. Performativity theory provides a theoretical framework for identifying the essential mutuality of the subjects of liturgy as they exercise their respective ministries. We now turn to an analytic that accounts for the actual liturgical performances of these subjects.

3. Analytic Schema. Liturgical proclamation is a distinctive activity whereby the saving acts of God in Christ Jesus through the Spirit are rendered present here and now in the intersection of the communication force of the presider and assembly. As only one type of liturgical proclamation, the homily cannot be isolated from the whole liturgical action. The homily actually derives its fullest meaning within the dynamic of the whole celebration. Two other proclamations within the shape of the same liturgical act help to break open the meaning of homily as proclamation.

We have already mentioned that the Gospel is also proclamation. The usual minister who proclaims the Gospel is a deacon,[16] and it is telling to recall that it was the deacons' role in the early Church to distribute Communion to those both present and absent and also to distribute the food gifts of the assembly to the poor.[17] Thus the proclamation of the Gospel leads to concrete action on behalf of the absent and poor, which carries the liturgical activity beyond the ritual moment and reminds us of what should be the relationships within the Christian community. Genuinely preached Good News is lived.

If the proclamation of the Gospel leads to (liturgical) service of the poor, to what does the homily as proclamation lead? In addition to proclaiming the homily, the other liturgical role of the presider-presbyter is the proclamation of the Eucharistic Prayer. This great thanksgiving sums up the salvific deeds of Christ Jesus, and in that very proclamation is present the living Bread for Christian Communion.

Since there is only one Christian proclamation—the Good News in Christ Jesus—we suggest a parallel between the liturgical performance of these ministers. Thus, the proclamation of the Gospel is to doing for others as the proclamation of the homily is to offering the Eucharistic Prayer. We might schematize this as follows:

> *Gospel Proclamation : Doing for others :: Homily Proclamation : Offering the Eucharistic Prayer.*

Objectifying the proclamation of the Gospel by taking care of the needy is an activity parallel to objectifying the proclamation of the homily by offering the Eucharistic Prayer. The differing communicative acts complement each other and serve to indicate the breadth of activity of Christian ministry for they all share the same content: to manifest the presence of Christ Jesus.

So far our analysis has focused on two liturgical ministers, deacon and presider. Recent scholarship has emphasized the liturgical ministry of the assembly[18] and so we might consider additionally the assembly's liturgical performance in light of our proposed schema. The clearest self-involving activity of the liturgical assembly is the "proclamation" of the acclamations. These reiterations of acceptance of the liturgical activity by the assembly lead to communion, a profound sign of the transformation into Christ that is the ultimate goal of the Christian life. To eat and drink the body and blood of Christ is to proclaim who we are and are ever more perfectly becoming until that day when Christ returns in final glory to bring to finality what will be. Communion is the most perfect sign of the content of Christian proclamation: the Body of Christ. If we add this to our schema from above, we have the following threefold set of parallel activities:

> *Gospel Proclamation : Doing for others :: Homily Proclamation : Offering the Eucharistic Prayer :: Acclamations : Communion.*

None of these ministers, nor their liturgical performances nor where they lead tells the whole story of the Eucharistic action; together they witness to a profound mystery of God's saving, personal, and Trinitarian presence.

Our analytical schema demonstrates the mutuality of the liturgical roles that ministers exercise. Rather than a hierarchical "one better or more important than another" that we have inherited from our historical development, Christian liturgical ministry is a complex of the intersection of originary experience and lived tradition that makes present the enduring meaning of God's various presences to and for the community. It stresses that all liturgical performance has a counterpart activity that carries the liturgical action into the everyday living of the subjects who are the liturgical assembly. It also underscores the mutual dependence the community shares; no single member is a sign of God's activity. But together the assembly embodies the vocation to carry on the salvific and redemptive work of the God of Israel and Jesus Christ and to have all the gifts for ministry that are needed to carry on that work.

Specific to the subject at hand, the homily as proclamation is hardly an "add-on" to liturgy wherein the preacher does the work of "application" for the hearers. Instead, the homily is a constituent component of a ritual that confronts the participants with the here and now and calls them to relate originary events and lived tradition as a two-sided coin pointing to the same content: the Paschal Mystery.

Evaluative Criteria

The proposal of an analytical schema such as the one we have made is helpful insofar as it promotes making connections and discerning relationships among what might appear at first glance to be disparate or improbable elements. We have been pursuing a perception of homily as proclamation, and have striven to place it in the context of the larger body of proclamatory activity that unfolds as a liturgical dynamic.[19]

Our interest has been to show how approaching homily as proclamation serves to shatter a dualistic path to faith and praxis insofar as authentic proclamatory activity connects locutionary, illocutionary, and perlocutionary aspects of communication. This synthesis of performative acts suggests a model whereby the homily draws us, through the lived faith experience of the preacher, into the content of the tradition experienced as an encounter with Jesus Christ, the Good News. This personal encounter challenges and shifts the gaze of the assembly toward new horizons of living their faith commitment. The homily may be described as a dynamic of the Word/lived faith experience of the preacher <—> a personal encounter with Jesus Christ <—> the Word/lived faith experience of the assembly. Faith and praxis meet both in the discourse between Word and lived experience and in the encounter between Christ and the subjects of liturgy.

Our interest, further, has been to show how the homily is always an *interpretive* discourse. Interpretation here does not refer to exegesis or any other study bearing on understanding the scripture selection, though that may well be a significant part of the homilist's—and, ideally, also the assembly's—preparation. As applied to homily, interpretation means catching the light the Word sheds on the meaning of lived experience and grasping how lived experience affords an insight into the immediacy of the Word.

Obviously, the preparation of homilies is no easy task. It is necessarily a self-involving undertaking that reaches to the very faith-core of the homilist. Realistically, to be effective the homily demands the preacher to lay bare his or her very faith life. Without an earnest faith and depth of prayer, preaching is impossible. It requires a commitment of time measured not by hours of study but by days of living *this* Word for *this* time and place.

There will be as many preaching styles as there are preachers if the Word, indeed, is spoken as a lived Word. Some homilists are "homey" and down-to-earth, and their lived faith comes through simple language and easily-recognized examples, not unlike the language of the parables. Some of the content in Mark's Gospel reflects a homey style; for example, Mark 14:51 brings a smile to our faces when we imagine the "certain young man" so in a hurry to desert the arrested Jesus that he "ran off naked." Some homilists are lyrical and poetic and the sheer beauty and eloquence of their language raises us to a heightened expectancy. For example, each Christmas we thrill at the beauty of Luke's annunciation and incarnation accounts. Some homilists are profound in expression and their depth of language-use draws us into the stillpoint of mystery. John, for example, stops us cold when we read (6:35): "I am the bread of life. Whoever comes to me will never be hungry, and whoever believes in me will never be thirsty." Effective use of stopping points and silence, questions, challenges, stream of consciousness, illustrations from literature and the theatre arts—these all can be techniques around which preachers build a style. To some extent, the selected text(s) for the day suggest a style. However, most homilists, over a period of time and practice, tend to develop a personal style that for them best communicates their encounter between Word and lived experience.

It would be impossible to develop a homiletic style that would meet the needs and expectations of each and every person in the pews. What can be a realistic expectation, nevertheless, is that a homily ring true with the lived faith of the preacher. If this comes through, no matter what the style, then the Word/lived experience/encounter dynamic of homiletic discourse can unfold.

At bottom line, certain observations are basic and form a backdrop against which all proclamatory activity can be measured. Although the lines may be somewhat blurred, we have divided the criteria according to the possible force of the communication.

Locutionary Criteria

> *Revelation of divine Presence
> *Annunciation of salvation
> *Dialectic of originary event/present remembrance
> *Dynamism of Paschal Mystery and its lived rhythm
> *Sacred encounter in which assembly is immersed

Illocutionary Criteria

> *Word of God to *this* assembly at *this* time and place
> *Impetus toward proclamation of praise and thanksgiving
> *Evocation of affections and freeing of conceptual clarity
> *Promise of eschatological fulfillment

Perlocutionary Criteria

> *Transformation of self-identity as Body of Christ
> *Intersection of divine and human activity
> *Link of liturgy and life
> *Summons to faith-decision
> *Assurance of liturgical communication
> *Critique of limits and misguided choices
> *Anticipation of utter human fidelity of response
> *It makes a difference in how we live

Certainly, this list of evaluative criteria is hardly exhaustive and, most likely, not every homily is able to meet all the implications of even these. Nor is meeting the demands of this list a good place to begin when preparing a homily. Evaluative criteria more aptly serve as a goal against which we might measure the attentiveness of both preacher and hearer of the Word. It suggests that homiletic proclamation can no longer be ignored, omitted, or considered to be an extraneous intrusion in the proclamation of the Word. Homily as proclamation is nothing less than our encounter with the Risen Christ, recognized in the breaking open of the lived faith experience of the homilist—a bread that nourishes and transforms the assembly's Christian living.

Notes

1. Edward Schillebeeckx, *The Church with a Human Face: A New and Expanded Theology of Ministry,* trans. John Bowden (New York: The Crossroad Publishing Company, 1985).

2. *Sacrosanctum Concilium* ("The Constitution on the Sacred Liturgy") §35.2.

3. That is, kerygmatic (Acts 2:14-36; 4:8b-22; 5:29-32; 14:15-17); parenetic (Acts 3:12-26; 13:46-47; 27:21-26); catechetical (Acts 7:2-53; 10:34-43; 13:16-41); evangelistic (Acts 17:22-31; 20:18-35); apologetic (Acts 22:3-21; 24:10-21; 26:2-29; 28:17-20; 28:25-29).

4. Space restraints prohibit showing examples of these characteristics in early Christian preaching. The reader is invited to examine examples of preaching in Acts (see Note 3, above) for textual evidence of these five characteristics.

5. See "dabar" in *Theological Dictionary of the Old Testament,* ed. Gerhard Kittel, trans. and ed. Geoffrey W. Bromiley, vol. 4 (Grand Rapids, Mich.: Eerdmans Publishing Company, 1967) 802–27.

6. See, for example, Mary Catherine Hilkert, "Naming Grace: A Theology of Proclamation," *Worship* 60 (1986) 434–49.

7. See, for just three examples, Donald D. Evans, *The Logic of Self-involvement: A Philosophical Study of Everyday Language with Special Reference to the Christian Use of Language about God as Creator* (New York: Herder and Herder, 1969); Jean Ladrière, "The Performativity of Liturgical Language," trans. J. Griffiths, *Concilium* 9-2 (1973) 50–62; and Roger Lundin, Anthony C. Thiselton, and Clarence Walhout, *The Responsibility of Hermeneutics* (Grand Rapids, Mich.: Wm. B. Eerdmans Publishing Co., 1985).

8. For one example, see James M. Schmitmeyer, *The Words of Worship: Presiding and Preaching at the Rites* (New York: Alba House, 1988) who studies and gives examples of homilies using reader-response theory.

9. This is a good example of Schillebeeckx's second aim at work: the experience of proclaiming (tradition) *precedes* any description (interpretation) of it.

10. See, for example, Paul Ricoeur, *Interpretation Theory: Discourse and the Surplus of Meaning* (Ft. Worth: The Texas Christian University Press, 1976) and especially the first essay, "Language as Discourse," 1–23.

11. See Mary Catherine Hilkert, "Naming Grace," 445: "Ultimately preaching is a matter of handing on the Christian story in such a way that the experience of grace—God's presence in ordinary human life—is communicated."

12. Walter J. Burghardt, S.J., "From Study to Proclamation" in *A New Look at Preaching,* ed. John Burke, O.P., Good News Studies 7 (Wilmington: Michael Glazier, Inc., 1983) 37.

13. "The Homily Fulfilled in Our Hearing," *Worship* 65 (1991) 34 and 35, respectively.

14. "Preaching in the Apostolic and Subapostolic Age" in *Preaching in the Patristic Age: Studies in Honor of Walter J. Burghardt, S.J.,* ed. David G. Hunter (New York: Paulist Press, 1989) 25.

15. See J.L. Austin, *How to Do Things With Words,* The William James Lectures Delivered at Harvard University in 1955 (Oxford: Clarendon Press, 1963). John R. Searle refined the theory in *Speech Acts: An Essay in the Philosophy of Language* (Cambridge: University Press, 1969).

16. See the *General Instruction of the Roman Missal,* §34. The presider reads (really, "proclaims") the Gospel only in the absence of a deacon or other ordained minister (which is, unfortunately, often the parish situation on Sundays).

17. See Justin Martyr, *First Apology,* §65 and 67. Although this latter paragraph says that the gifts are deposited with the president and he takes care that they are distributed to the needy, elsewhere (e.g. Ignatius' letter to the Trallians 2:3) there is implication that it was the deacons who were responsible for the actual distribution of gifts.

18. See, for example, the second essay, "The People Shout Amen: The Ministry of the Liturgical Assembly" in James Empereur, S.J., *Worship: Exploring the Sacred* (Washington, D.C.: The Pastoral Press, 1987) 11–19.

19. Our analysis has drawn upon the Eucharistic liturgy for its components. It would not be difficult to show a similar schema for baptism or other liturgical rites. I suggest that the homily functions differently when proclaimed in a liturgical context than when used elsewhere. This raises important questions that remain unaddressed: Who may preach and when? What competency is required for ordination? What constitutes *liturgy* and what are other quasi-liturgical, sacramental actions? Who is the subject of liturgy? Is the homily an optional or essential element of liturgy?

Chapter 10

General Intercessions

Joyce Ann Zimmerman, C.PP.S.

Manuals on growth in the spiritual life used to speak of four modes of prayer: praise, thanksgiving, adoration, and petition. The manuals would urge that personal prayer ought to reflect a balance among these modes of prayer. Informal discussions about prayer, however, would reveal that most of us had a hard time with the balance: We agreed that the largest part of our prayer was petition, with an occasional dose of gratitude thrown in; praise and adoration were mere formulae for us. Intercessory prayer seems to be a naturally human activity. Even the "unchurched" and those who don't consider themselves very religious often turn to God in times of need. Many more folks besides Roman Catholics invoke St. Anthony to help them find lost or misplaced articles or carry St. Christopher medals in their cars! St. Jude's patronage for those in difficulty seems happily to cross denominational boundaries!

Liturgy is essentially a prayer of praise and thanksgiving, often including a recitation of God's salvific deeds on our behalf. Nonetheless, it is no surprise that we find intercessory prayer as part of all liturgy, Jewish and Christian, and notice the close relationship between supplication and praise and thanksgiving. A few examples will help us see this relationship clearly.

The *berakot,* those great blessing prayers of Jewish liturgy and piety, show a remarkable movement from thanksgiving to intercession, reaching a climax in doxology (praise).[1] During the synagogue morning and evening services, the opening *berakot* were followed by a profession of faith (the *shema*), and then came the great "eighteen

blessings" (the *tefillah*), essentially a prayer of supplication introduced and concluded by a series of *berakot.* Another example: There
is a remarkable affinity between our Christian Our Father (which begins with three invocations of praise, includes four petitions, and has
a concluding doxology, the text of which we find in the *Didache* §8:2)
and the Jewish *kaddish* which concluded the synagogue service's
scripture readings[2] and follows the same praise-petition-doxology
pattern.

As to emerging Christian intercessory prayer practices, Justin
Martyr (mid-second century) mentions common prayers after the
baptism or preaching (§§65, 67). The Eucharistic prayer is the great
prayer of praise and thanksgiving for Christians. Even the earliest extant formularies include prayers of petition (often in litany form). The
anaphora (Eucharistic prayer or canon) in the *Liturgy of St. James* (Jerusalem, 5th c.) has very extensive intercessory prayer, remembering
everyone from the bishops and clergy to civil leaders to those with
various needs and praying for everything from dispersion of scandals
to abolition of war to good weather for the harvest.[3] So long as these
prayers were part of the *anaphora,* they retained the Jewish pattern
of thanksgiving-petition-praise. This pattern was broken when Gela-
sius (late 5th c.) introduced a litanic form in the West and moved the
intercessory prayer to the introductory rites (where it eventually was
reduced to a ninefold repetition of the peoples' response "Lord, have
mercy," which was further reduced to six invocations in the present
rites). Thus, for centuries in the Western Church we had all but lost
our Eucharistic intercessory prayer, except for the brief mementos of
the living and dead in the Roman Canon.[4]

The structural relationship of thanksgiving, petition, and praise
has its theological voice. Our constant lifting up of needs to God is a
forceful reminder of our "creatureliness" and of our dependence on
the creator God for everything we have. Ultimately, we humans are
not masters of the world, but God. Raising supplication to God is an
indirect way of praising God for all that has been given us and a way
of thanking God for those gifts. The question has been raised, "Why
ask God for what we need, when God knows our needs better than
we do?" One response is that supplication is an opportunity for us
to express our first relationship to God: creature to Creator. Further,
the general intercessions is sometimes called the "Prayer of the
Faithful" (see the *General Instruction of the Roman Missal* [hereafter,
GIRM], §45), and this offers further theological insight. These prayers
are not only an expression of our participation in the priesthood of
Christ, but they also express a solidarity with the whole Church and,
indeed, all the world.

The restoration of intercessory prayer to conclude the liturgy of the word has been perhaps the most easily accepted of the "innovations" incorporated in the revision of liturgical rites after the promulgation of *Sacrosanctum Concilium* ("The Constitution on the Sacred Liturgy"). However, their inclusion has not been without its pastoral problems and misunderstandings. The remainder of this chapter addresses some pastoral issues.

A Pastoral Approach to the General Intercessions

Probably one reason for the widespread acceptance of the general intercessions is that they supply an opportunity for the assembly to "personalize" a liturgy that still too often seems formal and removed. It is not unusual at a parish on Sunday morning to hear named those parishioners who have died during the past week (often complete with an announcement of the funeral arrangements) or to hear named those parishioners who are sick (often complete with diagnosis and prognosis).

This kind of information surely is worthy of our corporate attention. Further, we humans have a need to pray for and share our personal concerns with those close to us. The question is, Is this what the general intercessions at Sunday Eucharist are all about? This question raises the issue of different forms and needs of intercessory prayer in our lives. Many of us grew up praying for mommy and daddy, siblings and our pets, and for a new bike or whatever was on our mind at the time. When we became adults the categories might have changed, but the very personal nature of our prayer has not changed: We may still pray for aging parents, our troubled teenager, employment. To lay our needs before God during prayer seems as right as choosing to pray at all.

Intercessory prayer is an integral part of both personal/devotional prayer and liturgical prayer. Nonetheless, the history and documentary statements on the liturgical general intercessions show that they really function quite differently and have a different form from those prayers of petition we might utter at our times of need. Devotional intercessory prayer can be as specific as we wish to make it. It names our needs and in that very utterance we express our hope for being heard in an individual, personal way. On the other hand, the general intercessions at Sunday Eucharist is the prayer of an *assembly,* not of an individual. The challenge is to be general enough to unite this particular liturgical assembly with the whole Church and, at the same time, be specific enough to lead this particular assembly into meaningful prayer. The next several paragraphs offer a blueprint for a better pastoral understanding of the general intercessions at Sunday Eucharist and some suggestions for practical implementation. We limit our discussion to the general intercessions at Sunday Eucharist; individual/personal intercessory prayer and the intercessions during Liturgy of the Hours have their own particular form and will not be addressed in the following remarks.

Meaning

The general intercessions are a unit of liturgical prayer; as such they are essentially prayers of praise and thanksgiving as is all liturgical prayer. As we said above, by acknowledging our dependence on God, we worship God as the One who provides all good for us. The purpose, then, of liturgical general intercessions is far more significant than placing our *needs* before God (important as that is at times): it is really placing *ourselves* before God. This "offering" is an exercise of our baptismal priesthood and an "ordering" of this assembly towards union with the whole Church and world. These are called "general" intercessions because we intercede before God on behalf of all humanity. It is wholly a *liturgical* act that discloses for us our unique relationship to God and each other.

Prayerful participation in the general intercessions is one way to take seriously our baptismal commitment to live the Gospel. Living Christianity, then, is far more than "being good" and "going to church on Sunday." Our baptismal commitment implies a *conversion,* a new way of living with each other that includes a genuine concern for others' needs. It is telling that deacons in the early Church had a three-fold liturgical role: they proclaimed the Gospel, announced the intentions for the common prayers, and took the Eucharistic food to absent members and distributed to the needy the food contributions brought to the celebration. We might interpret all three of these actions as making the Good News concrete in the here-and-now: first, its proclamation to the assembly; second, its concretization in a kind of faith (i.e., "yes") response whereby the assembled people unite themselves to the whole Church and world; and then, third, its manifestation in charitable works. In other words, proclamation of the Good News is directly connected to action on behalf of others (especially those in particular need).

Forms and Structure

Intercessory prayer at Sunday Eucharist has taken different forms throughout its long and rich history, as we briefly indicated above.

Diptychs (lists of names; cf. the names of the living and dead in Eucharistic Prayer I) and litanies (the Lord Have Mercy, Lamb of God, and Litany of All Saints are three that still remain part of today's liturgies) are early prototypes. The general intercessions in their present form have their most immediate connection to the ancient form of intercessory prayer we pray at the solemn prayers during the Good Friday liturgy. The structure of this latter prayer comes from early intercessory prayer patterns: (1) invitation to pray by the presider; (2) announcement of a category of people and intention about them; (3) invitation to kneel; (4) silent prayer by all present; (5) invitation to rise; (6) collect (conclusion) by the presider.

If we omit the invitations to kneel and stand, this same structure serves well as a model for the general intercessions at Sunday Eucharist: (1) invitation to pray by the presider; (2) announcement of prayer intention (by deacon, cantor, or other person; see *GIRM* §47); (3) prayer (including common response and/or silent prayer; *GIRM* §47); and (4) collect (conclusion) by the presider. In practice, most parishes use a common response to the intercessions, but it may be pastorally effective to introduce a time for silence either before the common response or in place of it. Time for silent prayer allows room for specificity of individual intentions at the same time that the universal nature of liturgical intercessions is respected.

Categories

GIRM lists four specific categories for our liturgical intercessions: "(a) for the needs of the Church; (b) for public authorities and the salvation of the world; (c) for those oppressed by any need; (d) for the local community" (§46). Intentions in at least each of these four categories must be included, although there is nothing that prohibits intentions in other categories or more than one petition for each category. Common sense, however, does caution us that lengthy lists of petitions run the risk of diminishing the prayer. Let's look at these categories in greater detail.[5]

We pray first of all for the Church, who is the people of God—for every Christian of every denomination—around the world. All who are baptized or who are seeking baptism are recognized as our sisters and brothers in Jesus Christ. We pray for a growing unity among Christians at every level: They are all part of the "household of God" (Eph 2:19). We pray for believers who are being persecuted, and for their persecutors (Matt 5:44). We pray for members of the universal Church and for all our leaders and ministers. As well, we need to pray for our Church at the national, regional, and local levels. We pray also for other Christians in our community. These intentions may become more specific according to local needs: It is always important to pray for a growing unity among the Christians in our community and around the world (see John 17:20-23). Special celebrations such as weddings and funerals may include a number of petitions relating to the particular occasion.

Second, we pray for civil authorities, for nations, for the salvation of the whole world. 1 Timothy 2:1-4, 8 suggests that Christians pray for civil rulers so that believers—who were often in peril because they did not honor the gods of the pagan Roman empire—could live in peace and safety. (There are still countries in the world today where practicing Christians are in need of our prayers.) This area of our prayer could be expanded at times to all who serve the community in any form of government and public service, from city hall to school boards to public health to police and military and other services providing security. We need to pray for those who serve in the United Nations Organization as well as for all who work at the national, regional, and local levels of public service. The World Day of Prayer for Peace on January 1 is included in our liturgical prayers for the world. Similar occasions for community prayer could include the Week of Prayer for Unity Among Christians (in January), the World Day of Prayer in March, Earth Day, and the anniversary of Hiroshima (August 6). Most national churches provide a calendar of days on which we are invited to pray for special intentions and causes. Many of these days may be observed with members of other Christian churches.

Third, we pray for people in special need. We may pray for victims of natural disasters (storms, floods, avalanches, earthquakes), or of events caused by humans (wars, pollution, poor distribution of food). We may pray for those suffering from local disasters (such as fires, epidemics, unemployment) and major accidents. The true Christian spirit should lead us to back up our prayer for those in need by making our own donations, by volunteering our help in other practical ways, and by continuing our prayer throughout the week.

Fourth, we pray for the local community. Members of the assembly are invited to pray for themselves and for the needs of their local civic and ecclesial community. Through the district ministerial association, all the congregations in the area could be invited to pray for a particular intention or need on a specific Sunday.

The number of intentions would depend upon the format chosen and the occasion. The number of intentions would ordinarily not be more than one for each category. This is especially important if a brief silence is included after each intention. At least the four categories must be included to preserve the *universal* nature of this prayer. These categories touch on four important aspects of our relationship to others: Church, world, needy, and ourselves. We could even argue that any intention at all would fit under one of these four categories. Obviously, we cannot include all our prayer intentions at a single liturgy. It is better to have fewer intentions that invite real prayer, than many intentions that only promote boredom.

On special occasions, such as weddings or funerals or anniversaries, it is always good pastoral practice to include at least a fifth intention mentioning the special occasion or people involved. Sometimes even it is appropriate to cast all the intentions within the context of a special occasion, still keeping one intention in the four categories. For example, the intentions for a wedding might shape up something like this (these samples are necessarily generic; actual ones would include imagery from the scripture texts): (1) that Mary and John might witness to all the Church God's faithful covenant of love with us; (2) that all married couples might continue to grow in their fidelity to each other; (3) that those tempted to infidelity might be strengthened in their commitments; (4) that the family and friends of Mary and John here gathered might return home renewed in love by this celebration together; (5) that Mary and John will continue to grow in their love for each other as they grow together in the members of the assembly. Jesus continues to pray in us and through us (see Heb 7:25; Matt 18:20).

Formulation

There are basically three usual ways to formulate the intentions of the general intercessions: "For . . ." (name a category of *persons;* e.g., Church, all people of the world, those in need, ourselves); "That . . ." (name an intention; e.g., that God's reign may prevail); or—probably most common—a combination that takes the form "For . . . that . . ." (e.g., for the world, that God's reign may prevail). In general, well-written announcements of intentions are consistent in form, short, and open the assembly to prayer. Any one of these three formulations may lead to a response by the people (e.g., the popular "Let us pray to the Lord . . . Lord, hear our prayer") or invite silent time for prayer. A period of silent prayer after each announcement may be communally concluded with "Let us pray . . . Lord, hear our prayer."

Which formulation to use is determined by the shape of the intention themselves. The language and imagery of the announcements derive primarily from the Gospel and, secondarily, from the first reading and responsorial psalm. In other words, the general intercessions are shaped by the liturgy of the word that they conclude and are necessarily particular for each Sunday. When we draw on the imagery of the scripture texts, we are underscoring that proclamation of God's Word always leads to actions on behalf of others. The general intercessions draw us out of a "privatized religion" into a solidarity with all others.[6]

A very different kind of formulation may be suggested by some gospels. For example, the text of Matthew 25 on the last judgment ("Lord, when did we see you hungry and feed you . . .") lends itself nicely to a litany format. The petitions suggested by the Gospel (hungry, thirsty, naked, sick, imprisoned . . .) can be expanded to include intentions for victims of injustice, violence, peace, etc. This kind of a litany format is most effective when sung as a dialogue between cantor and assembly. Also, a period of silence would not be observed after each intention, but perhaps a brief silence might be added at the end of the litany and before the concluding prayer.

Should We Write Our Own Intercessions?

With the many books of general intercessions available as pastoral aids—some of them quite good, some of them questionable—it is very tempting for parish liturgy personnel to adopt one of these and use it on a regular basis. Especially since we stress the "general" character of this liturgical intercessory prayer may we be tempted to think "What's the difference? They're supposed to be *general* so it must be OK for all of us to use the same ones." Although announcing the intentions from a well-written pastoral aid may be better than using poorly written ones we've composed ourselves, the ideal is for each parish or liturgical community to write their own general intercessions. This, for two reasons.

First, though "general," these intentions remain those of a specific liturgical assembly. As such, over time and with practice a certain pattern develops in the prayer that is indicative of the spiritual depth and growth of the community. If pre-written intercessions are regularly used, not only is the challenge of delving into the corporate "soul" lost, but also the record over time of the community's depth and growth is not so readily at hand for evaluation.

Second, the specific concerns of a liturgical assembly need not be lost in the "general" character of the intercessions. If a parish is writing its own intercessions, they can still be "personal" without sacrificing the "general" character of this prayer. On the one hand, the general intercessions can't be a mere re-cap of the newspaper headlines or lead stories on the evening news. On the other hand, the general intercessions ought to reflect the real concerns of *this praying community.*

Who Writes the General Intercessions?

Even though most parishes have numerous liturgies on a weekend—and different celebrative styles mark them to respect the differing assemblies that gather—the general intercessions ought to be the same for all the Sunday Eucharistic celebrations. This, because it is the one parish (ideally) celebrating the one Eucharist. This means that only one set of intentions must be written for each Sunday, which suggests only one small (few enough in number to get the "job" done expeditiously; e.g., three to five persons) group of intention writers is needed. This group may be a subcommittee of the liturgy committee, may be the group of Sunday lectors, or another group who wishes to use this as an opportunity for faith sharing on the Sunday readings. In order to establish some kind of consistency, the same group should compose the intentions for a specific period of time; e.g., over a liturgical season. One group can learn from another group's compositions and thus all are enriched.

Cautions

It is important to have a good grasp of the structure, meaning, and function of the general intercessions in the Sunday Eucharist and also some sense of the format and categories. Even with this knowledge, several cautions ought to be kept always in mind:

1. *Intentions that are too general* (e.g., "Let us pray for everyone in need"), *very individualistic* (e.g., "Let us pray for Father Smith's special intentions"), *or too specific* (e.g., "Let us pray for Mrs. Smith who is the parish council president and who had a stroke this morning") *to lead the assembly to prayer.*

2. *Intentions that are "gimme" lists.*

3. *Intentions that are judgmental* (e.g., "Let us pray that all our teenagers stop taking drugs," which implies that all teenagers take drugs).

4. *Intentions that are meant to be informative* (which include hospital lists, announcements, thank you notices, etc.).

Challenges

When writing general intercessions, certain challenges emerge:

1. *Intentions are poetic utterances, open-ended, symbolic so they lead to prayer.* This requires a more "poetic" than didactic language

in the formulation of the intentions. They entice rather than teach; they awaken rather than identify; they arouse prayer rather than analyze data; they excite to action rather than bring satisfaction; they draw comfort rather than instill complacency.

2. *Intentions incorporate images drawn from the Gospel (and first reading and responsorial psalm).* When a group sits down to write the general intercessions for a particular Sunday, the "raw" data is already given in the Sunday lectionary. These images help shape the intentions. This assures that the intentions "belong to" the whole community and aren't just the concerns of the writers. Drawing on the scripture texts also helps us keep from too much repetition; new ideas for intentions arise from the scriptures.

3. *Retain the same formulation and response over a period of time (for example, during a given liturgical season).* As part of a larger ritual, the general intercessions also retain certain ritual characteristics. Repetition and familiarity are important here. If an assembly is fumbling with trying to recall their appropriate response (especially true when it is rather long and complex in composition), they can hardly be praying. The same response (either a formula, such as "Lord, hear our prayer," or a period of silent prayer) consistent throughout a liturgical season helps to unify this unit of liturgical prayer at the same time that it promotes familiarity. A change in response may cue the assembly to a change in liturgical time. Avoid the temptation of too much novelty which tends to break the familiarity of the ritual flow.

4. *Intentions and response, ideally, are sung.* Singing not only brings out the litany form of the intercessions, but it also allows a greater degree of participation by the whole person. Singing the general intercessions underscores the importance of this prayer and helps us bring the liturgy of the word to a fitting, solemn conclusion.

Procedure for Composing General Intercessions

Too often liturgy personnel are put off by the thought of composing their own general intercessions because previous attempts have resulted in time-consuming sessions. My experience with writing general intercessions with various groups is that a prayerful atmosphere and clear procedures ensure that about a half hour is all that is needed per Sunday. I have devised this simple method for writing general intercessions and have used it with various groups in different contexts.

1. *One person read aloud the Gospel, first reading, and responsorial psalm (in that order).* Even if only one person is preparing intercessions, it is still good to read aloud the texts.

2. *Read the texts aloud a second time. Ask the group to key into words and images that strike them during this second reading.* Sometimes I have the group quietly think about the words/images; at other times I have members of the group write down the words or images as they listen to the Gospel being prayerfully read for the second time. Sometimes I specify writing down only words or phrases that actually occur in the readings.

3. *On chalkboard, flip chart, or paper (if only one or two are writing the intercessions), write down the four categories of general intercessions, leaving plenty of room to write.* Again, the four categories are Church, world, needy, ourselves.

4. *Reflect on the key words or phrases noted in the texts. Ask anyone to propose an intention for any of the four categories,* drawing on the key words and phrases for imagery. At this point in the process, stress that we are not yet looking at language, format, etc. Simply throw out ideas. The recorder writes them down without comment and without editing them.

5. *Begin to refine and formulate the final intentions to be used.* At this point, a decision about the formulation (For . . . ; That . . . ; For . . . , that) needs to be made. Usually the four initial intentions given lead the group to a decision. If there is more emphasis on intention than categories of persons, use the "that" form; otherwise, use the "for" form. If the "For . . . that" form is used, be care that there isn't needless repetition (e.g., for the Church, that the Church . . .).

6. *Refine to final statements of intentions.* This step includes reading the intentions aloud to the group to hear how they sound; listening for metaphoric, poetic, open-ended language that draws into prayer (if the statement sets off "wild images," it needs to be refined further!); and checking for judgments and other "hidden agendas" that may still be contained in the statements of intentions. One final reading out loud is helpful; if the intention is not clear or the reader stumbles over words, rework the intention until it "sounds" right. After all, the assembly will *hear* the intentions, not be reading them.

7. *Decide on the response (short formula or silent prayer).* In most cases, this step is most important at change of liturgical seasons.

8. *Well in advance of the Eucharistic liturgy, give the statements to the deacon or cantor or other person who will announce them.* Like all

public activities, the announcement of the intentions of the general intercessions must be practiced (especially so if they are sung) if they are to be done well. It is important to pay attention to body language as an invitation to the assembly for response. It is also helpful to give the list of intentions to the presider, so he or she can formulate his or her invitation to prayer and concluding prayer according to the language and imagery of the particular set of intentions.

The point here is not to be a slave to procedure. Once a group or individual becomes familiar with a process for composing intercessions, they will personalize and simplify the process for themselves.

Getting Started

Sometimes all we need is a simple guide to accomplishing a task well, and a little nudge to get started. One practical way for a parish to make the transition toward writing its own general intercessions is to have the liturgy personnel review the purposes and limitations of the general intercessions. Then they might try their own hand at the step-by-step procedure outlined above. Feel free to modify the steps according to local needs. Familiarity with the procedure will probably have individuals skipping steps or combining steps. Sometimes an image in the scripture reading(s) is so startling that an intention just seems to "write itself." Practice writing intentions together until the group becomes comfortable with the process. When the liturgy personnel no longer need an outline of the procedure on a paper to manage to get through it, they most likely understand the process quite well. At this time they may in turn teach others in small groups to write the general intercessions for Sunday Eucharists. I have found it better to begin by writing intercessions in small groups, or even in groups of two. As the flow of writing comes easier, the weeks may be divided among individuals. One advantage, though, of writing them in groups of two or more is that this can become a time for faith sharing on the Sunday scriptures.

Conclusion

When we reflect on the historical origins, theological implications, and pastoral richness of the general intercessions, it seems appropriate to make the judgment that intercessory prayer ought to be included every time God's Word is proclaimed (whether public or private). Certainly, this is a norm for our Sunday celebrations. Equally important as including them, is a norm that the general intercessions are best composed by members of the liturgical community so that they reflect the concerns of that community. In this way can the assembly "own" their own impetus to reach out to others.

Sometimes the question arises about inviting the members of the assembly to spontaneously speak their intentions. This may or may not be a good practice. It would not be pastorally helpful if (1) the assembly is large and everyone cannot see the speaker and hear the intention; (2) the four categories are not respected; and (3) if the *universal* character of the intentions is not respected. Too frequently, opening the intentions to the assembly simply paves the way for "laundry lists." On the other hand, this may be a good practice when (1) the assembly is small enough so that the speaker can be seen and heard; and (2) the small assembly is knowledgeable about the intentions, and includes *universal* intentions in the four categories. My pastoral experience, however, has always shown that it is best to have prepared intentions.

The general intercessions conclude the liturgy of the word. Within the shape of the ritual itself they help us to begin to formulate how we will live the scripture challenges in the coming week. The general intercessions help us to remember that God's Word is always a lived Word, always a dynamic Word, always a Word enfleshed in our own deeds on behalf of others. Let this prayer well up in our hearts so that, like Jeremiah (20:9), the word is like a burning fire within and we cannot hold it in. We must act. We must speak God's Word. *Our* speaking God's Word is *doing* for others. The general intercessions are a challenge to us to carry forth God's Word into our daily lives.

Notes

1. See Louis Bouyer, *Eucharist: Theology and Spirituality of the Eucharistic Prayer,* trans. Charles Underhill Quinn (London/Notre Dame, Ind.: University of Notre Dame Press, 1968) 69. For a good introduction to the relationship of Jewish and Christian prayer, see Carmine DiSante, *Jewish Prayer: The Origins of Christian Liturgy,* trans. Matthew J. O'Connell (New York/Mahwah, N.J.: Paulist Press, 1991). See also Eugene J. Fisher, ed., *The Jewish Roots of Christian Liturgy* (New York/Mahwah, N.J.: Paulist Press, 1990).

2. See Bouyer, *Eucharist,* 78.

3. See R.C.D. Jasper and G.J. Cuming, *Prayers of the Eucharist: Early and Reformed,* 3rd revised edition (New York: Pueblo Publishing Company, 1987) 94–98.

4. For a more detailed history of intercessions, see Richard Mazziotta, "The General Intercessions," *liturgical ministry* 2 (Winter, 1993) 2–14. This entire issue is on the general intercessions.

5. I am indebted to Msgr. Patrick Byrne for some of the material in this exposition of these categories.

6. On the linguistic import and formulation of the general intercessions, see my "The General Intercessions: Yet Another Visit," *Worship* 65 (July, 1991) 306–19.

Chapter 11

Liturgical Spirituality: Living What We Sing About

James Dallen

Teacher and liturgical scholar Cipriano Vagaggini tells of a conversation between two ancient Palestinian ascetics in which one reveals to the other the sorry state of his spiritual life. Repeatedly he contrasts what he prays with how he lives, citing passage after passage from the psalms. Because of this inconsistency, the monk admits, his liturgy and prayer have become his shame. His confidant counters that David the psalmist was speaking all these things of himself. But the ascetic concludes, "Brother, brother what are you saying? Surely if we do not do what we sing about, we are on the road to perdition."[1]

The monk's conviction is central to liturgical spirituality: Life and liturgy must coincide. In the broadest sense, any spirituality which is in harmony with public worship could be considered liturgical. Usually, however, the relationship is explicit and prominent, with the Paschal Mystery celebrated in the liturgy shaping and orienting personal spirituality as it does the Church's spirituality. In this sense, Christian liturgical spirituality may be defined as a spirituality formed, informed, and oriented by communal ritual participation in the Paschal Mystery. Such spirituality is a recent topic in academic study, but its referent, the interrelation of liturgy and spirituality, is as old as Christianity.

Liturgical Spirituality in History

During Christianity's first centuries the community assembled for worship, particularly for Eucharist, and this was the basic "school"

169

for Christian spirituality. Converts were formed and transformed by initiation into the worshiping community. The faithful were formed as pray-ers through the repeated experience of communal worship.

Succeeding centuries continued to pay lip-service to the tag *lex orandi, lex credendi*—which implies a similar interaction between liturgy and spirituality—but spirituality's liturgical foundation gradually diminished after the fourth and fifth centuries. By the late Middle Ages liturgy was no longer recognized as central in Christian formation and spirituality, and spirituality developed independently of the liturgy. For the most part, liturgy came to be considered a compulsory ceremonial performed by the clergy and attended by the laity.

This false concept, largely the product of the baroque era,[2] reinforced the separation between liturgy and spirituality. At the very least, it made liturgical spirituality a clerical and religious spirituality with little apparent relevance for laity. Though liturgy and life continued to interact—a fact rarely acknowledged—their intimate relation was largely unrecognized because of the inadequate level of inclusive participation.[3]

Recognition of Liturgical Spirituality

Liturgical spirituality came to be acknowledged as a consequence of the liturgical movement. The reintegration of liturgy and spirituality was implicitly a major motivating force from the movement's nineteenth-century beginnings. The relationship between them gradually became a prominent topic in liturgical writings. The movement's orientation toward the revival of liturgical spirituality became clearer as it progressed and particularly as it was officially accepted and prompted liturgical reform. As a consequence of Vatican Council II's call for renewal and the experience of postconciliar reforms, liturgical spirituality has become a core theme in liturgical literature and a recognized area of study.

In its first phase, the liturgical movement was dominated by monastics and characterized by a romanticized and sentimentalized view of the Middle Ages. Prosper Guéranger (1805–1875), as an example, made the abbey of Solesmes a center of spirituality and of revitalized monastic liturgy modeled on the medieval Roman rite. His regard for the liturgy as source of contemplation and the heart of monastic life played a significant role in creating interest in liturgy's place in the spiritual life. Nevertheless, the antiquarian and monastic character of his work and that of others at the time kept it from having a widespread influence. Romantic sentiment and ceremonial aestheticism meant that liturgy and spirituality were only loosely associated. The state of medieval liturgy and spirituality hindered the perception of a closer relationship so long as the Middle Ages were the focus.

In its second phase, from the time of Pius X until World War II, the movement, still led by monastics such as Odo Casel, Lambert Beauduin, Pius Parsch, and Ildephonse Herwegen, became more theological and more pastoral. Historical interests shifted to the patristic era. The movement's leaders were concerned to provide a theological foundation for returning the liturgy to the people. Out of their concern for the pastoral implications of liturgical revival grew a realization of the need for liturgical reform so as to reintegrate liturgy and spirituality. In his 1903 motu proprio on church music *Tra le sollecitudini,* Pius X stated a fundamental principle: The true Christian spirit comes from active participation in the liturgy.

Odo Casel (1886–1948) made a major contribution to the necessary shift. From the perspective of his mystery-presence theory, spirituality is an assimilation to Christ in the liturgical realization of the mystery of Christ, not an individual quest and adventure guided by intellect, will, imagination, and sentiment.[4] In restoring the Paschal Mystery to a central position, with the Christian life flowing from the liturgical celebration of the mystery, Casel—whatever the historical and theological defects of his theory—provided a solid foundation for liturgical spirituality.

Works on liturgical spirituality began to appear at about the same time as Casel's patristic research. Romano Guardini was one of the first to argue for the liturgy as an objectively established norm for spirituality,[5] although Herwegen had earlier seen the medieval error in a turn from objective to subjective piety. Evelyn Underhill, already a prominent spiritual writer, presented the liturgy as formative of Christian consciousness and commitment, the source of spiritual guidance for the majority of Christians, because it is a corporate human response to God.[6] Dietrich von Hildebrand explored the formative and transformative power of the liturgy through the contact it makes possible with Christian values; e.g., communion and reverence.[7] Each helped to popularize liturgical spirituality as well as to provide historical, theological, and practical foundations for it.

The third phase of the liturgical movement, the period from World War II to the present, has been one of liturgical reform with a deep pastoral emphasis. Liturgical spirituality has been the explicit rationale for this liturgical reform. This is evident in Pius XII's reform interests[8] and in his encyclical *Mediator Dei.* It is even clearer in Vatican Council II's call for liturgical reform and renewal in order to revitalize

Christian life.[9] The process was motivated by the conviction that the liturgy provides the paradigm for Christian spirituality.[10] The research and catechesis that have accompanied it have been marked by that conviction.

Because of their strong pastoral interests, few liturgists writing in the postconciliar period have failed to deal with liturgy's relationship to life—hence, with liturgical spirituality. Historical studies have frequently correlated the state of the liturgy with the spirituality of the Christian people.[11] Works on liturgical theology are often practically indistinguishable from discussions of liturgical spirituality.[12] Even practical guides to appropriate celebration have used the impact on spirituality as their rationale.[13] Most significantly, the rubrics of the official liturgical books have, for the first time in history, acknowledged the presence and participation of the assembled people, called for more than proper ritual performance,[14] indicated the pastoral purpose of elements and rites, and offered options and guidelines for effective celebration.[15]

Major works dealing explicitly with liturgical spirituality have appeared in the course of this reform. Authors have not only produced spiritualities of the liturgy but have also reflected systematically on the intrinsic relationship between liturgy and spirituality and on the nature of liturgical spirituality. The first book-length treatments were published in the 1950s. We first look at them, then at recent authors, and close with a statement of topics currently prominent in the discussion of liturgical spirituality.

Classics of Liturgical Spirituality

Louis Bouyer, *Liturgical Piety*

Bouyer's approach to liturgical spirituality is primarily inspired by history, particularly Casel's mystery-presence theory based on patristic research. He develops a systematic theological understanding of the mystery, a focus that remains prominent in subsequent writers. His pastoral interests are evident throughout, although he provides little indication of how a revitalized liturgical experience of the mystery has an impact on Christian living. Controversial when published, his work is still timely in its essentials and anticipates several reforms initiated by the Council.

Bouyer's focal point is the mystery of Christ, lost sight of because of the distorted interpretation of liturgy produced by the baroque period and further obscured by the early liturgical movement's preoccupation with medievalism. He utilizes the work of Casel and subsequent students of the patristic era to show that the Paschal Mystery—the enactment in, by, and for the Church of Christ's saving act[16]—is the core of the liturgy. Attempting to avoid both a "false traditionalism" and a "rash modernism," Bouyer sees the permanent shape of the liturgy in the elements of communion, sacrifice, thanksgiving, and memorial, deeply permeated by the mystery. This mystery embodies the Church's conviction that its celebration is Christ's presence and Christ's action for salvation, "the one saving action of God in Christ throughout history."[17] The mystery is God's plan in history for our salvation, Christ's once-and-for-all *transitus*—a perfect past action which can never be repeated—fulfilled in the cross, embodied in the liturgical rite, and realized in us.

For Bouyer, the liturgy is clearly the work of all God's people, meeting together at God's call. The "hierarchical" character of the assembly is the primary effect of the *assembly's* new-covenant apostolicity, and the individual liturgies of all the participants are joined together. He surveys the Jewish origins of Christian Eucharist, the mystery proclaimed in the service of the Word and in the thanksgiving celebration. The mystery is both God's Word and human thanksgiving in God become human and in his whole Body. This mystery permeates the ordained ministries; the process of initiation into the mystery through baptism, confirmation, and penance; the expansion of the mystery through the blessings flowing from the Mass (nuptial blessing, the oil of the sick, and consecrations); the liturgical year; and the praise of the mystery in the Liturgy of the Hours.

Bouyer stresses that for early Christians, "the liturgy comprehended the whole prayer-life of the Church and of all Christians . . . [it] was not only a school of prayer, *the* school of prayer, but it *was* their prayer."[18] In noting the later development of Franciscan and Dominican spiritualities to fill the vacuum left by the fossilization of the liturgy, he shows how the liturgy was further obscured and concludes that various devotions develop only "when people are no longer in touch with the authentic spirit of the liturgy."[19] He calls for a liturgical revival to restore the liturgy's authentic spirit to the center of the Christian life.

Gabriel Braso, *Liturgy and Spirituality*[20]

Braso deals directly with spirituality throughout and is more systematically theological than Bouyer. He first explains the meaning and essential characteristics of Christian spirituality—*"the particular way of conceiving and of realizing the ideal of the Christian life"*[21]— and then identifies liturgical spirituality as the Church's spirituality.

He defines it as the spirituality "which seeks in its method and in its style of private sanctity (subjective piety, ascetical exercises, practice of the virtues, etc.) to imitate totally and exclusively the method and the style used by the Church in her official relations with God, that is, in her liturgy."[22] He considers this the spirituality most adequate and effective for achieving holiness.

Braso is also more systematic than Bouyer in his historical survey of the relationship between liturgy and spirituality (chapter 3). He gives extensive anecdotal evidence of the liturgical spirituality of the age of martyrs. He then describes the external splendor and interior decline in the Constantinian and early medieval periods. Finally, he narrates the decadence of liturgical spirituality in the late medieval and early modern period before telling of the renewal of liturgical spirituality in the course of the liturgical movement.

Chapter 4 presents a systematic analysis of the doctrinal foundations of the Church's public worship. Theology, however, is as often imposed on the liturgy as derived from it. As would be expected, his theology is that of the Thomistic revival, though with a consciousness of salvation history and a spirit derived from the patristic era. Worship is the honor owed to God, at once the glorification of God and the sanctification of those who engage in it. Such worship is both interior and exterior, both private and public. In Christian worship Christ—redeemer, sanctifier, and head of humanity—and the Church as Christ's Mystical Body are central. The liturgy is, at its heart, the exercise of Christ's priesthood perpetuated in the Church.

In chapter 5 he analyzes the characteristics of liturgical action in a similar fashion. He highlights the communitarian and hierarchical character of the liturgy and its sacramentality. For him the liturgy is the "temporal center of the unity of the divine plan"[23] and its "objectivity of expression"[24] is the basis for its central role in Christian formation and spirituality.

Chapter 6 analyzes the individual's contribution to the Church's public worship. Braso insists that the subjective (i.e., personal) element must inform liturgical prayer, even though the objective element must direct and orient it. Like Bouyer, Braso gives few concrete examples of liturgy's impact when he discusses the relationship of liturgical spirituality to the Christian life (chapter 7). He makes clear that liturgical spirituality does not reduce the Christian life to liturgical participation: Private spiritual activity prepares for the liturgy and makes possible the vital assimilation of the liturgy. Devotions are examined in some detail, primarily, it would seem, to show their harmony with the liturgy.[25]

Chapter 8, a new addition to the American edition, examines the interrelation of objective piety, subjective piety, and liturgical spirituality. The pre-eminence of the objective element is due to the fact that the mystery realizes the economy of salvation and is the object of faith. Thus, liturgical piety is to pray as the Church does and the Christian life is living according to liturgical spirituality. Chapter 9, on the life of worship and pastoral action, emphasizes again that the Paschal Mystery is at the center of the Christian life (but gives few concrete examples of its effect).

Cipriano Vagaggini, *Theological Dimensions of the Liturgy*[26]

Although this monumental work is not exclusively on liturgical spirituality, that topic is clearly central to the author's interests. Part Five is devoted to liturgy and life and its initial chapter (648–739) synthesizes Vagaggini's views on liturgical spirituality.

Like Braso, Vagaggini begins his treatment by clarifying the meaning of spirituality. For him spirituality is primarily concerned with the tendency toward perfection in the Christian life. Various elements give rise to diversity of spiritualities, but these spiritualities (if sound) are merely differing arrangements of the same elements according to particular necessities and tastes. "Liturgical spirituality is that spirituality in which the specific concretization and the proper synthetic relative ordering of the diverse elements common to every Catholic spirituality as a means toward Christian perfection are determined by the liturgy itself."[27] For Vagaggini, liturgical spirituality is more than participation in the liturgy, but all is "attuned to the spirit of the liturgy, is brought into relation with it, and is regulated [i.e., ordered and shaped] by it both quantitatively and qualitatively."[28]

Vagaggini's description of the general characteristics of liturgical spirituality is similar to Braso's, though more dynamic, less rigid, and more humane. The most noticeable characteristic, he says, is the strong accent on the ecclesial and communitarian aspect of salvation. (He does not stress the hierarchical element as Braso does.) Like Braso, he emphasizes the objective or "extroverted" character of liturgical spirituality, its focus on God rather than the self. But, unlike Braso, Vagaggini stresses that its attempt to achieve balance among the psychological faculties—its holistic character—is a significant characteristic. The sacramental starting-point integrates theocentric, Christocentric, dogmatic, ecclesial, and biblical perspectives. Finally, liturgical spirituality is Eucharistic.

Vagaggini's discussion of devotions ("extraliturgical forms of piety") is more nuanced than Braso's, though not as critical as

Bouyer's. The key criterion is "harmony" with the liturgy. Devotions are subordinated to the liturgy and defined by the spirit of the liturgy.

Vagaggini discusses liturgical spirituality in relation to two aspects of the striving for perfection, the ascetical and the mystical. In the context of discussing ascetical efforts, he gives special attention to discursive meditation (both in the liturgical action and outside it in a climate of liturgical spirituality) to show the "real possibility of personalization that is intrinsic to the liturgy."[29] Spiritual exercises and the effort to live virtuously are discussed in detail to show that liturgical spirituality, far from being confined to the liturgy, extends the spirit of the liturgy into the whole of life. Vagaggini, more than Bouyer, shows the practical relevance of liturgy to Christian living. While his treatment, particularly of the virtues, shows traces of the scholastic schema, it is, overall, much more successful than Braso's.

A basic issue in discussions between liturgical theologians and spiritual writers has been the compatibility of mystical experience—individual and interior—with liturgical spirituality—communal and sensual. The writings of the sixteenth-century mystics, John of the Cross and Teresa of Avila, seem to have little place for liturgy. However, Vagaggini offers extensive evidence from the writings of mystics who have dealt explicitly with liturgical prayer (Cassian, Marie of the Incarnation, Gertrude the Great) to show the basic compatibility—even the intrinsic correlation—of liturgical spirituality with mystical experience, including the prayer of quiet and contemplation. "When the interior union, which must be realized in every true and active participation in the liturgy, arrives at its perfection, it becomes at the same time contemplation or contemplative participation."[30]

More clearly than Braso, Vagaggini highlights that liturgical spirituality is not one spirituality among many but the spirituality of the Church, clearly distinguished from others. It is such because liturgy is the prayer of the Church. Moreover, "the liturgy is capable of being the center of a complete spiritual doctrine, and hence the pivotal point of a style of Christian life well adapted to the purpose of leading one to the highest state of perfection."[31]

Recent Authors on Liturgical Spirituality

The writings of several authors in the 1980s and 1990s show the growing maturity of liturgical spirituality as a distinct area of study. Others undoubtedly could, and should, be included, but we will focus on six American Catholics for practical reasons.[32]

Michael Downey

Although he rarely mentions liturgical spirituality explicitly, much of Downey's writing touches on the relationship between liturgy and spirituality but with a characteristic emphasis on spirituality's formative role. He puts the relationship between them most simply when he states: "We might say that the life of prayer and liturgy (contemplation) is surrender to the Spirit, while Christian moral life (action) is manifestation of the Spirit."[33] Thus, the unity of liturgy and spirituality is the presence of the Spirit. However, his perspective is from spirituality's side of the relationship. Apparently, the dynamism of the Spirit means that manifestation in life is primary, although this in turn calls for and leads to surrender in worship.

Liturgical spirituality may thus include practical implications of prayer and worship[34] but not in a fashion that would derive a spirituality *from* the liturgy. The relationship between liturgy and spirituality is reciprocal and one of critical correlation.[35] In this relationship sacramental liturgy provides a vision and perspective, not a collection of specifics.

What seems to be of most interest to Downey is spirituality's impact on liturgy. The spirituality of which he speaks, however, is liturgical in at least a broad sense, since it flows from a sacramental vision of life. Downey's work on Jean Vanier and the spirituality of l'Arche[36] establishes a crucial perspective, that of the weak, wounded, and forgotten elements within society and within the self and how these are to be brought before God in prayer and worship.[37] What emerges is the vision of a God revealed in weakness and vulnerability and suffering, surfacing "at the margins" of a life envisioned sacramentally. Recurrent topics in Downey's writings thus include worship between the holocausts (the Jewish holocaust and the threat of nuclear holocaust), the dead Christ, the relationship between liturgy and justice, and the need for lament to be explicit in liturgy.

Regis Duffy

Although Regis Duffy's *Real Presence: Worship, Sacraments, and Commitment*[38] does not attempt to analyze the relationship of liturgy and spirituality, it does deal with central issues of liturgical spirituality. In particular, Duffy is concerned with the fact that liturgical symbols often appear disconnected from commitment to authentic Christian living; i.e., from spirituality. He argues that sacramental ritual and community worship must function as symbols of transformation and renewed commitment and that the quality of participation must be gauged by life commitments.

Symbols call for participation—real presence—but they also clarify experience and thus allow for insight and change. *"Worship, rooted in the gratuity of God's justification, is tested by ecclesial and eschatological responsibility."*[39] This is because worship symbolizes both divine presence and our response to it and thereby calls us to commitments that are not merely private but ecclesial. In the liturgy, God's presence challenges our lack of presence, the praxis which misreads experience and fails to recognize the salvation present there. It challenges us, in other words, to recognize God's presence in our lives and to be present there ourselves in renewed commitment to mission and service. Liturgical intentionality is thus a way of seeing the meaning of God's action in our lives for the sake of others.[40]

Peter E. Fink

Most of Fink's writing is concerned in one way or another with liturgical spirituality. Two articles are particularly helpful in clarifying the interrelation of liturgy and spirituality.

In "Liturgical Prayer and Spiritual Growth"[41] Fink first insists that liturgy as prayer is not a product but a gathering of people who do certain things as dialogue with God. In all human activity those who do it are affected by it: we become what we do. What happens in liturgy and prayer is the visible and tangible side of grace and salvation. However, it does not happen instantaneously: sacraments are effective as processes of signifying. The passage from signification to effect spells out the process of spiritual growth as what we do gradually changes us and we live our way into a new kind of thinking. What happens to us—if we do it often and long enough—depends on the range of activities in which we take part, for liturgy is made up of many elements. Most importantly, the path of liturgical prayer transforms images and affections and behavior and enlarges our images of God and Christ and Church and selves. Ultimately we come to see as Christ sees, from within Christ.

"Liturgy and Spirituality: A Timely Intersection"[42] deals with what each offers the other. In first clarifying the meaning of spirituality, Fink takes issue with the dominant psychological paradigm that focuses on the self, on personal growth and fulfillment. Liturgy, he says, "stretches us to be for others" from initiation to burial and takes us where the psychological paradigm cannot, "into the mystery of God where the God-become-flesh is the center and where human life . . . is transformed into the divine."[43] In developing the liturgical side of Christian spirituality, he argues first that *"the language of all authentic Christian spirituality is public language and can-*

not be privatized without doing it violence" and then that *"every spirituality can and should intersect with the liturgy of the Church."*[44] Fink offers two conclusions. First, liturgy provides a paradigm for all spirituality: "The vision set forth in the Church's liturgy is the primary vision that must shape any authentic Christian spirituality and the primary context in which any specific spirituality must understand itself." Second, "the Church's liturgy sets forth a vision which is itself a spirituality, a journey into the mystery of God made human and the mystery of men and women transformed into the divine."[45]

Kevin W. Irwin

Part One of Irwin's *Liturgy, Prayer, and Spirituality*[46] focuses on distinctions and relationships among liturgy, prayer, and spirituality. Irwin starts with a discussion of faith and describes spirituality as "the experience of our relationship with God in faith and the ways in which we live out our faith."[47] Liturgy is the *Church's* spirituality because "it touches the lives of all Christians" and because it is the "community's response in faith to all that has been accomplished in Christ."[48] Liturgical prayer is formative of an incarnational spirituality that embraces all of life, a liturgical spirituality which helps us discover God manifesting and disclosing self in all of life.

In Part Two Irwin discusses various elements of liturgical prayer and their contribution to a liturgical spirituality. He begins with the fact that liturgy is a *corporate* work done in faith; conversion and ecclesiology are included in the discussion. He then focuses on the proclamation of the Word (readings, response, homily, and intercessions); communal participation in memory and hope in the Paschal Mystery of Jesus, past, present, and future; and the fact that liturgy is a *patterned* experience of ritual prayer (speaking, listening, movement, song, and silence). Two final chapters focus on the rhythm of liturgical time (especially feasts and seasons) and Trinitarian prayer (in terms of who is addressed and how the Trinity actualizes and effects the liturgical act).

Part Three draws out implications of the reformed liturgy for liturgical spirituality. The first and most important is that liturgy, the proclamation and enactment of the mystery of God incarnate in Jesus, is an experience of prayer and needs to be more clearly such. The second is that, while spirituality is broader than liturgy, what is celebrated in liturgy is to be lived, and liturgical prayer is to be extended into personal prayer. The third is that the interrelation of liturgy and life requires a commitment to mission, particularly work for justice.

Shawn Madigan

For Shawn Madigan, liturgical spirituality is broader than liturgy and embraces all of life, with liturgy providing meaning and direction for living. Madigan's approach to liturgical spirituality can be summed up in her statement that "Christians who live a liturgical spirituality experience the liturgical life of the Church as their source of spiritual direction."[49] Spiritual direction appears to function primarily as source of both nourishment and critique, and so the first chapter of *Spirituality Rooted in Liturgy*[50] explores how Christian spirituality is intrinsically a liturgical spirituality because it "originates, and is constantly renewed, through the liturgical celebration of the [paschal] mystery."[51] In the liturgical model of spiritual direction, the community is the subject and the liturgy calls the community to conversion. Many elements within the liturgy mediate Christ's presence, but the central reality is that the liturgy forms the community into the Paschal Mystery, which is always the focus. The liturgy is thus formative and foundational for the Christian life, lived in Christ for the transformation of the world.

The community, its worship, and its liturgical spirituality are always in a cultural context. Madigan explores aspects of this context by discussing variant worldviews and the contemporary American situation. Chapter 5 identifies two models of worship within two worldviews characterized by differences concerning organization of relationships (adult mutuality vs. symbolic kinship or hierarchical ordering), perception of the ideal (idealism vs. empiricism), and perception of time and history (continuous vs. linear). Chapter 6 ("Liturgical Spirituality: Conciliar Foundations") traces the presence of these two worldviews and models in the documents of Vatican II and concludes to two different ways of looking at liturgical spirituality.

Chapter 7 ("Christian Memory and Life Direction") discusses how communal memory affects imagining the future in the contemporary American context and chapter 8 carries this vision of the future into a dimension of ultimacy, concluding with a discussion of domestic spirituality that seems to regard the American family as a correlate of the house church. Chapter 9 ("House Church: Yesterday, Today, Tomorrow") looks at ancient and modern intentional communities or domestic churches and at liturgy and the particularization of liturgical spirituality in these contexts. Although Madigan's analysis is loosely sketched and in need of clarification at several points, it raises intriguing questions for further developing liturgical spirituality in the context of family and intentional communities.

Joyce Ann Zimmerman[52]

Zimmerman builds upon the link established between liturgy and life in liturgical spirituality by attempting an ontological grounding of the relationship between liturgy and life as a basis for dealing with questions of meaning (spirituality). In particular, she utilizes recent developments in the field which focus attention on the bond between liturgy and work for justice as a component of Christian mission. She denies a dualism between liturgy and life and contends that the deep dynamic structures of liturgy and Christian living are identical in that both express the Paschal Mystery. Her study is heavily philosophical and likely to daunt nonacademics, but it demonstrates that liturgical spirituality has achieved theological maturity and is not merely a useful form of pastoral catechesis.

The first part of the book details a theological and methodological framework. First, Zimmerman *shows* the link between liturgy and life by exploring critically the connection in scripture between "remembering" and the oppressed (chapter 1) and the late New Testament coincidence between liturgy and concern for the poor (chapter 2).

She then turns her attention to the deeper question of *why* this is so, using a postcritical method derived from French philosopher Paul Ricoeur's work that looks to the depth structure of texts and attempts to identify the underlying dynamic. Chapter 3 explains Ricoeur's methodology of textual hermeneutics and his concept of "meaningful human activity." Interpretation requires participation, connection to what is being interpreted (here, the tradition of Christian living communicating the originary event of the Paschal Mystery). It requires distanciation, a separation from the tradition, in order to analyze it objectively. (Zimmerman proposes that liturgy is such a distancing, a mirror of ideal Christian living. Rather than seeing liturgy as telling us how to live—an implicitly dualistic perspective—she sees Christian living as its content.) Thirdly, interpretation requires appropriation, and at this stage liturgy challenges us to accept new possibilities for self-understanding in living the Paschal Mystery. Her claim is that meaningful Christian living is living the Paschal Mystery; liturgy provides a vision, guides our choices, and impels us to interact with others in a manner that incarnates the Paschal Mystery.

Chapter 4 applies Ricoeur's hermeneutical method to Luke's description of the Lord's supper to produce a description of the Paschal Mystery. She concentrates on the "table talk," which conveys Luke's understanding of the meaning of the supper in relation to the passion and resurrection. She analyzes the text from two perspectives to bring out both a linear thematic dynamism and structure and a concentric dynamism and structure. She identifies a soteriological focus and an eschatological focus and a dialectic between "already" and "not yet." The meaning of the Paschal Mystery is then found, not in the past, but in the dialectic, the redemptive tension, between soteriology and eschatology, between the already and the not yet. Christians live out this dialectic in order to recognize themselves in the Jesus event.

Part Two, "Pastoral Interpretations," applies the methodology of Part One to liturgical experience in order to interpret the Paschal Mystery for contemporary Christian living. Here Zimmerman rethinks liturgical categories in order to present a pastorally oriented and theologically grounded liturgical spirituality supported by a consistent methodology. Ricoeur's three moments structure the hermeneutical process.

Participation: As Christians sharing a tradition, expressing our identity constitutes the tradition. Chapter 5 lays out foundational elements of Christian self-understanding from the participated tradition—Paschal Mystery (Jesus' death, resurrection, ascension, and sending of the Spirit, with the sending of the Spirit given special attention), baptism, Body of Christ, ministry of the assembly (including remarks on the priesthood of the faithful and the gifts of the Spirit), community (both liturgical and sociological), and prayer (including both liturgical prayer and devotional prayer). Liturgy celebrates that identity and life interprets liturgy.

Distanciation: The next three chapters critique this participation by exploring key dimensions of Christian living through particular liturgical moments of distanciation. Zimmerman uses a temporal rather than spatial organizational principle throughout. The Liturgy of the Hours is the daily expression of the Paschal Mystery dialectic (chapter 6). The Sunday Eucharist is the weekly fulfillment of the celebration of our daily life (chapter 7). The rhythm of the liturgical year is an integrating expression of the Paschal Mystery (chapter 8). Each (daily, weekly, yearly) moves beyond the other—paradoxically, into a more focused and simplified experience of the Paschal Mystery—facilitating a holistic experience.

Appropriation: In Chapter 9, Zimmerman presents a liturgical spirituality, a statement of Christian self-understanding, that chooses among the possibilities uncovered in the previous moment of distanciation. "To be Christian means to *live* a liturgical spirituality for that is how we define ourselves."[53] Liturgical spirituality integrates all Christian living, for both liturgy and life make present the Paschal Mystery and both express the soteriological-eschatological dynamic of the Paschal Mystery. The dialectic is experienced both ritually and temporally. It is not resolved but lived, to the point that it objectifies and makes present the Paschal Mystery when we are aware that the pole of the dialectic other than what we immediately experience is also operative. There is the same dialectic of liturgy and life: In liturgy we distance ourselves from life in order to enter into life more deeply. At the same time, the more deeply we express the Paschal Mystery in our lives, the more deeply we enter into liturgical celebration. Thus, there is no dualism between liturgy and justice: doing justice is at the core of our identity, for to live the Paschal Mystery is to be in right relationship, and liturgy, as the celebration of our identity, moves us to establish justice.

Zimmerman concludes by explaining basic principles operative in a liturgical spirituality. (1) Liturgical spirituality is a dialectic of interpretive moments. (2) The depth structure of Christian living is the same as the depth structure of Christian liturgy. (3) The Jesus event is originary to our tradition. (4) The Jesus event is communicated through a tradition by an authority (the Spirit) resting within the community. (5) *Koinonia* is constitutive of liturgical spirituality. (6) *Kerygma* is constitutive of liturgical spirituality. (7) *Metanoia* is constitutive of liturgical spirituality. (Surprisingly, Zimmerman does not mention *diakonia* or *martyria*, service and witness, since she emphasizes service and work for justice elsewhere.) Liturgy and life are not side-by-side and separate but grafted together onto God's life: "Liturgical spirituality interprets through living and celebrating the meaning of the Paschal Mystery from the depths of the One who dwells within."[54]

Emerging Themes

Few liturgical authors since World War II have failed to deal to some extent with liturgical spirituality and with liturgy's relation to life. This has especially been the case since Vatican Council II.[55] The classic works of liturgical spirituality from the 1950s lay solid historical, theological, and pastoral foundations. They argued convincingly that the liturgy is the basic school of Christian spirituality and that liturgical spirituality is the Church's official spirituality. They implied that liturgical spirituality is more complete and comprehensive than other spiritualities. They saw the special character of liturgical spirituality in its objectivity, its focus on the Paschal Mystery experienced communally and personally in liturgical celebration.

Though formed theologically in the scholastic modes of thought, these writers seemed to recognize that scholastic approaches and categories—developed in an era of liturgical decadence and a disintegrating liturgical community—were inadequate to deal successfully with liturgy and liturgical experience. Their efforts to expand beyond the scholastic thought forms—seen particularly in mining the patristic era for more appropriate resources and in integrating the salvation-history approach from the biblical movement—were not altogether successful. They were particularly deficient when it came to dealing with the existential richness of everyday life and liturgy's impact on it. These authors did affirm liturgy's formative value for Christian life and mission but were rarely specific except in discussing the traditional virtues.

However, leaders such as Virgil Michel united in their persons a passion for liturgy and a passion for social justice.[56] And since the 1970s the intersection of liturgy and ethics and particularly of liturgy and justice has emerged as a major area of interest, remedying an important lack in earlier liturgical spirituality and in *Sacrosanctum Concilium*. Though too extensive to treat here, that literature is part of the general field of liturgical spirituality. Specific justice issues, especially regarding language, sexism, and patriarchy, have generated intense interest and extensive literature, most of which is closely related to liturgical spirituality. In general, few treatments of liturgical spirituality fail to give prominence to liturgy and social justice.

Postconciliar authors dealing explicitly with the relationship of liturgy and spirituality and the nature of liturgical spirituality have several characteristics in common that distinguish them as a group from the classical authors. Although they build on and presuppose historical research, contemporary authors are less likely to take an historical approach. Popular spirituality is only beginning to be investigated, and a comprehensive history of liturgical spirituality is still to be written.

Although they take a systematic theological approach, contemporary writers show few signs of influence from scholastic theology. Their rationales for liturgical spirituality and the link between liturgy and life consequently tend to be more complete and more solidly founded in experience, but sometimes they are less systematic. Pastoral interests and the use of more contemporary philosophical and theological categories, as well as the social sciences, enable them to deal more successfully with liturgy's formative role in the day-to-day living of the Christian life. They are especially concerned to show the relevance of liturgy to life issues of justice and peace.

Interest in the transformative power of liturgy and liturgical symbol has led to an enriching dialogue with the social sciences. The work of anthropologists such as Mary Douglas and Victor Turner and the new field of ritual studies, where Ronald Grimes is a central figure, have been especially valuable to show the centrality of ritual to human life and the role of ritual in personal and social transformation.[57] This has added evidence and precision to the contention that Christian liturgy is paradigmatic for Christian living.

Recent writers have also explored the relevance of specific liturgical processes, elements, and symbols for communal and personal spirituality. The baptismal base of Christian spirituality and the role of initiation in Christian formation has been an area of interest.[58] The liturgy of the word and the formative character of listening to the proclamation of Scripture has been examined.[59] The relationship of the Eucharist,[60] the Eucharistic Prayer,[61] and the absence of Eucharist[62] to Christian spirituality, especially with regard to justice issues, has been a frequent topic. Other sacraments, including marriage[63] and penance,[64] have also received attention, as have environment and art[65] and liturgical time.[66] Symbols as varied as music, silence, and dance have been explored. In general, most major studies of sacraments and liturgy have given some attention to spirituality.

In addition to new interests, such as liturgy and ethics, liturgy and justice, and intentional communities,[67] most of the "classical" topics recur in contemporary literature. However, interest in inculturation and the positive value now placed on pluralism and multiculturalism mean more than toleration for popular devotions and piety[68] and there is a new appreciation of the varied forms of personal prayer.[69] The relationship of liturgy to contemplation and mysticism and traditional stages of prayer still draws interest,[70] as does the general theme of liturgy's relationship to life.[71] Most significantly, writers have continued to reflect on the mystery that is at the heart of Christian worship and is the synthesizing principle of liturgical spirituality[72] and on how liturgy is the Church's "school" of spirituality.[73]

Present and Future Directions

Twentieth-century liturgical reform has been motivated by the need to reintegrate liturgy and spirituality. When reform has been implemented with pastoral sensitivity and with attention to a broad-based renewal, that has generally happened, although even then some individuals' spirituality has been disrupted to an extent because of changing liturgical experience.[74] Particular reforms—demystification of the liturgy, adult lay ministers of both sexes, vernacular and inclusive languages, a more dialogic liturgy—have been the precondition for an imaginative relocation of the divine presence and a different valuation of ourselves in relation to a God differently imaged. The overall effect appears to have been, if not greater intersection of liturgy and life in all parishes, then at least a greater *desire* for it and a sharper consciousness of factors that hinder it.[75] At the same time, there has been a greater awareness of points of contrast and conflict between Christianity and American culture, factors which are a major issue in a liturgical spirituality.[76] In other words, the work of liturgical reform is only part of the Church's renewal process and only part of the reintegration of liturgy and spirituality.

To the extent that reintegration is being achieved, old dualisms and dichotomies are diminishing and even disappearing. As liturgy is the work and play of the assembled Christian community, so all Christians, not just a clerical and religious elite, are called to holiness through the diversity of their roles and lifestyles. As a communal spirituality, liturgical spirituality is other-oriented, not individualistic, but it is also as personal and varied as the members of the liturgical assembly, moving them inward as well as outward. Because liturgy is the prayer of the Church, liturgical spirituality is intrinsically ecclesial. Because that prayer is for the coming of God's rule on earth as in heaven, liturgical spirituality is oriented to the Church's communal mission, especially work for justice and peace, as well as to striving for holiness and grace. As that prayer is Trinitarian, so Christian life is a movement toward God through Christ in the Spirit. Liturgical spirituality is more holistic than many traditional spiritualities because liturgy is itself a bodily activity that requires interior commitment, thus integrating all the dimensions and faculties of human being. Incarnational and sacramental in its origin and expression, liturgical spirituality embraces all of life, recognizing the sacramental character of all reality. The cross is at its center, because it is focused on the Paschal Mystery, and so those who live a liturgical spirituality recognize that they are constantly called to join Christ in his movement from the sin of this world into the glory of God by a life of love and virtue in praise and thanksgiving to God.

Each of these characteristic features of liturgical spirituality is still a task to be accomplished both pastorally and academically. Liturgy is not yet fully experienced as the self-expression of an inclusive community. Spirituality still retains traces of a hierarchical, patriarchal, and elitist mentality. Liturgical spirituality needs to attend to the diversity of roles, functions, vocations, and lifestyles within liturgy and community, developing, for example, both domestic and marketplace orientations.

Liturgy needs to be more locally creative and allow for more personal expression while maintaining bonds of universal communion. Spirituality needs to be innovative within a continuity with the tradition. Thus, liturgical spirituality needs to follow through on its initial recognition of multiculturalism and the need for inculturation and to develop the place of the personal within the communitarian.

Ecclesial consciousness in liturgy and life must go deeper than institutional conformity to a mature adult collaboration and communion. Liturgical spirituality must move in the direction of a similar shared responsibility, including study of how liturgical participation fosters communal discernment and serves individuals as a means of communal spiritual direction.

Liturgical spirituality has in recent years developed the links between faith celebrated in worship and faith working for justice and peace. It must strengthen those links by incorporating the marginalized and suggesting ways in which those who gather for worship can also gather for mission and in both gatherings experience the holy presence of God. It needs to recognize as well such other elements of mission as evangelization, witness, catechesis, leadership formation, and forms of personal ministry. Attention to the rule and reign of God as future restoration as well as present reality should also help to counter the tendency toward self-preoccupation and complacency, cultural characteristics prominent in the New Age.

It must continue to explore and communicate the Trinitarian nature of the Christian God and Christian prayer to show how both are the practical basis of meaningful human life and activity. Liturgy and life in the likeness of the triune God are geared toward full, conscious, and active participation in a communion of persons and toward perfection through mutuality and self-gift. Liturgical spirituality attuned to the Trinity should be able to counter the tendency to believe that the ascent to God is only through descent into the self and that it is a private adventure.

The reformed liturgy has become increasingly verbal and verbose rather than sensual, even as spirituality has become more experiential and holistic. Liturgical spirituality needs to develop its holistic character and bring liturgy and spirituality together by giving attention to affectivity, intimacy, and sexuality in Christian worship and Christian living. It also needs to incorporate contemporary recognition of developmental factors in faith and personal growth, including the special character and role of children, the mentally and physically challenged, the aged, sexual minorities, and others. The place of silence in liturgy and of solitude in life need to be explored and fostered.

The incarnational and sacramental character of liturgical spirituality has been well developed in theory but should also enhance symbols and ritual in celebration. It also needs to promote the consciousness and development of the worldly character of liturgy and the liturgical character of everyday life.

The most important work that remains, of course, is to draw attention to how the Paschal Mystery is experienced in life and liturgy and to remove the obstacles that hinder its transforming power both in life and in liturgy, both in individuals and in the church community. The place given the Paschal Mystery is always a primary criterion for evaluating Christian spiritualities, but in liturgical spirituality ritual participation in the mystery is the primary source of religious experience and personal transformation. It provides a common center that prevents the fragmentation and drifting characteristic of many other spiritualities. Yet that experience risks diminishment as church authorities deprive Catholic Christians of the birthright of their baptism by keeping them from celebrating the Lord's supper on the Lord's day. At the same time, cultural individualism and narcissism turn Christians' attention away from the Paschal Mystery. Liturgical spirituality thus has a special responsibility to counter both ecclesiastical and cultural trends that call it into question.

Liturgy is the gathering of people who *do* certain things as rite and as prayer to express their identity. Liturgical spirituality not only flows from and leads to the liturgy, it is also formed by the spirit of the liturgy. It is communal in nature, founded in Scripture, focused on praise and thanksgiving, and oriented to action in the world to establish the right relationships that are rehearsed in celebration. Its forms often echo those of the liturgy and, in particular, fit with the temporal rhythms of the liturgy. In liturgy as in life the Spirit moves us inward and outward, through, with, and in Christ into the mystery of the triune God. But for that to happen we must be open to that action by engaging fully, consciously, and actively, personally and as a community, in both liturgy and in life. It is that to which liturgical spirituality calls us.

Notes

1. *Theological Dimensions of the Liturgy: A General Treatise on the Theology of the Liturgy,* trans. Leonard J. Doyle and W.A. Jurgens (Collegeville: The Liturgical Press, 1976) 703. Vagaggini borrows the story from 1. Hausherr, *Penthos. La doctrine de la componction dans l'Orient chrétien* (Rome: 1944).

2. For an analysis of baroque influence, see Louis Bouyer, *Liturgical Piety* (Notre Dame, Ind.: University of Notre Dame Press, 1955) 1–9.

3. The common assumption is that there was no liturgical spirituality in the late-medieval and counter-Reformation periods and little interaction between

liturgy and life. John Bossy, a social historian who has concentrated on the late medieval and early modern period, shows that liturgy has always had a key position in everyday religious life. See his "The Mass as Social Institution, 1200–1700" in *Past and Present*, no. 100 (1983) 29–61, and *Christianity in the West, 1400–1700* (New York: Oxford University Press, 1985), and Paul Post, "John Bossy and the Study of Liturgy" in *Omnes Circumadstantes: Contributions towards a History of the Role of the People in the Liturgy, Festschrift Presented to Herman Wegman*, eds. Charles Caspers and Mae Schneiders (Kampen: Kok, 1990) 31–50. In the same volume, see also Th. Clemens, "Liturgy and Piety in the Netherlands during the Seventeenth and Eighteenth Centuries," 197–217.

4. See his *The Mystery of Christian Worship* (Westminster, Md.: Newman, 1962). *Die Liturgie als Mysterienfeier* first appeared in 1922.

5. *The Spirit of the Liturgy* (New York: Sheed and Ward, 1953). This first appeared in German in 1920.

6. *Worship* (London: James Nisbet, 1936).

7. *Liturgy and Personality* (New York: Longmans, Green, 1943).

8. Annibale Bugnini, *The Reform of the Liturgy, 1948–1975* (Collegeville: The Liturgical Press, 1990) 7ff. Pius XII first stated his interest in such a reform in May 1946 and work began in October of that year. A commission established in May 1948 continued its work in secrecy for twelve years.

9. *Sacrosanctum Concilium* ("The Constitution on the Sacred Liturgy") §1.

10. Ibid., §§2, 10–12.

11. See, for example, Theodor Klauser, *A Short History of the Western Liturgy: An Account and Some Reflections*, 2nd edition (New York: Oxford University Press, 1979); J.A. Jungmann, *Public Prayer through the Centuries* (New York: Paulist Press, 1978).

12. See, for example, Gordon W. Lathrop, *Holy Things: A Liturgical Theology* (Minneapolis: Fortress, 1993).

13. See, for example, Gilbert Ostdiek, *Catechesis for Liturgy: A Program for Parish Involvement* (Washington, D.C.: Pastoral Press, 1986).

14. This was already explicitly stated in *Sacrosanctum Concilium*, §11.

15. Thomas Richstatter, *Liturgical Law: New Style, New Spirit* (Chicago: Franciscan Herald Press, 1977); R. Kevin Seasoltz, *New Liturgy, New Laws* (Collegeville: The Liturgical Press, 1980). This has been more evident in the Sacramentary than in the rituals. However, the new arrangements of the official liturgical books being prepared by ICEL make this clearer.

16. Bouyer, *Liturgical Piety*, 18. Casel's theory is further examined in chapter 7.

17. Ibid., 79–80.

18. Ibid., 243.

19. Ibid., 248.

20. Gabriel Braso, *Liturgy and Spirituality* (Collegeville: The Liturgical Press, 1971) is a revised and expanded second edition of *Liturgia y Espiritualidad* (Barcelona: 1956).

21. Braso, *Liturgy and Spirituality*, 3; emphasis in the original.

22. Ibid., 17.

23. Ibid., 126.

24. Ibid., 134–48.

25. Ibid., 194–208.

26. Vagaggini, *Theological Dimensions,* 648–803.

27. Ibid., 661.

28. Ibid., 663.

29. Ibid., 690.

30. Ibid., 734–735.

31. Ibid., 738.

32. This is not meant to deny significant contributions from outside the Catholic communion, even from churches not normally regarded as "liturgical." In particular, Eastern churches have generally maintained a spirituality centered on the liturgy and Eastern authors have made major contributions. Nevertheless, space restrictions require limitation. For representative Protestant and Eastern perspectives, see Don E. Saliers, *Worship and Spirituality* (Philadelphia: Westminster, 1984); Alexander Schmemann, *Liturgy and Life: Lectures and Essays on Christian Development through Liturgical Experience* (New York: Orthodox Church in America, 1974); Louis Weil, *Gathered to Pray: Understanding Liturgical Prayer* (Cambridge, Mass.: Cowley Publications, 1986); W. Jardine Grisbrooke, "Toward a Liturgical Spirituality," *Studia Liturgica* 17 (1987) 77–86; Robert E. Webber, "Worship and Spirituality," *Reformed Liturgy and Music* 20 (1986) 67–71. Philip H. Pfatteicher, *Liturgical Spirituality* (Valley Forge, Pa.: Trinity Press International, 1997). For surveys, with bibliography, see the essays by Niels K. Rasmussen and Boris Bobrinskoy in *Liturgie et Vie Spirituelle,* 83–87 and 88–107.

33. Michael Downey, *Clothed in Christ: The Sacraments and Christian Living* (New York: Crossroad, 1987) 128.

34. See especially Michael Downey, "Widening Contexts of Sacramental Worship" in *At the Margins: Spirituality and Liturgy* (Washington, D.C.: Pastoral Press, 1994) 187–208. This essay is a concise restatement of the thesis of *Clothed in Christ.*

35. Michael Downey, *At the Margins,* 211. The essay is "Liturgy's Form: Work of the Spirit."

36. Michael Downey, *A Blessed Weakness: The Spirit of Jean Vanier and l'Arche* (San Francisco: Harper and Row, 1986).

37. Michael Downey, *At the Margins,* vii–viii.

38. Regis Duffy, *Real Presence: Worship, Sacraments, and Commitment* (San Francisco: Harper and Row, 1982).

39. Ibid., 78; emphasis in the original.

40. Duffy also develops this in his "Formative Experience and Intentional Liturgy," *Studies in Formative Spirituality* 3, no. 3 (November 1982) 351–61. He uses the examples of Francis of Assisi and Thérèse of Lisieux to show how honest intentionality enables liturgical participation to be formative for holiness despite the inadequacy of the rituals participated in. See also Christopher Kiesling, "The Formative Influence of Liturgy," *Studies in Formative Spirituality* 3, no. 3 (November 1982) 377–85.

41. Peter E. Fink, *Worship* 55 (1981) 386–98.

42. Peter E. Fink, "Liturgical Spirituality: A Timely Intersection" in *Liturgy and Spirituality in Context: Perspectives on Prayer and Culture,* ed. Eleanor Bernstein (Collegeville: The Liturgical Press, 1990) 47–61. The two articles have been combined as chapter 9 in Fink's *Worship: Praying the Sacraments* (Washington, D.C.: Pastoral Press, 1991).

43. Fink, "Liturgy and Spirituality," 51–52.

44. Ibid., 56; emphasis in the original. Fink also speaks of what happens to liturgy when spiritual depth is not brought to it and how it can be taken over by a political paradigm: the spiritual side of the liturgy is that it is prayer.

45. Ibid., 61.

46. Kevin W. Irwin, *Liturgy, Prayer, and Spirituality* (New York: Paulist Press, 1984). See also his "Liturgy" in *The New Dictionary of Catholic Spirituality,* ed. Michael Downey (Collegeville: The Liturgical Press, 1993) 602–10.

47. Irwin, *Liturgy, Prayer, and Spirituality,* 13.

48. Ibid., 14–15.

49. Shawn Madigan, "Spirituality, Liturgical," in *The New Dictionary of Sacramental Worship* ed. Peter E. Fink (Collegeville: The Liturgical Press, 1990) 1224. Curiously, neither Madigan's article nor Irwin's (cited above, note 41) provides an overview of the field, either the history or the literature.

50. Shawn Madigan, *Spirituality Rooted in Liturgy* (Washington, D.C.: Pastoral Press, 1988).

51. Ibid., 2.

52. Joyce Ann Zimmerman, C.PP.S., *Liturgy As Living Faith: A Liturgical Spirituality* (Scranton: University of Scranton Press and London & Toronto: Associated University Presses, 1993).

53. Ibid., 129.

54. Ibid., 140.

55. Much of this literature is concerned with liturgical spirituality in a pastoral rather than academic manner or with developing a liturgical spirituality rather than reflecting on its nature. See, for example, Lawrence E. Mick, *To Live as We Worship* (Collegeville: The Liturgical Press, 1984) and Austin Fleming, *Preparing for Liturgy: A Theology and Spirituality* (Washington, D.C.: Pastoral Press, 1985).

56. See, for example, Kenneth Himes, "Eucharist and Justice: Assessing the Legacy of Virgil Michel," *Worship* 62 (1988) 201–24.

57. See, for example, Tom F. Driver, *The Magic of Ritual: Our Need for Liberating Rites that Transform Our Lives and Our Communities* (San Francisco: HarperSan Francisco, 1991).

58. Examples include Ronald Lewinski, "Rites of Initiation and Christian Spirituality" in *Spirituality and Prayer: Jewish and Christian Understandings,* eds. Leon Klenicki and Gabe Huck (New York: Paulist Press, 1983) 106–27; Frank C. Quinn, "The Sacraments of Initiation and Christian Life," *Spirituality Today* 34 (1982) 27–38; Richard E. Trutter, "A Paradigm for Christian Living: The Catechumenate," *Spirituality Today* 34 (1982) 18–26. Not directly concerned with liturgical spirituality but very helpful is Kilian McDonnell and

George T. Montague, *Christian Initiation and Baptism in the Holy Spirit: Evidence from the First Eight Centuries* (Collegeville: The Liturgical Press, 1991).

59. Among others, see Gerard Austin, "Spirit through Word" in *Called to Prayer: Liturgical Spirituality Today* (Collegeville: The Liturgical Press, 1986) 11–26.

60. E.g., Monika Hellwig, *The Eucharist and the Hunger of the World* (New York: Paulist Press, 1976); Roger Mahony, "The Eucharist and Social Justice," *Worship* 57 (1983) 52–61; R. Kevin Seasoltz, "Justice and the Eucharist," *Worship* 58 (1984) 507–25; Thomas Hopko, "Upon Us and Upon These Gifts: A Spirituality of the Eucharist," *Spiritual Life* 12 (1966) 87–94.

61. James Dallen, "Spirituality of Eucharistic Prayer," *Worship* 58 (1984) 359–72.

62. James Dallen, *The Dilemma of Priestless Sundays* (Chicago: Liturgy Training Publications, 1994).

63. Christopher Kiesling, "The Liturgy of Christian Marriage: Introduction to Marital Spirituality," *Spirituality Today* 34 (1982) 48–59.

64. James DaRen, "The Absence of a Ritual of Reconciliation in Celtic Penance" in *The Journey of Western Spirituality,* ed. A.W. Sadler, Annual Publication of the College Theology Society, 1980 (Chico, Calif.: Scholars Press, 1981) 79–105.

65. E.g,. Louis Weil, "The Arts: Language of the Spirit" in *Called to Prayer,* 69–81.

66. E.g., Thomas Keating, *The Mystery of Christ: The Liturgy as Spiritual Experience* (New York: Amity House, 1987); Mark G. Boyer, *Mystagogy: Liturgical Paschal Spirituality for Lent and Easter* (New York: Alba House, 1990). The periodical literature is abundant.

67. Paul J. Philibert, "Human Development and Sacramental Transformation," *Worship* 65 (1991) 522–39. See also Shawn Madigan, *Spirituality Rooted in Liturgy,* Chapters 7–9.

68. See, for example, Mary Collins, "Devotions and Renewal Movements: Spiritual Cousins of the Liturgy" in *Called to Prayer,* 47–68; Timothy Matovina, "Liturgy, Popular Rites, and Popular Spirituality," *Worship* 63 (1989) 351–61; Lawrence S. Cunningham, "Worship, Spirituality and Inculturation, American Style: Some Theses and Reflections," *Assembly* 17, no. 3 (April 1991) 518–521; Regis A. Duffy, *"Devotio Futura:* The Need for Post-Conciliar Devotions?" in *A Promise of Presence: Studies in Honor of David N. Power,* eds. Michael Downey and Richard Fragomeni (Washington, D.C.: Pastoral Press, 1992) 163–83.

69. Mark Searle, "On the Art of Lifting up the Heart: Liturgical Prayer Today," *Studies in Formative Spirituality* 3, no. 3 (November 1982) 399–410.

70. E.g., Louis John Cameli, "The Spirituality of Celebration," *Chicago Studies* 16 (1977) 63–74; Mary Collins, *Contemplative Participation: Sacrosanctum Concilium Twenty-Five Years Later* (Collegeville: The Liturgical Press, 1990), especially 75–85; Odilo Lechner, *"Mystik und Liturgie"* in *Liturgie zwischen Mystik und Politik: Österreichische Pastoraltagung 27–29 December 1990* (Wien: Herder, 1991) 81–89; Paul Grammont, *Liturgie et contemplation* in

Pierre Grelot et al., *Liturgie et Vie Spirituelle* (Paris: Beauchesne, 1977) 118–27; Emilie Griffin, "The Challenge to Interiority" in *Liturgy and Spirituality in Context*, 83–98.

71. Nathan Mitchell, "Spirituality of Christian Worship," *Spirituality Today* 34 (1982) 5–17.

72. Jean Corbon, *The Wellspring of Worship* (New York: Paulist Press, 1988); Robert Taft, "What Does Liturgy Do? Towards a Soteriology of Liturgical Celebration: Some Theses," *Worship* 66 (1992) 194–211; Germán Martínez, "Sacramental Mystery and Christian Spirituality," *Studies in Formative Spirituality* 3, no. 3 (November 1982) 387–97.

73. Gordon E. Truitt, "Liturgy as a School of Prayer: A Question," *Spiritual Life* 27, no. 1 (Spring 1981) 3–13; Roy Reed, "Liturgy as a School of Prayer: A Prologomenon," *Spiritual Life* 27, no. 1 (Spring 1981) 24–34.

74. See Robert Duggan, "Liturgical Spirituality and Liturgical Reform," *Spiritual Life* 27, no. 1 (Spring 1981) 46–53.

75. See especially Sandra Schneiders, "Liturgy and Spirituality—The Widening Gap," *Spirituality Today* 30 (1978) 196–210.

76. For excellent perspectives, see M. Francis Mannion, "Liturgy and the Present Crisis of Culture," and Mark Searle, "Private Religion, Individualistic Society, and Common Worship," both in *Liturgy and Spirituality in Context*, 1–26 and 27–46; and Richard R. Gaillardetz, "North American Culture and the Liturgical Life of the Church: The Separation of the Quests for Transcendence and Community," *Worship* 68 (1994) 403–10.

Chapter 12

Liturgy and Worship:
A Select Pastoral Bibliography

Joyce Ann Zimmerman, C.PP.S.

Some subject areas lend themselves nicely to a complete bibliography. Some areas are simply too extensive, and that is the case with liturgy and worship. The most complete liturgy bibliography has been compiled by the Institut de Bibliographie Liturgique in Leuven, Belgium but it is available in only a few libraries here in North America (e.g., The Catholic University in Washington, D.C. and the University of Notre Dame in Indiana). Unfortunately for scholars, the production of the index cards was discontinued at the end of 1987. After that date, the monks of Mont César Abbey in Leuven collaborate with the theology faculties of both the Katholieke Universiteit te Leuven and the Université Catholique de Louvain and continue the service in the yearly "Elenchus Bibliographicus" in *Ephemerides theologicae Lovanienses* and in the "Bulletin Bibliographique" in *Questions liturgiques.* Both of these periodicals are available in most theology libraries. Additionally, many books on liturgy include sometimes rather extensive bibliographies. Realistically, however, these bibliographies are of interest primarily to the liturgical scholar. The liturgical practitioner usually has neither the library resources nor the time to pursue these more scholarly publications, nor would it even be all that helpful.

This select pastoral bibliography on liturgy and worship has been carefully selected from among the virtually thousands of resources available in order to be a sensible aid. The general categories somewhat follow the chapter topics in this first part of the book. No attempt has been made to include all the references cited in the other eleven chapters of Part I, but those citations can serve as additional bibliographic suggestions. This bibliography lists what this writer considers the basic materials anyone working in pastoral liturgy ought to have on hand, or at least enjoy a working familiarity with the references. Most of the selections are not scholarly works, as such; they all are chosen because they embrace solid liturgical principles. Most of the books are not "how to" type references; instead, these suggestions are intended to further the theological and pastoral understanding of worship and liturgy for the reader. This bibliography would be an excellent basis for building a parish liturgical library, if one has not already been started. No denominational service books nor their respective commentaries have been included. It is assumed that anyone working in liturgy is already in possession of and thoroughly familiar with the service books they are using.

Copyright

Of all the resources included, one deserves special mention. Liturgical musicians are some of the more notorious violators of copyright laws (although recent lawsuits and a number of articles and printed warnings have alerted people to the problem). Unless something is in the public domain (and many hymns are), reprinting without the express permission of the copyright holder is illegal (and this includes making one copy of a text or music on a transparency for overhead projection). Many music publishers have tried to help parishes and liturgical communities by making available reprint licenses that are reasonably priced and can be renewed annually. For one-time reprinting (e.g., for a wedding worship aid), contact the music publisher; generally, the charge is quite low and sometimes permission is granted free of charge. A very helpful resource is FDLC's *copyright update: reprint permission policies of publishers of liturgical music and sacred scripture* (see the first section of the bibliography on reference works). The work has not been updated and re-released, but most of the publishers' policies are the same or very similar. An updated list of publisher addresses and phone numbers can be purchased from Church Music Publishers Association, P.O. Box 158992, Nashville, TN 37215, (615) 791-0173 for a nominal $2.00.

Professional Reading

Every parish liturgy budget ought to have a line item for professional reading materials. Each year books are purchased to build up a parish liturgy/worship library. The purpose of these professional materials is twofold. First, a parish liturgy library serves as resource material in the planning/preparing of liturgies and worship services. It also provides information for questions about liturgy or worship that arise. Further, these resources can help a parish begin to formulate and articulate a theology of liturgy and worship that is the basis out of which all decisions are made.

Second, a parish liturgy library can be a stimulus to the liturgy personnel to do ongoing professional reading. All too often, we expect our parishioners to grow in their understanding of worship (especially when we introduce something new), but we ourselves as the professionals have not moved beyond our formal education. As Church reaches a deeper self-understanding, so will liturgy necessarily grow and change. The only way to keep up with the advancements in liturgical theology is to read, read, read! (In addition to regularly attending professional update workshops and programs!) Most professional liturgists already have commitments that would fill a forty-eight hour day. Yet nothing is more important than setting aside at least some time each week (a minimum of at least an hour) for serious professional reading.

As mentioned, the following bibliography only lists books. Periodicals are a marvelous resource for professional updating, and every parish ought to subscribe to at least some. Since they come in "periodically," this can sometimes be a natural stimulus for professional reading, especially if the individual makes the resolution to read the periodical within two days after its arrival (we all know that our "to do" pile just keeps getting higher!). Since more parishes have limited budgets, I would suggest subscribing to at least one more challenging or scholarly periodical, one more pastoral or professional one (that would usually include liturgy planning helps and seasonal notes), and one that is denominational (in order to keep up with new regulations or recently published materials).

Pastoral Bibliography

Further comment on these sixteen selected areas of liturgical interest is hardly necessary. The bibliography is presented in list form; hopefully, this will be most useful to the reader, even serving as a "checklist" of owned/to be acquired resources.

1. Reference Works

Cantalamessa, Raniero, O.F.M. Cap. *Easter in the Early Church: An Anthology of Jewish and Early Christian Texts.* Translated by James M. Quigley, S.J., and Joseph T. Lienhard, S.J. Collegeville: The Liturgical Press, 1993.

Davies, J.G., ed. *The New Westminster Dictionary of Liturgy and Worship.* Philadelphia: The Westminster Press, 1986.

Federation of Diocesan Liturgical Commissions (FDLC). *copyright update: reprint permission policies of publishers of liturgical music and sacred scripture.* Washington, D.C.: FDLC, 1989.

Fink, Peter E., S.J., ed. *The New Dictionary of Sacramental Worship.* Collegeville: The Liturgical Press, 1990.

Flannery, Austin, O.P., gen. ed. *Vatican Council II: The Conciliar and Post Conciliar Documents.* New Revised Edition 1992. Northport, N.Y.: Costello Publishing Company, 1988.

ICEL. *Documents on the Liturgy 1963–1979: Conciliar, Papal, and Curial Texts.* Collegeville: The Liturgical Press, 1982.

Jasper, R.C.D. and Cuming, G.J., eds. *Prayers of the Eucharist: Early and Reformed.* New York: Pueblo, 1987.

Lang, Jovian P., O.F.M. *Dictionary of the Liturgy.* New York: Catholic Book Publishing Company, 1989.

Smolarski, Dennis C., S.J. *Liturgical Literacy: From Anamnesis to Worship.* New York/Mahwah, N.J.: Paulist Press, 1990.

Stuhlmueller, Carroll, gen. ed. *The Collegeville Pastoral Dictionary of Biblical Theology.* Collegeville: The Liturgical Press, 1996.

The Liturgy Documents: A Parish Resource. 3rd Edition. Chicago: Liturgy Training Publications, 1991.

Vatican Council II: The Conciliar and Post Conciliar Documents. Gen. ed. Austin Flannery, O.P. New revised edition. Northport, N.Y.: Costello Publishing Company, 1992.

2. General Books on Liturgy

Bell, Catherine. *Ritual Theory, Ritual Practice.* New York/Oxford: Oxford University Press, 1992.

Burkhart, John E. *Worship.* Philadelphia: Westminster, 1982.

Burson, Malcolm C., ed. *Worship Points the Way: Celebration of the Life and Work of Massey H. Shepherd, Jr.* New York: The Seabury Press, 1981.

Casel, Odo. *The Mystery of Christian Worship.* Trans. B. Neunheuser. Westminster, Md.: Newman Press, 1962.

Collins, Mary, O.S.B. *Worship: Renewal to Practice.* Washington, D.C.: The Pastoral Press, 1987.

Crichton, J.D. *The Once and Future Liturgy.* Dublin: Veritas, 1977.

DiSante, Carmine. *Jewish Prayer: The Origins of Christian Liturgy.* New York/Mahwah, N.J.: Paulist Press, 1985.

Empereur, James, S.J. *Worship: Exploring the Sacred.* Washington, D.C.: The Pastoral Press, 1987.

Fink, Peter E., S.J. *Worship: Praying the Sacraments.* Washington, D.C.: The Pastoral Press, 1991.

Fisher, Eugene J., ed. *The Jewish Roots of Christian Liturgy.* New York/Mahwah, N.J.: Paulist Press, 1990.

Freburger, William J. *Liturgy: Work of the People.* Mystic, Ct.: Twenty-Third Publications, 1984.

Frederick, John. *The Future of Liturgical Reform.* Wilton, Ct.: Morehouse-Barlow, 1987.

Gelineau, Joseph. *The Liturgy Today and Tomorrow.* Trans. Dinah Livingstone. London: Darton, Longman & Todd, 1978.

Irwin, Kevin W. *Liturgical Theology: A Primer.* American Essays in Liturgy. Collegeville: The Liturgical Press, 1990.

Kavanagh, Aidan. *Elements of Rite: A Handbook of Liturgical Style.* New York: Pueblo, 1982.

Kavanagh, Aidan. *On Liturgical Theology.* New York: Pueblo, 1985.

Lathrop, Gordon. *Holy Things: An Ecumenical Liturgical Theology.* Minneapolis: Fortress Press, 1993.

Lebon, Jean. *How to Understand the Liturgy.* Preface J.D. Crichton. New York: Crossroad, 1988.

Martimort, G.A.. *The Church at Prayer.* Four vols. Trans. M.J. O'Connell. Collegeville: The Liturgical Press, 1986.

Mitchell, Leonel L. *The Meaning of Ritual.* New York: Paulist, 1977.

Newman, David R. *Worship as Praise and Empowerment.* New York: The Pilgrim Press, 1988.

Saliers, Don E. *Worship Come to Its Senses.* Nashville: Abingdon Press, 1996.

Schauss, Hayyim. *The Jewish Festivals: History & Observance.* Trans. Samuel Jaffe. New York: Schocken Books, 1977 [1938].

Schmemann, Alexander. *Introduction to Liturgical Theology.* Trans. Asheleigh E. Moorhouse. London: Faith Press, 1966.

Searle, Mark. *Liturgy Made Simple.* Collegeville: The Liturgical Press, 1981.

Smolarski, Dennis C. *Sacred Mysteries: Sacramental Principles and Liturgical Practice.* New York/Mahwah, N.J.: Paulist Press, 1995.

Taft, Robert, S.J. *Beyond East and West: Principles in Liturgical Understanding.* Washington, D.C.: The Pastoral Press, 1984.

Underhill, Evelyn. *Worship.* New York: Crossroad, 1989 [1936].

White, James F. *Christian Worship in North America: A Retrospective: 1955–1995.* Collegeville: The Liturgical Press/A Pueblo Book, 1997.

White, James F. *Documents of Christian Worship: Descriptive and Interpretive Sources.* Louisville: Westminster/John Knox Press, 1992.

White, James F. *Introduction to Christian Worship.* Revised Edition. Nashville: Abingdon, 1990.

White, James F. *Protestant Worship: Traditions in Transition.* Louisville: Westminster/John Knox Press, 1989.

Willimon, W.H. *The Service of God: Christian Work and Worship.* Nashville: Abingdon Press, 1983.

3. History of Liturgy

Adam, Adolf. *Foundations of Liturgy: An Introduction to Its History and Practice.* Collegeville: The Liturgical Press, 1992.

Botte, Bernard. *From Silence to Participation: An Insider's View of Liturgical Renewal.* Trans. John Sullivan, O.C.D. Washington, D.C.: The Pastoral Press, 1988.

Cooke, Bernard. *Ministry to Word and Sacraments: History and Theology.* Philadelphia: Fortress Press, 1976.

Dix, Gregory. *The Shape of the Liturgy.* Additional notes P.V. Marshall. New York: The Seabury Press, 1982.

Jones, Cheslyn, Wainwright, Geoffrey, Yarnold, Edward, S.J., and Bradshaw, Paul, eds. *The Study of Liturgy.* Revised Edition. London: SPCK/New York: Oxford University Press, 1992 [1978].

Jungmann, Josef A., S.J. *The Early Liturgy: To the Time of Gregory the Great.* Trans. Francis A. Brunner, C.SS.R. Notre Dame, Ind.: University of Notre Dame Press, 1959.

Jungmann, Joseph A., S.J. *The Mass of the Roman Rite: Its Origins and Development.* Trans. Francis A. Brunner, C.SS.R. 2 vols. Westminster, Md.: Christian Classics, Inc., 1986 [1951].

Klauser, Theodor. *A Short History of the Western Liturgy: An Account and Some Reflections.* Second Edition. Trans. John Halliburton. Oxford: Oxford University Press, 1979.

Martos, Joseph. *Doors to the Sacred: A Historical Introduction to Sacraments in the Catholic Church.* Garden City, N.Y.: Image-Doubleday, 1982; expanded edition: Ligouri, Mo.: Triumph Books, 1991.

Maxwell, W. *A History of Christian Worship: An Outline of Its Development and Forms.* Foreword Robert G. Rayburn. Grand Rapids: Baker Book House, 1982.

Stevenson, Kenneth. *The First Rites: Worship in the Early Church.* Collegeville: The Liturgical Press, 1990.

Wegman, Herman. *Christian Worship in East and West: A Study Guide to Liturgical History.* Trans. Gordon W. Lathrop. New York: Pueblo, 1985.

White, James F. *A Brief History of Christian Worship.* Nashville: Abingdon Press, 1993.

4. Sacred Space, Symbols, Time

Boyer, Mark G. *The Liturgical Environment: What the Documents Say.* Collegeville: The Liturgical Press, 1990.

Buscemi, John. *Places for Devotion.* Meeting House Essays 4. Chicago: Liturgy Training Publications, 1993.

Clark, Keith. *Make Space, Make Symbols.* Notre Dame, Ind.: Ave Maria Press, 1979.

Debuyst, Frederic. *Modern Architecture and Christian Celebration.* Ecumenical Studies in Worship 18. Richmond, Va.: John Knox Press, 1968.

Dillistone, F.W. *Myth and Symbol.* London: SPCK, 1966.

Dunne, John S. *A Search for God in Time and Memory.* Notre Dame, Ind.: University of Notre Dame Press, 1977.

Environment and Art in Catholic Worship. Washington, D.C.: USCC, 1978.

Hatchett, Marion S. *Sanctifying Life, Time and Space: An Introduction to Liturgical Study.* New York: The Seabury Press, 1976.

Mauck, Marchita B. *Places for Worship: A Guide to Building and Renovating.* American Essays in Liturgy. Collegeville: The Liturgical Press, 1995.

Philippart, David. *Saving Signs, Wondrous Words.* Chicago: Liturgy Training Publications, 1996.

Richter, Klemens. *The Meaning of the Sacramental Symbols: Answers to Today's Questions.* Trans. L.M. Maloney. Collegeville: The Liturgical Press, 1990.

Rouet, Albert. *Liturgy and the Arts.* Collegeville: The Liturgical Press, 1997.

Ryan, John Barry. *Symbolism: The Language of Liturgy.* Washington, D.C.: FDLC, 1982.

Vosko, Richard S. *Designing Future Worship Spaces: The Mystery of a Common Vision.* Meeting House Essays 8. Chicago: Liturgy Training Publications, 1996.

5. Liturgical Year

Adam, Adolf. *The Liturgical Year: Its History and Its Meaning after the Reform of the Liturgy.* New York: Pueblo, 1981.

Berger, Rupert and Hollerweger, Hans, eds. *Celebrating the Easter Vigil.* Trans. Matthew J. O'Connell. New York: Pueblo, 1983.

Edwards, Tilden. *Sabbath Time: Understanding and Practice for Contemporary Christians.* Minneapolis: Seabury Press, 1982.

Guthrie, Clifton F., ed. *For All the Saints: A Calendar of Commemorations for United Methodists.* Akron, Ohio: OSL Publications, 1996.

Halmo, Joan. *Celebrating the Church Year with Young Children.* Collegeville: The Liturgical Press/Ottawa: Novalis, 1988.

Hickman, Hoyt L., Saliers, Don E., Stookey, Laurence Hull, and White, James F. *The New Handbook of the Christian Year.* Nashville: Abingdon, 1996.

Huck, Gabe. *The Three Days: Parish Prayer in the Paschal Triduum.* Chicago: Liturgy Training Publications, 1981.

Irwin, Kevin W. *Sunday Worship: A Planning Guide to Celebration.* New York: Paulist, 1983.

Martimort, A.G. *The Church at Prayer.* Vol. IV, *The Liturgy and Time.* Trans. M.J. O'Connell. Collegeville: The Liturgical Press, 1986.

Nocent A. *The Liturgical Year.* Four Volumes. Collegeville: The Liturgical Press, 1977.

Onley, Dan F. *Ordinary Time in the Parish.* Old Hickory, Tn.: Pastoral Arts Associates, 1982.

Onley, Dan F. *The Great Sunday: Fifty Days of Easter in Your Parish.* Old Hickory, Tn.: Pastoral Arts Associates, 1982.

Searle, Mark. *Sunday Morning: A Time for Worship.* Collegeville: The Liturgical Press, 1982.

Stookey, Laurence Hull. *Calendar: Christ's Time for the Year.* Nashville: Abingdon Press, 1996.

Talley, Thomas J. *The Origins of the Liturgical Year.* New York: Pueblo, 1986.

The Liturgical Year: Celebrating the Mystery of Christ and His Saints. Study Text 9. Secretariat: Bishops' Committee on the Liturgy. Washington, D.C.: United States Catholic Conference, 1985.

Wilde, James A., ed. *At That Time: Cycles and Season in the Life of a Christian.* Chicago: Liturgy Training Publications, 1989.
Winter Festivals. San Jose, Calif.: Resource Publications, 1986.

6. Initiation

Austin, Gerard. *The Rite of Confirmation: Anointing with the Spirit.* New York: Pueblo, 1985.
Christian Initiation Resources Reader: Volume III, Purification and Enlightenment. New York: William H. Sadlier, Inc., 1984.
Duggan, Robert D. and Kelly, Maureen A. *The Christian Initiation of Children: Hope for the Future.* New York/Mahwah, N.J.: Paulist Press, 1991.
Dujarier, Michel. *The Rites of Christian Initiation: Historical and Pastoral Reflections.* New York: Sadlier, 1979.
Huels, John M. *Catechumenate and the Law: A Pastoral and Canonical Commentary for the Church in the United States.* Chicago: Liturgy Training Publications, 1994.
Johnson, L.J. *Initiation and Conversion.* Collegeville: The Liturgical Press, 1985.
Johnson, M.E., ed. *Living Water, Sealing Spirit: Readings on Christian Initiation.* Collegeville: The Liturgical Press, 1995.
Kavanagh, Aidan. *The Baptismal Rites.* New York: Pueblo, 1982.
Kavanagh, Aidan. *Confirmation: Origins and Reform.* New York: Pueblo, 1988.
Larere, Philippe. *Baptism in Water and Baptism in the Spirit: A Biblical, Liturgical, and Theological Exposition.* Trans. Patrick Madigan, O.S.B. Collegeville: The Liturgical Press, 1993.
Made, Not Born: New Perspectives on Christian Initiation and the Catechumenate. Notre Dame, Ind.: University of Notre Dame Press, 1976.
Maldonado, Luis, and Power, David. *Structures of Initiation in Crisis.* Concilium 122. New York: Seabury, 1979.
Mitchell, Leonel L. *Worship: Initiation and the Churches.* Washington, D.C.: The Pastoral Press, 1991.
Osborne, Kenan B., O.F.M. *The Christian Sacraments of Initiation: Baptism, Confirmation, Eucharist.* New York/Mahwah, N.J.: Paulist Press, 1987.
Regan, David. *Experience the Mystery: Pastoral Possibilities for Christian Mystagogy.* Collegeville: The Liturgical Press, 1994.
RCIA and the Period of Postbaptismal Catechesis. Edited by National Liturgy Office. Canadian Studies in Liturgy 7. Ottawa: Canadian Conference of Catholic Bishops, 1996.
Searle, Mark. *Christening: The Making of Christians.* Leigh-on-Sea: Kevin Mayhew, 1977.
Stasiak, Kurt, O.S.B. *Return to Grace: A Theology for Infant Baptism.* Collegeville: The Liturgical Press, 1996.
Stookey, Laurence Hull. *Baptism: Christ's Act in the Church.* Nashville: Abingdon Press, 1982.
Tufano, Victoria M., ed. *Readings in the Christian Initiation of Children.* Introduction James W. Moudry. Chicago: Liturgy Training Publications, 1994.
Turner, Paul. *Sources of Confirmation from the Fathers through the Reformers.* Collegeville: The Liturgical Press, 1993.

202   *Joyce Ann Zimmerman, C.PP.S.*

Vincie, Catherine. *The Role of the Assembly in Christian Initiation.* Forum Essays Series. Chicago: Liturgical Training Publications, 1993.
Whitaker, E.C. *Documents of the Baptismal Liturgy.* London: SPCK, 1970.
Wilde, James A., ed. *Before and After Baptism: The Work of Teachers and Catechists.* Chicago: Liturgy Training Publications, 1988.
Wilde, James A., ed. *Commentaries: Rite of Christian Initiation of Adults.* Chicago: Liturgy Training Publications, 1988.
Yarnold, E.J. *The Awe-Inspiring Rite of Initiation: The Origins of the RCIA.* Collegeville: The Liturgical Press, 1995.

7. Eucharist

Emminghaus, J.H. *The Eucharist: Essence, Form, Celebration.* Collegeville: The Liturgical Press, 1978.
FDLC. *The Mystery of Faith: A Study of the Structural Elements of the Order of Mass.* Washington, D.C.: FDLC, 1994 [1981].
Fitzsimmons, John H. *Guide to the Lectionary.* Great Wakering, Essex, England: Mayhew-McCrimmon, 1981.
Griffiths, Alan. *Focus on the Eucharistic Prayer.* Leigh-on-Sea: Kevin-Mayhew Publishers, 1988.
Johnson, Lawrence J. *The Word & Eucharist Handbook.* San Jose, Calif.: Resource Publications, Inc., 1986.
Kwatera, Michael, O.S.B. *Preparing the General Intercessions.* Collegeville: The Liturgical Press, 1996.
LaVerdiere, Eugene, S.S.S. *The Eucharist in the New Testament and the Early Church.* Collegeville: The Liturgical Press, 1996.
Mazza, Enrico. *The Origins of the Eucharistic Prayer.* Trans. R.E. Lane. Collegeville: The Liturgical Press, 1995.
Mitchell, Nathan. *Cult and Controversy: The Worship of the Eucharist Outside Mass.* New York: Pueblo, 1982.
Powers, Joseph M., S.J. *Eucharistic Theology.* New York: Herder & Herder, 1967. See especially Chapter 1, "The Eucharist in the History of Doctrine and Theology."
Schmemann, Alexander. *The Eucharist: Sacrament of the Kingdom.* Crestwood, N.Y.: St. Vladimir's Seminary Press, 1988.
Seasoltz, R. Kevin, O.S.B., ed. *Living Bread, Saving Cup: Readings on the Eucharist.* Collegeville: The Liturgical Press, 1982.
Senn, Frank C., ed. *New Eucharistic Prayers: An Ecumenical Study of their Development and Structure.* New York/Mahwah, N.J.: Paulist Press, 1987.
Smolarski, Dennis C., S.J. *Eucharistia: A Study of the Eucharistic Prayer.* New York: Paulist, 1982.
Smolarski, Dennis C. *How Not to Say Mass.* New York: Paulist, 1986.
Stookey, Laurence Hull. *Eucharist: Christ's Feast with the Church.* Nashville: Abingdon Press, 1993.

8. Reconciliation

Dallen, James. *The Reconciling Community: The Rite of Penance.* New York: Pueblo, 1986.

Dudley, Martin and Rowell, Geoffrey, eds. *Confession and Absolution.* London: SPCK/Collegeville: The Liturgical Press, 1990.

Favazza, J.A. *The Order of Penitents: Historical Roots and Pastoral Future.* Collegeville: The Liturgical Press, 1988.

Gula, Richard M. *To Walk Together Again: The Sacrament of Reconciliation.* New York/Mahwah, N.J.: Paulist Press, 1984.

Guzie, Tad and McIlhon, J. *The Forgiveness of Sins.* Chicago: Thomas More Press, 1979.

Hellwig, Monika K. *Sign of Reconciliation and Conversion: The Sacrament of Penance for Our Times.* Message of the Sacraments 4. Wilmington: Michael Glazier, 1982.

Henchal, Michael J., ed. *Repentance and Reconciliation in the Church.* Collegeville: The Liturgical Press, 1987.

Kennedy, Robert J., ed. *Reconciliation: The Continuing Agenda.* Collegeville: The Liturgical Press, 1987.

Lopresti, James. *Penance: A Reform Proposal for the Rite.* American Essays in Liturgy 6. Washington, D.C.: The Pastoral Press, 1987.

Osborne, Kenan B. *Reconciliation and Justification: The Sacrament and Its Theology.* New York/Mahwah, N.J.: Paulist Press, 1990.

9. Care of the Sick and Dying/Funerals

Cuschieri, Andrew. *Anointing of the Sick: A Theological and Canonical Study.* Lanham Md./London: University Press of America, 1992.

Dudley, Martin and Rowell, Geoffrey, eds. *The Oil of Gladness: Anointing in the Christian Tradition.* London: SPCK/Collegeville: The Liturgical Press, 1993.

Empereur, James L. *Prophetic Anointing: God's Call to the Sick, the Elderly and the Dying.* Message of the Sacraments 7. Wilmington: Michael Glazier, 1982.

Fournier, William, and O'Malley, Sarah. *Age and Grace: Handbook of Programs for the Ministry to the Aging.* Collegeville: The Liturgical Press, 1980.

Gusmer, Charles W. *And You Visited Me: Sacramental Ministry to the Sick and Dying.* New York: Pueblo, 1984.

Marchal, Michael. *Parish Funerals.* Chicago: Liturgy Training Publications, 1987.

Oates, Wayne E. *Grief, Transition, and Loss: A Pastor's Practical Guide.* Minneapolis: Fortress Press, 1997.

Rutherford, Richard. *The Death of a Christian: The Rite of Funerals.* New York: Pueblo, 1980.

Ziegler, John J. *Let Them Anoint the Sick.* Collegeville: The Liturgical Press, 1987.

10. Marriage

Kasper, Walter. *Theology of Christian Marriage.* New York: Seabury Press/Crossroad, 1980.

Lawler, Michael G. *Secular Marriage, Christian Sacrament.* Mystic, Ct.: Twenty-Third Publications, 1985.

Mayendorff, J. *Marriage: An Orthodox Perspective.* New York: St. Vladimir's Seminary Press, 1971.

Schillebeeckx, Edward. *Marriage: Human Reality and Saving Mystery.* New York: Sheed & Ward, 1965.

Searle, Mark and Stevenson, Kenneth W. *Documents of the Marriage Liturgy.* Collegeville: The Liturgical Press, 1992.

Stevenson, Kenneth W. *Nuptial Blessing: A Study of Christian Marriage Rites.* Alcuin Club Collections 64. London: SPCK, 1982/New York: Oxford University Press, 1983.

Stevenson, Kenneth W. *To Join Together: The Rite of Marriage.* Studies in the Reformed Rites of the Catholic Church 5. New York: Pueblo, 1987.

Thomas, D.M. *Christian Marriage: A Journey Together.* Message of the Sacraments 5. Wilmington: Michael Glazier, 1983.

11. Orders/Ministry

Bausch, William J. *Ministry: Traditions, Tensions, Transitions.* Foreword Anthony Padovano. Mystic, Ct.: Twenty-Third Publications, 1982.

Bradshaw, Paul F. *Ordination Rites of the Ancient Churches of East and West.* New York: Pueblo, 1990.

Dunn, P. J. *Priesthood: A Re-examination of the Roman Catholic Theology of the Presbyterate.* New York: Alba House, 1990.

Echlin, E.P. *The Deacon in the Church: Past and Future.* New York: Alba House, 1971.

Hanson, Anthony. *Church, Sacraments and Ministry.* Mowbrays Library of Theology. Oxford: Alden Press, 1975.

Hovda, Robert W. *Strong, Loving and Wise: Presiding in Liturgy.* Foreword Godfrey Diekmann, O.S.B. Collegeville: The Liturgical Press, 1976.

Lawler, M.G. *A Theology of Ministry.* Kansas City, Mo.: Sheed & Ward, 1990.

Miguens, Manuel, O.F.M. *Church Ministries in New Testament Times.* Westminster, Md.: Christian Classics, 1976.

Mitchell, Nathan. *Mission and Ministry: History and Theology in the Sacrament of Order.* Message of the Sacraments 6. Wilmington: Michael Glazier, 1982.

O'Meara, Thomas F. *Theology of Ministry.* New York: Paulist Press, 1983.

Osborne, Kenan B. *Ministry. Lay Ministry in the Roman Catholic Church: Its History and Theology.* New York/Mahwah, N.J.: Paulist Press, 1993.

Osborne, Kenan B., O.F.M. *Priesthood: A History of the Ordained Ministry in the Roman Catholic Church.* New York: Paulist Press, 1988.

Porter, H. Boone. *Ordination Prayers of the Ancient Western Churches.* Alcuin Club Collections 39. London: SPCK, 1967.

Power, David N. *Ministers of Christ and His Church: The Theology of Priesthood.* London: G. Chapman, 1969.

Power, David N. *Gifts that Differ: Lay Ministries Established and Unestablished.* New York: Pueblo, 1985.

Rademacher, W.J. *Lay Ministry: A Theological, Spiritual and Pastoral Handbook.* New York: Crossroad, 1983.

Roles in the Liturgical Assembly. The Twenty-third Liturgical Conference, Serge. Trans. Matthew J. O'Connell. New York: Pueblo, 1981.

Schillebeeckx, Edward. *The Church with a Human Face: A New and Expanded Theology of Ministry.* New York: Crossroad, 1985.

Schreiter, Robert J. *Reconciliation: Mission and Ministry in a Changing Social Order.* Maryknoll, N.Y.: Orbis Books, 1992.

Whitehead, James D. and Whitehead, Evelyn E. *Method in Ministry: Theological Reflection and Christian Ministry.* Minneapolis: Seabury Press, 1980.

Wicks, R.J., ed. *Handbook of Spirituality for Ministers.* New York/Mahwah, N.J.: Paulist Press, 1995.

12. Preaching

Burghardt, Walter, S.J. *Preaching: The Art & the Craft.* New York: Paulist Press, 1987.

Burke, John, O.P. *A New Look at Preaching.* Wilmington: Michael Glazier, Inc., 1983.

Foley, Nadine, O.P., ed. *Preaching and the Non-Ordained: An Interdisciplinary Study.* Collegeville: The Liturgical Press, 1983.

McNulty, Frank J. *Preaching Better.* New York: Paulist Press, 1985.

Rueter, Alvin C. *Making Good Preaching Better: A Step-by-Step Guide to Scripture-Based, People-Centered Preaching.* Collegeville: The Liturgical Press, 1997.

Schmitmeyer, James M. *The Words of Worship: Presiding and Preaching at the Rites.* New York: Alba House, 1988.

Skudlarek, William. *The Word in Worship: Preaching in a Liturgical Context.* Nashville: Abingdon Press, 1981.

Sloyan, Gerard S. *Worshipful Preaching.* Philadelphia: Fortress Press, 1984.

Tisdale, Leonora Tubbs. *Preaching As Local Theology and Folk Art.* Minneapolis: Fortress Press, 1997.

13. Liturgy of the Hours

Bradshaw, Paul F. *Daily Prayer in the Early Church: A Study of the Origin and Early Development of the Divine Office.* New York: Oxford University Press, 1982.

Campbell, Stanislaus, F.S.C. *From Breviary to Liturgy of the Hours: The Structural Reform of the Roman Office, 1964–1971.* Collegeville: The Liturgical Press, 1995.

Crichton, J.D. *Christian Celebration: The Prayer of the Church.* London: Geoffrey Chapman, 1976.

Scotto, Dominic F., T.O.R. *Liturgy of the Hours: Its History and Its Importance as the Communal Prayer of the Church after the Liturgical Reform of Vatican II.* Petersham, Mass.: St. Bede's Publications, 1987.

Taft, Robert, S.J. *The Liturgy of the Hours in East and West: The Origins of the Divine Office and Its Meaning for Today.* Collegeville: The Liturgical Press, 1986.

Zimmerman, Joyce Ann, C.PP.S. *Morning and Evening: A Parish Celebration.* Chicago: Liturgy Training Publications, 1996.

14. Liturgical Spirituality

Austin, Gerard, O.P., et. al. *Called to Prayer: Liturgical Spirituality Today.* Collegeville: The Liturgical Press, 1986.

Bernstein, Eleanor, C.S.J., ed. *Liturgy and Spirituality in Context: Perspectives on Prayer and Culture.* Collegeville: The Liturgical Press, 1990.

Irwin, Kevin. *Liturgy, Prayer and Spirituality.* New York: Paulist, 1984.

Madigan, Shawn. *Spirituality Rooted in Liturgy.* Washington, D.C.: The Pastoral Press, 1988.

Saliers, Don E. *Worship and Spirituality.* 2nd Edition. Akron, Ohio: OSL Publications, 1994.

Zimmerman, Joyce Ann, C.PP.S. *Liturgy as Living Faith: A Liturgical Spirituality.* Scranton: University of Scranton Press/London and Toronto: Associated University Presses, 1993.

15. Inculturation

Chupungco, Anscar J. *Cultural Adaptation of the Liturgy.* New York: Paulist, 1982.

Chupungco, Anscar J. *Liturgical Inculturation: Sacramentals, Religiosity, and Catechesis.* Collegeville: The Liturgical Press, 1992.

Costen, Melva Wilson. *African American Christian Worship.* Nashville: Abingdon Press, 1993.

Francis, Mark R., C.S.V. *Liturgy in a Multicultural Community.* Collegeville: The Liturgical Press, 1991.

Power, David N., O.M.I. *Worship: Culture and Theology.* Washington, D.C.: The Pastoral Press, 1990.

Senn, Frank. *Christian Worship and Its Cultural Setting.* Philadelphia: Fortress, 1983.

16. Issues in Liturgy

A Blessing to Each Other: Cardinal Joseph Bernardin and Jewish-Catholic Dialogue. Foreword Cardinal Edward Cassidy. Introductions Herman Schaalman, Thomas A. Baima, John T. Pawlikowski, Daniel F. Montalbano. Chicago: Liturgy Training Publications, 1996.

Baldovin, John F., S.J. *Worship: City, Church and Renewal.* Washington, D.C.: The Pastoral Press, 1991.

Baptism, Eucharist and Ministry. Faith and Order Paper 111. Geneva: World Council of Churches, 1982. (The "BEM document.")

Dallen, James. *The Dilemma of Priestless Sundays.* Foreword Bishop William E. McManus. Chicago: Liturgy Training Publications, 1994.

Empereur, James L., S.J. and Kiesling, Christopher G., O.P. *The Liturgy that Does Justice.* Theology and Life Series 33. Collegeville: The Liturgical Press, 1990.

Foley, Edward, ed. *Developmental Disabilities and Sacramental Access: New Paradigms for Sacramental Encounters.* Collegeville: The Liturgical Press, 1994.

Gagne, Ronald, Kane, Thomas, VerEecke, Robert. *Introducing Dance in Christian Worship.* Intro. Carla DeSola. Bibliography by Gloria Weyman. Laurel, Md.: The Pastoral Press, 1984.

Hackett, Charles D. and Saliers, Don E. *The Lord Be With You: A Visual Manual for Presiding in Christian Worship.* Akron, Ohio: OSL Publications, 1990.

Henderson, J. Frank, Quinn, Kathleen, and Larson, Stephen. *Liturgy, Justice and the Reign of God: Integrating Vision and Practice.* New York/Mahwah, N.J.: Paulist Press, 1989.

Hellwig, Monika. *The Eucharist and the Hunger of the World.* New York: Paulist, 1976.

Huck, Gabe. *Liturgy Needs Community Needs Liturgy.* New York: Paulist Press, 1973.

Huels, John M. *Disputed Questions in the Liturgy Today.* Chicago: Liturgy Training Publications, 1988.

Huels, John M. *More Disputed Questions in the Liturgy.* Chicago: Liturgy Training Publications, 1996.

Hughes, Kathleen, R.S.C.J. and Francis, Mark R. C.S.V., eds. *Living No Longer for Ourselves: Liturgy and Justice in the Nineties.* Collegeville: The Liturgical Press, 1991.

Leonard, John K. and Mitchell, Nathan D. *The Postures of the Assembly during the Eucharistic Prayer.* Introduction John F. Baldovin. Chicago: Liturgy Training Publications, 1994.

Osborn, Linda. *Good Liturgy, Small Parishes.* Chicago: Liturgy Training Publications, 1996.

Pottebaum, Gerard A., Freeburg, Sister Paule, D.C., and Kelleher, Joyce M. *A Child Shall Lead Them: A Guide to Celebrating the Word with Children.* Cincinnati: Treehaus Communications, Inc., 1992.

Proctor-Smith, Marjorie. *In Her Own Rite: Constructing Feminist Liturgical Tradition.* Nashville: Abingdon Press, 1990.

Ramshaw, Gail. *Liturgical Language: Keeping It Metaphoric, Making It Inclusive.* American Essays in Liturgy. Collegeville: The Liturgical Press, 1996.

Searle, Mark. *Liturgy and Social Justice.* Collegeville: The Liturgical Press, 1980.

Uzukwu, Elochukwu E. C.S.Sp. *Worship As Body Language: Introduction to Christian Worship: An African Perspective.* Collegeville: The Liturgical Press, 1997.

Witherup, Ronald D., S.S. *A Liturgist's Guide to Inclusive Language.* Collegeville: The Liturgical Press, 1996.

Part II

Liturgical Music

Chapter 13

What Is Liturgical Music?

Robin A. Leaver

"Liturgical Music" is the term that is becoming the accepted designation for the music of worship in the Judeo-Christian tradition, the *Gebrauchsmusik* (functional music) of the gathered congregation (συναγωγή and ἐκκλησία, *synagogé* and *ecclesia*) at worship. The use of the term with this expanded meaning is a recent development. For example, such basic reference works as *The New Grove Dictionary of Music and Musicians* (1980) and *The New Harvard Dictionary of Music* (1986)[1] offer no entry under "Liturgical Music," whereas *The New Dictionary of Sacramental Worship* (1990)[2] does. This is not to imply that the *New Grove* and *New Harvard* dictionaries, along with other reference works, do not discuss the substance of "Liturgical Music," but they cover this material under different entries, most commonly "Church Music" (see further below). It is also significant to note that whereas the *New Grove* and the *New Harvard* dictionaries are musicological reference works, *The New Dictionary of Sacramental Worship* is an ecclesiastical and theological resource. This illustrates the fact that the pressure for the change in terminology has come mainly from those who have a fundamental concern with worshiping communities, both contemporary and historical. The terminology reflects the paradigm shift that has taken place in which questions of function, form, and liturgical significance are addressed before those that relate to phenomenology, philology, history, and musicology. Again, this should not be taken to mean that "Liturgical Music" only concerns the practice of music in worship to the exclusion of theoretical and historical inquiry. Indeed, the term "Liturgical Music" has

211

generated the cognate "Liturgical Musicology," a nomenclature that not only appears in recent publications[3] but is also being used to describe programs of graduate studies currently being planned. But this change is of substance and represents more than a semantic reinterpretation. The question of definition, "What is worship music?" has become secondary to the primary question, "What is worship music *for?*" Function and context determine form and content, therefore the substance and genre of worship music cannot be fully understood until its purpose and usage are established. The qualifier "Liturgical" in the term "Liturgical Music" clearly identifies the primary function of worship music, which determines its character and content. When such "Liturgical Music" is heard and studied outside of its context and usage it loses much of its integrity, significance, and essence because worship music cannot be fully understood outside the worship—liturgy in the broadest terms—for which it was intended.

The Function of Music in the Bible

This concern for the function of worship music, "*Liturgical* Music," is reflected in the similar shift that can be detected in biblical studies in relation to music. Until fairly recently the weight of these studies was on the historical and the philological. But there are signs that the function(s) of music in biblical terms is being given increasing attention.

The classic study in the English speaking world was *The Music of the Bible* by Sir John Stainer, first issued in 1879; reissued in 1914 with a substantial supplement by Francis William Galpin,[4] the noted authority on ancient instruments, who later wrote on the music of the Sumerians.[5] Stainer's book was almost entirely given over to a philological investigation into the various biblical terms for musical instruments, their iconography, and how they were played. Little attention was given to the function(s) of music in biblical terms. Stainer was a primary source used by later authors of articles on music in biblical dictionaries and handbooks, who similarly concentrated on the description of biblical instruments. This trend is detectable in more recent literature. One example is *Key Words in Church Music* (1978), edited by Carl Schalk, which includes an article on "Biblical Instruments,"[6] but no entry on the function of biblical music. There is however a sub-article, "Church [sic] Music History: Jewish"— which, incidentally, illustrates one of the problems that the term "Church Music" creates (see further below)—that gives an historical overview, again with a marked stress on instruments and only a passing reference to function.[7] Another example is the article "Music," in *The Interpreter's Dictionary of the Bible* by Eric Werner.[8] Again the emphasis is historical with a concentration on musical instruments, but questions of function are addressed, albeit briefly. The more recent *Anchor Bible Dictionary* (1992) has two articles on biblical music, the more substantial being "Musical Instruments,"[9] but the other, "Music in the Bible," does include a section on the "religious purposes" of biblical music.[10] This is an indication of the growing concern to identify and delineate the functions and usages of biblical music.[11]

The previous stress on the historical and philological rather than the functional and liturgical helped to perpetuate the myth that the synagogue in biblical times was a place of worship where the psalms were commonly and regularly sung. For example, both Schalk and Werner repeat the widely-held assumption that the worship of the synagogue included psalmody, and thus was the cradle for the singing of the early Christian Church. But the sources do not support the theory, rather the reverse. Recent scholarship has shown that the Jewish synagogue was essentially an educational institution in which there is no evidence of either worship or psalmody until some time after the destruction of the Temple in 70 A.D., and probably not before 200 A.D. Christian psalmody therefore has its roots not in the synagogue but in the liturgical psalmody of the Temple, which was an integral part of the sacrifices.[12]

This reinvestigation of the historical evidence has thus contributed to the shift away from the simple philological and phenomenological description to the liturgical and functional analysis of biblical music. It is no longer sufficient to know what it is; it is also necessary to know why it was created and how and where it was used. What is true of the liturgical music of the Bible is also true of such music of any historical period, including the liturgical music of our own day.

Changes in Terminology

The most common term for worship music has been "Church Music," but this is losing general currency because many see it as being too restrictive and exclusive to embrace the breadth of the differing manifestations of worship music, both historical and contemporary. Therefore various alternatives have come into use, the most frequent being: "Religious Music," "Sacred Music," "Pastoral Music," "Ritual Music," "Christian Ritual Music," and "Liturgical Music." But each alternative, while avoiding some of the narrower connotations of "Church Music," nevertheless creates its own problems.

"Church Music," notwithstanding its limitations, is still the most commonly used term for the music of worship. Part of the reason for its continued use is the related term for the one who leads such music: "Church Musician." "Religious Musician" is not a fortuitous expression because, while one hopes that all leaders of worship music are religious, it carries with it the notion that other musicians are therefore "irreligious." Similarly "Sacred Musician" implies an unacceptable "holier than thou" connotation. Although some churches use the designation "Minister" or "Director" of music, the term "Church Musician" continues by default. For example, Paul Westermeyer wanted to call his extremely useful book *"The Cantor,"* employing a term with a long history of use within German Lutheranism, and an even longer history in both Western Catholicism and Eastern Orthodoxy. But because of the general usage of "Church Music/Church Musician" he reluctantly had to settle for *The Church Musician.*[13]

As indicated above, many reference works continue to use the term "Church Music." *The New Harvard Dictionary of Music* has an entry on "Church Music," as well as one on "Anglican Church Music," but not on other denominational traditions. *The New Grove Dictionary of Music and Musicians* has an article on "Christian Church, Music of the Early,"[14] but no entries for later periods or denominational traditions of liturgical music, a deficiency rectified in *The New Grove Dictionary of American Music,*[15] and which will be fully addressed in the forthcoming revised edition of *New Grove.* The denominational entries in *AmeriGrove* confirm the preference for the term "Church Music" because it can be used to define the traditions of specific denominations or "churches": "Baptist Church, music of," "Episcopal Church, music of," "Lutheran Church, music of," "Methodist Church, music of," "Moravian Church, music of," "Roman Catholic Church, music of," etc. The term is workable when the focus is on historiography within a given tradition, but becomes less so when applied more broadly, and when function, context, and practice become primary concerns. Richard French's entry "Church Music," in *The New Harvard Dictionary of Music,* begins with the following definition:

> [Church Music is:] Music composed, adapted, or deemed suitable for church use, or for Christian worship, prayer, meditation, thanksgiving, or commemoration, public or private. Western church music has a distinctive character that differentiates it from other church musics and even from its own Judeo-Christian roots.[16]

While a good working definition, it nevertheless reveals some of the weaknesses of the term "Church Music." To begin with, as the second sentence acknowledges by implication, "Church Music" excludes the liturgical music traditions of both Eastern Orthodoxy and Judaism. This is a serious deficiency, since, even though Western liturgical music may well have developed in distinctive ways, it has common roots in both Jewish and Byzantine chant. As noted above in connection with Schalk's *Key Words in Church Music,* "Church" is not a broad enough term to embrace Jewish traditions and it is incongruous when the attempt is made to use it in this way. But "Church" also excludes the traditions of such groups as Shakers, the Society of Friends, or the Salvation Army, that have their own forms of worship music, but do not customarily speak in terms of "Church" for either the local congregation or the wider affiliation of congregations. Since "Church Music" has been the preferred term among English-speaking Protestants, but less so among Roman Catholics,[17] in recent years the term for many has come to mean *Protestant* "Church Music."[18] Further "Church" is a general term that does not indicate such specifics as function, context, and character of the music of worship. These are some of the reasons why other terms have been sought, definitions that avoid the problems that are seen to be inherent in the definition "Church Music."

"Religious Music" is a term preferred by some. It certainly avoids the exclusivity of "Church," and Jewish worship traditions can easily be embraced by it. But "Religious" is an extremely broad term that creates its own difficulties: all forms of religion are included under its umbrella, and not just those of the Judeo-Christian tradition. "Religious Music" is equally broad and includes all forms of religious music, whether or not they were intended for worship. The term thus embraces Gustav Holst's Hindu *Hymns from the Rig Veda,* his Gnostic *Hymn of Jesus,* a number of works by Edmund Rubbra, written under the influence of the composer's study of Buddhism and Tāoism, and many other works in which various composers, from Mozart and Beethoven to Messiaen and Tippett, have sought to express a variety of religious themes.[19] But most of these works, while undoubtedly being religious, cannot be considered as the functional music of worship.

"Sacred Music" is a fairly common term that is used in the attempt to find an alternative that avoids the breadth of "Religious Music" and the narrowness of "Church Music." However, the unqualified term is open to the same criticism as "Religious Music," since "Sacred" is a synonym of "Religious." But "Sacred Music" is usually restricted to mean either liturgical music *per se,* or music that in some way explores sacred themes in the general Judeo-Christian tradition. Thus many of the compositions of Penderecki, Gorecki, Tavener, and Pärt have to be classified as sacred music even though they

were not intended for liturgical use.[20] Significantly, many pieces of non-liturgical sacred music nevertheless have liturgical origins. For example, Passion music, which is now almost always heard in a concert setting, has its roots in the gospel narratives sung at Mass during Holy Week,[21] the Oratorio grew out of oratory devotions,[22] and concert masses are, of course, direct descendants of liturgical Mass settings. Even though the term has its ambiguities, "Sacred Music" is for many a happier term than "Church Music," which excludes Jewish traditions of liturgical music, as well as, by implication, the non-Protestant music of Roman Catholicism. It is for this reason that a number of academic institutions that provide music instruction across a wide denominational spectrum prefer "Sacred Music" to "Church Music." Examples include Yale University's Institute of Sacred Music and Rider University's Westminster Choir College which has its Sacred Music Department. But there also appears to be a more general shift away from "Church Music" to "Sacred Music." Thus instead of Bach's "church cantatas" there is a tendency to use "sacred cantatas,"[23] and genres of what in the past would have been labeled "Church Music" are classified as "Sacred Music."[24] But like "Church," "Sacred" does not indicate function and thus other alternatives have been sought.

"Pastoral Music" is a term widely used among Roman Catholics, who, in this country, have The National Association of Pastoral Musicians with its journal *Pastoral Music.* The qualifier "Pastoral" clearly emphasizes the function of music within the local parish. As the priest is also the pastor of his people, serving a variety of their needs, so "Pastoral Music" ministers to the worship needs of those people. The strength of the term is its suggestion that worship music is not important for its own sake but for its participation in the *diaconia* of the Church. Its weakness is that the word "Pastoral" is a general term that embraces the worship of the Church but is by no means confined to it.

"Ritual Music" has therefore been adopted as an alternative to "Pastoral Music" because it clearly associates the music of the Church with its rites, its liturgical actions. Again, it is the function of this music that is paramount: it is the music of the rites. But the bald term without qualification is somewhat broad and implies any religious ritual music, such as Hindu ritual songs,[25] the study of which might illuminate parallels in the music of Christian rituals of birth and death, but which would nevertheless remain on the periphery of the primary concern.

"Christian Ritual Music" is thus frequently employed instead of the more general term "Ritual Music."[26] It is the preferred term found

in the Universa Laus document *Music in Christian Celebration,*[27] and the ten-year report of *The Milwaukee Symposia for Church Composers.*[28] But it does not have wide usage and is somewhat narrowly drawn. As Edward Foley observes: "While I believe that 'Christian ritual music' is the most accurate technical term for discussing worship music in the Christian churches, as yet it does not have much currency outside of the academy." He therefore suggests that when one is taking a broader view, the term "Liturgical Music" is to be preferred, because it "does have the necessary currency, and is more inclusive, employed as it is by both Christians and Jews."[29]

"Liturgical Music" is thus the term that is increasingly becoming widely used to cover the whole range of the worship music of the Judeo-Christian tradition. It does, however, have a possible weakness. "Liturgy" in the past has been interpreted to mean only the text(s) of worship. Therefore the term "Liturgical Music" is in danger of being interpreted as the music of liturgical texts, which could be taken to imply only liturgical, monodic chant. It is for this reason that "Ritual Music" is the preferred alternative by some because of its stress on rite—words, actions, physical space, and music—rather than on text alone. But the contemporary use of "Liturgy" is not restricted to text and embraces all that is designated by "Rite," and used in this way "Liturgical Music" is the appropriate term for the music of worship.

The chapters that follow are explorations and explanations of liturgical music, its characteristics, forms, genres, contexts, and its purpose as a primary and integral component of worship.

Notes

1. *The New Grove Dictionary of Music and Musicians,* ed. Stanley Sadie, 20 vols. (London and New York: Macmillan, 1980), and *The New Harvard Dictionary of Music,* ed. Don Michael Randel (Cambridge, Mass.: Harvard University Press, 1986).

2. Edward Foley, "Liturgical Music," *The New Dictionary of Sacramental Worship,* ed. Peter Fink (Collegeville: The Liturgical Press, 1990), 854–70.

3. See the series edited by the present author, "Studies in Liturgical Musicology," published by Scarecrow Press, and such books as Edward Foley's *Ritual Music: Studies in Liturgical Musicology* (Beltsville, Md.: Pastoral Press, 1995).

4. John Stainer, *The Music of the Bible, with an Account of the Development of Modern Musical Instruments from Ancient Types,* new edition with additional illustrations and supplementary notes by Francis W. Galpin (London: Novello, 1914; reprint New York: Da Capo, 1970).

5. Francis W. Galpin, *The Music of the Sumerians and their Immediate Successors, the Babylonians and Assyrians* (Cambridge: Cambridge University Press, 1937; reprints: Strasbourg: Strasbourg University Press, 1955; New York: Da Capo, 1970; Freeport, N.Y.: Books for Libraries, 1970; Westport, Ct.: Greenwood, 1970; Baden-Baden: Koerner, 1972).

6. *Key Words in Church Music: Definition Essays on Concepts, Practices, and Movements of Thought in Church Music,* ed. Carl Schalk (St. Louis: Concordia, 1978) 26–29.

7. Ibid., 87–91.

8. Eric Werner, "Music," *The Interpreter's Dictionary of the Bible* (New York: Abingdon, 1962) 3:457–69; cf. Werner's later article "Jewish Music I. Liturgical," especially sections 3–6, *New Grove* 9:616–23.

9. Ivor H. Jones, "Musical Instruments," *The Anchor Bible Dictionary* (New York: Doubleday, 1992) 4:934–39.

10. Victor H. Matthews, "Music in the Bible," ibid., 4: 930–34, esp. 932–33.

11. To date the best summary of the functions of music in biblical terms is the comprehensive survey by P. Casetti, "Funktion der Musik in der Bibel," *Freiburger Zeitschrift für Philosophie und Theologie* 24 (1977) 366–89; an English translation is due to appear in *The Hymnology Annual* 4, to be published in 1998. The first substantial discussion of the integral function of music within the liturgical action of sacrifice is John W. Kleinig, *The Lord's Song: The Basis, Function and Significance of Choral Music in Chronicles* (Sheffield: JSOT Press, 1993); see also John W. Kleinig, "The Divine Institution of the Lord's Song in Chronicles," *Journal for the Study of the Old Testament* 55 (1992) 75–83. Mention should also be made of the broader study by Hans Seidel, *Musik in Altisrael: Untersuchungen zur Musikgeschichte und Musikpraxis Altisraels anhand biblischer und außerbiblischer Texte* (Frankfurt: Lang, 1989).

12. The basic literature includes: J.A. Smith, "The Ancient Synagogue, the Early Church, and Singing," *Music and Letters* 65 (1984): 1–16; J.A. Smith, "First-Century Christian Singing and its Relationship to Contemporary Jewish Song," *Music and Letters* 75 (1994) 1–15; James W. McKinnon, "On the Question of Psalmody in the Ancient Synagogue," *Early Music History* 6 (1986): 159–91; Paul F. Bradshaw, *The Search for the Origin of Christian Worship: Sources and Methods for the Study of Early Liturgy* (New York: Oxford University Press, 1992); and Heather A. McKay, *Sabbath and Synagogue: The Question of Sabbath Worship in Ancient Israel* (Leiden: E.J. Brill, 1994).

13. Paul Westermeyer, *The Church Musician: Revised Edition* (Minneapolis, Minn.: Augsburg Fortress, 1997). Originally published in 1988.

14. *New Grove* 4: 363–71, written by Christian Hannick.

15. *The New Grove Dictionary of American Music,* ed. H. Wiley Hitchcock and Stanley Sadie (New York: Macmillan, 1986), commonly designated *AmeriGrove.*

16. *New Harvard Dictionary of Music,* 166–69, here 166.

17. In German-speaking areas "Kirchenmusik" has not developed this Protestant connotation. It is either used as a general term or qualified thus: "Katholische Kirchenmusik (Roman Catholic), "Evangelische Kirchenmusik"

(Lutheran), "Reformierte Kirchenmusik" (Reformed/Calvinist). However, "Kirche" has the same exclusivity as the English "Church."

18. Although there is hesitation in Catholic usage, the term continues to be employed; see, for example, Virgil C. Funk, "The Future of Church Music," *Sung Liturgy: Toward 2000 AD,* ed. Virgil C. Funk (Washington, D.C.: Pastoral Press, 1991) 95–109.

19. See Robert William Sigismund Mendl, *The Divine Quest in Music* (New York: Philosophical Library, 1957).

20. These composers, especially Tavener and Pärt, have, of course, written liturgical music, but some of their concert pieces, even when based on chant forms, were not intended for performance within the context of worship.

21. See Robin A. Leaver, "Passion Music," *Passover and Easter: The Liturgical Structuring of a Sacred Season,* eds. Paul F. Bradshaw and Lawrence A. Hoffman, University of Notre Dame Press, forthcoming.

22. See Howard E. Smither, *A History of the Oratorio,* vol. 1 (Chapel Hill: University of North Carolina Press, 1977) 19–76.

23. For example, Melvin P. Unger, *Handbook to Bach's Sacred Cantata Texts* (Lanham, Md.: Scarecrow, 1996).

24. For example, Allen Perdue Britton, Irving Lowens and Richard Crawford, *American Sacred Music Imprints 1698–1810: A Bibliography* (Worcester: American Antiquarian Society, 1990).

25. See, for example, Stuart H. Blackburn, *Singing of Birth and Death: Texts in Performance* (Philadelphia: University of Pennsylvania Press, 1988).

26. Notice how Edward Foley qualifies the term in the title cited in note 3 above.

27. See Claude Duchesneau and Michel Veuthey, *Music and Liturgy: The Universa Laus Document and Commentary,* trans. Paul Inwood (Washington, D.C.: Pastoral Press, 1992).

28. *The Milwaukee Symposia for Church Composers: A Ten-Year Report* (Washington, D.C.: Pastoral Press, and Chicago: Liturgy Training Publications, 1992).

29. Edward Foley, "Liturgical Music: A Bibliographic Introduction to the Field," *liturgical ministry* 3 (1994) 130, n. 2.

Chapter 14

Liturgical Music as Music:
The Contribution of the Human Sciences

Jan Michael Joncas

Scholars have noted a series of correspondences between music and language. Both actualize fundamental human capacities to structure the world in symbolic forms. Both may occur in actual time ("played music" / "spoken language") or be fixed by forms of visual representation ("notated music" / "written language").[1] Both presuppose a culturally encoded and hierarchically structured reservoir of possible linguistic or musical events from which particular occurrences are chosen and created by performers or speakers. Just as a word can be broken down into its meaning-bearing components, so musical notes may be analyzed in terms of their acoustic properties. Just as words can be combined in various combinations to produce different types of sentences, sentences combined to produce paragraphs and paragraphs combined to produce a theme, so musical notes can be combined to produce melodies which in turn can be combined to produce more complex structures. Just as language encodes and displays a social world, so music enshrines and symbolizes cultural values.

Musical phenomena, as patterns of oscillation of air molecules set in motion by vibrating strings, air columns, or percussive surfaces, patterns that are in turn perceived and interpreted by humans, may be studied through the analysis of the physical characteristics of the sound produced: pitch, volume, duration, and timbre. The organization of musical sounds into complex structures in turn may be analyzed in terms of melody, harmony, counterpoint, texture, and form. The human sciences of psychology, sociology, anthropology (ethnomusicology), and semiotics in turn provide theoretical models for understanding this structuring of sound and silence as a cultural phenomenon. Engaging these analytic parameters and disciplines can assist liturgical musicians to understand the acoustic experience and cultural communication operative in worship.

1. Musical Sounds as Acoustic Phenomena

Pitch is a function of *frequency,* the number of times a vibrational pattern repeats itself per unit of time. Scientifically, frequency is measured in cycles per second or "Hertz" (abbreviated Hz): the faster the repetition of the pattern, the higher the frequency. Frequency is interpreted by the ear as pitch: the higher the frequency, the higher the pitch. (The Western standard of "A-440" means that the frequency of 440Hz produces the pitch identified as "A above middle C.") In addition to vibrating over its entire length, a string or column of air will also vibrate at a variety of fractional lengths (1:2, 2:3, 4:3, etc.). These secondary vibrations produce a series of softer pitches called the "partials" or "overtones," which the ear perceives as one compound sound. Human hearing is capable of perceiving frequencies between c. 20 and c. 20,000 Hz.

Volume is a function of *amplitude,* the amount of displacement of each air molecule produced by the vibrating string, air column, or percussive surface. The greater the displacement, the louder the volume. Note that frequency and amplitude describe different aspects of an acoustic event: a pitch may remain constant (have the same frequency) while growing louder or softer (varying amplitude) or, in contrast, a variety of pitches (different frequencies) may sound at the same volume (have the same amplitude).

Duration of musical sounds is conceptualized by patterns of *meter* and *rhythm.* Meter refers to a recurring pattern of strong and weak beats or pulses. "Symmetrical meter" is characteristic of Western music in the common practice period (ca. 1600–ca. 1900); it involves regularly recurring patterns of strong and weak accents arranged in sets of two ("duple meter"), three ("triple meter"), or combinations of two and three ("compound meter") pulses per unit. "Non-symmetrical meter" avoids recurring patterns of strong and weak accents; it characterizes some contemporary Western classical music and various forms of plainchant. Rhythm identifies the various arrangements of durations of pitch within a meter. Six "rhythmic modes," varying ways of organizing triple meter, appeared in European compositions of the thirteenth century. In the fourteenth century, "isorhythm" transformed the principle of the rhythmic modes to a rhythmic pattern repeated in a single part throughout a composition. Music associated with various dances exhibits characteristic rhythms in set meters (for example, waltz, minuet, mazurka, or polonaise rhythms).

As was noted above, a given pitch (determined by frequency) produces a variety of vibrational patterns (harmonic series). Sounds of the same pitch, amplitude, and duration but produced by different media can be distinguished on the basis of **timbre** or "tone color," since different sounding media cause characteristically different pitches in the harmonic series to be suppressed and others to be amplified for each fundamental. Thus each voice and instrument exhibits a characteristic timbre in producing a different vibrational pattern for a given pitch, amplitude, and duration.

Note that different cultures may identify aspects of each of these parameters as appropriate or inappropriate for worship. High pitched female ecstatic cries ("ullation") or microtonal cantillation patterns may be considered quite appropriate in some forms of African or Syrian worship but would be considered disruptive at British Anglican vespers. Organ registration deemed strong enough to lead congregational song by North American Lutherans is frequently considered too strident and loud by their Catholic confreres. Some have argued that only non-symmetrical meter is appropriate to Christian worship, since regularly recurring metrical patterns induce emotional and bodily reactions associated with profane activity. The passionate declamation of a gospel-song soloist would be considered an inappropriate timbre in which to execute Gregorian chant.

2. The Structuring of Musical Sounds

Melody is so complex and subtle a combination of elements that it practically defies definition. The arrangement of pitches in patterns of duration produces various melodic elements: *tunes* (easily recognized and remembered melodies such as folk or popular songs), *themes* (pitch arrangements used in sonatas, symphonies, themes and variations, and other forms of homophonic composition), *subjects* (pitch arrangements used in inventions, fugues, and other forms of contrapuntal composition), *motives* (short pitch arrangements lending themselves well to further transformation and development), *phrases* (basic units of pitch arrangement, usually consisting of two, four or eight measures, and giving a sense of completeness), and *periods* (combinations of two or more phrases). The *contour* (range, direction) and *motion* (tempo, rhythmic structure) of melodies can be analyzed, as well as the manipulation of melodic material through *sequence* (repetition of a melodic pattern at a new pitch level), *inversion* (changing the direction of the intervals of a melody), *retrograde motion* (playing the notes of a given melodic unit in reverse order), *retrograde inversion* (the combination of intervallic inversion and retrograde motion), *augmentation* and *diminution* (increasing or decreasing the durations of the original melodic unit).

Harmony is the simultaneous sounding and thus combination of notes, considered "vertically" (i.e., at points in time). Harmonic movement comprises a succession of "chords" (combinations of notes performed simultaneously). Given the varieties of scalar pitches and their organization, one can distinguish *modal* (employing chords comprising notes confined to the mode employed and its melodic organization), *diatonic* (employing chords confined to notes employed in the major or minor key in force), *chromatic* (employing chords in which some notes are extraneous to the major or minor key in force but with evidence of some underlying tonal center), *bitonal* (in which two melodies or successions of chords proceed in different keys), *polytonal* (in which more than two melodies or successions of chords proceed in multiple keys), *atonal* (in which no key center is observed), and *microtonal* (in which intervals smaller than the diatonic semitone are employed) scales and harmonies.

Counterpoint is the simultaneous sounding of streams of melody or harmony, considered "horizontally" (i.e., in duration over time). The term "counterpoint" is derived from the Latin phrase *punctus contra punctum,* literally "point against point" and meaning "note against note." *Organum* is a species of counterpoint in which each note of a given melody is matched by a note sounding at a fixed interval. Counterpoint is characterized by *parallel* (melodies mirroring one another at a fixed interval, usually a fourth or fifth), *contrary* (one melody rising when another descends and vice versa), and *oblique* (melody producing a variety of intervals over a drone) melodic motion. *Polyphony* proper is born when each melody or chord progression moves independently of the other(s). In *imitative* polyphony the various melodic or chordal lines share common patterns (motives), mirroring one another as in rounds, canons, and fugues; *nonimitative* polyphony, in contrast, does not employ such shared patterns.

In Western musical tradition four **textures** of music have been distinguished. *Monophony* occurs when one or more persons or groups perform an unaccompanied single-line melody at the same pitches; doubling the pitches at octave or double octave intervals moves in the direction of organum. *Heterophony* occurs when two or more persons or groups simultaneously perform different versions of the same melody. *Polyphony,* predominantly associated with counterpoint, occurs when two or more melodic lines are combined while avoiding simultaneous use of parallel rhythmic or melodic contours. *Homophony,* predominantly associated with harmony, occurs when attention is focused on a primary melodic line with the other notes being sounded having the secondary character of an accompaniment to the melodic line.

Musical **form** is the structural intelligibility of a particular musical event unfolding over time. Any of the preceding parameters or their combination may serve as the basis for organizing a musical form. Repetition and contrast provide the two fundamental characteristics for identifying musical form. *Repetition* reinforces in the listener a memory of what has already been heard and may arouse anticipation of what is to come. *Contrast* stimulates the listener's attention by confirming or frustrating the listener's anticipations. Both repetition and contrast function within complex cultural conventions organizing acoustic events.

Four fundamental categories for analyzing the relationship of repetition and contrast ground the analysis of musical form. *Exact repetition* simply reproduces the original acoustic event. Mantra-singing is an obvious religious use of exact repetition. *Variation* offers an elaboration of one element of the original acoustic event (for example, ornamenting the melody, altering the harmony, changing the rhythm). Cantillation of religious texts to recitation formulae and the singing of strophic hymnody are examples of variation employed in worship music: the melodic patterns remain fixed while the texts change. *Development* extracts certain components of the original acoustic event and combines them in new ways and with new material. A hymn-tune concertato in which each verse is sung by different vocal forces and harmonized in different ways represents a worship music form of this category. Finally, *contrast proper* presents material unrelated to the original acoustic event. The treatment of the "Hosanna in excelsis" as a choral movement in contrast to the "Benedictus qui venit in nomine Domini" as a soloist's aria in a concerted Mass setting of the Roman rite "Sanctus" demonstrates this category of musical form.

Musical forms are also sometimes characterized as free or fixed. *Free* musical forms do not exhibit regular patterns of repetition and contrast. In Western classical music a free musical form is often termed "through-composed" and is represented by such forms as fantasias, rhapsodies, nocturnes, and romances. Many graduals, offertories, and communions in the Gregorian chant tradition represent such "free" forms. *Fixed* musical forms are usually defined as binary, ternary, or mixed on the basis of structural contrast. *Binary* form consists of two balanced phrases or periods called statements and counter-statements (AB); these phrases or periods may be repeated or varied (AAB/AABB/AA¹BB¹). *Ternary* form consists of an initial phrase or period, followed by a contrasting phrase or period and concluding with a repetition of the initial phrase or period (ABA); varying phrases or periods produces the variety of *rondo* forms (ABA¹/ABACA/ABACADA/ABACABA). *Sonata-allegro* form consists of an Exposition of two contrasting themes, a Development of some aspect(s) of these themes in free form, a Recapitulation of the Exposition with some variation and a Coda to bring the form to a close. Since much music written for use in worship conforms to the exigencies of the ritual and the pattern of the texts, the forms discovered in the analysis of Western classical music do not always apply to the formal analysis of worship music, although there are exceptions. For example, a litany could be considered as a binary form involving minimal repetition and some musical settings of the "Kyrie eleison" exhibit rondo form.

3. Structured Musical Sound as Cultural Phenomena

Since music-making occurs as a cultural artifact, it is a human product susceptible to analysis by various human sciences. The data gained from such analyses assist liturgists and liturgical musicians in clarifying the contribution music makes in effective liturgical celebration. Here we will consider the study of music by four human sciences: psychology, sociology, anthropology (ethnomusicology), and semiotics.

Studies in **musical psychology** explore human capacities to perceive and interpret acoustic phenomena. They measure the range of tones and intensities, the patterns of rhythm and tempo, the qualities of timbre and texture, and the discriminations of pitch and volume that can be perceived by human hearing. They describe the human ability to organize musical perception: to identify a melody with its phrase components, to recognize harmonies and harmonic movement, to trace contrapuntal and polyphonic patterns, to perceive compositional structures. They map the various developmental stages individuals negotiate in developing musical appreciation, performance, and compositional skills.

These studies suggest various applications regarding the use of music in liturgy. Since music functions communicatively in Christian worship, the acoustic environment should enhance rather than inhibit such communication. Technical aspects of sound production and amplification should assist participants in perceiving and performing musical worship. Melodies, harmonies, and musical structures should be congruent with worship texts and actions if the participants are to engage in a unified ritual act. The various capabilities of (classes of) worshipers must be respected in devising musical programs for common worship (for example, music intended for congregational singing cannot exhibit the complexity one associates with concert performance; children's liturgical music must respect their capacities for vocal and instrumental production).

Select Bibliography on Musical Psychology

M. Clynes, ed., *Music, Mind and Brain: The Neuropsychology of Music* (New York: Plenum, 1982).

J. B. Davies, *The Psychology of Music* (Stanford: Stanford University Press, 1978).

D. Deutsch, ed., *The Psychology of Music* (New York: Academic, 1982).

C. Dreisoemer, *The Psychology of Liturgical Music* (Kirkwood, Mass.: Maryhurst, 1942).

S. Handel, *Listening: An Introduction to the Perception of Auditory Events* (Cambridge, Mass.: MIT Press, 1989).

M. R. Jones, and S. Holleran, eds., *Cognitive Bases of Musical Communication* (Washington, D.C.: American Psychological Association, 1991).

D. Raffman, *Language, Music, and Mind* (Cambridge, Mass.: MIT Press, 1993).

M. L. Serafine, *Music as Cognition: The Development of Thought in Sound* (New York: Columbia University Press, 1988).

R. Shuter-Dyson and C. Gabriel, *The Psychology of Musical Ability,* 2nd ed. (London: Methuen, 1981).

J. A. Sloboda, *The Musical Mind: The Cognitive Psychology of Music* (Oxford: Clarendon, 1985).

N. Spender and R. Shuter-Dyson, "Psychology of Music," *The New Grove Dictionary of Music and Musicians,* Stanley Sadie, ed., 20 vols. (London: Macmillan, 1980) 15:388–427.

T. J. Tighe and W. J. Dowling, eds., *Psychology and Music: The Understanding of Melody and Rhythm* (Hillsdale, N.J.: Erlbaum, 1992).

A. Storr, *Music and the Mind* (New York: Free Press, 1992).

Studies in **musical sociology** explore musical functions in various social groupings. Sometimes music is performed and listened to "for its own sake" (for example, in concert settings); sometimes it is performed and listened to as an accompaniment to related activity (for example, dance, epic poetry); sometimes it occurs as background to unrelated activity (for example, played as "background" during study or shopping). Music entertains both social elites and the common masses. Music may function to uphold certain cultural beliefs and values, helping to confer and maintain group identity (for example, patriotism reinforced by the singing of a national anthem). Music may also function to critique or subvert cultural beliefs and values, expressing and furthering the process of social change (for example, the use of "protest songs" in the civil rights movements of the United States or South Africa). Music may assist socialization (for example, many children's rhymes and chants encode both information and appropriate behaviors) and reflect social stratification (for example, "art music" associated with elites, "folk music" associated with lower classes).

These studies suggest various applications in the use of music in liturgy. Employing distinctive music in liturgy may promote religious identity but also suggests that religious identity has little or no relation to the wider culture; on the other hand, employing the musical styles of the surrounding culture in worship may blunt the distinctiveness of the liturgical act. The cultural codes surrounding the use of music in different social groupings (for example, a lullaby, a sea shanty, a wedding dance) constrain and bridge to the music-making at worship. In some societies (especially in the First World), a cultural shift from music-making to music-consuming is far advanced, with serious implications for liturgical music practice. The presence of worshipers of various ages, genders, socio-economic classes, and ethnic heritages at the same liturgical celebration provides opportunities for a genuinely transcultural experience of the Church but also poses problems of representation and coherence in the musical program.

Select Bibliography on Musical Sociology

T. W. Adorno, *Introduction to the Sociology of Music,* trans. E. B. Ashton (New York: Continuum, 1976).

H. Eisler, *Musik und Politik,* ed. G. Mayer (Munich: Rogner and Bernhard, 1973).

P. R. Farnsworth, *The Social Psychology of Music,* 2nd ed. (Ames, Iowa: Iowa State University Press, 1968).

K. G. Fellerer, *Sociologie der Kirchenmusik: Materialen zur Musik- und Religionssoziologie* (Köln: Westdeustcher Verlag, 1963).

P. J. Martin, *Sounds and Society: Themes in the Sociology of Music* (Manchester: Manchester University Press, 1995).

J. Shepherd, P. Virden, G. Vulliamy, and T. Wishart, *Whose Music? A Sociology of Musical Language* (London: Latimer, 1977).

I. Supicic, *Music in Society: A Guide to the Sociology of Music* (New York: Pendragon, 1987).

M. Weber, *The Rational and Social Foundations of Music* [orig. *Die rationalen un soziologischen Grundlagen der Musik,* 1921] (Carbondale, Il.: Southern Illinois University Press, 1958).

Studies in **musical anthropology** and **ethnomusicology** identify three musical "dialects" within the musical "language" of some cultures. *"Classical," "serious,"* or *"art"* music, composed and performed by trained professional musicians, is transmitted by notation demanding musical literacy; this musical dialect was originally developed under patronage by courts or religious establishments, but tends to be supported today by government subsidies, educational establishments, and devotees' contributions. *"Folk"* music, in contrast, composed by anonymous individuals and recreated in a process of communal elaboration, is transmitted orally and aurally rather than by written notation; it is generally performed in non-commercial settings by members of the community who are not highly trained musical specialists (although high degrees of instrumental and vocal skill may be in evidence). Finally, *"popular," "light,"* or *"entertainment"* music, composed by identifiable individuals, can be listened to and performed by those with some musical training, although not usually the depth of training needed for classical performance; this musical dialect is commercially marketed, disseminated by the mass media (in sheet music; on disks, tapes, and films; by radio, television, and public address transmission). It should be clear that the boundaries between these musical dialects vary from culture to culture and that a given piece may appear in more than one category (for example, as when Maurice Ravel's "Bolero," a classical piece of "art" music becomes associated with "entertainment" values by being incorporated into a motion-picture score or used as background music in a televised commercial).

Ethnomusicological studies challenge enthnocentrism in musicological theory. The presumption that music must "develop" from pentatonic, to modal, to diatonic, to chromatic, to microtonal scalar structures or from monody, to organum, to polyphony, to melody-cum-harmony betrays a particular evolutionary bias. Distinctions between "serious/artistic" and "entertainment/popular" music are unmasked by ethnomusicological studies not as ontological categories, but as particular cultural encodings. Cross-cultural music studies guarantee that no single era or tradition will be taken as normative for all liturgical music; rather, each epoch's musical monuments will be evaluated in terms of its ability to enable worshipers to engage its liturgical prayer.[2]

Select Bibliography on Musical Anthropology and Ethnomusicology

J. Blacking, *How Musical Is Man?* (London: Faber, 1976).
J. E. Kaemmer, *Music in Human Life: Anthropological Perspectives on Music* (Austin: University of Texas Press, 1993).
J. Kunst, *Ethnomusicology* (The Hague: Nijhoff, 1959).
A. Merriam, *The Anthropology of Music* (Evanston: Northwestern University Press, 1964).

H. Myers, *Ethnomusicology: An Introduction* (New York: Norton, 1992).

B. Nettl, and P. V. Bohlman, eds., *Comparative Musicology and Anthropology of Music: Essays on the History of Ethnomusicology* (Chicago: University of Chicago Press, 1991).

B. Nettl, *The Study of Ethnomusicology: Twenty-nine Issues and Concepts* (Chicago: University of Illinois Press, 1983).

A. B. Schuursma, *Ethnomusicology Research: A Select Annotated Bibliography* (New York: Garland, 1992).

M. Stokes, ed., *Ethnicity, Identity, and Music: The Musical Construction of Place* (Providence, R.I.: Berg, 1994).

Semiotics has made its own contribution to the study of music as a cultural phenomenon. Jean-Jacques Nattiez has developed a semiotic framework for exploring music as a sign-system. He suggests that researchers might concentrate on the processes by which music is generated ("poietics"), the processes by which music is employed ("esthesics"), or the residue abstracted from both of these processes ("immanent analysis"). A "global analysis" of music as sign-system would then involve: (1) analyzing what the composer/performer intends, either by correlating the written music or recorded performance with external evidence of performative intent such as diaries, interviews, etc. ("deductive poietics") or by extrapolating the composer/performer's intention from the repeated patterns of melody, harmony, timbre, volume, rhythm, etc. ("inductive poietics"); (2) analyzing what the auditor receives, either by correlating the perceived music with external evidence of thoughts and feelings in the auditor through interviews, etc. ("deductive esthesics") or by extrapolating from the written or recorded work what an auditor might be expected to perceive ("inductive esthesics"); (3) analyzing the musical artifact without reference to composer/performers' or auditors' intents ("neutral level"): an analysis of pitch, tonal, harmonic, timbre, volume, etc., relationships; and (4) correlating the results of the other three investigations.

While the application of semiotic theory to music is still in its infancy, Willem Marie Speelman (see below) has employed the theory of meaning developed by Algirdas Julien Greimas (1917–1992) and his Paris School to the musical and literary discourses yoked in liturgical songs. Speelman distinguishes the musical expression form from the musical content form and analyzes their relationships; similarly he distinguishes the literary expression form from the literary content form and analyzes their relationship; finally he explores how new meaning is generated in the yoking of text and music. The sheer complexity of musical semiotics and the technical terminology by which it is undertaken is daunting, but it provides a possible approach to identifying and understanding the multiple codes operative in any liturgical event.

Select Bibliography on Musical Semiotics

C. Boilès, "Processes of Musical Semiosis," *Yearbook of Traditional Music* 14 (1982) 24–44.

J. M. Joncas, "Liturgical Musicology and Musical Semiotics: Theoretical Foundations and Analytic Techniques," *Ecclesia Orans* 8/2 (1991) 181–206.

J. M. Joncas, "Semiotics and the Analysis of Liturgical Music," *liturgical ministry* 3 (1994) 144–54.

D. Lidov, "Music," *Encyclopedic Dictionary of Semiotics,* ed. T. A. Sebeok, 3 vols. (Berlin-New York- Amsterdam: Mouton de Gruyter, 1986) 1: 577–87.

R. Monelle, *Linguistics and Semiotics in Music* (Reading, U.K.: Harwood, 1992).

J.-J. Nattiez, "Reflections on the Development of Semiology in Music," *Music Analysis* 8 (1989) 21–75.

J.-J. Nattiez, *Musical Discourse: Toward a Semiology of Music* (Princeton: Princeton University Press, 1990).

N. Ruwet, "Methods of Analysis in Musicology," trans. and introduced by Mark Everist, *Music Analysis* 6 (1987) 3–36.

W. M. Speelman, *The Generation of Meaning in Liturgical Songs: A Semiotic Analysis of Five Liturgical Songs as Syncretic Discourses* (Kampen: Kok, 1995).

G. Stefani, *Introduzione alla semiotica della musica* (Palermo: Sellerio, 1976).

G. Stefani, *L'espressione vocale e musicale nella liturgia: gesti—riti—repertori* (Torino-Leumann: ElleDiCi, 1967).

Fundamentally, the human sciences provide descriptions of musical events and explanatory frameworks for how these events function in human society. They do not provide normative statements of the adequacy and appropriateness, the congruence and coherence of musical events for Christian worship. Establishing such criteria is the task of historical, philosophical, and theological disciplines informed by the contribution of the human sciences.

Notes

1. This is reflected, for example, in the title of Richard Taruskin's *Text and Act: Essays on Music and Performance* (New York: Oxford University Press, 1995).

2. See further chapter 22.

Chapter 15

Liturgical Music:
Its Forms and Functions

Raymond F. Glover

An understanding of the form and function of liturgical music is ideally attained when considered within the context of the two major forms of worship found in liturgical churches, the Daily Office and the Eucharist or Holy Communion. Contemporary forms of these services based on historic models share many common characteristics. This review will be written from an Anglican/Episcopal perspective and will use as its basic liturgical and musical resources the Book of Common Prayer 1979 of the Episcopal Church and *The Hymnal 1982* (1985).

The worship of the Anglican Church finds its roots buried deeply in the classic Catholic, liturgical tradition of the early Celtic and English Church. Contemporary forms of Anglican liturgical worship, like those of every other twentieth-century liturgical church, reflect very clearly the reforms and revisions brought about by the liturgical movement that has swept across the world for at least the last one hundred years. Its worship forms, although modified, will therefore be found to be compatible with those used in other liturgical churches.[1]

Note: Texts of liturgical rites historically fall into two categories: *propers,* texts that change with the season, feast, day of the week, or time in the day in which a particular service is celebrated, and *ordinary,* texts which are fixed or constant. Propers would include certain prayers, readings, prefaces of the Eucharistic Prayer, and hymns. The ordinary includes canticles of the Daily Offices and the *Kyrie,*

Gloria in excelsis, Credo, Sanctus, and *Agnus Dei* of Holy Communion or the Mass. In contemporary forms of the Office and the Eucharist many of the texts of the ordinary, with the exception for Episcopalians of the *Sanctus,* are variable. (For example, see *The Holy Eucharist, The Entrance Rite*).

The Daily Office

The Daily Offices or daily services of contemporary Western liturgical churches find their roots in the daily services of monastic communities, primarily those of the Benedictine Order founded by Benedict of Nursia (ca. 540). The *Rule of St. Benedict* divided the day into nine segments, each having its proper liturgy. These segments, called Offices or Hours, are: Vigils, Matins, Lauds, Prime, Terce, Sext, None, Vespers, and Compline.

Vigil: A service held just before dawn.

Matins: The first morning Office, begun at the crowing of the cock. It can, however, mean several different things according to the time and place historically in which it is used. In medieval texts it sometimes means the morning vigil; in the Benedictine rite, the service after the vigil; sometimes the services of vigil, lauds, and on occasion, prime recited together.

Lauds: Matins is followed by Lauds and begins at dawn. Its name is derived from the Psalms 148, 149, and 150 whose Latin *incipits* (opening or introductory phrases) are *Laudate Dominum.*

Prime: Following Lauds, at the first hour of the day (approximately 6 a.m., in our contemporary method of determining time), is *Prime (prima hora),* the first of the "Little Hours" (services first developed by monks to mark the hours of the day set aside by Jews and early Christians for private devotions). The order of texts of each of these services is identical.

Following *Prime* (at approximately 9 a.m., 12 noon, and 3 p.m.), are the three other "Little Hours": *Terce,* the third hour *(hora tertia); Sext,* the sixth hour *(hora sexta),* and *None,* the ninth hour *(hora nona).*

Vespers: In monastic rites this is the primary evening service.

Compline: This service is recited just before retiring.

These services share in common the singing of psalms, canticles, versicles, and a hymn; readings from the Bible; and prayers.

Today, as stated above, the daily services of liturgical churches are based on these earlier monastic Offices and include the same basic liturgical/musical elements i.e., scripture, prayers, psalms, canticles, and hymns.

Morning and Evening Prayer

At the time of the Reformation in England, Archbishop Thomas Cranmer (1489–1556) reduced the number of daily services to two, Morning Prayer, or *matins,* and Evening Prayer, or *vespers.* For Morning Prayer he used elements taken from the Latin rites of *matins, lauds* and *prime* and for the Evening Office, elements from *vespers* and *compline.* Over the years of Prayer Book revision in both England and the United States, the structure of the daily Offices for Anglicans has remained basically the same, although various components within each Office have changed. For example, in the most recent revision of the Prayer Book of the Episcopal Church, the Noonday Office, based on the liturgies for *terce, sext,* and *none,* dropped by Archbishop Cranmer at the Reformation, has been restored, as has the Office of *Compline.*

For pastoral reasons the present Book of Common Prayer of the Episcopal Church contains two rites of the Offices of Morning and Evening Prayer: Rite I continues the traditional, Elizabethan form of the language of the Offices, while Rite II offers contemporary language forms. Noonday Prayer and *Compline* are found only in contemporary language forms.

Preces. According to the Book of Common Prayer the first musical settings of the liturgical text of the Offices are those of the *Opening Preces* (from the Latin *preces,* meaning petitions). Preces are *versicles* and *responses,* verses of various psalms sung in dialogue between the officiant, sometimes called the *precentor* (a Latin term for the one who leads or sings first or, alternatively, *cantor,* one who sings) and the people. The opening preces at both Morning and Evening Prayer introduce the psalmody for the day. The Invitatory portion of Evening Prayer in the Book of Common Prayer uses a different text than that at Morning Prayer. However, both are invitations to praise the Lord and are followed by the *Gloria Patri,* "Glory to the Father, the Son and the Holy Spirit." Except during Lent the *Gloria Patri* may be followed by *Alleluia* (Praise the Lord!). In the cathedral tradition of the Anglican Church, especially in England, the musical settings of these texts may be quite elaborate, in which case the responses are sung by the choir on behalf of the people. Settings appropriate for use by a congregation are found in *The Hymnal 1982.*

Invitatory Psalm or Canticle. The opening preces at the daily Offices are followed by the singing of an *Invitatory Psalm* or *Canticle,* or, in the case of Evening Prayer, a hymn. At Morning Prayer there is a choice of one of two psalms: Psalm 95, the *Venite,* "Come, let us sing to the Lord," or Psalm 100, the *Jubilate Deo,* "Be joyful in the Lord all you lands," or the *Pascha nostrum,* "Christ our passover has been sacrificed for us," a canticle of invitation. It is identified as a *canticle,* a term which distinguishes biblical songs from the psalms. At Evening Prayer, rather than an invitatory psalm or canticle, the ancient Greek hymn sung at the lighting of the lamps, *Phos Hilaron,* "O gracious Light, pure brightness of the everliving Father in heaven," is sung. *The Hymnal 1982* contains both plainsong and contemporary settings of this Prayer Book text and a rubric gives permission for the use of metrical settings of the ancient Greek hymn, of which several are found in *The Hymnal,* or of "some other suitable hymn."

Antiphons. Although the texts of both Psalms 95 and 100 are general in nature they may be made specific to a particular day or season in the liturgical year through the use of antiphons, refrains sung at the beginning and end of the psalm, or with Psalm 95 at the beginning and end and between groups of verses, or in psalm 100 at the beginning and after every verse. For example, in Advent the text of the invitatory antiphon is, "Our King and Savior now draws near: Come let us adore him" making the text of Psalm 95 more specific to the season. Musical settings in either *plainsong* or *Anglican chant* (harmonized chant) of the Prayer Book antiphons for the use by a congregation with the Morning Prayer Invitatory Psalms are found in the Appendix section of Volume I of the Accompaniment edition, Service Music of *The Hymnal 1982*.[2] (For more detailed directions on the performance practice of singing canticles with antiphons, see Antiphonal and Responsorial Recitation, below.)

The Psalter. The choice of psalms, readings, and collects (prayers) at the Prayer Book Offices of Morning and Evening Prayer varies with the day in the liturgical year on which they are used. The listing of the proper psalm and readings for these Offices is found in *The Daily Office Lectionary,* a schedule arranged in a two-year cycle of psalms and lessons to be read on specific days and occasions. Since the First Book of Common Prayer in 1549 there have been many revisions of Prayer Book lectionaries. The current lectionary for use by Episcopalians arranges the order of psalms over a seven-week period. Generally they are read "in course," that is, in numerical order, but with a sensitivity to the time of the day, the day of the week, or season of the year when they are being read. For example, a psalm that includes a reference to night would not be assigned to a morning office. The traditional monthly reading of the Psalter, however, is also permissible. Directions for this use are found in the Prayer Book

Psalter. Musical settings for the Prayer Book Psalms suitable for use by a congregation called Simplified Anglican Chant are found in *The Hymnal 1982*.[3] Other settings are available in *The Plainsong Psalter,* which includes antiphons proper to particular days and seasons and others of a general nature suitable for use at other times, and *The Anglican Chant Psalter*.[4]

The psalms at the Offices may be sung in several ways. Directions as found in the Book of Common Prayer (p. 582) are as follows:

> *Direct Recitation:* "the reading or chanting of a whole psalm, or portion of a psalm in unison." The Prayer Book suggests, "It is particularly appropriate for the Psalm verses suggested in the lectionary for use between the Lessons at the Eucharist, when the verses are recited rather than sung, and may often be found a satisfactory method of chanting them."
>
> *Antiphonal recitation:* "the verse-by-verse alternation between groups of singers or readers, e.g., between choir and congregation, or between one side of the congregation and the other. The alternate recitation concludes either with the Gloria Patri, or with a refrain (called antiphon) recited in unison. This is probably the most satisfying method for reciting the psalms in the Daily Office."
>
> *Responsorial recitation:* "the name given to a method of psalmody in which the verses of a psalm are sung by a solo voice, with the choir and congregation singing a refrain after each verse or group of verses. This was the traditional method of singing the Venite, and the restoration of Invitatory Antiphons for the Venite makes possible a recovery of this form of sacred song in the Daily Office. It was also a traditional manner of chanting the psalms between the Lessons at the Eucharist, and it is increasingly favored by modern composers."
>
> *Responsive recitation:* "the method which is most frequently used in Episcopal churches, the minister alternating with the congregation, verse by verse."

Canticles. In the monastic tradition proper canticles assigned for use at particular Offices on particular days functioned as responses to readings and, as such, their musical settings were reflective or contemplative in nature. Although the present Prayer Book of the Episcopal Church allows for a flexible use of canticles at the Offices, their function is still considered to be as responses to readings and in *The Hymnal 1982* their musical settings are generally reflective or contemplative in nature. For places such as school, seminary chapels, where the Office canticles are sung daily, the Book of Common Prayer includes lists of "Suggested Canticles at Morning Prayer" and "Suggested Canticles at Evening Prayer."[5] This usage more closely parallels ancient monastic practice where the use of particular canticles had a fixed relationship with specific Offices and particular days of the week.

Canticles, as stated above, are, with two exceptions, biblical songs. The exceptions, which are technically prose hymns, are the *Te Deum*, "We praise thee, O God," (traditional translation), or "You are God" (contemporary translation), and the *Gloria in excelsis*, "Glory be to God on high" (traditional translation), or "Glory to God in the highest" (contemporary setting).[6]

Rubrics in the Book of Common Prayer allow the interchangeable use of any of the canticles at both rites of the Daily Offices.[7] The *Magnificat* and *Nunc dimittis*, the traditional Evening Prayer canticles, however, are printed with the Evening Offices as they have been since 1549, expressing what is perhaps the use preferred by the commission that prepared the Book of Common Prayer 1979. *The Hymnal 1982* offers a rich variety of musical settings for the Prayer Book forms of canticle texts in plainsong, Anglican chant, and contemporary styles. In addition, over the centuries, primarily in England, composers have composed a wealth of anthem settings of the canticles, primarily the *Te Deum laudamus, Gloria in Excelsis, Magnificat,* and *Nunc dimittis.* As with the choral settings of the preces, these anthem settings of the canticles are sung by the choir on behalf of the people. Contemporary American composers are also composing anthem-like settings of the canticles, many of which are set for use by choir and congregation and employ a variety of musical instruments in addition to, or with the organ.

Although historically the Prayer Book forms of the psalms and canticles are non-metrical in nature, strophic and metrical settings are also authorized for use.[8] Musical settings of these metrical texts are available among the hymns in *The Hymnal 1982* and in other publications.[9]

The Apostles Creed, the Lord's Prayer, and the Collects. The order for a choral setting of the Daily Offices continues with the recitation of the Apostles Creed, usually on a monotone, and the fixed Office collects (prayers). They are introduced with the singing in the form of a versicle and response of the historic salutation, "The Lord be with you. *And with thy spirit,*" or, in Rite II, *"And also with you."* The officiant continues the service with the invitation to prayer, "Let us pray," which is immediately followed by the Lord's Prayer sung on a monotone or, in the cathedral tradition, to a choral setting. The *Suffrages,* a form of *preces,* or versicles and responses follow. Like the opening preces that open the Office, they are a series of petitions using texts from the psalms. Several settings in contemporary forms of historic plainsong are available in *The Hymnal 1982,* or in harmonized choral settings by contemporary American composers. *The Hymnal* offers two different settings of Suffrages *B* at Evening Prayer. They use the two tones (melodic formulas used for the singing of historic chant) that are available for the singing of the Office collects.[10] Tone 1 is based on a contemporary form of chant found in some editions of the Roman Missal. Tone II is the formula for singing the collects prepared for use with the Book of Common Prayer, 1928.[11] The tone used for the singing of the collects determines the tone for the singing of the suffrage, e.g., if the collect is sung to Tone II then Suffrages *B,* Tone II would be sung.

Following the singing of the fixed Office collects at both Morning and Evening Prayer a rubric permits the singing of a hymn or anthem (on Office Hymn see below), and the use of authorized intercessions and thanksgivings, a concluding versicle and response, "Let us bless the Lord. *Thanks be to God,"* and the Grace. Musical settings of the latter for general use and one for use in Easter Season for both rites of the Daily Offices are found in *The Hymnal 1982.*[12] The text is the same for both rites of both Offices and is set to traditional plainsong.

The Noonday Office. The most recent revision of the Book of Common Prayer of the Episcopal Church has been enriched through the inclusion of three ancient Office liturgies. The first is "An Order of Service for Noonday,"[13] based on and retaining the basic structure of the monastic "little hours" of *terce, sext,* and *none.* Although designed for use at the noon hour, with careful selection of hymns, psalms, readings, and collects, it can be made appropriate for use at any of the "little hours": 9 a.m., 12 noon, or 4 p.m.[14]

An Order of Service for the Evening. This service, new to the Prayer Book of the Episcopal Church, is modeled after a congregational service common to the fourth and fifth centuries. The service opens with the church in darkness with a service of light which includes a greeting, the option of a short lesson, a prayer for light, the *Phos Hilaron,* or some other appropriate hymn, and the optional use of an anthem at the candle lighting, the *lucernarium.* Plainsong settings of this can be found in the first volumes of the Accompaniment Edition of *The Hymnal 1982.*[15]

The revival of monastic orders in the Anglican Church and the restored use of the ancient Office liturgies including *Compline* and the popular use of this Office in the years before World War II at conferences and retreats led to its inclusion in the Book of Common Prayer, 1979 of the Episcopal Church. Like "An Order of Worship for Noonday," the Prayer Book service of *Compline* follows the classic order for the rite and uses contemporary adaptations of historic plainsong settings of the texts.[16]

The Office Hymn. Although the congregational singing of hymns was not a part of the liturgical tradition of Roman Catholics until after Vatican II, hymns have had a long history of use by monastics in their celebration of the Daily Offices.[17]

In the *Rule of St. Benedict* it was required that a hymn be sung in each of the offices, although no specific text was listed. Over time the placement of these hymns within the offices on particular days and seasons in the various monastic orders became fixed and this pattern of use continues to this day. Because of the vast number of office hymns and the limited number of meters used in their composition, it is common for the same tune to be used for many of these texts.

With the rediscovery of early Latin hymns by John Mason Neale and others in the nineteenth century, these ancient hymns are now found in the hymnals of many contemporary congregations. It is also important to note that some of these ancient Latin texts were the basis of chorales which Martin Luther prepared for use by his reformed congregations. For example, his Advent text, "Savior of the nations, come!" is based on a text attributed to Ambrose, *"Veni redemptor gentium."*[18]

Resources for Use of the Daily Offices in Other Liturgical Churches

The Lutheran Church. *The Lutheran Book of Worship* (1978) contains the liturgical texts and a contemporary musical setting for Morning and Evening Prayer and Prayer at the Close of Day. A three-year lectionary of Prayers of the Day, Psalms, and Lessons is also included, which is followed by a collection of Petitions, Intercessions, and Thanksgivings.[19]

The psalms are pointed to be sung to contemporary unison settings created specifically for congregational use, with directions for "Singing the Psalms."[20] Music for eight different tones or melodies of single chant (intended for use with each single verse of the psalm) and double chant (for use with consecutive pairs of verses of a psalm) are given. Suggestions are made concerning the importance of selecting tones that suit the mood of the text, and there is a direction concerning the use of certain tones with canticles which are pointed for use with these or similar tones. These musical settings have proved to be very serviceable and have been included in publications of other Protestant denominations.

It was the intent of the Anglican Archbishop Thomas Cranmer that the Eucharist be the primary service on the Lord's day and the Offices of Morning and Evening Prayer the liturgies for daily worship. As daily worship there was no need in the Offices for either an offering or a sermon. Cranmer's intent is still the pattern of use for the present revision of the Prayer Book of the Episcopal Church. The Lutheran structure of the Office, however, makes it suitable for use as the principal service on the Lord's day or on some other occasion permitting the option of an offering, "during which a hymn, psalm, or anthem may be sung"; a hymn; a sermon followed by a prayer; and the Benediction.

The Roman Catholic Church. Although there is no official, authorized hymnal for use in the Roman Catholic Church, hymnals have been published for use by members of this denomination.[21] These collections, in addition to a large section of hymns and service music intended for use at Eucharist, contain services for Morning and Evening Prayer with musical settings utilizing contemporary and historic chant of Office hymns, versicles and responses, psalms, canticles, and prayers.

The Holy Eucharist

Although a pattern for daily worship is found in both the Old and New Testaments, for example, in the Psalms where there are references of prayer offered at particular times of the day, the institution of the Eucharist, also called Holy Communion, the Mass, and the Lord's supper is very clearly articulated by Jesus Christ in the synoptic Gospels of the New Testament: Matthew (26:26-30), Mark (14:22-26), and Luke (22:14-20) and in Paul's first Epistle to the Corinthians (11:23-26). Rooted in Jewish worship patterns and a passover meal, or a meal related to the Passover, the classic shape of the Eucharist was achieved over a period of at least four centuries of development.

The Liturgy of the Word

The opening part of the Eucharist, the liturgy of the word, *synaxis,* has deep roots in Jewish synagogue tradition and for early Christians was held on Sunday morning separate from the Eucharistic meal held in the evening. The primitive liturgy of the word, for example, opened with a greeting of Jewish origins, "The Lord be with you" (Ruth 2:4) or "peace to you" *(Shalom).* The response of the people was, as it is today, "and also with you," thus continuing the

Jewish construction of parallelism. Following the greetings, lessons were read interspersed with Psalms; the Bishop delivered a sermon which was followed by the dismissal of the *catechumens* (persons preparing for Baptism); then came intercessory prayers of the faithful; and if the synaxis was a separate event, the dismissal of the faithful was its conclusion.

Changes in the synaxis from the primitive simplicity of the early Church came at different times in different parts of the Roman Empire where Christians gathered for worship. Major changes, however, came with the establishment of the Constantinian church, the gradual breakdown of the Roman Empire and the division in the fifth century of the Christian Church into its two distinct parts, Eastern and Western. By the eighth century the synaxis in the Roman rite achieved a pattern, or structure, that we can easily recognize:

> Entrance chant, by 340 C.E., a Psalm with antiphons or refrains, *Introit.*
>
> Litany with *Kyrie* responses, replaced under Pope Gregory (ca. 595 C.E.), by the *Kyrie eleison, Christ eleison, Kyrie eleison* (Lord, have mercy upon us, Christ, have mercy upon us, Lord, have mercy upon us).
>
> Hymn, *Gloria in excelsis,* about 500 C.E., at first reserved for a bishop.
>
> Greeting and prayer (collect)
>
> Lections, by the fourth century three: Old Testament, Apostolic writings, and the Gospel. (The Old Testament lesson was dropped first in the East in the fifth century and in the West by the seventh.)
>
> Chants between readings: a Psalm *(Gradual)* between the first two and an *Alleluia* before the Gospel. After the establishment of Lent in the early part of the fourth century, the *Alleluia* was replaced by a *Tract* (Psalm verses sung without antiphons or refrains).
>
> Sermon
>
> Dismissals, lost between the fifth and sixth centuries
>
> Prayers
>
> The Creed, introduced by Charlemagne in the eighth century, but not added in Rome until the eleventh century and then reserved for Sundays and greater feasts.

The Middle Ages saw continued change in the Eucharistic rite, many of them corruptions that made the Mass fair game for the reformers of the fifteenth and sixteenth centuries who changed the Eucharist in an attempt to rid it of the liturgical and theological corruptions and excesses that had accrued over the previous seven or eight centuries.

The twentieth century has also been a time of change resulting from the work of the liturgical movement that began in Europe in the late nineteenth century. Through liturgical renewal, churches of many denominations around the world have sought to restore the Eucharist to a shape that reflects that of the early Church, primarily that of the apostolic tradition of Hippolytus, the third-century Bishop of Rome. The goal of this movement was to regain the vitality of the liturgy of the early Church and thus to bring new vitality to the liturgical and spiritual life of the twentieth-century Church. The liturgical movement is very much an ecumenical effort; as a result the shape of the revised Eucharist found in liturgical churches around the world is common to all. The most recent revision of the Eucharist as found in the Book of Common Prayer of the Episcopal Church will be used here as our model, since its structure conforms to the historic model discussed above.

The Entrance Rite. The entrance rite, although reflecting recent trends in liturgical revision, is felt by some liturgical scholars to be cluttered, for it includes material that in some ways is repetitive. For example, an opening Psalm (introit), hymn, or anthem is followed almost immediately (except in Lent) by the ancient hymn, *Gloria in excelsis* or some other song of praise.

The entrance psalm, called an introit, as noted above, was added to the liturgy of the word in the fourth century. A psalm sung antiphonally with congregational antiphons or refrains, it covered the entrance of the liturgical ministers into the church. Over time the verses of the psalm were greatly diminished in number and the musical settings of the verses and the antiphons, although beautiful, attained a degree of difficulty that precluded their being sung by the people. Since one of the goals of the liturgical movement is the restoration of congregational involvement, rubrics in the present Prayer Book allow the use of a hymn in place of a psalm. If a hymn is used, its text should reflect the season of the liturgical year or the particular day within the season in which the Eucharist is being celebrated. For example, one of the major festivals—Easter, Christmas, Epiphany, or Ascension—would call for hymns whose texts amplified the themes of these feasts. The rubric also allows the singing of an anthem whose text should be appropriate to the day or season.[22]

After a seasonal opening acclamation and a prayer in Rite I, the *Kyrie eleison,* in either Greek or English, "Lord, have mercy upon us," or the *Trisagion,* "Holy God, Holy Immortal One, have mercy upon us" is sung or said (for musical settings see below). The hymn, *Gloria in excelsis,* follows or, as the rubrics state, "some other song of praise in addition to, or in place of the preceding. . . ." In Rite II the rubrics permit the omission of the prayer after the acclamation and the immediate singing of the *Gloria in excelsis,* or some other song of praise. On other occasions, especially during Lent and on weekdays the *Kyrie* in either Greek or English, or the *Trisagion* is used. Various musical settings of these liturgical texts can be found in *The Hymnal 1982.*[23]

Other alternate "songs of praise" are the Office Canticles. This optional use is both practical and pastoral, especially for congregations that at one time used Morning Prayer as the principal service on the Lord's day, but, because they now celebrate the Eucharist each Sunday, no longer sing the canticles. To facilitate this alternate usage a "Canticle Use Chart" is given.[24] The entrance rite may be preceded by a penitential rite,[25] which may include an opening hymn, psalm, or anthem; the opening Acclamation; the Exhortation or homily; a reading of the *Decalogue* (the Ten Commandments), with *Kyrie* response; a brief reading of scripture; and confession and absolution. A rubric states that "When this Order is used at the beginning of the Liturgy, the service continues with the *Kyrie eleison,* the *Trisagion,* or the *Gloria in excelsis.*"[26] The entrance rite is completed with the reading or singing of the Collect of the Day. Sources for directions for singing the collect are listed above.

The Lessons. The reading of three lessons, one each from the Old Testament, the New Testament, and the Gospels, a practice of the early Church, has been restored as an option in the Eucharist of the Episcopal Church, following the reforms of the Second Vatican Council. Historically, the readings from the New Testament and from the Gospel were often sung. Directions for this use with the ancient lesson and Gospel tones may be found in *The Holy Eucharist: Altar Edition.*[27]

The Gradual Psalm. The psalm sung between readings is historically identified as the *gradual,* a term derived from the Latin word, *gradus,* or step of the *ambo,* or lectern, from which it was sung. As a responsorial psalm (see above), the gradual psalm verses are sung by a cantor and the antiphon by the congregation. Like the introit, the verses of the gradual psalm were over time diminished in number and, with the antiphon, set to musical settings that were very ornate and appropriate for singing by a soloist and a trained choir. When three lessons are used, the gradual psalm is usually sung between the readings from the Old and New Testaments.

The restoration of the gradual psalm to the Eucharist has assured its expanded use in liturgical churches of many denominations and is an inspiration for composers to create responsorial settings suitable for use by a choir and congregation.[28]

The Alleluia. Historically, an Alleluia was sung in anticipation of the reading of the Gospel. Like the introit and gradual psalms, the psalm verses, or later other scriptural or non-scriptural texts associated with the alleluia, were reduced in number and the musical setting became more ornate, including a long, elaborate wordless melody on the syllable "ah" of the final alleluia. During Lent the Alleluia is replaced by the Tract (see above).

The Sequence Hymn. Although congregational hymn singing is a major characteristic of reformed liturgies, congregational hymns were never a part of the Eucharistic liturgy in the Roman Rite until after Vatican II. They did, however, appear as part of paraliturgical events such as festive outdoor processions, popular devotions, and in the form of popular carols. The one exception is the *sequence,* a hymn sung after the Alleluia that first appeared in the Eucharist of the Roman Church in the last half of the ninth century, though it was not sung by the congregation at large. It developed from the setting syllabically of a text to the long wordless melody, *jubilus,* of the Alleluia. It eventually took the form of a metrical hymn, most of which have texts in which "verses grouped into pairs with an equal number of syllables, and these in turn are reflected by paired phrases in the music."[29] Popular primarily in Northern Europe, only four sequence hymns were retained in the revision of the Roman missal under Pope Pius V: *Victimae paschali* for Easter, *Veni Sancti Spiritus* for Pentecost, *Lauda Sion Salvatorum* for Corpus Christi, and *Dies irae* (suppressed by Vatican II) for the requiem Mass.[30]

The Nicene Creed. The Book of Common Prayer 1979 restores the ancient practice of using the Creed on Sundays and other Major Feasts. At other times its use is optional. The Book of Common Prayer text of the Creed appears in two forms: first, a contemporary translation developed by the International Consultation on Ecumenical Texts (ICET) Prayer Book and, second, a traditional form.[31] Musical settings, mostly chant, are found in *The Hymnal 1982.*[32]

Prayers of the People. Early forms of the Eucharist (second century) included Prayers of the People said after the sermon and the dismissal of the catechumens. Revision of liturgical rites in many denominations finds the restoration of these prayers to their ancient position after the sermon. The Book of Common Prayer in Rite I includes the traditional Prayer for the Whole State of Christ's Church from the 1549 edition, with optional congregational responses, and six different forms in Rite II. *The Hymnal 1982* contains a variety of musical settings for these prayer forms.[33]

The liturgy of the word concludes with the peace, a restoration of the ancient "Kiss of Peace," symbolic of the reconciliation between members of the congregation.[34]

The Liturgy of the Table: The Holy Communion

The Liturgy of the Table opens with the offertory at which time a rubric directs that "representatives of the congregation bring the people's offering of bread and wine, and money or other gifts, to the deacon or celebrant,"[35] thus restoring the pattern of early liturgies when people brought bread and wine of their own making and, if financially possible, monetary or other gifts for care of the needy. In the present liturgy of the Episcopal Church, the offering of gifts may be preceded by the reading of an appropriate sentence from Scripture, and may be accompanied by the singing of a hymn, psalm, or anthem.[36] It is at this point that an appropriate canticle might be sung.[37]

The Great Thanksgiving. The roots of the Eucharistic Prayer, or Great Thanksgiving, are found in the practice of Jewish blessings said over the bread and wine at meals. As at a Jewish meal, members of the congregation are first invited to enter into prayer with the traditional salutation, "The Lord be with you." The celebrant continues with an invitation asking the people to "Lift up your hearts," to which they respond, "We lift them up unto the Lord" (Rite I), or "We lift them to the Lord" (Rite II). The celebrant expands the invitations, "Let us give thanks unto our Lord" or "Let us give thanks to the Lord our God," to which the people give assent by saying, "It is meet and right so to do," or, "It is right to give him thanks and praise." This opening dialogue, the *Sursum corda* (Lift up your hearts), is followed in the Eucharistic meal by a preface containing a variable portion of "proper" text which relates the prayer to the Lord's day or a particular season or other occasion in the liturgical year.[38] It leads directly to the great congregational hymn, *Sanctus* ("Holy, holy, holy Lord") whose text is that of the seraphim heard by Isaiah in his vision (Is. 6:1-3), and their song before the throne of God in Revelation 4:8.

In the earliest years of the Christian Church the text of Great Thanksgiving was improvised by the celebrant and, from the fourth century up until the present day, always includes the scriptural words of institution. In the traditional Rite I form of the Eucharist, two forms of the text of Great Thanksgiving are available. Four are available in the contemporary Rite II Eucharist.[39]

The traditional, ancient, and universally used musical forms of the *Sursum corda* are found in *The Hymnal 1982*,[40] together with a very rich and musically varied collection of *Sanctus* settings, especially that of the Rite II, contemporary, ICET form.[41]

In the Book of Common Prayer Eucharistic prayers, A, B, and D, Memorial Acclamations are offered by celebrant and people and are given musical forms.[42]

Historically, the entire Great Thanksgiving was sung, although only remnants of the historic chant form remain. In an effort to restore this practice *The Hymnal 1982* includes two settings of Eucharistic Prayer C: a chant setting by Howard Galley[43]; and a contemporary setting by Richard Proulx.[44] Full music settings for use with Roman Catholic settings of the Prayer of Thanksgiving are also available.

Before the distribution of the bread and wine, a *Fraction anthem* or *confractorium* (anthem sung during the breaking of the bread) is sung. Added in the seventh century to the Roman rite this is the *Agnus Dei* (Lamb of God). Other Western rites used other texts appropriate to a particular feast or season such as the *Pascha nostrum* ("Christ our Passover"), appropriate to the Fifty days of Easter or other non-penitential occasions. Fraction anthem texts appear with a variety of musical settings.[45]

Early Eucharistic rites ended with a dismissal. In the Roman rite this was *"Ite, missa est,"* "the Mass is ended." As a result of the modern liturgical movement, dismissals have been restored in contemporary forms of the Eucharist of all denominations. Today, however, as the members of the congregation are sent out into the world a more direct command is proclaimed: for example, "Let us go forth in the name of Christ," or "Go in peace to love and serve the Lord." To these directives the people reply, "Thanks be to God." In the season of Easter these versicles and responses may be ended with the exclamation, "Alleluia."[46]

In the Rite I Eucharist of the Episcopal Church, before the dismissal, a blessing is given by the bishop or the priest. In Rite II this is an option. Musical settings of the various forms of blessings are found in the Altar Book and congregational responses to the Episcopal blessing (given by a bishop) are found in *The Hymnal 1982*.[47]

One of the distinguishing characteristics of the service music section of *The Hymnal 1982* is its organization which breaks the traditional, historic pattern in which all the parts of the ordinary by a composer or in a particular style, such as historic chant, were printed as a unit. Now the structure is described as "mix and match," and is based on the principle that musicians should be free to select those settings that are appropriate to the musical skills of their congregations. However, if desired, it is possible to find all the components of the ordinary by one composer or in historic chant.

Resources for the Eucharist in Other Liturgical Churches

The sweep of the liturgical movement through liturgical churches around the world has been so great that no denomination has been left untouched. Because of this, denominations continue to produce rich resources of music to accompany the renewed rites, especially that of the Eucharist. Because this essay is a brief survey, only a limited coverage of the resources of music for Eucharist in the Lutheran and Roman Catholic churches is possible.

The Lutheran Church. The Lutheran Book of Worship includes three settings of Holy Communion. They are "user friendly" in that each is printed with the complete liturgical text and their corresponding musical settings. A 1995 supplement, *With One Voice*,[48] contains three additional settings. *The Book of Worship* includes musical settings suitable for use by a congregation for the *Kyrie;* hymns of praise, the *Gloria in excelsis* in the ICET translation and "This is the feast of victory for our God;" an Alleluia and Lenten verse to be sung before the reading of the Gospel; congregational acclamations for use before and after the reading of the Gospel; an offertory; a setting of the *Sursum corda* (contemporary in settings one and four, and historic chant in settings two and three), and *Sanctus;* the doxology at the end of the Great Thanksgiving; the *Agnus Dei;* and two post-communion canticles, "Thank the Lord and sing his praise," or the *Nunc dimittis;* and the blessing. In the Lutheran rite an entrance hymn or psalm is sung before the "minister greets the congregation."[49] However, the Creed, Lord's prayer and dismissal are said. The use of the Gradual Psalm is not an option in the Lutheran Rite and the musical settings are those mentioned above under "Resources for Use of the Daily Offices in Other Liturgical Churches." An outline is included for a "Chorale Service of Holy Communion" following "the tradition of Luther's German Mass in which parts of the liturgy for Holy Communion are replaced with hymns."[50] Many of the suggested hymns are translations from the Latin ordinary by Martin Luther and others.

Like the Eucharist of the Episcopal Church, *The Lutheran Book of Worship* offers rubrics for optional use: for example, "A Brief Order of

Confession and Forgiveness [to] be used before [the] service"; an ending of the service when there is no Communion including a musical setting of an offertory psalm and rubrics about concluding prayers; two forms of the Great Thanksgiving; and permission to use "Hymns and other music . . . during the ministration of Communion."

The settings in the 1995 supplement, *With One Voice,* offer further choices, including additional forms of the text of the Great Thanksgiving. Settings four and five are complete musical settings, while setting six[51] "follows the model of Martin Luther's Chorale Service and suggests the insertion of service music from a wide variety of sources to be used for the principal musical elements."[52] The suggested hymns are from a wide spectrum of cultural and historic sources. There is also a "Service of Word and Prayer," the *synaxis.*[53]

Another distinctive feature of this supplement is a statement that lists and describes the four major divisions of the liturgy: Gathering, Word, Meal, and Sending. In the three settings of the Holy Communion which follow, bold headings mark these divisions.[54] At numbers 601 to 625 in the supplement are additional settings of service music in a wide variety of styles: historic plainsong and Orthodox chant; settings by contemporary composers; and others coming from a variety of cultures: Ghana, Hispanic, Native American, South African, Caribbean, and Celtic.[55]

The Roman Catholic Church. Although there is no official hymnal of the Roman Catholic Church in the United States, composers and publishers have been unbelievably prolific in making available for their people vast resources of music for Eucharist. We will limit our review to the three resources mentioned above in the section, "Resources for Use of the Daily Offices in Other Liturgical Churches."

Worship: Third Edition, also published in Singers and Accompaniment editions, contains a separate section headed "Mass."[56] This contains The Order of Mass with settings from several different sources: historic chant, adaptations of music from an earlier time, and works by contemporary composers; three additional musical settings, Setting One, "A Community Mass" by Richard Proulx, Setting Two, "Mass of the Bells" by Alexander Peloquin, and Setting Three, "New Plainsong," by David Hurd (also found in *The Hymnal 1982*); additional musical settings of service music; and *Cantus Missae,* the Mass in Latin with historic chant settings. With this publication, as with *The Hymnal 1982,* it is therefore possible to sing a setting of the ordinary by one composer, or to select a variety of settings suitable to the needs of a particular congregation. Settings are also available for the Mass at a marriage and for a funeral. Among its many other resources

Worship: Third Edition, contains psalm responses for a variety of rites; and a section entitled Lectionary includes the readings for the three-year Eucharistic lectionary and other feasts of the Church with congregational responses for the proper psalms.

Hymns, Psalms and Spiritual Canticles is an equally rich resource. It contains orders for the Mass in English and Latin. The Masses in English use historic chant melodies as well as contemporary settings for the Creed, the Prayers of the Faithful, the Eucharistic Prayer including the *Sanctus,* Memorial Acclamations, The Lord's Prayer, the *Agnus Dei,* the blessing, and the dismissal. The formula for singing the Gospel uses historic chant. Settings of the ordinary by Theodore Marier and others are also included. The Latin Mass uses historic chant and contemporary settings of parts of the ordinary for use by the congregation and choir. Gospel acclamations with proper psalm verses set to plainsong psalm tones for each of the three years of the lectionary and Alleluias with suggestions for suitable sentences of scriptures are also included.

After a large section of hymns in *Hymns, Psalms and Spiritual Canticles* appear settings of responsorial psalms and three other scriptural texts with antiphons.

With the exception of settings of the Mass ordinary—*Gloria in excelsis, Credo, Sanctus, Pater Noster,* and *Agnus Dei*—all the texts in *The Catholic Liturgy Book* are in English. The collection includes seasonal acclamations, alleluias, memorial acclamations, the Great Amen, greetings, sacramentaries, *Kyrie eleison* (Greek and English), *Gloria in excelsis,* the creed, the *Sursum corda, Sanctus,* the Lord's Prayer, *Agnus Dei,* blessings and a dismissal. An Appendix includes chants and acclamations for the Mass on special occasions such as Ash Wednesday, Holy Week, and the funeral Mass. The musical settings of the Latin portions of the ordinary use historic chant melodies, while the remainder are essentially settings by contemporary composers.

Notes

1. For further information see Raymond F. Glover, ed., *The Hymnal 1982 Companion,* vol. 2: *Service Music and Biographies* (New York: Church Hymnal Corporation, 1994).

2. Anglican chant: S 289, Rite I and S 293, Rite II. Plainsong: S 290–S 292, Rite I and S 294, Rite II.

3. Accompaniment Edition of *The Hymnal: Service Music,* S 408–S 416.

4. *The Plainsong Psalter* (New York: Church Hymnal Corporation, 1988), and *The Anglican Chant Psalter* (New York: Church Hymnal Corporation, 1987).

Texts for use with the psalms are found in *The Office Book,* ed. Howard Galley (New York: Seabury 1980).

5. *The Book of Common Prayer,* 144–45.

6. In the following listings, where two translations are given, the first will be
a traditional translation and the second, a contemporary translation. Of the
canticles in current Prayer Book use, five are continued from pre-reformation
monastic use: *Te Deum laudamus, Benedicite omnia opera* (A Song of Creation, "O all ye works of the Lord, bless ye the Lord" or "Glorify the Lord, all
you works of the Lord"), *Benedictus Dominus Deus* (The Song of Zechariah,
"Blessed be the Lord God of Israel," or "Blessed [blest] be the Lord, the God
of Israel"), *Magnificat* (The Song of Mary, "My soul doth magnify the Lord,"
and "My soul proclaims the glory of the Lord"), and *Nunc dimittis* (The Song
of Simeon, "Lord, now lettest thou thy servant depart in peace" and "Lord,
you have fulfilled your word"). The Book of Common Prayer, 1549, assigned
three of these canticles at Morning Prayer; *Te Deum laudamus,* which during
Lent was replaced by the *Benedicite omnia opera;* and the *Benedictus Dominus Deus,* and two at Evening Prayer, *Magnificat* and *Nunc dimittis.* Over the
centuries of Prayer Book revision the number of canticles and their place in
the offices has changed. The present Prayer Book of the Episcopal Church
authorizes twenty-one texts: 1–7, traditional Prayer Book texts with translations from the Great Bible of Miles Coverdale (1488–1569), repeated among
those at 12–21 with contemporary translations. The texts of numbers 8–11,
and 14, 18, and 19 are new to the Book of Common Prayer. They include: The
Song of Moses, *Cantemus Domino,* "I will sing unto the Lord"; The First Song
of Isaiah, *Ecce Deus,* "Surely it is God who saves me"; The Second Song of Isaiah, *Quaerite Dominum,* "Seek the Lord while he wills to be found"; The Third
Song of Isaiah, *Surge, illuminare,* "Arise, shine, for your light has come"; A Song
of Penitence, *Kyrie Pantokrator,* "O Lord and Ruler of the Hosts of heaven";
A Song to the Lamb, *Dignus es,* "Splendor and honor and kingly power"; and
The Song of the Redeemed, *Magna et mirabilia,* "O ruler of the universe, Lord
God."

7. *The Book of Common Prayer,* 47, 65, 84, and 119.

8. See additional directions, *The Book of Common Prayer,* 141, where permission is given for the use of metrical forms of the psalms and canticles as
alternatives to the prose versions.

9. To facilitate the use of metrical forms of psalms and Canticles, the Accompaniment Edition of *The Hymnal: Service Music,* vol. 1:679–81, contains
two practical resources, "Metrical Psalms and Hymns based on Psalms," and
"Hymns based on Canticles and other Liturgical Texts."

10. For directions on singing collects, see the Accompaniment Edition of
The Hymnal: Service Music, S 447 and S 448.

11. First published in *The Choral Service* (New York: H. W. Gray, 1927).

12. *The Hymnal 1982,* S 24, S 25, S 31, S 32, S 54, S 55, S 65, and S 66.

13. *The Book of Common Prayer,* 103–7.

14. The Appendix of the Accompaniment Edition of *The Hymnal: Service
Music,* S 296–S 304, contains settings for all the sung texts of the Office set to
traditional plainsong melodies adapted from settings used in *Compline.*

15. Ibid., S 305–S 320. Prayer Book rubrics give several choices for concluding the service; *The Book of Common Prayer,* 112.

16. The Appendix of the Accompaniment Edition of *The Hymnal: Service Music,* S 321–S 337.

17. See chapters 19 and 20.

18. *The Hymnal 1982,* Nos. 54–55.

19. *The Lutheran Book of Worship* (Minneapolis: Augsburg, 1978) 13–53.

20. Ibid., 215–91.

21. Recent examples include: *Worship: Third Edition* (Chicago: GIA, 1986), *Hymns, Psalms and Spiritual Canticles* (Boston: Archdiocesan Choir School Publishing, 1983) and *The Catholic Liturgy Book* (Baltimore: Helicon, 1975).

22. See the discussions of the Psalter above and Gradual Psalms below for sources of musical settings of psalms used as introits.

23. Opening Acclamations, S 76–S 83; Greek *Kyrie,* appropriate for both rites, S 84–S 89, and in the Appendix, S 356–S 359; English *Kyrie,* Rite I, S 90–S 93, and Rite II, S 94–S 98; *Gloria in excelsis,* S 201–S 204, S 272–S 281; and the *Trisagion,* S 98–S 102, and S 360 in the Appendix.

24. S 355 in the Appendix of the Accompaniment Edition of *The Hymnal 1982.*

25. *The Book of Common Prayer,* Rite I, 316–21; Rite II, 351–53.

26. Ibid., 321.

27. *The Holy Eucharist: Altar Edition* (New York: Church Hymnal Corporation, 1977) 221–25.

28. They include: *Gradual Psalms, Alleluia Verses and Tracts,* Parts I–VI (New York: Church Hymnal Corporation, 1980–89; James Barrett, *The Psalmnary: Gradual Psalms for Cantor and Congregation* (Missoula, MT: The Hymnary Press, 1986); Betty Pulkingham, *Celebrate the Church Year with Psalms and Canticles* (Pacific, Mo.: Cathedral Music Press, 1988); Betty Pulkingham and Kevin Hackett, *The Celebration Psalter,* 3 vols. (Pacific, Mo.: Cathedral Music Press, 1992); *The Psalter-Psalms & Canticles for Singing* (Louisville: Westminster/Knox, 1993); and various collections by Joseph Gelineau: *24 Psalms and a Canticle* (Chicago: GIA, 1958), *30 Psalms and Two Canticles* (Chicago: GIA, 1962), *20 Psalms and Three Canticles* (Chicago: GIA, 1967), *Forty-one Grail/Gelineau Psalms, 1993 Revised Grail Psalter* (Chicago: GIA, 1995).

29. Keith A. Falconer, "The Development of Plainchant to the Counter Reformation," in *The Hymnal 1982 Companion,* ed. Raymond F. Glover (New York: Church Hymnal Corporation, 1990–94) 1:167.

30. Some of these, such as *Victime paschali* and *Lauda Sion,* can be found in *The Hymnal 1982;* see Nos. 183 and 320.

31. *The Book of Common Prayer,* 326–377 and 358.

32. The traditional form of the Creed in historic chant, S 103; contemporary forms set to chant, S 104 and in the Appendix S 361; a contemporary musical setting is S 105.

33. S 106–S 109, Appendix, S 362–S 363.

34. Musical settings are found in *The Hymnal* at S 110 and S 111.

35. *The Book of Common Prayer,* 333, 361.

36. Ibid., 343–44, 376.

37. See the Canticle Use Chart, Appendix, S 355.

38. See *The Book of Common Prayer,* 344–49 and 377–82.

39. For a more detailed description of eucharistic prayers, particularly that portion which follows the *Sanctus,* see *The Hymnal 1982 Companion,* 2:83–87.

40. S 112 (Rite I) and S 120 (Rite II).

41. S 113–S 117 (Rite I), S 121–S 131, and Appendix S 364 and S 365 (Rite II).

42. S 132–S 142. The doxology that ends the Eucharist, The Great Amen and the Lord's Prayer are set to traditional chant, S 118 and S 119 (Rite I), S 142, 143, and S 148 (Rite II). Additional settings of the Great Amen are S 144–S 147, and settings of the contemporary, ICET translation of the Lord's Prayer are S 149 and S 150.

43. Appendix S 369, intended for use with the setting of the *Sanctus,* S 125.

44. Appendix 370, intended for use with his setting of the *Sanctus,* S 125.

45. "Christ our passover," S 154–S 156; *Agnus dei,* Rite I (O Lamb of God), S 157–S 159; Rite II (Lamb of God), S 160–S 163, Appendix, S 373 and S 374; (Jesus, Lamb of God), S 164–S 166; and other texts, S 169–S 172.

46. Musical settings of dismissals are S 174–S 176.

47. See *The Holy Eucharist: Altar Edition,* 232–33; *The Hymnal 1982,* S 173.

48. *With One Voice* (Minneapolis: Augsburg Fortress, 1995).

49. *Lutheran Book of Worship,* 57.

50. Ibid., 120.

51. *With One Voice,* 42–45.

52. Ibid., Introduction, 4.

53. Ibid., 46–53.

54. A similar use of headings is found in *The Book of Common Prayer* of the Episcopal Church.

55. Both the *Lutheran Book of Worship* and its supplement, *With One Voice,* are published in Pew and Accompaniment Editions. Supportive publications for the worship of the Lutheran Church include Philip H. Pfatteicher and Carlos R. Messerli, *Manual on the Liturgy, Lutheran Book of Worship* (Minneapolis: Augsburg, 1979), and *Lutheran Book of Worship, Minister's Desk Edition* (Minneapolis: Augsburg, 1979).

56. *Worship: Third Edition,* 229–340.

Chapter 16

Liturgical Music as Liturgy

William T. Flynn

Rembert Weakland, the Roman Catholic Archbishop of Milwaukee and an accomplished musician, was once asked, "How should one go about becoming a church musician?" His answer, which many church musicians will instinctively applaud, was this: "First, you must become a musician." It is obvious that Weakland's concern was with assuring a certain standard of musical competency. Although such a concern is of great importance, focusing on it might obscure another important and methodologically prior issue: namely, what is the purpose or goal that liturgical music serves that ought to influence the standards we apply both in judging specific musical creations and in determining what constitutes musical competency.

The principal reason that it is difficult to address questions about music in the church is that there is little cultural consensus on the purpose or goal of music-making. Nevertheless, most of the competing viewpoints state the purpose of music in one of two ways. The first of these is the claim that music is created primarily to support social practices. For example, most music-making in the United States might be explained as serving the goal of providing entertainment, and it is often the case that parishioners arrive at their preferences in church music based on this viewpoint. The second (often taken by professional musicians) contends that the goal of music-making is simply to produce the music, arguing that only by being itself can an art express what it has to say.

Both of these characterizations of the purpose of music have been supported by an impressive array of philosophical arguments,[1] but each of them requires considerable modification to be of use in articulating a theology of liturgical music. The reason for this is that liturgical music is part of enacted worship—that is, part of the praise of God as it is brought to expression in worship and as it extends into Christian living—thus, as a part of Christian life, music-making has the primary goal of doxology. Since this goal is made possible through Christ, and is appropriated, lived out, and witnessed to by the Church in the power of the Holy Spirit, the context of worship should define what musical competency means for the Church.

The basic notion of liturgical music as doxology can retain what is valuable in the two (secular) ideas of the goals of music referred to above, since each of them identifies an important function of music that is not necessarily in conflict with God's purposes for humanity, but which may actually help support the doxological direction of the Church's life. The idea that music serves social practices is not incompatible with liturgical music, since all of the social practices of the Church also have doxology as a goal. For this reason, the specific ways that music interacts with the other features of worship can help clarify and demonstrate ways for the Church to evaluate and express its corporate belief. Most often, it is when music comes into some kind of tension with other elements of worship that questions concerning its purpose arise. To demonstrate this, the first section of this chapter investigates relationships of our words and music to the Word of God. The idea that it is the music itself that is of primary importance is also not incompatible with liturgical music. Music which has been judged to be efficacious (that is, that the Church has evaluated and found to be fulfilling its goal of doxology) can feed theological reflection, because through it God's Word has become present to us. As an example of this, some of the ways in which liturgical music has been considered an image of the corporate and communal nature of the Church are explored in the second half of this chapter. Such imagery shows how our understanding of our relationships to God and to one another can be brought into focus and interpreted through music.

I. The Word of God, Our Words, and Music

Theologically speaking, one could contend that music is both more than and less than the word. Music is less than the word, in that the *logos* of God incarnate as Jesus Christ is witnessed to in the words of Scripture, which are normative for all subsequent witness. Music may be more than the word, in that Scripture must be proclaimed, that is, it must be effectively delivered. In so far as words are used in a rhetorically effective way, they acquire a certain musicality, and as this musicality is heightened into musical utterance the power of the delivery can be increased. Although we now tend to think of music as a relatively independent art form, the early Church correctly emphasized the closeness between music and words. Even when there is no pitched music, words may exhibit musical features such as structured timbre through alliteration, assonance, and rhyme, and structured rhythm through accent and meter. Furthermore, words in languages unfamiliar to the worshiper (like *Alleluia,* or *Amen*) are valued principally because of their musical features.[2] Writers in the patristic period were so aware of these features of spoken words that it was difficult for them to make a sharp distinction between music and rhetoric. For example, Augustine's six books *On Music* never discuss pitch, but instead examine the rhythms and meters inherent in the natural flow of spoken Latin.[3] These musical forms of ornamentation were not only acknowledged as a feature of the language, but were also valued as aids to the powers of concentration, attention and memory. Without such aids, the power of words to communicate anything was thought to be severely restricted.

Since music was considered an inherent feature of words, patristic authors like Augustine located tensions between music and words by examining the ways that any musical ornamentation might help or hinder one's understanding and appropriating the words' meaning. Augustine, in analyzing music's rhetorical functions in the liturgy, concluded that their mutual compatibility depends on factors relating to the complexity of the melody and its rhetorical interaction with the words, as well as upon the listener's subjective reactions to both the words and the music.[4] To the extent that the music supported the words, it was judged effective; to the extent that it drew attention to itself (or even to the extent that some might sin by paying more attention to it than to the words of Scripture), it could be judged detrimental. It is important to note, however, that Augustine was analyzing the musical items of a fifth-century liturgy, which consisted primarily of settings of portions of the psalms which were chosen for their typological reference to Christ. Not only was music restricted to scriptural texts, but the texts themselves were clearly identified by Augustine's community as related to the Word of God. For this reason, their understanding the meaning of the texts would help them to keep the doxological direction of worship clear. Even though Augustine acknowledged that his own church's musical style could detract from a listener's understanding of the words, he decided that melodic singing ought to be retained because such dangers were outweighed by the benefits of the music in helping the congregation to appropriate the words.

A different level of tension is inherent in hymns, which balance structured words with structured music. The text of a hymn is already complicated by the musical elements of its poetic structure, and therefore its structure increases the potential for distracting from the text's meaning.[5] Furthermore, even if a hymn is directly based on Scripture, the words need to be substantially reworked to fit the rhythmic and metrical schemes of a language different from the original. Indications of the tensions between the text and its own musical features as well as between the text and tune can be seen in the constant revision of hymn-texts and discussions of the objective musical requirements of hymn-tunes. Most discussions of hymn texts tend to center around the need to have clear correspondence to the Word of God as Scripture, and most discussions of hymn tunes tend to center on the need to help the congregation to proclaim the Word effectively. Implicit in such discussions is the idea that a good hymn should achieve a balance of words and music that is experienced within a community as a clear proclamation of the truths of Scripture. In short, a hymn has the same theological requirements as a good sermon, but achieves its rhetorical goals through 'musical' text combined with music that proclaims that text effectively.

On Augustine's terms, wordless music would seem to pose an even greater problem than texted music, since its relationship to the Word of God is necessarily more remote. Although there are no clear references to the use of wordless music in the liturgy during the first five centuries, Augustine was able to interpret one type of "pure" music (jubilation) as praise of God. In his commentary on Psalm 33:3,[6] he spoke favorably of a type of wordless song sung by the workers in the harvest and by others who engage in arduous occupations, saying that this *jubilus* is something which signifies that the heart labors with a joy it cannot utter. "And whom does jubilation befit but the ineffable God?"[7] This issue was practically encountered in the liturgy only as instruments were (very) gradually accepted into worship in the West. In the history of Western liturgy, three prominent functions of instruments have evolved. First, in their accompanimental function, instruments have occasionally heightened the possible tensions between music and words: since music takes on a more sophisticated structure when instruments are used, it can more readily draw attention to itself. Nevertheless, the words can still indicate the goal of the music. Second, even in their solo function instruments tend to be tied to words, either by substituting for choir or congregation on the alternate verses of a hymn (historically in the Mass ordinary with the instrumental music being directly based on the chant which would have carried the words), or by being associated with a well-known tune and text, as in the Protestant chorale or hymn prelude. Even though the text is not sung, it is supposed to be the common property of the worshipers who are expected to associate it with the instrumental music. Third, free instrumental pieces (those not associated with specific words) can be tied to important liturgical actions, such as processions or the elevation of the elements. The total context of the worship service may be seen to provide the necessary reference to doxology. Practically, instruments may be seen as a useful extension of human capabilities given in creation, and may be seen as an example of humanity bringing some portion of God's creation into a correct (doxological) relationship with God.

As the tensions between our words and music and the Word of God are addressed and resolved in the liturgy, the practices of the Church are constantly shaped in the direction of doxology. Often as the shaping of the liturgy fits them to their goal, the resulting forms achieve a relative stability and are recognized as particularly suitable. For this reason, the musical repertory of the church can become an important means of transmitting the faith and a source of theological reflection.

II. Music as an Icon of Worship

From the discussion above, it can be seen that both human words and human music play a role in expressing and thus representing the Word of God made known and offered to us through Christ. To the extent that music is able to represent the Word, it must function as some kind of mediation of Christ, because whatever music presents to us is only made present through the music. This means that there is an important truth in the professional musician's notion that the proper goal of music is the music itself.

However, this poses a theological problem: how can forms of human communication represent or be expressive of God, and how do such representations relate to our fundamental experience of God in Christ? It is possible to argue that "pure" music (by its reconciling contrasts such as tension and release, motion and stasis, and preparation and fulfillment) presents a human notion of salvation which is in some way analogous to Christ's salvation (in which we are reconciled with God).[8] But, such an analogy of salvation tends (in the end) to emphasize the distinction between God and humanity rather than their relationship precisely because analogies are *human* creations. We might better understand God's relationship to forms of human communication if we understand God's relationship to humanity to have a Trinitarian pattern.[9] If any human communication can represent or be expressive of God, God the Father must graciously create the very possibility of our expressing his salvation through Christ. In the Holy Spirit we can recognize the truth of the scriptural account of God's coming to us. Likewise, in the Holy Spirit, we may also be able to represent this truth through our forms of communication. In this way we can understand God as active even in our making of analogies, and therefore as present to us through our human forms of communication. Such a view places music on the same level as human words, and therefore, in exactly the same relationship to the Word of God as preaching and prayer, but not on the same level as Scripture.

In this view Scripture is foundational in three ways, two of which are unique and the third which is shared with other forms of human communication: first, as the best *historical* witness to God's coming as a particular human being at a particular time and place; second, as language that has been canonized (found indispensable) by the Church; third, as communication about God that has been and continues to be especially efficacious. At this third (sacramental) level, other human words about God are regularly admitted into worship, where a less formal process of judgment decides for or against their efficacy. Although such communication about God is not "canonical" (being open to change, revision, and restatement), it is "sacramental" to the extent that God is present through it. At this same level, music about God is potentially as efficacious and potentially as fallible as speech about God, and is open to the same process of testing in worship: it never becomes "canonical" but it may be such a useful sign that it remains in the repertory indefinitely.

This means that music ought to be tested for its conformity to God's salvation within the worship of the Church, which is worship in the Holy Spirit. Music which has passed this test is rightly honored, since through it, God's salvation has been proclaimed. This means that the musical tradition of a Church has an essential part to play in forming and keeping alive a Church's memory of its true response to God. Thus, the musical tradition of a Church can serve as an image of the worship of the Church itself, feeding back into theological reflection, and helping us to understand what we celebrate.

One of the most prominent images of worship developed in Christian tradition depends on two musical metaphors: musical harmony and unison singing. Both of these are related to the idea of worship as constitutive of a community which is in communion with God. Although our conceptions of what constitutes "harmony" in music have changed along with changes in musical style, most styles have achieved a balance between their various elements which can serve as an image of a unity which encompasses all diversities. Furthermore, this balance of various elements constitutes an agreement that enables the music as a whole to be directed to the same goal: praise of God. This direction of thought is implicit in the New Testament and was extensively developed during the patristic period. In Romans 15:5-6, Paul prays that "the God of patience and encouragement grant that you live in harmony with each other, in accord with Christ Jesus, so that together with one mouth you may glorify the God and Father of our Lord Jesus Christ."[10] Clement of Alexandria gave an even stronger Christological focus to this image of Christian community by developing the musical metaphor explicitly. For Clement, the Church is in complete *symphonia* (agreement or harmony) because it is led by Jesus: "The union of many, which the divine harmony has called forth out of a medley of sounds and division, becomes one symphony, following the one leader of the choir and teacher, the Word, resting in that same truth and crying out: 'Abba, Father.'"[11] Origen linked the idea of concord in Matthew 18:19-20 with the promise of Christ's presence to those who assemble in his name, contending that the harmony of those so assembled "makes room for the Son of God to be present."[12] Ambrose combined the insights of these interpretations in his commentary on the parable of the prodigal son: in Luke 15:25, the word *symphonia* (music) is used to describe the celebration ordered by the father upon the son's return. According to Ambrose, this "merry-making" fittingly included music, which points to the harmony restored between the father and the son. Furthermore, Ambrose gave an example of what this harmony is like by referring to the music in his own church: "For this is a symphony, when there resounds in the church a united concord of differing ages and abilities as if of diverse strings; the psalm is responded to, the Amen is said."[13] The unison singing by the whole congregation at these points in the service was, for Ambrose, an image of the unity between God and humanity established through Christ. Johannes Quasten, in his book *Music and Worship in Pagan and Christian Antiquity,* makes an important point concerning the nature of the unity described by patristic authors:[14] the community represented by singing was not only an image of earthly community, but was also a participation of the earthly community in heavenly worship, and therefore in the life of God. Quasten notes that patristic commentators would often prove this by referring to the preface to the Eucharistic Prayer where the congregation is invited to join in the singing of the Sanctus with all the angels, archangels, cherubim, and seraphim.[15]

Perhaps unison congregational singing is one of the most compelling images of musical community available to the Church, as the passages cited above suggest. This is because, as Ambrose pointed out, such singing unites all ages and abilities. However, one should also note that this does not prohibit the exercise of a more specialized musical ministry. For example, both of the items mentioned by Ambrose are responses (the first is a response to the psalm and the second a response to prayer) and the person to whom the congregation responded exercised a specialized musical ministry. (In Ambrose's example, the cantor sang the verses of the psalm in a melodious and elaborate style to which the congregation would respond with a refrain).[16] It is also possible for the congregation to respond appropriately to music without making its own musical response; just as a sermon does not require a functional response in words, a motet or cantata does not require a functional response in song. The congregation appropriately responds by paying attention to the sermon's or the music's message. If the congregation is participating largely by listening, the people must be able to understand both the musical style and the music's function in the rite. For example, in the medieval Church, the congregation typically made only the most rudimentary musical responses (amens, greetings, some litanies), while most of the music was sung by clergy or choir. However, the music was still considered to be one of the principal ways that the whole of the Church was united, since it was commonly interpreted as being expressive of heavenly joy.[17] On the other hand, if a congregation's functional role in the service (in both words and music) diminishes too radically, it becomes more difficult for the participants to think of musical harmony as a unity that embraces all gifts and abilities. By the sixteenth century, it is clear that neither the Reformers nor the Roman Catholic Church hierarchy thought that the music was functioning completely successfully. Luther and Calvin tried to restore an important place for congregational song, while the Council of Trent adopted the Anglican and Lutheran position that chorally sung words should be intelligible (and therefore available to those listening to the music). Both the perception of a problem with the music of the Church and the goal of ensuring a properly corporate response to the music was common to both groups. It seems clear that although the ways that music expresses the unity in Christ vary as musical styles and liturgies vary, the goals and evaluation of liturgical music remain fairly stable. Thus, music ought to enable the Church to respond to the Word of God with one voice. Furthermore, this enabling can also take place by enhancing congregational responses with musical elaboration which is beyond the musical capability of the ordinary individual. In addition, there ought to be some place for music in which the congregation participates through active listening and meditation.

When the corporate nature of faith is meant to be most clearly expressed, congregational song is in order. When the congregation is meant to respond, solo or choral singing which invokes that response is in order. When the focus is upon reflecting or meditating upon the mysteries of the faith, a more 'professional' and perhaps even complex music is appropriate.[18]

The last of these points explains why the tension between offering the most accomplished and complex music that we can achieve and fulfilling other requirements of the liturgy is felt so strongly by church musicians who tend to conceive of music-making as their liturgical vocation. Church musicians might justly consider that even their most sophisticated technical accomplishments serve the worship service. J. S. Bach, for instance, seems to have considered his most complex and abstruse music to have been really his most religious.[19] This was because he was able to believe that the prayer with which he started most of his compositions ("Jesus, help!") had been answered in its working out, and he was able to believe that the prayer with which he ended his compositions (that the music be directed solely to the glory of God) might also be answered in the liturgy. If music is to serve as an image of heavenly worship, there is a natural tendency on the part of composers to attempt to create the most glorious music conceivable. There is also a duty to re-create such music as competently as possible if it is used in worship. Although it would be inappropriate to give this kind of music a dominant place in the liturgy (since it would tend to substitute for properly corporate response), it is still important to find a proper place for the best that musicians have to offer.

This brings us back to our opening concern: how do we decide upon standards of musical competency? First, it cannot be emphasized too much that it is only through use in worship that music and musicianship can be tested for its efficacy. Therefore the principal locus for developing our ideas of musical competence ought to be the church service itself. This does not mean that the Church cannot serve, and be served by, people who are formed by very different ideas about musical competency. The practical experience of providing music for worship can reorient and shape both musicians and music. Our various experiences of praising God in song provide a context that enables us to respond to, and to test, different forms and fit them for worship. This means that the Church itself must arrive at its standards through the testing of music and musicianship in the liturgy. Lively discussion about music in a church is a sign that such testing is going on. Second, the Church ought to take the responsibility to ensure that the musical and ministerial skills which have proved themselves beneficial to the liturgy are passed on to those who wish to fulfill their musical vocation in the Church. The teaching of the history of liturgical music is an essential part of this task, for the intersection between music and ministry is part of that history. Third, the Church ought to examine all of those whom it entrusts with its liturgical ministry and require them to develop the musical, theological, and ministerial skills that the liturgy demands. This means that the Church has an interest and a duty in training all liturgical ministers: a basic understanding of music is essential for those in sacramental or preaching ministries, and a basic theological education is essential for those in musical ministries. Finally, the Church needs to respond to music theologically: the most important judgment about a music's efficacy is whether God has graciously been present through it. Such a judgment is never easy, since the Holy Spirit is present to the Church *kenotically,* through the same self-emptying that enabled the Son to be present to the world. However, it is the experience of the Church that such a presence has been known and continues to be known through music in worship, and it is the duty of the Church to claim and celebrate whenever we find *God with us.*

Notes

Note: References to patristic texts are given according to J. P. Migne's editions: *Patrologiae cursus completus, series latina, (PL),* 221 vols. (Paris: Migne, 1844–64) and *Patrologiae cursus completus, series greca, (PG),* 162 vols. (Paris: Migne, 1857–66), followed by a reference to an English translation. Most of the translations are found in the excellent edition of James McKinnon, *Music in Early Christian Literature* (Cambridge: Cambridge University Press, 1987).

1. For an interesting summary of some of these arguments, see Edward Foley, *Music in Ritual: A Pre-Theological Investigation* (Washington, D.C.: Pastoral Press, 1984). The most important debate missing from Foley's summary is that between Walter Benjamin and T. W. Adorno; see especially, Benjamin's essay, "The Work of Art in the Age of Mechanical Reproduction," *Illuminations* (New York: Schocken, 1985) 217–51, and Adorno's *Aesthetic Theory* (New York: Methuen, 1986). The most interesting sociological account of contemporary music-making can be found in Pierre Bordieu's *Distinction: A Social Critique of the Judgment of Taste* (Cambridge: Harvard University Press, 1984).

2. Joseph Gelineau makes the point that words used as liturgical acclamations, such as *Alleluia, Maranatha, Kyrie eleison,* and *Amen,* tend not to be translated; see his "Music and Singing in the Liturgy," *The Study of Liturgy,* eds. Cheslyn Jones, Geoffrey Wainwright, and Edward Yarnold (New York: Oxford University Press, 1978) 449–54.

3. Augustine, *De Musica, PL* 32:1081–1194; trans. R. C. Taliaferro, *The Fathers of the Church, a New Translation: Writings of Saint Augustine*, vol. 2 (New York: Cima, 1947) 153–379.

4. Augustine's most sophisticated examination of liturgical music can be found in *Confessions* X, 33; *PL* 32:799–800; McKinnon, 154 (no. 352).

5. Note, for example, how the rhythm, meter, and rhyme make the syntax of Psalm 23 much less clear than the prose model: "The Lord is my shepherd; I shall not want. He maketh me to lie down in green pastures: he leadeth me beside the still waters" (King James Bible) compared with, "The Lord's my shepherd, I'll not want; I He makes me down to lie I In pastures green; He leadeth me I The quiet waters by" (Scottish Psalter, 1650).

6. Augustine, *In Psalmum* 32; *PL* 36:283; McKinnon, 156–57 (no. 356).

7. Although many musicologists have identified such descriptions with the *Alleluia* in the Roman liturgy, there is no evidence of this being the case. Furthermore, the *Alleluia* can hardly be considered to be textless. If one could establish a connection between a reference to the *jubilus* and the practice of glossolalia, one might be able to argue that such discussions could describe liturgical practices; however, up to now, no one has been able to do this.

8. Sociologists have suggested that ritual expresses and forms a group identity by mediating between the structures supportive of, or destructive of, human community. The most notable of these "structures" is the tension between life and death. This argument has been carefully related to the sacraments by George Worgul, Jr. in *From Magic to Metaphor* (New York: Paulist Press, 1980). Such accounts, however, generally have the problems with analogy outlined in the main text of this chapter. (Incidentally, Western music has developed an impressive array of techniques which could help create analogies of structural tensions, the most impressive of which is, perhaps, functional tonality.)

9. For an account of the problems with *analogia entis* (analogy of being) see Eberhard Jüngel, *God as Mystery of the World* (Grand Rapids: Eerdmans, 1983) 261–309. Jüngel essentially holds a "sacramental" view of language, although he rejects the classical terminology as bound up in the problems of the *analogia entis*. The rest of my paragraph (above) develops his discussion of *analogia fidei* (analogy of faith) as applied to music, avoiding the problems inherent in discussing music as symbol (see for instance, Foley, *Music in Ritual*, referred to in note 1 above for a summary of the problems).

10. McKinnon, 14 (no. 7). It is uncertain whether Paul was referring to singing in this passage, but later commentators developed the musical parallels.

11. Clement of Alexandria, *Protrepticus*, 9. Both the Greek and an English translation appear in Johannes Quasten, *Music and Worship in Christian and Pagan Antiquity* (Washington, D.C.: Pastoral Press, 1983) 67 and 102.

12. Origen, *Commentary on the Gospel of Matthew* 16:1; *PG* 13:1181–88; McKinnon, 39–40 (no. 70).

13. Ambrose, *Expositio evangelii secundum Lucam*, 7:238; *PL* 15:1763; McKinnon, 129 (no. 284).

14. Quasten, *Music and Worship*, 66–72.

15. For example, see Cyril (or John?) of Jerusalem, *Mystagogical Catechesis*, 5:6; *PG* 33:1113; McKinnon, 76 (no. 157). Note that Cyril conflates Isaiah's vision (Isa. 6:3) with John's vision (Rev. 4:8ff.) by specifically attributing Isaiah's vision to the power of the Holy Spirit (cf. Rev. 4:2). Isaiah's vision of God is given a Christological turn in the Revelation account, since the Lamb is the recipient of the song.

16. Ambrose, *De interpretatione Job et David*, 4:6, 23–24; *PL* 14:821; McKinnon, 129 (no. 284). Ambrose is the first Western author to use a technical term related to the minor ministerial order which we now call cantor. (Presumably this office was new to the West, since Ambrose uses the Greek term *psaltes*). A good discussion of the musical style (new to Western churches) can be found in James McKinnon's "The Fourth-Century Origin of the Gradual," *Early Music History* 7 (1987) 91–106; see also, Edward Foley, "The Cantor in Historical Perspective," *Worship* 56 (1982) 194–213, especially 202–3. The office of cantor probably originated as a lay ministry, in which individual members of a congregation would offer a hymn, a lesson, a tongue or an interpretation (cf. 1 Cor. 14:26). Since there is no clear indication in any of Paul's letters that the congregation did any unison singing, the individual offerings encouraged by Paul would have depended entirely on the relative musical sophistication of the person who was singing. Paul's letter emphasizes that all of these offerings are for the building up of the Church, and it is clear that already in New Testament times certain practices (uninterpreted tongues, for example) were considered detrimental to such edification.

17. The following quote from the eleventh-century liturgical commentary of John of Avranches, *De officiis ecclesiasticis* (*PL*, 147:35) is typical:

> At feasts, the cantor gives the water covered with a linen cloth to the deacon, which the deacon mixes with wine: for by the sweet music *[modulatione]* of the cantor, the people are inflamed with pious devotion and divine love, and thus run to the Lord, and one body in Christ is made. By the wine, Christ [is expressed]; by the water, the people; by the linen covering the water, the labor of singing *[modulationis]* of the cantors, through which the people are freed from their private thoughts: for by weaving labor is expressed. The water mixed with wine [signifies] the people joined with Christ; the wine without the water is Christ, the water without the wine, the people without Christ.

18. The most complete and helpful guidelines relating to the role of the choir in worship have been developed by the U.S. Roman Catholic Bishops' Committee on the Liturgy. These can be found in two documents: "Music in Catholic Worship," 1972 and "Liturgical Music Today," 1983. Both are available in *The Liturgy Documents*, 3rd ed., ed. Mary Ann Simcoe (Chicago: Liturgy Training Publications, 1991). Although directed to the Roman Catholic liturgy, these guidelines have many scriptural, liturgical, theological, and cultural insights which are adaptable for other liturgies.

19. See, for instance, the discussion of Bach's *Clavierübung III* by Peter Williams in *The Organ Music of J.S. Bach,* vol. 2 (Cambridge: Cambridge University Press, 1980) 175–225; Günther Stiller, *J.S. Bach and Liturgical Life in Leipzig* (St. Louis: Concordia, 1984) 254; and Robin A. Leaver, "Bach's 'Clavierübung III': Some Historical and Theological Considerations," *The Organ Yearbook* 6 (1975) 17–32.

Chapter 17

Liturgical Music as Prayer

Kathleen Harmon, S.N.D. de N.

All the elements of liturgy, tangible and intangible, share one over-riding function: to help us to pray, and specifically to pray as the community who has come together to enact the mystery of Christ's life, death, and resurrection. This statement says a great deal about the nature of liturgy as prayer, as communal, and as paschal mystery-oriented. It also says something significant about the elements of liturgy, that their purpose is to support prayer that is communal and that is focused on the Paschal Mystery.

The purpose of this chapter is to examine the role of music in relation to this function *vis-à-vis* liturgical prayer. I must begin, however, with a prior question, the answer to which lies at the heart of our vocation as liturgical musicians. In our ministry are we dealing with liturgical music *and* prayer, or with liturgical music *as* prayer?

Is liturgical music prayer? We all know that it can be, that there are times in the course of worship when the singing of the community envelops us with awareness of the presence of God, or the music of an instrument touches us with paradoxical feelings of humility and awe, or the silence of the assembly is heard as the audible sound of surrender[1] to the mystery which is both Christ and Church.

But we also know that music can have a disastrously centrifugal effect on liturgy, throwing us more quickly and further off-center than any other element, and this because of its very centripetal capacity to draw us into itself.[2] We all have known times when we were so enamored of our own doing of the music that it impeded our ability to surrender to the real action of the liturgy. The seductive power of the music anesthetized us to deeper possibilities of response. And how often has the "high" we have experienced from liturgy been because of the beat and/or decibel level of the music instead of from the sense of renewed surrender to the death-resurrection demands of Christian living?

Perhaps the most honest way to answer the question of whether or not liturgical music is prayer is to say that it certainly is *meant* to be. Answering this way squares us off face to face with our own death-resurrection demands: how do we musicians allow liturgical music to be faithful to itself?

We must begin by examining what it is about the nature of music which allows it to be prayer, and specifically liturgical prayer. The format of this chapter will follow this route. I will begin by looking at prayer in a generic sense. Next I will examine aspects of liturgical prayer which make it distinct from individual, private prayer. What I will be developing is a specific formulation about liturgical prayer that can act as a framework for an understanding of liturgical music as prayer. I will then explore what it is about music, and specifically sung music,[3] that makes it so apt for liturgical prayer. What I will be investigating are those overlaps between the nature of liturgical prayer and the nature of music which make them such natural partners in the liturgical enterprise. These overlaps have to do with the substance of prayer as personal presence, as communion, and as transformation through surrender to the Paschal Mystery, and with the natural capacity of music to embody these realities.

Prayer

In a generic sense prayer can be defined as attention to the presence of God. God's presence is free gift. So is our ability to pay attention to that presence when, amid our myriad distractions, blocks, and fears, we recognize it. The divine presence to which we attend may take many forms, from a constantly felt awareness of God's nearness to the paradoxical sense of God's complete absence. It is not the sense of God's nearness which constitutes prayer, but rather the fidelity of our attention which chooses to trust that, near or distant, God remains God-with-us and God-for-us.

Yet we know from experience that our attention is an elusive commodity. We may pay attention out of only the corner of our awareness, or we may split our attention across a multitude of stimuli, or we may choose to focus our attention completely on a single object. In authentic prayer our attention is fully focused on the presence of God. There is a quality to this attention which filters through the distractions which come and go during prayer so that we hear God speaking even through them.

Paying attention to the presence of God means making a conscious choice to do so. There is a difference between a being present which is purely spatial, a mere physical "being there" and a presence which is a personal "being with," "being for," "being in."[4] We can only enter this second level of presence when we choose to situate ourselves "in reference to another person through conscious acts of knowing and loving."[5] Prayer requires the "*art* of cultivating that presence."[6]

Paradoxically, this kind of personal presence to the other generates clearer self-awareness and identity, and is a necessary part of healthy personality growth and of Christian development.[7] When things which are present to each other only spatially move too close together, they lose their separate identities.[8] When hydrogen and oxygen mix, for example, they lose themselves in water; when blue and yellow meet, they become green. Maintaining the integrity of identity requires keeping distance. In the realm of personal presence, on the other hand, communion generates differentiation and is a prerequisite for discovering authentic identity.[9] We achieve selfhood through the conscious choice to be lovingly present, to pay attention. In making ourselves present to the other we become present to ourselves.

When this personal presence is to God in prayer the identity we discover within ourselves is that of Christ. Through the working of the Holy Spirit prayer becomes the fusing of our attentiveness with the attentiveness of Christ. As Peter Fink points out, "Christ's own prayer is the privileged prayer that shapes and guides all Christian prayer."[10] The consciousness with which we attend to God becomes the consciousness of Christ. From the Old Testament story of Israel we know that the God who is ever-present to us is one who continually calls and saves the people. From the New Testament revelation of Jesus Christ we know that this God is also *Abba.* As we grow in prayer what characterizes our consciousness is tender regard for *Abba,* and a growing desire to bring all others into *Abba's* salvific embrace.

Because prayer is a conscious act of presence which generates identity it is deeply personal. Because it turns us outward toward all the other members of the human family, it is innately communal.[11] Its authenticity is evidenced by a growing transformation of our attitudes and behaviors in the direction of wider and deeper openness, compassion, forgiveness, and communion.

What also becomes clear in the course of such prayer is that the way to salvation lies only through the path of death.[12] To find life we must surrender in trust to the presence of God in and beyond death. Such is no easy choice, as it was not for Jesus, but Christian prayer is precisely the gradual and ongoing making of this choice. The decision is none other than the growing willingness, on both the personal and the communal planes, to surrender with and as Christ to the reality of the Paschal Mystery in our lives.

Prayer, then, is conscious attention to the presence of *Abba* who calls us with Christ toward and into the Paschal Mystery. Prayer is that willing attentiveness whereby our consciousness is transformed into the consciousness of Christ, a consciousness which awakens both the most deeply personal and intuitively communal aspects of our selfhood. It is moreover, even when private, always at its foundation liturgical.[13]

Liturgical Prayer

Since all Christian prayer is by nature both personal and communal, what is the difference between individual prayer and liturgical? The difference is not one of disparity but of two modalities which stand in dialectic relationship to one another.[14] In general, individual prayer is unstructured, spontaneous, and determined by the existential needs of the individual who is praying. Liturgical prayer, on the other hand, is structured, formalized, and determined by pre-existing ecclesial patterns. What they share in common is the deeply personal element of attentiveness to the presence of God.[15] This deeply personal element is an opening of self, a listening to *Abba* which inevitably opens the self to neighbor. Where the two forms of prayer differ is in modality: while one is the individual paying attention, the other is the community of the Church paying attention. Both modalities are necessary for the fullness of Christian surrender to the Paschal Mystery.[16] Individual prayer involves private reflection on the ways in which my life is engaged in the Paschal Mystery. Liturgical prayer is communal, public, ritual enactment of that mystery.

Both individual and liturgical prayer are acts which "practice" salvation.[17] They train us in those attitudes and behaviors which are necessary for surrender to the Paschal Mystery, values such as gratitude, contrition, trust, surrender, and hope. Our transformation in Christ lies in the practicing of these "affections," and in the gradual reshaping of self, attitude, and behavior which comes from such discipline.[18]

But however intimately both modalities of prayer are related, liturgical prayer does hold primacy of place, both as foundation and as completion of all Christian prayer.[19] Liturgical prayer remains the source of and condition for the holiness of the Church, first because of the formative power of public ritual, second because of the necessity of public profession for the authenticity of faith, and finally because of the nature of Church as Body of Christ. It is as the Body assembled for liturgical prayer that the Church most strongly constitutes herself as Church.[20] As the liturgical assembly the Church is the body visibly united in communal enactment of the Paschal Mystery. It is the reality of assembly that is central. What happens here is not collective prayer, where a group gathers to share individual prayer, but liturgical prayer where the Church gathers to lift up the one prayer of Christ. And in this one prayer of Christ we both learn and we practice that we do not pass through the Paschal Mystery alone, either as an isolated experience or for an isolated purpose. Rather, we die and rise precisely in relation to one another. "We are never alone when we embrace the responsibilities of the Paschal Mystery dynamic. We are members of the Body of Christ and share in its collective strength as a mutual embrace."[21] It is the nexus of my dying and rising with the dying and rising of all the members of the Church which is the genius of liturgical prayer. And commitment to this nexus is a core element of our public profession of Christian faith.

This discussion of individual and liturgical prayer points out their shared elements as well as their dynamic relationship. Both are intensely personal and innately communal. Both are necessary for full Christian living. Yet liturgical prayer stands as the foundation and completion of individual prayer, not as the aggregate of individual voicings, but as the public, ritualized expression of the essentially communal nature of all Christian prayer as shared participation in the mystery of Christ's paschal surrender to *Abba*. In the public assembly of liturgical prayer the Church makes tangible, to herself and to the world, the relational reality of surrender to the Paschal Mystery.

Once we understand liturgical prayer in this light we can begin to see what is the natural connection between liturgical prayer and music, especially song.

Music as Liturgical Prayer

Here we will examine the nature of music in terms of its natural relationship to personal presence, to personal and communal transformation, and to participation in the Paschal Mystery. As these capabilities are overlapping rather than discrete, my treatment of them will also overlap somewhat. My method will be to extrapolate on ideas concerning sound and music developed by Walter J. Ong[22] and David Burrows[23] to see what insights can be gained from their work for our understanding of the relationship between music and liturgical prayer. Ong deals with the relationship of sound and word to personal presence and communication; Burrows also deals with these notions, but carries them further into the specific realm of sound which is music. For him music is doorway to a field of awareness and communion not available through speech alone. This is furthermore a field which transforms our use of sound/words as tools of control and barriers of defense into sound/song which obliterates all barriers in the creation of a single unity.

Sound and the Communication of Personal Presence

Ong elaborates on the unique capacity of sound to communicate presence. Sound always reveals presence, even when its source is unseen.[24] We know, for example, of the presence of a nearby creek by the sound of its babbling; we know of the presence of a baby in the apartment next door by the sound of its crying. Sound furthermore always manifests the operation of power.[25] The babbling of the creek tells us of water in motion; the crying of the baby tells us of the exertion of diaphragm and lungs (and on a deeper level, of the will of the baby) to wield influence over the behavior of others.

In addition to communicating presence sound also always manifests interiority.[26] This is so because the nature of a specific sound is determined by interior relationships within the source generating the sound. The tone of a violin, for example, is determined by resonances occurring within its interior—the size and shape of its inner cavity as well as the internal properties of its wood and strings. Its appearance—what we see—never reveals its true quality; only what we hear when its component parts are set into play with one another can tell us that. The same is true of the quality of a human voice, that unique internal timbre which marks identity as clearly as does a fingerprint.

Communication and interiority are the hand and glove of sound's capacity to unite separate bodies, because sound communicates precisely by binding interiorities together.[27] Sound is a consequence of an interior manifesting itself[28] and each manifestation unleashes physical waves which set off reciprocating vibrations within the interiors of all the other objects they touch, entering and engaging their response, even unwittingly, and even across great distances.

It is the nature of these sound waves to obliterate sensations of distances and difference. Sound is not blocked by physical barriers, such as furniture or pillars, but oozes around these, intent on its journey outward from its source. As the sound enters our hearing it sets up responding vibrations within us, dissipating our sense of separateness from its source. Sound acts as a vast "vibrant connective tissue"[29] which involves us, consciously or not, in what "the source of the sound is going through."[30] To hear sound, then, is necessarily to become involved with something outside of self which is entering self in an active and activating way. The result is a deep mutual interpenetration that generates communion. "Listening is necessarily participation, stressing commonality with the source rather than difference from it."[31]

When the sound that we hear is word, we know that the presence it manifests is personal.[32] Word alone reveals thought, will, desire, dream, pain, joy, all those intangibles that the impersonal can neither know nor express. Because sound as voice reveals person it "conveys presence as nothing else does."[33] Human voice "manifests the actual use of power by the most interior of interiors, a person."[34] Addressing/communicating with other persons, then, is both a participation in our own inwardness and in theirs.[35] And it is a participation in the mutuality of power. "Thus because of the very nature of sound as such, voice has a kind of primacy in the formation of true communities. . . ."[36]

Song and Liturgical Prayer

When we apply the above insights about sound and word to singing in liturgy we discover that song is the most powerful human way we have of entering, manifesting, and communicating the personal presence that is required in liturgical prayer. The act of liturgical singing is a manifestation of our presence in two ways: first, as that inherent property of sound which always reveals presence and interiority; and second, as revelation about how we are choosing here and now to orient that interiority.

> We cannot choose to have no visual appearance. . . . But we can choose to have no auditory appearance at all simply by remaining silent, and this imparts a special quality to the moment when we do commit ourselves to speech, or song, or any other sound. The voice strikes out beyond the way things are; it is always a performance reaching beyond the self-evident, a manifestation of will and intention.[37]

Singing in liturgy reveals our disposition of soul toward participation with the Church in communal surrender to the Paschal Mystery. Because it is such a revelation of presence and of interiority singing is the most deeply individualized contribution to liturgical worship which we can make.[38] (Perhaps this is one reason why some persons are so shy about singing in the liturgy; they intuit what is at stake and are not yet ready to make the commitment.)

Since all sound, however, reveals and communicates interiority, why is the mere recitation of words not sufficient to the goal of liturgy; why is singing the norm? The answer lies in the nature of the physical process of singing and its effect on self-awareness and body presence. Singing naturally integrates the body in a kinesthetic sensation of flow which is generated by the cycle of inhaling and exhaling in connection with phonation. When singing the body first receives breath, then releases it in a single circular-like movement which flows back upon itself over and over again. Although this is also true when we speak, the kinesthetic sensation of the circling of breath, with its sense of continuous flow, is more pronounced when we are singing. Singing generates a sensation of swelling or of expansion of self which, along with the sensation of connectedness with breath, the source of life, and with movement through and with this breath, builds within us a palpable sense of our own presence.[39] We know that we are here, that we are alive, that we are connected, and that we are powerful.

Furthermore, sound which is song bears a peculiar "quality of resonant presence."[40] This is so because song originates deeper within the body than speech, at the larynx where initial phonation produces vowels rather than consonants. Vowels are unstopped sounds which can be prolonged and elaborated by the breath in ways that consonants, the speech articulating sounds formed by the tongue at teeth and lips, cannot.[41] Singing deepens our awareness of interiority because it "elaborates the resonance of the body's center."[42] In a way we can say that we have more to give when we sing.

When we sing in liturgy we also choose to transform our use of power. When we sing we focus and concentrate our breath in such as way that we "animate the space around [us] with what is literally an expression, a pushing outward of [our] energy,"[43] but we do so in a way that is not confrontational or controlling but participative and communitarian.[44] The sense of increased autonomy which is generated by the body's expansion through breath in singing is transmuted into a sense of collective identity in the experience of communal singing. This transformation happens because communal singing simultaneously demands both sounding and listening, both receiving and giving, both self-awareness and attention to what is outside of self, both an inviting in and a giving out, all dialectics which are naturally paralleled by the cycle of inhaling and exhaling breath (of common air, of which there is plenty to go around), which moves in and out in a continuous, autonomic, communal loop. What is received is the interiority of the others who are the Church, in all their variation and differences from us, and what is given back is our own deepest interiority: both our uniquely personal vocal timbre, and our uniquely personal will to participate in this common endeavor, the being together of Church.[45]

Thus, more than any other activity of liturgy, singing manifests our personal presence and our disposition to participate with this here-and-now assembled Church in the paschal dying and rising of Christ. Through singing we announce that we are here and that we are choosing to be here in an active, participative, liturgical way: when we sing we become the ecclesial body at prayer.

Song as Transformation

There are further notions about the ontology of sound and of music which David Burrows has to contribute to our investigation of the relationship between music and liturgical prayer. In addition to giving a detailed explication of the unitive power of the voice, he also examines its disunitive properties. He then proceeds to demonstrate how music counteracts these disunitive elements by moving us into a realm of awareness where we experience the union of self with all things.

Voice segregates individuals first of all because of its link with semantic reference and the limits these references necessarily place on communication. To say the word "rose," for example, is to make present to our minds what may be physically absent to our senses, and it is through this intangible form of "making present" that we are brought into closer communication. Yet we remain separated by the fact that there will be as many disparate images of "rose" present in the room as there are participants in the conversation. Without a specific rose in front of us our minds scatter in multiple directions, each chasing its own perfect idealization. It may be ontologically true that "a rose is a rose is a rose," but this is never the case for us noetically.

Music, by contrast, unites us because of its very lack of semantic reference, by what Burrows calls its "protosemiotic" status. Music "is not essentially in the business of representing things beyond itself."[46] Even when tied to words in song, music maintains the upper hand in gaining our attention simply because taking it in "involves one cognitive operation less than does understanding speech."[47] Liturgically speaking this means that music can focus our attention more quickly than mere speech can. Through music we become present more easily to that speechless realm within one another where the struggle with semantic overload is at rest, and the peacefulness of simple presence is communication.

A second and more significant way that voice and speech divide us results from the natural origin of all sound in a force/resistance dialectic.[48] Wind whistles only when it meets the resistance of a crack in the eaves; a crystal glass only sings when we rub our finger along its lip. Likewise, vocalization only occurs when the force of the diaphragm pushes breath against the resistance of the vocal folds in our larynx. Burrows theorizes that this "dialogue between diaphragm and larynx can be thought of as a symbolic displacement to the body's interior of the interface between self and world."[49] Vocalization expressed in speech, then, manifests two levels of the force/resistance dialectic, that of the body's internal pushing of breath through its vocal mechanism, and that of the self's external bid for control over the confronting world.[50] The operation of power which, as Ong pointed out, sound always manifests, becomes for Burrows more than the physical exertion of energy. It is the psychic effort at control and domination.

Through music, however, our need to confront and control outside reality is transformed into a sense of communion with it. To grasp this point, we must first understand Burrows' model of the three fields of human action.[51] Each field deals with the orientation of self within a center-periphery scheme. Field 1—that of the body—is sense limited, time and space specific, and deals with physical peripheries that are here-and-now. The primary operative sense in Field 1 is vision; what we see is what we get.

Field 2 is that of the mind, where time and space are unspecific, where we "see" what is not here-and-now, and where we deal with intangible psychical edges that are "past, future, and elsewhere." In Field 2 we are aware that there is more, that there is a reality beyond appearances which we enter through the doorway of thought and speech.

Field 3 is the realm of the spirit (used here by Burrows not as a theological term but as "the sense of self as diffused through the full range of awareness") where the sense of self becomes contiguous with all reality, where peripheries no longer exist because "everything becomes center." In Field 2 limits on the world of here-and-now are stretched to the edges of our capacity to think, to remember, to imagine. In Field 3 all limits disappear as barriers between the center (self) and the periphery (other, world, cosmos) dissipate in an awareness of the oneness of self with the whole of things.

It is through our faculties of thought and speech that we come into contact with realities far beyond the remotest capabilities of our physical reach. But it is through the avenues of ritual and art[52] that we enter Field 3 and discover that even the most distant reality is very close to home. Above all it is "sound shaped into music" which gives us access to Field 3.[53] More than any other art form, music is the doorway to mystic union.

Song and Paschal Mystery

When we look more closely at the origins of sound in its force/resistance dialectic we discover a paradox in the ritual-musical movement into Field 3 about the death-resurrection demands of participation in the liturgy. In order for control and confrontation to yield to communion, resistance must surrender. This is what happens when we enter Field 3. Barriers melt. This is also what happens when song takes over the body, both as individual and as assembly.[54] Because breath moves, barriers melt.

Yet in order for the breath which is moving to produce song, resistance must hold ground. Sound only occurs through confrontation with resistance. Remove the resistance and the sound disappears. Similarly, the choice to participate with the Church in the communal enactment of the Paschal Mystery occurs only through conscious confrontation with the factors within ourselves which resist this participation. We desire both to be present and to absent ourselves, to communicate and to remain withdrawn. These ambivalences are a normal part of human existence, and we bring them to every liturgical celebration. Remove these resistances and the decision to participate in liturgy disintegrates because this choice has no meaning, no reality, outside of the reality of freedom and will.

The marvel of music, and particularly of song which is such an embodied form of communal participation, is that its very doing—the very creating of communal song—is a coalescing of the force/resistance dialectic with the resistance-free flow of Field 3. Neither dissipates, neither our force/resistance struggle without which there can be no choice and no song, nor our real, existential experience of authentic communion.

Participation in liturgy does not erase who we are, rather it embraces us in all our paradoxical reality. Liturgical singing both reveals this to us and practices it in us. This is so because the transformation brought about through surrender to the Paschal Mystery has the same character as the transformation brought about through participation in communal song. Neither eradicates our struggle with resistance but uses this very resistance to work out our salvation. We become in the process not sinless and perfect, but even more beautifully forgiven and human. And this is precisely how, in Christ, we are able to be present to one another, and to become the one Body.

This is how and where we know the embrace of *Abba* and the unlimited stretch of that embrace. This is the core of both the Church and of prayer.

Conclusion

We come full circle back to our starting question: is liturgical music, and specifically sung liturgical music, prayer? We answered earlier that it is certainly *meant* to be. In the subsequent sections we attempted to demonstrate how this could be so by aligning substantive elements of prayer with essential dynamics in music: both reveal and communicate personal presence; both engender communion; both transform through a Paschal Mystery dialectic.

Yet it remains true that music can be, and often is, a stumbling block to this prayer. Thus we arrive again at our secondary but no less important question: how do we musicians allow liturgical music to be faithful to itself? We do so primarily through our own consciously chosen fidelities: to prayer, to Church, to liturgy. And the doorways to this faithfulness are those offered to us by the very nature of music itself.

We need to use the power inherent in music to make us personally present and to transform us. The music itself can make us aware of our resistances to grace in such a way that these resistances can then be made available to the Paschal Mystery process. These resistances include, for example, our persistent temptation to use music as a mirror in which we gaze at our own glory; our desires, often unconscious, to use music as a means of control over others by manipulating the emotions of the assembly, even when these emotions are religious;[55] and our frequently easy acquiescence to the seductively superficial in music. Yet music's very capacity to be prayer, and especially that liturgical prayer which embodies communal surrender to the Paschal Mystery, is our avenue of redemption.

We must "practice" salvation precisely within the realm where we are most called to salvation, within our personhood as musicians and our vocation as musical ministers. In the prolonged, ongoing, disciplined process of making music we are offered the opportunity to confront ourselves and to undergo transformation. We are also offered the opportunity both to discover and to help create the Church at prayer. We must follow this opportunity, for it comes from Christ, and we must invite our congregations, choirs, and cantors to do the same.

Notes

1. Credit for this image belongs to Dianne Skubby, C.PP.S., participant in Liturgy in a Formative Environment (L.I.F.E. '96) July 21–August 2, 1996, Holy Family Retreat House, Oxley, Ontario.

2. See Joseph Gelineau, "The Importance of Prayer for the Musician," *Pastoral Music in Practice 5: The Pastoral Musician,* ed. Virgil Funk (Washington, D.C.: Pastoral Press, 1990) 76.

3. Although instrumental music also plays its part in liturgical prayer, this chapter will consider primarily sung music. Some of the content can be applied to instrumental liturgical music, but a full consideration of its role would require a more broadly oriented discussion than is possible here.

4. J. R. Sheets, "Personal and Liturgical Prayer," *Worship* 47 (1973) 406.

5. Ibid., 406.

6. Ibid., 413.

7. See Dietrich von Hildebrand, *Liturgy and Personality,* rev. ed. (Baltimore: Helicon, 1960), chapter 7, where he describes progressive degrees of "awakenedness," from a general inclination toward values, to a consciousness of the moral demands made by these values and of one's capacity in freedom to say yes or no to these demands, to a deep inner openness to God and God's presence in one's life. He asserts that this third level is essential for the development of authentic Christian personality.

8. Sheets, "Personal and Liturgical Prayer," 406.

9. Ibid., 406.

10. Peter E. Fink, "Public and Private Moments in Christian Prayer," *Worship* 58 (1984) 486; see also 412: "The prime analogue of all Christian prayer is Christ."

11. "It is important to grasp that we turn toward each other and outward to all people, not by abandoning the personal journey, but *precisely as part of it*. . . . To divorce either the personal or the communal from the pursuit and discovery of God is to remove them both from the realm of Christian prayer"; Fink, "Moments in Christian Prayer," 492–93.

12. "In the New Testament . . . God's presence is revealed to be a paschal presence. It has come about through the passion, death, and resurrection of Christ. This constitutes a new mode of being present. At the same time, it asks for a new type of response. Paschal presence asks for the reciprocity of paschal response. . . ."; Sheets, "Personal and Liturgical Prayer," 411.

13. David L. Fleming, S.J., points out that even in private spiritual direction "there is necessarily present a prior liturgical setting—the Christian community at worship—in which both parties [i.e., director and directee] are situated and formed. . . . A liturgical spirituality is the foundational spirituality of the church, since it always puts us in contact with some aspect of celebrating the paschal mystery which identifies all Christians with Christ"; David L. Fleming, "Spiritual Direction and Liturgy," *New Dictionary of Sacramental Worship,* ed. Peter E. Fink (Collegeville: The Liturgical Press, 1990) 1221.

14. Fink develops the thesis that ". . . the public, communal form of [Christ's/our] prayer is the *context* of the personal form, and the personal form is the *content* of the communal"; Fink, "Moments in Prayer," 488.

15. ". . . personal prayer takes on a certain 'otherness' when it becomes liturgical, an otherness which increases rather than diminishes its personal character"; Sheets, "Personal and Liturgical Prayer," 414.

16. Thus Pius XII could say in *Mediator Dei,* "Unquestionably, liturgical prayer . . . is superior in excellence to private prayers. But this superior worth does not at all imply contrast or incompatibility between these two kinds of prayer. For both merge harmoniously in the single spirit which animates them, 'Christ is all and in all.' Both tend to the same objective: until Christ be formed in us" (#37).

17. See Don E. Saliers, *The Soul in Paraphrase: Prayer and the Religious Affections.* 2nd ed. (Cleveland: OSL Publications, 1991); see also Mark Searle, "Ritual and Music: A Theory of Liturgy and Implications for Music," *Assembly* 12 (1986) 314–17.

18. "Learning to pray is opening oneself to a new way of being; to be formed in a language which shapes and expresses the deep emotions for which we are never quite prepared, and which we would never sustain by our own powers. And . . . 'meaning' what we pray is linked with entering into the way of life such belief-laden affections call forth"; Saliers, *Soul in Paraphrase,* 28.

19. Full and active participation in the liturgy "is the primary and indispensable source from which the faithful are to derive the true Christian spirit"; *Sacrosanctum Concilium,* #14.

20. "For the liturgy, 'making the work of our redemption a present actuality,' most of all in the divine sacrifice of the Eucharist, is the outstanding means whereby the faithful may express in their lives and manifest to others the mystery of Christ and the real nature of the true Church"; *Sacrosanctum Concilium,* #2.

21. Joyce Ann Zimmerman, C.PP.S., *Liturgy as Living Faith: A Liturgical Spirituality* (Scranton: University of Scranton Press, 1993) 137; see also 137–38, where Zimmerman states: "No one person is the Body of Christ, but together we are members of the one Body with Christ as Head. . . . This suggests that an individual is more than just 'one among many'; an individual holds the Body in the palm of her/his hand by the works s/he performs. Each of us is responsible for the whole Body. Each is co-author of the Christian text, the living document we call 'liturgy.'"

22. Walter J. Ong, S.J., *The Presence of the Word* (New Haven: Yale University Press, 1967).

23. David Burrows, *Sound, Speech, and Music* (Amherst: University of Massachusetts Press, 1990).

24. Ong, *Presence of the Word,* 111–15.

25. Ibid., 112.

26. Ibid., 117–18.

27. Ibid., 125.

28. Ibid., 117.

29. Burrows, *Sound, Speech, and Music,* 24.

30. Ibid., 24.

31. Ibid., 29.

32. Ong, *Presence of the Word,* 114.

33. Ibid., 114.

34. Ibid., 163.

35. Even silence, as entrance into one's own deepest interior, becomes a doorway for communication: "Religious silence . . . undertaken in union with others and out of regard for God and all mankind [sic] . . . constitutes a kind of communication and encounter"; Ong, *Presence of the Word,* 126.

36. Ibid., 124.

37. Burrows, *Sound, Speech, and Music,* 31.

38. "In singing, a man [sic] becomes, as it were, a pouring-out and a gift, because song, compounded of the breath which he breathes out from his inmost self and of the sound of his voice which cannot be held or imprisoned, is the free expression of himself, the manifestation of his interior being and the gratuitous giving of his personality. . . . Song is the living portrayal of spiritual self-giving. It is the gift of love whereby a man sets himself free in a joyous abandonment and complete affirmation, knowing that precisely there, where he seems to lose himself, is in fact where he finds and expresses himself to the full"; Joseph Gelineau, *Voices and Instruments in Christian Worship,* trans. Clifford Howell (Collegeville: The Liturgical Press, 1964) 17.

39. Burrows, *Sound, Speech, and Music,* 89–90; see also 20: "The singers themselves have the sensation of expanding, in attenuated form, into surrounding space and filling it."

40. Ibid., 81.

41. Ibid., 64–65.

42. Ibid., 64.

43. Ibid., 109.

44. Ibid., 68. Although Burrows here speaks specifically of polyphonic singing, where text overlaps and sometimes even collides, his point that the "participants' sense of autonomy shades over into a collective identity" is applicable to all communal singing.

45. See also Michel Veuthey's commentary on the *Universa Laus* document: "While listening to oneself singing, everyone hears each other singing, and this can become the moment when an intense communal experience takes place"; *Music and Liturgy: The Universa Laus Document and Commentary,* trans. Paul Inwood (Washington, D.C.: Pastoral Press, 1992) 72.

46. Burrows, *Sound, Speech, and Music,* 71. Burrows' argument for the nonreferential nature of music is at variance with the thinking of those who speak of music's symbolic role in the liturgy. See, for example, Joseph Gelineau, *Voices and Instruments in Christian Worship* (Collegeville: The Liturgical Press, 1964); Claude Duchesneau and Michel Veuthey, *Music and Liturgy: The Universa Laus Document and Commentary,* trans. Paul Inwood (Washington, D.C.: Pastoral Press, 1992); *The Milwaukee Symposia for Church Composers*

(Washington, D.C.: Pastoral Press and Chicago: Liturgy Training Publications, 1992), as well as the standard church documents on liturgical music. Burrows' viewpoint, as well as his lengthy discussion in chapters 4 and 5 about music and words, contributes an intriguingly differing viewpoint to the ongoing debate about which should predominate in worship, music or text.

47. Burrows, *Sound, Speech, and Music,* 88.

48. Ibid., 23.

49. Ibid., 30.

50. Ibid., 36–37.

51. Ibid., 5–9.

52. Ibid., 8.

53. Ibid., 122.

54. "Significantly absent from absorption in a song is a sense of otherness populated by others, an out-there oppositional world"; Ibid., 76.

55. Searle points out that there is a difference between music which makes us "feel religious" and music which "makes us religious," and that the goal of liturgy is not an emotional state, but the assumption of the roles and relational attitudes which the liturgical rite proposes. He goes on to make the plea, "Why are we putting so much time, energy and money into producing new music instead of training people in liturgical prayer?" Searle, "Ritual and Music," 317.

Chapter 18

Liturgical Music as Corporate Song 1: Hymnody in Reformation Churches

Robin A. Leaver

Introduction

Most of the mainline, non-Catholic churches that are frequently embraced by the term "Protestant" are in large measure the product of the reforms of the sixteenth century. However, in recent history the term Protestant has been disavowed by some denominational groupings, making the term less all-embracing than it once was. For this reason in this chapter the term "Reformation Churches" is preferred to "Protestant Churches." It is more accurate, since, on the one hand, essentially only Lutherans "protested" at the Diet of Speyer in 1529 and were first called "Protestants," and on the other hand, many more denominational groupings than Lutherans can claim similar origins in the wider reform movement of the sixteenth century.

In older literature the sixteenth-century phenomenon of ecclesiastical, political, and theological reform is usually designated by the singular "Reformation." But this movement for reform did not manifest itself uniformly in every European country that was touched by it. Thus in more recent literature the tendency is to define this era of change in the plural and to speak of the "Reformations" of the sixteenth century. For example, Christopher Haigh entitled his recent book not the *English Reformation*, but the *English Reformations*,[1] arguing that there were different reformations occurring simultaneously in England: in religion, in politics, and in society.[2] Even within a single area there were differences in the "reformations" of religion. Thus in the British Isles, Anglicanism developed in England and Presbyterianism in Scotland; in Germany Lutheranism was augmented first by various branches of the Radical Reformation, then by Calvinism. Further, German Lutheranism developed somewhat differently in those areas where High German was spoken, compared with Low German areas; and in Switzerland the German-speaking Reformed churches, centered in Zurich, developed different emphases from the French-speaking Reformed churches, centered in Geneva. These differences were reflected in the various patterns of worship that were established by these Reformation churches and also in the different approaches to congregational hymnody/psalmody within their reformed patterns of worship. Although most Reformation churches were united in a common use of congregational song in worship,[3] different hymnic traditions were established, traditions that, with the passage of time, were augmented and expanded from within, and cross-fertilized from without by the importation of hymnic forms from other traditions.[4]

Pre-Reformation Traditions

Vernacular religious song was not the invention of the Reformation era. There was a long European history of such songs,[5] including English carols,[6] Dutch *geestelijke liederen,*[7] Italian *lauda spirituales,*[8] and German *leisen.*[9] Luther knew of and utilized the para-liturgical German *leisen* that were closely associated with the liturgy and the festivals of the Church year. Examples include the fifteenth-century *Wir glauben all an einen Gott,* based on the Creed, the fourteenth-century *Gelobet seist du, Jesu Christ* (Christmas Day), the twelfth-century *Christ ist erstanden* (Easter Day), textually and musically related to the Easter sequence *Victimœ paschali laudes,* and the thirteenth-century *Nun bitten wir den Heiligen Geist* (Feast of Pentecost), all of which, with others, Luther revised and expanded. But whereas previous generations had sung these *leisen* extra-liturgically, after Mass on the respective festivals, Luther directed that the new evangelical hymns—whether they were re-workings of older material or newly-created—should be sung intra-liturgically, that is, within the reformed Mass by the congregation at large.

Luther's liturgical use of vernacular hymnody had been anticipated by the Bohemian Brethren, the followers of Jan Hus, who had sung Czech hymns in worship during the fifteenth century. German-speaking Bohemian Brethren translated many of these Czech hymns into their own language, issuing them in a hymnal published in Prague as early as 1501.[10] Other collections of German versions of Czech hymns were *Ein New Gesengbuchlen* (Jungbunzlau, 1531), edited by Michael Weisse,[11] and *Ein Gesangbuch der Brüder inn Behemen und Werherrn* (Nuremberg, 1544), edited by Johann Horn:[12] hymns from both collections were utilized by Lutherans in Wittenberg and elsewhere.

The Latin hymns of the daily office were also influential in the development of Lutheran hymnody. Manuscript and printed *Hymnaria*, although designed for use by clergy and choirs, nevertheless provided a model for later Lutheran collections of vernacular congregational hymns, since many of these German hymns, like the earlier Latin office hymns, were intended to be sung during the primary seasons of the Church year.

Lutheran Tradition

The theological imperative for congregational hymnody came from Luther's understanding of the doctrine of the royal priesthood of all believers, which stood in contradistinction to the particular priesthood of Catholicism. Although it took five years after the debate concerning indulgences of 1517 for Luther to make the connection between the doctrine and the practice, once he had linked the two he saw that unison congregational song was a powerful demonstration of the doctrine of universal priesthood, since every member of the congregation was involved in the activity. But Luther was also aware of the practice of the early Church. In the *Formula missae* of 1523 he wrote: "I also wish that we had as many songs as possible in the vernacular which the people could sing during mass, immediately after the gradual and also after the Sanctus and Agnus Dei. For who doubts that originally all the people sang these which now only the choir sings?"[13]

Before the end of 1523, the year that the *Formula missae* was published, Luther and his colleagues began creating a basic corpus of congregational song for Reformation worship, both ecclesiastical and domestic. They revised and reworked old German *leisen;* translated Latin office hymns into the vernacular, and modified, where necessary, their associated plainsong melodies; created *contrafacta,* either by rewriting pre-existing religious folksongs, or by supplying folk melodies with new "evangelical" texts; and wrote newly-created hymns, both texts and tunes. These "new" hymns were first published on broadsides, but, beginning with the so-called *Achtliederbuch* (a small hymnal of just eight hymns published in Nuremberg in 1524), an extraordinary number of hymnals was published, with and without music, in German-speaking lands over the next quarter of a century—at least 500 different hymnals.

Even before he and his colleagues had really begun to assemble a basic corpus of vernacular congregational song, Luther saw the primary function of such singing in liturgical terms. In the *Formula missae,* following the passage cited above, he wrote: "Poets are wanting among us, or not yet known, who could compose evangelical and spiritual songs, as Paul calls them [Col. 3:16], worthy to be used in the church of God [after the Gradual and also after the Sanctus and Agnus Dei, etc.]."[14] Sufficient progress had been made over the ensuing two years that when Luther drew up his vernacular liturgy towards the end of 1525—the *Deutsche Messe,* published in Wittenberg early in 1526[15]—there was a sufficient number of hymns available in Wittenberg for congregational use. Thus he was not only able to refer to hymns but also to include some texts, with tunes, within the document. He retained the traditional structure of the Mass but, as in the *Formula missae,* the content was theologically reinterpreted. The five parts of the traditional ordinary were retained, except that in the *Deutsche Messe* Luther developed the principle that the congregation could sing them in hymnic forms. In the course of time a complete sequence of "ordinary" hymns became customary: *Kyrie, Gott Vater in ewigkeit* (Kyrie), *Allein Gott in der Höh sei Ehr* (Gloria), *Wir glauben all an einen Gott* (Credo), *Jesaja dem Propheten das geschah* (Sanctus), *Christe, du Lamm Gottes,* or *O Lamm Gottes, unschuldig* (Agnus Dei).

The new congregational hymns were not only to be liturgical but biblical as well. In the initial months when Luther and his colleagues were writing their earliest hymns, the reformer created a new genre that was to have enormous significance for hymnic congregational participation in Reformation churches: the psalm-hymn, or metrical psalm, that is, the biblical psalm in the vernacular rendered into a strophic and rhymed form. Towards the end of 1523 Luther wrote thus to Georg Spalatin:

> Following the example of the prophets and fathers of the church, I intend to make vernacular psalms for the people, that is, spiritual songs so that the Word of God even by means of song may live among the people. Everywhere we are looking for poets. Now since you are so skillful and eloquent in German, I would like to ask you to work with us in this and to turn a psalm into a hymn as in the enclosed example of my work [Psalm 130: *Aus tiefer Not schrei ich zu dir*]. But I would like you to avoid new-fangled, fancied words and to use expressions simple and common enough for the people to understand yet pure and fitting. The meaning should also be clear and as close as possible to the psalm. Irrespective of the exact wording, one must freely render the sense by suitable words.[16]

Luther wrote no less than five metrical psalms during this earliest period of writing, 1523–1524: *Ach Gott, vom Himmel sieh darein* (Psalm 12), *Es spricht der Unweisen Mund wohl* (Psalm 14), *Es wollt uns Gott genädig sein* (Psalm 67), *Wär Gott nicht mit uns diese Zeit* (Psalm 124), and *Aus tiefer Not schrei ich zu dir* (Psalm 130)—all in the same metre. *Wohl dem, der in Gottes Furcht steht* (Psalm 128) and *Ein feste Burg ist unser Gott* (Psalm 46) were written later, in 1525 and 1528/29 respectively.

Other Lutherans followed Luther's example and wrote metrical psalms, thus establishing the genre that was to become almost universal in the churches of the Reformation, especially those that were Reformed in their theology.

Evangelical Tradition

The Reformation in Strassburg, the leading city of Alsace situated on the borders between France and Germany, though influenced by Wittenberg Lutheranism, nevertheless charted a somewhat independent course with regard to theological and ecclesiastical reforms. These reforms were certainly "evangelical," but not consistently Lutheran and not yet Reformed, in the sense of later Calvinism. During the first period of hymn-writing by Luther and his colleagues, 1523–25, these German Lutheran hymns, especially the metrical psalms, were republished in Strassburg soon after their first appearance in Wittenberg.[17] But there were two significant differences. First, the Wittenberg hymns were given new "Strassburg" tunes, composed or edited by Mathias Greiter and Wolfgang Dachstein, respectively cantor and organist of Strassburg cathedral. Second, additional congregational songs written by various Strassburgers were added to those of the Wittenbergers. Congregational singing was taken seriously in the city and area of Strassburg. In his 1543 Catechism Martin Bucer, the leading reformer of the city and surrounding area, included a whole section on the importance of participation in the "Kirchengesang," congregational hymnody, which he saw as second only to participation in corporate prayer in the worship assembly.[18]

The contents of the Strassburg hymnals published in the 1520s and 1530s demonstrate a growing marked preference for metrical psalms, a fact that was to have far-reaching consequences, not only for the later hymnals and psalters published in Strassburg, but also for the development of Genevan psalters. This later Calvinist psalmody had its genesis in the metrical psalmody of Strassburg. In 1537 Jean Calvin was called by Bucer to minister to the relatively small group of French-speaking Protestants in Strassburg. It was here that

Calvin encountered German metrical psalms and was stimulated to create French metrical psalms to be sung to the same melodies used by the German congregations in Strassburg. These were published as *Aulcuns pseaumes et cantiques* (Strasbourg, 1539), the first fruit of what was to become the French Genevan Psalter.

Reformed Traditions

The character of the Swiss Reformed churches was in large measure shaped by the two primary languages of the cantons: German and French. The churches of the German-speaking cantons were focused on Zwingli (and later Bullinger) in Zurich, and the French-speaking cantons on Calvin in Geneva. Each language-group developed specific theological emphases, patterns of worship, and different conclusions with regard to the practice of congregational song.

Zwinglian

Ulrich Zwingli, probably the most musically gifted of the sixteenth-century reformers, paradoxically excluded music from the churches in Zurich. A principal reason for this action was Zwingli's theological understanding of the nature of worship.[19] He saw outward observances as of little value when compared to the inner spiritual life, which he regarded as the essence of Christianity. Outward rites and gestures with ceremonial music, such as in the Roman Mass, obscured the essence of true worship.[20] Although he did accept the principle of corporate speech, as opposed to corporate song, for the public worship of the churches of Zurich, the introduction of the practice was disallowed by the Zurich magistracy.[21] However, Zwingli's exclusion of corporate song and other music from public worship has been misunderstood as a prohibition of all music from all worship.[22] To the contrary, music was important in his own devotional life and he is known to have written both words and music for at least three religious songs: the *Pestlied,* a metrical version of Psalm 69, and the *Kappeler Lied.*[23] He also believed that music had important secular functions, especially in education, and made provisions for the study of music in his reformed curricula for the schools attached to the Zurich churches. Although he gave a role to music in the secular sphere, and also in the realm of private devotion, he nevertheless excluded the possibility of music in public worship. Hymnody was therefore not generally admitted into the worship of those churches that were among the first to adopt Zwinglian theology and practice. In the churches of Zurich all music was excluded from worship for the remainder of the century,[24] Zwingli's non-musical ecclesiastical agenda being continued by his successor, Heinrich Bullinger. Thus in 1561, when drafting the Second Helvetic Confession (not published until 1566), Bullinger included the following somewhat defensive statement: "If there are churches which have a true and proper sermon [*orationem* = service of worship] but no singing, they ought not to be condemned. For all the churches do not have the advantage of singing."[25] The reason for his defensiveness on the issue was the growing influence of Genevan psalmody, which caused the churches following the Zurich model to become exceptions rather than the rule in Reformed Switzerland.

Calvinist

Calvin's 1539 Strassburg collection of congregational songs included nineteen metrical psalms, of which six were written by Calvin himself, and the remainder by Clement Marot, poet to the French court, whose psalm-versions had not hitherto appeared in print. Calvin returned to Geneva in 1541 and a year later issued his Genevan liturgy, *La Forme des prieres et chantz ecclesiastiques* (Geneva, 1542), which also included an expanded version of his Strassburg psalter, containing more metrical psalms by Marot. Calvin's goal was to produce the complete biblical psalter rendered into rhyme and metre, the principle being to render accurately the substance of the biblical text in vernacular verse. Marot continued to work with Calvin on the project, indeed, the French poet not only wrote more metrical psalms but also produced other versifications that replaced Calvin's earlier examples. After Marot's death in 1544 Calvin turned to Theodore Beza to continue the work on a complete French metrical psalter. Within a few years, eighty-three psalms had been completed and the important and influential edition of the French psalter could be published: *Pseaumes octante trois de David* (Geneva, 1551), for which Louis Bourgeois was the musical editor.[26] The objective of a complete psalter was eventually realized in *Les Pseaumes mis en rime, Par Clement Marot, & Theodore Beza* (Geneva, 1562). It contained all 150 psalms, written in 110 different metres, with 125 tunes edited by Claude Goudimel.[27] It is difficult to overestimate the influence of these Genevan psalters, since virtually every European language-group, one way or another, emulated them by producing other vernacular collections of metrical psalms during the following century. Significant psalters following the French Genevan model were produced in English, Dutch, German, various East European languages, and even in Russian in the early eighteenth century.

Anglican

The general European religious environment influenced the rise and development of English metrical psalmody. In England, during the reign of Henry VIII, Lutheran hymns and psalms were translated into English in the mid-1530s by Miles Coverdale who published them as *Goostly psalmes and spirituall songes* (London, ca. 1535). Fifteen of the forty-one texts were metrical psalms, a foretaste of what was to develop later. Coverdale's collection was ordered to be burned, since its contents were too Lutheran. Thus the promising beginning that *Goostly psalmes* represented never matured, although one of its translations was later used, almost *verbatim*, by Cranmer in drawing up the burial service for the 1549 Prayer Book, and at least two of the melodies were later refashioned into English metrical psalm tunes.[28]

After Henry VIII's death in 1547 a new beginning of vernacular psalmody was made. Thomas Sternhold, a personal courtier to both Henry VIII and his successor Edward VI, wrote poetic versions of the psalms, which were reported to have circulated in manuscript and at the English Court. Early in the reign of Edward VI, when the Reformation ideals were openly pursued, nineteen of Sternhold's metrical psalms were published as *Certayne Psalmes chosen out of the Psalter of David, and Drawen into Englishe metre by Thomas Sternhold grome of ye Kynges Maiesties Roobes* (London, ca. 1547). Sternhold continued work on writing metrical psalms, with the intention of completing the psalter, but died soon after his psalms first appeared in print. After his death an expanded edition of his psalms was edited by John Hopkins: *Al such psalmes of David as T. Sternhold didde in his life time draw into English metre. Newly emprinted* (London, 1549). An additional eighteen versions by Sternhold were included, and Hopkins contributed a further seven, making a total of forty-four metrical psalms. This small collection proved to be popular and at least ten reprints, dated between 1550 and 1554, are extant, implying that they were widely sung, at least in London, during the reign of Edward VI.

During the Marian years, 1553–1558, when the English church reverted to Catholicism and the Roman Mass, Sternhold's psalter was expanded in various English Protestant exile congregations in Germany and Switzerland. In Strassburg the Sternhold and Hopkins metrical psalms were augmented by English translations of Luther's *Vater unser im Himmelreich* and *Erhalt uns, Herr, bei deinem Wort*. In Wesel a new edition of Sternhold and Hopkins was printed by Hugh Singleton, *Psalmes of David in Metre* (Wesel, ca. 1555/56), an expanded edition which, in addition to the basic corpus of forty-four Sternhold and

Hopkins metrical psalms, included seven psalm versions by William Whittingham, who had been in Frankfurt before moving to Geneva (see further below). The Wesel English psalter also included a number of metrical canticles: five anonymous, one by Whittingham, the Strassburg translation of Luther's "Lord's Prayer" hymn, and five by William Samuel, one of the two assistant ministers of the English exile congregation in Wesel. In Frankfurt a split occurred within the exile congregation, one party favoring Prayer Book worship and the other demanding a form more akin to the French liturgy of Calvin in Geneva. Ultimately the Prayer Book party remained in Frankfurt, while the others, including William Whittingham and (later) John Knox, migrated to Geneva. Soon after arriving in the city, Whittingham published (February 1556) the Calvinistic liturgy that had been drafted in Frankfurt. It included a modified and expanded version of the Sternhold and Hopkins psalter with its own title page: *One and fiftie Psalmes of David In Englishe metre, whereof .37. were made by Thomas Sternholde: and the rest by others. Conferred with the hebrewe, and in certeyn places corrected as the sens of the Prophete required* (Geneva, 1556). The revisions were made in accordance with Calvinist ideals: the biblical text of the psalm was primary and poetry secondary. Rhyme and metre were acceptable but poetic paraphrase was not. The versions of Sternhold and Hopkins had therefore to be "conferred with the Hebrew" and corrected accordingly. At least three further editions of the Anglo-Genevan psalter were issued between 1558 and 1560, with additional psalms by Whittingham, Pullain, and Kethe. The no longer extant 1559 edition was probably the first to include Kethe's version of Ps. 100, "All people that on earth do dwell," the oldest metrical psalm and also the oldest congregational song in the English-speaking world that has been sung continuously since its first appearance.

Following the death of Mary towards the end of 1558, her half-sister Elizabeth I succeeded to the English throne and the Reformation in England was begun again. English exiles abroad were now free to return. Among other things, they brought with them their experience of continental hymn and psalm singing, as well as the psalters they had used in their exile congregations. Thus a complex pattern of psalter publication was embarked upon in London between 1559 and 1562. The basic corpus of metrical psalms of Sternhold and Hopkins, in their revised Genevan versions, were supplemented by: more psalms by Sternhold, discovered after his death; more contributed by Hopkins (who had survived the Marian years), and a number of other Elizabethan writers; and various metrical hymns and canticles that originated in Strassburg, Wesel, Frankfurt, and Geneva were also incorporated at the beginning and the end of the evolving English psalter.[29]

In September 1562 the first complete English metrical psalter was published: *The Whole Book of Psalmes, collected into Englysh metre by T. Starnhold I. Hopkins & others: conferred with the Ebrue, with apt Notes to synge them withal* (London, 1562). Apart from one or two adjustments which were made over the following year or so,[30] the English metrical psalter was now complete. It then ran through an extremely numerous sequence of editions, being reprinted again and again, in some years several times, throughout the next three centuries. Indeed, the Sternhold and Hopkins psalter or, as it was later known, the *Old Version,* remained in print well into the nineteenth century in England. It proved to be the foundation-stone on which the English tradition of metrical psalmody and hymnody was built.

Puritan, Presbyterian, and Independent

In Scotland, under the leadership of John Knox who had been in exile in both Frankfurt and Geneva, the Reformation developed in a Genevan direction. The Anglo-Genevan liturgy of 1556 was reprinted with only minor revisions in Edinburgh in 1564, and the complete metrical psalter that was issued with it was basically the eighty-seven psalms from last revision of the Anglo-Genevan psalter of 1560, with the remainder taken from the English psalter of 1562: *The C.L. psalmes of David in English metre* (Edinburgh, 1564).[31] The greater number of psalms from the Anglo-Genevan psalters made the Scottish psalter closer to the Franco-Genevan tradition, especially with regard to tunes, than its English counterpart.

The more extreme Puritans found Elizabethan England too unsympathetic to their views. After the Dutch Calvinist Reformation at the end of the 1570s many cities of the Netherlands were more amenable, especially Middleburg, Leiden, and Amsterdam. In Middleburg, towards the end of the sixteenth century, a number of imprints of both the English and Scottish psalters were produced for these exile congregations.[32] In the early seventeenth century a new metrical psalter was produced for English-speaking Separatists abroad: Henry Ainsworth, *The Book of Psalmes, Englished in both Prose and Metre* (Amsterdam, 1612). Ainsworth's aim was to produce metrical versions that were more faithful to the Biblical psalms than *The Whole Book of Psalms* of Sternhold and Hopkins, and written in as many of the metres of Calvin's psalter as possible, so that more of the rugged Genevan psalm tunes could be sung by English Puritans and Separatists. Some of the English Separatists in the Netherlands, together with others from England (later known collectively as "the Pilgrim Fathers"), sailed to the New World on the *Mayflower*, arriving in the New World in December 1620. The psalms they took with them were those of the metrical psalter of Henry Ainsworth. Thus congregational song in English-speaking North America at this time was metrical psalmody, either the psalms of Sternhold and Hopkins, preferred by Anglicans and some Puritans (later known as Independents, and later still as Congregationalists), or the psalms of Ainsworth, the psalter of the Separatists.

In the congregations of the Bay Company the psalms of Sternhold and Hopkins were considered to be inaccurate renderings of the biblical texts, and the psalms of Ainsworth, with their many different metres, too difficult to sing. Thus the so-called "Bay Psalm Book" was created, the first book of any kind to be published in British North America: *The Whole Book of Psalms Faithfully Translated into English Metre* ([Cambridge, Mass.] 1640). The key words on the title page "Faithfully Translated," the equivalent of "conferred with the Hebrew" on the title page of Sternhold and Hopkins, expressed the Calvinistic concern for literal accuracy, and was expounded in the final paragraph of the preface to the Bay Psalm Book:

> If therefore the verses are not always so smooth and elegant as some may desire or expect; let them consider that God's Altar needs not our polishings: Ex. 20. For we have respected rather a plain translation, than to smooth our verses with the sweetness of any paraphrase, and so have attended conscience rather than elegance, fidelity rather than poetry, in translating the Hebrew words into English language, and David's poetry into English metre; that so we may sing in Sion the Lord's songs of praise according to his own will; until he take us from hence, and wipe away all our tears, & bid us enter into our Master's joy to sing eternal Alleluias.[33]

Over the following century the Bay Psalm Book was revised, reprinted, and widely used not only in New England, but also in England and Scotland, where it was reprinted a number of times.

Radical Traditions

The Anabaptists of the sixteenth century, the representatives of the so-called Radical Reformation, were the forerunners of the later Baptist tradition and included such groups as Mennonites, Hutterites, and Swiss Brethren. The Anabaptists were persecuted and treated with suspicion by Catholics and Protestants alike. Some of their members were summarily executed in particularly barbarous ways. To honor the memory of these Anabaptist saints, narrative songs re-counting their sufferings and faith were written and sung by their co-religionists.[34] The earliest song that Luther is known to have written was in the nature of one of these martyr songs. In July 1523 he re-ceived the news that two young friars from the Augustinian mon-astery in Antwerp had been burned at the stake in Brussels as "Lutherans." In response and in the narrative style of popular folk-songs Luther wrote a "new song," *Ein neues Lied wir heben an.*[35] In it the martyrdom of the two men is described and their faith and wit-ness commended. There may be a connection between Luther's mar-tyr song and those of the Anabaptists, since they post-date Luther's; at the very least they share many common features with the then current narrative ballad. A number of Dutch martyr songs were writ-ten by David Joris and his followers between 1529 and 1536 to cele-brate the lives and deaths of executed Anabaptists. These were later collected together and issued by Joris as *Een Geestelijck Liedt-Boecxken,* perhaps published around 1540 or at some later date. The Swiss Brethren produced a hymnal in 1564, *Etliche schöne Christliche Gesang,* which was later incorporated into the *Aussbund* of 1583, the principal hymnal of the Anabaptist tradition, especially the Men-nonites. It is still in use, textually unchanged, in some American Men-nonite communities today.

Later Movements and Influences

Metrical Psalmody Renewed

When the seventeenth century was giving way to the eighteenth cen-tury, there were three important factors that led to a renewal of the singing of metrical psalms that were to have far-reaching conse-quences in Britain and British America: the metrical psalms of Tate and Brady, the change to "regular singing," and the radical psalms of Isaac Watts.

In England in the latter part of the seventeenth century there was a growing dissatisfaction with the poetic limitations of the metrical psalms of Sternhold and Hopkins. The Stationers Company of Lon-don not only held the copyright to the *Old Version,* they also had an effective veto on any other version of the psalms. To circumvent the Stationers Company, Nicholas Brady, a chaplain to King William III, and Nathan Tate, the Poet-Laureate, applied for, and were granted, Royal permission to publish *A New Version of the Psalms of David in English Metre, fitted for Publick Use* (London, 1696). Their choice of *"New Version"* meant that the psalter of Sternhold and Hopkins would thereafter be referred to as the *Old Version*. But before the *New Version* could be established in public worship its authors withdrew it in response to considerable criticism. Over the next two years Tate and Brady reworked their psalms, some of them being substantially revised, and reissued them in 1698. But even some of these revisions were criticized so that the authors undertook one final revision before the definitive edition was published later the same year, 1698.[36]

The first church that is reported to have sung the new psalms was St. Martin-in-the-Fields, London, in January 1699. Eventually the *New Version* of Tate and Brady became acceptable to many Church of England congregations, but it never completely displaced the *Old Version*. By and large in rural England the psalms of the *Old Version* continued to be the main form of congregational psalmody in the worship of the churches, in some places until fairly late in the nineteenth century, but in urban England the *New Version* was generally the preferred psalter. Although Tate and Brady accepted the Calvinist principle of rendering the biblical psalms in strophic verse, they were also concerned with doing so with a greater sense of poetry.

The Bishop of London commended the *New Version* for use in the churches served by his clergy. Since his episcopal oversight extended beyond the boundaries of the diocese of London to include all Anglican churches of the British colonies, this commendation had far-reaching consequences. In particular it was a major factor in the extensive use of Tate and Brady texts within and beyond Anglicanism in British North America throughout the eighteenth and early nineteenth centuries.

Hard on the heels of these poetic concerns came a far-reaching musical revolution. Until this time the performance practice of psalmody was "lining out," that is, the congregation singing line by line, repeating them after the clerk or cantor. But this kind of call and response singing did not make too much sense when every line of every psalm was effectively sung twice, and where members of the congregation had to suspend their understanding while waiting for the next line that was essential to the meaning of the line they had just sung. At the beginning of the eighteenth century there was therefore a movement to displace "usual singing" (lining-out, singing line by line) by "regular singing" (stanza by stanza). With regular singing came two far-reaching developments. First was the production of new tune-books that introduced new tunes and therefore the basic repertoire of the old psalm tunes was significantly expanded. Second, the rise of the singing master, who not only sold the new tunebooks but also created parish singing schools to teach the new way of singing, that is by reading the notes in the tune-book rather than echoing the lining out of the parish clerk. It was a development that was to have far-reaching consequences on the hymnic development of the eighteenth century, especially Methodist hymnody.

The singing school tradition had a longer life in America, influencing the emergence of New England composers such as William Billing, Lewis Edson, and others in the early national period of the United States of America and continuing well into the nineteenth century.

Isaac Watts was brought up as a Dissenter or Independent, a denominational affiliation that was later known as Congregationalism, and later became an ordained minister. Early in life he had begun to write metrical psalms and paraphrases in the attempt to improve on what he was called upon to sing Sunday by Sunday. Eventually these congregational songs were published. The first edition of *Hymns and Spiritual Songs* (London, 1707) included a number of metrical psalms but they were withdrawn from later editions because by this time he was working on a metrical psalter, which was eventually issued as *The Psalms of David Imitated in the Language of the New Testament, And Applied to the Christian State and Worship* (London, 1719). "Imitated in the Language of the New Testament" contrasted with "conferred with the Hebrew" of the title page of the *Old Version,* and represented a significant hermeneutical and theological shift.[37] The authors of both the *Old* and *New Versions* strived to put the substance of the Hebrew psalms as accurately as possible into English verse. In contrast Watts specifically interpreted these Old Testament songs by incorporating the substance of New Testament teaching into them. In his preface to *The Psalms of David Imitated* he explained his purpose and method:

> I have not been so curious and exact in striving every where to express the antient [sic] Sense and Meaning of David, but have rather exprest myself as I may suppose *David* would have done, had he lived in the days of *Christianity.* And by this means perhaps I have sometimes hit upon the true intent of the Spirit of God in those Verses farther and clearer than *David* himself could ever discover, as St. *Peter* encourages me to hope. 1 *Pet.* 1:11,12. . . . In all places I have kept my grand Design in view, and that is *to teach my Author to speak like a Christian.*[38]

Watts had been anticipated by Luther who had introduced New Testament teaching into his version of Psalm 46, *Ein feste Burg,* but in the English-speaking world this new hermeneutic was revolutionary. Although many voices were raised against "Watts Whims," their perceptive poetry made it impossible to ignore them. In the course of time they were not only widely accepted but frequently imitated.

The revolution that Watts brought about was his insistence that Christian congregational song cannot be confined to the Old Testament psalms, but must embrace the totality of Scripture. In doing so he laid the foundation on which later English hymnody would be built. At the same time he exposed weaknesses in the old metrical psalm tradition. The success of Watts's psalms and hymns eventually brought about the disintegration of the almost monolithic tradition of English metrical psalmody, which, though it continued for a few generations, was almost finally stifled by the increasing volume of hymn and hymnal production of the nineteenth century. Watts' success was in his use of an almost exclusively monosyllabic language to create epigrammatic opening lines and lofty thoughts in connected stanzas. He contributed numerous "classic" hymns to English hymnody, among them "I'll praise my Maker while I've breath," "Jesus shall reign where'er the sun," "Nature with open volume stands," "Our God, our help in ages past," and "When I survey the wondrous cross."

The hymns and psalms of Isaac Watts were widely sung by American Congregationalists and Presbyterians, among others, throughout the eighteenth century, a practice that continued after the American Revolution with the texts suitably revised (together with additional psalms and hymns) by Joel Barlow, Timothy Dwight, and others.[39]

Pietism and the Evangelical Revival

German Pietism, which flourished at the end of the seventeenth and the beginning of the eighteenth century, grew out of the combined influences of English Puritan devotional writings and the effects of the devastation of the Thirty Years War during the first half of the seventeenth century. *The Practice of Piety* by Lewis Bayly, published in the early 1600s,[40] was extremely widely read not only in English but in several other European languages including German. Its spirituality caught the spirit of the era, especially in Germany where the effects of war, famine, and disease created a subjective religious response, as can be seen in the poetry of Martin Opitz and the hymnody of Martin Rinckart *(Nun danket alle Gott)*, Johann Heerman *(Herzliebster Jesu)*, Tobias Clausnitzer *(Liebster Jesu, wir sind hier)*, and, especially, Paul Gerhardt *(Befiehl du deine Wege, Nun ruhen alle wälder,* and *O Haupt voll Blut* ["O Sacred Head"]). The new hymns were set to new melodies that were lighter and more expressive than the older chorale tunes that had become slow and ponderous by this time. Many of the new tunes were written by Johann Crüger[41] and Johann Georg Ebeling, successively organists of the Nikolaikirche, Berlin, where Paul Gerhardt was the pastor.

These subjective hymn texts and freer hymn tunes became the model for the hymn-writers and composers of later Lutheran Pietism, when its existence was formalized following the publication of Philip Spener's *Pia Desideria* (1675). Under the leadership of Spener's successor August Hermann Francke, the movement called for a continuation of what they saw as Luther's incomplete Reformation. All remnants of Roman Catholic theology and liturgy were to be eliminated from public worship, and private worship was to be exemplified by personal devotion built on fervent prayer and intensive Bible study. Further, the only music of public worship should be the newer type of hymns, with their subjective texts and livelier tunes, that these Pietists were already singing in their private worship. The Pietist hymnal was Johann Anastasius Freylinghausen's *Neues Geistreiches Gesangbuch*, first published in Halle in 1704. It was reprinted numerous times, reaching its 19th edition by 1759; a second part issued in 1714 went through four editions by 1733; and the two parts, comprising some 1600 hymns, were issued in one volume in 1741, being reprinted in 1771.[42] This collection not only became the hymnal of German Lutheran Pietism, it also became a primary resource for both Moravianism, as reconstituted by Count Nikolas von Zinzendorf in 1722, and Methodism under the Wesley brothers, John and Charles.

John Wesley encountered Moravian hymn-singing on board the ship *Simmonds* on his way to Georgia, October 1735-February 1736. He translated some of these German hymns sung by the Moravian missionaries and they were subsequently included in his *Collection of Psalms and Hymns* (Charleston, 1737). After their experiences of conversion (or assurance) in London, May 1738, the two brothers, Charles and John Wesley, created and directed the continuing intensification of hymn-singing in the emerging Methodist movement.[43] Charles began writing what was to prove to be an astonishing output of hymn texts in a variety of poetic forms, metres, and images.[44] In common with the embryonic Moravian communities in England, the Methodists in the 1740s are reported to have sung the "swift German" tunes of the Freyinghausen type.[45]

Beginning in 1738, John and Charles Wesley issued many different collections of hymns, almost exclusively made up of texts by Charles, culminating in *A Collection of Hymns for the People Called Methodists* (London, 1780) which provided the basic anthology of hymns for later Methodism. Through these publications the English-speaking world was introduced to a whole range of hymnody that has become part of the basic corpus of English hymns. Among these hymns are: "Christ whose Glory fills the Skies," "Hark! the herald Angels sing," "Hail the Day that sees him rise," "Love Divine, all loves excelling," "O for a thousand tongues to sing," "Rejoice the Lord is King," "Ye servants of God," among many others. Such hymns were taken over in many other hymnals of the later eighteenth century, among the most influential being: George Whitefield's *A Collection of Hymns for Social Worship, more particularly design'd for the use of the Tabernacle Congregation in London* (London, 1753), Martin Madan's *A Collection of Psalms and Hymns, Extracted from Various Authors* [the Lock Hospital hymn book] (London, 1760), Augustus Toplady's *Psalms and Hymns for Public and Private Worship* (London, 1776), and *A Select Collection of Hymns to be universally sung in all the Countess of Huntingdon's Chapels* ["Collected by her Ladyship"] (London, 1780). Another influential collection was *Olney Hymns* (London, 1779) that contained only the hymns of John Newton and William Cowper and disseminated such hymns as "Amazing grace," "How sweet the name of Jesus sounds," "O for a closer walk with God," and "God moves in a mysterious way." This remarkable hymnodic output of the Evangelical Revival of the eighteenth century spilled over into the following century and laid the foundation for the developments of the following century, which were equally as remarkable but in different ways.

Nineteenth-Century Movements

At the beginning of the nineteenth century there were several different influences and movements that contributed to the on-going development of hymnody in the churches that had their origins in the Reformations of the sixteenth century.

First, there was the consolidation of the evangelical movement in camp meeting revivalism that was the outgrowth of the Scottish Presbyterian practice of annual Eucharistic celebrations.[46] At these non-Eucharistic camp meetings a new style of hymnody was developed. The evangelical hymns of the eighteenth century, especially those of Watts and Wesley, were extended by repetitive refrains added to the end of each stanza, and/or to the end of each line within a stanza. A lighter musical style that could be quickly picked up at first hearing was created for these expanded hymn-texts. In the course of time a significant sequence of camp meeting hymnals was published. Ultimately the camp meeting hymn style would be incorporated into the later Sunday school hymnals and eventually evolve into the gospel hymn.

Second, particularly in the southern states of America, folk hymns that had hitherto been transmitted orally began to appear in tunebooks, many of them in shape-notes, in the early decades of the century. Among them was *The Sacred Harp*, first published in 1844, which created a singing tradition that continues today. Although Henry Ward Beecher included some of these tunes in his *Plymouth Collection* (New York, 1855), it was not until the twentieth century that these tunes entered into mainline denominational hymnals.

Third, from the second decade of the century Lowell Mason undertook to reform congregational hymnody in the United States. He was concerned that most congregations did not sing very much: in rural churches the congregation tended to be replaced by the choirs of singing schools who sang fuging-tunes, and in urban churches by paid quartets of singers. Mason saw that a musical reform was necessary if congregations were to be encouraged to sing. They needed simple and straightforward tunes, but not the light and sometimes extravagant tunes that had been generated by the evangelical revival of the previous century. Hymn tunes had to be "good" music so he borrowed the philosophy and practice of William Gardiner, who had published *Sacred Melodies from Haydn, Mozart and Beethoven: Adapted to the Best English Poets* (2 vols., London, 1812–15). Music from the "best" contemporary (or near contemporary) composers was adapted into hymn tunes. Gardiner was not the first to make such adaptations—some eighteenth-century tunebooks had included adapted versions of arias and choruses from the oratorios of Handel and Haydn—but he was the first to exploit the technique as a matter of principle. Lowell Mason, however, out-Gardinered Gardiner by producing an extremely large number of adapted tunes in a dazzling sequence of tune-books. Beginning with *The Boston Handel and Haydn Society Collection of Church Music* (Boston, 1822), and ending with *Carmina Sacra Enlarged: The American Tune Book* (Boston, 1869), he issued approaching forty different collections of church music, mostly devoted to congregational hymnody, that were reprinted and revised numerous times.[47] These tune-books encouraged others, notably Thomas Hastings and William Bradbury, to produce other collections. They were also quarried by later hymnal editors, and a significant number of Lowell Mason tunes are still to be found in contemporary American hymnals.

Fourth, there was the discovery that, contrary to popular belief, hymns, as opposed to metrical psalms, were not illegal in the worship of the Church of England. In a famous ecclesiastical court case, brought by the members of St. Paul's Church, Sheffield, against their incumbent, Thomas Cotterill, who had produced an anthology of congregational song in which hymns outnumbered 150 metrical psalms by more than two-to-one, it was shown that the Church of England had never concluded that metrical psalms were the only legitimate congregational songs for Anglican worship.[48] The aftermath of the court case was that, at the request of the Archbishop of York, Cotterill produced a new edition of his hymnal in which the hymns approximately equaled the number of metrical psalms: *A Selection of Psalms and Hymns for the Use of Saint Paul's Church in Sheffield* (London, 1820). Included at the beginning of the small volume was a commendation written by the Archbishop of York. The result of the court case, the Archbishop's commendation of the collection, and the fact that the publisher also made available editions with a generic title page that omitted reference to St. Paul's Sheffield, ensured a wide dissemination of the *Selection* and encouraged the production of similar volumes. During the next generation many such locally-produced hymnals appeared.

Fifth, there was the Oxford Movement that was to exert an all-pervasive influence on the patterns and content of worship far beyond the boundaries of England or Anglicanism. It was essentially a reform movement with the aim of revitalizing the Church of England by examining its spiritual nature and historical roots, a movement that increasingly moved towards Catholic doctrine and practice. The principal leaders were John Henry Newman, John Keble, R. H. Froude, and E. B. Pusey, who together, from 1834, edited and wrote *Tracts for the Times,* hence the other name for the movement: Tractarianism. Many of the tracts were liturgical and some specifically drew attention to Latin hymnody. Thus Newman's Tract 75, *On the Roman Breviary as Embodying the Substance of the Devotional Services of the Catholic Church* (1836), included fourteen Latin hymns in translation. Newman later published an anthology of Latin hymns from the Roman and Paris breviaries as *Hymni ecclesiae* (Oxford, 1838). The ideal of the Tractarians was for the English church to adopt, in translation, the Latin hymns of the liturgy from which the Book of Common Prayer was substantially created. Edward Caswall published *Lyra Catholica* (London, 1849), a collection of translations from the Roman missal and breviary, and John Mason Neale, with Thomas Helmore, produced *The Hymnal Noted* (London, 1851–56), a comprehensive hymnal of translated Latin hymns, with plainsong notation, to be used in conjunction with the English Prayer Book services. Neale also published further translations of Latin hymnody and others from Greek sources, together with a few original hymns. Although the ideal of singing only translated Latin hymns in the English church was never realized, these translations were widely used and a good many of them remain in current hymnals.

The Tractarian Movement also led, indirectly, to other translations. There were those who reacted to the Tractarian idealization of late medieval Catholicism and looked to European Protestantism instead.

German Protestantism was in the public eye: Queen Victoria was married to Albert of Saxe-Coburg; Mendelssohn, whose music made significant use of the German chorale, was frequently in the United Kingdom; and there was a growing awareness of the music of J.S. Bach, who was seen as the quintessential Protestant composer. For those out of sympathy with the Catholic emphases of the Oxford Movement, the German Protestant chorale became a viable prospect. Thus Frances Elizabeth Cox published translations of German hymns in *Hymns from the German* (London, 1841; revised and enlarged 1864), and Arthur Tozer Russell's translations appeared in two collections: *Hymns for Public Worship and Private Devotion* (London, 1848), published for the London German Hospital, and *Psalms and Hymns, Partly Original, Partly Selected, for the Use of the Church of England* (London, 1851). But the most significant translator of German hymns was Catherine Winkworth who, between 1855 and 1869, published almost four hundred translations of German hymns.[49] Her first collection was issued as *Lyra Germanica* (London, 1855), and a second series followed in 1858. Five years later she collaborated with two musicians to produce *The Chorale Book for England* (London, 1863), and her last collection containing translations was *The Christian Singers of Germany* (London, 1869). Some of her translations have become classic English hymns in their own right, among them, "Comfort, comfort ye my people," "Praise to the Lord, the Almighty," and "Now thank we all our God." Catherine Winkworth's translations of German hymns have been used more extensively in American hymnals than in British counterparts, especially those produced by Lutheran bodies in the final quarter of the nineteenth century when many congregations were beginning to move from German to English as the language for worship.

The most important hymnological outcome of the Oxford Movement was the creation of *Hymns Ancient & Modern,* the cooperative product of a number of Tractarian clergy.[50] The editorial committee was chaired by Sir Henry W. Baker; John Keble and John Mason Neale were appointed advisers; and William Henry Monk, Organist and Director of Music at King's College, London, oversaw the music. After a number of trial compilations were given restricted circulation in 1859–60, the words-only edition of *Hymns Ancient & Modern for Use in the Service of the Church* was published in time to be used on Advent Sunday 1860, with the full music edition appearing the following year. Between 1861 and 1868, when a *Supplement* was issued, four and a half million copies of the basic edition were sold. The original edition with its supplement also crossed the Atlantic, being reprinted at least fourteen times in New York and Philadelphia between 1866 and 1888.[51] In 1869 it was decided that a revised and enlarged edition of the hymnal was needed. Theologically and ecclesiastically the revision was much broader in scope than the original Tractarian hymnal had been, and incorporated more of contemporary writing, thus proportionately reducing the influence of translated Latin hymnody. Similarly, the presence of John Stainer on the music committee ensured that the predominant style became the somewhat self-indulgent, chromatic four-part harmony, with a propensity for seventh-chords, that has come to be recognized as "the Victorian hymn tune."[52] The revised and expanded edition was issued in 1875. A supplement was added in 1889, which further broadened the total content of the hymnal. *Hymns Ancient & Modern* thus quickly became the most important and influential collection of the nineteenth century. It was extensively used by hymnal editors throughout the English-speaking world and was the primary model for the many denominational hymnals published on both sides of the Atlantic in the final quarter of the nineteenth century, and continued to exert a marked influence on twentieth-century hymnals.

Sixth, there was the phenomenon of gospel hymnody. As indicated above, gospel hymnody developed from the camp meeting style as it evolved through the Sunday school movement. Between 1840 and 1870 an astonishing sequence of Sunday school hymnals was published. Among the most influential were those of William Bradbury, notably *The Golden Chain* (1861) and *The Golden Shower* (1862), which were frequently reprinted. The gospel hymn finally emerged as an identifiable genre during the final quarter of the century with the evangelistic enterprises of organizations such as the YMCA and of individuals such as Dwight L. Moody. Although primarily an American phenomenon, gospel hymnody nevertheless had an important early British dimension. Ira Sankey first published his gospel hymns *Sacred Songs and Solos* (London, 1873), a sixteen-page pamphlet, for use during Moody's revivalist meetings in Great Britain. The basic collection was expanded and continued to be available in Britain at the same time as its American counterpart: *Gospel Hymns and Sacred Songs* (New York, 1875), an amalgam of Sankey's pieces in the genre and those of P.P. Bliss that had been published in *Gospel Songs* (Cincinnati, 1874). There were many imitators and numerous collections were published. The genre is probably best epitomized in the gospel hymns of the prolific Fanny Crosby.

Twentieth-Century Developments

The Reformation churches in the twentieth century have continued the development of inherited hymnodic traditions in many and varied ways—as well as pursuing new directions, such as the notable expansion from the narrow confines of monoculturism into the broader concerns of multiculturalism, the exploration of gender and linguistic issues, etc.—but space precludes an adequate investigation here.[53] Nevertheless some of the major influences can be charted, at least in outline.

The first half of the century, devastated by two World Wars, disorientated first by the Wall Street crash and then the great depression, created a conservative mind-set. The hymnody of the period was therefore characterized primarily by a conservation of the familiar. New hymnals were produced but their orientation was a backward-looking continuation of the major strands of nineteenth-century traditions. That is not to say that new hymns were not being written and published, but these "twentieth-century" hymns were generally written in the older styles. There were exceptions, such as Henry Emerson Fosdick's "God of grace and God of glory," but few gained entry into the regular hymnals until after the 1950s and 1960s. The themes of the hymns that were written during the first half of the century reflected various concerns of the age. In the aftermath of the First World War, peace themes were prominent; the deprivations of the post-depression years fostered the "social gospel" of liberal Protestantism which was reflected in many of the hymns of the period; the beginnings of the ecumenical movement, which eventually led to the formation of the World Council of Churches, gave rise to hymns that expressed the fundamental unity of faith of world-wide Christianity; and after the testing of the hydrogen-bomb in the late 1940s, when it became painfully clear that humanity now had the expertise to destroy itself, hymn-writers such as Albert Bayly expressed a new perspective on the need for the human race to depend on the providence of God.

The iconoclastic 1960s proved to be a watershed with regard to the creation of new hymnody. The last thirty years have seen an unprecedented period of hymn-writing in a variety of textual and musical styles, and an almost bewildering sequence of hymnal publication. On the one hand, there has been the British Hymn Explosion, whose leading writers and composers have been Fred Pratt Green, Fred Kaan, Brian Wren, Erik Routley, Peter Cutts, among many others, and the American Hymnal Explosion, in which every major denominational grouping has already produced its own hymnals, or has plans to do so. The former has already been fairly fully described and analyzed,[54] but the latter has yet to receive the attention it deserves.

One of the most (some would say *the*) significant ecumenical developments of the twentieth century has been the liturgical movement. The Catholic Church played a leading role in this movement which proved to be of catalytic importance with regard to its own reformation of worship initiated by the Second Vatican Council. But these reforms have had an impact on the older Reformation churches. For example, the introduction of the three-year lectionary outside Catholicism has materially effected a greater biblicism among those traditions that prided themselves on their biblicity! That is because the wider biblical spread of the lectionary revealed whole areas that had not been covered hitherto in "Protestant" hymnody, especially in the English-speaking world, thus stimulating hymn writing on these neglected biblical themes. But not only has much of contemporary hymnody become more biblical, it has also become more "liturgical" in its usage. Thus as Catholicism has been embracing the "Protestant" hymn in its worship, many Reformation churches have been singing their hymns within a "Catholic" liturgical structure. In the latter part of the twentieth century we are therefore seeing a reinforcement of the insights of Tractarian Anglicans, Genevan Calvinists, and Wittenberg Lutherans, who all, one way or another, saw congregational song not as incidental to worship but rather as part of its liturgical substance.

Notes

1. Christopher Haigh, *English Reformations: Religion, Politics, and Society under the Tudors* (Oxford: Clarendon Press, 1993).

2. See further, Robin A. Leaver, *Elisabeth Creutziger, the Magdeburg Enchiridion, 1536, & Reformation Theology. The Kessler Reformation Lecture, Pitts Theology Library, October 18, 1994* (Atlanta: Pitts Theology Library, Emory University, 1995).

3. See Robin A. Leaver, "'Then the Whole Congregation Sings': The Sung Word in Reformation Worship," *The Drew Gateway* 60/1 (Fall 1990) 55–73. A survey of sixteenth century hymnody can be found in the first chapter of Robin A. Leaver, *"Goostly psalmes and spirituall songes": English and Dutch Metrical Psalms from Coverdale to Utenhove 1535–1566.* (Oxford: Clarendon, 1991); and Robin A. Leaver, "Hymnals," *Oxford Encyclopedia of the Reformation,* ed. Hans J. Hillerbrand, 4 vols. (New York: Oxford University Press, 1996) 2:286–89.

4. Basic studies include: Louis F. Benson, *The English Hymn: Its Development and Use in Worship* [1915] (Richmond: Knox, 1962); Harry Eskew and Hugh McElrath, *Sing With Understanding: An Introduction to Christian Hymnody,* 2nd ed. (Nashville: Church Street Press, 1995). The introductory essays in the first volume of *The Hymnal 1982 Companion,* ed. Raymond Glover (New York: Church Hymnal Corporation, 1990–1995), 3 vols. in 4, offer a

comprehensive survey from an Episcopalian perspective; Carlton R. Young, *My Great Redeemer's Praise: An Introduction to Christian Hymns* (Akron: OSL Publications, 1995) is written from a Methodist viewpoint; Harry Eskew, David W. Music and Paul A. Richardson, *Singing Baptists: Studies in Baptist Hymnody in America* (Nashville: Church Street Press, 1994) is a collection of essays on important Baptist composers, hymn writers, and tunebooks; Erik Routley, *Christian Hymns Observed* (Princeton: Prestige, 1982), is a brief tour-de-force written from the unique and perceptive perspectives of Erik Routley; Robin A. Leaver, "Hymnals, Hymnal Companions, and Collection Development" *MLA Notes* 47 (December, 1990) 331–54, is essentially a bibliography of historical and background handbooks and companions to a wide range of denominational/confessional hymnals. For specific hymn texts and tunes see the historical anthologies edited by Erik Routley: *A Panorama of Christian Hymnody* (Collegeville: The Liturgical Press, 1979) and *The Music of Christian Hymns* (Chicago: GIA, 1981).

5. On the general background, see Patrick S. Diehl, *The Medieval European Religious Lyric: An Ars Poetica* (Berkeley: University of California Press, 1985).

6. See Richard Greene, *Early English Carols,* rev. ed. (Oxford: Clarendon Press, 1977); John Stevens, *Words and Music in the Middle Ages: Song, Narrative, Dance, and Drama, 1050–1350* (Cambridge: Cambridge University Press, 1986); Hugh Keyte and Andrew Parrott, *The New Oxford Book of Carols* (Oxford: Oxford University Press, 1992); see also Rosemary Woolf, *English Religious Lyric in the Middle Ages* (Oxford: Clarendon Press, 1968).

7. See J.A.N. Knuttel, *Het geestelijk lied in de Nederlanden voor de kerkhervorming* (Rotterdam: Brusse, 1906; reprint Groningen: Bouma, 1974).

8. See F. Liuzzi, *La lauda e I primordi della melodia italiana* (Rome: Libreria della Statu, 1934); Cyrilla Barr, *The Monophonic Lauda and the Lay Religious Confraternities of Tuscany and Umbria in the Late Middle Ages* (Kalamazoo: Medieval Institute, 1988).

9. See Johannes Riedel, "Leisen Formulae: Their Polyphonic Settings in the Renaissance and Reformation," Ph.D. dissertation (University of Southern California, 1953).

10. The hymnal went through at least five further editions by 1561.

11. It was reprinted in Ulm at least four times by 1541.

12. Reprinted thirteen times by 1611.

13. *Luther's Works: American Edition,* ed. Jaroslav Pelikan and Helmut T. Lehmann (St. Louis and Philadelphia: Concordia & Fortress, 1955–86) [hereafter cited as LW] 53:36.

14. Ibid.

15. *Martin Luther Deutsche Messe 1526* [Facsimile], ed. Johannes Wolf (Kassel: Bärenreiter, 1934); LW 53:61–90.

16. LW 53:221.

17. Strassburg at this time was in a predominantly German-speaking area.

18. *Martin Bucers Katechismen aus den Jahren 1534, 1537, 1543,* ed. Robert Stupperich [*Martin Bucers Deutsche Schriften,* Bd. 6/3] (Gütersloh: Mohn, 1987) 257.

19. See, for example: Markus Jenny, *Zwinglis Stellung zur Musik im Gottesdienst* (Zurich: Zwingli Verlag, 1966).

20. See Charles Garside, *Zwingli and the Arts* (New Haven: Yale University Press, 1966; reprint New York: Da Capo, 1981) *passim,* but see the summaries on pp. 37 and 75.

21. See Bard Thompson, ed., *Liturgies of the Western Church* (Cleveland: World Books, 1961; reprint Philadelphia: Fortress, 1981) 142.

22. See the corrective essay by A. Casper Honders, "The Reformers on Church Music," *Pulpit, Table, and Song: Essays in Celebration of Howard G. Hageman,* eds. Heather Elkins and Edward C. Zaragoza (Lanham, Md.: Scarecrow, 1996) 46–52.

23. See especially the three contributions by Markus Jenny: "The Hymns of Zwingli and Luther: A Comparison," *Cantors at the Crossroads: Essays on Church Music in Honor of Walter E. Buszin,* ed. Johannes Riedel (St. Louis: Concordia, 1967) 45–63; "Die Lieder Zwinglis," *Jahrbuch für Liturgik und Hymnologie* 14 (1969) 63–102; *Luther, Zwingli, Calvin in ihren Liedern* (Zurich: Theologischer Verlag, 1983) 175–214.

24. See Hannes Reimann, *Die Einführung des Kirchengesangs in der Zürcher Kirche nach der Reformation* (Zurich: Zwingli Verlag, 1959).

25. Arthur C. Cochrane, ed. *Reformed Confessions of the 16th Century* (Philadelphia: Westminster, 1966) 290–91.

26. A number of tunes from this psalter have found their way into English use, among them OLD 124TH, TOULON, and OLD 100TH.

27. See Pierre Pidoux, *Le Psautier Huguenot du XVIe siècle,* 2 vols. (Basel: Bärenreiter, 1962); Waldo Seldon Pratt, *The Music of the French Psalter of 1562: A Historical Survey and Analysis* (New York: Columbia University Press, 1939; reprint New York: AMS Press, 1966).

28. For details see Leaver, *Goostly psalmes,* chap. 2.

29. For details see ibid., chap. 7.

30. For example, the *Whole Book of Psalms* of 1562 had included the version of Ps. 100 by Hopkins, rather than Kethe's "All people that on earth do dwell"; from 1563 Kethe version of the psalm was preferred to that of Hopkins.

31. See Miller Patrick, *Four Centuries of Scottish Psalmody* (London: Oxford University Press, 1949).

32. See Nicholas Temperley, "Middleburg Psalms," *Studies in Bibliography: Papers of the Bibliographical Society of the University of Virginia,* 30 (1977) 162–70.

33. The *Bay Psalm Book: A Facsimile Reprint of the First Edition 1640,* ed. Zoltán Haraszti (Chicago: University of Chicago Press, 1956) [14–15].

34. See Rudolf Wolkan, *Die Lieder der Wiedertäufer: Ein Beitrag zur deutschen und niederländischen Literatur-und Kirchengeschichte* (Berlin: Behr, 1903; reprint Nieuwkoop: de Graaf, 1965).

35. LW 53:214–16.

36. On the background and the significance of the psalms of Tate and Brady, see Robin A. Leaver, "The Failure that Succeeded: The *New Version* of Tate and Brady," *The Hymn* 48/4 (Oct. 1997) 22–31.

37. See further, Robin A. Leaver, "Isaac Watts's Hermeneutical Principles and the Decline of Metrical Psalmody," *Churchman* 92 (1978) 56–60.

38. Isaac Watts, *The Psalms of David Imitated in the Language of the New Testament, And apply'd to the Christian State and Worship* (London, 1719), xix–xx; see also Watts' letter to Cotton Mather of Boston, written in March the previous year; cited in Henry W. Foote, *Three Centuries of American Hymnody* (Cambridge, MA: Harvard University Press, 1940; reprint, with additions, [n.p.]: Archon, 1968) 66–67.

39. See Rochelle A. Stackhouse, *The Language of the Psalms in Worship: American Revisions of Watts' Psalter* (Lanham, Md.: Scarecrow, 1997).

40. The earliest extant edition is the third of 1613.

41. A significant number of Crüger's hymn tunes were self-consciously modeled on Genevan psalm-tunes; see, Siegrfried Fornançon, "Johann Crüger und der Genfer Psalter," *Jahrbuch für Liturgik und Hymnologie 1* (1955) 115–20.

42. On the publication history, see Dianne Marie McMullen, "The Geistrieches Gesangbuch of Johann Anastasius Freylinghausen (1670–1739): A German Pietist Hymnal," Ph.D. dissertation (University of Michigan, 1987) 29–32.

43. In these middle years of the eighteenth century, and for much of the following generation, both Charles and John Wesley ensured that Methodism was essentially an Anglican movement; see Robin A. Leaver, "Charles Wesley and Anglicanism," *Charles Wesley: Poet and Theologian*, ed. S. T. Kimbrough (Nashville: Kingswood, 1992) 157–75, 241–43.

44. See the introduction of Frank Baker, ed., *Representative Verse of Charles Wesley* (London: Epworth, 1962) ix–lxi. Many of these evangelical "Methodist" hymns express a highly developed Eucharistic theology; see J. Ernest Rattenbury, *The Eucharistic Hymns of John and Charles Wesley* (London: Epworth, 1948).

45. On the common corpus of German tunes sung by Moravians and Methodists, see Robin A. Leaver "Lampe's Tunes," *Hymns on the Great Festivals and Other Occasions: Hymn Texts by Charles Wesley and Samuel Wesley, Jr., Music by John Frederick Lampe*, facsimile (1746) with introduction by Carleton R. Young, Frank Baker, Robin A. Leaver, and ST Kimbrough, Jr. (Madison, N.J.: Charles Wesley Society, 1996) 31–44. SWIFT GERMAN was the name John Wesley gave to a German tune included in his "Foundery" tune book of 1742.

46. See Leigh Eric Schmidt, *Holy Fairs: Scottish Communions and American Revivals in the Early Modern Period* (Princeton: Princeton University Press, 1989).

47. See further Carol A. Pemberton, *Lowell Mason: His Life and Work* (Ann Arbor: UMI Research Press, 1985).

48. For the background, see Thomas K. McCart, *The Matter and Manner of Praise: The Controversial Evolution of Hymnody in the Church of England, 1760–1840* (Lanham, Md.: Scarecrow, 1998).

49. They are listed in Robin A. Leaver, *Catherine Winkworth: the Influence of Her Translations on English Hymnody* (St. Louis: Concordia, 1978) 85–134.

50. On the background see: W. K. Lowther Clarke, *A Hundred Years of Hymns Ancient and Modern* (London: Clowes, 1960); Susan Drain, *The Anglican Church in Nineteenth Century Britain: Hymns Ancient and Modern (1860–1875)* (Lewiston, N.Y.: Mellen, 1989).

51. See James Brumm, "The Mysterious American Odyssey of Hymns A & M," *The Hymn Society of Great Britain and Ireland Bulletin,* 12/ 2 (April 1988) 24–26.

52. See Nicholas Temperley, *The Music of the English Parish Church,* 1 (Cambridge: Cambridge University Press, 1983) 303–10.

53. See, for example: Robin A. Leaver, "British Hymnody, 1900–1950," *The Hymnal 1982 Companion,* ed. R. F. Glover (New York: The Church Hymnal Corporation 1991), 1:474–504; David Farr, "Protestant Hymn-Singing in the United States, 1916–1943: Affirming an Ecumenical Heritage," ibid., 1:505–554; Russell Schulz-Widmer, "Hymnody in the United States Since 1950," ibid., 1:600–630; Robin A. Leaver, "Renewal in Hymnody," *Lutheran Quarterly* 6 (1992) 359–83; Robin A. Leaver, "Are Hymns Theological by Design or Default?" *New Mercersburg Review* 18 (Autumn 1995) 12–33.

54. The basic literature includes: Alan Dunstan, *The Hymn Explosion* (Croydon: Royal School of Church Music, 1981); Ian Fraser, "Beginnings at Dunblane," *Duty and Delight: Routley Remembered,* ed. Robin A. Leaver and James H. Litton (Carol Stream: Hope, 1985) 171–90; Robin A. Leaver, "British Hymnody Since 1950," *Hymnal 1982 Companion,* ed. Glover, 1:555–99; Alan Luff, "The Hymn Explosion after 25 Years," *The Hymn* 46/2 (April 1995) 6–15.

Chapter 19

Liturgical Music as Corporate Song 2: Problems of Hymnody in Catholic Worship

Frank C. Quinn, O.P.

There is some ambivalence concerning the use of hymns in Roman Catholic liturgy, especially in the Mass. On the one hand there is the publication of Catholic "hymnals" like *Worship,* subtitled "A Hymnal and Service Book for Roman Catholics."[1] Containing well over four hundred hymns, one would suppose that this is the standard form music takes in Catholic worship. And yet in *Liturgical Music Today,* a document issued by the Bishops' Committee on the Liturgy, there is at best grudging acceptance of hymns in the Mass:

> While the responsorial form of singing is especially suitable for processions, the metrical hymn can *also fulfill* the function of the entrance song. If, however, a metrical hymn with several verses is selected, its form should be respected. The progression of text and music must be allowed to play out its course and achieve its purpose musically and poetically. In other words, the hymn should not be ended indiscriminately at the end of the procession. For this same reason, metrical hymns *may not be the most suitable choices* to accompany the preparation of the gifts and altar at the Eucharist, since the music should not extend past the time necessary for the ritual [italics added].[2]

Ten years later another document simply denied the value of hymns at processional moments in Catholic worship:

> This kind of music [hymns] can be well suited to those moments when singing is all we do (for example, a song of praise after communion) but seldom lends itself to accompany actions (for example, a communion procession).[3]

How different the approach to hymns in Protestant worship:

> . . . in Protestant worship, hymns often are the proclamation, and they "carry" the liturgy . . . [Hymns are,] as John Wesley reminds us in the eighteenth century, "a little body of . . . practical divinity." That is, hymns help form and express the truths of Christian faith in our lives, and, for good or for ill, constitute a tacit repertoire of proclamation.[4]

This attitude towards hymnody is even more pronounced in the Lutheran churches:

> . . . it is a commonplace to observe that a great contribution of the Lutheran Reformation was the restoration of congregational singing. But what is usually less noted is that Luther's desire for the active participation of the congregation through hymnody was a result of his concern that the people participate actively *in the singing of the liturgy.* For much of Protestantism today hymns may best be described as general Christian songs loosely attached to worship, but for Luther the congregational hymn was a vehicle for involving the faithful *in the singing of the liturgy.*[5]

The Hymn

In this paper the word "hymn" is used to designate a musical form "consisting of a number of stanzas sung to the same melodic line."[6] The stanzas themselves are usually rhymed and the individual strophes are usually four or more lines in length. The word "hymn," strictly speaking, refers to the text, the music being called the hymn "tune." Modern hymn tunes are also named, either from the text (such as RESONET IN LAUDIBUS), or after the composer (such as MOZART), by reference to some event or feeling (such as RESIGNATION) or locale (for example, REGENT SQUARE), or for some other reason.

Parenthetically, it should be noted that the word "hymn" has and can refer to much more than metrical, strophic songs. It can be used, for example, in the same general way that the word "song" is used. In the scriptures we hear of "psalms and hymns and spiritual songs" (Col. 3:16). In this context it seems unlikely that "hymns" refers to a strophic song.[7] The word seems to fit larger lyrical forms still found in the New Testament, such as the Gospel canticles (the *Benedictus, Magnificat,* and *Nunc Dimittis*), as well as certain of the Old Testament psalms. It also applies to such *psalmoi idiotikoi* (private, not inspired, psalms) as the *Gloria in excelsis,* and the *Te Deum.* From the third century we have a strophic hymn still sung in evening prayer today, the famed *Phos Hilaron,* although the three stanzas of this hymn are not metrical.[8] Around the same time metrical hymnody began to appear[9]; this form was utilized by Ambrose of Milan in the late fourth century.[10]

Hymns in Pre-Vatican II Worship

Several of these early "hymns" are found in Catholic liturgical rites today. For example, the Gospel canticles are an unchangeable feature of the Roman Catholic Liturgy of the Hours. The *Gloria in excelsis,* though originally a prose hymn found in Byzantine Morning Prayer *(Orthros),* found its way into the Western celebration of the Eucharist. But unlike the Eastern liturgies, in which various hymnic forms proliferated, even in the Eucharist, in the Western rites they are not all that common.

Metrical hymns became part of the Liturgy of the Hours in the thirteenth century. The only prose hymn that remains an integral element in Eucharistic celebrations is, as noted above, the *Gloria in excelsis.* This sung text, known also as the "greater doxology," began to be added to the opening rites of the Mass, following on the *Kyrie eleison,* in the sixth century. It is instructive to note that it is located within the opening rites at a moment when nothing else is going on. In other words the *Gloria* is simply sung while the congregation is standing. It is its own ritual unit.[11]

It would be misleading, however, to pass by another type of hymn that was very much part of the Eucharistic liturgy for a good seven centuries. From the ninth century until the Council of Trent in the sixteenth century the sequence gained popularity in the Mass. The texts could be metrical or non-metrical, unrhymed or rhymed. The fact that some 4500 sequences were created in the Middle Ages and early Renaissance is testimony, as Richard H. Hoppin has noted, "of the enthusiasm with which religious writers and composers seized every opportunity for self-expression that the liturgical practice of the time allowed."[12] Because Trent drastically reduced the number of sequences allowed in the Mass, and Vatican II even more so,[13] our appreciation of this particular form of liturgical expression is much attenuated. However, such tropes "formed a normal and even integral part of the liturgy."[14]

Besides sequences, placed, like the *Gloria,* at a point in the liturgy where they themselves more or less formed the ritual unit, metrical hymnody as we know it never became a regular element in the Western Roman Catholic Eucharist. The reason for this was that other musical forms were found more suitable for processions and for those ritual moments for which the strophic hymn form would not work, such as moments of acclamatory praise.

Excepting the Liturgy of the Hours, then, metrical hymns had little role in official Catholic worship. This does not mean that various kinds of metrical songs were not sung elsewhere. On the contrary: by the high Middle Ages, while liturgical music was sung by schola and cantor, the people were not to be denied their voice, at least outside the official liturgy. Note, for example, carols in England and *Laude* in Italy and France.[15]

> Such music was sung outside the liturgy—at the door of the church, so to speak. This dichotomy between official liturgical and popular religious music remained in force until the twentieth century, and to some extent the distinction still holds.[16]

With the sixteenth century reformers, hymns began to play a larger role in worship. Although Luther wanted to keep the Latin chants, still he also wanted the people to join in with their own song, the strophic hymn.[17] This development occurred at the same time that printing made possible the dissemination of many different hymns. Before this, as in the Liturgy of the Hours, hymns were used over entire seasons. This made it possible for the worshipers to memorize a text; thus, even the illiterate could join in song. To promulgate a number of hymns, two things were required: printing and literacy.

As is well known, the Roman reaction to Protestant reformers was not to add new musical forms to official public worship. Rather, there was some attempt to purify the Latin chants and insist that the polyphonic music be intelligible. In any case, none of this music was intended for the congregation. As a consequence, the issue of hymns in Catholic worship, particularly with regard to the Mass, did not arise. The musical forms for liturgy were already in place and served the rite in an appropriate fashion: the processional chants, the *Graduale,* and the *Alleluia* were responsorial in origin; the ritual music for the ordinary of the Mass—*Kyrie, Gloria, Credo, Sanctus, Benedictus,* and *Agnus dei*—although consisting of a number of musical forms, such as acclamation and litany, in their current chant forms might better be characterized as songs.

Catholics did sing hymns, not in public liturgical services but in devotional rites. These prayer occasions, more than the official liturgy, spoke to the peoples' feelings. Here strophic hymns played a role. Unlike the hymns for the hours, which were not so much directed to individual feelings but rather expressed time of day or liturgical feast or season and, furthermore, were in Latin, devotional hymns payed little attention to liturgical proprieties. For example, they were addressed directly to the saint being honored; their purpose was to move the emotions of the worshiper. Many were also in the vernacular. Finally, their theological content was minimal, excepting such hymns taken from earlier liturgical sources, such as the *Tantum ergo* at benediction. For the most part, little of this music was fit for liturgical usage. As a consequence, with the insistence on the peoples' musical participation in the liturgy after Vatican II there was little music from the Catholic past that could be recycled for use by congregations, especially once texts were to be sung in the vernacular. Much music was, therefore, "borrowed" from Protestant churches.

The Return to Popular Participation in the Twentieth Century

One reason for discussing hymns in Catholic worship, even though, as we have tried to show, such musical forms are not generally found in sacramental rites, is because it is the nature of the hymn to be communal song—and the Roman Catholic Church has emphasized again and again in the twentieth century the fact that popular participation is essential to liturgical celebration. One of the issues, then, is what music will enable such participation. It would seem that the hymn form would be most suitable. Note how Edward Foley describes that hymn form known as the Lutheran chorale:

> More than any other [musical] form, the chorale says "we"! There is no assembly and other here, nor is there any leadership outside the assembly. There is simply assembly. Ecclesiologically such music defines the assembly and only the assembly in the singing of the chorale as the subject of the liturgy. . . . This is not music designed for specialists, ministers with special training or people with special gifts.[18]

It is rather curious that most of the official Roman Catholic statements on liturgical music that were promulgated before Vatican II stress a two-fold approach to popular participation in the liturgy. The first is to get the people to sing sacred songs (i.e., hymns). After they have become accustomed to singing, they could then be weaned away from such songs, especially those in the vernacular, and be taught to sing Latin Gregorian chant. In this way they would finally achieve the goal of popular musical participation, that is, they would finally sing "liturgically!"

Participatio actuosa was first insisted upon by Pius X in his *Motu proprio* of 22 November 1904.[19] This demand became the guiding principle for all the pontiffs writing after him.[20] As noted above, for Pius X and his successors popular participation in the liturgy was to be accomplished through the renewal of Gregorian chant, the song proper to the Roman Church.[21] Supposedly, by fostering chant and teaching the congregation to sing it, liturgical renewal would be made possible. Up to and including the *Sacrosanctum Concilium* of Vatican II[22] the main thrust of official documents on sacred music was, *mutatis mutandis,* to ensure the survival of the chant and to assume that it was possible for congregations to take part in it.

Other musical styles were allowed in the liturgy. Pius X singled out renaissance polyphony[23]; Roman pontiffs writing after him did the same thing. New sacred music was to be allowed on the model of earlier music.[24] In terms of instruments the organ was claimed as the instrument of the Roman Catholic Church.[25] Other instruments were only allowed if they exhibited the proper dignity.[26]

It is true that the popes, especially Pius XII, spoke encouragingly of popular religious music, a music that could be (and would be) in the vernacular.[27] There was already a tradition of such music in some national churches, such as the German and Polish churches. But the use of such music in rites that were "liturgical" rather than being "pious exercises" was heavily restricted.[28] In order to allow such music into the liturgy—Pius XII did realize that this was a necessary vehicle for popular participation—the Pope and the Congregation of Rites distinguished several kinds of Masses. First there was the sung Mass, itself divided into the solemn Mass and the high Mass or *missa cantata* in which all music was liturgical and thus in Latin. Then there was the *missa lecta,* the "read" Mass. In this latter form the Mass could admit of vernacular, popular music, as well as the spoken Latin dialogue with the presider (giving us the so-called "dialogue" Mass). It is important to note, however, that such music was not, strictly speaking, "liturgical."[29]

It was through this process of getting the people to participate musically in the low Mass by the singing of popular songs that metrical hymns entered Roman Catholic Eucharistic liturgy in the twentieth century. Although not formally "liturgical" at that time, such distinctions were lost on actual congregations. If they were singing at liturgy, they were singing at liturgy, similar to their singing at popular devotions. The downside was that, since there was no liturgical place for metrical hymns in the Western Roman Mass, the popular songs of the people were substituted for the processional moments of the Mass, what Robert Taft has spoken of as the "soft parts" of the liturgy.[30] This meant that the supposedly popular songs were not sung as part of the more important liturgical units. As a consequence of this,

> . . . because of the emphasis on the "four hymn mass," and despite the fact that closed, strophic forms do not generally function as well at processional moments as do open forms [such as responsorial or litanic forms], . . . it has taken years for many pastoral musicians to understand the importance of the ritual music that is integral to the liturgy of the word and the Eucharist. . . . We have [only] gradually come to realize that *music planning must begin with the heart of the rite* and not with peripheral elements.[31]

Vatican II and Beyond

With "The Constitution on the Sacred Liturgy" there is a change in the official view as to what is "liturgical" music. First, and most importantly, despite vehement opposition, paragraph 113 of chapter 6 speaks of the importance of all taking part in the rite as pertaining to the more noble aspect of liturgical celebration. It repudiates the first draft of this number, which originally read:

> Forma nobilior celebrationis liturgicae est Liturgica sollemnis [=liturgy with the three ministries of priest, deacon, and subdeacon], *lingua latina celebrata,* cum participatione populi [Italics added].[32]

Without the changes from the first to the final draft, the norm for the Eucharist would today be a Mass celebrated in Latin. Although several paragraphs continue to speak of preserving the treasury of sacred music (*CSL* 114) and the need to preserve the chant (*CSL* 116), such preservation is subordinated to the need for the assembly's participation as described in the important paragraph 30:

> To promote active participation, the people should be encouraged to take part by means of acclamations, responses, psalmody, antiphons, and songs, as well as by actions, gestures, and bearing. And at the proper times all should observe a reverent silence.[33]

Paragraph 118 brings up the issue, discussed by Pius XII and the Congregation of Rites in its 1958 *Instruction on Music in the Liturgy,*[34] of popular religious song. The text reads:

> The people's own religious songs are to be encouraged with care so that in sacred devotions *as well as during services of the liturgy itself,* in keeping with rubrical norms and requirements, the faithful may raise their voices in song [italics added].

Although the framers of this paragraph intended these words to be read in terms of the norms for religious songs established by the Congregation of Rites in 1958[35]—that is, that such songs were not really "liturgical"—the interpretation of this paragraph has gone far beyond such assumptions. Through this paragraph, popular religious song, in the vernacular, and thus including metrical hymns, has not only become liturgical music, but has become the song of the liturgy, brushing the former "treasury of sacred music" aside.

As a consequence of Vatican II the desire of previous twentieth century pontiffs for popular participation in the liturgy was made possible through the turn toward the vernacular. As one author has noted:

> The history of Church music will be permanently changed by the far-reaching results of Vatican II's Constitution on the Sacred Liturgy. Never again in the Western Church will there be the uniformity of practice that prevailed until December 4, 1963, when important disciplines were fundamentally altered. The two prominent points which became the bases of these really radical interjections were the introduction of the vernacular languages into the liturgy and the mandate that the congregation must henceforth take an active part in worship.[36]

Chapter 6 of "The Constitution on the Sacred Liturgy" was interpreted by an Instruction from the Sacred Congregation of Rites in 1967.[37] This constitution emphasized participation in the liturgy and vernacular song. Its statements on the Church's treasury of music and the use of Latin are thus to be interpreted in light of the principle of participation.[38] Nothing is said in this document about metrical hymns in the Eucharist. The only statement which would seem open to such usage is found in no. 36, which states: "Sometimes it is even quite appropriate to have other songs at the beginning, at the presentation of the gifts, and at the communion, as well as at the end of Mass." Of course, this paragraph simply formalizes what had been allowed by the 1958 Instruction.

Lucien Deiss, in his book *Spirit and Song of the New Liturgy*,[39] examined the Vatican II statements on music in the liturgy and the need for implementing the assembly's participation. Although his examination of musical forms focuses in the main on those forms that had evolved in Catholic sacramental worship, he does mention metrical hymns or strophic songs. For example, he allows that some hymns might be used as entrance songs (133). He disapproves of the use of hymns at the Communion procession: "The congregation's singing would not be natural and spontaneous and therefore the procession would not 'flow'" (154). He allows the singing of a "hymn" after Communion (as permitted by the *General Instruction of the Roman Missal*) and speaks of the concluding hymn (207–8). In neither case does he deal with the issue of the metrical or strophic hymn as such.

As just noted the *General Instruction of the Roman Missal* does speak of the possibility of a hymn being sung after Communion:

> After communion, the priest and people may spend some time in silent prayer. If desired, a hymn, psalm, or other song of praise may be sung by the entire congregation.[40]

The mention of a hymn at this point in the liturgy indicates the possibility of a metrical hymn being sung as a rite in itself, as is the *Gloria,* and not, as is usually the case in Catholic worship, as music accompanying an action, ordinarily a procession.

The first more or less official American statement on post-Vatican II liturgical music and the need for popular participation was *Music in Catholic Worship.*[41] This document has had a strong impact in the training of music ministers. But it really does not speak to the issue of metrical hymns as such. As we have already noted above, the 1982 document *Liturgical Music Today* did treat metrical hymns but with a good deal of caution. A more positive approach to the hymn as such is that taken by the Milwaukee report. Part of paragraph 41 was already quoted above, relative to what not to do. But this same paragraph challenges us to be sensitive to the use of different musical forms in liturgy, such as the strophic form:

> The structure of the music should match the structure of the ritual to which it is joined. A strophic hymn, for example, can be considered a self-enclosed form. Once one begins singing a strophe, the normal musical conclusion is to sing all the way to the end of the strophe. And normally one moves directly from strophe to strophe. This kind of music can be well suited to those moments when singing is all we do (for example, a song of praise after communion) but seldom lends itself to accompany actions (for example, a communion procession).[42]

Singing Hymns in Catholic Worship Today

It should be clear by now that official Catholic statements take little account of the metrical hymn. It is a song that, except for the Liturgy of the Hours, has little role in official Catholic ritual. Because of this, it is perhaps all the more surprising that in actual practice Catholics sing a goodly number of metrical hymns in their worship. Encouraged by the 1958 Instruction from the Congregation of Rites, as noted above, congregations were encouraged to sing and their song was generally located at processional moments in the mass. With the promulgation of "The Constitution on the Sacred Liturgy," such song became "liturgical." Publishers began printing hymnals for use by Catholics. Excepting some few Catholic hymns, particularly those in honor of Mary or the saints, they found available hymns in Protestant hymnals and service books (thus perhaps the anguish of some that Catholic worship was becoming "Protestant"). As is evident from the major U.S. and Canadian Catholic hymnals,[43] in the 90s hymns are fully ensconced in Catholic sacramental practice.

At the time that hymns were becoming part of Catholic worship, another movement, the so-called "folk" movement, began to provide music for worship in the late 60s. Generally speaking, the forms created by folk groups belonged to the responsorial genre, with a refrain for the congregation and verses for cantors. Other kinds of ritual music, such as the music for the Eucharistic acclamations, was composed according to patterns of folk music or in more traditional chorale/hymn style (think of the popular "Holy" from the St. Louis Jesuits in contrast to the "Holy" in Richard Proulx's *Community Mass,* both composed about the same time, at the end of the 1960s).

The contrast between hymn style and folk style led some to speak of more formal as against less formal liturgies, as well as to create different Eucharistic opportunities on Sundays for those who wanted an "older" form of worship as against a "newer." What few asked were ritual questions about how music was to be used in liturgy.[44] Thus hymns in Catholic worship continued to be employed at processional moments when, sometimes, even the congregation was moving. Hymns actually began appearing as entrance songs at weddings and ordinations although what the congregation really wanted to do was to watch the bride or ordinand processing into the church!

Today, thirty-some years after Vatican II, Catholic music making has matured. New generations of composers in the so-called folk tradition have provided Catholic parishes with a richer musical fare, including a number of fine metrical hymns. The hymns published in Catholic hymnals demonstrate a more careful evaluation of text and tune. In the past twenty or so years there has been an explosion of hymn and hymn tune writing, even among Catholics. As the Methodist liturgist Don Saliers notes:

> Congregational hymn singing is still relatively new to Roman Catholic parishes, but a new interest in the range and depth of hymns is being encouraged by ecumenical sharing and by the appearance of

excellent new hymn collections over the past twenty years. While hymns are the typical liturgical song of the churches of the Reformation, there is little doubt now that hymns are finding their way into the liturgical life of Roman Catholic parishes in a new and vital way.[45]

Questions about Practice

Questions remain concerning actual practice with regard to hymns in Catholic worship. Such questions may be dealt with under two major headings: location and performance.

First, location. As we have seen, although metrical hymns have generally entered Catholic liturgy at processional points—and such use affects our appreciation for, and even our performance of, metrical songs—the place for hymns in liturgical rites should ordinarily be moments when such communal and "closed" forms can function as individual ritual units. This is the reason why the prose hymn *Gloria in excelsis* is part of the opening rites; it does not occur during a particular processional moment or while something else is going on. It is a rite unto itself. The new location for singing a hymn after Communion rubricated by the *General Instruction of the Roman Missal* also occurs at a moment when nothing else is going on. One can focus on both text and tune. There are really no other "official" locations for metrical hymns in the Catholic Eucharist.

If a parish were to employ hymns by reference to what their Protestant neighbors were doing they might wait to sing an opening song until the procession was complete and all could sing together; they would also sing a final hymn before anyone processed out (although this function may now be actually filled by the optional post-communion song). Furthermore, a Catholic parish might imitate their neighbors by singing a gospel hymn, in other words, a hymn related to the lectionary readings of the day and coming before the homily.[46] Many contemporary hymns fit the liturgy of the word and really do not work well in other locations since such hymns of the day are based upon hearing the scriptures and responding to them in song.[47]

Secondly, with regard to performance, one must question the way hymns are accompanied and sung in many parishes. One discovers very quickly, when attending services in other Christian churches, that both musicians and congregations approach the music and texts of hymns with great seriousness and that different approaches to hymn singing as well as hymn accompaniment are found in the different churches. One might, for example, speak of a Lutheran approach to hymn singing in contrast to an Episcopal approach. Organists may vary accompaniments to each stanza of a hymn, following the meaning of the text; choir and congregation may alternate different stanzas, as in a more developed hymn concertato form; the soprano section of the choir may add a descant on the final stanza, etc. The point is, the way a hymn is to be performed is not simply revealed on the page of a hymnal. *Performance needs to be prepared ahead of time.* When one turns to performance of hymns in many Catholic churches one often finds a casual carelessness with regard to sloppy tempos, the use of only a few stanzas of the hymn, or the lack of necessary variation in singing and accompaniment occasioned by the meaning of the text and by the need for variety in performance. In other words, quite often Catholic singing of hymns is unutterably pedestrian and boring: it does not enliven the faith of the assembly. Certainly one of the reasons for this is the fact that metrical hymns entered Catholic liturgy as accompaniments to processions. Normally, processional music ends when the procession is over. Many Catholic parishes got used to ending a hymn at the end of a procession, paying little if any attention to the meaning of the text.

There is confusion here between what is meant by an entrance song and an opening or gathering song. This confusion has existed since the new *Ordo missae* was promulgated in 1969. Historically, the introit was a song sung by the choir during the entrance of the clergy. A modern opening or gathering song is music sung by the congregation as they engage in the liturgical celebration. It would seem that two functions, and thus two musical forms, are being confused here.

Parenthetically, I might note that the service where Catholics would accustom themselves to sing hymns as an important element in the ritual and in their entirety is in the Liturgy of the Hours. Here the hymn is a moment of praise and thanksgiving. No one would think of *not* singing the entire hymn! But the Liturgy of the Hours is foreign to Catholics; ordinarily, most do not have the chance to learn from the Hours that hymn singing is a ritual unto itself. Furthermore, even those who regularly celebrate the Hours do not always recognize that those hymns are different than hymns for other liturgical rites, that office hymns have reference to time and season and feast, not to some other sacramental rite.[48]

The Future

Since Catholic sacramental worship is a worship that calls for procession and movement, there will always be a place for musical forms which best accompany a procession. And no matter present practice, hymns may not be the answer. But since metrical songs can be performed in a number of ways, if the musician is conscious of the purpose of a rite and how song is part of that rite, some of the problems of hymn singing at this moment might be overcome. But it should be noted that many of the best new hymns demand the attention of the assembly; thus, they need their own space, so to speak.

Future developments in the liturgy will see the issuance of a series of entrance and Communion antiphons with the new edition of the ICEL Sacramentary. These antiphons are translated into a rhythmic English which can readily be set to music. Psalm verses will also be appointed so that the musical form of these antiphons is responsorial, a form fitting processional moments in liturgy. If this attempt to restore the entrance and Communion antiphons to the Eucharist as sung forms succeeds over the next decade, then the use of hymns at these points might be diminished.

Along with a more intentional approach to sung texts, there is also an increasing awareness of the possibility of singing ritual texts, such as the dialogues between presider and people, the prayers, especially the Eucharistic prayer, the Our Father, etc. This approach may well occupy a parish's attention more than in the past. All of this should make us more aware of how music fits into Catholic liturgy. It should also cause us to ask questions about how we employ different musical forms in liturgy. Perhaps it might lead to greater respect for the music we use. And, in terms of metrical songs—actually so much more varied than this paper might suggest, each song being an epiphany of a time, a culture, and a people—conceivably we might get beyond the "four-hymn Mass" syndrome and employ such music with respect for our assembly's needs, love for the music we actually sing, and full dedication to the Christ we celebrate in and within every liturgical act.

Notes

1. *Worship: Third Edition* (Chicago: GIA, 1986).

2. *Liturgical Music Today: A Statement of the Bishops' Committee on the Liturgy on the Tenth Anniversary of Music in Catholic Worship* (Washington, D.C.: United States Catholic Conference, 1982) no. 19.

3. *The Milwaukee Symposia for Church Composers: A Ten-Year Report, July 9, 1992* (Chicago: Liturgical Training Publications, 1992) 41.

4. Don E. Saliers, "Proclamation: Hymns and the Song of God's People," *Proceedings of the North American Academy of Liturgy, Annual Meeting Washington, D.C., 2–5 January, 1992* (Valparaiso: North American Academy of Liturgy, 1992) 86. See also chapter 19.

5. Carl F. Schalk, *Luther on Music: Paradigms of Praise* (St. Louis: Concordia, 1967) 41.

6. Ibid.

7. Edward Foley explains hymn in the New Testament as "any praise of God (or Christ) that employs what Kroll calls 'heightened speech'"; Edward Foley, *Foundations of Christian Music: The Music of Pre-Constantinian Christianity* (Bramcote: Grove, 1992) 55, n. 1.

8. For a discussion of Psalms, Canticles, etc., see chapter 15.

9. See Foley, *Foundation of Christian Music*, 51–84.

10. On the early use of hymns, see chapter 20.

11. On the issue of ritual units and placement of music in Christian worship, see Frank C. Quinn, "Music in Catholic Worship: The Effect of Ritual on Music and Music on Ritual," *Proceedings of the Annual Meeting of the North American Academy of Liturgy, Nashville, 2–5 January, 1989* (Valparaiso: North American Academy of Liturgy, 1989) 161–76.

12. Richard H. Hoppin, *Medieval Music* (New York: Norton, 1978) 155. Hoppin reminds us that sequences came into being as a "special kind of trope," dependent on the Gospel Acclamation (the Alleluia) for their location. "Recent objections to this classification [that is, as tropes] stress the fact that the sequences rapidly became, if it was not from the very beginning, an independent composition, complete in itself textually and musically. . . . It is not to say, however, that sequences were born from a different impulse than those that produced other kinds of tropes. With relatively few exceptions, the sequence remained a liturgical appendage to the Alleluia or in some cases, perhaps, the chants that were traditionally extended by the addition of lengthy melismas" (154–155).

13. Today, there remain only two sequences required to be read or sung at the Eucharistic liturgy, *Victimae paschali* at Easter and *Veni, sancte spiritus* at Pentecost, and two sequences permitted to be sung, the *Lauda Sion* for Corpus Christi and *Stabat Mater* for the feast of the Seven Dolors of the Blessed Virgin Mary.

14. Hoppin, *Medieval Music*, 154.

15. See Erik Routley, *The Music of Christian Hymns* (Chicago: GIA, 1981) 17–20.

16. Frank C. Quinn, "The New State of Music in the Liturgy," *Liturgy* 3/3 (1983) 47.

17. See Chapter 18.

18. Edward Foley, *Ritual Music: Studies in Liturgical Musicology* (Beltsville, Md.: Pastoral Press, 1995) 165.

19. *Motu proprio, Tra le sollecitudini,* 22 November 1904, § 1; Robert Hayburn, *Papal Legislation on Sacred Music, 95 A.D. to 1977 A.D.* (Collegeville: The Liturgical Press, 1979) 223–24.

20. The most important statements, following on the *Motu proprio* of Pius X, are: The Apostolic Constitution on Sacred Music of Pius XI, *Divini cultus sanctitarem,* 20 December 1928; the encyclical of Pius XII on sacred music, *Musicae sacrae disciplina,* 25 November 1955; and the *Instruction on Sacred Music and Liturgy* from the Sacred Congregation of Rites, 3 September 1958.

21. *Tra le sollecitudini,* §3; Hayburn, *Papal Legislation on Sacred Music,* 224–25.

22. Second Vatican Council, "The Constitution on the Sacred Liturgy," *Sacrosanctum Concilium,* 4 December 1963.

23. *Tra le sollecitudini,* §4; Hayburn, *Papal Legislation on Sacred Music,* 225.

24. See *Musicae sacrae disciplina* (hereafter *MSD*) 55–56.

25. *MSD,* 58. It is rather ironic that the instrument best suited for accompanying hymns, specifically Lutheran chorales, that is, music not considered to be an official part of the Roman Catholic liturgy, was elevated to such a status in a church that claimed unaccompanied monody as its fundamental patrimony.

26. *Tra le sollecitudini,* §15–16; Hayburn, *Papal Legislation on Sacred Music,* 228–29.

27. *MSD,* 36–37.

28. *Instruction on Sacred Music and Liturgy,* 14b

29. Ibid., 3.

30. Robert Taft, "The Structural Analysis of Liturgical Units: An Essay in Methodology," *Beyond East and West: Problems in Liturgical Understanding* (Washington, D.C.: Pastoral Press, 1984) 160–61.

31. Quinn, "The New State of Music in the Liturgy," 168–69.

32. "The more noble form of liturgical celebration is the solemn liturgy, celebrated in Latin, with the participation of the people." The first draft may be found in *Acta synodalia sacrosancti concilii oecumenici Vaticani II, I: Periodus prima, pars II, Sessio publoica I: Congregationes generales X–XVIII* (Vatican: Polyglot, 1970) 461–66.

33. Note that the word "hymn" is not used to describe the kind of music the people sing.

34. *MSD,* 62–66; *Instruction on Music in the Liturgy,* 51–53.

35. *Instruction on Music in the Liturgy,* 13–15.

36. Hayburn, *Papal Legislation on Sacred Music,* 20–21.

37. SC Rites, *Instruction Musicam sacram,* On Music in the Liturgy, 5 March 1967.

38. See No. 50, which reiterates the statement found in "The Constitution on the Liturgy," number 116, that "Gregorian chant has pride of place, all other things being equal." The latter clause subordinates chant and the use of Latin to participation and the need for the vernacular.

39. Lucien Deiss, *Spirit and Song of the New Liturgy,* New Revised Edition (Cincinnati: World Library, 1976). The first edition appeared in 1970.

40. 38 SC Divine Worship, *General Instruction of the Roman Missal,* 4th ed., 27 March 1975, No. 56j; see also no. 122.

41. Bishops' Committee on the Liturgy, *Music in Catholic Worship* (Washington, D.C.: United States Catholic Conference, 1983). The first edition was published in 1982.

42. *The Milwaukee Symposia,* 41.

43. According to Kevin Irwin, such a development ignores the differences between Catholic and Protestant worship: "It is important to explore how

whatever (style of) music is used in liturgy ought to cohere in style and text with the intended purpose(s) of the rite at issue. For example, this is to raise the question of the adequacy of using hymns in the Eucharistic liturgy. Here the classic understanding of the way hymns function differently in Roman Catholic and Protestant churches comes to the fore. . . . Specifically, we wish to critique at least the overuse of hymns in Roman Catholic Eucharist. Historically, hymns came into many liturgies at the Reformation, precisely because the Roman liturgy's use of Latin made liturgical music inaccessible for the assembly's participation. In our opinion they now need to be evaluated across denominational lines in terms of their legitimacy within the Eucharistic rite itself and then for the value that should be placed on them as theological sources"; *Context and Text: Method in Liturgical Theology* (Collegeville: The Liturgical Press, 1994) 237; for a full analysis of the problem with hymns in Catholic Eucharistic liturgy, according to Kevin Irwin, see esp. 235–46.

44. It should be clear by now that this author is approaching the question of hymns in Catholic eucharistic liturgy from the perspective of the "ritual-functional" paradigm. In other words, the question is one of how a particular musical form operates in liturgy; see Francis Mannion, "Paradigms in American Catholic Church Music," *Worship* 70 (1996) 116.

45. Saliers, "Proclamation," 86.

46. It must be noted, however, that the liturgy of the word is highly structured in Catholic worship, with response psalm and gospel acclamation, Nicene creed and intercessions. One needs to be cautious in introducing further elements without modifying the ritual at hand.

47. Several collections of such lectionary hymns have recently appeared, for example, from Thomas H. Troeger and Carol Doran: *New Hymns for the Lectionary* (New York: Oxford University Press, 1986), and *New Hymns for the Life of the Church* (New York: Oxford University Press, 1992).

48. This was one of the reasons for compiling the *Hymnal for the Hours* (Chicago: GIA, 1989), that is, to provide hymns that suited the different hours of the office, since no other such collection existed in English.

Chapter 20

Liturgical Music as Corporate Song 3: Opportunities for Hymnody in Catholic Worship

Michael James Molloy

The problem of hymnody within the Eucharistic liturgy of the Catholic Church may well be described as trying to make a square peg fit a round hole. Some of the hymnic points of angularity have been identified in the previous chapter; this chapter is primarily concerned with the function and use of hymnody within the Eucharist. If hymnody is to continue within our liturgies, then there must be: (1) a clear rationalization for its liturgical function; (2) a realization of how the hymnic form can exercise that function; and (3) some concept of the process, whether it should be constant or variable. In short, we will examine the when, where, why, and how of liturgical hymnody.

The status of hymn singing in the Catholic Church today is the result of several processes, all of which have had impact on the liturgical praxis of the individual worshiping community. The most ancient hymnic influence in the Church derives from the hymns used in the Divine Office as found in the Roman Breviary. Indeed, this vast resource has been the source of much hymnody throughout the history of the Christian Church—Roman and non-Roman alike. The music used at devotions and other such para-liturgical events also have had an enormous impact on the experience of hymnody within the Church. The "Low Mass" or Dialogue Mass of the pre-Vatican II Church involved a minimum of congregational participation (especially when compared to the ideal post Vatican II liturgy), and often the only music at these liturgies were hymns sung at the entrance procession, offertory, Communion, and recessional. Finally, the influence of the hymnic repertoire and practices of other traditions have been particularly influential in contemporary parishes, especially in pluralistic cultures where Catholics and non-Catholics live in harmony.[1]

The Early Use of Hymns

The earliest examples of hymnody are scriptural, the most obvious being the psalms and canticles. Of course, these do not rhyme, nor do they have a strophic metrical structure. They were, however, sung texts, although we do not have any musical or paleographic record as to indicate the sound of the music. The terms "psalms, hymns, and spiritual songs" referred to by St. Paul may be interpreted as loose synonyms used interchangeably. However, it is also possible that hymns and spiritual songs may have referred to other texts, and that spiritual songs might well have been improvised sung prayer at domestic liturgies. From a modern perspective it is helpful (albeit somewhat anachronistic) to distinguish three types of texts sung in the early Church: (1) psalms; (2) canticles or odes, psalm-like poems found in other books of the Bible (for example, Exodus 15, Habakkuk); and (3) hymns, that is, non-scriptural compositions of any kind.[2]

As the Church moved from comparatively simple domestic worship to the more complex worship patterns of basilicas, there was a restructuring of the liturgy to reflect or adapt to the imperial space. It can be argued that whereas the early domestic liturgies were more a reflection of the worship of the Jewish home rather than that of the Temple (prior to its destruction), particularly regarding music and ceremonial, the move into the basilicas restored a sense of the splendor of the worship of the Temple. The larger acoustic space required a more professional approach to music making, which also led to the development of choirs.

As the liturgy of the Church evolved, there was a variety and diversity of practice throughout the early Christian world. Although the celebration of the Eucharist and the observance of the Hours can be seen as a constant, there were any number of variations upon a theme. In the early centuries, unlike the East, the West did not receive the free, non-scriptural hymn into its liturgy with eagerness.[3] Hymns in the Roman rite were at the periphery, variable songs for liturgical movement drawn from scriptural compositions.

The hymnody of the early Latin Church had its greatest exponent in the person of St. Ambrose (ca. 340–397). Although Ambrose cannot lay claim to being the earliest hymn writer, he was the first to recognize the effective use of the hymn as a means of evangelization against the proponents of the Arian heresy.[4] Ambrosian hymns and chant existed prior to Roman chant, and may have been influenced by Jewish chant, the music of the Greeks, or contemporary folk music since these were the musical forms that early Christians would have experienced. Whereas Ambrose opened the door for the use of hymns in the Western world, it was St. Benedict who continued and expanded the process by the widespread use of his Rule, which prescribed an exact system of liturgical offices for monastic communities. Hymns were required for the succession of canonical hours, and, as the liturgical calendar developed, the various ecclesiastical seasons, feast days, and saints days all collected their appropriate hymns.[5]

In the course of time three categories of Latin hymns became evident: (1) Office hymns, which as noted above were specified texts according to the hour and liturgical season, or sanctoral feast; (2) sequences and other tropes,[6] and (3) quasi-liturgical, non- liturgical, and popular hymns used for processions and other such occasions.[7] The sequence was really the only place within the Mass for the singing of poetic texts.[8] Hymns had assumed a regular liturgical function.

In 506, the Council of Agde in southern France, which had concerned itself primarily with matters of discipline, decreed that hymns should be sung morning and evening, and at the conclusions of matins, vespers, and Masses.[9] There has always been a struggle within the Church concerning the use of nonscriptural hymns. In 563 the Council of Braga decreed that except for the psalms or other biblical passages from the Old and New Testaments, no poetic compositions, that is, hymns, could be sung in liturgical gatherings. The concern was to prevent heretical doctrines from entering the Church through the poetic compositions.[10] The need for such legislation is usually indicative of a practice that was getting out of control and was in need of corrective measures. Thus, it could be assumed that hymnody was achieving a certain degree of popularity within the Church.

With the increasing complexity of poetic and musical form, together with the decreasing use of Latin by the people, the nature of the Latin hymn changed from a vehicle for popular expression to something reserved for the almost exclusive use of monastic communities and cathedral churches.[11] The Latinization of the Mass was complete, so that most were unable to respond to the Latin chants, which increasingly became the domain of the choir. The use of hymns "outside" the Church at missions, pilgrimages, processions, etc., was the only way the people could participate musically.[12] Macaronic verse (the vernacular mixed with Latin phrases) became popular out-

side the Church. Although this activity had been forbidden by ecclesiastical decree it became very popular and is the genus for the ever-
popular carol form.[13] Thus a group of hymns of special interest, not
necessarily related to any particular occasion, became popular. These
hymns were not the more formal categories of Office hymn, or sequence, but were dedicated to an extra-liturgical purpose. From these
categories in the early evolution of the hymn, it becomes clear that it
is in hymns that it is possible to perceive most clearly the role of culture in the development of liturgical music, since hymns embody the
poetic spirit and lyrical talent of the people.[14]

The Council of Trent

The Council of Trent (1545–1563) was of paramount significance in
the shaping of general ecclesiastical usages and in the reform of the
worship and music of the Church. It did not concern itself with the
exact details of musical and stylistic problems, but rather with fundamental attitudes on its use in the liturgy.[15] Two matters addressed
by the Council which had an impact upon the role of hymnody in the
liturgy involved the curtailment of liturgical texts, and the insertion
of non-churchly songs into the liturgy.[16] As a result of the Council of
Trent, the number of sequences was reduced to four (later five) in
order to purify the rites. Although hymns remained an important
part of the Divine Office, the result was that for the Post-Tridentine
Church hymnody had no place within the Eucharistic liturgy.

In 1563, previous to the convening of the Council, the bishop of
Vienne, France, had sent to Pope Paul III a document containing suggestions for discussion at the Council. He was very critical of Protestant hymnody, which he felt was contrary to the authority of the
Pope, and the tradition and doctrine of the Church. In addition to his
attack on the emerging hymnic tradition of the Protestant traditions
he goes on to say:

> Nothing may be read or sung in church unless it is taken from Sa-
> cred Scripture, or is at least in accord with it, or not in disagree-
> ment with it. It must be serious in tone without exciting laughter, in
> whatever language this is accustomed to be read or sung.[17]

Thus hymnody was essentially excluded from the Eucharistic liturgy, with the only exceptions being the four or five remaining sequences.[18] Thus in 1665, in a document aimed specifically at the
Diocese of Rome (again, likely in order to curb abuses), Pope Alexander VII stated:

> It is enjoined that nothing be said at Mass but the words prescribed by the Roman Missal, not only in the offices of the day but also on the solemnities of saints.[19]

Nineteenth- and Early-Twentieth-Century Developments

The glorious repertoire of Latin hymns was therefore destined to remain unknown to the vast majority of Catholics. It was not until the nineteenth century—as a result of the Anglican Oxford Movement—that these hymns were translated into English, largely through the efforts of John Mason Neale (1818–1866), and Edward Caswall (1814–1878). There is a certain irony in the fact that the treasury of Latin hymns became known, not through the inheritors of the tradition, but as a result of a non-Catholic movement endeavoring to determine its own liturgical heritage. Many of these texts are better known today by Protestants rather than Catholics, and indeed many uninformed Catholics would automatically assume that these texts were foreign to the Catholic liturgical tradition.[20]

Where Catholic hymnody did continue was in extra-liturgical activities such as devotions, Benediction, processions, novenas, etc. The hymns that became popular for these ceremonies were largely of a sentimental, pietistic nature, although there are examples of some traditional Latin texts, particularly of Thomas Aquinas (*O Salutaris* and *Tantum Ergo*), which were used at Benediction.

In commenting on a nineteenth-century collection of hymns by Rev. Frederick W. Faber (1814–1863), which included "Mother of Mercy, day by day," "Jesus My Lord My God My All," and "Faith of Our Fathers," Cardinal Wiseman characterized them

> as of so mixed a character that we could almost regret his choice of a title (hymns) which sets them more strikingly in contrast with the authorized hymns of the Church. Many of them are evidently not constructed for use in public worship, they are expressions of an individual, and even of a particular mind, which will have response in a devout heart, but which could not be introduced into a mixed congregation without danger of forcing the feeling, in some instances, into an unnatural state. Some of them represent sentiments of piety and contrition which on the lips of the casual worshiper would be unreal; . . . while all but a few are more subjective in their character than we should fancy suitable to public worship, even as outlets of informal and auxiliary devotion.[21]

The state of Catholic hymnody was not much improved at the end of the nineteenth century when hymnal editor and composer Dr. A.

Edmonde Tozer (1857–1910) commented in the preface to an 1898 hymnal

> The common practice . . . has been to look upon the English Hymn as something of no great importance—a kind of "stop gap" in the interval that exists between Vespers and the Sermon, or while the altar is being prepared for the rite of Benediction—and to pay no heed as how it should be sung, or by whom. I venture to think that this is a low view to take of the matter which, if properly approached, can be made a great means of devotion to the congregation.[22]

In an institution as vast as the Roman Catholic Church it would be naive to expect that there would be strict uniformity in all areas. Such was also the case with hymnody. Certain traditions, particularly in the German and Polish Church, had a strong tradition of hymnody, as was witnessed when many emigrated to North America bringing their traditions with them. Many of the older and more popular Catholic hymns are indeed of German origin, such as "Holy God We Praise Thy Name" *(Grosser Gott)* and "O God Almighty Father" *(Gott Vater sei gepreisen).*

The turn of the century saw a renewed interest in the music of the Church, particularly through the leadership of Pope Pius X (1903–1914). His *Motu Proprio* of November 22, 1903 is considered a landmark of ecclesiastical legislation in the area of liturgical music. One of the objectives of the *Motu Proprio* was to purge the Church of the increasing influence of theatrical and operatic compositional style which was pervading the music written for liturgical use. A musician himself, Pius sought to restore Gregorian chant and classic polyphony to its previous position of preeminence in the Church. The language of the liturgy remained Latin and it was forbidden for anything to be sung in the vernacular during solemn liturgical functions, as well as the parts, either proper or common, of the Mass and the Office:

> . . . on great feasts Gregorian chant may be used in turn with so-called *falso bordone* chant, or with verses composed in the same suitable style. It may even be permitted to sing a whole psalm in figured music sometimes, as long as the proper form of singing psalms is not lost, that is . . . alternately, either with new melodies or with those taken from or modeled on Gregorian chant. Psalms sung in the manner called *di concerto* are therefore absolutely forbidden. The hymns of the Church must also keep their traditional form. It is not lawful, for instance to compose a *Tantum Ergo* so that the first verse be a romance, an air or an adagio, and the *Genitori* an allegro.[23]

Although Pius' intentions were noble, there was certainly no flowering of chant and polyphony within the North American Church. The low Mass with its lack of music became the norm, although it was not considered to be the ideal form. Pope Pius XII (1939–1958) in his encyclical *Mediator Dei,* promulgated on November 20, 1947, in promoting the participation of the people in the liturgy, stated

> This can be done . . . when for instance the whole congregation in accordance with the rules of the liturgy, either answer the priest in an orderly and fitting manner, or sing hymns suitable to the different parts of the Mass, or do both, or finally when they answer the prayers of the minister of Jesus Christ and also sing the liturgical chant.[24]

Later, in the same encyclical, he promotes the active and popular singing of Gregorian chant by the congregation: "If . . . this is done, it will not happen that the congregation *hardly ever or only in a low murmur* answer the prayers in Latin or the vernacular" [italics added].[25]

The encyclical *Musicae sacrae disciplina* of December 25, 1955 seems to give greater credence to the role of the hymn in the celebrations of the Church:

> We must also hold in honor that music which is not primarily a part of the sacred liturgy, but which by its power and purpose greatly aids religion. This music is therefore rightly called religious music. . . . As experience shows [this music] can exercise great and salutary force and power on the souls of the faithful, both when it is used in churches during non-liturgical services and ceremonies, or when it is used outside churches at various solemnities and celebrations.
>
> The tunes of these hymns, which are often sung . . . [in the vernacular], are memorized with almost no effort or labor . . . Hence these popular religious hymns are of great help to the Catholic apostolate and should be carefully cultivated and promoted.[26]

Although it was still not permitted to sing non-liturgical texts in the Mass, in those areas where that had been the custom from "time immemorial," the practice was allowed to continue if it was not prudently possible to remove the tradition.[27]

One of the last documents issued under the authority of Pius XII before his death in 1958 was the Instruction of September 3 of that year, in which the participation of the congregation was one of its most important concerns. This Instruction grants a certain degree of sanction to the role of the vernacular hymn within the low Mass and can be seen to be leading the way toward the musical reforms of Vatican II.

> In a *read* Mass, the priest celebrant, his ministers and the faithful who participate directly in the liturgical functions with the celebrant must pronounce in a clear voice those parts of the Mass which apply to them and may use only the Latin language. Then if the faithful wish to add some popular prayers or hymns to this *direct* liturgical participation, according to local custom, this may be done in the vernacular.

> Popular religious song has a place in all the solemnities of Christian life . . . it has an even nobler part to play in all the "pious exercises" performed inside and outside the church and is sometimes admitted in liturgical functions themselves. . . .[28]

Although the so-called "hymn sandwich" approach to the musical treatment of the liturgy was gaining in legitimacy, it would be inaccurate to say that Catholics were "singing the Mass," but rather were singing "during the Mass." The four hymns at the entrance, offertory, Communion, and recessional hardly involved the people in the liturgical action, were generally seen as accompaniment or "filler" to cover processions, and thus were dispensed with easily. It was through this process of encouraging people to participate musically in the low Mass by the singing of popular songs that metrical hymns entered Roman Catholic liturgy in the twentieth century. Although in the language of the time, and not formally "liturgical," such distinctions had little effect on congregations. They were singing at Mass just as they sang at devotions, without any cognizance of the liturgical distinctions between the two, even though these hymns were not an integral part of the liturgical action.

Vatican II

The reforms of Vatican II called for a more conscious and active participation of the faithful in the liturgical action. Almost immediately the liturgy was transformed. The "Instruction on Music in the Liturgy," *Musicam Sacram,* of March 5, 1967, established clear criteria for the use of music within the liturgy and established three progressive degrees of solemnity involving the musical participation of the priest and the people. To the first degree belongs the chants of the priest, in dialogue with the people, the opening prayer, prayer over the gifts, preface and sanctus, gospel acclamation, Lord's Prayer, prayer after Communion, and final dismissal. The second degree adds the Ordinary of the Mass (Kyrie, Gloria, Agnus Dei), the profession of faith and the general intercessions. The third degree involves the songs for entrance and Communion, responsorial psalm, and songs for the presentation of the gifts.[29] It is obvious that hymnody is still not considered essential to the solemn celebration of the liturgy.

Unfortunately, the initial musical response to Vatican II involved vernacular hymnody. There had already been some practice of singing hymns at the liturgy, or perhaps more precisely, of hearing the choir sing the hymns at Mass, so that is where the first efforts were concentrated. The existing repertoire of Catholic hymnody, comprised of devotional, Office, and seasonal hymns was not particularly well suited for the Eucharistic liturgy. Therefore much music was borrowed from Protestant churches where hymns had been sung successfully for centuries. This material, however, was viewed as foreign, and regarded suspiciously by Catholics with a limited ecumenical sense and to many, in the mood of the sixties, represented an anachronistic archaism that had no relevance in the contemporary Church.

As the full impact of the reforms of Vatican II came to be realized and implemented, energy was properly directed towards those elements in the liturgy which were in need of a proper musical setting. Acclamations are now sung, psalms are chanted responsorially, and there are even some priests who sing their prayers in dialogue with the assembly.

Unfortunately, hymns are still receiving short shrift as easily dispensable items that are considered to be accretions to the liturgy. Part of the problem rests with the nature of hymnody itself. The texts have several stanzas and often appear to be longer than needed. In fact, hymns are used in the liturgy at points where the rubrics call for short, repeatable antiphons. The hymnic form and the liturgical form and function seem to be at odds with each other, and we are faced with the problem of trying to force a square peg into a round hole. Given this seeming contradiction in function, is it possible to sing hymns in the liturgy?

The entrance procession is often too short to accommodate the singing of a hymn. Likewise, time is also a factor during the preparation of the gifts. It is very difficult to sing a hymn during Communion, especially if one is carrying a hymn book, and receiving the host in the hand! At the end of Mass why sing a hymn after the priest has dismissed everyone? The ultimate contradiction is for the presider and ministers to leave the church while the assembly is still singing. If the priest is not going to stay and sing, why should anyone else?

The solution lies not in simple pre- and proscriptions as to where or where not to sing hymns, but rather in the realization of the function of music within the liturgy and its integrity within the ritual act. In *Liturgical Music Today,* the Bishops' Committee on the Liturgy states that:

> (9) The various functions of sung prayer must be distinguished within liturgical rites. Sometimes the song is meant to accompany ritual actions. In such cases the song is not independent but serves, rather, to support the prayer of the assembly when an action requires a longer period of time. . . . The music enriches the moments and keeps it from becoming burdensome.
>
> (10) At other places in the liturgical action the sung prayer itself is a constituent element of the rite. While it is being prayed no other ritual action is being performed.
>
> (11) Beyond determining the moments when song is needed, the musical form employed must match its liturgical function.[30]

Universa Laus is an international group of liturgical musicians whose mission is to understand and communicate ever more clearly and deeply how liturgy works, and how music works within liturgy. To that end they have posited a number of guidelines or points of reference concerning music and liturgy. With regard to ritual function, guideline 7.4 states:

> [T]he role of music in the liturgy extends well beyond what one can see of how well it works. Like every symbolic sign, music "refers" to something beyond itself. It opens the door to the indefinable realm of meanings and reactions.[31]

Commenting on this, Michel Veuthey writes

> [T]hese problems, however, do not resolve themselves as easily as . . . would lead one to believe since, with art, we are always faced with multiple imponderables.
>
> In fact we can distinguish two orders of functionality. First, we must clearly define what we are aiming at by the use of a particular musical element, and we must try to ascertain if the achieved result corresponds to what was intended. But this search for a precise goal leaves the door open for a second category of effects, greatly varied in their nature and often very difficult to perceive and to measure. This symbolical function of music . . . constitutes one of music's most important roles.[32]

Therefore, it is of primary importance when preparing for liturgy to determine the nature of the ritual act, and the way in which music will function within the ritual act.

> The vocation of the participants in the assembly is to enter wholeheartedly into the musical action and to be fully involved in it,

when the celebration calls for it. When and if these conditions are met, singing and instrumental music will truly and genuinely be ritual on the printed page and as actually performed. And the ritual character of singing will be concrete, not abstract; they will both be music "appropriate for" the rites in which they are used.[33]

Music *for* the liturgy must be music *in* the liturgy, a music that fits the ritual action like a glove, but in order to accomplish this the rite must be understood.[34] There is a danger in regarding congregational song as a functional accompaniment to a ritual action. If the song is "done well," then it is entirely possible that the people have been caught up in something other than the action. The sung prayer should be a constituent element of the rite, not an add-on or accretion. Within the contemporary Church there has been a grudging acceptance of hymns.[35] This is indicative of a lack of insight as to the purpose and nature of the music in conjunction with the ritual act.

In looking again at the entrance rite, it is necessary to determine the nature of the ritual action. If the entrance hymn is meant to accompany the ministers on their journey to the altar, then the liturgical focus becomes centered on those few individuals. On the other hand, if the nature of the entrance hymn is truly that of gathering, as is implied in the appellation "gathering song," then the focus must be on the community gathering to celebrate. In this case, the music becomes the ritual event, not only the procession. Therefore it is not necessary to end the hymn when the presider reaches the altar. Rather, the hymn should constitute an act of praise on the part of the gathered community, of which the priest and the other liturgical ministers are members, and in which they participate. There must be a synchronicity between the expectation and execution of the ritual act and its music. If they do not share the same mutual objectives, and work towards the same result, then the character of the music as well as the ritual act will be compromised.

The use of the hymn form at these times is very important. The back and forth nature of responsorial song is essentially a dialogue, a "you and me" construction. Hymn singing, on the other hand, says "us" standing together, united in belief.[36] Hymn singing is a unitive form and is ideal for gathering the community into one.

One of the reasons that Catholic singing of hymns has become so boring and pedestrian is that they basically serve as accompaniment to processions. In the Roman Catholic liturgy as it is now popularly celebrated there is no such thing as an extended, splendid moment of communal praise. Hymns of praise have become subordinated to the relatively insignificant activities they accompany.[37] If the hymn itself were conceived as a ritual act, then the hymn could receive the kind of musical treatment it deserves. If the hymn is viewed as a poetic structure with a number of stanzas constituting the whole, then the performance of the hymn should include all of those stanzas. The organist, or other musicians could then plan the performance of the hymn effectively so that varied harmonizations could be used on some stanzas, descants could be used, instruments could be added, stanzas could be sung antiphonally between various groups, etc. This is impossible to achieve if no one is sure if two, three, or four stanzas of the hymn are to be sung. In situations where it is felt that a certain hymn has too many verses, it is better to choose a different hymn, than to compromise the integrity of that text.

Music for the preparation of the gifts constitutes more of a dilemma, in that the ritual act which the music "accompanies" has a more forward direction. If the music takes too long, the flow of the liturgy has been disturbed. Also, when a hymn (or any other form of congregational music) simply accompanies the ritual action, then the priest in his role of leadership is not participating with the rest of the assembly, and thereby is removing himself from the community as it celebrates in song. This rite can be adequately performed without music. So too, choral, instrumental, or vocal music may serve the liturgy better at this juncture than congregational song, which would distract the attention of the assembly away from the ritual action. It *is* possible for hymns to be sung at this point in the liturgy, but again the synchronicity of the rite and the music must be in harmony with each other. Texts need not deal exclusively with bread and wine, or offering, but could also be a point of reflection on the homily and scriptural texts, or music and text appropriate to the liturgical season.

As mentioned above, it is almost impossible to sing a hymn during the Communion procession, but this could provide another opportunity for instrumental or choral music. Congregational music used for the Communion procession must be such that it is easily memorized and sung by people who are moving, without hymnals in hand.[38] Again the synchronicity of music and rite will accomplish the liturgical objective.

A more appropriate moment for congregational song would be a hymn or song of thanksgiving after Communion. This hymn could be an act of praise, or remembrance, and indeed need not be as restricted by text or aesthetic as are other moments in the liturgy. Music for inward reflection or hymns of exuberant praise are equally viable depending on the overall character of the celebration. This moment need not be restricted to congregational music. There may well be times when other forms of musical expression are in order. A general rule of thumb could be that the hymn be the usual musical form at this liturgical point, but that practice need not be restricted to the one form, and that on occasion, and with proper planning, a variety of musical and performing styles may be employed. Again the underlying principle would be the synchronicity of music and rite.

As alluded to earlier, the recessional hymn provides certain challenges which make it out of character with the closing rites. It seems ludicrous to ask people to remain and sing a hymn after they have been dismissed by the priest. "The Mass is over, but. . . ." This is one of those points in the liturgy where hymns really do not belong. It may be more appropriate to place increased emphasis on the song after Communion as a response of the people to the Eucharist, or to direct their attention to the final blessing and commissioning. If such is the case that a particular recessional hymn is desired, then it must be executed so that the hymn is an act of praise by the entire community. The presider and ministers should remain in the sanctuary and sing. The procession from the sanctuary should be planned so that the presider reaches the back of the church at the end of the hymn. A suitable organ or instrumental postlude may be a more appropriate and easily executed option. Overall, again, the music and rite must be synchronous.

Hymns do have an important part to play in the liturgical life of the Church, but in most cases it is necessary to carefully plan and evaluate their use. A well planned variety in the musical options of the liturgy should be encouraged, not feared. There is of necessity a connection between the liturgies of succeeding generations. There are no clean breaks with the remembered and experienced past. New rituals and formulas will end up saying the same as the old unless the consciousness of the worshiper is changed.[39] As with much of the liturgy, catechesis is important so that the people not only know what is going to happen next, but understand why, and what their role is in the liturgical/ritual act.

Just as theology cannot ignore the historical development of doctrine from the early Church to the present, so too our musical life will not be healthy if it is expected to operate in a historical vacuum, cut off from its past.[40] Hymnody is an important link with our past, ranging from the pre-Vatican II Church back through to Apostolic times. If we are to be true to our Christian roots and heritage, then hymnody must be an important constituent element of liturgical worship. A square peg can fit a round hole if the dimensions of both shapes are able to accommodate each other.[41] The circle and the square superimposed over each other create a much more interesting geometric shape.

APPENDIX

Early Latin Hymn Texts as found in translation in *Worship III*

Ambrose (c. 340–397)
372	*Veni redemptor gentium*	Savior of the Nations Come

Prudentius (348–c. 413)
398	*Corde natus ex Parentis*	Of the Father's Love Begotten

Gregory the Great (c. 540–604)
420	*Ex more docti mystico*	Again We Keep This Solemn Feast
4	*Nocte surgentes*	Father We Thank Thee
422	*Clarum decus jejunte*	The Glory of These Forty Days

Fortunatis (c. 540–c. 610)
405	*Quem terra, pontus,*	The God Whom Earth and Sea and Sky
435	*Vexilla regis*	The Royal Banners Forward Go
437	*Pange lingua, gloriosi*	Sing My Tongue, the Song of Triumph
444	*Salva festa dies*	Hail Thee Festival Day

Theodulph of Orleans (c.760–c.821)
428	*Gloria laus et honor*	All Glory Laud and Honor

Rabanus Maurus (c. 776–856)
475	*Veni creator Spiritus*	O Holy Spirit by Whose Breath
482	*Veni creator Spiritus*	Come Holy Ghost

Bernard of Clairvaux (c. 1091–1153)
434	*Salve caput cruentatum*	O Sacred Head
605	*Jesu delcedo cordium*	O Jesus Joy of Loving Hearts

Thomas Aquinas (1227–1274)
489	*Adoro te devote*	God With Hidden Majesty
757	*O salutaris*	O Saving Victim
758	*Tantum ergo*	Come Adore

Notes

1. In those countries which are primarily Catholic, with a very low proportion of Protestants, the influence of Protestant hymnody would obviously not be as great.

2. Margot Fassler and Peter Jeffery, "Christian Liturgical Music from the Bible to the Renaissance," *Sacred Sound and Social Change: Liturgical Music in Jewish and Christian Experience,* eds. Lawrence Hoffman and Janet Walton (Notre Dame, Ind.: University of Notre Dame Press, 1992) 85–86.

3. Vernon Perdue-Davis, *A Primer of Ancient Hymnody* (Boston: Schirmer, 1968) 31.

4. Ruth Ellis Messenger, *The Medieval Latin Hymn* (Washington, D.C.: Capital, 1953) 2.

5. Cecil Northcott, *Hymns in Christian Worship: The Use of Hymns in the Life of the Church* (London: Lutterworth, 1964) 20.

6. Tropes were textual and melodic elaborations of chants, both Ordinary and Proper.

7. Perdue-Davis, *Ancient Hymnody,* 33.

8. By the time of the Council of Trent in the mid-sixteenth century, they were of such a proliferation that there were sequences for almost every day of the church year; see *Key Words in Church Music,* ed. Carl Schalk (St. Louis: Concordia, House, 1978) 327.

9. Samuel Willoughby Duffield, *The Latin Hymn-Writers and their Hymns* (New York: Funk and Wagnalls, 1889) 47.

10. Anscar J. Chupungo, *Worship: Progress and Tradition* (Beltsville, Md.: The Pastoral Press, 1995) 82–83.

11. Schalk, *Key Words,* 193.

12. Messenger, *Latin Hymn,* 26.

13. Ibid., 58.

14. Chapungco, *Worship,* 84.

15. Hayburn, *Papal Legislation on Sacred Music,* 25.

16. The use of non-churchly songs was a concern especially regarding the use of secular melodies within the polyphonic settings of the text of the Ordinary of the Mass.

17. Hayburn, *Papal Legislation on Sacred Music,* 26.

18. The *Gloria in excelsis* as a canticle could be regarded as a hymn of praise, but its structure without strophes or rhyme places it outside of the commonly accepted hymnic form.

19. Hayburn, *Papal Legislation on Sacred Music,* 78.

20. The Appendix at the end of this chapter lists a number of ancient Latin texts found in translation in the hymnal *Worship III.*

21. J. Vincent Higginson, *History of American Catholic Hymnals: Survey and Background* ([s.l.]: Hymn Society of America, 1982) 55.

22. Ibid., 148.

23. Hayburn, *Papal Legislation on Sacred Music,* 227–29.

24. Ibid., 338.

25. Ibid., 340.

26. Ibid., 350.

27. Ibid., 351.

28. Ibid., 359, 367.

29. *Documents on the Liturgy 1963–1979: Conciliar, Papal, and Curial Texts* (Collegeville: The Liturgical Press, 1982) 1298 [art. 4150].

30. *The Liturgy Documents: A Parish Resource,* ed. Mary Ann Simcoe (Chicago: Liturgy Training Publications, 1985) 247.

31. Claude Duchesneau and Michel Veuthey, *Music and Liturgy: The Universal Laus Document and Commentary,* trans. Paul Inwood. (Washington, D.C.: Pastoral Press, 1988) 23.

32. Duchesneau and Veuthey, *Music and Liturgy,* 87.

33. Eugenio Costa, "Music at the Crossroads: Liturgy and Culture," *Sung Liturgy: Toward 2000 A.D.,* ed. Virgil C. Funk (Washington, D.C.: Pastoral Press, 1991) 71.

34. Costa, "Music at the Crossroads," 68.

35. When speaking of hymns in the contemporary liturgy, I am referring to the term generically, without making distinctions between "traditional" hymns and those in the so-called "folk" idiom.

36. Edward Foley, "Theater, Concert, or Liturgy: What Difference Does it Make?" *Sung Liturgy: Toward 2000 A.D.,* 83.

37. Carl Dehne, S.J. "Roman Catholic Popular Devotions," *Christians at Prayer,* ed. John Gallen, S.J. (Notre Dame: University of Notre Dame Press, 1977) 95.

38. The music of Taizé comes to mind as particularly well suited for this procession.

39. Dehne, "Popular Devotions," 84.

40. Fassler and Jeffery, *Sacred Sound,* 116.

41. Technically, if the hypotenuse of the triangle, formed by two adjacent sides of the square, is equal to the diameter of the circle.

Chapter 21

Liturgical Music as Homily and Hermeneutic

Robin A. Leaver

Liturgical music has both interpretive and proclamatory functions that are not always understood or recognized. Those congregations that support a choral tradition perhaps understand and recognize these functions more readily than those where liturgical music is purely congregational, especially over the past thirty years or so when choral music within the worshiping community has at best been tolerated, and at worse treated with suspicion and even hostility. But this is not a new problem.[1]

From the Reformation and Counter-Reformation of the sixteenth century until today the question of choral music in worship has been under almost continual debate. In contrast to polyphonic excesses in medieval liturgical music, in which liturgical texts were deluged beneath successive waves of choral texture, Calvin and others of Reformed theological sensibilities rejected all forms of multi-voiced choral music in favor of the simple unison of congregational song. Within Catholicism there were also voices of criticism, notably from humanists such as Erasmus of Rotterdam, who registered discontent with the over-elaborate choral music of the Mass. Thus, later in the sixteenth century, the Council of Trent decreed a simplification of liturgical choral music. The Tridentine model was the basic homophonic style of Palestrina, which avoided text overlay and paid attention to the declamation of the liturgical text.

These two responses to choral music were thus different: one pursued a policy of *elimination*, while the other advocated a *change of style*. Calvinism and Catholicism in the sixteenth century, therefore, developed two opposing approaches to choral music. Calvinism rejected choral music and in its place substituted congregational song. Catholicism did not suppress choral music as such but did deliberately reject both the concept and the practice of the people's song at Mass. In more recent times there have been opposite tendencies within the two traditions. On the one hand, following the Second Vatican Council, Catholicism has adopted the Reformation ideal of vernacular liturgy, within which congregational song is an important and integral part. On the other hand, largely since the nineteenth century, churches in the Reformed tradition have come to terms with choral music in worship. Today, for example, many Presbyterian churches have sizable choirs accustomed to singing an anthem on most Sundays.

Looking at the Catholic Church, one must conclude that the great gains of the Second Vatican Council have also brought with them some unfortunate consequences. One is the loss, in many parishes, of the distinctive Catholic choral tradition. Although the Second Vatican Council did not intend that the Latin Mass should be totally replaced by vernacular forms, in practice this is exactly what happened. The disappearance of the Latin Mass brought about the demise of the choral music associated with it. Thus, in the place of choral settings of the Mass various forms of congregational versions, as well as responsorial psalms and hymns, frequently led by amplified cantors and acoustic guitars, are widely heard.

Looking at the non-Catholic churches that share a common heritage in the Reformation of the sixteenth century, one must admit that although choral music does retain a place in a good many churches, there is also a mood that favors congregational song to the detriment of choral music in worship—unless it is in a blatant entertainment style—which is treated with suspicion. The music of the congregation is thought to be more authentic or appropriate in contradistinction to the sectional or specialized music of the choir. In a sense it is a result of the contemporary emphasis on a democratic theology—both Catholic and Protestant alike—which has the basic premise that true worship, and therefore all music of worship, if it is to be *for* the people, must be done *by* the people—*all* the people and *all* the time.

But this assertion is not a new one: it has been heard in almost every generation. For example, the following appeared in *The Presbyterian* in 1855:

> When shall "all the people" in our congregations begin to "praise God?" Not so long as church music is regarded as a thing to be done

by proxy. We have no disposition to enter upon a crusade against choirs, but we beg leave to protest against the monopoly of this delightful part of the service by the handful who may occupy the end gallery. If choirs will lead the congregation, we have not a word against them; but if they undertake to do as proxies, what the people are required to do for themselves, we think it the sooner such an arrangement is dispensed with the better. How lamentable a travesty on the music of the sanctuary is that where a whole congregation sit mute, whilst the gallery orchestra exhibits its science![2]

If the choir replaces the singing of the congregation then something is wrong with the theology of worship, but equally there are theological objections to the proposition that the democracy of worship demands that the choir's only role is to support the congregation. Certainly worship is for everyone within the gathered community of faith who should be involved in every aspect of it. But this does not mean that all the people must be obviously and demonstrably active in every part of the service of worship. Public worship is not continuously the same from beginning to end. It is—or should be—a variegated experience, an activity of ebb and flow, with periods of sound and silence, of speaking and listening, praying and praising, and so forth. A congregation does not have to be on its feet singing all the time. The sermon is not a period of inactivity on the part of the congregation, or at least, it should not be. A sermon, rightly given and rightly received, may not evoke a sound from the worshipers but each of their hearts and minds will be stimulated and actuated by the import of the spiritual truth of what is being said. Independent choral music—rightly understood, and in addition to congregational song—can also have the same homiletic purpose in a service of worship. It gives the worshiper time to think, to pray, to meditate on the themes of the day or celebration.

In theory this homiletic function of choral music is accorded an intellectual assent, but in practice it is frequently denied. If a planned service is deemed too long then it is the anthem that is truncated or eliminated, rarely the sermon. Similarly, clergy frequently state that the anthem undermines worship by rendering the congregation passive and mute. But the same clergy would never apply the same logic to their sermons, to which their congregations must submit in deferential silence. Why is there a preference given to verbal proclamation over musical proclamation? Usually because neither the liturgical function of preaching nor the homiletic function of music in worship is really understood or appreciated.

Although other musical forms could have been explored, such as the Catholic motet, the Lutheran cantata, and the Reformed psalm setting, the Anglican anthem will be the focus of the following paragraphs in order to demonstrate the homiletic functions of liturgical music.

The Anthem as Homily

The Anglican anthem has its roots in the late-medieval Marian polyphonic antiphon that was customarily sung in English cathedrals and collegiate chapels after vespers (or after compline, if the two offices were sung successively one after the other). At the end of the office the choir would process to Lady Chapel and sing a polyphonic Marian antiphon before a statue of the Virgin. With the introduction of the Book of Common Prayer in 1549 the practice was transmuted into the singing of an "anthem" (an Old English term derived from "antiphon") at the end of the office of evensong. In this Anglican usage a biblical rather than a Marian text, frequently taken from the psalms, was employed and, like the earlier practice, the anthem was sung after the office had concluded, that is, after the Third Collect, "Lighten our darkness, we beseech thee, O Lord." The practice is confirmed by the rubric added at this juncture in the 1662 *Book of Common Prayer:* "In Quires & places where they sing here followeth ye Anthem."[3] Thus the anthem in the Anglican choral tradition was established. There are many studies that examine the Anglican anthem, its various forms and styles, major periods of development and the primary and secondary composers of the genre,[4] but there have been relatively few investigations of its homiletic function, presumably, at least in earlier generations, because it was assumed to be self-evident.[5]

In English cathedrals and collegiate chapels, today as in the past, there is usually no sermon (or homily) at choral evensong. This is because it already has a homily, a homily in sound rather than a homily in words alone. The anthem in Anglican choral evensong has a homiletic purpose. There is other music in choral evensong, of course, but the anthem functions differently. At the beginning the organ voluntary directs the thoughts and prayers of the congregation by setting the mood of the worship. The psalms that follow, sung to Anglican chant, are partly praise, partly prayer. The Magnificat and Nunc Dimittis are praiseful and prayerful responses to the two lessons. Then, after the suffrages and collects,[6] comes the anthem, the sermon in sound. This is eloquent preaching, sometimes by earlier and at other times by contemporary composers. In the case of earlier composers their music speaks to individual worshipers far beyond the span of their own lives, and long after the tongues of the preachers they have heard in their lifetimes have long been stilled.

In biblical terms these composers are like Abel who died, "but through his faith still speaks" (Heb 11:4), and continue to preach beyond their generations through their music. The subject of their preaching is, in the words of Hebrews 12:24: "Jesus, the mediator of a new covenant . . . the sprinkled blood that speaks a better word than the blood of Abel."

There is documentary evidence, such as letters, diaries, journals, and other writings from many different historical periods that witness to the effect certain anthems, sermons in sound, had on the attending worshiper. One of the most significant and interesting source is the *Journal* of John Wesley, especially some of the entries for May 1738.

The formative spiritual experience of John Wesley's life was his "conversion" that not only gave new direction to his subsequent ministry but also marked the birth of what was to become Methodism, even though the term had been coined some time earlier. It has been variously described as his "conversion," "experience of assurance," or the "Aldersgate experience," although he himself referred to it as his "experience of justification." The occasion is recorded in Wesley's *Journal*, published in 1740, and much discussion in biographical and theological studies has centered on how he described what happened on the evening of Wednesday, May 24, 1738, in a passage that has been quoted again and again:

> In the evening, I went very unwillingly to a society in Aldersgate Street [London], where one was reading Luther's Preface to the Epistle to the Romans. About a quarter before nine, while he was describing the change which God works in the heart through faith in Christ, I felt my heart strangely warmed. I felt I did trust in Christ, Christ alone for salvation; and an assurance was given me that he had taken away *my* sins, even *mine,* and saved *me* from the law of sin and death.[7]

John Wesley's experience in the Aldersgate chapel is, of course, not to be underestimated, but what he recorded as happening earlier the same day is not always taken into account, and yet it was part of his spiritual enlightenment of that day:

> In the afternoon I was asked to go to St. Paul's [Cathedral, London]. The anthem was "Out of the deep have I called unto thee, O Lord: Lord, hear my voice. O let thine ears consider well the voice of my complaint. If thou, Lord, will be extreme to mark what is done amiss, O Lord, who may abide it? For there is mercy with thee; therefore thou shalt be feared. . . . O Israel trust in the Lord, for with the Lord there is mercy and with him is plenteous redemption. And he shall redeem Israel from all his sins."[8]

The text is Psalm 130, verses 1-4, 7-8 in the version found in the 1662 *Book of Common Prayer*. Earlier in the service Psalm 119, verses 1–32, the psalm appointed for the 24th evening, would have been sung to Anglican chant, therefore Wesley was not mistaken when he referred to the psalm as the text of the anthem. That he should record the words in detail and at length in his *Journal* is a measure of the impact they had on him. But he did not hear the words alone; there were conveyed to him in the musical form of an anthem, a homiletic exposition of the psalm in melody, rhythm, and harmony. But the *Journal* also records that he attended choral evensong in St. Paul's Cathedral on the two following days, and the texts of the anthems he heard are also recorded in the *Journal:*

> Thursday, May 25. Being again in St. Paul's in the afternoon, I could taste the good word of God in the anthem, which began, "My song shall be always of the loving-kindness of the Lord: with my mouth will I ever be showing forth thy truth from one generation to another."

> Friday, May 26. My soul continued in peace, but yet in heaviness because of manifold temptations. I asked Mr. Töltschig the Moravian what to do. He said, You must not fight with them as you did before, but flee from them the moment they appear, and take shelter in the wounds of Jesus. The same I learned also from the afternoon anthem, which was, "My soul truly waiteth still upon God; for of him cometh my salvation. He verily is my strength and my salvation; he is my defense, so that I shall not greatly fall . . . O put your trust in him alway, ye people; pour out your hearts before him, for God is our hope."[9]

Again Wesley quotes the Prayer Book versions of Psalm 89, verse 1, and Psalm 62, verses 1-2, 8, respectively, and similarly both psalms are clearly anthem texts since the Prayer Book directs various sections of Psalm 119 as the proper psalms for the 25th and 26th evenings of the month.

Over these three days, when Wesley was coming to terms with his new spiritual awareness and understanding, a succession of three anthems sung at evensong in St. Paul's Cathedral made a deep impression on him. Although there is no documentary evidence giving the detail of the music of these services,[10] it is nevertheless possible to identify the most likely anthems he heard on each of these three days in May 1738.

The organist of St. Paul's Cathedral at the time was Dr. Maurice Greene, who had been appointed twenty years earlier in 1718. From 1727 he was simultaneously one of the composers and organists of the Chapel Royal, and from 1730, professor of music at Cambridge.[11] The music that Wesley heard was presumably chosen and directed by Greene. The identity of the first anthem, heard in the afternoon before Wesley's Aldersgate experience, has been the subject of discussion over the years, particularly among musicians. Sir Frederick Bridge, organist of Westminster Abbey between 1882 and 1912, favored Henry Purcell's "Out of the Deep,"[12] but this has to be ruled out because only the first 7 verses are set and Wesley specifically includes verse 8 in his *Journal* entry. Other possibilities are the two settings included by John Barnard, a minor canon of St. Paul's, in his *Selected Church Musick* (1641): one by Thomas Morley and the other by Adrian Batten.[13] But many copies of Barnard's anthology were destroyed during the Civil War and very few were available in the post-Restoration period. The two settings of Psalm 130 by Morley and Batten can therefore be disregarded as possible anthems heard by Wesley in 1738. Sir John Dykes Bower, organist of St. Paul's Cathedral from 1936 to 1967,[14] suggested that the identity of the setting that Wesley heard was by William Croft, an opinion endorsed by Martin Schmidt, Erik Routley, and Ian Spink.[15]

William Croft, organist of Westminster Abbey and, like Greene, of the Chapel Royal,[16] published a collection of his church compositions, *Musica Sacra* (1724),[17] which included the verse anthem "Anthem a 2 Voi[ces], Psalm the 130th," that is, "Out of the Deep," for bass and countertenor solos, four-part choir, with organ accompaniment.[18] As Maurice Greene was one of the subscribers to Croft's volumes,[19] Croft's anthem was most likely the setting of Psalm 130 that Wesley heard on Wednesday afternoon in St. Paul's, before his Aldersgate experience in the evening.

At evensong on the following day, Thursday, May 25, he heard an anthem that began with the opening words of Psalm 89. This was almost certainly composed by Henry Purcell, another musician of the Chapel Royal, the verse anthem, "My song shall be alway of the lovingkindness of the Lord" (Ps 89:1, 5-10, 14-15).[20] The anthem is found in the late seventeenth-century manuscript part-books at St. Paul's Cathedral, that were once owned by the Rev. John Gostling, Subdean of St. Paul's and "priest in ordinary" of the Chapel Royal, famed for his brilliant bass voice.[21] It is also found in Gostling's manuscript collection of anthems in score,[22] and in print in Henry Playford's *Harmonia Sacra* (1703).[23] It therefore seems that this anthem by Purcell was the one Wesley heard on the day following his Aldersgate experience.[24]

On the second day following his Aldersgate experience, Friday, May 26, 1738, Wesley was presumably again in St. Paul's for evensong.[25] This time he heard an anthem on Psalm 62, verses 1-2 and 8.

Maurice Greene's verse anthem, "My soul truly waiteth still upon God," for solo bass and choir, composed in 1720 and eventually published in Greene's *Forty Select Anthems* (1743)[26] would seem to be the most likely anthem that Wesley heard.

Although without further documentary evidence one cannot be absolutely certain that these were the anthems Wesley heard on the two days following his Aldersgate experience in May 1738, they nevertheless appear to be the most likely possibilities. What is certain is that they, together with Croft's "Out of the Deep," were of the common type of verse anthem that was popular at the time, and that Purcell, Croft, and Greene were leading composers of the genre.

Wesley was later critical of some aspects of the Anglican anthem, especially when overindulged, such as the repetition of "the same words, contrary to all sense and reason, six or eight or ten times over."[27] But at other times he recorded that he was moved by the power and effectiveness of various forms of religious music, such as Charles Avison's *Ruth,* which he heard in the Lock Hospital chapel in 1765,[28] or Handel's *Messiah* he heard in Bristol Cathedral in 1758,[29] or the worship of Exeter Cathedral he attended in 1762: ". . . the whole service was performed with great seriousness and decency . . . and the music of 'Glory to God in the highest,' I think exceeded the *Messiah* itself."[30]

Although Wesley did not comment on the music of the three anthems he heard on successive days in May 1738, the fact that he recorded their texts at length in his *Journal* at least indicates something of the impact they made on him. The homiletic power of the sermons in sound was therefore a not insignificant factor in his life-changing experience in the Aldersgate Street chapel, since he heard one of them earlier in the same day and the others on successive days as he was coming to terms with what had happened to him.

The first anthem he heard in St. Paul's Cathedral at evensong in the afternoon of Wednesday, May 24, was almost certainly Croft's setting of Psalm 130. The text is significant, given Wesley's spiritual condition: "Out of the deep have I called to thee, Lord." Croft's long verse anthem in b minor begins with the solo bass voice singing the opening words of the psalm. There is a marked ornamented stress on "called" and a long, agitated cry over two and a half measures on the vocative "O [Lord]," with the words "Lord, hear my voice," being repeated. Later the solo countertenor and bass have overlapping voice parts that stress the words "there is mercy with thee." At length the tutti choir echoes the solo voices with the words "O Israel, trust in the Lord: For with the Lord there is mercy, and with him is plenteous redemption." Here the musical setting places an emphasis on the words "trust in the Lord." The anthem concludes with the choir singing "And he shall redeem Israel from all his sins," which ends in a quiet and untroubled B major.[31] Here is a powerful sermon in which musical and verbal rhetoric expounded the need to call upon the Lord for mercy and redemption, which Wesley was moved to do later that day in the Aldersgate Street Chapel. Although Wesley only mentions the immediate influence of Luther's preface to the Epistle to the Romans, his Aldersgate experience owed perhaps as much to Croft's musical homiletics he heard in St. Paul's Cathedral earlier in the day.

On the day following his Aldersgate experience John Wesley most likely heard Henry Purcell's setting of Psalm 89, another lengthy verse anthem. Wesley recorded in his *Journal:* "Being again in St. Paul's in the afternoon, I could taste the good word of God in the anthem, which began, 'My song shall be alway of the lovingkindness of the Lord: with my mouth will I be ever showing forth thy truth from one generation to another.'" Purcell's verse anthem is a long, virtuosic bass solo that is punctuated by a seven measure "Alleluia" for four-part choir, heard after verse 8 and again after verse 15. It is essentially a flowing G major "song" of joy in the mercy of God, with melodic flourishes on such words as "loving[kindness]," "generations," and "wondrous." At verse 10 the composer employs a number of compositional techniques to illustrate the text: "Thou rulest the raging of the sea: thou stillest the waves thereof when they arise." The tempo is quickened[32] and the solo voice and its accompaniment make audible waves of running sixteenth-notes for the "raging of the sea."[33] However, at the words "stillest the waves" (heard five times) the musical waves are "stilled" by the repetition of four notes on the same pitch. It is a striking compositional device that accords with Wesley's alternation between agitated fearfulness and calm assurance that he records in his *Journal* entries of these few days.

On Friday, May 26, John Wesley almost certainly heard Maurice Greene's verse anthem on Psalm 62, "My soul truly waiteth still upon God." The first part of the first verse is set as a tranquil D major *adagio.* The solo bass begins with a rising and falling melodic line above a static pedal-point, illustrating the concept of "waiting." At measure 8 the tempo changes to *andante vivace* and a spirited version of the opening rising and falling figure is first heard in the organ part, then is echoed by the solo voice: "for of him cometh my salvation." Following verse 8, "O put your trust in him alway, ye people: pour out your hearts before him, for God is our hope," there is a rush of *allegro* "Alleluias," the solo voice alternating with four-part choir. There is an affinity between the anthem by Greene, which speaks of "waiting" on God, and the similar advice Wesley had received from the Moravian Töltschig the same day that he heard the anthem.

It is clear that hearing these three anthems made a deep impression on John Wesley, important enough for him to record their texts on successive days in his *Journal*. They are examples of the homiletic power anthems, and similar liturgical music, can have on individual worshipers. Church musicians and clergy need to think through together the implications of the homiletic function of such music. Both need to recognize that these settings are no less sermons than the verbal homilies heard from pulpits. That they are preached from the alternative ambos of organ bench and choir stall should not mislead them into thinking that their function is other than homiletic.

Liturgical Music as Hermeneutic

While some genres of liturgical music have a direct homiletic function, others have an indirect role. Here one should speak more of hermeneutics than homiletics. Liturgical music functions homiletically when it is an independent genre, such as an anthem or motet; it functions hermeneutically when it adds an interpretive dimension to the liturgy.

Liturgical music as hermeneutic has many more manifestations than does liturgical music as homily. The following examples are a representative sampling of the different ways liturgical music adds a further stratum of meaning to liturgical worship that cannot be supplied by any other means.

Among the most obvious examples of liturgical music operating as hermeneutic are the seasonal Gregorian chant settings of the ordinary of the Mass. One of the first things a student of liturgy learns is the unchanging nature of the traditional ordinary: *Kyrie, Gloria, Credo, Sanctus, Agnus Dei*. But this needs qualifying. Although the text remained unchanged, the associated chant *did* change according to the season or celebration. Thus *Missa XI* was sung on the general Sundays throughout the year; *Missa XVII* on the Sundays in Advent and Lent; *Missa XVIII* on weekdays in Advent and Lent; and *Missa I* in the Easter season.[34] In a similar way that the changing colors of liturgical vestments and paraments were a visual hermeneutic of the different feasts, fasts, observations, and celebrations of the church year, the changing chant of the ordinary was an aural hermeneutic indicating the same changes. On Easter day the introit *Resurrexit* signaled the celebration of the resurrection, but so did the following *Kyrie paschale,* because its different chant melody was only sung during the Easter season. The same kind of musical hermeneutic is employed in

Anglican choral evensong, when choral settings of versicles and responses are chosen to reflect the day or season, such as minor mode settings for Lent and major mode settings for Easter. Similarly, the Missouri synod's hymnal, *Lutheran Worship,* assigns simplified psalm tones according to the liturgical season, so that the congregational psalms at Divine Service are sung to a Dorian psalm tone during Advent, an Ionian psalm tone for the psalms of the Christmas season, Lydian for Epiphany, and so on throughout the church year.[35] The individual melodies mark the changing seasons and celebrations.

When polyphonic settings of the ordinary developed they were settings of the chant melodies of the Gregorian *Missae* sung at the various seasons and celebrations of the church year. By the fourteenth century such settings by different composers were gathered together according to genre (*Kyrie, Gloria,* etc.) in manuscript collections. Following the example of Marchaut's *Messe de Nostre Dame,* written in the mid-fourteenth century, composers began to write complete polyphonic settings of all five parts of the ordinary (sometimes with an additional setting of the *Ite missa est*) to be sung together at one celebration of the Mass. This in turn led to the development of the cyclic Mass during the fifteenth century. A cyclic Mass comprises polyphonic settings of the ordinary in which every section has the same melody as the *cantus firmus.* Thus the use of a common melody throughout the sections of the Mass gave to the liturgical celebration a unifying dimension it would not otherwise have. Although in many cases it was a compositional rather than an audible hermeneutic (the long notes of the *cantus firmus* often make it difficult to hear the melodic contour), a cyclic Mass nevertheless added an interpretive element to the liturgical rite. For example, if the *cantus firmus* for every section of a polyphonic Mass was the antiphon for the second vespers of the Annunciation, *Ecce ancilla Domini,* a unitive motive was added to the liturgical celebration of the Mass on the feast of the Annunciation. But the same Mass could also be sung on other Marian feasts and have a similar hermeneutical function.

This unitive musical hermeneutic can have a contemporary resonance, if clergy and musicians are thoughtful in their liturgical planning. The same congregational refrain could be sung as a response during the entrance rite, in the responsorial psalm, perhaps during the intercessions, and following the benediction. The repeated melody throughout the rite creates a unitive element within the celebration. The use of the same melodic/harmonic Amen[36] throughout the rite is another example.

There is a further unitive musical hermeneutic to be found in the traditional chant of the Mass, the melodic formulae sung by the celebrant at the beginning and end of the Eucharistic canon: the preface at the beginning and the *Pater noster* at the end. Thus the Eucharistic Prayer is framed by the same melodic forms which create an audible unity to this part of the Mass and provides an aural link between the offertory and Communion.[37]

In the medieval Mass most of the canon was spoken in an inaudible whisper and therefore what the people heard was essentially the *Sanctus* framed by the preface and *Pater noster,* which were sung to the same melodic formulae. When Luther eliminated the canon from his Latin evangelical Mass and replaced it by the *Verba testamenti* alone, he recognized and retained the musical connection between the preface and *Pater noster.* Indeed, he expanded the connection by suggesting that the *Verba testamenti* should be sung by the celebrant to the same melodic forms as the preface and *Pater noster.* In the *Formula missae* of 1523 he wrote of the *Verba:* "I wish these words of Christ—with a brief pause after the preface—to be recited in the same tone in which the Lord's Prayer is chanted elsewhere in the canon so that those who are present may be able to hear them."[38] For Luther the sequence of preface, *Verba,* and Lord's Prayer are to be interpreted as a unity, a unity that is audible through the use of the same chant form throughout.[39]

In the *Deutsche Messe* of 1526, Luther developed further his concept of musical hermeneutics and created audible connections between parallel pieces within the liturgical order. First, in this vernacular liturgy the two prayers for mercy, the *Kyrie* and the German *Agnus Dei (Christe, du Lamm Gottes),* are based on the same melodic material, in fact their incipits are identical. This melodic connection between the *Kyrie* and German *Agnus Dei* in Luther's *Deutsche Messe* allowed later Lutheran composers to create some complex but not obscure musical hermeneutics, Johann Sebastian Bach being preeminent. The gospel for *Estomihi,* the Sunday before Lent, was Luke 18:31-43, which includes the passage of the blind man who calls for mercy from Jesus as he passes by with his disciples. In two *Estomihi* cantatas (BWV 23 and 127) Bach makes use of *Christe, du Lamm Gottes* melody in a similar way: from within the vocal and orchestral texture the melody is heard as an additional element. The text of the second movement of Cantata 23 is based on the words of wrestling Jacob in Genesis 32:26: "I will not let you go until you bless me." Here the tenor sings on behalf of each member of the worshiping congregation: a request to the Savior not to leave without imparting his blessing. But from within the orchestra another message is heard from the unison oboes and first violins who together play, in augmentation, the first melodic line of the German *Agnus Dei, Christe, du Lamm Gottes, der trägst die Sünd' der Welt, erbarm dich unser,* though the words are not heard, only the melody. Similarly, the opening movement of Cantata 127 also introduces the same melody in counterpoint with the melody for Paul Eber's hymn "Herr Jesu Christ, wahr' Mensch und Gott," on which the cantata is based. Segments of the *Christe, du Lamm Gottes* melody are carried successively in the orchestral accompaniment, first by violins, then oboes, then flutes, then violins again. But there is a deliberate ambiguity that Bach is exploiting in both cases. Since Luther's Kyrie and *Christe, du Lamm Gottes* have the same melodic first line, the Leipzig congregations could not be sure which melody they were hearing. But whether it was the *Kyrie* or the German *Agnus* the import was the same: a prayer for mercy, "eleison" or "erbarm dich unser." It is only as more of both movements are heard that it becomes clear that Bach is using the *Christe, du Lamm Gottes* melody. Again, in both movements Bach's intention is to draw attention to the blind man of the gospel pericope who cries to Jesus for mercy, and the connection is made purely through the music for only the melody, without the associated text, is heard from within the orchestral accompaniment.[40] It is a sophisticated hermeneutic that links each cantata with the liturgical context within which it is heard, but it was made possible by Luther's creativity in musically linking these parallel liturgical prayers.

A second musical parallel found in Luther's *Deutsche Messe* is between the gospel of the day and the *Verba testamenti,* two items of liturgical proclamation in the vernacular liturgy, which are given the same melodic formulae. Again, as with the linkage between the *Kyrie* and German *Agnus Dei,* the use of these common melodic forms interpreted to the worshipers the connections, theological and functional, between the different parts of the liturgy.[41] It is the music that interprets the meaning of the liturgy at these points to the attending worshipers. But Luther's starting point for both these examples appears to have been the unitive connection between the preface and the *Pater noster* of the traditional chant surrounding the canon of the Mass. But in the case of the connections between the gospel of the day and the *Verba testamenti,* Luther adapted and developed another example of musical hermeneutics in older chant forms: the passion tones heard during Holy Week.

In the Mass the passion narratives were chanted by the single voice of the deacon, who customarily sang the Gospel. The individual voices of the evangelist and Jesus, and the corporate voices of the disciples and others were distinguished by different pitches of the basic reciting tone. For example, the voice of the evangelist was pitched in the tenor range, and the voice of Jesus was usually a third lower. But the different "speakers" were conveyed by alternate pitches, with various melodic punctuation formulae for each person or group, and sung by the deacon alone. These different pitches thus constitute a musical hermeneutic whereby the different speakers in the passion narrative are distinguished from each other, the lowest being reserved for the voice of Jesus. The worshipers could clearly recognize the different speakers, especially the voice of Jesus, by the different reciting tones at different pitches. Later it became customary for the passion narratives to be sung by different voices representing the *dramatis personae,* and by the fifteenth century the widespread practice was to use three singers.[42]

What Luther did in the *Deutsche Messe* was to accept the principle of the traditional passion tones, heard only during Holy Week, and create evangelical gospel tones that would be heard every Sunday and festival. Further, he used the same tones for the *Verba testamenti.* Thus in his vernacular liturgy the proclamation of the Gospel in the gospel pericope and the *Verba* were both sung to the same melodic forms. Through this musical hermeneutic Luther intended the worshipers to listen for the voice of Jesus Sunday by Sunday both in the Gospel for the day and the *Verba.* Here the hermeneutic of music was used to create a symmetrical structure[43] and also to give the liturgical celebration a further dimension of meaning.

Another level of musical hermeneutics can be seen in a number of Magnificat settings by sixteenth century Lutheran composers, in which the verses are sung alternately in monodic chant and polyphony. The alternate polyphonic verses of the Latin vespers canticle are juxtaposed with other texts such as *In dulci jubilo, O Maria reine Magd,* and *Resonet in laudibus,* or its German version *Joseph, lieber Joseph mein.*[44] But the connection is made by the intertwining of the associated melodies, with those of the Christmas pieces working in counterpoint with the respective plainsong psalm tone, the *cantus firmus* on which the polyphony is based. The Christmas "carols" interpret the Magnificat for the celebration of the Feast of the Nativity, linking Mary's song of conception with these songs of the nativity of Christ. Particularly striking is the conjunction of *Sicut locutus est* ("As he promised to our forefathers, Abraham and his seed for ever") with *Joseph, lieber Joseph mein*[45] in the anonymous *Magnificat sexti toni.*[46] Joseph is thus symbolically numbered with the "forefathers," and the nuclear Holy Family, Mary, Joseph, and Jesus, are brought together in a way that is not found in the Magnificat text alone. Through the hermeneutic of the juxtaposed melodies, with their associated texts, the celebration of vespers at Christmas was focused for the worshipers, who would have immediately recognized these Christmas melodies.

In later Lutheran practice, instead of intertwining such melodies within the polyphonic texture of settings of the Magnificat, it was customary to insert Latin and German "chorales" at certain points of the text of the canticle. Such settings can be found by such composers as Michael Praetorius, Johann Kuhnau, and, supremely, Johann Sebastian Bach, whose E-flat Magnificat included such chorale "interpolations."[47] But it was the functioning of a similar musical hermeneutic: the vespers canticle was interpreted specifically for the celebration of the feast of the Incarnation.

Another, more recent example of musical hermeneutics in a Magnificat setting is *A New Magnificat* by Carolyn Jennings, first published in 1981.[48] It combines the Song of Hannah (1 Sam 2) with the Song of Mary (Luke 1). The two mothers, one from each of the two testaments, sing to each other: Mary is represented by a soprano and Hannah by an alto. The two biblical songs, which have similar themes, are brought together: the graciousness of God's salvation is proclaimed from the two testaments, the one interpreting the other, but it is the musical form that is the vehicle of the hermeneutic.

The connection between Incarnation and Atonement is a theme of Charles Wesley's famous Christmas hymn "Hark! The herald angels sing." The sixth stanza reads:

> Mild he lays his Glory by,
> Born—that man no more may die,
> Born—to raise the Sons of Earth
> Born—to give them Second Birth

It is not stated how the Incarnation would eradicate death, raise humanity one by one, and give them second birth. The implication is that Christ was born to die and rise again, but it is not explicitly asserted in Wesley's hymn. The connection is supplied by the tune Wesley originally had in mind for his text, that is, EASTER HYMN, with its added Alleluias at the end of each line.[49] The tune was already popular in Wesley's day with the text that first appeared with it in *Lyra Davidica* of 1708, "Jesus Christ is risen today," a translation of *Surrexit Christus hodie* via German.[50] The tune was widely sung and recognized as having strong "resurrection" associations. By choosing this resurrection melody for his incarnation hymn Wesley was employing a musical hermeneutic to supply explicitly what was implicit in his text, salvation in the birth, death and resurrection of Christ.[51]

Another incarnation-atonement hermeneutic is found in Bach's *Christmas Oratorio* (BWV 248), a cycle of six cantatas composed for liturgical use on various days between Christmas day, and the Feast of the Epiphany. The first (no. 5) and the last chorale (no. 64) of the complete work are set to the melody of *Herzlich tut mich verlangen,* otherwise known as the "Passion Chorale." Again it is the melody that establishes the birth, death, resurrection hermeneutic, a connection that is underlined both by the text of the concluding chorale (no. 64) as well as its celebratory orchestral accompaniment:

> Now are you well avenged
> on the host of your foes,
> for Christ has broken
> all that was against you.
> Death, devil, sin and hell
> are thoroughly defeated,
> and the human race is
> reinstated by God.

As the examples given in this chapter demonstrate, liturgical music has both interpretive and proclamatory functions. Many composers, and some theologians, have understood and recognized these functions and have incorporated them into the liturgical orders and the liturgical music they created. We still need composers and liturgists to cooperate with each other to generate new forms of liturgical music that have homiletic and hermeneutic dimensions. We also need informed clergy and musicians who are able to let such liturgical music preach and interpret to the gathered community of faith the multilayered significance of the rite.

Notes

1. A few of the following paragraphs are revisions of material in my article "Choral Music in Worship," *Reformed Liturgy & Music* 23 (1989) 66–68.

2. *The Presbyterian,* Saturday, March 3, 1855, under the heading "Congregational Singing."

3. See *The Durham Book: Being the First Draft of the Revision of the Book of Common Prayer in 1661,* ed. G. J. Cuming (London: Alcuin, 1975) 82.

4. Basic studies include: John S. Bumpus, *A History of English Cathedral Music, 1549–1889,* 2 vols. (New York: Pott, 1908); Edmund H. Fellowes, *English Cathedral Music from Edward VI to Edward VII,* 5th ed., rev. J. A. Westrup (London: Methuen, 1969); Christopher Dearnley, *English Church Music, 1650–1750* (New York: Oxford University Press, 1970); Kenneth R. Long, *The Music of the English Church* (London: Hodder & Stoughton, 1972); Peter le Huray, *Music and the Reformation in England, 1549–1660* (Cambridge: Cambridge University Press, 1978); Erik Routley, *A Short History of English Church Music,* with additional material by Lionel Dakers (Carol Stream, Il.: Hope, 1997).

5. An exception is Stephen Plank, who draws attention to the Anglican anthem as homily by a detailed examination of Henry Purcell's large-scale

verse anthem "They that go down to the sea in ships"; Stephen Plank, *"The Way to Heavens Doore": An Introduction to Liturgical Process and Musical Style* (Metuchen: Scarecrow, 1994) 142–49; see the whole of Plank's chapter 5, "Liturgical Music as Homily," 128–63.

6. On Anglican/Episcopalian usage of canticles, suffrages, etc., see generally chapter 15 above.

7. *The Works of John Wesley,* ed. Frank Baker, et al., 34 vols. (Oxford: Clarendon, 1975–) [*Journals and Diaries,* eds. W. Reginald Ward and Richard P. Heitzenrater, vols. 18–24] 18:249–50.

8. Ibid., 18: 249.

9. Ibid., 250, 251.

10. See Carlton R. Young, *Music of the Heart: John and Charles Wesley on Music and Musicians* (Carol Stream, Ill.: Hope, 1995) 53.

11. See Watkins Shaw, *The Succession of Organists of the Chapel Royal and the Cathedrals of England and Wales from c. 1538* (Oxford: Clarendon Press, 1991) 176–77.

12. Franklin B. Zimmermann, *Henry Purcell 1659–1695: An Analytical Catalogue of His Music* (London: St. Martin's Press, 1963) No. 45. Bridge's conjecture was taken over in the Curnock edition of Wesley's journal: *The Journal of the Rev. John Wesley, A.M.,* ed. Nehemiah Curnock, 8 vols. (London: Epworth, 1909–16) 1:472, n. 1.

13. John Barnard, *Selected Church Musick, consisting of Services and Anthems, such as are now used in the Cathedrall and Collegiat Churches of this Kingdome* (London: Griffin, 1641; facsimile, Farnborough: Gregg, 1971).

14. See Shaw, *Succession of Organists,* 181.

15. Martin Schmidt, *John Wesley: A Theological Biography,* trans. Norman Goldhawk, 2 vols. (Nashville: Abingdon, 1962–66) 1:262; Erik Routley, *The Musical Wesleys* (London: Jenkins, 1968) 26–27; and Ian Spink, *Restoration Cathedral Music 1660–1714* (Oxford: Clarendon, 1995) 182.

16. Shaw, *Succession of Organists,* 10.

17. William Croft, *Musica Sacra: Or, Select Anthems in Score, consisting of 2, 3, 4, 5, 6, 7 and 8 parts,* 2 vols. (London: Walsh, 1724; reissued in 1732).

18. Croft, *Musica Sacra* 1:40–48.

19. Prefatory material in Croft, *Musica Sacra* 1:[vi]; see Shaw, *Succession of Organists,* 176.

20. Zimmermann, *Henry Purcell,* no. 31.

21. Under the date of January 28, 1685, the diarist John Evelyn recorded: "I also heard . . . sing before his Majesty . . . privately, That stupendious base Gosling"; *The Diary of John Evelyn,* ed. E. S. de Beer, 6 vols. (Oxford: Clarendon, 1955), 4:404.

22. See the facsimile, *The Gostling Manuscript: Compiled by John Gostling,* foreword by Franklin B. Zimmermann (Austin: University of Texas Press, 1977) Choral Anthems, fol. 125–29.

23. Henry Playford, *Harmonia Sacra; or Divine Hymns and Dialogues . . . The first book. The 2d edition . . . also four . . . anthems of the late Mr. Henry Purcell's, never before printed* (London: Pearson, 1703); the anthem is also

found in book 2 of the third edition of 1714, and in book 1 of another reissue in 1726.

24. Wesley would have heard the verse anthem accompanied by the organ, as is implied in *The Gostling Manuscript,* where it is included with "Choral Anthems," rather than with "Orchestral Anthems." However, the version published by Playford has four-part string accompaniment, with an opening "Symphony" and ritornelli, which are not found in *The Gostling Manuscript* version; see Henry Playford, *Harmonia Sacra . . . The First Book* (London: Pearson, 1726) 121–30.

25. Wesley does not mention St. Paul's, only the anthem. But given that he had attended evensong in the cathedral on the previous two days it is most likely that he heard this anthem, as the others, in St. Paul's.

26. Maurice Greene, *Forty Select Anthems in Score, Composed for 1, 2, 3, 4, 5, 6, 7 and 8 Voices,* 2 vols. (London: Walsh, 1743). "Solo Anthem Psalm LXII" 2:114–19.

27. *Journal,* 9 August 1768. *The Works of John Wesley,* 22:152.

28. *Journal,* 13 February 1765. Ibid., 21:499.

29. *Journal,* 17 August 1758. Ibid., 21:161. Wesley added: "I doubt if that congregation was ever so serious at a sermon as they were during this performance. In many parts, especially several of the choruses, it exceeded my expectation."

30. *Journal,* 29 August 1762. Ibid., 21:387.

31. See Spink, *Restoration Cathedral Music,* 182–84, esp. musical examples 37a-c. Austin Lovelace's arrangement of Croft's *Out of the Deep* (New York: Abingdon, 1963) is much abbreviated and Croft's melodic lines are curtailed and simplified.

32. In the Gostling manuscript it is marked "quick Time" and "Faster"; *The Gostling Manuscript,* fols. 127–28.

33. See Spink, *Restoration Cathedral Music,* 164–65, esp. musical examples 31a-c.

34. See "The Ordinary Chants of the Mass," *Liber usualis* (Tournai: Desclée, 1934; and later editions) 11–94.

35. *Lutheran Worship* (St. Louis: Concordia, 1982) 10–123; for an explanation of these simplified psalm tones, see Paul G. Bunjes, "The Musical Carriage for the Psalms," *Lutheran Worship: History and Practice,* ed. Fred L. Precht (St. Louis: Concordia, 1993) 477–87.

36. Some hymnals give selections of "Amens"; for example, *The United Methodist Hymnal* (Nashville: United Methodist Publishing House, 1989) nos. 897–904.

37. See *Liber cantualis* (Paris-Tournai, 1978) nos. 16 and 20. For the two items within the context of the medieval Mass of Easter Day, see Richard Hoppin, ed., *Anthology of Medieval Music* (New York: Norton, 1978) nos. 16 and 18.

38. *Luther's Works: American Edition,* eds. Jaroslav Pelikan and Helmut T. Lehmann (St. Louis: Concordia, and Philadelphia: Fortress Press, 1955–1986) 53:28.

39. In his *Deutsch-evangelisch Messe* (1524) Thomas Müntzer appears to have followed Luther's suggestion in the *Formula missae* by giving the three items the same melodic forms; see Thomas Müntzer, *Schriften und Briefe: Kritische Gesamtausgabe*, eds. Paul Kirn and Günther Franz (Gütersloh: Mohn, 1968) 174–79. However Müntzer's sequence is not as symmetrical as that of Luther because the former gives the Sanctus in the traditional position following the preface, whereas the latter directs that the Sanctus should be sung later, during the distribution of Communion.

40. Bach also juxtaposes a three-voice, fugal Kyrie, the *Christe, du Lamm Gottes* melody and the Kyrie from the end of Luther's German litany of 1529 in the single *Kyrie* movement (BWV 233a), which was later modified and incorporated into his Mass in F (BWV 233); see further Robin A. Leaver, "Bach and the German *Agnus Dei*," *A Bach Tribute: Essays in Honor of William H. Scheide*, eds. Paul Brainard and Ray Robinson (Kassel: Bärenreiter, 1993) 163–71, and "*Agnus dei* Compositions of J. S. Bach: Some Liturgical and Theological Perspectives," *Das Blut Jesu und die Lehre von der Versöhnung im Werk Johann Sebastian Bachs*, ed. Albert A. Clement (Amsterdam: The Royal Netherlands Academy of Arts and Sciences, 1995) 233–49.

41. See further, Robin A. Leaver, "Theological Consistency, Liturgical Integrity, and Musical Hermeneutic in Luther's Liturgical Reforms," *Lutheran Quarterly* 9 (1995) 117–38.

42. See further, Robin A. Leaver, "Passion Music," *Passover and Easter: The Liturgical Structuring of a Sacred Season [Two Liturgical Traditions 5]*, eds. Paul F. Bradshaw and Lawrence A. Hoffman, forthcoming from the University of Notre Dame Press.

43. Leaver, "Luther's Liturgical Reforms," 124–29.

44. See *Drei Weinachtsmagnificat* [one by Johannes Hähnel (Galliculus), and two anonymous], ed. Winfried Kirsch [*Das Chorwerk* 85] (Wolfenbüttel: Möseler, [1961]).

45. For an English translation of the German text, see *The New Oxford Book of Carols*, eds. Hugh Keyte and Andrew Parrott (Oxford: Oxford University Press, 1992), no. 55[IV].

46. *Drei Weinachtsmagnificat*, 6.

47. See Robert M. Cammerota, "The Sources of the Christmas Interpolations in J. S. Bach's Magnificat in E-flat Major (BWV 243a)," *Current Musicology* 36 (1983) 79–99.

48. It has been re-issued with a revised text: Carolyn Jennings, *A New Magnificat* (Minneapolis: Augsburg, 1993).

49. In [John Wesley], *A Collection of Tunes Set to Music, As they are commonly Sung at the Foundery* (London: Pearson, 1742), 11, the tune is called SALISBURY and appears with Charles Wesley's Easter hymn, "Christ the Lord is ris'n today" (see further note 51 below). In the Methodist tune book edited by Thomas Butts, *Harmonia Sacra* (London: Butts, ca. 1756), 17, the tune is given with "Hark how all the Welkin rings" (Wesley's original first line) under the heading "For Christmas Day"; see Nelson F. Adams, "The Musical Sources of John Wesley's Tunebooks: the Genealogy of 148 Tunes," DSM dissertation (Union Seminary, New York, 1973) 85.

50. See *The Hymnal 1982 Companion,* ed. Raymond F. Glover, 3 vols. in 4 (New York: Church Hymnal Corporation, 1990–94) 3:415–19 (no. 207).

51. That this was Wesley's intention appears confirmed by the fact that "Hark! The herald angels sing" was the first of three consecutive hymns in the same meter in *Hymns and Sacred Poems* (1739), as if they were three parts of the same hymn, and therefore sung to the same tune: *Hymn for Christmas* ("Hark! the herald angels sing"), *Hymn for Easter Day* ("Christ the Lord is ris'n today"), and *Hymn for Ascension Day* ("Hail the day that sees him rise"); see Frank Baker, ed., *Representative Verse of Charles Wesley* (London: Epworth, 1962) 12–17.

Chapter 22

Liturgical Music, Culturally Tuned

Mark P. Bangert

For anyone acquainted with Western music history, liturgical music designates a rather commonly accepted repertoire of music made distinct by its content and purpose. Knowledge about non-traditional Christian ritual music is less secure. Yet, sizable and significant practices of liturgical music continue to emerge across the world as the Christian Gospel and liturgical shape undergo contextualization, that is, the rooting of the Gospel in a specific culture and the subsequent dialog which such rooting engenders. These processes need to be recognized and understood. But first questions of definition have to be addressed.

Definitions

One description of culture instructs us to think of it as an "ensemble of customs, laws, values, and rituals which give symbolic expression to the social dimensions of life commonly held by a group of people."[1] Music often displays customs, values, and rituals—in fact is their prime embodiment. When the Gospel is brought to a people with a distinct culture it will be shaped by its values and patterns in order to express the meanings and purposes of the Gospel, a process, Ansgar Chapungco suggests, is preferably called "inculturation."[2] The Gospel thus undergoes cultural intonation as it were, it becomes culturally tuned as do the variety of responses to it. Inculturated Gospel gives birth to culturally tuned liturgical music.

When a person from one culture deliberately works to live in and understand another culture, and does that somewhat successfully, that person can be considered a "cross cultural" individual, someone who is able to live in two cultures as measured by the people of the cultures themselves.[3] Christians, and this includes Christian musicians, do not necessarily have an easier time of this than others, for cross cultural living is profoundly difficult for anyone. Occasionally cross cultural or bi-cultural individuals extend their reach to yet another culture or two at which time they become "multicultural," a term and concept which has unfortunately taken a beating because of its use to advance various political causes.

One final culture-related term needs attention. Because a given culture sometimes employs values and practices at odds with the Christian Gospel (for example, gender discrimination), inculturation of the Gospel shows a countercultural energy in order to clear away all that which might confuse the Gospel's purposes and meaning. Such energy is not new to the Church; liturgical music history is full of ecclesiastical mandates and theological warnings beginning in the fourth century with John Chrysostom and continuing up to the present day with some Indian Christian leaders pressing for reconsideration of classical sitar music in worship since the instrument represents the Brahmin class.[4]

A cursory rehearsal of definitions indicates that a tour through culturally tuned liturgical music is not without issues and difficulties, some of which clearly pertain to the practice of liturgical music as a whole. But those should not deter departure, although a few other preliminary concerns might cause a slight delay.

First, it helps to think of music in the plural: as there are cultures, so there are cultural musics. Many of these cultural musics are oral traditions in progress, which is why some African church musicians pay little attention to notated forms of the songs. Because repertoires keep evolving and are mostly not written down, descriptions and analyses of these musical systems come with difficulty. Second, one must be honest here: culturally-tuned liturgical musics do not exist in a vacuum. In China, Thailand, Africa, nearly everywhere for that matter, the ubiquitous "Walkman" or "Discman" brokers Western popular music to large segments of the world's population, in some cases threatening local cultural musics if not intimating their demise. Third and something of a counter indication, cultural musics are being brought to the megamarketplace, there to be mated with others, so that the offspring, known as "world music" also clamors for attention by all the world's peoples.[5] It's not yet clear how these new styles will affect liturgical music.

Whatever one might think of the culturally tuned music which reaches home's shores, such music evolves in complicated ways. A romantic view of things would have us believe that these musics, like their practitioners, develop in a vacuum, untouched by the cultural flow we know. But globalization has emerged here, too, since nearly everyone on this planet today lives in two cultures simultaneously: a primary culture in which adherents by birth preserve some older heritages such as home life, cooking, music, etc.; globalization as a secondary culture makes an impact on each of these primary cultures through its web of world markets, mass media, technology, and the Internet itself.[6]

This kind of global tug-of-war affects music especially since music is such an immediate and strong indication of social change. Since secondary culture easily gains an upper hand among the young of various ethnic groups, the ancient arts are threatened. This poses a dilemma for Christian musicians, those inside the culture and those outside. Insofar that these musics represent artifacts worthy of preservation, or, to express it another way, because they are distinct gifts from a people whom God has created and nurtured, do we mutually have a responsibility to provide ways to care for these arts ecologically and to preserve them (as well as the people who give them birth)? Some would urge committed assent to such care. Others, while not minimizing the importance of these individual musics, would suggest that musics come and go and it is not ours to interfere. Fragility is nevertheless integral to culturally tuned music, and one cannot easily stand idly by.

Borders

So what musics are we talking about here? Some ethnomusicologists (those who study and perform the music of ethnic groups) categorize the musics of the world by differentiating five major musical systems: Persian, Chinese, Indonesian, Indian (as in Asia), and Graeco-Roman-European. These are singled out because each has a substantial recorded history supported by theoretical writings of depth and clarity.[7] Here our concern is not with hoary pasts nor with categories proposed by scholars with non-coinciding interests. Rather, culturally tuned liturgical music contained in recent Western hymnals suggests borders which delineate four major repertoires which are supported with written collections and with descriptive material though in some cases quite minimal. Yet, such organizing remains tenuous since most of this music is no more than fifty years old.

In the following pages, then, we will focus on four major repertoires, each in its own way gathering up several cultural musics in itself: African, African-American, Latino-Hispanic, and Asian. A general discussion of these repertoires, sources, and characteristics leads to some consideration of the performance challenges these musics provide for today's church musician, and provokes a preliminary dialog with dearly held canons of liturgical music.

Some repertoires are not treated here, for example, Native American, east European, music of the Eastern Orthodox Churches, European-American, Australian, and Sami (formerly known as Laplanders)—just to name a few. In some instances the vastness of materials prohibits a fair and useful discussion, as is the case with the European-American grouping. Besides, that repertoire is known rather well by the average musical church person. In other cases, the paucity of available information encourages meaningless evaluations, while at the same time provides impetus for immediate research.

Finally, it should be noted that none of these four musical groupings is without its own art music. The Fisk Jubilee singers long ago provided concert versions of spirituals. The Javanese and Balinese gamelan is in some senses art music. The Asian Institute for Liturgy and Music in Manila has published and produced large-scale musicals which parallel Masses of the concert tradition in concept, and the *Missa Luba* from thirty years ago,[8] while growing from actual Mass celebrations, nevertheless today looks more like a captured musical moment for listening consumption. Overall art music is at a minimum, however, and that alone is refreshing, for the centering of energy on music of the common tongue urges all church musicians to give attention to the integral and fruitful relationships between struggling missionary churches and people's music.

Repertoires at a Glance

Africa

When in the latter part of the nineteenth century European missionaries came to Africa, they brought with them liturgical and musical resources from home. Converted Africans were invited to sing the hymnody and liturgical music of Anglicans, Presbyterians, Methodists, and Lutherans, usually according to versions currently popular back home. Translations were made, of course, but often the musical stresses of a tune forced unusual textual accents which in the case of those peoples who used tone languages provided alternate, if not contrary, meanings. Four-part harmony, foundational to both the hymnody of the missionary churches and to the marches of the colonialist military, became the dominant sound of this transplanted liturgical music. For sixteenth-century Lutheran hymns the missionaries offered the isometric versions of the tunes widely used in Europe at the time, and modeled the slow tempos typical of the age.[9] Continuing deep respect for the missionaries and for the transplanted tradition provides enough motivation to perpetuate these practices and even to honor them as central elements of African liturgical music.

The history of African Christian music is older than all that, however. Recent studies in Ethiopian chant have uncovered a complex system and repertoire of music.[10] In other areas of Africa, efforts by Roman Catholics which predate the great Protestant missionary initiatives resulted in various manifestations of the historic chant repertoire. More recently "The Constitution on the Sacred Liturgy" from Vatican II offered new directions which energized both Roman Catholics and Protestants. Theological and liturgical bases for indigenous liturgical and musical work set free what was already waiting to be born, namely culturally tuned liturgy and music. The fruits of these fresh perspectives have been rich.

The *Missa Luba,* while bearing signs of art music, modeled what could be done and in many cases was being done everywhere. In Zaire reformers reshaped the rite taking seriously the culture of those using it. Some efforts received more press than others, but across denominational lines centers emerged which generated distinct musical direction and materials. In Kenya Roman Catholic leaders supported musical developments which eventuated in the production of *Atukuzwe Mungo,*[11] a sizable collection of service music which contains many local contributions. Churches in Ghana, Nigeria, and Tanzania have published parallel hymn collections for use by local parishes.[12] Official books such as these often contain representations of European hymnody as a sign of what still is loved by many African Christians. Howard Olson, a Lutheran missionary to Tanzania, collected local inculturated songs from the various Tanzanian dioceses, translated many of them, and then in 1968 edited them as *Tumshangilie Mungo,*[13] a continuing popular source for European and American publishers. Missionary Tom Colvin has brokered songs from Malawi for use among western churches.[14] The Church of Sweden served as a conduit for songs from both South Africa[15] and Zimbabwe since its missionaries in those countries took a strong interest in indigenous liturgical music. At the Kwanangoma music/church music school in Bulawayo, Zimbabwe, Olof Axelsson and others fostered local creativity including the manufacture of Zimbabwan xylophones and mbiras (thumb pianos) and the publication of religious and secular songs through the services of Swedish printers.[16] That school has subsequently been taken over by the Zimbabwan government. Finally this token list must include the Magnet church music school at Ruhija (Bukoba), Tanzania, which has graduated several hundred musicians who work inconspicuously at inculturating liturgical music across a good part of eastern and central Africa.

Centralized activity such as this indicates projects nurtured by official intent, and certainly helps to ventilate the African musical spirit. But this is only part of the story. Just like sixteenth- and seventeenth-century European cantors, the local African church musician sets the pace. New music emerges from the individual parishes. Sometimes songs result from improvisatory sessions arranged by choir directors. Manuals exist to guide the process.[17] At regional choir festivals dozens of singers activate their tape recorders to capture a new piece sung by another choir. Often in transition it is altered according to local needs and habits. Still other songs derive from secular tunes fitted with new text. In this kind of context musical memory is essential to singer and leader alike, for very little is written down. Local hives of creativity shape the culturally tuned liturgical music in Africa today and most of it is unavailable through printed resources. In non-African hymnals, acknowledgments which read "As taught to . . . by . . ." are as much a statement of frustration about the ability to identify sources in this gushing of creativity as they are a sign of the outpouring of song coming from growing numbers of converts.

Getting inside this culturally tuned music is made easier by some grasp of its peculiarities. If there is one thing we all seem to know about this repertoire, that would be its strong rhythmic foundation. Where there is African music there are drums, we think. Yet, in parts of Zimbabwe the *mbira* is the chief instrument and drums play a much smaller role, a sign that while some generalities are possible, it is wrong, Francis Bebey writes, "to imagine that all African music necessarily has a particular role or function."[18] After all, Africa is a large continent and holds cultures as diverse as Egyptians and Pygmies.

Yet some generalities are possible. African music is outdoor music, often because its dance-based structure assumes contact with the earth. Scale systems and intervalic distances vary from region to region, which makes it difficult to posit continent-wide tonal characteristics. Non-Western tunings are sometimes more noticeable in instrumental music than in vocal music. While in some pieces tonal centers are noticeable, it is more common for songs to begin at one place, usually in a high register, and descend, sometimes in a ladder of thirds, to finish at another. Harmony is accidental, often in parallel fourths, or in simple imitation of hymnic chordal structure. As was mentioned above, military bands were permanent fixtures for both the Germans and the English who occupied large parts of Africa before nationalization efforts; hence whistles, ornate batons, and marching often enter church music performance as indigenized characteristics. Formal structure of much of the music revolves around the call/response pattern in its many variations. This serves basic impulses to improvise (in the call part) and to keep the music accessible (in the response part) to all in the community. Together with antiphonal formations, the call/response pattern serves well to manifest liturgical needs of Christian communities.

Even though drums and drumming are not ubiquitous, rhythmic features deserve a little fuller discussion. In general it is useful to think of African rhythmic impulses as parallel to European inclinations to polyphony, that is, in Africa one experiences a kind of "polyphony of rhythms." But that is not to suggest that African rhythmic practices are so unusual that they must be thought of as "non-Western," an African scholar has recently cautioned.[19] Rather, rhythmic sensibilities are significantly developed, though even that varies from community to community. Ewe drum ensembles from Nigeria demonstrate both complex planned relationships among the participants and carefully assigned roles. What seems to be widespread are the practices of divisive rhythm, in which basic beats are divided into two or three units, and additive rhythm, in which groups of smaller pulses are strung together, two plus three, plus five, etc.[20] In various ways both practices are present also in the European tradition. African rhythmic conceptions in many areas thrive on the layering principle, which is achieved by stacking various contrary rhythmic units, or by so-called "apart playing," two instruments playing the same pattern but at canonic-like intervals.[21] Both stacking and apart playing yield complexity, and by their very nature resist freezing through notation. Nevertheless, to facilitate Western use of these repertoires, basic notated patterns are often offered in print but should be considered as dispensable doorways to true participatory expressions.

The uniqueness of African rhythmic approaches probably lies in assumed purposes and conceptions. It is said that there always need to be at least two rhythms in any given piece, because rhythm is a means to community and participation.[22] Multiplicity of rhythms here implies a culture which is receptive to pluralism, whose silences invite participation rather than signaling time for personal withdrawal. That musical characteristics like this are closely related to a much deeper social outlook is a factor which needs further consideration.

Even as non-religious music in Africa serves many purposes, for example, songs to deliver litigation, songs to praise someone, so liturgical music serves a variety of intentions, especially those repertoires disconnected from prescribed ritual text. Songs of this kind are often endearing in their naivete, show obvious signs of improvisation and planned accessibility, and reflect clearly the circumstances in which they originated. Texts derive from a noticeable wonder at the newly-heard promises of the Christian message and from a consequent love for favorite sections from the Bible.

African-American

Consideration of African-American liturgical music as a separate category of culturally tuned music might appear imbalanced to some. Indeed, accepted canons of scholarship well into the twentieth century were aimed to convince one of the dependence of African-American music upon European repertoires. But less biased research into the origins of spirituals and so-called gospel music has unveiled a musical development which is profoundly African in its foundations though surely influenced by its new world surroundings. Foundational Africanisms have been cataloged by Portia Maultsby:

1) predominance of group participation;
2) emphasis on body language and dress, both of which lift up the liveliness of this music, its emotional intensity, and authenticity;
3) attention to the expressiveness of vocal timbre;
4) importance of improvisation, privileging reinterpretation over correct performance;
5) commitment to topical music as a means of social commentary.[23]

Africanisms set into the North American social scene lead one to consider spirituals and Gospel as a distinct culturally tuned music which awaits its long-overdue attention. Maultsby's chart (see fig. 1) helps one visualize the complex development of African-American music. In spite of a variety of attending influences there is a direct line from what she calls "Folk Spirituals" to various manifestations of Gospel. The intricate interdependencies in sub-repertoires can be helped by a few details. Spirituals and work songs are related, for instance, and sharing in that relationship too are the ring shouts, a kind of round dance which embodies textual material either sacred or secular. Boundaries between sacred and secular are in all respects indistinct. As shouts became less important, their inherent urges towards movement were given new avenues of expression by turn of the century, mid-south Pentecostals, who were encouraged in large

The Evolution of African American Music

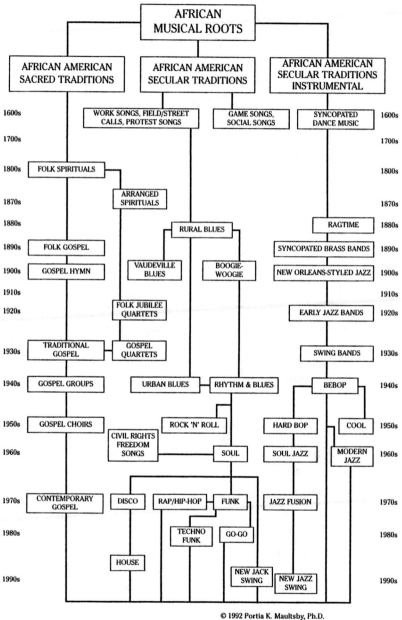

Figure 1

congregational gatherings to adorn their singing with clapping, body-swaying, stomping, and shouting.[24]

While Gospel developed alongside post-civil war social changes, roots predate the conflict. We learn that slaves took opportunity to worship by themselves either in place of, or in addition to, their often expected presence in the balconies of white churches. By themselves they exercised their improvisatory prowess by reworking or inventing spirituals which sometimes included musical and textual phrases heard in white worship. There were other opportunities for them to adopt and adapt the music of their surroundings. African-Americans often attended the camp meetings so popular in the early 1800s. At these events they probably heard the European-Americans sing "Watt's" hymns, perhaps joining in their renditions. But because the slaves were often set apart spatially for these gatherings their own work songs and sorrow songs were also sung, all of these musical experiences then tapped to shape the spiritual.

Early Gospel was built on the foundations of the spiritual. It was marked at the latter part of the nineteenth century by texts which were slightly more sophisticated than the spirituals, by large doses of colorful imagery, and by some recognition of so-called "white" Gospel such as the hymns of Fanny Crosby and others. In a word, Gospel possesses a little brighter view of life since slavery is, officially at least, in the past. The Holiness groups and Pentecostals, particularly the Azuza Street Revival in Los Angeles 1906–09, provide gospel hymnody with new theological accents. Pentecostals also brought to Gospel the addition of instruments whereas Baptist groups continued to render the music in a vocal mode. After 1930 African-American Baptist congregations embraced Gospel as a staple in their liturgical music programs, often lifting up the Gospel Quartet as the most important medium of delivery.

Some scholars date contemporary Gospel to a 1969 hit recording of "O Happy Day," by Edwin Hawkins, though the Maultsby chart shows several influences which brought that style to birth. Since the sixties cross fertilization between Gospel and popular music has been considerable. Contemporary Gospel is urban music, intensely personal in its religious expression, and most at home in evangelical Protestant churches.

Nevertheless significant contemporary collections of African-American music, such as *Lead Me, Guide Me* and *Lift Every Voice II*, both prepared within strong Western liturgical churches, exemplify the marriage of the Gospel style with traditional liturgical text. Contents of these books attend to the acknowledged leaders in Gospel music: Charles Tindley (1851–1933), talented hymnist and pastor of

East Calvary Methodist Episcopal Church in Philadelphia; Thomas Dorsey (b. 1899), a person who incorporates vividly the blending of sacred-secular musical relationships and a promoter of gospel choirs; and James Cleveland (b. 1932) who brought a blues style to gospel singing.

Stylistically, one can expect from this repertoire of music numerous manifestations of the Africanisms described by Maultsby. In addition it is rich with quartal harmony and chromaticisms, designed to be accompanied by piano or organ and, via Pentecostal influence, adorned with tambourine. Melodies are often syncopated and in performance versions rich with "blues" notes, or bent intonation. When used in contemporary liturgical situations, Gospel appears to some as overly performance oriented, but further examination of its characteristics leads to a deep appreciation for its own liturgical context.[25] It is said that any hymn can be accompanied in gospel style, but for those whose keyboard experience with that style is minimal, some contemporary hymnals now provide assistance.[26]

Latino-Hispanic

Both terms have been used to describe this repertoire of music. Choice depends upon what particular emphasis is desired. Latino is used in North America to differentiate this particular culture from others. The term Hispanic designates all those peoples, whether in North America or not, who have experienced some form of Iberian influence in their respective cultures. In this context, either term refers to liturgical music which is integrally bound up with the peoples from Central and South America. Within that vast repertoire there is music which derives from the following diverse origins, all of which continue to be represented in one way or another in the North American experiences of this music: (1) native or Amerindian music, that is, music which derives from those Central or South American cultures which have long occupied those lands; (2) Hispanic music, that is, music which comes directly from Iberian sources or from a mixture of Iberian and local musics, also known as Mestizo music; (3) music which results from cross fertilization of local characteristics and Africanisms, as Maultsby calls them, the music sometimes described as *criolla*.[27] The influences of *criolla* are dominant in the liturgical music of Puerto Ricans, particularly those converted to Pentecostal movements in New York and Florida.

During the seventeenth and eighteenth centuries Franciscan missionaries, working in what is now New Mexico, taught the natives there what they had learned about music and helped them to sing

Gregorian chant, European polyphonic music, and traditional Spanish religious music. In spite of the fact that so much of this music was taught in Spanish without singable translations, the natives responded well to it. *Villancicos, aguinaldos* (Christmas songs), *alabados* and *alabanzas* (general praise songs) continued to be used and loved in southwest North America as were folk plays like *Los Pastores* (the shepherds) and the music which accompanied them, particularly the *Posada* which portrayed the story of holy family in search of lodging.[28] Much of that music and contemporary parallels which fill out the requirements of the genre have solid places in today's repertoire of Hispanic liturgical music.

Diversity within the Hispanic repertoire makes generalizations risky. Puerto Rican examples employ the use of the congas, reflecting African rhythmic contributions, and often feature layered rhythms. Music from the Southwest has its own characteristics, as we have seen. Because of immigration patterns, the Midwest gives prominence to Mexican liturgical music, particularly the folk-inspired music of the late nineteenth and early twentieth centuries. Here one finds the use of regional styles, particularly those associated with the poor, and the so-called *conjunto* scoring with small accordion, twelve string guitar, and bass. Folk ballads in the *corridos* style are employed to convey biblical narratives. Mexican examples show the influence of the polka rhythm, which together with other dances from the European dance halls was adopted by Latinos for their own purposes.

Hispanic Christians frequently come from humble and poor backgrounds. Music is circulated not via printed sources but by oral transmission. In addition to a small but growing collection of hymns (many also in English translation), which are now showing up in standard hymnbooks, there is an increasing amount of Hispanic liturgical music being made available through published materials. *Flor y Canto* for Roman Catholics is a sizable book containing psalms, hymns, and settings of liturgical texts. *Libro de Liturgia y Cantico* (1998) for Lutherans has similar contents. Complimenting these materials are many supporting titles published by Oregon Catholic Press and G.I.A.[29] Protestants and Roman Catholics alike from both Central and South America show an increasing commitment to publishing this vast collection of liturgical music.

It has been said that the very title *Flor y Canto* (Flower and Song) conveys the heart of Hispanic piety and therefore its music, for both flower and song grow from fertile ground and are dependent upon the nurture of God. Imagery is rich in Hispanic music, often fresh, vigorous, and dynamic. Song texts rely on strophe/refrain patterns (*estrofa/estribillo*) and are not restricted by rhyming schemes. When combined with music the syllabic style predominates though often, much to the consternation of the uninitiated, more than one syllable is required on a given note. Iberian influences in the music show up in the use of the guitar and dance-based rhythmic structures. Over 1000 dances have been cataloged by scholars of Iberian music,[30] and many of these are used for liturgical music. It is typical for this music that tunes move quickly from major to minor modality and just as quickly from 3/4 to 6/8 time.[31] Favorite instruments are the guitar, accordion, bass, flute, trumpet, and percussion instruments such as the guiro and tambourine. Caribbean examples assume the use of congas and moraccas. For nearly the entire repertoire the employment of instruments is essential, so some of the more recent collections have included directions for performance practice.

Asia

Describing the culturally tuned liturgical music of Asia "at a glance" is close to impossible, if not simply foolish, because Asia is so vast and diverse. Three of the five major musical systems of the world have their homes in Asia. Diversity not only dominates the region, it shows up within the countries considered. In India, for instance, the music of the north (sometimes referred to as "Hindustani") differs in concept and detail from music in the south ("Carnaitic"), and in the far northeast of the country the music of smaller cultural subgroups like the Mizo bears little resemblance to mainstream music elsewhere. Further complications derive from the tight relationships between musical types and social class. Sitar music in India, for instance, has traditionally belonged to classes other than the poor, so its use within liturgical situations raises difficult issues for some people. National repertoires therefore are nuanced by geographical and social borders.

Because Asia is home to such a variety of peoples and nations, each in its own stage of rejecting or conforming to secondary Western culture, culturally tuned liturgical music occurs with varying intensity. In Japan, for instance, Western music, both classical and popular, is an established fixture, so attention by the Japanese to their own musical heritage is minimal. China has ignored its indigenous music in order to advance unencumbered allegiance to socialistic agendas, though the Church is supporting efforts to revive and nurture the old musical patterns of the culture. On the other hand, individuals from Thailand, India, Bali, and regions of the Philippines and Taiwan have encountered less resistance in their efforts to employ traditional cultural ways for Christian worship.

Deliberate work in developing various liturgical musics began about thirty-five to forty years ago. Such a program receives help from two centers of research and training. The first of these came into existence as an Indian response to the guidelines proposed in "The Constitution of the Sacred Liturgy" (Vatican II). Roman Catholics established the National Biblical, Catechetical, and Liturgical Center in Bangalore in the 1960s to explore the complex relationships between culture and worship. While music is not the chief aim of its careful and sometimes daring experimental work, musical matters typify overall issues of liturgical inculturation.[32] Because of its persistent dedication the Center has promoted indigenous music in such a way that many Indian Protestants have also benefited from its endeavors.

Of greater regional influence has been the Asian Institute of Liturgy and Music located in Manila, the Philippines. Founded in the early 1980s as an adjunct program of St. Andrew's Episcopal Seminary, the faculty of AILM serve a truly ecumenical clientele by providing their students with a thorough understanding of the various regional musics and by urging them to return to their own countries in order there to develop, foster, and promote culturally tuned liturgical musics. Hundreds of students have responded to such a commission. Following the example of ethnomusicologist I-to Loh, past professor at AILM, these students also bring to the school collections of melodies and songs from their individual local traditions. The school's founder, Francisco Feliciano, has realized the importance of this raw material and so has initiated a sizable publishing operation to make this music available to others.[33]

It can be said that students from AILM have missionized church musical Asia, providing too by their example support and encouragement for similar efforts in culturally tuned liturgical music. Notable among these are inculturation successes on the island of Bali. The founding of the Protestant Church of Bali in the early 1940's largely came about because of local efforts at missionizing the people. Since its inception the church has always had a strong sense of independence. Responding to the leadership of its past bishop, Wayan Mastra, parishes have attempted to utilize local musical media, the most spectacular of which is the gamelan. The gamelan is an orchestra of about twenty instruments, made from bronze, iron, and wood. Except for a few drums and the large gongs, each of these instruments consists of a kind of xylophone or metallophone and is given specific melodies or patterns to play. Key to the music of the gamelan is the layering of rhythms, all related, but graded in complexity, the lower pitched instruments having the slower rhythms. The instruments are tuned to fit into the entire orchestra, but each orchestra has its own unique

tuning conforming loosely to larger schemes of intervalic relationships. It is a grand sound, clock-like, and frequently employed to work
in partnership with dancers—also used by these Balinese Christians
in their liturgical meetings.

As a result of more recent missionary efforts in northeast Thailand the Covenant Church has established Christian parishes in and
nearby the city of Udon Thani. Local leaders of the church, not bur-
dened with colonialist tendencies of missionary work, determined
from the beginning that worship in these parishes should be fully responsive to the culture of the area. Their care in these matters led
the missionaries and local leaders alike to replace the sermon with
Bible studies since Thai people are more attentive to dialogical structures of learning, and to the establishment of a cultural music center
in order to harness its potential for worship.

Here, too, AILM graduates have been at work. It became clear to
both missionaries and musicians, the latter trained at AILM, that
three kinds of local music could serve their liturgical needs. Folk
songs, still in the memory and use of the people, were put to use by
outfitting them with new texts and by disseminating them on tape to
the small house churches. The simplicity of texts enabled quick learning and continued use. Second, the musicians reworked an old ballad form called *maw lum* whose purpose it was to tell the stories
which preserved the history and myths of the people. In Christian
hands the *maw lum* took on the more specific purpose of presenting
the narratives of Christmas, Easter, and other events surrounding
the life of Christ. More recently, an ancient form of chant called the
leh has been pressed into service. For Thai people the *leh* functioned
as a solemn rehearsal of the deeds of the ancestors complete with
opportunities for the listener to respond at regular intervals. Thai
Christian musicians have now begun to press the *leh* into service to
the liturgy, giving it the task of recounting the lives of Abraham and
other Old Testament figures.

Most of these musical forms call for Thai instruments: the *ching
chap*, a small hand cymbal which marks phrases; drums; the *ranat
ek*, a xylophone; and the *khaen*, a kind of mouth organ made from
bamboo pipes. Local tunings usually prevail. That means a scale of
seven equidistant steps each at 171.4 cents—slightly smaller than a
Western major second. Melodic progression evolves from a vocal
style which features glides from one syllable or note to the next. Heterophony, or varying simultaneous deliveries by voices and instruments of a singular melody, is at the center of performance practice.

Culturally tuned liturgical music in India presents yet another variation of inculturation among Christians in Asia. Since "The Constitution

on the Sacred Liturgy" (1965) from Vatican II, Indian Roman Catholics at the National Biblical, Cathechetical, and Liturgical Center in Bangalore have sought to develop a truly Indian musical expression for use in their liturgical life. As it turns out that task has been complicated by profound differences in musical development between north and south India, by the solo orientation of much of Indian music, by the localization of certain musics in social classes, and by the extremely intricate structures of Indian music.

Now, years later, the music most popular among the worshipers, both those Roman Catholic and those Protestant, are the so-called "lyric," which is a stanzaic song not unlike a Western hymn, and the *bhajan,* also strophic but much simpler to learn. The *bhajan* has been used for centuries by Hindus for purposes of meditation. While for some the line between what is Indian and what is Hindu sometimes blurs, the *bhajan* has grown in popularity among Christians because it does not require books (the leader lines out the sections of the strophe), and because it serves the meditative inclinations of the people.

Both the lyric and the *bhajan* characteristically come to life with accompaniment by local instruments. Most common are small bells; the harmonium, a small hand-pumped reed organ actually introduced by missionaries but now considered indigenous; sometimes the sitar; and usually the *tabla,* a pair of small hand drums which give Indian music its typical sound.

When used by local Christians these songs display shadings and ornaments which reflect the complexities of Indian music theory. Classically, melodies are built from material selected from dozens of intervalic possibilities. Selection occurs at various levels. The smallest interval is called a *sruti* which ranges from 22–90 cents, any one of these variances smaller than a western minor second at 100 cents. Quickly ascending through other levels of the melodic construction process, one arrives at melodic germs which are individually called a *raga.* An improvising singer, composer, or sitar player gains public recognition by how many *ragas* are known. Thousands exist, making the task considerable. While the ordinary singer knows little of these intricacies, the overall effect of the music reflects persistent practices and shadings tied to these principles.

Overviews of Bali, Thailand, and India indicate the diversity of culturally tuned music in the Asian region. Even a passing acquaintance with some of these repertoires provides a Western liturgical musician either with a creeping sense of inadequacy which can often lead to despair and imposition of musical blinders or to an overwhelming desire to explore what these fledgling efforts mean in an ecumenical Church.

Taken as a whole, culturally tuned liturgical music has already entered the standard hymn repertoires of Western denominations, so what used to be a subtle nudge to go next steps is no longer subtle. Some of these musical nudges we now consider in the next section.

Learning Again How to Make Cents

For Western liturgical musicians the convention of an equidistant twelve tone scale is so entrenched that the possibility of other than 100-cent half-step intervals seems to question the very rational foundations of music. Intervals of 171.4 cents (Thailand), or of 22, 66, or 90 cents (India), or of 240 cents (Indonesia) not only relativize our own working suppositions but are also signs which bring into relief certain practices long thought to be integral to Western liturgical music. These signs also solicit new attitudes about what liturgical music is all about.

Another look at some African vocal music, for instance, tells us that it has no clear tonal center or implies one which seems at first to be unlikely. But medieval chant repertoires sometimes behave in a similar way. The predominance of Western music in one of two modes, both transposable of course to eleven other pitches, makes bland the more colorful possibilities of compositional structuring based on at least eight modes of the classic medieval system. Culturally tuned music may be calling us to repertoires both old and new which break away from the harmonic molds of the last 250 years.

There may be a similar call to evaluate our dependence upon the keyboard with its conventional tuning. Frozen sizing for intervals is not a characteristic of culturally tuned music, nor has it been for Western music. The well-tempered tunings of the seventeenth century which via transposition enabled different intervallic relationships in the major scale provided nuanced shadings. In more recent times it is characteristic of singers, string and wind players to raise or lower certain pitches according to their current function in a scale. Such accepted practices ought to help the contemporary liturgical musician to be more tolerant of variations in pitch so typical of assembly singing if not recognize it as a welcomed manifestation of musical tendencies across the world.

Pitch is not the only variation the world's peoples of God offer the professional liturgical musician. Learned versions of a tune, which may differ from official printed or played versions, or the common tendency to sing a raised seventh in modal tunes create a kind of heterophony of hymnic praise. It may never have been different in the worship assemblies of Christians. In fact, heterophony could well be a musical inclination shared with peoples of many other cultures. Heterophony does point to the strength of monody and so alerts us to pay attention to the beauty of personalized unity in melody rather than to prettiness of harmony and of our own notions of perfection.

The Balinese, most African, and Thai instrumentalists remind us that rhythm and the sometimes open invitation to join in its elaboration are constituent elements of large and diverse repertoires of Christian liturgical music. Increasingly this rhythm-based music resonates also in the Western world. African choirs are warmly received world-wide precisely because of their unselfconscious investment in dance-based rhythm. But this characteristic is not entirely foreign to the Western musical tradition. Late eighteenth-century isometric versions of earlier Lutheran hymnody mask the origins of some of these German chorales in folk music and dance. It is possible to see how layered rhythms and additive rhythms have been a part of the Western tradition all along. When fears of the dance and dance-based music emerge they function generally as reliable barometers of the level and intensity of liturgical participation by the people who gather. The African drum calls us to our humanity and to many of our own cultural traditions.

Culturally tuned liturgical music invites contemporary Christians to the dance and to other nuanced liturgical action. For instance, the Indian *bhajan* carries and prompts meditation from its singer. It does so in a simple monodic form with texts focusing on the many names of God. Together with other examples of such music (for example, the meditative mantras from the Taizé community), the *bhajan* serves to provide relief from successions of programmed liturgical text and action, not to replace the specified but rather to complement it. Not just another hymn, the *bhajan* resonates with a long history of meditative music in Christian worship which includes the psalms, hymn-based organ music, and portions of the hymn repertoire which are meant for private usage.

Much of culturally tuned music, liturgical or otherwise, gets transmitted from one group to another via oral/aural means. In the process tunes, harmonies, performing forces, instrumentation, and sometimes rhythmic frameworks undergo transformation. For considerable numbers of people vitally interested and invested in culturally tuned music, cross cultural transformation of repertoires is understood to be a necessary and natural process. For them there is no correct performance, there is no ideal version of the piece which requires freezing in notation or in recording. Western preoccupations with performance practice, period instruments, delivery of ornamentation, etc., prejudice useful cross cultural experiences of other music. But even as we are not offended by J. S. Bach's arrangements of Vivaldi's music for instance, we should not hesitate to employ percussion substitutions for African liturgical music when *kayambas*[34] and *hoshos*[35] are unavailable, nor should we worry if our realizations of African-American Gospel sound just a little stiff. Translations differ from transliterations, and our "stiff" translations may more accurately take on the authenticity of the original were we to get at the heart of the music we gratefully experience, that is, to be enriched by the people whose music is graciously shared. And that brings us to still more challenging reflections prompted by familiarity with culturally tuned liturgical music.

Repitching the Venerable Canons

Growing familiarity with culturally tuned music taxes our musical abilities and asks us to open the door on our working assumptions, on the venerable canons which tune our thinking about music in general and about liturgical music in particular. No one is forced to respond. Indeed, some may prefer to keep that door closed because to open it causes discomfort if not the need to repitch both thought and practice. But the venerable canons have been repitched before (as in the move from metrical psalmody to the hymns of Isaac Watts), and new tunings have usually meant bursts of creativity and new energy for the Church. Whether or not culturally tuned liturgical music will occasion such blessed upheaval remains to be seen; for those ready to alter the pitch, here are three observations which could lead to new temperaments.

First, new repertoires of liturgical music are often measured, consciously or unconsciously, against what are thought to be timeless, pristine specimens of ideal church music, for example, the chant of the great abbeys and cathedrals, the *organum* of Notre Dame in Paris, the polyphony of the Sistine Chapel, the cantatas of Leipzig's Bach, the carols of Kings College, etc. The historians of church music, who too often get their subject confused with the history of music according to surviving documents, want to convince us that these arguably unusual samplings derive from geographical centers which have somehow gotten it right. "It" is difficult to define, but "it" plainly gets mixed up with impressive spaces, attention to liturgical detail, great music, professionalism, and pleasing presentations. Culturally tuned musics derive from contexts frequently oblivious to "it" if not unmoved by the characteristics attributed to "it." Were we to examine *these* classic specimens in greater detail we will discover that while they too evolve from impressive spaces (the outdoors of Africa!), local professionalism and pleasing presentations are other forces which give them shape. Reflecting on the shared characteristics of culturally tuned musics, Per Harling advances four twentieth-century movements which he thinks shape this music,[36] and which—for those who have ears to hear—make the old canons sound flat. First, Harling proposes, the Christian ecumenical movement has solicited a lively sense of the globalization of Christianity and a willingness, perhaps desire, to investigate common roots and traditions. Second, the missionary movement, in turn, forces questions about inculturation and the sharing of one another's gifts. Third, the liturgical movement has challenged people to recover the communal nature of worship, the active participation of all the people and the inculturation of the liturgy. Finally, the charismatic movement, one of the engines powering the missionary movement, also has helped to make comfortable for many people more spontaneous expressions of the faith in worship. In other words, culturally tuned liturgical music responds to a sense of the whole Church, to the core structures and energies of worship, to the impulse to move out into the world, and to the confessed power of the Holy Spirit. None of this automatically rules out the continuing importance of that confluence of interests thought to have birthed the great specimens of church music. Users of culturally tuned music, however, will recognize an accompanying clear but tacit invitation to draw close to the movements which energize this music and to respond with some kind of commitment.

Of these four influences the charismatic dimension causes some worshipers and musicians the greatest sense of uneasiness. The liturgical musics of the Balinese and Africans, for example, are simple, unpretentious, and reflect the unguarded Pentecost-like response of the newly baptized. These are musics which have little patience for privatism, but rather solicit immediate participation and bodily involvement. That may challenge the newcomer unbearably. Yet, such discomfort may drive all liturgical musicians in search of those essential elements of music which shape the common vocation of those who invite the muse into the liturgy.

Second, when aesthetic concerns are introduced into conversations about traditional liturgical music, parties in the discussion often turn to matters of form, meaning, in music, its origins, and sometimes its typology (for example, a triad represents the Trinity, etc.). Usually these conversations are meant to discover what it is that bestows "greatness" upon our favorite church music repertoires, or to synthesize a formula for generating more. Unfortunately, theories of beauty are sometimes used to keep whole repertoires from worshiping groups. What's more unfortunate is that such theories deal only with matters of form, harmonic vocabulary, or aspects of performance. Studies of world music, sacred and secular, yield alternative ways to think about music and thereby provide a path out of the aesthetic morass in which we frequently find ourselves. Ethnomusicologist Alan Merriam is an exemplary advocate in this respect. From his broad experience he ventures a three-fold formula for analyzing and apprehending all music. Any musical experience consists of the musical concept, the musical event itself, and the attending behavioral circumstances.[37] Insofar that his definition is meant to be all inclusive, we are being asked here to think about liturgical music in new ways.

Now, if one approaches culturally tuned musics with questions shaped by Merriam's proposal, how might notions about church music be repitched? At the heart of Merriam's view are questions that have to do with the social meanings and patterns of the music making process itself; as this or that music occurs, he would want us to ask: How are things going? What else is happening when a choir sings? Who is active, who is not? Does the music call forth active participation or communal involvement? Does it prejudice the professional or the amateur? If music is a way of processing information, or if it is social communication at a deep level, what is being processed? These kinds of questions not only get us closer to the heart of *liturgical* music but they also shed light on the vocation of the musical leader, who in some cultures is asked to be as attentive to the social processes surrounding the musical event as to the music itself. Preoccupations with traditional aesthetic concerns tend to disembody music, if one takes Merriam seriously, and have helped to direct our attention to product rather than to process. Repitching the sacred canons so as to attend to the behavioral aspects of church music will lead to redefinitions of the church musical vocation. That will lead to significant changes in curricular design for the preparation of church musicians, surely incorporating intense training in liturgical community and participation.

Third, whatever motivates one to enter the world of culturally tuned music—whether it be a kind of naïve inquisitiveness, a way to preserve one's musical occupation, or an avenue for exercising one's intentions about living as a globalized person—one leaves with significantly different perspectives and commitments, that is, if one permits the music to do its job. It is, of course, possible to resist the music's deeper invitations or to feign the behavioral involvement the music expects. This culturally tuned music, however, is never satisfied to be taken as an artifact, for it is meant to be a bridge or a doorway to the people whose music it is. Cross cultural musical experiences inevitably carry one to the people who make this music, to their unique gifts, to their views of the world, to their unique experiences of God, and to their unique understandings of the Christian faith. The gifts of such a conversion process far outweigh the confusion which it causes in one's participation in cross cultural or multicultural adventures.

Multicultural projects, also those attached to the goals of liturgical music, are sometimes the children of Western ideals. To engage in culturally tuned music, however, requires a kind of disarming, so that the exchange is on equal footing. Embraced by the people and embracing the people makes it quite clear that the point is not to amass repertoires for use "back home";[38] the point is not to impress others with a newly-found ability to "do Gospel"; the point is not even to expand the listening ability of the pew-bound whom liturgical musicians serve. Rather, culturally tuned musics make it possible for people to share both music and lives, and to be mutually engaged in processes by which faith and Church are perceived by all in new ways. Behind culturally tuned musics are people, hurts, oppressions, and offers of healing, all waiting for attention through and beyond the music. Ultimately the aim of entering the world of culturally tuned liturgical music is the world itself as God envisions it. With that goal in mind, those who cross cultural lines will be helped to avoid the plundering of other people's gifts which have been so graciously and widely distributed like seasonings for the cuisine of spiritual life.

Notes

1. Gregory Baum, "Two Question Marks: Inculturation and Multiculturalism," *Christianity and Cultures,* eds. Norbert Greinacher and Norbert Mette, *Concilium* 1994/2 (1994) 102.

2. Anscar Chapungco, "Liturgical Inculturation and the Search for Unity," *So We Believe,* eds. Thomas Best and Dagmar Heller (Geneva: WCC Publications, 1995) 56–58.

3. Margaret Pusch, ed., *Multicultural Education: A Cross Cultural Training Approach* (La Grange, Il.: Intercultural Network, 1979) 6–7, 17–20.

4. Interview with Yashoda, a sister and chief musician at the National Biblical, Catechetical, and Liturgical Center in Bangalore, India, December 9, 1993.

5. Tony Mitchell observes that "in a very real sense the music of South America, Africa, and Asia is being mined as a raw resource" to be reassembled for sale but only as an array of "surfaces"; "World Music and the Popular

Music Industry: An Australian View," *Ethnomusicology* 37 (1993) 309–38, here 335–36.

6. Baum, "Two Question Marks," 104–5.

7. I-to Loh, "Asian 'Traditional' Church Music," lecture notes (Chicago, June 13–16, 1993).

8. Les Troubadours du Roi Baudouin, Father Haazen, director, *Missa Luba,* Philips PCC 206.

9. See Georg Feder, "Decline and Restoration," Friedrich Blume, *Protestant Church Music: A History* (New York: Norton, 1974) 336–47.

10. Kay Kaufman Shelemay and Peter Jeffrey, eds., *Ethiopian Christian Liturgical Chant,* vol. 1 (Madison: A-R Editions, 1993). See also the ample contributions to African music history in *Africa,* ed. Ruth M. Stone, vol. 1 of *The Garland Encyclopedia of World Music* (New York: Garland, 1998).

11. *Atukuzwe Mungo* (Bologna, Italy, 1981), a book of service music for Roman Catholics who speak Swahili.

12. J. O. Ajibola, ed., *Orin Yoruba* (Lagos, Nigeria, 1974), *Ghana Praise* (Accra, Ghana, 1979), and *Mwimbieni Bwana,* for Kanisa La Kiinjili La Kilutheri Tanzania (Vèllingby, Sweden: Svenska Tryckcentralen, 1988).

13. Howard Olson, ed., *Tumshangilie Mungo,* 6th ed. (Nairobi, Kenya: Printfast Kenya, 1987).

14. Tom Colvin, ed., *Fill Us With Your Love, and Other Hymns from Africa* (Carol Stream, Il.: Hope, 1983).

15. See Anders Nygren, ed., *Freedom Is Coming* (Uppsala: KM; and Ft. Lauderdale: Walton, 1984).

16. Anna Sjögren, ed., *Sjung med Afrika,* 3 vols. (Stockholm: Gehrman, 1982–84).

17. D. Dargie, *Workshops for Composing Local Church Music* [Training for Community Ministries 40] (Lady Frere, Transkei, South Africa: Lumko Missiological Institute, 1983).

18. Francis Bebey, *African Music,* trans. Josephine Bennett (New York: Hill, 1975) 125.

19. Kofi Agawu, "The Invention of 'African Rhythm,'" *Journal of the American Musicological Society* 48 (1995) 387.

20. J. H. Kwabena Nketia, *The Music of Africa* (New York: Norton, 1974) 128.

21. Ibid., 133.

22. John Miller Chernoff, *African Rhythm and African Sensibility* (Chicago: University of Chicago Press, 1979) 42–45.

23. Portia K. Maultsby, "Africanisms in African-American Music," *Africanisms in American Culture,* ed. Joseph E. Holloway (Bloomington: Indiana University Press, 1990) 186–96.

24. Harry Eskew, James C. Downey and Horace Boyer, "Gospel Music," *New Grove Dictionary of American Music* [commonly designated *Ameri-Grove*], eds. H. Wiley Hitchcock and Stanley Sadie (New York: Macmillan, 1986) 2:248–61.

25. See Melva Wilson Costen, *African American Christian Worship* (Nashville: Abingdon, 1993) *passim.*

26. See *With One Voice, Accompaniment Edition* (Minneapolis: Augsburg Fortress, 1995) for example, no. 699.

27. Thomas Turino, "Music in Latin America," *Excursions in World Music*, eds. Bruno Nettl and Philip V. Bohlman (Englewood Cliffs: Prentice Hall, 1992) 238.

28. Gerard H. Béhague, "Hispanic-American Music," *AmeriGrove* 2:395–98.

29. Oregon Catholic Press is located in Portland (5536 NE Hassalo, 97213) and GIA is located in Chicago (7404 Mason Ave., 60638).

30. Martin Cunningham, "Spain, § II, 6: Folk Music, Dance" *New Grove Dictionary of Music*, ed. Stanley Sadie, 20 vols. (London: Macmillan, 1980) 17: 797–99.

31. The use of 3/4 and 6/8 meters can be simultaneous or sequential and is particularly characteristic of the ubiquitous Mexican "son"; Turino, "Music in Latin America," 249–50.

32. Questions about indigenous Indian spirituality, for instance, lead immediately to the *bhajan*, a strophic song used for meditation on the names of the deity.

33. See, for instance, *The Mountains Ring Out Their Joy*, ed. Ronald H. Walcott [AILM Collection of Asian Church Music 7] (Manila: Asian Institute for Liturgy and Music, 1987), Christian music from Cordilleras of northern Philippines.

34. Hollow flat rattles often made from stalks of grass and filled with dried seeds.

35. Gourd rattles not unlike maracas.

36. *Worshiping Ecumenically*, ed. Per Harling (Geneva: WCC Publications, 1995) 2–3.

37. Alan Merriam, *The Anthropology of Music* (Evanston: Northwestern University Press, 1964) 32.

38. Much has been written recently concerning the ethics connected to the expansion of world music; see the introduction and the chapter by Steven Feld in *The Traffic in Culture: Refiguring Art and Anthropology*, eds. George E. Marcus and Fred R. Myers (Berkeley: The University of California Press, 1995).

Chapter 23

Liturgical Musical Formation

Don E. Saliers

Music is the language of the soul made audible. This definition gives an immediate depth to our subject. Intuitively we sense that something profoundly inward is touched and seeks expression in and through music. The deepest human yearnings and feelings seem to be available to us in the hearing and singing of certain songs and compositions. With this definition we hear an accent on inwardness seeking expression. Intuitively this seems apt, especially when we think of spontaneity in moving from inner impulse toward outward audibility in form.

But for all its evocative power, this definition may mislead us as well. For music is also something which *shapes* our inward sense of life, and gives us a common language with which we share emotions not otherwise experienced. This is a key feature of ritual music. Music in Christian worship serves more than the expression of felt emotion. Texts set to music carry the words into the bodily memory of the assembly. As we shall discover, music which serves the worship of God has to do with the formation of faith. Far from being a matter of simple ornamentation or "emotive" enhancing of worship, certain forms of music are intrinsic to the Christian assembly's act of worship. This essay explores how music both shapes and expresses religious affections, and in so doing, forms congregational faith experience.

Music and the Word of God

Several years ago I had occasion to teach a setting of a new ICEL liturgical translation of Psalm 95. The antiphon was "Listen today to God's voice, harden no heart, harden no heart."[1] The musical form was a minor ostinato over which the cantor sings the verses. I was suddenly struck by a question once asked by Frank Burch Brown in a paper dealing with the music of Mozart: "Can music voice what God wants humans to hear?" That question lies at the heart of our explorations. It can be asked of music as such, but it is crucial to matters of church music—especially in contemporary American culture. This question is about the very conditions for the possibility of divine self-communication in and through the liturgical assembly's experience of sound.

In Christian worship music is a servant of the Word of God, especially so in most Protestant traditions. Earlier Augustine pondered his own ambivalence toward the musical praying of the psalms he experienced under Ambrose. In his *Confessions* we overhear his attraction to the sound that made him weep, yet that he knows also may distract him from the Word itself. The suspicion of music has also been part of Christian liturgical tradition, again surfacing in the Protestant Reformation with the so-called "left wing" traditions represented most austerely by Quaker silence. The sensual character of music and its emotional power over human beings was noticed especially in the neo-Platonic strands of Christian sensibility and theology. Is the Word of God in public worship deepened or obscured by the musical forms and their performative character? Should we be surprised if the answer is "both"?

Those of us familiar with the classical Western traditions in which music is understood as serving the Word think immediately of hymns, psalms, canticles, cantatas, oratorios, and the variants thereof. Luther, for whom music was second only to the very Word of God among God's gift to humankind, chose at the outset to create a singing assembly with hymns and liturgical song of freer composition, such as his setting of his Isaiahan *Sanctus*. Luther, and the first generation of Lutheran composers, combined the late medieval legacy of the *cantus firmus* of plainsong melody with fresh vernacular texts, joining these with the rhythmic vitality of carol and secular song traditions (as from the Meister- and Minnesingers) in a new body of song for the Church. Calvin and the Reformed tradition chose to stay wedded to Scripture as such, giving us a fine if somewhat restricted range of sounding God's Word in metrical psalmody. Watts and Wesley came, of course, to open this tradition up in unanticipated ways, creating a broader range of human experience of God in psalm paraphrases and in the full-blown experiential power of "first person" evangelical hymns.

It was Zwingli and others of the left-wing Reformation who carried forward the earlier ambivalence toward the use of music to articulate and express the Word. Zwingli, an accomplished poet and gifted musician who wrote the famous Plague Song in a four-voiced polyphonic setting, banned music completely from public worship scarcely three years later. His is one of the most dramatic examples of the sustained ambivalence which worries about the "aesthetic" and sensual powers of sound as distracting from the Word of God. It was precisely Zwingli's aesthetic sensibility which led him to prohibit its use in the worship of God. For, like Augustine and others before him, the power of music could obscure and even subvert the "hearing" of what God has to say. Only in the "true stillness"—unmixed with the potentially seductive and non-discursive sounds of melody, harmony, rhythm, and timbre—could the voice of God be heard and acted upon.

This tension between flesh and Spirit, between the sacred and the aesthetic means, between the sensually "sounded" and the inwardly heard, is rooted in the biblical prophets. Any convincing case for music as the bearer of God's voice must come to terms with the prophetic side of the biblical and Christian tradition. The suspicion that music may serve idolatry, injustice, or religious self-deception must be faced if we are to give a truthful account of how music shapes and expresses authentic religious experience. This can and must be distinguished from a metaphysical dualism of flesh and Spirit or of body and soul. It is one thing to say with Amos: "Take away from me the noise of your songs; to the melody of your harps I will not listen. But let justice roll down like waters. . . ." (Amos 5:23-24). It is another to say with Augustine: "Sometimes I go to the point of wishing that all the melodies of the pleasant songs to which David's Psalter is adapted should be banished both from my ears and those of the Church as well" (*Confessions,* Book VIII). The first objection is generated by the abuse of music in worship; the second from an ambivalent suspicion of what music itself is.

Such worries might well be dismissed as belonging to the parochial concerns of the Church. Music which serves the worship of God is only a small band on the great spectrum of music which shapes and gives expression to human feeling and emotion. It may well be that it is more *outside* than inside the narrow confines of church music that the voice of God is heard—there mediated through larger, complex forms such as oratorio and opera. Even in such a rambunctious piece as Leonard Bernstein's *Mass,* whatever judgment history will make about its specific musical quality, we confront a new dimension of what God has to say to a contemporary world in which "things get broken." The musical iconoclasm therein sounded has a great deal to do with re-hearing the prophetic denunciation of a social order which refuses to listen for God—even in its religious rituals.

Our present cultural ethos challenges us to think in fresh ways about the relations between music, whether texted or not, and the spirituality of listening for God. This is the heart of musical liturgy. We turn first to features of liturgy that are intrinsically musical. Then we will explore how music may be said to form human communities in the pattern of affections related to listening for God.

Intrinsic Musical Dimensions of Liturgy

Anyone who is attentive to a particular congregation's liturgy over time becomes acutely aware of the acoustical dimensions of various acts of worship. Public prayer, as in the intercessions or unison collects, or in the reciting of psalms, has pitch, intensity, rhythm, and color. The same is true of the reading of Scripture. The difference between reading a passage with understanding and simply muddling through it is characteristically a musical difference, where inflection and cadence, pitch and pacing communicate the semantic content of the text vibrantly or poorly. So each element of a service of worship is "performed" in a specific manner, for good or for ill. In particular traditions, the sound of praying, reading, and especially of preaching, has everything to do with whether or not something is "heard" and received as authentic. This means that particular traditions, whether liturgically "high" or "low," carry with them a performance practice. Congregations have tacit understandings of what constitutes integrity and authenticity in the "realization" of the texts. While the performance practice is not entirely acoustical, my point is simply that the "music" of the act is intrinsic to its sense and its significance for the assembly.

This implies that, at some level, music is never an "ornament" to worship. If many of the basic acts or units of a worship service carry with them certain associated acoustical qualities and patterns, then music is not something we "insert" or "apply" to liturgy. Rather, music which serves the worship of God is itself an embodied form of praying, proclaiming, and listening. Since liturgy involves speaking, listening, movement and rest, attunement to the pace, pitch, tone, and shape of the sound is crucial to participation. Even to think of the "role" of music in worship is slightly misleading. It is not that there is something already *there* called the liturgy to which we add something else called music. While this may be a commonplace view, it is misleading. Even in those traditions where the music is not related to what comes before and after in the service, it becomes an element in the over-all perceptual experience.

My proposal is therefore that music is *integral* to Christian liturgical worship. This is part of our concern for the integrity of the spiritually formative power of worship. To clarify this we must raise questions about the use and abuse of musical forms and performance practices in relation to the content of worship. If worship is to glorify God and sanctify what is human and creaturely, then musical judgments are ingredient in assessing the adequacy of our worship.

This leads us to the central concern of this essay: the formative power of music in liturgy. When we are engaged in worshiping God, the words are not merely "dressed out" in sound; rather, we are formed in and give expression to those emotions and dispositions which govern the life of faith. Thus musical forms—especially though not exclusively texted musical forms—articulate communal emotions which the particular attributes of God and aspects of human life before God require. In this way the pattern of our experience of faith as shaped by our common assemblies around the Word of God, the table of Eucharist, and the font of baptism is deeply related to the particular range and style of musical forms employed. To persist in using tensionless, easy-listening music will, over time, produce tensionless spirituality. To have a steady diet of music which is pompous, romantically self-assertive, or grandiose will affect and effect a pompous or self-indulgent ethos of prayer and participation.

Fred Pratt Green, in one of the best hymn texts of recent vintage, has penned the following stanza:

> How often making music we have found
> A new dimension in the world of sound
> As our music moved us to a more profound
> Alleluia![2]

Everyone sensible to music has had an experience when, suddenly or slowly, in listening to ordered sound, one "understands" something with a clarity that shocks. I am not speaking solely of the "felt emotions" at the time, though that is surely involved; rather, I speak of the state of receptive awareness to existence, to the world. Recently in listening to Mahler's Fifth Symphony, I had such an experience. It is what T.S. Eliot refers to in the Quartets: ". . . music heard so deeply that you are the music while the music lasts." But this has also occurred in singing "For All the Saints . . ." or "I Will Arise and Go to Jesus" from the Appalachian traditions.

My point is simply that, whether we are deeply moved to the poignancy and vulnerability of life, or to grief, or to great ecstasy, music has the capability of providing a way of understanding the world in and through sound. That is, music gives us a kind of grasp of life, a taste and sense of life that we cannot have without the music. And here the question of "wordless music versus music with texts" is set aside for the moment.

Why are we so moved by music that we are inclined to speak of it, or at least, of such experiences of it, as "religious"? Why are we inclined to speak of music as the "language of the soul made audible"? It is, I think, because ordered sound uses what is sensual and sensible falling upon the ear to articulate that which we cannot express discursively—simply with words. Any "hearing of the divine" is part of this approach to the inexpressible. What is most important to us, that which lies most deeply hidden from our ordinary non-musical daily existence, requires music to be understood. Music, in its greater capacities, illuminates the deeper connections and patterns by which we understand life as sheer gratuity—as gift.

This does not mean that only harmonious, well-ordered music— perhaps especially with texts such as Haydn's *Creation*—has this capacity. Quite the contrary, it is required sounding the contrasts of harmony and dissonance, or the beautiful and the painful, that we grasp the totality of life this way. This is what Karl Barth has in mind when extolling Mozart: he has the sense of the fullness of creation in both darkness and light.[3]

Music, Mystery, and Liturgical Action

There is, however, another feature of music, whether texted or wordless, which contributes to the connection between hearing it deeply and "religious experience." As Suzanne Langer long since has taught us in *Feeling and Form*,[4] music gives us the very patterning of the human sentience. The whole way in which music employs pitch, rhythm, melodic and harmonic forms, dissonance, and so on provides us with a non-discursive symbolism of our life. So the very temporality of music is revelatory of our temporality: tensions, climaxes, releases, serenities, dissonance and consonance— only in and through well-crafted or deeply shared common forms of ordered sound can we receive back our way of affectively being in the world. In this sense one might be led to speak of the "sacramentality" of music. Haven't we all had the experience of not hearing a work until our lives matured? Suddenly we come back to Palestrina or to Penderecki or to Duke Ellington, and hear it as if for the first time.

If the first dimension is music's approach to the inexpressible (things too finely or exquisitely there for words alone), the second dimension is its capability of giving us the very shape of our emotional life in the world. We come to know something of ourselves and the givenness of the world more intimately because music is just such a non-discursive symbol. Then, in the rare occasions where texts and music form are so powerfully fused—as in Bach's *b-minor Mass* or Mahler's *Das Lied von der Erde* or in "What Wondrous Love Is This," we behold the larger mysteries and totality of our being. This is what Schleiermacher was searching for in the aesthetic side of his theology: an awareness of the sense (the *Gefühlen*) of absolute dependence upon a Source.

A third dimension is also involved in exploring the relation between music and specific texts and liturgical rites. Communal musical form and practice is historically and culturally intertwined in our common religious traditions, and especially within Christianity, with worship, with ritual, with praise, with the articulation of sacred texts. So we return to the specific relationships between music forms and the Word of God in Scripture and in living tradition. Our very conception of God could not be what it is (in all its varieties) without the musical articulation and expression of it in living worship. The Byzantine rites, the Jewish festival liturgies, the Moravian love feasts, the Wesleyan meetings—none of these could be what they are without music. Having once heard certain texts which are honored as God's Word to humankind set to music, we can never un-hear them! Think of the influence, to cite one example, of Handel's *Messiah* on our hearing and understanding texts of prophecy from Isaiah, or of I Corinthians, or of the texts of the canticles in the Apocalypse of St. John.

We should not take for granted the fact that, in hearing certain music, we also hear the texts. I think it a fitting parable for our inquiry that Alzheimer's patients will, up to the end, respond to songs from childhood. This is the depth of music's role in our lives, and why non-discursive sound fuses with sounds from traditions who listen for God to speak. Quite obviously, however, we can also silence the hearing of God as well. If the music itself is self-serving, pompous, thoughtlessly crafted and performed, its power to "speak" is diminished. When texts set to music are tensionless, banal and without poetic multivalence, then the music itself is diminished. Significant form is required for the speaking and the hearing.

Professor Brown's observations concerning Mozart kept leading me back to the *Alleluia* of Fred Pratt Green's hymn text. It is in sounding the *Alleluia,* the praise of the Creator before whom they say the morning stars sang together, that we come to know our humanity.

Let me summarize the three major dimensions of this mystery of listening for and hearing the voice of God in and through music.

First, religious awareness of life points inevitably toward the inexpressible, that which is beyond the merely rational and the discursively expressed. Music, attentive to its own best resources can and does lead us to the apprehension of the inarticulate mystery of a sense of temporal being.

Secondly, I suggest that music, as Langer and others have claimed, presents us with the very pattern of how we have affective being in the world; the morphology of our deepest emotional connection with things. Music is a non-discursive symbolism whose power to form and to express us before the divine unlocks a consent to being. And finally, music has been linked with heightened speech and ritual activity in sacred ceremony and worship. In some contexts we can say that the music is the ritual gesture itself. It is the very way we confess or praise: *Kyrie!* or *Gloria!*

From these preliminary reflections certain trajectories emerge for further inquiry. This last point opens a complex set of issues concerning ritual music. We should, I think, pursue much more thoroughly the relationship between music and bodily memory, between the psycho-physiology of sound in the ritual context and commonly held images of self, world, and divine. To cite one example, why is the sound of drumming so crucial in specific African ritual contexts? Or, why does the very shape and sound of plainsong carry a sense of prayerful attentiveness? Could these matters be linked to the symbolic presentation of the embodied self and community, resonating and breathing the specific character of how the holy is to be encountered?

Finally, if we are to explore more adequately how music is related both to religious experience and to theology as "knowledge of God," we must note the rich variety of ways in which music asks questions of us. The analogies and disanalogies between music and language (with semantic content, referentiality, etc.) will come clear by taking up instances of music which force us to silence about our presumptive knowledge of the world.

There is a permanent tension within the Christian theological tradition, shared by others as well, between the aesthetic and the holy, the cultic and the prophetic. All biblical religion that is authentic wrestles with these tensions. But only by studying where music forms and expresses human beings in the depth of awe, fear, gratitude, suffering, and joy, can we hear an echo of why and how we might construe music as "theological." And yet, in the biblical tradition, we know that God is enthroned on the sung praises of Israel. "When adoration leaves no room for pride, it is as though the whole creation cried, *Alleluia!*"

Musical Formation of Sacramental Life

At the outset I focused upon musical formation of our capacities to listen for God. The Word of God permeates liturgical action. Thus musical settings of the psalms, canticles, various prayers and prayer responsories, and the hymns are specific ways in which congregations learn to "sound" the texts. The power of such formation should never be taken for granted, nor should it be abused. Over time, the activity of singing imprints the descriptions of the divine in creation and history and ascriptions to God voiced in praise, confession, lamentation, and thanksgiving on the body of the faithful. The access to the life-significance of the texts is often by a recalling of the melody or harmonic setting. So we find ourselves drawn to awareness of God in various parts of our life by the musical memory, or by the "overhearing" of the tune which suddenly floods our awareness with the way the wedding of words and music connect our present experience with the divine.

But the same must be said of sacramental formation. When we sing the "ordinaries" of the Eucharistic liturgy we are not simply expressing piety. Rather, the singing is itself ritual action. Sung acclamations are ways of congregational solidarity with the prayers of great thanksgiving, both at the Lord's table and at the font of baptism. Here again, when the setting brings out the intentionality of the ritual action of praising God for creation, for redemptive history, and for the promised future in Christ the words are more than words. Music offered during the Communion of the people, whether in congregational song or in choral or instrumental forms, is part of the symbolic liturgical action. This is why the education of the assembly in a durable and ample body of ritual music is essential to spiritual formation in and through the liturgical assembly.

As Joseph Gelineau observed, the problems of a singing assembly in its prayer and sacramental celebrations "bring out in an exemplary manner nearly all the problems involved in celebrating [the liturgy] as a common symbolic action."[5]

The formation of a community into a common symbolic action requires participation in the musical forms which animate and make present the experienced meaning of the ritual actions. The assembly's formation in integral and integrated musical repertoire is a theological activity, not merely an "aesthetic" enhancement.

This leads us to risk the practical liturgical judgments which are required in order to promote faithful liturgy. The musical forms themselves must be congruent with the prayer-action and the ritual acts. This does not lead to uniformity in musical idiom. If the liturgy is to

be faithfully celebrated over time in various seasons and festivals—
each with their own appropriate communication, then a variety of
musical idioms and styles are to be cultivated. Sacramental formation calls out for the combination of durable ritual music and theo-
logical/biblical and culturally-grounded hymnody.

"Carols are songs with a religious impulse that are simple, hilari-
ous, popular, and modern."[6] Thus begins the preface to *The Oxford
Book of Carols.* Percy Dearmer ends this preface by observing that
people crowd into churches at festivals such as Christmas, "largely
because the hymns for those occasions are full of a sound hilarity."[7]
This feature of the wedding of text and tune in the musical forms
known as carols has always combined accessible, dance-like rhythms
and meters with sincere and accessible language. Genuine folk song
traditions have contributed to the sense of musical connection between popular piety and the gathered worship of the Church. We
might regard the expression "sound hilarity" as a pun denoting both
hilarity that is appropriate to the text and particular occasions, as
well as exploring or "sounding" the *hilaritas* which is part of the gre-
garious joy Christian faith contains. I think immediately of the neglected Easter carol which begins, "The whole bright world rejoices
now, *hilariter, hilariter.*"[8]

It is no accident that many persons who know little else of Christian hymnody are quite familiar with the carols, due in part in our
culture to their astonishing commercialization. But it is their form
and musical language which is the point here. Their origins show
them to be related to narratives, ballads, folk-poetry, and bodily rhythms for the musically untutored. Like other musical forms that have
found their way from "outside" to "inside" the liturgy, carols provide
bridges between sentiment and discourse in everyday life to a sense
of the sacred. This accounts for their vivacity and for a certain important ambiguity in reference. The carol allows Christian communities to perceive connections between human vitalities and the
sacrality of divine worship, while knowing that they hint at the expression of human exuberance and sorrow without the divine referent—as in carols for the seasons in nature or in human lives.

Occasionally, in all this singing, the songs of earth and heaven
meet. These are times and places when the significance of singing together is suddenly revealed, whether inside or outside church. One
such occasion occurred for me in 1985, during an ecumenical gathering at the Orthodox Center outside Geneva, Switzerland. Among
those participating in the liturgy of Holy Week and Easter were several from behind the Iron Curtain—from Romania, Russian, East Germany, and Czechoslovakia, as well as from Ethiopia and several

English-speaking countries. We were invited to attend the great Easter Vigil in one of the several churches grouped together there, which included a French-speaking Greek Orthodox, a Russian Orthodox, and the small expatriate Romanian congregation I chose to attend. Shortly after midnight, as each liturgy concluded, we poured out of our respective church buildings into the chill, starry night singing in several languages, "Christ is risen!" while the bells sounded the Easter morning air. It was as though we stood—from so many different cultures, languages, and liturgical traditions—at the very center of the cosmos, singing and receiving the song in which heaven and earth had embraced.[9]

Notes

1. The musical setting by Christopher Willcock, S.J. is found in the *ICEL Psalter Project* (Washington, D.C.: Bishops' Committee on the Liturgy, 1983).

2. *The Hymns and Ballads of Fred Pratt Green*, ed. Bernard Braley (Carol Stream, Il.: Hope, 1982) No. 39.

3. See Karl Barth, *Wolfgang Amadeus Mozart*, trans. Clarence K. Pott (Grand Rapids: Eerdmans, 1986).

4. Suzanne Langer, *Feeling and Form: A Theory of Art* (New York: Scribner, 1953), esp. chapter 3, on music as the symbolic presentation of feeling, and chapter 8, on the musical matrix, which develop themes first found in her *Philosophy in a New Key* (New York: Harvard University Press, 1948).

5. Joseph Gelineau, *Liturgy Today and Tomorrow* (New York: Paulist Press, 1977) 94.

6. *The Oxford Book of Carols*, ed. Percy Dearmer, Ralph Vaughan Williams, Martin Shaw (London: Oxford University Press, 1928) v.

7. Ibid., xix. This was precisely the reason for the publication of this carol-book—to restore this element to Christian worship throughout the year.

8. Ibid., no. 96.

9. This paragraph is from "Singing Our Lives," my essay in *Practicing Our Faith: A Way of Life for a Searching People*. Ed. by Dorothy C. Bass (San Francisco: Jossey-Bass, 1997) 189.

Chapter 24

Liturgical Music as Anamnesis[1]

Robin A. Leaver

Contemporary American society suffers from corporate amnesia, ambivalent sensibilities, and mounting insecurities. This is particularly marked in people who were born after 1965, the baby-boomers' children—the baby-boomlets—whose parents were the products of the iconoclastic sixties. These thirty-year-olds face the prospect, or the actuality, of becoming parents themselves with a mixture of foreboding and dread, because the past does not mean much to them—it was essentially ignored by their parents who were concerned only with the here-and-now of the sixties counter-culture, which was antithetical at almost every point to the culture into which they themselves had been born. To many of these baby-boomlets life appears to be rootless and groundless, and the prospect of the future new millennium frightens them to death. They are a generation seeking a spirituality that is different from the spirituality their parents searched for. New Age spirituality seeks tranquility and serenity in a clean world of perfect ecological balance, aspirations that contrast starkly with the noisy, messy, and chaotic spirituality embraced by their parents in the sixties and seventies. New Age music with its bland explorations of ethereal sound, and the music of minimalism with its subtleties of small incremental changes over an incredibly slow-moving harmonic rhythm, are diametrically opposite in aural terms to the raucous, high-decibel rock, hard rock, and the other popular music of the previous generation.

American culture at the end of the twentieth century is much more complex than it was thirty years ago. Then there was a simple dichotomy between those who were "with it" and those who were, by definition, "without it," the tension between the lifestyles portrayed by Doris Day, on the one hand, and Timothy Leary on the other. But now our culture has become much more complex, fluid and disparate, a mosaic of bewildering diversity, as even a quick surf on the Internet clearly demonstrates. We live in a changing culture that is hardly monolithic, or even "bi-lithic." It is a dynamic rather than a static culture, a culture in process, embracing an ever-widening range of possibility for life, work, leisure, artistic expression, and, of course, music, along with everything else.

Herein lies one of the dilemmas for our age. Much of the current leadership of the churches has a mind-set that is out of step with what is happening in our culture today, a mind-set that nevertheless thinks of itself as up-to-date with matters of popular culture. Many of the national, denominational leaders of the churches—the bishops, presiding ministers, denominational administrators, seminary professors, their staffs, and associates—are in themselves products of the 1960s. Similarly, many of the parish clergy are either direct products of the sixties, or they are indirect products in that they were trained in seminaries by professors who were strongly influenced by the sixties. They are products of this era, whether they espoused the spirit of the age or reacted against it.

Of course, there were some very good things that came out of that period of reform and revolution, and we continue to reap the benefits. The civil rights movement, the concern for social justice, the concern that our democracy should be open and available for all, and so on. These were significant and positive gains. But there were also significant negative losses. In many cases, the concern for reform very quickly degenerated into the quest of change for change's sake.

Although specific agendas have altered, the principles behind them have remained very much the same: worship must be "relevant"—that mighty shibboleth of the sixties—and understandable to everyone, even if they have only just walked through a church door for the first time in their lives. Language has to be of the every-day type—prosaic, mundane, and obvious—because what we have to say has to be instantly comprehensible. Ritual, it is argued, distances people from people, and people from God and, therefore, it ought to be de-ritualized. Thus at the beginning of worship "The Lord be with you" is replaced by "Good morning. How are you feeling today?" Similarly, music is treated essentially as a propaganda tool and therefore has to be immediately accessible to make people "feel good," and thereby pre-conditioned to receive the message we have for them to hear. Worship in many of our churches is a one-dimensional "happening" in the present tense, with an amnesic unawareness of the past, and a myopic denial of the future: it starts and finishes, occupying a finite amount of time, but does not have a sense of direction, of pilgrimage, of spiritual journeying.

Although frequently assumed to be up-to-date and very contemporary, these approaches to worship were set thirty years ago, as the secular iconoclasm of the sixties became the model for a reaction against traditionalism in the churches. But some would want to object and make the point: "Isn't this exactly what the theological and liturgical term *anamnesis* means? Making the past present. In this case it is the spirit of the sixties *then* that is being made present in the nineties *now.*" Further, some musicians, who would not want to regard themselves as products of the sixties, would want to assert something similar: "If *anamnesis* means making the past present, then that is exactly what I do when I play the music of Bach in worship Sunday by Sunday—and I wouldn't perform anything else." But no. Neither point of view expresses what *anamnesis* means. Instead, each represents a selective *anamnesis,* the remembrance of a period of time that we have determined to repristinate in the present, be it the 1960s, the 1720s, or some other era. But in theology and liturgy *anamnesis* is always the result of God's choosing and action in redemption, as in the creation of Israel in the crossing of the Red Sea, and in the creation of the new Israel in the red blood of the cross. Under both covenants the *anamnesis* depends on God's initiative, not ours, and in both the experience of *anamnesis* is focused in a fellowship meal, of a Passover lamb in the case of the former, of the Passover Lamb in the case of the latter.

Part of our dilemma is that worship and worship-music are frequently understood only as practical matters. It is part of the mindset inherited from the sixties: "Deal with the practical issues first. What seems to be working in other churches? They seem to be successful. Let's keep up with these ecclesiastical Jones's and do what they are doing." So it has been practical matters first, then modifying the liturgical practice to suit, then, lastly, checking on what the theological issues might be. But when we do this, we are either ignoring our memories, or our memories are defective, or our memories have never been adequately formed.

There is a corporate amnesia from which we all suffer to some degree or another, an amnesia that approximates closely to the nature of sin. As there are sins of omission and sins of commission, there is an amnesia by default and an amnesia by design. There are some things we do not remember because the information has never been written on the hard drives of our minds. And there are other things we do not remember because they have been deliberately erased from our memories.

Amnesia by Default

There are some things we do not remember because the information has never entered into our memories. I received my initial theological education in the sixties. True it was in England rather than in this country, but I have since discovered that my experience is very similar to those who went through seminaries here. Much of that theological education centered on biblical studies. We were subjected to in-depth studies of the history of Israel, the message of the prophets, the distinctive theological emphases of both Testaments with a particular stress on the theology of redemption and reconciliation. In these studies we were taken, in great detail, through the complex minutiae of the sacrificial system of the Old Testament. But in all this intensity of the study of sacrifice, not once was it mentioned that an indispensable element of biblical sacrifice was music. At that time I learned nothing of the indissoluble connection between the offering of sacrifice and the offering of musical praise.[2] The fault is not in the biblical record, because the connection is clearly there. The fault is rather in the commentators, the biblical scholars and teachers, who bring a basic presupposition to the task of the interpretation of scripture: the hermeneutic that music, and especially music in worship, is a peripheral, non-fundamental concern in biblical theology. So music is largely ignored in biblical studies. Many translations of the Bible, which otherwise strive for accuracy, are incredibly inexact when it comes to musical matters. For example, 1 Samuel 16:23 states very clearly that David played the Kinnor "with his hand," but in some modern translations the phrase is treated as tautology and simply omitted. The statement is simply rendered as "David played the Kinnor [translated either as "harp" or "lyre"]." But first the effect of David's playing of the Kinnor should be considered, that it had a therapeutic effect on Saul and the evil spirit departed from him. Second, it needs to be remembered that the Kinnor was usually played with a pick, or plectrum. Thus the phrase "played with his hand" (rather than with a pick), implies a change in performance practice, a softer, less jangly sound, which must have had something to do with the soothing of the soul of Saul. But biblical scholars and translators are generally not musicians, so they miss the point. They suffer from amnesia in this area because the information is missing from their memory-bank; if it is not there it cannot be recalled.

More serious is the way in which biblical sacrifice is treated in the seminaries, for what I experienced in the sixties has been normative in most seminaries over the past thirty years, and remains current today. The musical element of sacrifice may be mentioned in passing, but is usually ignored.

The topic of music in the Bible is extensive and space preludes an extended study here,[3] but consider these few instances. First, 1 Chronicles 25:1-7 [NRSV]:

> David . . . set apart for the service [of the tabernacle] the sons of Asaph, and of Heman, and of Jeduthun, who should prophesy with lyres, harps, and cymbals . . . the sons of Asaph, under the direction of Asaph, who prophesied under the direction of the king [that is, David] . . . the sons of Jeduthun . . . who prophesied with the lyre in thanksgiving and praise to the Lord. . . . All these were the sons of Heman the king's seer. . . . They were all under the direction of their father for the music in the house of the Lord with cymbals, harps, and lyres for the service of the house of God. Asaph, Jeduthun, and Heman were under the order of the king. They and their kindred, who were trained in singing to the Lord, all of whom were skillful, numbered two hundred eighty-eight.

Here it is quite plainly stated that for the worship of the Temple there were three families of musicians who in turn lead the music of the worship of the house of God. Notice first, that they were not well-meaning amateurs who did this in their spare time. It was rather a full-time occupation, closely akin to the ministry of the priests who prepared the sacrifices. Further, it is specifically stated that these musicians were all skillful and trained in singing and in the necessary musical accompaniment. Notice second, that this singing and playing is described as prophesy. In other words, the special musicians who were set apart for the worship of the tabernacle, and later the Temple, were as much prophets as were the great prophetic figures of the Old Testament. Through the music of psalmody they proclaimed the word of God, like the prophets, and simultaneously led the people's prayers and praises. This is hardly an insignificant role for music in worship, nor is this music-making anything approaching a disposable optional-extra, or even a mere propaganda tool. But the idea that musicians in worship exercise both priestly and prophetic functions is a matter that not many clergy, and other church leaders, have come to terms with. It never enters their minds to think this way because there is nothing in their memories that would make this connection.

A second fundamental passage is 2 Chronicles 23:18:

> Jehoiada assigned the care of the house of the Lord to the Levitical priests whom David had organized to be in charge of the house of the Lord, to offer burnt offerings to the Lord, as it is written in the law of Moses, with rejoicing and with singing, according to the order of David.

Here is made plain the connection between sacrifice and music, between offering and psalmody: "burnt offerings" are to be sacrificed to the Lord "with singing." That connection is made even more explicit a few chapters later, in 2 Chronicles 29:27-29:

> Then Hezekiah commanded that the burnt offering be offered on the altar. When the burnt offering began, the song to the Lord began also, and the trumpets, accompanied by the instruments of King David of Israel. The whole assembly worshiped, the singers sang, and the trumpeters sounded; all this continued until the burnt offering was finished. When the offering was finished, the king and all who were present with him bowed down and worshiped.

Here it is made abundantly clear that the offering of sacrifice and singing of psalms were not two actions, one more important than the other, but rather one combined action of two equal parts: the offering of the sacrificial victim and the offering of musical praise, two integral aspects of the one activity. This is stated again and again in the parallelism of the poetry of the psalms, as the following two examples illustrate:

> Psalm 27:6. . . . I will offer . . . sacrifices with shouts of joy; I will sing and make melody to the LORD.
> Psalm 43:4. Then I will go to the altar of God, to God my exceeding joy; and I will praise you with the harp, O God, my God.

All these passages are emphatic in declaring that this temple music-making—the singing of the psalms with instrumental accompaniment—was not brought to an end until the particular sacrifice had been completely consumed.

There is also the witness of the Dead Sea scrolls. In the Psalms Scroll (Qumrân Cave 11), there is a document that summarizes David's psalmic activity. It states that David composed a grand total of 4,050 psalms and songs. Of these, 3,600 were general psalms, 82 were psalms for the fasts and festivals of the year, and 364 special daily psalms, which are described as "songs to sing before the altar over the whole-burnt *tamid* offering every day, for all the days of the year."[4]

It was this fundamental connection between sacrifice and psalmody, the two components of the one action, that led the later rabbis—looking back on the temple worship that had then been lost—to make the incredible and staggering pronouncement that if there was no music of psalmody then the sacrifices were invalid and ineffective because they were incomplete. The offering of the sacrifice and the offering of music were two vital parts of the one activity. These rabbis did not suffer from a default amnesia because they had been taught the fullness of biblical teaching on sacrifice. But now among many of our church leaders, seminary professors, and clergy amnesia appears to be an endemic disease. How can the theory and practice of worship and worship-music be put into a proper perspective when there is this corporate default amnesia that unbalances the perception of what the issues really are? There is an irony here in that in many other respects the churches have become increasingly more biblical over the past thirty years, notably in the wide use of the common three-year lectionary that has opened up our worship to a broader biblical content, and the consequential explosion of new hymnody and church music that explore biblical themes and issues that the lectionary exposed, themes and issues that were either poorly represented or non-existent in earlier hymnody and church music. But on the broader issues of worship and worship-music, the biblical perspectives are not remembered because the information has never really been entered into the individual and collective memories.

Amnesia by Design

There are some things we do not remember because they have been deliberately erased from our memories.

There is a current, fairly widespread, ecclesiastical fashion that insists that the quality of a congregation is to be determined by the increasing numbers of its members. It is not a biblical notion, though its proponents would want to claim that it is. A much more persuasive argument could be made to show that biblical theology enshrines the opposite: that there is spiritual power in smaller rather than larger numbers. Gideon prevailed because of a diminishing rather than an increasing number of men in his army; David was specifically reprimanded by God when he attempted to count heads, to take a census of the people of Israel; he was reprimanded because he was in danger of trusting in his numerical strength rather than God; and the whole of the doctrine of the remnant in the prophetic writings of the Old Testament implies that God does great things with small resources, rather than the other way around. But the fashion persists that the quality of a church is to be measured by the fullness thereof.

A successful church is a full church. For many this becomes the controlling principle for everything that a particular church does. Pressure is brought to bear on the church musician, who is often trapped between a minister who is anxious to lead a growing church, and a congregation that is more concerned to judge its success by following what other churches are doing, rather than by working out its own pilgrimage before God, "with fear and trembling."

Enter the Church Growth movement, the knight in shining armor, with all the right equipment and tactical know-how, that offers to make it all available to beleaguered ministers who, under pressure from denominational headquarters and from their own congregations, are desperate to make their churches grow. It is not the motive—"the world for Christ"—that is suspect, it is the methodology: "Do what we tell you, and you will be successful and your church will grow."

Music is high on the Church Growth agenda, indeed, one of its major tenets is that traditional "church" music is positively harmful. It is frequently stated by Church Growth gurus that unless and until the respective minister has eliminated all such music from the worship of his or her church, there can be no growth. It is argued that the music of Bach, Buxtehude, Pachelbel, Stanford, Parry, Sowerby, Willan, Hurd, Proulx, Hillert, and all the rest is a primary hindrance to church growth—it should therefore be eliminated from worship, at a stroke, and if the church musician objects he or she should be fired. What has been characterized as "good" music by musicians in the church is portrayed as "bad" music by the proponents of the movement, who argue that it needs replacing by more suitable music. By this is meant the lowest-common-denominator music, simplistic and soloistic, strongly reminiscent of commercial advertizing jingles. It is contended that only such music has a place in the worship of the churches, because, if they are to grow, then only an easy popular style should be used, a style that approximates to what most people are familiar with in the market-place of life.

The argument resounds with redolent echoes of the sixties. For example, in the early sixties I was serving a parish in South London. Billy Graham was coming to England for one of his Greater London Crusades and a meeting was held for several hundred leaders of church-based youth groups in the London area. It was largely an informational meeting, for members of the team to explain how the crusade was to operate and what was being done especially for young people. At the question time at the end, I had the temerity to ask why the crusade used only one kind of music, when young people in Britain had an interest in a wider range of music. I pointed out that every night for around three months each summer there were the

Promenade Concerts at the Royal Albert Hall at which a high proportion of the audience was predominantly made up (and still is) of young people. The music in these concerts covered a wide range of classical and contemporary music. I therefore asked the crusade to consider broadening its range of music style so that such young people might be encouraged to attend. The response to my questioning was simple and direct: "Such serious music is too intellectual and lacking in emotion for most people. Our concern is with the majority, so we use a musical style that will appeal to most people." One of the problems with this argument is that the Gospel is perverted by the suggestion that it is only for the majority and not for all.

Some thirty years later, however, the Church Growth movement uses the same basic argument, but with a significant shift in its application. In the mid-sixties it was used in relation to evangelism in a secular setting, evangelism in an exhibition hall or sports arena. Worship was seen to be a different activity. But in the course of the last thirty years there has been a blurring of the distinction between worship and evangelism so that worship for many churches has been transmuted into evangelism. Therefore what was once applied to evangelism in a secular setting is now applied to worship in a specific religious setting. Worship has become evangelism and traditional liturgical music, specifically composed to serve the rite and to express and convey a sense of worship, awe and wonder, has been displaced by evangelistic music that can only shout its billboard messages of propaganda.[5]

Liturgical music stresses the vertical relationship between us and God; evangelistic music stresses the horizontal relationship between us and others. Thus God-directed music has been replaced by human-directed music. The distinction between worship and evangelism has been forgotten because the Church Growth camp and others have been at pains to erase the evidence from our minds—to produce amnesia by design.

When the understanding of music in worship is thus attenuated by such amnesia, the experience of worship is also diminished—it lacks the perspectives of biblical theology and the insights of long traditions of liturgical music. When the role of music is reduced to propaganda, or persuasion, or becomes the tribal songs of demarcation of the "authentically Christian," or when one style of music, historical or contemporary, is decreed to be the *only* valid style, then worship has become anthropocentric rather than theocentric—with the primary concern being to please ourselves and others rather than to worship at God's good pleasure. Further, the limitations caused by human amnesia obscure that Divine amnesia by which God chooses to forget sin, for the sake of Christ. Our memories therefore need to be reformatted to learn or relearn the *anamnesis,* the "not forgetting," of Christian theology and liturgy, and how it relates to music.

Anamnesis and Its Implications

Music—its styles, forms and idioms—is not the problem in contemporary worship, though many pretend that it is. Music in worship is frequently symptomatic of other maladies. A primary ailment is the way in which contemporary secular culture has been allowed to set the agenda for the worship and ministry of the churches, at the expense of specific Christian culture, which is thereby rejected. Thus the model of the pastoral minister is no longer the Suffering Servant, but the C.E.O. of business and commerce; the Via Crucis has been displaced by the Via Madison Avenue; evangelism, in the sense of D.T. Niles of "one beggar telling another beggar where to find bread," has become high-pressure marketing; preaching is modeled on the radio-mike techniques of talk-show hosts; music is reduced to the level of commercial jingles; and theology is parceled up into digestible sound-bites.

The principal problem with this contemporary reductionism is that it has lost touch with the sacramental. Indeed, this latter amnesia is both the essence and the particularity of much of the American experience.[6] Early nineteenth-century revivalism had its roots in the sacrament of the supper but it quickly lost its sacramental origins. As a number of church historians have recently shown,[7] this tent-meeting revivalism grew out of the "Holy Fairs," the open-air communions, of Scottish Presbyterianism. It had the preaching for repentance, the congregational singing, and the long, hortatory prayers, but the specific sacramental actions and elements were omitted. There was a gathering but no meal; there was the imperative to receive Christ, but no elements of bread and wine; there was an altar-call but no altar. It was the story without the meal, the Haggadah without the Passover, the Gospel without the Eucharist.

Two fundamental elements of Eucharistic worship are enshrined in the two Greek terms *anamnesis* and *epiclesis,* the "not-forgetting" of God's redemptive acts in the past, and the invocation of the Spirit of God in the present. These two realities may be expressed in different ways but are to be found in differing traditions. In the Catholic Mass, Episcopalian, Lutheran, and other modern liturgies, both *anamnesis* and *epiclesis* will be found in a Eucharistic Prayer. But both will also be found in the Lord's supper of the Reformed tradition.

Calvin's prayer for illumination before the sermon is just as much an *epiclesis,* the invocation of the Holy Spirit, as is found in traditional Eucharistic prayers. Similarly, the use of the words of institution from 1 Corinthians 11, with the words "Do this in remembrance of me," are in themselves an *anamnesis.*

When the sacramental element is lost, worship becomes overly didactic, wordy, and ordinary, a mirror-image of the contemporary world in which we live. But this one-dimensional, static approach to worship in the present tense needs to be expanded into a three-dimensional experience: of the past we have received, of the present we now share, as we look towards the infinity into which we are being drawn. Music has a unique power to express and convey all three dimensions simultaneously in our worship. But before we can perceive and experience this, we must recover a sense of perspective by digging into the biblical understanding of liturgical music.

First, we have to learn again what Luther meant by saying that "Music is next to theology." Catholics need to read what Edward Foley has written about "Martin Luther: A Model Pastoral Musician,"[8] and Protestants need to review Carl Schalk's booklet *Luther on Music: Paradigms of Praise,*[9] because for Luther, though he did not use the exact formula of words, music is the *viva voce evangelii,* the living voice of the Gospel. This is the biblical theology of music as proclamation, prophecy, the bearer of the word from God.

Second, we have to come to terms with the music of the Old Covenant. There is a fine study of the role of music in temple worship, a revised dissertation, by the Australian biblical scholar, John W. Kleinig. This book, *The Lord's Song: The Basis, Function and Significance of Choral Music in Chronicles,*[10] is the first major study to address the issue. Here the intimate connection between sacrifice and psalmody is dealt with in detail. But what is fascinating is how Kleinig came to write it. He says that the "book began more by accident than design." I had some small part in its genesis. He read my book, *J. S. Bach and Scripture: Glosses from the Calov Bible Commentary,*[11] where he found references to the marginal comments Bach wrote into his personal Bible commentary, comments that were written beside passages in 1 and 2 Chronicles, comments that refer to music. Alongside 1 Chronicles 28:21 Bach wrote: "NB. Splendid proof that, besides other arrangements of the service of worship, music too was instituted by the Spirit of God through David." Against 2 Chronicles 5:13 Bach wrote: "NB. Where there is devotional music, God with his grace is always present." It should give pause for reflection that a composer from the past should have sufficient biblical insight to influence a contemporary biblical scholar to undertake a study of the role of music in the liturgical actions of the Temple. What is significant is that Bach understood that *anamnesis* and *epiclesis* should always be kept together. The remembrance of the past is made a present reality by the Spirit of God and music has a primary role. Thus a true biblical theology of music will also see it as a component of sacrifice, a sacramental element that accompanies God's grace.

Third, we have to come to terms with the music of the New Covenant. Long before Geoffrey Wainwright wrote his seminal systematic theology from the perspective of *Doxology*,[12] Martin Franzmann, poet, theologian, and New Testament scholar, was preaching that "Theology is doxology, theology must sing." In that sermon, published in 1966, Franzmann went on to explain that our music in the present tense, if it is to be biblical, must also be eschatological, an anticipation of that future song at the heavenly banquet.[13] Thomas Seel's recent book, *A Theology of Music for Worship Derived from the Book of Revelation*,[14] is an exploration of the same theme, the doxological function of music in worship in New Testament terms. Franzmann's sermon should be read for inspiration and Thomas Seel's study for information. A true biblical theology of music will see music as a component of what is yet to be, that the liturgical music of the present is therefore the doxological anticipation of the consummation of the end time.

Music has a unique power to express and convey simultaneously all three dimensions, past, present, and future, in our worship. It is therefore more than a conveyor-belt for words and ideas, more than an effective mechanism for propaganda. In an address given at Princeton University not long before he died, the Canadian novelist Robertson Davies spoke about the careless way we treat words. He said, we throw them around without much thought, but we need to remember that they are like sharp razor blades. Similarly, we tend to throw music around with little thought, harming ourselves and others, as well as music itself, by trivializing something that has the power to uplift, ennoble and inspire.

What is somewhat paradoxical is that many outside the churches recognize this, while many within the churches do not. In our culture at large there is a quest for spiritual music, music that is different from what is generally meant by "the music of popular culture." There is the wide variety of New Age music that explores multiple levels of spirituality. There is the Gregorian chant phenomenon that really is astonishing. Then there is the surprising popularity of the music of Gerecki, Pärt, and Tavener, music that is inspired to a greater or lesser degree by ancient chant forms, but which could only have been written in these latter years of the twentieth century.

Some of the interest can be dismissed as modish and faddish, but that does not explain away the phenomenon. Just based on the sheer numbers of CDs sold, and the fact that recording companies like Sony have introduced a section in their catalogues devoted to new spiritual music, there clearly has been a substantial shift in the diversity of the music of our culture.[15]

But many of the leaders of the churches have not caught up with these changes and are still trying to be "relevant" and "with it" by using the fashions of a previous generation. In the late fifties and early sixties Geoffrey Beaumont and the others of Twentieth Century Church Light Music Group thought they were bringing the music of the Church right up-to-date with their *Twentieth-Century Folk Mass,* and "contemporary" hymn tunes. They insisted that their music style was on the cutting edge of modernity. But when you listened to it critically, it was not in the popular style of the late fifties but rather the softer Broadway style of the thirties. Similarly, in the seventies, when the charismatic movement was moving into mainline denominations, great stress was placed on the "newness" of the work of the Spirit. Yet this contemporary spirituality was usually expressed in the "old" language of the King James Version and the style of the music was clearly stuck in the late nineteenth century.[16] And much of contemporary Christian music, as John Ferguson has observed, "is not contemporary at all, since it was written, say twenty years ago, and even if written more recently, sounds like pop music of twenty years ago—sort of warmed over Carpenters."[17] When the Church pursues the musical styles of popular culture as a vehicle for its message, it finds itself promoting what is by then out-of-date.

The communications guru of the sixties, Marshall McCluhan, was not always taken as seriously as he should have been. One of his sayings was "The Medium is the Message." It was a concept that Bishop Pike of California took up in his expositions of religionless religion, thereby discrediting the concept for many. But it needs revisiting. "The Medium is the Message" is a shorthand way of expressing the truth that it is not simply the substance of a message but how that message is received that makes an impression on people. "The end justifies the means" was decried as the immoral concept of communism, but it has become an acceptable working agenda for Christian evangelism. If the end is bringing individuals within the sound of the Gospel, then whatever means is available can and should be used. In the case of music, any popular style can be used, so long as it gets a hearing for the grace of God in Christ. But the argument needs to be evaluated before being accepted. Marshall McCluhan needs to be heard again, and the implications of what is being proposed should be carefully considered. "The Medium is the Message." It is not only the substance of the message but how that message is conveyed that conditions how people hear. If a disposable, popular musical style is being used to convey the Christian message, is not the implied message that the Gospel is somehow disposable, too?[18] By using a musical style that has a serious amnesia-defect—it is forgotten when new styles come along—are we not introducing an element of obsolescence into the Gospel we preach? Proponents will protest and say that is of course is not what they intend to convey. But, again, another saying of McCluhan needs to be called to mind: "It is not what you say but what people hear." We know that we have said something very clearly to someone else, and yet when they tell us what they heard us say, we are horrified by the mis-communication that has occurred. Something other than what we intended, and actually said, was heard, another meaning was conveyed to that other person. "It is not what you say but what people hear." In the churches, by deliberately choosing popular music styles simply because they are popular music styles (or are perceived to be), we are guilty of the charge of attempting to manipulate the spiritual lives of others. We know the effect we want to create, so we use a particular style of music in order to move people in the way we have pre-determined that they should be moved. This is the music of the "cheap grace" that Dietrich Bonhoeffer speaks about in his perceptive book, one of the classics of twentieth-century Christianity, *The Cost of Discipleship*.[19]

But when I read the New Testament I do not find that peoples' lives were touched and changed because of the techniques that the apostles invented. On the contrary, the Book of Acts, which is, rightly, often referred to as the Acts of the Spirit, is full of the actions of the Holy Spirit, and it is the Apostles and disciples who have to extend themselves in order to catch up with where the Spirit had already been at work, leading, guiding and changing peoples lives. This is the "costly grace" that Dietrich Bonhoeffer speaks about in *The Cost of Discipleship,* and we need to use the kind of music in our worship that will convey this "costly grace."

To use a particular musical style in worship or evangelism to obtain a desired result is to attempt to confine the activity of God within the limitations of our own thinking and experience. We therefore need a paradigm shift—instead of being preoccupied with the forms of music, we should pay much more attention to the functions of music. Form follows function rather than the other way around. Form follows function in the sense of Shaker furniture, or Frank Lloyd Wright architecture. So should it be with the music of the Church. It is a question of balance, symmetry, proportion, function, that combination that produces a profound simplicity in sound—like the ebb and flow of plainchant; like the integrity of the African-American spiritual; like the hymn tune "Amazing Grace"; like the stark intensity of the music of Arvo Pärt; or even in the complexity of a choral fugue by Bach, because the intricacy is built up from the essential simplicity of the fugal subject.

The primary function of liturgical music is to facilitate worship, not to mirror the culture in which we now live. It may well do the latter, too, but as a by-product rather than a goal. Liturgical music should lift up our hearts and minds beyond the mundaneness that makes up too much of our lives; it should raise our spirits to worship, adore and thank the God who has created us, who redeems us, who sustains us. Liturgical music is *anamnesis,* the celebration of the "presentness" of God's presence with the community of faith at worship.

Notes

1. An earlier form of this chapter was given as the keynote address at the Third AGO Seminary Musicians Conference at General Theological Seminary, New York, July 6, 1996, and then as a lecture at the Centennial Convention of the American Guild of Organists in New York, July 8, 1996.

2. Some years after I completed my theological studies H. H. Rowley's *Worship in Ancient Israel: Its Forms and Meaning* (London: SPCK, 1967) was published. It included a chapter entitled "Psalmody and Music," but was mostly concerned with the psalm studies of Gunkel and Mowinckel, especially enthronement psalms, rather than the connections between sacrifice and psalmody.

3. Some of the primary literature is cited in note 11 of chapter 13 above.

4. J. A. Sanders, *The Psalms Scroll of Qumrân Cave 11 (11QPsa)* (Oxford: Clarendon, 1965) 92.

5. "Are there truly two kinds of musical expression, one identified as sacred and the other as non-sacred and appropriate only for secular occasions? If the composer-musician is careless, clumsy, or impious, and mixes the two expressions, how will the religious leaders protect the faithful from this abuse of the worship service? If the religious message is confused, diluted, or . . . replaced by an irreligious meaning, either explicit or implied in the sounds of the music, this propaganda has failed"; Arnold Perris, *Music as Propaganda: Art to Persuade, Art to Control* (Westport, Ct.: Greenwood, 1985) 124.

6. Historical studies include: A. James Reichley, *Religion in American Public Life* (Washington: Brookings Institute, 1985); R. Laurence Moore, *Selling God: American Religion in the Marketplace of Culture* (New York: Oxford University Press, 1994); see also E. Digby Baltzell, *Puritan Boston and Quaker Philadelphia: Two Protestant Ethics and the Spirit of Class Authority and Leadership* (New York: Free Press, 1979). Contemporary studies include: Phillip L.

Berman, *The Search for Meaning: Americans Talk About What They Believe and Why* (New York: Ballentine, 1990); and the analyses of Robert Wuthnow, *The Restructuring of American Religion* (Princeton: Princeton University Press, 1988), *The Struggle for America's Soul: Evangelicals, Liberals, and Secularism* (Grand Rapids: Eerdmans, 1989), *Producing the Sacred: An Essay on Public Religion* (Urbana: University of Illinois Press, 1994), and *God and Mammon in America* (New York: Macmillan, 1996).

7. See, for example: Marilyn Westerkamp, *Scots-Irish Piety and the Great Awakening, 1625–1760* (New York: Oxford University Press, 1988); Leigh Eric Schmidt, *Holy Fairs: Scottish Communions and American Revivals in the Early Modern Period* (Princeton: Princeton University Press, 1989); and Paul K. Conklin, *Cane Ridge: America's Pentecost* (Madison: University of Wisconsin Press, 1990).

8. Edward Foley, *Ritual Music: Studies in Liturgical Musicology* (Beltville: Pastoral Press, 1995) 89–106.

9. Carl Schalk, *Luther on Music: Paradigms of Praise* (St. Louis: Concordia, 1988).

10. John W. Kleinig, *The Lord's Song: The Basis, Function and Significance of Choral Music in Chronicles* (Sheffield: Sheffield Academic Press, 1993).

11. Robin A. Leaver, *J. S. Bach and Scripture: Glosses from the Calov Bible Commentary* (St. Louis: Concordia, 1985).

12. Geoffrey Wainwright, *Doxology: the Praise of God in Worship, Doctrine, and Life; a Systematic Theology* (New York: Oxford University Press, 1980).

13. See Robin A. Leaver, *Come to the Feast: The Original and Translated Hymns of Martin H. Franzmann* (St. Louis: Morning Star, 1994) 137–40.

14. Thomas Seel, *A Theology of Music for Worship Derived from the Book of Revelation* (Metuchen, N.J.: Scarecrow, 1995).

15. Recent research has shown that young people, contrary to conventional wisdom, are suspicious of contemporary music styles being used in a specific religious context; see Barbara Resch, "Adolescents' Attitudes towards the Appropriateness of Religious Music," D.M.E. dissertation (Indiana University, 1996).

16. See Robin A. Leaver, "British Hymnody Since 1950," *The Hymnal 1982 Companion,* ed. Raymond Glover, 3 vols. in 4 (New York: Church Hymnal Corporation, 1990–94) 1:555–99, esp. 558–60.

17. John Ferguson, "Lutheran Church Music: Today and Tomorrow," *Cross Accents: Journal of the Association of Lutheran Church Musicians* 6 (1995) 25.

18. "The musical style is a shaper of the message, and only at our peril do we divorce the lyrics from the medium that conveys them"; Calvin Stapelt, "It's How You Say It," *The Reformed Journal* 36 (1986) 7–8.

19. Dietrich Bonhoeffer, *The Cost of Discipleship,* trans. R. H. Fuller, 2nd ed., rev., Irmgard Booth (New York: Macmillan, 1959).

Chapter 25

Liturgical Music: A Bibliographic Essay

Edward Foley, Capuchin

Introduction

The field of liturgical music is a vast and far-ranging one, diversely partitioned, studied, and presented. Unlike some other subdisciplines of liturgics, there is little standardization in the study of liturgical music, and syllabi for courses of study in the area often cover very different terrain employing a variety of methods.[1] There is barely agreement on the appropriate language for accessing the field,[2] as symbolized by the many dictionaries on the topic that are diversely titled and arranged. Examples include:

Joseph Robert Carroll, *Compendium of Liturgical Musical Terms* (Toledo: Gregorian Institute of America, 1964).

James Robert Davidson, *A Dictionary of Protestant Church Music* (Metuchen, N.J.: Scarecrow, 1975).

Utto Kornmüller, *Lexikon der kirchlichen Tonkunst* (Regensburg: Coppenrath, 1870 [corrected and expanded 1891–1895]; reprint, Hildesheim: Olms, 1975).

Salomon Kümmerle, *Enzyklopädie der evangelischen Kirchenmusik,* 4 vols. (Gütersloh: Bertelsmann, 1888–1895; reprint, Hildesheim: Olms, 1974).

Hans Musch, *Musik im Gottesdienst* (Regensburg: Bosse, 1975).

Joseph Ortique, *Dictionnaire liturgique, historique et theorique de plainchant et de musique d'église* (Paris: Migne, 1853; reprint, New York: Da Capo, 1971).

Jacques Porte, *Encyclopédie des musiques sacrées,* 4 vols. (Paris: Editions Lagergerie, 1968–1970).

David Poultney, *Dictionary of Western Church Music* (Chicago: American Library Association, 1991).

Carl Schalk, *Key Words in Church Music* (St. Louis: Concordia, 1978).

G.-W. Stubbins, *A Dictionary of Church Music* (London: Epworth Press, 1949).
E. Valentin and F. Hofmann, *Die Evangelische Kirchenmusik. Handbuch für Studium und Praxis* (Regensburg: Bosse, 1967).
Andreas Weissenbäck, *Sacra Musica: Lexikon der katholischen Kirchenmusik* (Klosterneuburg: Augustinus Druck, 1937).
A new ecumenical dictionary that I am editing is entitled *Worship Music: A Concise Dictionary* (Collegeville: The Liturgical Press, forthcoming).

While there is little standardization in the field, there are a few recurring methods and areas of interest in the field—some more prevalent than others—which dictate something of the content of an introductory survey such as this. The three most important of these are (1) historical studies, (2) theological reflections upon the relationship between music and worship or faith, and (3) the recent turn to non-traditional methods—often borrowed from the social sciences—to examine liturgical music ritually and culturally.

While there are innumerable other areas of interest that could occupy us, we will focus on these three. While my perspective is Roman Catholic and my own cultural lens that of the dominant culture, I will attempt to map these areas ecumenically and cross-culturally, with special attention to their influence on Judaism and Western Christianity in the U.S. Since this essay is intended to be an introduction to the field, it is designed as a bibliographic essay, with selective references to works that are important because of the quality of their scholarship, the relevance of the topic, or the uniqueness of their perspective. It is hoped that such referencing will help to balance my own presuppositions, which will inevitably permeate the essay.

General bibliographies include:

Israel Adler, *The Study of Jewish Music: A Bibliographic Guide,* Yuval Monograph Series 10 (Jerusalem: Manges Press, Hebrew University, 1995).
Irene V. Jackson, *Afro-American Religious Music: A Bibliography and a Catalogue of Gospel Music* (Westport, Ct.: Greenwood, 1979).
Bard Thompson, *A Bibliography of Christian Worship* (Metuchen, N.J.: Scarecrow, 1989) 656–739.
Walter Buszin, Theodore Finney, and Donald McCorkle, *A Bibliography on Music and the Church* (New York: National Council of the Churches of Christ, 1958).
Irene Heskes, *The Resource Book of Jewish Music: A Bibliographical and Topical Guide* (Westport, Ct.: Greenwood, 1985).
Martin Rössler, *Bibliographie der deutschen Liedpredigt* (Nieuwkoop: de Graaf, 1976).
Alfred Sendry, *Bibliography of Jewish Music* (New York: Columbia University Press, 1951).
Gino Stefani, "Bibliographie fondamentale de musicologie liturgique," *La Maison-Dieu* 108 (1971) 175–89.

Pasquale Troìa, "Panorama Bibliografico Internazionale su Musica e Biblia," *La Musica e la Biblia: Atti del Convegno Internazionale di Studi promosso da Biblia e dall'Accademia Musicale Chigiana, Siena 24–26 agosto 1990,* ed. Pasquale Troìa (Roma: Garamond, 1992) 395–476.

Richard von Ende, *Church Music: An International Bibliography* (Metuchen, N.J.: Scarecrow, 1980).

Albert Weisser, *Bibliography of Publications and Other Resources on Jewish Music* (New York: National Jewish Music Council, 1969).

Paul Yeats-Edwards, *English Church Music: A Bibliography* (London: White Lion, 1975).

More specific bibliographies will be noted throughout the essay.

1. Historical Studies

Just as initial studies in liturgics showed a preference for the historical method, so does this approach dominate most earlier as well as many contemporary studies of liturgical music.

General Histories

Books and Articles. The standard single-volume general history of music in English is:

Donald J. Grout and Claude V. Palisca, *A History of Western Music,* 5th ed. (New York: Norton, 1995).

Of the multi-volume works on the history of Western music, three of the best in English are:

The New Oxford History of Music, 10 vols. (London: Oxford University Press, 1954–), currently being reissued in revised and newly-written volumes.

Prentice Hall History of Music Series, 10 vols., ed. H. Wiley Hitchcock (Englewood Cliffs, N.J.: Prentice Hall, 1965–).

Music and Society, 8 vols., ed. Stanley Sadie (Englewood Cliffs, N.J.: Prentice Hall, 1989–1994).

Apart from such general histories of Western art music, which contain much information on liturgical music, there is an abundance of general works on the history of liturgical music. Three well-known examples available in English are:

Friedrich Blume, *Protestant Music: A History* (New York: Norton, 1974 [1965]).

A. Z. Idelsohn, *Jewish Music in Its Historical Development* (New York: Schocken, 1967 [1929]).

Karl Gustav Fellerer, *The History of Catholic Church Music* (Baltimore: Helicon Press, 1961 [1949]; reprint, Westport, Ct.: Greenwood, 1979). More extensive is Fellerer's *Geschichte der katholischen Kirchenmusik,* 2 vols. (Kassel: Bärenreiter, 1972).

Other studies include:

Ch. L. Etherington, *Protestant Worship Music. Its History and Practice* (New York: Holt-Rinehart-Winston, 1962).

Paul Huot-Pleuroux, *Histoire de la musique religieuse des origines à nos jours* (Paris: Presses Universitaires, 1957).

Paul Hume, *Catholic Church Music* (New York: Dodd, Mead, 1956).

Frits Mehrtens, *Kerk & Muziek,* 2 vols. ('s-Gravenhage: Boekencentrum, 1961).

William Carroll Rice, *A Concise History of Church Music* (New York: Abingdon, 1964).

Alec Robertson, *Christian Music* (New York: Hawthorn, 1961).

Hans Sabel, *Die liturgischen Gesänge der katholischen Kirche* (Wolfenbüttel: Möseler, 1965).

Alfred Sendry, *Music in Ancient Israel* (New York: Philosophical Library, 1969).

Oskar Söhngen, *Musica sacra zwischen Gestern und Morgen,* 2 Aufl. (Göttingen: Vandenhoeck & Ruprecht, 1981).

Otto Ursprung, *Die katholische Kirchenmusik* (Potsdam: Athenaion, 1931).

Eric Werner, *The Sacred Bridge,* 2 vols. (New York: Columbia University Press, 1959; New York: KTAV Publishing House, 1984).

There are a few significant difficulties with these and similar works. The first is that the sheer amount of current scholarship on a given topic makes it very difficult for any single author to provide a competent overview of such a vast field. Consequently, the various entries in a multi-volume, or smaller-scale dictionaries such as those listed below, are sometimes a better source of historical information than single-volume, general histories of liturgical music:

Die Musik in Geschichte und Gegenwart (MGG), ed. Friedrich Blume, 17 vols. (Kassel: Bärenreiter, 1949–86). A new edition, which will ultimately comprise 20 vols. is currently being issued.

The New Grove Dictionary of Music and Musicians (NGDMM), ed. Stanley Sadie, 20 vols. (New York: Norton, 1980), a revised edition is in preparation.

The New Grove Dictionary of American Music, eds. H. Wiley Hitchcock and Stanley Sadie, 4 vols. (New York: Norton, 1986).

The New Harvard Dictionary of Music, ed. Don Michael Randel (Cambridge, Mass.: Belknap, 1986).

The New Oxford Companion to Music, ed. Denis Arnold, 2 vols. (Oxford-New York: Oxford University Press, 1983).

The Oxford Dictionary of Music, ed. Michael Kennedy (Oxford: Oxford University Press, 1994).

There are also some very good survey articles on the history of liturgical music that are a good place for the uninitiated to begin their study:

Margot Fassler and Peter Jeffery, "Christian Liturgical Music from the Bible to the Renaissance," *Two Liturgical Traditions*, vol. 3: *Sacred Sound and Social Change: Liturgical Music in Jewish and Christian Experience,* eds. Lawrence A. Hoffman and Janet Walton (Notre Dame, Ind.: University of Notre Dame Press, 1992) 84–123.
Joseph Gelineau, "Music and Singing in the Liturgy," *The Study of Liturgy,* ed. Cheslyn Jones, et al., rev. ed. (New York: Oxford University Press, 1992) 493–507.

A second difficulty with books on the history of liturgical music is that, given the reality of the sociology of knowledge today, our information about a given field such as liturgical music doubles almost every ten years. Consequently, much of the historical nuancing in many of the standard works on liturgical music is eclipsed or significantly challenged even before such are widely distributed. The ground breaking work in the history of liturgical music—as is true in other disciplines—often appears in various scholarly journals. These need to be consulted by the serious student of liturgical music. A sampling of current journals and yearbooks includes:

Black Sacred Music (Durham)
Bulletin of the Hymn Society of Great Britain and Ireland (Redhill)
Il Canto dell'Assemblea (Torino)
Église qui chante (Paris)
Étude grégoriennes (Solesmes)
The Hymn (Boston)
Jahrbuch für Liturgik und Hymnologie (originally Kassel, now Göttingen)
Journal of Jewish Music and Liturgy (New York)
Kirchen-musikalisches Jahrbuch (Regensburg)
Der Kirchenmusiker (Berlin)
Musik und Altar (Freiburg im Br.)
Musik und Gottesdienst (Zürich)
Musica Judaica (New York)
Musik und Kirche (Kassel)
Plainsong and Medieval Music (Cambridge)
Reformed Liturgy and Music (Philadelphia)
Revue grégorienne (Paris)

There is no single, comprehensive list of music journals or journals on liturgical, sacred, or church music. Three basic resources on music periodicals are:

The Music Index (Detroit: Information Service, 1949–).

RILM [*Répertoire international de litérature musicale*] *Abstracts of Music Literature* (Flushing, N.Y.: New York RILM, 1967–).

Bibliographie des Musikschrifttums (Leipzig: Staatliches Institut für deutsche Musikforschung, 1936–1939; Frankfurt a.M.: Institut für Musikforschung, 1950–).

A final difficulty with many general histories of liturgical music— and this is also true of many of the dictionary and survey articles—is that they are often more histories of the music than of the musical-liturgical event. Thus a book will often enumerate which musical works were employed in worship, or offer extended analysis of that music, but seldom analyze how the music interacted with the rite, how it was experienced by those who heard it or those who performed it, or how it was considered theologically or in terms of its spirituality. For example, there are many histories that discuss Mozart's (d. 1791) Masses, *Requiem,* and other "sacred" compositions. Seldom, however, do these works examine how or even if such works were employed in worship. Consequently, many histories are not histories of "liturgical music" properly speaking, but of the music which was, in some way, connected to the church or synagogue. One notable exception is Solange Corbin's *L'église à la conquête de sa musique* (Paris: Gallimard, 1960), of which an English translation and revision is currently underway.

Manuscripts, editions, and recordings. Besides writings about the history of liturgical music, there are three other important genres of sources for this history. Prior to the invention of printing by movable type in the 1450s, all written music appeared in manuscript form. Even after Gutenberg's invention, it took some time for music to be printed. In 1457 a *Psalterium* was printed by Johanna Fust and Peter Schöffer—associates of Gutenberg—but in this work only the staves were printed, while the notes were written by hand. The earliest known book of printed music appears to be a German gradual, possibly from 1473. On the history of music printing, see:

A. Hyatt King, *Four Hundred Years of Music Printing,* 2nd ed. (London: British Museum, 1968).

Kathi Meyer-Baer, *Liturgical Music Incunabula* (London: The Bibliographical Society, 1962) a useful resource for identifying printed liturgical music before 1500 *(incunabula).*

Suzanne Haïk-Vantoura alleges to have deciphered one of the Masoretic systems (the Tiberian) of accents *te'amin,* dating from the

9th century C.E. She claims that this system of accents reflects a musical system that developed before the emergence of Christianity that can be reconstructed today:

Suzanne Haïk-Vantoura *The Music of the Bible Revealed*, trans. Dennis Weber, ed. John Wheeler (Berkeley, Calif.: Bibal Pres, 1991); a recording of her transcription, *La musique de la bible revélée*, is available (HMA 190989).

Notwithstanding such claims to have deciphered exactly the notation in manuscripts previous to the 10th century, it is only Daseian notation—appearing around 900 C.E.—which is the first nonalphabetic Western European notation that can be so deciphered.

The basic resource for identifying music manuscripts is *Répertoire international des sources musicales* (RISM), a joint project of the International Association of Music Libraries and the International Musicological Society begun in 1952. The two German publishers of RISM are Bärenreiter in Kassel and Henle in Munich:

Manuscripts of Polyphonic Music, 11th–early 14th Century [RISM, ser. B, vol. 4:1], ed. Gilbert Reaney (Munich: Henle, 1969).
Manuscripts of Polyphonic Music (c. 1320–1400) [RISM ser. B, vol. 4:2]. Ed. Gilbert Reaney (Munich: Henle, 1969).
Manuscripts of Polyphonic Music. Supplement 1 to RISM B IV¹⁻² The British Isles, 1100–1400, ed. Andrew Wathey (Munich: Henle, 1993).
Tropen- und Sequenzen-handschriften [RISM, ser. B, vol. 5:1], ed. Heinrich Hausmann (Munich: Henle, 1964).
Music Manuscripts 1600–1800 [RISM, ser. A, pt. II] (Kassel: Bärenreiter, 1986), 2 microfiches and 16-page pamphlet. The RISM-US Music Manuscripts Database is available as a special database being developed in HOLLIS, the Harvard University online library catalogue. The database is the U.S. contribution to the international project RISM Series A/II, a world-wide inventory of music manuscripts, ca. 1580–1825. When complete the database will contain the bibliographic records of the many thousands of music manuscripts in American libraries.

Besides manuscripts, there are many printed editions of individual liturgical musical manuscripts as well as historical (critical)[3] editions of the works of individual composers compiled from multiple manuscripts available today. Guides for accessing these editions include:

Anna Heyer, *Historical Sets, Collected Editions, and Monuments of Music*, 3rd ed. (Chicago: American Library Association, 1980), a new edition is in preparation.
Sydney R. Charles, *A Handbook of Music and Music Literature in Sets and Series* (New York: Free Press, 1972).

The most important collection for Jewish music in general, and Jewish liturgical music in particular, continues to be Abraham Z. Idelsohn's *Hebräische-orientalischer Melodienschatz*, 10 vols. (Leipzig: Breitkopf & Härtel, 1914–32; English version: KTAV Publishing House, 1973). There is no collection of such singular importance for Christian liturgical music.

Notable monuments for the latter include various editions of the collected works of important composers, collections of liturgical music from specific eras or geographic areas, and more broadly defined collections of liturgical import. A sampling of collected works of individual composers includes:

J.S. Bach: Werke, ed. Bach Gesellschaft (Leipzig: Breitkopf & Härtel, 1851–1899).

Neue Bach-Ausgabe, ed. Johann-Sebastian Bach-Institut, Göttingen, and Bach-Archiv, Leipzig (Kassel: Bärenreiter, 1954–).

William Billings, *Complete Works,* ed. Karl Kroeger (Charlottesville: University Press of Virginia, 1978–1990).

Josquin Deprez, *Werken,* ed. A. Smijers, et al. (Amsterdam: G. Alsbach—Leipzig: Kistner & Siegel, 1922–69).

Guillaume Dufay, *Opera omnia,* ed. G. De Van and Heinrich Besseler (Rome: American Institute of Musicology, 1947–49, 1951–66).

Giovanni Gabrieli, *Opera omnia,* ed. Denis Arnold (Rome: American Institute of Musicology, 1956–).

Guillaume de Machaut, *Oeuvres complètes* (Paris: Le droict chemin de musique, 1977).

Giovanni Pierluigi da Palestrina, *Le opere complete,* ed. R. Casimiri, et al. (Rome: Edizione Fratelli Scalera, 1939–65, 1973–).

Heinrich Schütz, *Sämtliche Werke,* ed. Heinrich Schütz Gesellschaft (Kassel: Bärenreiter, 1955–).

Heinrich Schütz, *Stuttgarter Schütz-Ausgabe,* ed. Günther Graulich, et al. (Neuhausen-Stuttgart: Hänssler-Verlag, 1971–).

Representative collections of liturgical music from specific eras or geographic areas include:

Knud Jeppesen, *Italia sacra musica* (Copenhagen: Hansen, 1962).

Fernando Liuzzi, *La Lauda e i primordi della melodia italiana,* 2 vols. (Rome: La libreria dello stato, 1935).

Monumenta liturgiae polychoralis sanctae ecclesiae romanae, ser. I–IV, ed. Laurentius Feininger (Rome/Trento: Societas Universalis Sanctae Ceciliae, 1950–1968).

Monumenta monodica medii aevi, ed. Bruno Stäblein (Kassel: Bärenreiter, 1954–).

Monumenta polyphonae liturgicae sanctae ecclesiae romanae, ser. I–II, ed. Laurence Feininger (Rome/Trento: Societas Universalis Sanctae Ceciliae, 1947–).

Felipe Pedrell, *Hispaniae schola musica sacra* (Barcelona: Juan Baptista Pujol, 1894–98).

Hanna Stäblein-Harder, *Fourteenth-Century Mass Music in France* (Rome: American Institute of Musicology, 1962).

Tudor Church Music, ed. Edmund Fellowes, et al. (London: Oxford University Press, 1922–29).

More broadly defined collections of liturgical import include:

Monumenta musicae sacrae, ed. Dom René Jean Herbert (Macon: Protat Frères, 1952–81).

Wilhelm Bäumker, *Das katholische Kirchenlied* (Freiburg: Herder, 1883–1911; reprint, Hildesheim: Olms, 1962).

Charles van den Borren, *Polyphonia sacra,* rev. ed. (University Park, PA: Pennsylvania State University Press, 1963).

François Delsarte, *Archives du chant* (Paris: Delsarte, 1860–70).

Paléographie musicale, 21 vols. in 2 series (Solesmes: Imprimerie St. Pierre, Tournai Desclée, 1989– ; reprint, Bern: H. Lang, 1969–).

Karl Proske, *Musica divina* (Regensburg: Pustet, 1853–76).

Yvonne Rokseth, *Motets du XIIIe siècle* (Paris: L'Oiseau-Lyre, 1936).

Johannes Zahn, *Die Melodien der deutschen evangelsichen Kirchenlieder* (Gütersloh: Mohn, 1889–93; reprint, Hildesheim: Olms, 1963).

Finally, those interested in music of any type, including liturgical music, require resources that demonstrate that music is not notation on a page, but a sonic event. Recordings are invaluable in studying or teaching the history of liturgical music. Discographies describe and catalogue recordings. Recordings of most liturgical, sacred, or religious music composed before the twentieth century are categorized as "classical." One useful guide to discographies about this music is Michael H. Gray and Gerald D. Gibson's *Classical Music, 1925–1975* (New York: Bowker, 1977), which is a bibliography of discographies.[4] Another important resource for medieval, Renaissance, and baroque music—much of which would be considered liturgical—is Trevor Croucher's *Early Music Discography: from Plainsong to the Sons of Bach* (Phoenix: Oryx, 1981). Resource Publications in San Jose, Calif., annually publishes a series of *Christian Music Directories,* one of which is subtitled *Recorded Music,* listing recordings of contemporary Christian liturgical, sacred, and religious music. *Schwann Opus* is a widely-used quarterly journal, which lists "classical" recordings currently on the market.[5] The elasticity of the recording industries and markets has spawned the development of new electronic resources for accessing recorded music. One of the better of these is a quarterly CD-rom service entitled *Music Library,*[6] whose contents are copied from the OCLC[7] online Union Catalogue and consists of all types of musical sound recordings from all time periods, including LPs, 45s, cassettes, tape reels, CDs, and piano rolls. Another such resource—available in book format, on CD-rom, or through Internet—is the *All Music Guide*.[8] *Notes,* the quarterly journal of the Music Library Association, includes a substantial "Index to CD Reviews" in each issue.

Focused Histories

Even more numerous than general historical works are the many studies that focus on particular times, places, or people in the history of liturgical music. The history of Western music is commonly divided into six or seven discrete segments.[9] Sometimes the general divisions of Western music are followed for studying liturgical music. Often, however, these prove problematic for chronicling worship music, and various authors construct different schemes for the periodization of liturgical music.

Judaism. In Judaism, for example, the music of the Bible is an important historical subdivision of the field. Thus there are various monographs, important articles on the subject in many biblical dictionaries and commentaries, as well as entries in the standard musical dictionaries noted above, and Jewish dictionaries and encyclopedias. Monographs and major articles include:

Bathya Bayer, *The Material Relics of Music in Ancient Palestine and Its Environs* (Tel Aviv: Israel Music Institute, 1963).

Abraham Wolf Binder, *Biblical Chant* (New York: Philosophical Library, 1959).

Wolfgang Blissenbach, *Musik in Bibel und Gemeinde* (Erzhausen: Leuchter-Verlag, 1975).

P. Casetti, "Funktion der Musik in der Bibel," *Freiburger Zeitschrift für Philosophie und Theologie* 24 (1977) 366–89. An English translation appears in *The Hymnology Annual* 4, published in 1997.

John W. Kleinig, *The Lord's Song: The Basis, Function and Significance of Choral Music in Chronicles* (Shefflield, England: JSOT Press, 1993).

Sigmund Mowinckel, *The Psalms in Israel's Worship,* trans. D. R. Ap-Thomas (Oxford: Blackwell, 1962).

Hans Seidel, *Musik in Altisrael: Untersuchungen zur Musikgeschichte und Musikpraxis Altisraels anhand biblischer und ausser-biblischer Text* (Frankfurt am Main & New York: Lang, 1989).

Alfred Sendrey, *Music in Ancient Israel,* cited above.

J.A. Smith, "Which Psalms Were Sung in the Temple?" *Music and Letters* 71 (1990) 167–86.

Representative important articles in biblical dictionaries include:

Edith Gerson-Kiwi, "Musique dans la bible," *Dictionnaire de la Bible,* supp. 5 (Paris: Letouzey & Ané, 1957).
Eric Werner, "Music," *Interpreter's Dictionary of the Bible,* ed. George A. Buttrick, 4 vols. (New York-Nashville: Abingdon, 1962) 3:457–69.
Ivor Jones, "Musical Instruments," *Anchor Bible Dictionary,* ed. David Noel Freedman, 4 vols. (New York: Doubleday, 1992) 4:934–39.
Victor H. Matthews, "Music in the Bible," *Anchor Bible Dictionary,* ed. David Noel Freedman, 4 vols. (New York: Doubleday, 1992) 4:930–34.

There are many valuable articles in:

Encyclopaedia Judaica (EJ), eds. Cecil Roth and Geoffrey Wigoder, 16 vols. (Jerusalem: Keter Publishing, 1972).
Various entries in NGDMM, such as "Jewish Music, I. Liturgical," by Eric Werner, et al. (9:614–34).
Entries in Macy Nulman, *Concise Encyclopedia of Jewish Music* (New York: McGraw-Hill, 1975).
Two forthcoming volumes are likely to be valuable here: the *Dictionary of Biblical Judaism,* edited by Jacob Neusner from Macmillan, and the *Dictionary of the Jewish Religion,* edited by R. J. Zwi Werblowsky and Geoffrey Wigoder from Oxford.[10]

Other fruitful sources of information on biblical music are key publications on the worship of Ancient Israel, such as:

H. H. Rowley, *Worship in Ancient Israel: Its Forms and Meaning* (London: SPCK, 1967) 176–212.

The rise of the synagogue usually serves as the delineating factor for setting a second major period of Jewish music. Though disputed, it appears that that synagogue arose in first or second century before Christ. For the origins of the synagogue see:

Ancient Synagogues: The State of Research, ed. Jacob Neusner, et al. (Chico, Calif.: Scholars Press, 1981), especially the contributions by Joseph Gutman, "Synagogue Origins: Theories and Facts," and Marilyn Chiat, "First Century Synagoguges: Methodological Problems."
Heather A. McKay, *Sabbath and Synagogue: The Question of Sabbath Worship in Ancient Israel* (Leiden: E.J. Brill, 1994).

This extensive period of the synagogue is often divided: the early period extends to the year 1000 C.E., the later period after that year. The synagogue period post-1000 C.E. is further subdivided in terms of two emerging traditions in Judaism: Ashkenazic and Sephardic.

Notable monographs include:

Hanoch Avenary, *The Ashkenazi Tradition of Biblical Chant between 1500 and 1900* (Tel Aviv: Tel Aviv University, 1978).

Hanoch Avenary, *Hebrew Hymn Tunes: The Rise and Development of a Musical Tradition* (Tel Aviv: Israel Music Institute, 1971).

Alfred Sendrey, *Music of the Jews in the Diaspora (up to 1800)* (New York: Yoseloff, 1970).

Eric Werner, *The Sacred Bridge,* 2 vols., as cited above. Appropriate cautions about Werner's work are outlined in Peter Jeffery, "Werner's Sacred Bridge, vol. 2: A Review Essay," *Jewish Quarterly Review* 77 (1987) 283–98.

Eric Werner, *A Voice Still Heard: The Sacred Song of the Ashkenazi Jews* (University Park, Pa.: Pennsylvania State University Press, 1976).

Dictionary and encyclopedia entries provide information on key developments such as the metrical prayer-poems known as piyyutim and the rise of the hazzan. Liturgical studies that shed some light on the music of the synagogue are:

Joseph Heinemann, *Prayer in the Talmud* (Berlin and New York: De Gruyter, 1977).

Lawrence Hoffman, *The Canonization of the Synagogue Service* (Notre Dame, Ind.: University of Notre Dame Press, 1979).

Ismar Elbogen, *Jewish Liturgy* (Philadelphia: The Jewish Publication Society, 1993), is also of value, though it needs to be read with caution.

Much scholarly literature on synagogue music has appeared across the spectrum of periodic literature. A sampling includes:

Higini Anglès, "La musique juive dans l'Espagne médiévale," *Yuval* 1 (1968) 48–64.

Hanoch Avenary, "Contacts between Church and Synagogue Music," *Proceedings of the World Jewish Congress on Jewish Music* [Jerusalem 1978] (Tel Aviv, 1982) 89–107.

Joseph A. Levine, "Toward Defining the Jewish Prayer Modes with Particular Emphasis on the Adonay Malakh Mode," *Musica Judaica* 3 (1980–81) 13–41.

James McKinnon, "On the Question of Psalmody in the Ancient Synagogue," *Early Music History* 6 (1986) 159–91.

Baruch David Schreiber, "The Woman's Voice in the Synagogue," *Journal of Jewish Music and Liturgy* 7 (1984–1985) 27–32.

Avigdor Shinan, "Sermons, Targums and the Reading from Scripture in the Ancient Synagogue," *The Synagogue in Late Antiquity,* ed. Lee I. Levin (Philadelphia, 1987) 97–100.

Johanna Spector, "Chant and Cantillation," *Musica Judaica* 9 (1986–1987) 1–21.

Max Wohlberg, "The History of the Musical Modes of the Ashkenazic Synagogue and Their Usage," *Journal of Synagogue Music* 4:1-2 (April, 1972) 46–61.

There are also a number of theoretical works from this period, and a body of accompanying literature, some of which will be discussed below.

The nineteenth-century reforms in Judaism provide the focus for delineating a third major period in Jewish liturgical music. There are fewer monographs or individual articles on this period than the previous two. Two articles in *Sacred Sound and Social Change:* Geoffrey Goldberg, "Jewish Liturgical Music in the Wake of Nineteenth-Century Reform," (pp. 59–83); and Benjie-Ellen Schiller, "The Hymnal as an Index of Musical Change in Reform Synagogues," (pp. 187–212) provide a helpful overview of some of the developments and literature on this era.

Christianity. The New Testament period (1st century) is one of the Christian eras least considered by musical scholars—partly because there is little that could properly be isolated as "music" in the New Testament.[11] The studies by scriptural and other scholars on the general topic of music in the New Testament include:[12]

Gerhard Delling, *Worship in the New Testament,* trans. Percy Scott (Philadelphia: Westminster, 1962), especially chapters 5 and 6.

Franz Josef Dölger, *Sol Salutis: Beget und Gesang in christlichen Altertum, mit besonderer Rücksicht auf die Ostung in Gebet und Liturgie,* 3. Aufl. (Münster: Aschendorff, 1972).

J.A. Smith, "The Ancient Synagogue, the Early Church and Singing," *Music and Letters* 65 (1984) 1–16.

J.A. Smith, "First Century Christian Singing and its Relationship to Contemporary Jewish Religious Song," *Music and Letters* 75 (1994) 1–15.

William Sheppard Smith, *Musical Aspects of the New Testament* (Amsterdam: Uitgeverij w. Ten Have N.V., 1962).

Samuel Terrien, *The Magnificat: Musicians as Biblical Interpreters* (Mahwah, N.J.: Paulist Press, 1994).

Such scholars have also given us numerous studies on particular texts, or of "musical" genres—especially hymnody—suggested by the New Testament, for example:

Klaus Berger, "Das Canticum Simeonis (Lk 2:29–32)," *Novum Testamentum* (1985) 27–39.

Reinhard Deichgräber, *Gotteshymnus und Christushymnus in der frühen Christenheit* (Göttingen: Vandenhoeck & Ruprecht, 1967).

Pierre Grelot, "Le Cantique de Siméon Luc 2.29–32," *Revue Biblique* 93 (1986) 481–509.

Michael Lattke, *Hymnus: Materialien zu einer Geschichte der antiken Hymnologie,* Novum Testamentum et Orbis Antiquus 19 (Fribourg: Editions Universitaires, 1991).

F. Manns, "Un hymne judéo-chrétien: Philippiens 2, 6–11," *Euntes Docete* 29 (1976) 259–290.

Ralph P. Martin, *Carmen Christi* (Cambridge: Cambridge University Press, 1967).

W. Richardson, "Liturgical Order and Glossolalia in 1 Cor. 14:26c-33a," *New Testament Studies* 32 (1986) 144–53.

Máximo Brioso Sanchez, *Aspectos y problemas del himno cristiano primitivo* (Salamanca: Consejo Superior de Investigaciones Cientificas, 1972).

Jack Sanders, *The New Testament Christological Hymns* (Cambridge: Cambridge University Press, 1971).

R. Schnackenburg, "Logos-Hymnus und johannischer Prolog," *Biblische Zeitschrift* ns 1 (1957) 69–109.

Klaus Wengst, *Christologische Formeln und Lieder des Urchristentums* (Gütersloh: Mohn, 1972).

G. Wilhelmi, "Der Versöhnen-Hymnus in Eph. 2:14ff," *Zeitschrift für neutestamentliche Wissenschaft* 78 (1987) 145–52.

General histories of Western music usually say very little about Christian worship music until Ambrose (d. 397). One of the better general treatments of the era of the early Church (c. 100–600) is Giulio Cattin's *Music of the Middle Ages I* (Cambridge: Cambridge University Press, 1984). Other studies, in addition to previously cited works, include:

E. Foley, *Foundations of Christian Music,* 2nd rev. ed. (Collegeville, Minn.: The Liturgical Press, 1996).

C. Hannick, "Christian Church, music of the early," *NGDMM* 4:363–71

A.W.J. Holleman, "Early Christian Liturgical Music," *Studia Liturgica* 8 (1972) 185–92.

James McKinnon, "Christian Antiquity," *Antiquity and the Middle Ages: From Ancient Greece to the 15th Century,* ed. James McKinnon (Englewood Cliffs, N.J.: Prentice Hall, 1991) 68–87.

Johannes Quasten, *Music and Worship in Pagan and Christian Antiquity,* trans. Boniface Ramsey (Washington, D.C.: NPM Publications, 1983 [1929, rev. 1973]).

Bruno Stäblein, "Frühchristliche Musik," *MGG* 4:1036–1064.

Gino Stefani, "L'expressione vocale nella liturgia primitiva," *Ephemerides Liturgicae* 84 (1970) 97–112.

One of the better collections of patristic texts on music is James McKinnon's *Music in Early Christian Literature* (Cambridge University Press, 1987). Other studies include:

Théodore Gérold, *Les Pères de l'église et la musique* (Paris: Alcan, 1931; reprint, Genève: Minkoff, 1973).

Robert Skeris, *Chroma Theoi,* Catholic Church Music Associates 1 (Altötting: Coppenrath, 1976).

There are significant studies on various musical forms from this period, especially hymnody and psalmody:

Hymnody:

James H. Charlesworth, *The First Christian Hymnbook: The Odes of Solomon* (New York: Crossroad, 1993).

Jacques Fontaine, "Les Origines de l'hymnodie chrétienne latine," *La Maison-Dieu* 161 (1985) 33–74.

Josef Kroll, *Die Christliche Hymnodik bis zu Klemens von Alexandreia* (Darmstadt: Wissenschaftliche Buchgesellschaft, 1968 [1921]).

J.M. Robinson, "Die Hodajot-Formel in Gebet und Hymnus des Frühchristentums," *Apophoreta: Festschrift für Ernst Haenschen,* ed. W. Eltester and F.H. Kettler (Berlin: Töpelmann, 1964).

Gottfried Schille, *Frühchristliche Hymnen* (Berlin: Evangelische Verlagsanstalt, 1965).

E. R. Smothers, "Phos Hilaron," *Recherches de science religieuse* 19 (1929) 266–84.

Psalmody:

J. Dyer, "Monastic Psalmody of the Middle Ages," *Revue Bénédictine* 99 (1989) 41–74.

Everett Ferguson, "Psalm-singing at the Eucharist: A Liturgical Controversy in the Fourth Century," *Austin Seminary Bulletin* 98 (1983) 52–77.

Balthasar Fischer, "Der liturgische Gebrauch der Psalmen im altchristlichen Gottesdienst, darfgestellet am ältesten bezeugten Beispiel: Jerusalem, 5. Jahrhundert," *Liturgie und Dichtung: ein interdisziplinäres Kompendium,* eds. Hansjakolo Becker und Reiner Kaczynski, 2 vols. (St. Ottilien: EOS Verlag Erzabtei, 1983) 1:303–13.

Joseph Gelineau, "Les psaulmes a l'époque patristique," *La Maison-Dieu* 135 (1978) 99–116.

Peter Jeffery, "The Introduction of Psalmody into the Roman Mass by Pope Celestine," *Archiv für Liturgiewissenschaft* 26 (1984) 147–65.

Helmut Leeb, *Die Psalmodie bei Ambrosius* (Wien: Herder, 1967), a classic study.

Some monographs examine the contributions of important individuals in this era. Examples include:

Ephrem the Syrian: Hymns, trans. and intro. Kathleen McVey, pref. John Meyendorff, The Classics of Western Spirituality (New York: Paulist Press, 1989).

Richard L. LaCroix, *Augustine on Music* (Lewiston, N.Y.: Mellen, 1988).

More numerous are articles examining a wide variety of topics such as the role of instruments in early Christian music and the role of the cantor:

J. Dyer, "Augustine and the 'Hymni ante oblatium,' the Earliest Offertory Chants?" *Revue des études Augustiniennes* 27 (1981) 85–99.

Margot E. Fassler, "The Office of the Cantor in Early Western Monastic Rules and Customaries: A Preliminary Investigation," *Early Music History* 5 (1985) 29–51.

Edward Foley, "The Cantor in Historical Perspective," *Worship* 56 (1982) 194–213; revised version in Edward Foley, *Ritual Music: Studies in Liturgical Musicology* (Beltsville, Md.: Pastoral Press, 1995).

A. Holleman, "The Oxyrhynchus Papyrus 1786 and the Relationship between Ancient Greek and Early Christian Music," *Vigiliae christianae* 26 (1972) 1–17.

James McKinnon, "The Church Fathers and Musical Instruments," Ph.D. dissertation, Columbia University (1965).

James McKinnon, "The Meaning of the Patristic Polemic Against Musical Instruments," *Current Musicology* 1 (1965) 69–82.

Since this era also witnesses the rise of the Byzantine liturgy and its distinctive music, there is significant study of this repertoire as well as the distinctive repertoires of Rome, Jerusalem and other centers of worship:

General Studies:

Dimitri Conomos, *Byzantine Hymnography and Byzantine Chant* (Brookline, Mass.: Classical Folia Editions, 1984).

Andrew Hughes, *Medieval Music: The Sixth Liberal Art* (H-MM) rev. ed. (Toronto: University of Toronto Press, 1980) bibliography, nn. 390–475.

Oxford History of Byzantium, ed. Alexander Kazhdan, 3 vols. (New York: Oxford University Press, 1991) respective entries.

Oliver Strunk, ed., *Essays on Music in the Byzantine World* (New York: Norton, 1977).

Josef Szövérffy, *A Guide to Byzantine Hymnography: A Classified Bibliography of Texts and Studies,* 2 vols. (Brookline, Mass.: Classical Folia Editions, 1978–79).

Egon Wellesz, *Eastern Elements in Western Chant* (Copenhagen: Munksgaard, 1947).

Egon Wellesz, *A History of Byzantine Music and Hymnography,* 2nd ed. (Oxford: Clarendon Press, 1961).

See also key works on the history of the Byzantine liturgy, such as:

Hans-Joachim Schulz, *The Byzantine Liturgy,* trans. Matthew J. O'Connell (New York: Pueblo, 1986).

Robert Taft, *The Great Entrance* (Rome: Pont. Institutum Studiorum Orientalium, 1978); as well as other studies by Taft.

Rome:

Paul F. Cutter, *Musical Sources of the Old-Roman Mass,* Musicological Studies and Documents 36 (Stuttgart: American Institute of Musicology, 1979).

Paul F. Cutter, "The Question of the 'Old Roman' Chant: a Reappraisal," *Acta Musicologica* 39 (1967) 2–20.

Paul F. Cutter, "Oral Transmission of the Old-Roman Responsories?" *Musical Quarterly* 62 (1976) 182–94.

Helmut Hucke, "Gregorian and Old Roman Chant," *NGDMM* 7: 693–97.

See also relevant references in H-MM, nn. 605–31.

Jerusalem:

Peter Jeffery, "The Earliest Christian Chant Repertory Recovered: The Georgian Witnesses to Jerusalem Chant," *JAMS* 47 (1994) 1–38.

Peter Jeffery, *Liturgy and Chant in Early Christian Jerusalem: The Sources and Influence of a Seminal Tradition,* forthcoming.

Peter Jeffery, "The Lost Chant Tradition of Early Christian Jerusalem: Some Possible Melodic Survivals in Byzantine and Latin Chant Repertories," *Early Music History* 11 (1992) 151–90.

Peter Jeffery, "The Sunday Office of Seventh-Century Jerusalem in the Georgian Chantbook (Iadgari): A Preliminary Report," *Studia Liturgica* 21 (1991) 52–75.

Helmut Leeb, *Die Gesänge im Gemeinegottesdienst von Jerusalem vom 5. bis 8. Jahrhundert* (Vienna: Herder, 1970).

Histories of Western music often date the Middle Ages from 500 to 1430, followed by the Renaissance (1430 to 1600). From the viewpoint of liturgical music, it may be preferable to consider the liturgical-musical continuity between these two periods by speaking of the early Middle Ages (7th to 12th centuries) and the late Middle Ages (13th to the mid-16th centuries). A good overview, especially of the early Middle Ages, is provided in Richard Crocker and David Hiley, *Early Middle Ages to 1300,* New Oxford History of Music II, 2nd ed. (New York: Oxford University Press, 1994). See also the introductory bibliography on Ambrosian, Aquileain, Beneventa, Mozarabic, and Gallican chant in Cattin, *Music of the Middles Ages I,* 217–219; the relevant articles in NGDMM; and the bibliography in H-MM. Other general introductions include:

John Caldwell, *Medieval Music* (Bloomington, Ind.: Indiana University Press, 1978).

Cattin, *Music of the Middle Ages I,* cited above.

F. A. Gallo, *Music of the Middle Ages II* (New York: Cambridge University Press, 1985).

Richard Hoppin, *Medieval Music* (New York: Norton, 1978).

Gustav Reese, *Music in the Middle Ages* (New York: Norton, 1940).

Albert Seay, *Music in the Medieval World,* 2nd ed. (Englewood Cliffs, N.J.: Prentice Hall, 1975).

Jeremy Yudkin, *Music in Medieval Europe* (Englewood Cliffs, N.J.: Prentice Hall, 1989).

The best annotated bibliography for this period is in H-MM.

Parts of the late Middle Ages are often treated in histories of Western music as the Renaissance. General introductions include:

Heinrich Besseler, *Die Musik des Mittelalters und der Renaissance* (Potsdam: Athenaion, 1931).

Howard Mayer Brown, *Music in the Renaissance* (Englewood Cliffs, N.J.: Prentice-Hall, 1976).

Friedrich Blume, *Renaissance and Baroque Music: A Comprehensive Survey,* trans. M.D. Herter Norton (New York: Norton, 1967).

Anselm Hughes and Gerald Abraham, eds., *Ars Nova and Renaissance 1300–1540,* New Oxford History of Music III (London: Oxford University Press, 1960).

André Pirro, *Histoire de la musique de la fin XIVe siècle à la fin du XVIe* (Paris: Laurens, 1940).

Gustav Reese, *Music in the Renaissance,* rev. ed. (New York: Norton, 1959).

Particular studies with relevance to liturgical music of this era include:

Hugh Benham, *Latin Church Music in England, c. 1460–1575* (London: Barrie & Jenkins, 1977).

Douglas Bush, "The Liturgical Use of the Organ in German Regions Prior to the Protestant Reformation," Ph.D. dissertation, University of Texas (1982).

Susan Rankin and David Hiley, eds., *Music in the Medieval English Liturgy* (New York: Oxford University Press, 1993).

There are numerous theorists who write about music during this era, and the principal writers in the West are listed, with accompanying bibliography, in H-MM, nn. 900–1016.

As important for the history of liturgical music are the various ecclesiastical instructions on how music is to be employed in worship. The best source for this material is André Pons, *Droit ecclésiastique et musique sacrée,* 4 vols. (St. Maurice: Éditions de l'oeuvre St. Augustin, 1959–61). See also:

Robert Hayburn, *Papal Legislation on Sacred Music* (Collegeville: The Liturgical Press, 1979).

Fiorenzo Romita, *Codex Iuris Musicae Sacrae* (Rome: Desclée, 1952).

Fiorenzo Romita, *Ius Musicae Liturgicae: Dissertatio Historico-Iuridica,* 2nd ed. (Rome: Ephemerides Liturgicae, 1947).

The major topic in the early Middle Ages vis-à-vis liturgical music is plainchant. David Hiley's *Western Plainchant: A Handbook* (Oxford: Clarendon, 1993) is the best single-volume introduction to the topic. Especially valuable is his substantial bibliography (xxxii–xcvii); see also, H-MM particularly nn. 476–714. A key issue in this area is the origin of Gregorian chant and especially its relationship to Old Roman chant. Peter Jeffery rehearses most of the relevant material on this issue in *Reenvisioning Past Musical Cultures: Ethnomusicology in the Study of Gregorian Chant* (Chicago and London: The University of Chicago Press, 1992).[13]

A major area of study in the late Middle Ages is polyphony and its effects upon the liturgical text. A good introductory article is Marion Gushee, "The Polyphonic Music of the Medieval Monastery, Cathedral and University," *Antiquity and the Middle Ages: From Ancient Greece to the 15th Century,* pp. 143–69. Consult the general histories on the Middle Ages [or Renaissance] and the various dictionary articles on conductus, organum, motet, polyphony, and polytextuality. Richard Hoppin's *Medieval Music* is unusually good regarding medieval liturgical polyphony (chapters. 8–10, 14, 16–17). An important edition is the previously cited *Fourteenth-Century Mass Music in France* as are the various volumes in *Polyphonic Music of the Fourteenth Century* (Monaco: l'Oiseau Lyre, 1956–). Specific places and individuals of note in this vast topic include: St. Martial, Notre Dame (Leonin [d. 1201] and Perotin [fl. c. 1200]), Machaut, Dunstable (d. 1453?), Binchois (d. 1460), Dufay (d. 1474), and Deprez (d. 1521). Consult H-MM (nn. 1335–1748) for further bibliography. From a liturgical music perspective this would include Palestrina (d. 1594) and the Council of Trent (1545–1563) for, although they chronologically overlap into the next period, musically and liturgically they are more backward than forward looking, and could be considered the culmination of the late medieval period.

Palestrina:
Herbert Andrews, *An Introduction to the Technique of Palestrina* (London: Novello, 1959).
Malcolm Boyd, *Palestrina's Style: A Practical Introduction* (London: Oxford University Press, 1973).
Knud Jeppesen, *The Style of Palestrina and the Dissonance,* 2nd ed., trans. Margaret W. Hamerick (Copenhagen: Munksgaard, 1946; reprint ed., New York: Dover, 1970), the classic work.
Jerome Roche, *Palestrina* (New York: Oxford University Press, 1971).

Council of Trent:
Karl Gustav Fellerer, "Church Music and the Council of Trent," *Musical Quarterly* 39 (1953) 576–94.
Hugo Leichentritt, "The Reform of Trent and its Effect on Music," *The Musical Quarterly* 30 (1944) 319–28.
Raphael Molitor, *Die nachtridentinische Choralreform zu Rom,* 2 vols. (Hildesheim: Olms, 1967 [1901–2]).

Another key topic is the development of Latin hymnody: a splendid introduction, in an important series *(Typologie des sources du moyen âge occidental)* is Josef Szövérffy, *Latin Hymns* (Turnhout: Brepols, 1989). A key collection is *Analecta hymnica medii aevi*, 55 vols. (Leipzig: Reisland, 1886–1922; reprint, New York: Johnson, 1961). See also:

Helmut Gneuss, *Hymnar und Hymnen in englischen Mittelalter* (Tübigen: Niemeyer, 1968).

James Mearns, *Early Latin Hymnaries: An Index of Hymns in Hymnaries before 1100* (Cambridge: Cambridge University Press, 1913).

Alain Michel, *In Hymnis et canticus: culture et beauté dans l'hymnique chrétienne latine* (Louvain: Publications Universitaires, 1976).

Bruno Stäblein, ed., *Monumenta monodica medii aevi*, vol. I: *Hymnen* (Kassel: Bärenreiter, 1956).

Josef Szövérffy, *Die Annalen der lateinischen Hymnendichtung: Ein Handbuch*, 2 vols. (Berlin: Schmidt, 1964–65).

Not to be overlooked are the popular religious songs, especially of the laity, such as the *cantio, cantique,* carol, *Geisslerlied, lauda, Leise,* and *Ruf,* as well as the expansion of musical-liturgical forms at this time:

Popular Religious Song:

Higini Anglès, "The various forms of Chant sung by the Faithful in the Ancient Roman Liturgy," *Scripta Musicologica*, 3 vols., ed. José Lópey-Calo (Rome: Edizioni Storia e Letteratura) 1:57–75.

Cyrilla Barr, *The Monophonic Lauda and the Lay Religious Confraternities of Tuscany and Umbria in the Late Middle Ages* (Kalamazoo: Medieval Institute, 1988).

Blake McDowell Wilson, *Music and Merchants: The Laudesi Companies of Republican Florence* (New York: Oxford University Press, 1992).

José Romeu Figeras, "La canción popular navidena, fuente de un misterio dramático de técnica medieval," *Anuario Musical* 19 (1964) 167–84.

Johannes Janota, *Studien zu Funktion und Typus des deutschen geistlichen Liedes im Mittelalters* (München: Beck, 1968).

Walther Lipphardt, "'Laus tibi Christe'—'Ach du armer Judas,' Untersuchungen zum ältesten deutschen Passionslied," *Jahrbuch für Liturgik und Hymnologie* 6 (1961) 71–100.

Johannes Riedel, *Leise Settings of the Renaissance and Reformation Era* (Madison: A-R Editions, 1980).

Anthony Ruff, "A Millenium of Congregational Song," *Pastoral Music* 21:3 (1997) 11–15.

W. Wiora, "The Origins of German Spiritual Folk Song: Comparative Methods in a historical study," *Ethnomusicology* 8 (1964).

See also, H-MM, nn. 1313a–1334, and 1816–1848; and relevant entires in various dictionaries and encyclopedias.

Musical-Liturgical Forms:

Most notably clausulae, motets, prosulas, sequences, and tropes. Besides the many studies on these forms, important editions of these works are to be found in *Analecta hymnica medii aevi*, especially vols. 47 and 49 (tropes), and 53–55 (sequences); and *Corpus troporum*, eds. Ritva Jonsson et al. (Stockholm: Almqvist & Miksell, 1975–). Numerous other collections and individual publications are detailed in *The New Harvard Dictionary of Music*, s.v. "sources (pre-1500)"; also, H-MM, e.g. tropes (nn. 715–83) and "Notre Dame and the thirteenth-century motet" (nn. 1390–1494).

The Reform and Counterreform (16th–19th centuries) was a period of unusual musical-liturgical ferment. There is no single volume that adequately summarizes the period. Most general histories give more attention to "sacred" non-liturgical music of this period—especially for Roman Catholicism—than to music actually employed in the rites. In multi-volume works on the history of Western music, information on this period is often scattered across numerous volumes. For Protestant liturgical music, Blume's *Protestant Music: A History* (1974 [1965]) remains a useful guide; Fellerer's 2nd volume of *Geschichte der katholischen Kirchenmusik* is similarly useful for the music of the Roman Catholic Counterreform. A handy introduction to the music of the Protestant Reformation is Robin A. Leaver's "Christian Liturgical Music in the Wake of the Protestant Reformation," *Sacred Sound and Social Change*, pp. 124–44; and Robert Stevenson, *Patterns of Protestant Church Music* (Durham: Duke University Press, 1953). Also, see Konrad Ameln, et al. eds. *Handbuch der deutschen evangelischen Kirchenmusik*, 3 vols. (Göttingen: Vandenhoeck & Ruprecht, 1930–76).

Among the many valuable monographs on this period is Anthony Lewis and Nigel Fortune's *Opera and Church Music 1630–1750* (New York: Oxford University Press, 1986). Others include:

Conrad Donakowski, *A Muse for the Masses: Ritual and Music in an Age of Democratic Revolution* (Chicago: University of Chicago Press, 1977).
Arthur Hutchings, *Church Music in the Nineteenth Century* (London: Jenkins, 1967; reprint ed., Westport, Ct.: Greenwood, 1977).
Paul Nettl, *Luther and Music*, trans. F. Best and R. Wood (Philadelphia: Muhlenberg, 1948).
Johannes Riedel, ed., *Cantors at the Crossroads* (St. Louis: Concordia, 1963).
Carl Schalk, *Luther on Music: Paradigms of Praise* (St. Louis: Concordia, 1988).
Gino Stefani, *Musica e religione nell'Italia barocca* (Palermo: Flaccovio, 1975).
Elwyn Wienandt, *Choral Music of the Church* (New York: Free Press, 1965).

There are numerous parallels between the broad categories of Protestant[14] and Roman Catholic worship music during this period. These include the introduction of concerto style composition for worship, the growth of instrumental music in the liturgy,—in particular, the organ—and the development of new vocal forms such as the cantata, oratorio, and passion music.

Instrumental Music in General:
Both in combination with voices, as well as independent instrumental compositions such as the *canzona* and *sonata da chiesa.* Besides the various entries in the *NGDMM,* as well as the expansion of some of these articles in *New Grove Dictionary of Musical Instruments,* ed. Stanley Sadie, 3 vols. (London: Macmillan, 1984), see the fine overview article "Performing Practice" by Howard Brown, et al., and the accompanying bibliography in the latter (3:34–61); also, H-MM, nn. 318–76 and 1947–1953a.
Eleanor Selfridge-Field, *Venetian Instrumental Music from Gabrieli to Vivaldi* (New York: Praeger, 1975).
Eleanor Selfridge-Field and Alexander Silbiger, "The Roman Frescobaldi Tradition, c. 1640–1670," *Journal of the American Musicological Society* 33 (1980) 42–87.

Organ:
Willi Apel, *The History of Keyboard Music,* trans. and rev. Hans Tischler (Bloomington: Indiana University Press, 1972).
Edward Higginbottom, "French Classical Organ Music and Liturgy," *Proceedings of the Royal Musical Association* 103 (1976–77) 19–40.
Peter Williams, *The European Organ, 1450–1850,* 2nd ed. (Bloomington: Indiana University Press, 1978).
Peter Williams, *A New History of the Organ* (Bloomington: Indiana University Press, 1980).
On the liturgical use of the organ previous to this period, see: Peter Williams, *The Organ in Western Culture, 750–1250* (New York: Cambridge University Press, 1993).
See also the article in *NGDMM.*

Choral Music:
Besides the previously cited dictionaries and general works on this era, see:
H. Wiley Hitchcock, "The Latin Oratorios of Marc-Antoine Charpentier," *The Musical Quarterly* 41 (1955) 41–65.
Robin A. Leaver, "Passion Music," *Passover and Easter: The Liturgical Structuring of a Sacred Season,* in *Two Liturgical Traditions,* vol. 5, ed. Paul F. Bradshaw and Lawrence A. Hoffman, forthcoming.
Günther Schmidt, "Grundsätzliche Bermerkungen zur Geschichte der Passionshistorie," *Archiv für Musikwissenschaft* 17 (1960) 100–25.
Basil Smallmann, *The Background of Passion Music,* 2nd rev. ed. (New York: Dover, 1970).

Vernacular metrical psalmody and hymnody are especially important for emerging Protestantism. There are fewer general works on the former; Erik Routley's *The Music of Christian Hymns* (Chicago: GIA, 1981) offers a good overview of Reformation psalmody (28–58), including many musical examples. See also:

Leonard Ellinwood, "Tallis' Tunes and Tudor Psalmody," *Musica Disciplina* 2 (1948) 189–203.
Robin A. Leaver, *Goostly Psalmes and Spirituall Songes: English and Dutch Metrical Psalms from Coverdale to Utenhove, 1535–1566* (New York: Oxford University Press, 1991).
Millar Patrick, *Four Centuries of Scottish Psalmody* (London: Oxford University Press, 1949).
Pierre Pidoux, *Le psautier huguenot*, 2 vols. (Basel: Bärenreiter, 1962).
W. S. Pratt, *The Music of the French Psalter of 1562: A Historical Survey and Analysis* (New York: Columbia University Press, 1959).
Cecil Roper, "The Strassbourg French Psalters, 1539–1553," DMA dissertation, University of Southern California (1972).

The general works on hymnody are more plentiful, including various bibliographies, dictionaries, and hymnal companions:

Bibliographies:
Keith C. Clark, *A Selective Bibliography for the Study of Hymns 1980* (Springfield, Oh.: Hymn Society of America, 1980).
Ruth Ellis Messenger, *A Short Bibliography for the Study of Hymns* (New York: Hymn Society of America, 1964).
See also major sections in the various general bibliographies (e.g., Thompson) already cited.

Dictionaries:
John Julian, *Dictionary of Hymnody,* 2 vols. (Grand Rapids: Eerdmans, 1985 [1907]), the standard work.
Katherine Smith Diehl, *Hymns and Tunes: An Index* (New York: Scarecrow, 1966).

Hymnal Companions:
Robin A. Leaver, "Hymnals, Hymnal Companions, and Collection Development," *MLA Notes* 47 (December 1990) 331–54.

The hymns of many reformers are available in various editions, and there are numerous specific studies on various aspects of Reformation hymnody:

Martin Luther, *Liturgy and Hymns,* ed. Ulrich Leopold [*Luther's Works,* vol. 53] (Philadelphia: Fortress, 1965).
Isaac Watts, *Hymns and Spiritual Songs, 1707–1748,* ed. Selma Bishop (London: Faith, 1962).

John and Charles Wesley, *John and Charles Wesley: Selected Prayers, Hymns, Sermons, Letters and Treatises,* Frank Whaling, ed. (New York: Paulist Press, 1981).

Maurice Frost, *English and Scottish Psalm and Hymn Tunes, c. 1543–1677* (London: SPCK and OUP, 1953).

Robin A. Leaver, *The Liturgy and Music: A Study of the Use of the Hymn in Two Liturgical Traditions,* Grove Liturgical Study 6 (Bramcote Nottingham: Grove, 1976).

Madeleine Forell Marshall and Janet Todd, *English Congregational Hymns in the Eighteenth Century* (Lexington, KY: University Press of Kentucky, 1982).

Wilhelm Mützell, *Geistliche Lieder der Evangelischen Kirchen* (Hildesheim: Olms, 1975)

Edna Parks, *Early English Hymns: An Index* (Metuchen, N.J.: Scarecrow, 1972).

J. Ernest Rattenbury, *The Eucharistic Hymns of John and Charles Wesley* (London: Epworth, 1948; reprint ed., Cleveland: OSL Publications, 1991).

Johannes Riedel, *The Lutheran Chorale: Its Basic Traditions* (Minneapolis: Augsburg, 1967).

Samuel J. Rogal, *A General Introduction to Hymnody and Congregational Song* (Metuchen, N.J.: Scarecrow, 1991).

Howard C. Smith, *Scandinavian Hymnody from the Reformation to the Present* (Metuchen, N.J.: Scarecrow, 1987).

While many of the above cited sources also document the hymnic developments in Roman Catholicism, more particular to its musical-liturgical history in this era was the revival of Gregorian chant, especially symbolized in the Caecilian movement. In addition to the appropriate reference work articles, as well as the relevant sections in Fellerer, Hayburn, etc., see:

Johannes Overath, ed., *Musicae sacrae ministerium: Beiträge zur Geschichte der kirchenmusikalischen Erneuerung im XIX. Jahrhundert* (Köln: Luthe-Druck, 1962).

Ronald Damian, "A Historical Study of the Caecilian Movement in the U.S.," DMA dissertation, Catholic University of America (1984).

There are a host of important liturgical composers during these centuries and many other luminaries who also write some liturgical or sacred music. Aside from those already mentioned, some notables are Orlando Di Lasso (d. 1594), William Byrd (d. 1623), Orlando Gibbons (d. 1625), Girolamo Frescobaldi (d. 1643), Giacomo Carissimi (d. 1674), Henry Purcell (d. 1695), Dietrich Buxtehude (d. 1707), Arcangelo Corelli (d. 1713), François Couperin (d. 1733), Antonio Vivaldi (d. 1741), Georg Frideric Handel (d. 1759), Georg Phillipp Telemann (d. 1767), Wolfgang Amadeus Mozart (d. 1791), Franz Joseph Haydn (d. 1809), Franz Schubert (d. 1828), and Charles Gounod (d. 1893).

The musical-liturgical giant of this era is Johann Sebastian Bach. The literature about him and his music is daunting. An outstanding introduction to the liturgical Bach is Günther Stiller's *Johann Sebastian Bach and Liturgical Life in Leipzig*, ed. Robin A. Leaver (St. Louis: Concordia, 1984), and one should also note Jaroslav Pelikan's splendid *Bach Among the Theologians* (Philadelphia: Fortress, 1986).

Finally, it was during this period that liturgical music developed in various churches in the United States. A good introduction to this study is Victor Gebauer's "'Look Again!' Writing about America Church Music," *Currents in Theology and Mission* 16:3 (1989) 180–86. Also, see the various denominational entries in *The New Grove Dictionary of American Music*, eds. H. Wiley Hitchcock and Stanley Sadie, 4 vols. (New York: Macmillan Press, 1986); as well as the section on "American Psalmody and Hymnody" in Terry Miller's *Folk Music in America: A Reference Guide* (New York: Garland, 1986) 229–52. Other useful works include:

Allen Perdue Britton and Irving Lowens, completed by Richard Crawford, *American Sacred Music Imprints 1698–1910: A Bibliography* (Worchester: American Antiquarian Society, 1990).
Albert Christ-Janer, et al., *American Hymns Old and New* (New York: Columbia University Press, 1980).
Buell E. Cobb, *The Sacred Harp: A Tradition and Its Music* (Athens: University of Georgia Press, 1978).
Leonard Ellinwood, *The History of American Church Music* (New York: Morehouse-Gorham, 1953).
Henry W. Foote, *Three Centuries of American Hymnody* (Hamden, Ct.: Shoestring Press, 1961 [1940]).
Hamilton MacDougall, *Early New England Psalmody, 1620–1820* (New York: Da Capo, 1969 [1940]).
Robert Stevenson, *Protestant Church Music in America* (New York: Norton, 1966).

The twentieth century has been a period with few parallels with regard to the amount of scholarship, legislation, composition, and change in liturgical music. While there has been much historical writing in this century, there are few general works on the history of liturgical music in this era. The writings of Erik Routley provide something of an introduction to this period, for example, *Twentieth Century Church Music* (New York: Oxford University Press, 1964). See also:

Ernesto Moneta Caglio, "Dom André Mocquereau e la restaurazione del Canto Gregoriano," *Musica Sacra: Rivista Bismestrale* 84 (1960) 2–17, 34–49, 98–117, 130–42, 162–72; 85 (1961) 8–20, 34–46, 68–87, 151–59; 86 (1962) 70–84, 108–18; 87 (1963) 4–16, 38–50, 75–85.

Philipp Harnoncourt, "Katholische Kirchenmusik vom Cäcilianismus bis zur Gegenwart," *Traditionen und Reformen in der Kirchenmusik: Festschrift für Konrad Ameln zum 75. Geburtstag am 6. Juli 1974,* ed. Gerhard Schuhmacher (Kassel: Bärenreiter) 78–133.

Jean-Yves Hameline, "Le son de l'histoire: Chant et musique dans la restauration catholique," *La Maison-Dieu* 131/3 (1977) 5–47.

Klaus Rohring, *Neue Musik in der Welt des Christentums* (München: Kaiser, 1975).

Oskar Sohngen, *Die Erneuerungskräfte der Kirchenmusik unserer Tage* (Berlin: Evangelische Verlagsanstalt, 1949).

There has been a great deal of writing, especially among Roman Catholics, about the liturgical-musical developments which have occurred since the Second Vatican Council (1963–65). For example:

William Bauman, "Church Music in America: Vatican II to '82," *Pastoral Music* 7/3 (1983) 30–33.

Jean Beilliard and François Picard, eds., *Le Musique sacrée après la réforme liturgique, décisions, directives, orientations* (Paris: Centurion, 1967).

Virgil Funk, "Enculturation, Style and the Sacred-Secular Debate," *Sacred Sound and Social Change,* 314–23.

Joseph Gelineau, "The Music of Christian communities, twenty years after the Council," *Music and Liturgy* 10 (1984) 82–90.

Helmut Hucke, "Musical requirements of liturgical reform," *The Church Worships, Concilium* 12 (New York: Paulist Press, 1966) 45–80.

Bernard Huijbers, "Liturgical Music after the Second Vatican Council," *Symbol and Art in Worship, Concilium* 132 (New York: Seabury, 1980) 101–11.

Francis P. Schmitt, *Church Music Transgressed: Reflections on "Reform"* (New York: Seabury, 1977).

Some of the key issues of this era—the role of culture, the nature of ritual music, and the theology of liturgical music—will be addressed below. Other central developments for Roman Catholics include the spate of legislation and other documents on liturgical music in this century, while key for many Protestant communities has been the publication of new hymnals.

The two best sources for official documentation for Roman Catholics are R. Kevin Seasoltz, *The New Liturgy: 1903–1965* (New York: Herder, 1966), and *Documents on the Liturgy 1963–1979* (Collegeville: Liturgical Press, 1982). Additional documentation for U.S. Roman Catholics is found in Elizabeth Hoffman, ed., *The Liturgy Documents,* 3rd ed. (Chicago: Liturgy Training Publications, 1991). A sampling of the literature on these documents includes:

Akademie für Musik und darstellend Kunst, *Die Kirchenmusik und das II. Vatikanische Konzil* (Graz: Styria, 1965).

Ilario Alcini, *Pio X e la musica* (Rome: Associazione Italiana di Santa Cecilia, 1956).

Associazione Italiana di Santa Cecilia, *L'enciclia Musicae Sacrae Disciplina di Sua Santità Pio XII* (Rome: Associazione Italiana di Santa Cecilia per la Musica Sacra, 1957).

A. Duclos, *Sa Santeté Pie X et la musique religieuse* (Rome: Desclée, 1905).

Edward Foley, "Music in Catholic Worship: A Critical Reappraisal," *Liturgy* 90 (February–March 1991) 8–12.

Aloys Hanin, *La législation ecclésiastique en matière de musique religieuse* (Paris: Desclée, 1933).

Robert F. Hayburn, "St. Pius X and the Vatican Edition of the Chant Books," DMA dissertation, University of Southern California (1964).

J. Michael Joncas, "Re-Reading *Musicam Sacram:* Twenty-Five Years of Development in Roman Rite Liturgical Music," *Worship* 66 (1992) 212–31.

Tómas de Manzarrata, *La música sagrada a la luz de los documentos pontificos* (Madrid: Editorial Coculsa, 1968).

Johanna Schell, "Asthetische Probleme der Kirchenmusik im Lichte der Enzyklika Pius' XII *Musicae Sacrae Disciplina,*" doctoral dissertation, Berlin (1961).

Three other unofficial documents from this period are the *Universa Laus Guidelines, The Milwaukee Symposia for Church Composers: A Ten-Year Report,* and the *Snowbird Document.* Literature includes:

"The Music of Christian Ritual: Universa Laus Guidelines 1980," *The Bulletin of Universa Laus* 30 (1980) 4–15.

Felice Rainoldi, "Le document Universa Laus 1980 dans l'histoire de la musique de l'église," *La Maison-Dieu* 145:1 (1981) 25–48.

Claude Duchesneau and Michael Veuthey, *Music and Liturgy: The Universa Laus Document and Commentary,* trans. Paul Inwood (Washington, D.C.: Pastoral Press, 1992).

Edward Foley, "From Music in Catholic Worship to the 'Milwaukee Document,'" Foley *Ritual Music,* 127–44.

Edward Foley, "The Ritual-Musical Function of Music: From Assisi to Snowbird, " *Pastoral Music* 21/3 (1997) 17–21.

Francis Kline, "The Snowbird Statement on Catholic Liturgical Music," *Worship* 71 (1997) 221–36.

Recent Protestant hymnals in the U.S., together with respective literature, include:

Episcopal: *The New Hymnal* (1916–18), *Hymnal* (1940), and *Hymnal* (1982); resources for the latter include Robert Klepper's *A Concordance of the Hymnal 1982* (Metuchen, N.J.: Scarecrow, 1989); and *The Hymnal Companion,* ed. Raymond Glover, 3 vols. in 4 (New York: The Church Hymnal Corporation, 1990–1994).

Lutheran: *Common Service Book* (1917), *Service Book and Hymnal* (1958), *Lutheran Book of Worship* (1979), and *Lutheran Worship* (1982); resources for the LBW include Marilyn Stulken's *Hymnal Companion to the Lutheran Book of Worship* (Philadelphia: Fortress, 1979).

Methodist: *The Methodist Hymnal* (1905), *The Methodist Hymnal* (1935), *Book of Worship* (1944), *Hymnal* (1960), *The United Methodist Hymnal* (1989). Resources for the latter include Carlton R. Young, *The Companion to the United Methodist Hymnal* (Nashville: Abingdon, 1993).

Presbyterian: *New Psalms and Hymns* (1901), *The Presbyterian Hymnal* (1927), *The Hymnal* (1933), *The Hymnbook* (1955), and *The Presbyterian Hymnal* (1990). Resources for the latter include LindaJo H. McKim's *The Presbyterian Hymnal Companion* (Louisville: Westminster/Knox, 1993).

2. Theological Studies

Besides studies of the history of liturgical music there is a growing body of literature about liturgical music that is of a more overtly theological nature. The caution here is that historical works about liturgical music are also "theological," but usually implicitly. There is no such thing as purely "objective" history—all history is interpretive; any history of the liturgy or liturgical music is, likewise, interpretive and consequently theological to some degree. For a discussion of the theological implications of historical or descriptive studies, see Don Browning, *Fundamental Practical Theology* (Philadelphia: Fortress, 1991).

While there are few conventions for organizing this material, one useful way to divide this material is to distinguish between theological reflections: (1) on the nature of music and sound itself, (2) on the role of music in worship, and (3) on the relationship between music and texts.

On the Nature of Music/Sound

In some respects, much of our earliest material about music in the Judaeo-Christian tradition could be considered under this category. There is no generic word in Biblical Hebrew for "music," and music *per se* was not the point of theological speculation. There was an awareness in ancient Judaism and emerging Christianity, however, that public worship required a heightened auditory environment— especially in the proclamation of sacred texts.[15] Music was valued by the rabbis because of its capacity for enabling the praise of angels and of people.[16] Under the influence of Neo-Platonism, later Jewish writers, such as the 10th century philosopher Sa'adya in *Emunot vedeot* and Joseph Aknin (d. 1220) in his *Tibb al-Nufus,* acknowledged the power of music to move the spirit, and the innate ethical implications of music and its rhythms. See:

Hanoch Avenary, "A Geniza find of Sa'adya's Psalm-preface and its Musical Aspects," *Hebrew Union College Annual* 39 (1968) 145ff.
Henry G. Farmer, *Sa'adyah Gaon on the Influence of Music* (London: Probsthain, 1943).
Kalman Bland, "Medieval Jewish Aesthetics," *Journal of the History of Ideas* 54 (1993) 533–59.
Amnon Shiloah, *The Dimension of Music in Islamic and Jewish Culture* (Brookfield, Vt.: Variorum, 1993).
Eric Werner and I. Sonne, "The Philosophy and Theory of Music in Judeo-Arabic Literature," *Hebrew Union College Annual* 16 (1941) 251–319, and 17 (1942–3) 511–72.

The great philosopher Maimonides (d. 1204)—not unlike some Christian counterparts of the same era—was severely distressed at the power of music and poetry to distract the worshiper. See, for example:

B. Cohen, "The Responsum of Maimonides Concerning Music," *Jewish Musical Journal* 2 (1935) 3ff.
H. G. Farmer, "Maimonides on Listening to Music," *Journal of the Royal Asiatic Society,* 3rd ser., 45 (1933) 867ff.

The positive power of music was emphasized by the Kabbahlistic mystics who stressed music's vital role in contemplation:

Judith Eisenstein, "The Mystical Strain in Jewish Liturgical Music," *Sacred Sound,* ed. Irwin (see below) 35–54.

In Christianity, as well, many of the musical allusions or writings about music in the early church are implicit reflections on music or sound as vehicles or obstacles to the self-communication of God and the assent of the soul to that gracious self-communication. For example, see the writings from the Alexandrian school, especially Clement (d. c. 215) and Origen (d. c. 254); for a collection of the relevant texts, see Skeris, *Chroma Theoi,* pp. 54–93.

While *De utilitate hymnorum* by Niceta of Remesiana (d. after 414) contains some instruction on musical performance in worship, it is essentially a pastoral-theological reflection on the value of singing hymns and psalms. For this text, see:

Klaus Gamber, ed., *Textus patristici et liturgici I* (Regensburg: Pustet, 1964) 93–100.
C. Turner, "Niceta of Remesiana II. Introduction and Text of *De psalmodiae bono,*" *Journal of Theological Studies* 24 (1922–23) 225–50.

While ordinarily classified as one of the "philosophical" works of his youth, Augustine's (d. 430) *De musica*—especially book six—also needs to be considered for its theological reflections on rhythm, and the manner of ascent from mutable numbers to the immutable number, who is God. See, for example:

A. D. Kresteff, "Musica Disciplina and Musica Sonora," *Journal of Research in Music Education* 10 (1962) 13–29.

Ubaldo Pizzani, "Spunti escatologici nel 'De musica' di S. Agostino," *Augustinianum* 18 (1978) 209–18.

Robert O'Connell, *Art and the Christian Intelligence in St. Augustine* (Cambridge, Mass.: Harvard University Press, 1978) 178–88.

Also notable is the philosophical work of Boethius (d. 525), *De institutione musica*, in which he asserts—as did the Greeks before him—that music is intimately related to morality:

Boethius, *Fundamentals of Music*, trans. Calvin Bower, ed. Claude V. Palisca (New Haven: Yale University Press, 1989), the best available translation.

Henry Chadwick, *Boethius: The Consolation of Music, Logic, Theology, and Philosophy* (Oxford: Clarendon, 1983).

Finally, many ecclesiastical instructions, from John XXII's (d. 1334) *Docta sanctorum patrum* to Pius X's (d. 1914) *Tra le sollicitudini*—while usually providing pastoral instruction—also include theological reflections on the nature of music itself, as well as thoughts about the relationship of music to the rites.

There have been a number of contemporary attempts to articulate a general theology of music or liturgical music—such as my own "Toward a Sound Theology," *Studia Liturgica* 23:2 (1993), 121–39:

Charles Cleall, *Music and Holiness* (London: Epworth, 1964).

William Edgar, *Taking Note of Music* (London: SPCK, 1986).

Edward Foley, "Liturgical Music as Theological Discourse," *Artwork as Revelation*, ed. Stephen Happel (Washington, D.C.: Catholic University Press of America, forthcoming).

P. Froger, "Symbolism de la musique liturgique," *La Maison-Dieu* 22 (1950) 146–53.

Paul W. Hoon, "The Relation of Theology and Music in Worship," *Union Seminary Quarterly Review* 11:2 (1956) 33–43.

Judith Marie Kubicki, "The Role of Music as Ritual Symbol in Roman Catholic Liturgy," *Worship* 69 (1997) 427–46.

Maria-Judith Krahe, "Psalmen, Hymen und Lieder, wie der Geist sie eingibt: Doxologie als Ursprung und Ziel aller Theologie," *Liturgie und Dichtung II*, ed. Hansjacob Becker and Reiner Kaczynski (St. Ottilien: EOS Verlag, 1983) 923–57.

Winfried Kurzschenkel, *Die theologische Bestimmung der Musik: neuere Beiträge zur Deutung und Wertung des Musizierens im christlichen Leben* (Trier: Paulinus-Verlag, 1971).

Robin A. Leaver, *The Theological Character of Music in Worship* (St. Louis: Concordia, 1989).

Gerardus van der Leeuw, "Music and Religion," *Sacred and Profane Beauty: The Holy in Art,* trans. David Green (New York: Holt, Rinehart and Winston, 1963) 211–62.

Emil Martin, *Une Muse en péril: essai sur la musique et le sacré* (Paris: Fayard, 1968).

Alfred Pike, *A Theology of Music* (Toledo: GIA, 1953).

Erik Routley, *Church Music and the Christian Faith* (Carol Stream, Il.: Agape, 1978).

Erik Routley, *Church Music and Theology* (Philadelphia: Fortress, 1965 [1959]).

Thomas Allen Seel, *A Theology of Music for Worship Derived from the Book of Revelation* (Metuchen, N.J.: Scarecrow, 1995).

Victoria Sirota, "An Exploration of Music as Theology," *The Arts in Religious and Theological Studies* 5:3 (Summer 1993) 24–28.

Oskar Söhngen, "Fundamental Considerations for a Theology of Music," *The Musical Heritage of the Church,* ed. Theodore Hoelty-Nickel (St. Louis: Concordia, 1954) 4:7–16.

Oskar Söhngen, "Music and Theology: A Systematic Approach," *Sacred Sound,* ed. Joyce Irwin (Chico, Calif.: Scholars Press, 1983) 1–19.

Oskar Söhngen, *Theologie der Musik* (Kassel: Stauda Verlag, 1967).

Jay W. Wilkey, "Prolegomena to a Theology of Music," *Review and Expositor* 69 (1972) 507–17.

Jon Michael Spencer has even advocated the recognition of a specific discipline for addressing music and theology, which he calls "theomusicology," as in his *Theological Music: Introduction to Theo-musicology* (Westport, Ct.: Greenwood, 1991), and the journal *Black Sacred Music: A Journal of Theomusicology,* published by Duke University Press, which Spencer edits. The search for appropriate language in which to speak about music theologically, or its role in worship, is further symbolized in the literature that raises questions about the very concept of liturgical, religious, or sacred music. A recent article that raises such questions is Claude Duchesneau's "Musique sacrée, musique d'église, musique liturgique: changement de mentalité" in *Notitiae,* n. 256, 23:11 (1987) 1189–99. See also:

Lois Ibsen al Faruqi, "What Makes 'Religious Music' Religious?" *Sacred Sound,* ed. Irwin, 21–34.

Helmut Hucke, "Le problème de la musique religieuse," *La Maison-Dieu* 108 (1971) 7–20.

James Reilly, "What is Liturgical Music?" *The Caecilia* 66 (1939) 325–28, 369–72.

Nicolas Schalz, "La notion de musique sacrée: une tradition récente," *La Maison-Dieu* 108 (1971) 32–57.

Nicolas Schalz, "Musique sacrée: Naissance et évolution d'un concept," *La Maison-Dieu* 161:1 (1985) 87–104.

Gino Stefani, "Il mito della 'musica sacra': origini e ideologia," *Nuova Rivista Musicale Italiana* 10 (1976) 23–40.

Gino Stefani, "Musica sacra e regía liturgica," *Nuova Rivista Musicale Italiana* 1 (1967) 744–57.

While most of the writing on the interplay between music and theology has an implicit religious or denominational perspective, some works are explicit in their attempt to articulate a theology of music for a specific denomination. Besides Roman Catholics, such as Miriam Therese Winter, *Why Sing? Toward a Theology of Catholic Church Music* (Washington, D.C.: Pastoral Press, 1984), this trend is especially apparent among some Protestants as exemplified in Joyce Irwin's "Shifting Alliances: The Struggle for a Lutheran Theology of Music," *Sacred Sound,* pp. 55–69:

Walter E. Buszin, *The Doctrine of Universal Priesthood and Its Influence upon the Liturgies and Music of the Lutheran Church* (St. Louis: Concordia, 1946).

Theodore Hoelty-Nickel, "A Philosophy of Lutheran Church Music," *The Musical Heritage of the Church* 6 (1963) 113–22.

Markus Jenny, *Die Zukunft des evangelischen Kirkengesangs* (Zurich: Theologischer Verlag, 1970).

Two related historical studies are:

Charles Garside, "Some Attitudes of the Major Reformers toward the Role of Music in the Liturgy," *McCormick Quarterly* 21 (1967) 151–68.

Markus Jenny, "The Hymns of Zwingli and Luther: A Comparison," *Cantors at the Crossroads,* ed. Johannes Riedel (St. Louis: Concordia Publishing House, 1967) 45–63.

Music and the Rites

For the liturgical theologian, systematic reflection on sound or music requires such reflections to take seriously the rites themselves. This means, for example, considering the liturgical-theological dynamics between worship and its music. One such classic work in Roman Catholicism, written on the brink of the Second Vatican Council, is Joseph Gelineau, *Voices and Instruments in Christian Worship,* trans. Clifford Howell (Collegeville: The Liturgical Press, 1964). Some of Gelineau's further thinking and work is summarized in Charles Pottie's *A More Profound Alleluia: Gelineau and Routley on Music in Christian*

Worship (Washington, D.C.: Pastoral Press, 1984). An important post-conciliar work in this genre is Bernard Huijbers, *The Performing Audience*, 2nd ed. (Phoenix: North American Liturgy Resources, 1974) 93. See also:

Eugenio Costa, "La réflexion post conciliaire sur le chant et la musique dans la liturgie," *La Maison-Dieu* 108 (1971) 21–31.

Lucien Deiss, *Spirit and Song of the New Liturgy,* rev. ed. (Cincinnati: World Library, 1976).

Claude Duchesneau, Paul Bardon, and Jean Lebon, *L'important, c'est la musique! Essai sur la musique dans la liturgie* (Paris: Cerf, 1977).

Frank Quinn, "Music in Catholic Worship: The Effect of Ritual on Music and Music on Ritual," *Proceedings of the Annual Meeting of the North American Academy of Liturgy* (1989) 161–76.

Mark Searle, "Ritual & Music: A Theory of Liturgy and Implications for Music," *Assembly* 12 (1986) 314–17.

J. Michael Joncas, *From Sacred Song to Ritual Music* (Collegeville: The Liturgical Press, 1997).

Some studies in this category have focused on particular liturgical units, and considered the implications of music in these specific subdivisions of the rite. Mary McGann and I attempted such a study in our *Music and the Eucharistic Prayer* (Washington, D.C.: Pastoral Press, 1988); see also *Pastoral Music* 15:4 (1991), an entire issue on the communion rite. Some principles on the relationship between worship structures and music are explored in *The Milwaukee Symposia on Church Music,* nn. 37–44. For a more extended study of the relationship between music and liturgical structures, see my "Musical Forms, Referential Meaning and Belief" in *Ritual Music* (1995).

There has also been some inquiry about the theological implications of various genres of liturgical-musical forms; see, for example, the entire issue 12:6 of *Pastoral Music* (1988) on the "litany." There has been a similar concern with regard to hymnody. This was a frequent focus of discussion at the Milwaukee Symposia for Church Composers, and the topic for the Music Study Group of the North American Academy of Liturgy meeting in 1989. One public exchange by Roman Catholics over the issue included:

Joseph Swain, "An Apology for the Hymn," *America* 156:19 [23 May 1987] 421–23.

Kevin Irwin, "Musical Contretemps," *America* 156:23 [13 June 1987] 492.

Frank Quinn, "Music in Catholic Worship: The Effect of Ritual on Music and Music on Ritual," previously cited.

See also chapters 20 and 21 of the present volume.

The Interplay of Music and Texts

Another area of inquiry, related to the previous concern about the relationship between music and the rite, focuses on the intersection of text and music in worship. Apart from historical studies that analyze the treatment of texts by one composer or another, there are a limited number of more theological works that explore the faith dimensions of the text, and the influence of the music on the same. Noteworthy is Eugene Brand's unpublished dissertation from the University of Heidelberg (1959), "The Liturgical Function of Music: Music in its relationship to the Texts of the Liturgy." Also see the appropriate sections in works like Deiss' *Spirit and Song of the Liturgy* or Gelineau's *Voices and Instruments in Christian Worship,* as well as Walter E. Buszin, *Theology and Church Music as Bearers of the Verbum Dei* (St. Louis: Concordia, 1959), and Erik Routley, *Words, Music and the Church* (Nashville: Abingdon, 1968).

More recently, as part of the larger discussion about the translation of texts and issues of inclusivity, there has been significant writing about the appropriate language for worship and worship song, both in terms of inclusivity as well as poetics. Reflections from well-respected text writers, such as Thomas Troeger and Brian Wren have enriched this discussion:

Thomas Troeger, "Theological Considerations for Poetic Texts Used by the Assembly," *Worship* 59:5 (1985) 404–12.

Brian Wren, *What Language Shall I Borrow: God Talk in Worship—A Male Response to Feminist Theology* (New York: Crossroad, 1990).

More general works on inclusive language tackle some of the questions related to language for our worship song. For an introduction, see:

Teresa Berger, "Liturgical Language: Inclusivity and Exclusivity," *Studia Liturgica* 18 (1988) 132–41.

Mary Collins, "Inclusive Language: A Cultural and Theological Question," *Worship: Renewal to Practice* (Washington, D.C.: Pastoral Press, 1987) 197–214.

Frank Henderson, "ICEL and Inclusive Language," *Shaping English Liturgy,* eds. Peter Finn and James Schellman (Washington, D.C.: Pastoral Press, 1991) 257–78.

Elizabeth Johnson, *She Who Is: The Mystery of God in Feminist Theological Discourse* (New York: Crossroad, 1992).

Gail Ramshaw-Schmidt, *Worship: Searching for Language* (Washington, D.C.: Pastoral Press, 1988).

Works more specifically related to language for worship music include:

The introduction to the International Commission on English in the Liturgy's *Consultation on a Liturgical Psalter* (Washington, D.C.: ICEL, 1984).

Gracia Grindal, "Inclusive Language in Hymns: A Reevaluation," *Currents in Theology and Mission* 16:3 (1989) 187–93.

Erik Routley, "Gender of God: A Contribution to the Conversation," *Worship* 56 (1982) 231–39.

Such discussions raise some larger questions about the pastoral-theological responsibilities of composers and text writers in the shaping of worship music. See, for example:

Eugene Brand, "Word and Tone: A Challenge to the Composer," *Sacred Music* 93 (1966) 132–39.

Deirdre Brown, "The Contemporary Composer and Liturgical Reform," *Worship* 61 (1987) 16–25.

Carol Doran and Thomas H. Troeger, "Writing Hymns as a Theologically Informed Artistic Discipline," *Hymn* 36:2 (1985) 7–11.

Edward Foley, "On the 'Breath of Dawn' and other Metaphors," *Pastoral Music* (April–May, 1981) 23–25.

3. Pastoral and Cultural Studies

Apart from historical studies, or systematic reflections on the relationship between faith and music in general—or liturgical music, in particular—there have also emerged a variety of new approaches to considering worship music, largely borrowed from the social sciences. This evolution is reliant upon precedents in musicology over the past century, as well as later, parallel developments in the field of liturgy.

Musicologically, the late 19th and early 20th centuries were a time of diverse developments in the methods for the study of music. Some pioneered musical research from the perspectives of psychology:

Karl Stumpf, *Tonpsychologie* (Leipzig: Hirzel, 1883–90).
Carl Seashore, *Psychology of Music* (New York: McGraw-Hill, 1938).

A good introduction to the field is provided by John Booth Davies, *The Psychology of Music* (Stanford: Stanford University Press, 1978) or, the more recent John Sloboda, *The Musical Mind: The Cognitive Psychology of Music* (Oxford: Oxford University Press, 1985).

Others approached music from the viewpoint of sociology or anthropology. The first systematic attempt at a sociology of music was Max Weber's *Die rationalen und soziologischen Grundlagen der Musik*, dating from 1911 but not published until 1921; an English edition, by Don Martindale et al., appeared as *The Rational and Social Foundations of Music* (Carbondale: Southern Illinois University Press, 1958). Theodor Adorno, especially his *Introduction to the Sociology of Music,* trans. E. B. Ashton (New York: Continuum, 1989 [1962]), and Hanns Eisler, whose works are collected in *Musik und Politik,* ed. Günther Mayer (Munich: Rogner & Bernhard, 1973), are also important figures. The standard anthropological work is Alan Merriam, *The Anthropology of Music* (Evanston: Northwestern University Press, 1964), especially the summary and bibliography on the historical interface between music and cultural anthropology.

Musical studies employing methods from these varying disciplines spawned many of the new fields of inquiry. Of special import for liturgical music is the field of ethnomusicology (originally "comparative musicology"). On the distinction between comparative musicology and ethnomusicology, see:

Alan Merriam, "Definitions of 'Comparative Musicology' and 'Ethno-musicology': an Historical-Theoretical Perspective," *Ethnomusicology* 21 (1977) 189–204.

Kay Kaufman Shelemay, ed. *Ethnomusicology: History, Definitions and Scope* (New York: Garland, 1992), a useful collection.

While initially focused on music of non-Western cultures, there have been recent efforts within ethnomusicological circles to study the music of any culture. Of particular interest to some has been the study of music in ritual, which is now a common track of presentations at the annual meeting of the Society for Ethnomusicology. A recent published example of such study is Kenneth George, "Music-Making, Ritual and Gender in a Southeast Asian Hill Society," *Ethnomusicology* 37:1 (1993) 1–27.

Within the study of liturgy over the past few decades there has been a noticeable influence of psychology, anthropology, ethnology, and other social sciences. Gilbert Ostdiek provides a splendid overview of these developments in his recent article "Ritual and Transformation: Reflections on Liturgy and the Social Sciences," *Liturgical Ministry* 2 (1993) 38–48. A memorable articulation of the need for such methodological shifts was Mark Searle's 1983 vice-presidential address to the North American Academy of Liturgy, in which he outlined a new branch of liturgical scholarship, which he called "pastoral liturgical studies": "New Tasks, New Methods: The Emergence of Pastoral Liturgical Studies," *Worship* 57 (1983) 291–308. Since that time, the recently defined field of ritual studies has emerged which, in large measure, has taken up the concerns outlined by Searle. A key figure in this discipline is Ronald Grimes, for example, his *Reading, Writing, and Ritualizing: Ritual in Fictive, Liturgical, and Public*

Places (Washington, D.C.: Pastoral Press, 1993). Nathan Mitchell provides an introduction to Grimes' other major writings as well as an excellent overview of the field of ritual studies in *Liturgy Digest* 1:1 (1993).

The influence of the social sciences on the study of music, and their parallel ascendancy in liturgical studies—as well as the new work in ritual studies—has begun to affect the study, and even the production and publication of liturgical music. See, for example:

Charles Dreisoerner, *The Psychology of Liturgical Music* (Kirkwood, Mass.: Maryhurst, 1942).
Karl Gustav Fellerer, *Soziologie der Kirchenmusik: Materialen zur Musik- und Religionssoziologie* (Köln: Westdeutscher Verlag, 1963).
Edward Foley, "Ethnomusicology," *Pastoral Music* 14:6 (1990) 37–41.
Edward Foley, "Liturgical Musicology Redux," *Worship* 64 (1990) 264–68.
Edward Foley, *Music in Ritual: A Pre-Theological Investigation* (Washington, D.C.: Pastoral Press, 1984).
Note also the increased publication of African-American, Hispanic, and other ethnically identified hymnals in the past decade (see further below).

Of particular importance is the concern about varied cultural expressions of liturgical music and the development of appropriate frameworks for understanding and evaluating this music. A related concern is creating an experience-based method for ascertaining through field work how music actually functions in worship and faith.

Culture and Worship Music

The worship music of Jews and Christians, like that of other world religions, is culturally conditioned—a fact not always readily recognized. One common presupposition about worship music is the alleged superiority of certain works or a body of works that originated from a particularly prized era, geographic location, or composer. The hymns of Charles Wesley are an example of this in Methodism. The reverse is the development of indigenous hymnody, for example, as discussed by Robin A. Leaver, "Theological Dimensions of Mission Hymnody: The Counterpoint of Cult and Culture," *Worship* 62 (1988) 316–31. Such music has often been exported outside its culture of origin, and sometimes imposed regardless of the cultural tastes or standards of the receiving culture. Pius X's claim about the superiority of Gregorian chant in the previously cited *Tra le sollicitudini* is a classic example of this in Roman Catholicism. It is especially through the influence of cultural anthropology and ethnomusicology that such practices are being studied and challenged.

One example is the section on "Cross-Cultural Music Making" in the *Milwaukee Symposia for Church Composers* (nn. 56–63), which relies on this discipline in its challenge to traditional standards for evaluating worship music.

The number of studies—as compared with "reports"—of non-traditional music in Christianity and Judaism is small but growing. Some of these studies are of a more reflective or theological nature, such as:

James Cone, "Black Spirituals: A Theological Interpretation," in *Music and the Experience of God,* eds. Mary Collins et al., (Edinburgh: Clark, 1989) 41–51.
James Cone, *The Spirituals and the Blues* (Maryknoll: Orbis, 1991 [1972]).
Louis-Charles Harvey, "Black Gospel Music and Black Theology," *The Journal of Religious Thought* 43:2 (1986) 19–37.
I-To Loh, "Contemporary Issues in Inculturation, Arts and Liturgy: Music," unpublished paper presented at 12th International Societas Liturgica Conference (York, England: 14–19 August 1989).
Gino Stefani, "Musica, liturgia, cultura," *Nuova Rivista Musicale Italiana* 14 (1980) 479–96.

Other works—many of them the product of university study—are based on field observation, such as Stephen Frederick Duncan, "Christian *bhajans:* A Study of the Uses of Indigenous Music in the Rites of the Catholic Church on the Subcontinent of India Since the Second Vatican Council with Particular Attention to *Bhajan* and *Kirtan,*" Ph.D. dissertation, Memphis State University (1991).

African-American music has received the bulk of such attention in the U.S. One important scholar in this area is Mellonee Burnim:

Mellonee Burnim, "The Black Gospel Music Tradition: A Complex of Ideology, Aesthetic, and Behavior," *More than Dancing,* ed. Irene V. Jackson (Westport, Ct.: Greenwood, 1985).
Mellonee Burnim, "The Black Gospel Music Tradition: Symbol of Tenacity," Ph.D. dissertation, Indiana University (1980).
Mellonee Burnim, "Culture Bearer and Tradition Bearer: An Ethnomusicologist's Research on Gospel Music," *Ethnomusicology* 29 (1985) 432–447.
Mellonee Burnim, "Gospel Music Research," *Black Perspective in Music* (1980) 63–70.
Mellonee Burnim, "The Nature of African American Music: A Chronology," *Currents in Theology and Mission* 21:2 (1994) 93–104.
Mellonee Burnim, "The Performance of Black Gospel Music as Transformation," *Music and the Experience of God,* 52–61.

See also:

Mark Bangert, "Black Gospel and Spirituals: A Primer," *Currents in Theology and Mission* 16:3 (1989) 173–79.

Jacqueline Cogdell DjeDje, "Change and Differentiation: The Adoption of Black American Gospel Music in the Catholic Church," *Ethnomusicology* 30 (1986) 223–52.

Jacqueline Cogdell DjeDje, "An Expression of Black Identity: The Use of Gospel Music in a Los Angeles Catholic Church," *The Western Journal of Black Studies* 7:3 (1983) 148–60.

Irene V. Jackson, *Afro-American Religious Music: A Bibliography and a Catalogue of Gospel Music* (Westport, Ct.: Greenwood, 1979), an older guide which retains some value.

Irene V. Jackson, "Music among Blacks in the Episcopal Church: Some Preliminary Considerations," *More than Dancing: Essays on Afro-American Music and Musicians,* ed. Irene V. Jackson (Westport Ct.: Greenwood, 1985).

Portia Maultsby, "Afro-American Religious Music: 1619–1861," Ph.D. dissertation, University of Wisconsin (1974).

Portia Maultsby, "The Use and Performance of Hymnody, Spirituals and Gospels in the Black Church," *The Western Journal of Black Studies* 7:3 (1983) 161–71.

Elkin Sithole, "The Role of Gospel Music in the Black Churches of Chicago," Ph.D. dissertation, Queens University, New York (1976).

Jon Michael Spencer, *Black Hymnody: A Hymnological History of the African-American Church* (Knoxville: University of Tennessee Press, 1992).

Jon Michael Spencer, *Protest and Praise: Sacred Music of Black Religion* (Minneapolis: Fortress, 1990).

Wyatt T. Walker, *Somebody's Calling My Name: Black Sacred Music and Social Changes* (Valley Forge, Pa.: Judson, 1979).

There is less scholarly work on the current ritual music of Hispanics in this country. An exception is Steven Harry Cornelius, "The Convergence of Power: An Investigation into the Music Liturgy of Santeria in New York City," Ph.D. dissertation, University of California Los Angeles (1989); and there are some studies of music of the Spanish missions in North America. For example:

Wanda Jean Madsen, "Mexican Mission Music: A Descriptive Analysis of Two Seventeenth Century Chant Books," DMA dissertation, University of Oklahoma (1984).

Linda Popp, "Music in the early Evangelization of Mexico," *Missiology* 8 (1980) 61–69.

Owen Francis da Silva, *Mission Music of California* (Los Angeles: Warren Lewis, 1941).

A growing awareness of the value of these non-dominant cultural expressions has led to the inclusion of a sampling of "non-traditional" worship music in some recent major hymnals, as well as the publication of particular hymnals—especially for African-Americans and Hispanics—in this country. The former include *Lift Every Voice and*

Sing (1981), *Songs of Sion* (1981), *Lead Me, Guide Me* (1987), and *Lift Every Voice and Sing II* (1993). The latter include *Celebremos* (1979) and *Flor y Canto* (1989). Besides such hymnals for African Americans and Hispanics, the Methodist church published *Hymns from the Four Winds* (1983) for Asian-Americans.

Field Work and Liturgical Music

There is—and always has been—a variety of opinions about worship music and how it should function in worship. A sometimes amusing collection is Elwyn Wienandt's *Opinions on Church Music: Comments and Reports from Four-and-a-Half Centuries* (Waco, TX: Baylor University Press, 1974). The development of field methods in anthropology and ethnomusicology, as well as the use of such methods in ritual and liturgical studies, have spurred some investigators to explore news ways for understanding how music does function in worship. See, for example:

Margaret Mary Kelleher, "Hermeneutics in the Study of Liturgical Performance," *Worship* 67 (1993) 292–318.
Margaret Mary Kelleher, "The Communion Rite: A Study of Roman Catholic Liturgical Performance," *Journal of Ritual Studies* 5:2 (1991) 99–122, a field study report.

Most of these studies to date—and there are few of them—have been conducted by ethnomusicologists or anthropologists, who often do not ask the theological question in their work, such as:

DjeDje, "Change and Differentiation: The Adoption of Black American Gospel Music in the Catholic Church," cited above.
Brett Stutton, "Speech, Chant and Song: Patterns of Language and Action in a Southern Church," *Diversity of Gifts: Field Studies in Southern Religion* (Urbana: University of Illinois Press, 1988).

A few studies have been conducted by liturgists or musicians with little experience or training in field work in consultation with experts from the social sciences. For example, Edward Foley and Mary McGann, "Why Do Congregations Sing?" *Proceedings of the North American Academy of Liturgy* (1990) 87–97; also, the Lilly funded study of music programs in Episcopal and United Methodist churches in southern New England by Linda Clark (the description and findings were published in a series of reports issued from the Boston University School of Theology where Dr. Clark teaches). Prof. Don Saliers of Emory University is currently in the midst of a similar project. We look forward to the publication of his findings.

An unusual collaboration between liturgists and social scientists was the *Notre Dame Study of Catholic Parish Life,* which gave some attention to worship and its music. These findings by Mark Searle and David Leege were published at Notre Dame as two fascicles of the larger report: "The Celebration of Liturgy in the Parishes," *Notre Dame Study of Catholic Parish Life,* Report 5 (1985); and "Of Piety and Planning: Liturgy, the Parishioners and the Professionals," *Notre Dame Study of Catholic Parish Life,* Report 6 (1985). Unfortunately, the specifically musical data was very difficult to retrieve from this study. See my discussion of this study in "When American Roman Catholics Sing," *Worship* 63 (1989) 98–112; also, the entire issue of *Pastoral Music* entitled "Music and Song: Notre Dame Study of Catholic Parish Life," 10:6 (1986).

While there is certainly further need for historical and theological studies of worship music, this author believes that further field work in liturgical music—and the employment of disciplines such as semiotics for the interpretation of the data collected from such field work—are critical for the advancement of the field today. As this introduction itself demonstrates, historical studies dominate the field. It is necessary to balance those efforts, so that we not only acquire adequate knowledge of the liturgical music in our past, but develop our understanding for how it can serve our worship in the future.

Notes

1. See, for example, *Teaching Seminarians Music: Course Descriptions from Nine Seminaries,* ed. Anthony DiCello (Washington, D.C.: NPM Publications, 1991).

2. See chapter 13.

3. Critical editions in music are a late nineteenth-century development.

4. See also the more general work by Brian Rust, *Brian Rust's Guide to Discography* (Westport, Ct.: Greenwood, 1980).

5. *Schwann Spectrum* is the quarterly which lists "popular" recordings currently available. Both are published by Stereophile, 208 Delgado St., Santa Fe, NM 87501.

6. Available from SilverPlatter, 10 River Ridge Dr., Norwood, MA 02062 (telephone: 617-769-2599).

7. Acronym for the Online Computer Library Center (originally, the Ohio College Library Center).

8. Available from Miller Freeman Inc., 600 Harrison St., San Francisco, CA 94107 (telephone: 415-905-2470).

9. For example, Ancient (Greek antiquity to 500 c.e.), medieval (500–1430), Renaissance (1430–1600), baroque (1600–1750), classical (1750–1825), romantic (1825 to early 20th century) and modern (20th century).

10. I am grateful to Prof. Lawrence Hoffman for these references.

11. See Edward Foley, *Foundations of Christian Music: The Music of Pre-Constantinian Christianity* (Collegeville: The Liturgical Press, 1996), especially chapter 1.

12. There are many good articles in various biblical dictionaries and commentaries, including the 10 vol. *Theological Dictionary of the New Testament,* eds. Gerhard Kittel and Gerhard Friedrich, trans. Geoffrey W. Bromiley (Grand Rapids: Eerdmans, 1964).

13. Unfortunately, Jeffery's inability to be self-critical about his own presuppositions sometimes results in a skewed representation of the facts, especially regarding thoughts on Gregorian chant amongst those he calls "pastoral musicians" (present author included, 77, 83). Suffice it to say that, from my perspective, the decline in congregational singing within the liturgy during the Middle Ages was not a "result" of the emergence of Gregorian chant (thus, no simple cause-effect relationship as Jeffery seems to posit as the "pastoral" version of history); rather, the ascendancy of the Gregorian repertoire as well as the decline in congregational singing were both symptoms of much larger ecclesiological and theological developments in the medieval West, especially the monasticization of the Church and the theological assertion of the superiority of the monk (and eventually the priest) over the baptized.

See the substantial and critical review by the musicologist Leo Treitler, "Sinners and Singers: A Morality Tale," *JAMS* 47 (1994) 136–71; but compare the somewhat different response in the review of ethnomusicologist Richard Widdess in *Music and Letters* 75 (1994) 58–60.

14. James White subdivides "Protestant worship" into nine traditions: Lutheran, Reformed, Anabaptism, Anglican, Separatist and Puritan, Quaker, Methodist, Frontier, and Pentecostal, in *Protestant Worship: Traditions in Transition* (Louisville: Westminster/ Knox, 1989).

15. See my *Foundations of Christian Music,* chapters 2–4 for a further examination of this concept.

16. In the Babylonian Talmud, see Hagiga 2.12b, Erubin 2.21a, and Sanhedrin 11.91b.

Contributors

John F. Baldovin, S.J. is an associate professor of historical and liturgical theology at the Jesuit School of Theology, Berkeley. His publications include *Worship: City, Church and Renewal* (1991).

Mark P. Bangert is professor of worship and church music at the Lutheran School of Theology, Chicago. He is a member of the global study team "Worship and Culture" of the Lutheran World Federation. He is the author of "Dynamics of Liturgy and World Musics" in *Worship and Culture in Dialogue,* edited by S. Anita Stauffer (1994).

Patrick Byrne is a presbyter of the Roman Catholic Diocese of Peterborough in Ontario now serving as an associate pastor in St. Mary's, Lindsey, Ontario. From 1972 to 1987 he edited the *National Bulletin on Liturgy* and many liturgical books in Canada, including two national hymnals, *Catholic Book of Worship II* (1980) and *Catholic Book of Worship III* (1994).

William Cieslak, O.F.M. Cap. is president of Franciscan School of Theology, Berkeley, where he also professor of liturgical theology; he is a member of the St. Joseph Capuchin Province. His publications include *Console One Another* (1990).

James Dallen is professor of religious studies at Gonzaga University in Spokane and specializes in liturgy and sacraments. He is a presbyter of the diocese of Salina, Kansas. Among his publications is *The Dilemma of Priestless Sundays* (1994).

Austin H. Fleming is a presbyter of the Archdiocese of Boston and pastor of Our Lady Help of Christians parish in Concord, Massachusetts. His publications include *Preparing for Liturgy, Parish Weddings,* and *Prayerbook for Engaged Couples.*

William T. Flynn is assistant professor of music and liturgy at Emory University, Atlanta. His study of the medieval sequence, *Medieval Music as Scripture Exegesis,* is forthcoming.

Edward Foley, O.F.M. Cap. is professor of liturgy and music at Catholic Theological Union, Chicago. He is the author of a number of books, including *Ritual Music: Studies in Liturgical Musicology* (1995).

Joseph J. Fortuna is assistant professor of liturgy and sacramental theology at St. Mary Seminary, Diocese of Cleveland, Ohio and pastor of Ascension of Our Lord Church in Cleveland. He published "Contributing Credibly to a Sacramental Theology of Liberation" in *A Promise of Presence* (1992).

Raymond F. Glover is professor of music and chapel organist at Virginia Theological Seminary, Alexandria. He was the general editor of the Episcopal *Hymnal 1982* and *The Hymnal 1982 Companion* (1990–94).

Kathleen Harmon, S.N.D. de N. is director of music for the Institute for Liturgical Ministry. She contributes the music notes column for *Liturgical Ministry*, and is the composer of liturgical settings in *Pray without Ceasing: Prayer for Morning and Evening* (1993) and *Morning and Evening Prayer* (1996).

Jan Michael Joncas is assistant professor of theology at the University of St. Thomas, St. Paul, Minnesota. He is composer and editor of liturgical music and the author of *From Sacred Song to Ritual Music: Twentieth-Century Understandings of Roman Catholic Worship Music* (1997).

Robin A. Leaver is professor of sacred music at Westminster Choir College of Rider University, Princeton, and visiting professor of liturgy at Drew University, Madison, New Jersey. He has written widely on liturgy and music and is the editor of the series of monographs *Studies in Liturgical Musicology* and co-editor of the series *Drew University Studies in Liturgy*.

Michael James Molloy is a music teacher and music director of Centenary-Queen Square United Church, Saint John, New Brunswick, Canada. He is completing a Ph.D. in liturgical studies at Drew University.

Frank C. Quinn, O.P. is professor of liturgical theology at the Aquinas Institute of Theology, St. Louis. He is a noted teacher, liturgical consultant, and contributor to liturgical journals.

Don E. Saliers is professor of theology and worship and director of the sacred music program at Emory University, Atlanta. His books include *Worship and Spirituality* (1993), *Worship and Theology* (1994), and *Worship Come to Its Senses* (1996).

Mary M. Schaefer is professor of Christian worship and spirituality at the ecumenical Atlantic School of Theology, Halifax, Nova Scotia. Particular areas of research are theology of liturgy, history and theology of Eucharist and ministry, and liturgical architecture.

Thomas J. Talley, retired, was professor of liturgics at the General Theological Seminary in New York City. His publications include *The Origins of the Liturgical Year* (1986) and *Worship: Reforming Tradition* (1990).

Joyce Ann Zimmerman, C.PP.S. is director of the Institute for Liturgical Ministry and the founding editor of *Liturgical Ministry*. Her publications include *Liturgy as Living Faith: A Liturgical Spirituality* (1993), *Pray without Ceasing: Prayer for Morning and Evening* (1993), and *Morning and Evening: A Parish Celebration* (1996).